World Cinema

World Cinema: A Critical Introduction is a comprehensive yet accessible guide to film industries across the globe. From the 1980s onwards, new technologies and increased globalization have radically altered the landscape in which films are distributed and exhibited. Films range from the large-scale industries of India, Hollywood, and Asia, to the small productions in Bhutan and Morocco. They are seen in multiplexes, palatial art cinemas in Cannes, traveling theaters in rural India, and on millions of hand-held mobile screens.

Authors Deshpande and Mazaj have developed a method of charting this new world cinema that makes room for divergent perspectives, traditions, and positions, while also revealing their interconnectedness and relationships of meaning. In doing so, they bring together a broad range of issues and examples—theoretical concepts, viewing and production practices, film festivals, large industries such as Nollywood and Bollywood, and smaller and emerging film cultures—into a systemic yet flexible map of world cinema.

The multi-layered approach of this book aims to do justice to the depth, dynamism, and complexity of the phenomenon of world cinema. For students looking to films outside of their immediate context, this book offers a blueprint that will enable them to transform a casual encounter with a film into a systematic inquiry into world cinema.

Shekhar Deshpande is Professor and Founding Chair of Media and Communication Department at Arcadia University, where he held the Frank and Evelyn Steinbrucker Endowed Chair from 2005–2008. He teaches a broad variety of courses in film theory and analysis, critical theory, cultural studies, and world cinema. His writings have appeared in *Senses of Cinema*, *Studies in European Cinema*, *Seminar*, and *Widescreen*. He is the author of the forthcoming *Anthology Film and World Cinema*.

Meta Mazaj is Senior Lecturer in Cinema and Media Studies at the University of Pennsylvania. She has taught world cinema in both large lecture classes and smaller, discussion-oriented seminars. Her articles on Eastern European cinema, Balkan cinema, and small and marginal cinema have appeared in *Cineaste*, *Studies in Eastern European Cinema*, and *Situations: Project of the Radical Imagination*. She is the author of *Once Upon a Time There Was a Country: National and Cynicism in the Post-1990s Balkan Cinema* (2008), and co-editor, with Timothy Corrigan and Patricia White, of *Critical Visions in Film Theory: Classic and Contemporary Readings* (2010).

World Cinema

A Critical Introduction

**Shekhar Deshpande and
Meta Mazaj**

Routledge
Taylor & Francis Group

LONDON AND NEW YORK

First published 2018
by Routledge
2 Park Square, Milton Park, Abingdon, Oxon OX14 4RN

and by Routledge
711 Third Avenue, New York, NY 10017

Routledge is an imprint of the Taylor & Francis Group, an informa business

British Library Cataloguing-in-Publication Data
A catalogue record for this book is available from the British Library

Library of Congress Cataloging-in-Publication Data
Names: Deshpande, Shekhar A., 1953- author. | Mazaj, Meta, 1971- author.
Title: World cinema : a critical introduction / Shekhar Deshpande and
    Meta Mazaj.
Description: New York : Routledge, 2018. | Includes index.
Identifiers: LCCN 2017033821| ISBN 9780415783569
    (hardback : alk. paper) | ISBN 9780415783576 (pbk. : alk. paper) |
    ISBN 9780203129500 (ebook)
Subjects: LCSH: Motion pictures—History. | Motion pictures.
Classification: LCC PN1993.5.A1 D465 2018 | DDC 791.4309—dc23
LC record available at https://lccn.loc.gov/2017033821

ISBN: 978-0-415-78356-9 (hbk)
ISBN: 978-0-415-78357-6 (pbk)
ISBN: 978-0-203-12950-0 (ebk)

Typeset in Bembo
by Swales & Willis Ltd, Exeter, Devon, UK

Printed and bound in Great Britain
by Bell and Bain Ltd, Glasgow

Every effort has been made to contact copyright holders. Please advise the publisher of any errors or omissions, and these will be corrected in subsequent editions.

To Taja, Roheen, and Nakul

May your world be as enjoyable, nourishing, and cosmopolitan as world cinema!

Contents

Illustrations

Tables

Disclaimer

While every effort has been made to trace copyright holders and obtain permission, this has not been possible in all cases. Any omissions brought to our attention will be remedied in future editions.

Acknowledgements

If it takes a village to raise a child, it takes a lot more to complete a book. First, there is a more distant yet familiar transnational community of scholars and filmmakers who have already laid essential pathways to think about world cinema. A project such as this one is indebted to their thoughtful, creative foundations, and their rigor and richness of knowledge. Then there is a closer and warmer community of colleagues and friends whose unstinting support, intellectual nourishment, and continuous encouragement made this a project a reality. Together, these communities constitute a world outside of which this book would be inconceivable.

We owe our deepest gratitude to Natalie Foster, Senior Editor at Routledge, who shepherded this ambitious endeavor from its earliest stages to completion. Her patience, kindness, and support on many levels were an important constant throughout this long and dizzyingly complex process. We are grateful to our fantastic editorial team at Routledge for their inspirational work: Sheni Kruger, Kitty Imbert, and Jennifer Vennall, as well as our production team, especially Tom Cole and Andrew Melvin.

We entrusted the first draft of the completed manuscript to Anna Corrigan, a terrific reader and superb editor; we offer her a special bouquet of gratitude. Thanks also to the anonymous readers of the manuscript, who expressed enthusiastic endorsement of the project and offered valuable advice.

The book benefited greatly from numerous interactions and conversations over the years with colleagues, filmmakers, and friends who share our passion for world cinema. In 2014, Diane Carson and William Costanzo invited us to contribute to *Cinema Journal*'s Teaching Dossier "New Approaches to Teaching World Cinema," putting our pedagogical ideas to the test in light of their own wisdom and experiences. We have learned so much through conversations with Geoffrey Gilmore; his illuminating vision, experience, and fresh insights into global independent filmmaking and distribution contributed to our own navigation through the complex landscape of world cinema. Onookome Okome at the University of Alberta, and the late Akpor Otebele, brought us closer to Nollywood through many inspiring, eye-opening conversations, and a wealth of knowledge about African cinema.

Thanks to Bela and Parag Amladi, Dev Benegal, K. Hariharan, Bikas Mishra, and Nandita Dutta for their friendship, warmth, inspiring conversations, and shared cinephilia, and for being our comrade spectators of world cinema. Shekhar is grateful to his friend Ramiah Shankar for countless hours of conversation, co-spectatorship, and feverishly passionate cinephilia. Each cinematic encounter is still laced with fond memories of him. A big bow also to Feruzi Anjirbag and Anjoo Daswani, the original "BFFs" before it became fashionable. Special and heartfelt thanks must go to our very dear friends Alessandra Mirra and Peter Lešnik for many movie marathons, interminable conversations about world cinema, and unreserved enthusiasm for the project. Iggy Cortez, our brilliant interlocutor on Asian cinema, was always there to refresh and re-examine our assumptions.

Students in our world cinema classes have been invaluable in shaping our ideas over the years. Much more than good sounding boards for our pedagogy and conceptual models, it was their feedback and our exchanges with them that allowed us to bring to life the often-abstract ideas about world cinema. Shekhar would especially like to thank Jedidah Flores and Christine Acurantes for being such committed, engaged world cinema students. Thanks also to Jay Slott at the interlibrary desk, and Studio Supervisor Christine Kemp, for her help with web projects, particularly the Nollywood site. Our student research assistants provided us with valuable assistance in many stages of the project. We thank every one of them, but especially Dylan Hansen-Fliedner, Jay Jadick, Jennifer Morganroth, and Jacob Mattis. A special thank you goes to Gary Kafer, who came on board the Nollywood web project, boosting it with his incredible research skills, brilliant insights, and phenomenal writing.

We benefited immensely from our cinematic and social encounters at various international film festivals: the International Film Festival of Rotterdam, Cannes Film Festival, International Short Film Festival in Oberhausen, International Film Festival of Kerala, Sarajevo Film Festival, and Tribeca Film Festival, among others. We tip our hats to the organizers, filmmakers, and friends at these events who did so much for a deeper immersion in the worlds of cinema.

We are deeply grateful for a generative and warm environment provided by our colleagues. Shekhar would particularly like to thank JoAnn Weiner, Barry O'Connor, Norah Shultz, Hugh Grady, and Pradyumna Chauhan, whose support and friendship have been invaluable over the years. Meta considers herself truly fortunate to be part of the Cinema and Media Studies program at Penn, which is undoubtedly the most intellectually stimulating, encouraging, collegial, and fun place in the world. Timothy Corrigan, Karen Redrobe, Peter Decherney, Rahul Mukherjee, and Kathy DeMarco Van Cleve are an enviably amazing and inspirational group, a dream-team of colleagues, and their consistent, unwavering support, generosity, and warm friendship are deeply appreciated every single day. Our ship is masterfully steered by Nicola Gentili, a *metteur-en-scène* for many a cinematic, academic, social, and culinary event in our lives. A warm, kind, and generous friend, Nicola is indistinguishable from our own family.

Deeply heartfelt thanks also to Patricia White, who has been an ally, friend, interlocutor at conference panels, incisive reader and editor of our chapter drafts, passionate supporter, and simply an eloquent, spirited figure of inspiration. So lucky to have a friend-navigator in you!

Last but not least, all of this would be meaningless without our close and extended families. Shekhar remembers his grandfather Narasimha Vinayak Kulkarni, a versatile attorney and a pioneer in traveling tent cinemas in the 1940s India, who offered indelible primal scenes of cinephilia in his childhood. This moment requires recognition of an interminable debt to his mother, Kusum Kulkarni, a feminist out-of-her-time, whose incredible courage and perseverance made his life possible. She made him a citizen of the world, opening up the worlds of films, books, and the arts at a time when such influence was rare and precious. Meta's parents, Mirjam and Dušan Mazaj, your unconditional love and support has meant everything! Our fuzzy and warm companions, Lea and Zoe (biggest slow cinema fans!), loved nothing more than for us to sit still and watch long films in their company. Their expansive occupation of the desk-space was likely meant to claim some credit for the book. Taja, having endured what surely feels like a lifelong, endless project to her, patiently sat through and absorbed numerous films that she could have refused, often responding in sharp barbs, subtle compliments, and forthright discernment. A stunning creative artist in some phases of this project, she can easily claim to be one of the youngest and well-versed spectators of world cinema. Roheen, Nakul, and Taja were the sweetest, most tolerant partners in this process, encouraging and reminding us what really matters.

Introduction

"Watching world cinema connects us to something bigger," said Chris Hamel when introducing the World Cinema Weekend organized by Gateway to promote filmmaking around the world (quoted in Mikesell, 2017). "Something bigger," an abstract designation, is nevertheless an apt way to describe the increasing dimensions of world cinema. In its second century, cinema is "bigger," more vibrant, and more global than ever. Film production is burgeoning in all corners of the globe with a wide variety of styles, formats, and technologies. New technologies, new means of distribution, and the proliferation of film festivals have expanded and made filmmakers' sphere of activity "bigger." Film viewers, too, have available to them "bigger," broader choices of films from different cultures, and various platforms through which to access and watch them. The spheres of filmmaking and film viewing are more flexible, more diverse, and closer to each other, marking a cosmopolitan experience embedded in one part of the world yet reaching out for the as-yet unknown and unseen. The term "world cinema" merely names an undisputable reality of the experience of film practitioners, viewers, critics, students, teachers, and scholars. It is a complex cultural and commercial phenomenon with the power to create and connect disparate worlds. The rising acceptance and popularity of the term "world cinema" is therefore a welcome development, accommodating within it a broadening plurality of voices.

As we complete the writing of this stage of a book on world cinema, a paradoxical version of reality is unfolding before our eyes. Myopic forces in the West demand isolationism, insisting on hierarchy instead of dignity among human beings, and crude nationalism attempts to weaken the forces that have brought cultures together. The burden of the current moment poses great dangers to the consciousness cultivated over the past several decades toward cosmopolitanism, even though visions of cosmopolitanism are hardly rosy and acutely aware of the unequal power relations, histories of colonialism, and domination that have defined cross-border and cross-cultural relations. The critical voice carefully nurtured in this cosmopolitan vision of the world now seems drowned by loud pronouncements of derision and exclusion of others.

Yet, it is precisely in moments like these that we must insist with greater resolve on enacting the promise of world cinema that to circulate and watch films from outside of our cultural walls helps us recognize plurality and seek egalitarianism in thought and practice. Practices embedded in world cinema, world literature, and other cross-border art forms carry a powerful potential to build a front against the narrow forces that assert isolationism and superiority over others. To echo Walter Benjamin's words, it is to "bring about a real state of emergency" against authoritarianism and divisiveness. The vibrant, heuristic energy in producing, watching, and thinking about world cinema has to be sustained to do justice to the struggle of filmmakers, to a wide-eyed desire of viewers and students to be exposed to a variety of films, and to all the veins and capillaries of commerce and technology that allow for cross-border traffic of cinematic expression. A continued state of emergency must be in place to welcome strangers' images into our own worlds.

Often slippery and contentious, the currency of the term shows that world cinema is a reality, at the very least denoting a recognition that cinema is a global phenomenon that is produced around the world and circulates in nearly all its corners. Understanding the dimensions of such a global enterprise that contains a plurality of voices, positions, and perspectives is not an easy task, and it smacks of ambitions bound to fall short of their reach. While considering the multitude of cinemas as world cinema is certainly a democratic and inclusive gesture, it risks turning into a vast generality if no coordinates are offered to understand the phenomenon. Thus, to comprehend world cinema is to map it and to identify the pathways to navigate through it. The task of mapping the complex landscape of world cinema is the primary challenge of this book.

To begin this task, we turn to insights from Jorge Luis Borges's fable, "On Exactitude in Science" (1998). In this brief tale, Borges imagines an empire whose cartographers strove to create a perfect map of the world in all its detail and complexity; a representation so exact and vast that it "coincided point for point" with the actual territory. By promising complete coverage, however, such an unwieldy map turned out to be useless and too cumbersome for future generations, ending up in fragments and ruins, its still-discernible shreds a testament both to the vast ambitions and failures of the project. Borges showed in his lyrical wit the hubris of representing totality where the empire tries to map the world in its own image. Writing in hindsight, from the point of view of the future, outside and after the empire's collapse, Borges is aware of the absurdity of a map that tries to take over the territory and replace it. For him, "exactitude" is a false science. More useful is a map made from selection and reduction that can show something relevant about the world without blanketing it. The goal of any method of representation should be not coverage but fleshing out the relations between the parts and the whole. This is a fundamental principle of our approach in this book—that world cinema is not a totality, but rather a grasp, a representation of that totality with defined coordinates.

Among multiple models of mapping world cinema proposed in film studies, one of the most influential and exemplary models is Dudley Andrew's "An Atlas of World Cinema," where world cinema is approached in the form of an atlas, further systematized through maps, zones, and networks (2006). Andrew's multitude of maps—political, demographic, linguistic, topographical, and orientation maps—chart cinemas around the world cautiously and selectively, developing along the way criteria for navigating the cinematic world, although his presumed cartographer is still anchored in the West. Andrew values the wide cross-border circulation of films that open up unfamiliar worlds to students. The pedagogical value of his model comes from the need to provide a "different orientation to unfamiliar terrain," putting in place a recognition that the complexity of world cinema requires multiple perspectives (2006: 19).

Andrew (2010) later increases the dynamism of his model in two steps. First, he accepts Franco Moretti's proposition for world literature that global knowledge is better understood as a dynamic system, where each component develops and maintains itself in an energetic relationship with other elements, each affecting the other. To think of world cinema as a system where each component is in a dynamic relationship with the others provides an improvement over fragmentary and self-contained insights of earlier decades in film studies. The singular gift of the systems approach comes from its flexibility in approaching the smallest component to show its dynamic relationship to the largest and most powerful one. A second step that energizes Andrew's model comes from the added dimension of time in systemic changes. The trans-border, cross-cultural transactions of cinemas take place in a world of differentiated conditions, where global experience is shared across different time zones and through jet lags. The map of world cinema thus has a dynamic across the axes of time, as films travel and viewers receive them beyond their borders.

It is no secret that in cinema (as in many other spheres), the empire envisioned by Borges's fable that blankets the world and shapes it in its own view is represented by the West, especially its most dominant cinematic expression, Hollywood. In the face of Hollywood's power aligned with its capital, and the reach of its vision forming the borders of the world, the impetus behind developing a concept of world cinema comes in part as resistance to the self-proclaimed ambitions of Hollywood to equate itself with world cinema. Eurocentrism undergirds not just the dominance of Hollywood but also academic discourse, which arises from the embers of the same soil and provides an air of legitimacy to its patrons. In one of the most comprehensive and groundbreaking attempts to "unthink Eurocentrism" and challenge the dominant perspective of the West, Ella Shohat and Robert Stam (1994) tuned into a world radically altered after the demise of colonialism. They do not see the world as simply a negation of Eurocentric paradigms, but rather in its pluralistic fertility and the heterogeneous ways of thinking and seeing that reign from Africa to Asia, from India to the indigenous cultures of the world. Their clarion call to "de-center" the world still echoes in various fields, from literary studies and anthropology to film studies and the debates on world cinema, and *Unthinking Eurocentrism* has rightfully been seen as the first and key textbook on world cinema. Indeed, the emergence of world cinema as a discipline owes much to its impassioned advocacy of polycentric perspectives.

Following Shohat and Stam's foundations of polycentric multiculturalism, *Theorizing World Cinema* (2012) by Lúcia Nagib, Chris Perriam, and Rajinder Dudrah provides a positive definition of world cinema by recognizing and putting on equal footing multiple cinemas around the world, where Hollywood is merely one cinematic expression among many that are all interconnected. Comparative film history of world cinema illustrates that various cinemas emerge and become influential in different places and different moments in history. Nagib et al. guide scholars to emphatically recognize a multi-centered world that includes Hollywood and its interactive dependence on other cinemas. Several academic studies of world cinema, panels at academic conferences, journals, and websites concur with the proposition of presenting a multi-centered world, yet this proposition presents a quandary about how such a multi-centered world should be mapped. Most of these efforts fall short of the promise, invoking the effort and ideas behind it without putting them into practice. It seems impossible indeed to navigate a world where the unseen should remain satisfied with a promise but not a place.

Building our effort on the foundations built by Andrew, Nagib et al., and Shohat and Stam, we go beyond the promise of de-centering the world to show what such a map may look like and how it can be conceived. Too often, adapting a polycentric perspective works as an idealist aim, rarely practiced in the actual mapping that gives voices to different perspectives. Fragmented studies of various parts of world cinema assembled together in a survey-like manner, no matter how thorough and exhaustive, still show a gap between the promise and practice. This book develops a method of studying world cinema, a method of mapping a truly multi-centered world that not only makes room for divergent perspectives, traditions, and positions in world cinema, but also charts their interconnectedness and relationships of meaning.

Taking Borges's caution seriously, ours is not an exhaustive map in terms of coverage; rather, it is a representation of the layered topography of world cinema, produced through selection and reduction without attempting to blanket the world. As such, the map is open for others to re-chart or expand. Although our examples come from very diverse production contexts—they include major, smaller, emerging film industries, films circulating both in art house and commercial networks, as well as those outside of formal networks—our main, although not exclusive, focus is on fiction feature films. This is not to say that animation, documentary, short film, or other film forms present a less important or vital site of world cinema. In fact, crucial and transformative developments have taken place since the 1980s in the production, circulation, and exhibition of animated films, short films, and documentaries across the world. The focus on fiction feature films is therefore partly just that—a focus—but it is also justified because feature films' circulation and influence in popular culture elucidate the nodes and lines that connect specific cinema sites to their global context more clearly. Once traced, we hope these highlighted connections can serve as an invitation for others to include other forms and areas of production in an expanded map of world cinema.

The contemporary moment

The current phase of world cinema begins sometime in the late 1980s, when tectonic changes in geopolitical situations affect filmmaking industries in profound ways, and when the new technologies and global networks of distribution and exhibition radically alter the landscape in which films circulate. In some parts of the world, changes took place before the 1980s, while in other parts the main transformations have occurred since the 1990s. Whether dictatorships gave way to democracies or neo-colonial regimes loosened their grip, these changes were worldwide. We elaborate on the specific aspects of these changes in different parts of the book but, broadly conceived, they bear the following main features:

- Neoliberal economic policies in various guises, from free trade to marketization of all cultural production, created conditions that transformed film production, circulation, and exhibition. Fewer and fewer parts of the world faced restrictions and imposition of borders familiar in the earlier decades after the Second World War. While the effects of neoliberal policies were highly uneven and varied in different parts of the world, it is important to link them to the same global system set in place since the 1980s.
- New technologies, from digital to the web, increased and transformed the practices of cinema, from production, distribution, and exhibition to reception. Films that were inaccessible in distant parts of the world now moved across borders with greater ease, expanding the cinema audience, redefining cine-literacy, and offering new opportunities and exposure to new filmmakers. Cheaper, more accessible technology, combined with expanded international networks of financing, radically widened the zones of production and enabled more filmmakers and emerging film industries to enter the global circulation of films.
- Globalization after the 1980s may seem like it marches without political ideologies, but it has profound political implications. The global flow of capital and new technologies allowed the already-powerful industries in the West to embellish their

productions with flair and spectacle, and strengthen their dominant position in the film market. The combination of free capital and new technologies created conditions for globalization, a phenomenon that brought the world together, but with uneven flows of influence, where the powerful asserted their position more effectively while the powerless witnessed the distressing gap that separated them from the wealth and resources out of their reach. The study of any element of world cinema is deeply affected by the vectors of this global dynamic; therefore, all cinemas must be seen as interdependent and connected to a larger socioeconomic system rather than as isolated entities.

The periodization used in our work is marked by the three features outlined above, which were absent in either geopolitical conditions or in cinematic production of the earlier decades. For example, the national cinema approach practiced widely in earlier models of world cinema conceived world cinema as little more than an aggregate collection of various national cinemas, approached in relative isolation and without a systemic connectedness. The overwhelming influence of globalization eclipses such approaches, opening up the borders of a nation in economic and cultural terms. The framework of this book thus moves beyond both the fragmentary concept of international film (revolving around coverage and aggregates of national cinemas), the divisive notion of "foreign" film (falling back on the world division between *us* and *them*), or the instantly-generalizing concept of global cinema.

We need to emphasize in the strongest possible terms that our focus on "new world cinema" after the 1980s is not to be mistaken for the amnesia of film history of earlier decades. In many ways, "world cinema" is as old as cinema itself. Films have always circulated across borders and viewers have encountered "foreign" films in all parts of the world. Our project is not to negate the fundamentally transnational nature of film, but rather to respond to a radically different set of relationships and discourses that have emerged after the age of globalization. If we take a global view of the conditions of production and circulation of films after the tumultuous events of the late 1980s, it is clear that cinema, like other cultural forms, began a radical transformation. Many of our older conceptions, such as the centrality of Hollywood, the dominance of the national cinema model, the distinctions between art cinema and popular cinema, or the role of Third World cinema, acquired new coordinates. To be mindful of this rupture is to account for the responsiveness of academic discourses to the changing conditions around us. We accept that the gaps in our model are likely to be addressed by others or that it is possible to write an account of world cinema before and after the 1980s. We hope that the turn toward perspectives developed here will set markers for future comparative studies.

We propose three levels of approaching the new world cinema. The first, a **polycentric** level, shows the comparative strength and influence of five cinematic centers. The polycentric perspective defies the idea of a single center (most frequently Hollywood or European art cinema), presenting a field of uneven and constantly shifting "hot-spots" that gain prominence at different points of history, from Hollywood to Bollywood and Nollywood, from European to Asian cinema—each significant in its own moment and context. Second, world cinema is **polymorphic**, an interconnected assemblage of various forms: national, transnational, postcolonial, diasporic, small and minor cinemas. These traditional paradigms, far from being obsolete, still provide a necessary framework but now have to be reoriented or reconfigured from different vantage points and within the larger context of world cinema. For example, Estonian cinema as national cinema

is simultaneously local/national (both in its address and circulation) and a part of world cinema, suggesting alliances and utterances in a global context. Finally, world cinema is **polyvalent**, requiring an understanding of how each film is viewed and interpreted differently in different parts of the world. A film that travels across national and cultural borders is not dictated by a definitive or dominant interpretation, let alone one produced by Western theoretical models. Watching a film from a certain position in the world generates an interpretation that bears the imprint of the viewing conditions and the viewer. A polyvalent perspective thus requires an awareness of a geopolitical orientation, a "perspective of perspective," or the fact that "every film is a foreign film somewhere" (Egoyan & Balfour, 2004: 22).

Polycentric world cinema

In most open definitions, world cinema is the cinema of the world, without a center. We understand polycentrism not as an absence of, but rather an uneven and constantly shifting multiplicity of cinematic power centers that gain prominence at different points in history and different topographic zones. A center in world cinema presents substantial activity in its comparative influence on other cinemas, characterized by the following distinguishing features:

- A high level of cinematic activity, and a significant strength in the annual film production. Although numbers do not tell the story in terms of influence, the sheer size of the industries, as well as the sizes of their audiences, such as those of Indian cinema, Nollywood, or Asian cinemas, cannot be ignored.
- A formation of their own spheres of influence; substantial cultural and/or cinematic influence outside of its borders. Each one of the centers, besides its strong production numbers, produces films that circulate in other parts of the world and have considerable influence on other film cultures, diasporic cultures, as well as on cinematic styles of its filmmakers.
- The creation of independent perspectives and scholarship on their own cinemas, a distinct theoretical-philosophical-cultural approach to the image, thus representing de-centering also in terms of Western film studies and philosophy. European film theory has formulated dominant paradigms for perceiving and analyzing images, now enshrined in much of the Anglo-American film studies. Other centers boast similar traditions, which remain inaccessible partly due to lack of translation but also a lack of attention to alternative theoretical models and approaches to image-study. A truly de-centering enterprise must also bring Western academic theory into focus to make room for multiple models that emerge from other cinematic traditions.

Following these criteria, we find that along with Hollywood's power, Indian cinema, Asian cinema, Nigerian cinema or Nollywood, and European cinema present other cinematic centers, offering only one kind of a collective snapshot of world cinema since the 1980s. Indian cinema, with 1,600–2,000 films produced annually, is one such significant center, its distribution covering large territories from West to South East Asia, with a greater share now taken by its diasporic audiences in North America, Africa, and Far East Asia. Nollywood, producing well over 1,000 titles a year, forms another center, not merely because of its numbers, unique aesthetic, and circulation, but also because of its complex influence on African cinema in general. A similar case can be made about Asian cinema (Japanese, Chinese, Taiwanese, Hong Kong, and South Korean cinemas) that, while exerting influence over Asia, also has a significant influence on others, both popular and art cinemas around the world, including on Hollywood and European cinema. Mapping world cinema through such centers does not eclipse their internal diversity and complexity, nor should it consider these centers as isolated from each other. Power among them is not equal, and their differentiated status speaks of a number of factors such as financial power, aesthetic influence, cultural reach, technological dissemination, and a range of complex influences of political and social histories.

It is important to note that the model/map proposed in the book follows the principle of *mapping by representation*, rather than exhaustive inclusion. A model of Asian or European cinema, for instance, does not accommodate a detailed account of particular cinemas within a center (for example Taiwanese, or Hungarian). A way around the problem of grasping the totality in its expansive essence, Borges's tale tells us, is to approach it in terms of microcosms that bear a relation to the whole. That breadth has its limits is a known pedagogical lesson in world and comparative literature programs. Breadth may be a desired goal of broad intellectual inquiry but in effect, any learning exercise cannot fully grasp the landscape by accumulating content from one end to the other. Instead, an attempt to "think globally" is to understand the power relations between different parts. The idea of "world systems" itself invokes a totality approached through the examination of the dynamic between its constitutive parts. Kristin Ross's enduring insight into teaching world literature is that to study multiple fields of knowledge is to focus on the networks of relations, relative visibilities, and structures of power across various realms of interests and topics (1993). If a cumulative model always leaves gaps and promises that cannot be fulfilled, a representational model of world literature, Ross argues, aims to engage in the process of constituting its object without presuming the elements making that totality.

Our mapping of world cinema through multiple centers points to a similar method that begins to grasp the complexity of world cinema, rather than present a total sum of its components. If some parts of world cinema are not given an extensive treatment, it is because the criteria proposed here leave room to apprehend their existence through other methods. For instance, a strong case can be made for Latin American cinema as another one of the cinematic centers. Latin American cinema boasts an impressive regional profile, stylistic diversity, and connections to many cinemas around the world. With different yet connected manifestations in Brazil, Argentina, or Cuba, the Third Cinema movement in the 1960s and 1970s brought Latin American cinema to worldwide attention and was a major influence on the cinematic and theoretical developments elsewhere in the world. It explored film language in radical new ways and presented a formidable—ideological and cinematic—alternative to both the dominant Hollywood cinema and the European new waves.

However, in a constellation that we identify as the "new world cinema" after the tumultuous events of the 1980s, the relative profile and influence of Latin American cinema remains diffused. The regional and political promise of Third Cinema, which was diverse but nevertheless unified and operating under international solidarity, is now dispersed across various cinematic developments around the world. Its revolutionary practices and aesthetics, its critique from below of the conditions of postcoloniality, its positioning of the "aesthetics of garbage" (Stam, 2003) as resistance to the dominant discourses, have been absorbed into the unique idiom of Nollywood cinema. As we argue in the chapter on Nollywood, Third Cinema's militant and oppositional aesthetics of trash are re-positioned and transformed in Nollywood into an aesthetic rooted in popular culture. On the other hand, the political project of Third Cinema has been taken up by various practices of subversive aesthetic, from experimental film and anthology film to different minor cinema movements that foreground issues of class, gender, race, or ethnicity. There is no doubt that Latin American cinema remains a significant and vibrant part of contemporary world cinema, but its post-1980s developments—from the resurgence of popular genre cinemas and the renaissance of Argentinian cinema to the revival of the Mexican film industry and the strong emergence of women's cinema in various Latin American countries—are best approached through our polymorphic model, as a transnational cinema of the region that displays a complex dynamism of national, regional, and global identities on the levels of production, circulation, and textual negotiation.

Despite this position, our polycentric model by no means forecloses the possibility of students, teachers, or scholars making a case for Latin American cinema as one of the cinematic centers. The energy generated by their efforts will be a major step ahead of the current uncertainty and abstraction in the meaning of world cinema. The three criteria we propose in polycentrism (strength in numbers, realms of transnational influence, and indigenous theoretical traditions) are only a step toward theorizing the phenomenon of polycentrism. As Jacques Rancière points out in *The Ignorant Schoolmaster* (1991), the beginning of the inquiry is not the promise of knowledge; it is only an entry into exploration. The aim of proposing a polycentric model is to destabilize, once and for all, the hegemony of the Eurocentric model, with tangible steps toward identifying a vision of world cinema that is not confined to a single, privileged vantage point.

Finally, although our polycentric model includes five centers (Hollywood, European cinema, Indian cinema and Bollywood, Nollywood, and Asian cinema), *the book provides extensive accounts of only three of these cinemas*: Indian cinema and Bollywood, Nigerian cinema/Nollywood, and Asian cinema. Because of the limited scope of the book format, European and American cinema/Hollywood do not appear in the book. The exclusion may appear startling and to contradict our position that world cinema cannot be a concept defined in opposition to Hollywood, Europe, or the West. But as we began mapping, we found that the accounts of these cinemas as significant and powerful players in world cinema (not as mere alternatives to Hollywood or European cinema) are absent in the studies of world cinema. While the scholarship on these cinemas is extensive, Indian cinema/ Bollywood, Nigerian cinema/Nollywood, and Asian cinemas are studied in isolation and without a comparative framework, despite the fact that they provide a formidable front of their own, based on their strength, reach, and ingenuity in cinematic traditions. If we change our perspective from Eurocentric film studies to any of these other centers, it becomes clear that in terms of presence, influence, and power, these cinemas are second to none. Their diasporic strength is immeasurable after the 1980s, defying the notions of national cinemas and challenging a generalizing notion of transnational cinema. We found that expansive accounts of these cinemas, an actual treatment of them as power centers, had to be accommodated in the book—and seemed more urgent than a more superficial account of all five centers—at the expense of European and American/Hollywood cinemas (which have been traditionally assumed and approached as centers). Despite this gap, we hope that a polycentric map and the specific criteria proposed here will encourage students to include and extend their studies to European and American/Hollywood cinemas as additional centers of world cinema.

Polymorphic world cinema

Students, teachers, and scholars may find that a polycentric model of five centers does not include multiple other cinemas in the world. It is meant to focus on the most influential centers of activity, and as such does not include many other formations and cinemas of the world, for which we need a different way of conceiving totality. For example, most smaller national, regional, or ethnic cinemas, such as Cuban, Malaysian, Romanian, Estonian, or Indonesian cinema, need to be examined in their own right. Many of these cinemas transformed, expanded, and made themselves visible after the events of the 1980s, and they are important players on the world cinema stage. World cinema, particularly after globalization, is a vast and interconnected entity. It is impossible for anyone to understand the totality and its complexity in a single attempt. This may be one of the reasons why the very mention of world cinema raises eyebrows. The idea of understanding a vast system from our own limited space in the world is a daunting task indeed, yet we claim to provide access to that totality. To address the state of bewilderment about the vastness of world cinema is to use multiple approaches to look at totality.

The paradox may be best addressed through an old tale, "The Elephant in the Dark," also known as "Blind Men and an Elephant." It is an old Indian parable, told by the Sufi poet Rumi among others, disseminated through many parts of the world, and absorbed into many different cultural traditions. The story describes a group of men standing in the dark (or blind men) who touch an elephant to learn what it is like. Each visitor is asked to describe the creature after touching a certain part. "The creature is like a waterspout"; says one, feeling the elephant's trunk. "It is a pillar," says the other, touching its legs. None of the individual descriptions are in agreement with others, but taken together they nevertheless produce a large creature with some features. The tale offers a popular lesson that reality is never entirely comprehensible since all we have is a limited perspective on this reality. Transposed onto the perception of world cinema, a creature of unknown dimensions, all we have to describe it are multiple, often incongruous perspectives. In film studies, there are many forms of cinematic models and paradigms. Some prefer to see cinema through the lens of a nation; others believe this national framework is obsolete and has been surpassed by transnational approaches; still others prefer gender, ethnicity, or other categories as primary frameworks. Some models focus on cinemas that are small in size or marginal in their position in relation to the behemoths around them. All of these perspectives and categories of analysis constitute a part of our polymorphic approach, each exists in its own sphere, and each provides a partial image of the totality. The tale of an elephant tells us that at some point, however, we need to bring these multiple perspectives together to arrive at a larger image. National cinemas, for example, are imbricated simultaneously in local and global contexts; or, small cinemas are increasingly implicated in transnational relationships of production and multiple narratives, with their "smallness" a contextual significance as well as a geo-cultural identity.

The polymorphic level of analysis recasts some of the existing models in film studies to orient them to a systemic, interconnected vision of world cinema, where various parts are related to a totality that is grasped as a complex, uneven and dispersed formation—not a generalized universality. In their introduction to *Cinema at the Periphery* (2010), Dina Iordanova, David Martin-Jones, and Belén Vidal advocate for a view of world cinema seen from the periphery. Rejecting a binary, oppositional view of centers and margins, the dominant and the powerless, they ask that we shift our perspective. Conceived from the periphery, world cinema appears quite different, the canons disappear, and various local practices assume focal points. The previously unseen becomes seen. In a similar gesture, a polymorphic model asks that we adjust our perspective with an awareness of totality. Thus, we take some traditional categories of analysis—national, transnational, diasporic, small, women's cinema—and rather than proclaim them obsolete, show how they can be recognized in their fluidity and a renewed configuration in the systemic construction of world cinema. Each of the models places an emphasis on a specific perspective and position held by the observer, but also emphasizes its interconnections within a larger system.

The most enduring, although often eagerly dismissed, category of national cinema allows us to focus on industries or cinemas that struggle to maintain a distinct identity even in the age of globalization. We argue that the national still maintains its importance, but now as a locus from which to examine its relationship to world cinema. Similarly, small cinema is a concept born out of the desire to safeguard the cinemas of smaller nations and sizes whose relative significance is threatened either by the forces of globalization or other political and economic forces. These two categories are grouped under the national level of polymorphism. Part of the narrative of world cinema includes a movement from the once-dominant national cinema model to the ubiquitous transnational cinema model. But transnationalism indicates more than simply a transformation of national cinema into a broader, global configuration; it also includes a complex transformation of categories such as postcolonial, diasporic, or women's cinema, which are sometimes dispersed and sometimes nestled within another (national) cinema. Avoiding transnational as a slippery category, we deploy the concept of critical transnationalism, which allows for a clearer delineation of relationships on various axes of identification such as colonialism, ethnicity, race, or gender.

Polyvalent world cinema

It is axiomatic wisdom that films are perceived differently in different parts of the world, that each interpretation is the product of a subjective position. From reception theory to postcolonial theory, a recognition that different interpretations are products of a complex set of conditions is a given. When we accept that world cinema circulates freely across borders and influences viewers in different parts of the world, we are tacitly accepting that films acquire different meanings in different contexts. A mere admission of this fact on a global scale first challenges the hegemony of interpretations produced by academic discourses in the West then complicates the picture of understanding the numerous ways in which films are watched, absorbed, and interpreted, questioning the simultaneity and homogeneity often assumed in the global circulation of images. While it is impossible to track varying interpretations of films across the world, it is important to be aware of this polyvalence, the fact that every film, no matter how global its claim, embodies a specific geopolitical orientation, and that every viewer is situated differently.

As we suggest in the first chapter, polyvalence is not so much about uncovering suppressed voices, either in the filmmaking or academic sphere, as it is about *reorientation*, seeing the world from a different perspective to bracket commonplace assumptions about meanings and relationships between films. Given both the dominance of Western academic discourse in film studies and the difficulty of gaining access to scholarship on some of these cinemas (often due to lack of translation), the task of allowing for the full articulation of these polyphonic voices is often an impossible one, but efforts in this direction are an essential part of world cinema. Part of this exercise includes not privileging any reading of films or cinema over others and tuning into the vibrant but often ignored voices in other parts of the world.

Since the first and primary encounter of a viewer with world cinema is through individual films, the process of mapping often begins with watching specific films, which are then examined, as Andrew suggests, as a map, while being placed on a map (2006: 24). Thus, establishing the film's coordinates on the map of world cinema is also about locating the orientation that is inscribed in the film itself, recognizing how a film from a different corner of the world orients us to its place in the world, and what the world looks like from its perspective. This double process of cognitive mapping, whereby a film simultaneously exhibits its relation to world cinema, as it is also an embedded map of the world itself, *begins* with a polyvalent view, an awareness of how the viewers, as well as a given film, are situated in a specific context. Only with this awareness can we begin to successfully chart a film's relationships within a systemic totality of world cinema and ask questions about its positioning: How does a film achieve its visibility? What are the mechanisms that affect its discourses of recognition? What are the financial, social, institutional, and cultural networks associated with the film?

Teaching world cinema

Instructors who teach world cinema are often "faced with a considerable dilemma in simply determining the object of study," and this terminological instability plagues textbooks as well as scholarly material in the field of world cinema (Talbott, 2014). While there are numerous ways of approaching the study of world cinema, or its specific elements, the organization of this book follows a logic that we believe best represents the pressing issues in the field of world cinema, as well as one that brings different cinemas, contexts, and debates surrounding them into a productive and systematic dialogue. Our polycentric, polymorphic, and polyvalent maps both systematize a vast and often indeterminate object of study and emphasize that the study of world cinema has to begin with specific films. Film viewing is a world-making activity, a gesture toward "worlding" that attempts to comprehend the expanse and the limits of the world seen from one's locus. A map of world cinema is thus a map that presents "the global as a local utterance, for any attempt to represent 'the world' inevitably bespeaks the mapmaker's own placement" (Cooppan, 2001).

These two broad principles—to reduce the terminological instability, and to place the viewer/student and her encounter with specific films at the center of mapping/understanding world cinema—guide the structure of the book. We begin with conceptual issues, followed by extensive accounts of three different cinematic centers, and polymorphic configurations of various paradigms—which teachers, students and scholars can deploy in a variety of classes, contexts, and approaches.

Chapter 1 offers a conceptual framework that navigates existing and emerging ideas in the field of world cinema, situated firmly in the context of its world literature and world music precedents. This chapter should allow students to gain an understanding of world cinema as a concept. Discussing some of the dominant theoretical perspectives in film studies, the chapter outlines a clear definition of world cinema as a polycentric, polymorphic, and polyvalent formation. Since all cinemas are shaped in some way or other by the forces of globalization and neoliberal economy, it is possible to construct a comparative model where world cinema is no longer everything for the sake of everything, but a systemic multiplicity of cinemas from around the world.

Chapter 2 traces different, and unevenly developed, practices and habits of watching films around the world, examining a potent confluence of technological changes and cultural discourses that inform the ways in which we encounter films, whether it is in movie theaters (multiplex cinemas, art house cinemas, traveling theaters, film societies), on television, through physical media (VHS, VCD, DVD), or via smaller, portable screens. It also addresses other issues related to watching world cinema, such as piracy, with its various industrial and social manifestations, and subtitling. Despite new technologies that have radically changed the way we watch films, we find that theater persists as one of the most important forms of viewing, even as it is in decline in some countries or is being transformed by digital technology.

Chapter 3 offers an account of the main production models around the world. Film production since the 1980s is distinguished from earlier periods by a slow fading of the national-industry model and an emergence of various models of local, regional, and transnational collaborations. Based on our proposition of the five cinematic centers, we provide five different paradigms of production, exploring emerging transnational, global, and regional production patterns. The US dominates the production of films based on its ability to inject capital and offer the most lucrative distribution market. The European Union model, the most well-developed and formalized model of transnational structures with organizations such as the MEDIA Programme and Eurimages, shapes film production through formal alliances and the stability of state support. Asian countries offer far less formal but strong financial structures buoyed by the increasing power of distribution markets in China, South Korea, and Japan. Production patterns in India are increasingly formalized while those in the Nollywood film industry remain informal and unorganized, but generate significant revenues for the domestic, regional, and diasporic markets.

Chapter 4 addresses the most salient feature of world cinema after the 1980s: the global boom and influence of international film festivals, which have become one of the biggest growth industries. The diversity and expansion of film festivals are as daunting as their multidimensional role in shaping world cinema. Film festivals have consolidated the once marginal role of art cinema into one of the strongest and most influential modes of filmmaking. While the chapter acknowledges the complicated web of functions performed by film festivals, our emphasis is on the crucial role that festivals have played in the production of knowledge that guides our understanding of world cinema. This chapter explores the ways in which festivals are not only exhibition and distribution platforms, but play an active role in *shaping* the very landscape of world cinema, and by implication our understanding of it.

A course in world cinema, we hope, will include aspects set out in the first section of the book to form a conceptual framework that accommodates various manifestations of world cinema, from local to global, art cinema to popular cinemas. An illustration of how world cinema exists in different parts of the world, from modes of watching and producing film to exhibition, should build a useful foundation that allows students to access each cinema in relation to worldwide developments. With this conceptual model in place, we proceed with extensive accounts of three cinematic centers—Indian cinema and Bollywood, Nigerian cinema and Nollywood, and Asian cinema—that discuss in a substantive way the varied dynamic of each center, both its internal as well as cross-border influence and its interconnections to other cinemas. Learning from the accrued wisdom in world literature and world cinema courses at various universities, a course in world cinema may approach polycentrism through a study of one or two cinematic centers; that is, teaching by example rather than coverage. The criteria provided for identifying a center here serve as a basis for comparison between different cinemas rather than a fixed and hermetic strategy of classification.

In the section on polymorphic world cinema, specific case studies are approached through various national and transnational manifestations or paradigms—diasporic cinema, small cinema, women's cinema—not only to offer an overview of these frameworks used in the study of world cinema, but to show how they can be grasped in broader, global spheres of influence. Individual case studies are discussed less through the films' narrative or formal meanings or as instances of particular paradigms, but as utterances existing in a network of various local and global forces (economic, institutional, cultural) that determine their position on the map of world cinema, which may be prominent, marginal, or invisible.

The final chapter, on polyvalence, is an equally significant step in a course on world cinema. Recognizing that films are always "read" from the vantage point of the viewer's position in the world, it reinforces the de-centering project of the book. No longer should cinema studies consider interpretations and scholarship from the West as more valid or legitimate than others. Efforts at "de-Westernizing" must develop an awareness that every interpretation, every theoretical model, is specifically situated and bespeaks a particular view of the world.

As scholars, our aim was to do justice to the depth, dynamism, and complexity of the phenomenon of world cinema. We have also found this structure and proposed model useful and productive as teachers, and have been successfully using it in our world cinema classes. However, we believe that the flexibility and openness of the model allows the book to be deployed in various contexts. Whether it is a class on world cinema structured around different case studies than those found in a book, a class that focuses on a particular national cinema, a class on film festivals, or a class on specific world cinema auteurs, the book offers a blueprint, a way of mapping, that will enable a teacher or student to situate and map any specific cinema site they want to explore to its global coordinates.

Bibliography

Andrew, Dudley. (2006). "An Atlas of World Cinema." In Stephanie Dennison & Song Hwee Lim (eds), *Remapping World Cinema*. New York, NY: Wallflower, pp. 19–29.

Andrew, Dudley. (2010). "Time Zones and Jetlag: The Phases of World Cinema." In Nataša Ďurovičova & Kathleen Newman (eds), *World Cinema, Transnational Perspectives*. New York, NY: Routledge, pp. 59–89.

Borges, Jorge Luis. (1998). "On Exactitude in Science." In *Jorge Luis Borges: Collected Fictions*. Trans. Andrew Hurley. New York, NY: Penguin Books.

Cooppan, Vilasini. (2001). "World Literature and Global Theory: Comparative Literature for the New Millennium." *Symplokē* 9(1/2), pp. 15–43.

Egoyan, Atom & Ian Balfour. (2004). "Introduction." In *Subtitles: On the Foreignness of Film*. Cambridge, MA: The MIT Press, pp. 21–32.

Iordanova, Dina, David Martin-Jones & Belén Vidal (eds). (2010). *Cinema at the Periphery*. Detroit, MI: Wayne State University Press.

Mikesell, Terry. (2017). "Gateway to Screen Films from 11 Countries as Part of World Cinema Weekend." *Columbus Dispatch* (January 31). Available at: www.dispatch.com/entertainmentlife/20170131/gateway-to-screen-films-from-11-countries-as-part-of-world-cinema-weekend. Accessed March 5, 2017.

Nagib, Lúcia, Chris Perriam & Rajinder Dudrah (eds). (2012). *Theorizing World Cinema*. New York, NY: I.B. Tauris.

Rancière, Jacques. (1991). *The Ignorant Schoolmaster: Five Lessons in Intellectual Emancipation*. Trans. Kristin Ross. Stanford, CA: Stanford University Press.

Ross, Kristin. (1993). "The World Literature and Cultural Studies." *Critical Inquiry* 19(4), pp. 666–676.

Shohat, Ella & Robert Stam. (1994). *Unthinking Eurocentrism: Multiculturalism and the Media*. New York, NY: Routledge.

Stam, Robert. (2003). "Beyond Third Cinema: The Aesthetics of Hybridity." In Anthony R. Guneratne & Wimal Dissanayake (eds), *Rethinking Third Cinema*. New York, NY: Routledge, pp. 1–29.

Talbott, Michael. (2014). "What is World Cinema? Structuring the Course." *Cinema Journal Teaching Dossier* 2(1). Available at: www.teachingmedia.org/world-cinema-structuring-course. Accessed March 8, 2017.

1 What is world cinema?

Cinema, an international medium since its birth, has only recently assumed a worldwide reach and presence. Watching films from different parts of the world has been for most people a limited activity, situated mostly in urban centers where images could traffic freely through cine-clubs, film societies, and art house cinemas that cultivated spectatorship for international film. Films from France, Italy, Japan, Spain, Sweden, and Russia with directors such as Akira Kurosawa, Andrei Tarkovsky, Jean-Luc Godard, François Truffaut, Ingmar Bergman, Federico Fellini, Robert Bresson, Yasujiro Ozu, and Satyajit Ray developed a distinct culture of "foreign film" with an art house aesthetic that appealed to cine-literate audiences. While always alive for avid filmgoers in cities where films could be screened, world cinema was nevertheless a rather narrow and specialized realm.

The experiences of watching, producing, and distributing films have changed dramatically since the 1980s. Several factors that we outline in the introduction have contributed to this sea change in the landscape of cinema. The sustained geopolitical changes after the end of the Cold War have unleashed economic, cultural, and technological forces of globalization, unsettled the previous configuration of national borders, and played a major role in the transformation of what we grasp as the world. The film viewers' world has expanded into new realms, with broader choices of films from different cultures, and numerous platforms through which to access and view them. New technologies and means of distribution and proliferating international, local, and regional film festivals have redefined and expanded filmmakers' spheres of activity, charting a deeply complex territory for world cinema. Filmmakers and film viewers find themselves closer to each other, in more flexible and diverse environments, generating a different energy for cinema.

World cinema is no longer an isolated sphere of privileged film aficionados but a set of interactions and discourses that affects all aspects of cinema: the way we make it, the way we watch it, and the way we think and write about it. Before world cinema, two other art forms, literature and music, have charted a similar territory of cross-border traffic and horizons for listeners and readers. World cinema has much to learn from the successes and limitations of world literature and world music in the age of globalization, lessons which also show us that *world* cinema is a more suitable term than *international*, *global*, or *foreign* to grasp cinema's distinctness in alignment with other cultural developments.

The antecedents: world literature and world music

When poet and writer Johann Wolfgang von Goethe remarked in 1827 that "the epoch of world literature (*Weltliteratur*) is at hand, and everyone must strive to hasten its approach," he was suggesting that it was possible to read and learn from literature outside of one's own context (quoted in Damrosch, 2003: 2). It was a remarkably prescient statement at the moment when literature, then a distinctly national form, was beginning to travel across borders. It was also a statement of hope from Goethe, who envisioned national and European literature crossing geographical and cultural boundaries into a worldwide exchange. World literature or *Weltliteratur*, Goethe thought, would emerge through the vigorous interaction of national literatures, opening up doors to writers and readers beyond their established cultural spaces. Given the limitations of translation and lack of methods for circulation, it was a utopian vision at the time, but over the next two centuries, as modes of translation and exchanges became commonplace, his vision became a reality.

A proponent of Goethe's vision, David Damrosch looks at the current epoch as a cease-less transaction of literature across national borders: "I take world literature to encompass all literary works that circulate beyond their culture of origin, either in translation or in their original language" (2003: 4). World literature for him is not merely an "infinite and ungraspable" collection of works but "rather a mode of circulation and of reading, a mode that is as applicable to individual works as to bodies of material, available for reading established classics and new discoveries alike" (2003: 5). This simultaneous recognition of world literature as an expansive concept that also needs systematization or mapping allows literary scholar Franco Moretti to apply the world-systems approach to the study of world literature and show that literature is "one and unequal" or "one world literary system of inter-related literatures" (2000: 55). Given the fundamental orientation of literature toward the nation as well as toward the new realities of merging literatures, the national and world literature can co-exist.

In Moretti's world-systems approach, each component interacts with and affects other components. A system of world literature incorporates national literatures like it includes other modes of interaction across a diverse collection of languages and cultures. Moretti proposes two metaphors to illustrate how these interactions take place—that of a tree for national literatures and waves for world literatures: "National literature for people who see trees; world literature for people who see waves" (2000: 57).[1] The metaphor of a *tree* represents a homology between the nations and literatures of their languages. National literatures grow with a distinct linguistic identity that has genealogical roots related to its heritage, as branches are related to trees. They can be identified in their close proximity to each other, in languages and cultures, nurturing each other's development, and grow-ing in interdependence. His metaphor of a *wave*, on the other hand, depicts the influence of one literature on its adjacent cultures within their sphere of interaction. It illustrates the growth of literatures well beyond the proximity of national or linguistic affinities. Importantly, a world-systems approach does not deny the existence of national or local literatures but situates and connects them to broader spheres of world literatures that are not immune from influences beyond their borders. It also incorporates a wider range of literatures with varying degrees of status and visibility, since it considers world literature not as an object, but rather as a methodological problem, a matter of mapping relations and structures of visibility between literatures. To think of the world as an interactive system of constituent parts without privileging one component over the other challenges, among other things, the dominant Eurocentrism in the studies of literature.[2] It is true that questions of translation and hegemony of certain languages pose fundamental problems and present a vexing issue for world literature to accomplish its goals (Apter, 2013). Much of the debates in world literature regarding modes of circulation, reading, cross-border traffic, and wider audiences are shared with the goals of world cinema. However, cinema poses a distinct advantage over world literature for the commonality of its visual languages and its accelerated world traffic, despite the issues of translation and subtitling (addressed in Chapter 2).

Once world literature is configured through a world-systems approach, the question of representation and accountability for its plural voices becomes an urgent concern, since the representation of minorities against hegemonic voices must be reconciled with an understanding of the totality of world literature (Spivak, 2003; Damrosch & Spivak, 2011). Given this dilemma, how can one approach the study of world literature? Should we include all minorities, all the multiplicity of voices, or should we instead illustrate how various literatures reconcile with the totality from their own respective positions? In her insightful work on this issue, Kristin Ross (1993) argues against a cumulative approach insofar as it merely recreates the hierarchy of the hegemonic Western literature to world literature while allowing for token representation of other voices. In this approach, minority voices are included as mere gestures toward inclusiveness and have no effect on the existing systemic configuration. Instead, she proposes an allegorical approach where each example stands for itself, and where one studies the specific example's relationships to and negotiation with the totality and its hegemonic voices. For example, a study of Nigerian literature, rather than just an inclusion in world literature, becomes in Ross's model a figure, an allegorical example of how a minority voice negotiates its place in a larger system, marking its strength and its repression by others. This relational model is more productive and ultimately more comprehensive than an all-inclusive approach, since it helps us understand a specific phenomenon in its systemic totality, as a manifestation of relationship to world literature, without prioritizing one over the other.

Learning by example thus becomes more important than learning by content. For world cinema, this lesson demonstrates that each film, each national or regional cinema, is to be examined as a formation in itself, with its own values, while it can also be read as a paradigm for approaching other examples. Learning about world cinema cannot be an exercise in taking up all the cinemas of the world, but rather a strategy where each specific cinema is studied as part of a larger, dynamic organism.

Unlike world literature, the concept of world music owes its genesis to a more recent past. World music is an immediate and instant product of the globalization of market forces and their appropriation for the consumer tastes in the West. In the 1980s, a vast variety of musical traditions from different countries gained visibility for listeners and connoisseurs in the Western marketplace. Brazilian samba, West African rock, Hindi pop or Turkish Roma/Gypsy, previously popular and visible only in limited contexts, now became a fixed presence in record stores in major cities. Each musical form had a small constituency generated by a select group of artists. These diverse "ethnic," "folk," and "international" musical traditions were grouped together under the label of "world music," separating them from jazz, pop, rock, and the blues, which had a more substantial musical output and a larger number of listeners.

To the discerning listener, however, it was quite clear that only select artists appeared again and again under the rubric of world music, and they owed their visibility to massive and glamorous publicity efforts by record labels. It was a marketplace that generated the category of world music, combining ethnic music from various music traditions and catering to the taste of Western consumer. Once created, indigenous musicians stepped up to create music that appealed to this taste. In the West, musicians supported by capital positioned themselves to produce and market world music, patronizing artists of their choice from various traditions around the world. Peter Gabriel, for example, co-founded the WOMAD (World of Music, Art, and Dance) festival in 1982 and continued to produce and market world music through his Real World Records label. The *Graceland* album, a collaboration between Paul Simon and the South African group Ladysmith Black Mambazo, achieved impressive commercial success and stirred many debates on the commercialization of African music. In 1990, the magazine *Billboard* established a bi-weekly World Music chart that would list the fifteen top-selling albums in this new genre. A plethora of specialized publishers and vendors emerged, with names such as Music of the World, World Music Institute, and World Music Enterprises. While their patronage was welcome in that they offered support to local music traditions, their larger effect was to suppress the diversity and shape world music to the taste of a Western consumer.

While world music was more about an attempt to showcase the hegemonic tastes of the West than about representing the musical diversity of the world on its own terms, it in turn shaped specific expectations about local and regional music styles, and influenced the kind of music that was produced in different corners of the world. Artists from Africa and Asia needed patronage from the West, and in the absence of any other support systems in their own countries, it became increasingly difficult to resist the temptations of world music. As Turkish scholar Koray Değirmenci (2010) observes with his example of Turkish music, the power of world music threatened to reshape indigenous musical diversity within Istanbul itself. Ethnomusicologists expressed the fear that the force of multi-national industry would make world music homogeneous and not only transform indigenous musical styles but banish them into oblivion.

At the same time, the very idea of world music signified a larger listening community and the possibility that with the ever-expanding realm of musical tastes and styles, rich and remote traditions of music could reach wider audiences. It opened up the opportunities for collaborations between artists of different countries, a vision that Goethe had embraced for world literature. When film scholar Teresa Hoefert de Turégano (2012) weighs the similarity of world cinema with world music, she hopes that world cinema gains inspiration from its musical counterpart and forges collaborations between different cinemas. Thus, the concept of world music presents us with a double bind that is also instructive for world cinema: if by "world music" we mean cross-fertilization of traditions and a support of local music traditions with international capital, world cinema, too, can gain much from such exchanges and interactions. But if world cinema is merely a category of producing and presenting films from around the world for the eager viewer positioned in the West, then in effect the concept becomes a project of colonization and an example of appropriation by the dominant forces of the market.

International, foreign, global, or world cinema

Until now, students, teachers, and scholars have approached the study of films made in different parts of the world under the rubrics of international, foreign, and global cinemas. To understand the configuration of new world cinema and the massive transformations that have taken place in the development of world cinema, we must locate the meaning, usage, and limitations of the terms that preempt *world cinema*.

Borrowed from the field of international relations and law, *international* denotes an approach that focuses on relations between units or areas. *International film* points to a collection of national or regional cinemas, each as an independent and distinctive formation with its own history and trajectory. There is little hint of exchanges or interactions between these specific units. At best, it is seen as a survey of films from various parts of the world, suggesting, as Andrew says, "a distant gaze, panoptically monitoring the foreign for our convenience and use" (2006: 19). What is included in the scope of the international is merely the choice of an interlocutor, without paying attention to the dynamic of the interaction between elements. For Nicole Brenez, the notion of the international retains its currency because it signifies international solidarity desired by the left. Indeed, for her, "internationalism" is an essential dynamic in the history of politically engaged cinema and its connection to internationalist movements, from 1930s Spain and colonial Africa in the 1950s to contemporary movements such as Occupy Wall Street (Brenez & Foreman, 2012). For Galt and Schoonover, however, a brief attempt to politicize the circulation of films outside of national borders does not rescue the generally nascent meaning of the term "international," which remains outmoded and limited in its selective gestures (2010a: 12). Despite these limitations, the term "international cinema" retains currency in film festivals, and remains a popular designation for most film festivals whose programming suggests a wider, expansive scope of the presented films. Interestingly, despite the fact that many film festivals from Busan to Rotterdam call themselves "international film festivals," they avoid the term in their programming and use the label of "world cinema" in order to distinguish films that are considered new or different from other parts of programming.

The category of "foreign film" is even more problematic as it circulates in various ways. Andrew observes that it was a category of convenience used in the early days of film studies courses that allowed instructors to include films from wider but flexible contexts outside of their own (2006: 19). In many parts of the world, *foreign film* is simply a designation that refers to films outside of one's national or regional context. The term endures in the public sphere, in journalism and the media as a short-hand to speak of films found in art house venues, outside of mainstream cinema. Generally stubborn to change its ways, the popular press has not recognized the parochialism of the term that separates the domain of the familiar and the unfamiliar, of *us* versus *them*. Even publications like the *New York Times* and *L.A. Times* in the US, and *The Guardian* and *The Telegraph* in the UK, which provide generous space for films from other parts of the world, indiscriminately deploy the term "foreign," thus betraying their claims to liberal cosmopolitanism. In some sense, nationalism is implicit in the continued use of *foreign* in the case of the press as well as organizations with international posture. The Academy of Motion Picture Arts and Sciences in the US, for example, separates international cinema with the designation of Foreign Language Films. In colloquial terms, its main award is still known as "the foreign film Oscar," and non-American films are referred to as "foreign films."[3] In France, the Oscar equivalent is known as the César Award for Best Foreign Film (*César du meilleur film étranger*). In the UK, the British Academy of Film and Television Arts (BAFTA) awards sensibly break from this tendency and use "Films Not in the English Language," deftly separating Anglo-American films from the rest of the fare. The use of this term and its problematic implications are particularly visible in the case of the U.S. academy and its outdated and rigid selection process. Its one-country, one-nomination system not only segregates all films not in English, but eliminates much quality work, opens the competition up to influence by political consideration rather than artistic merit (a system that the festivals got rid of in the 1960s), and discriminates in large part against co-productions that are an integral part of world cinema. A continued use of the term "foreign" underscores this inertia in the face of changed circumstances and a stubborn Eurocentric myopia. It is time to leave this obsolete term as we recognize and respect the multi-vocal diversity of different cultures around us.

On the face of it, the recent usage of *global cinema* represents an improvement over earlier terms, and a recognition of the "global village" as foretold by Marshall McLuhan (1994) nearly half-a-century ago. In the context of cinema, the term is used to account for the new state of mobility of films, wider circuits of production, distribution, and reception, and an overall increase in convergence and accessibility of all kinds of media. But, in effect, the term's usage suggests less a totality of cinema than a particular sphere of world cinema.

The term appears perhaps most systematically in the edited volume *Global Art Cinema* by Galt and Schoonover (2010b), which includes definitive statements on various aspects of art cinema that circulate on a global scale. There are three implied levels of meaning in the book's conceptualization of global cinema. The first, perhaps most obvious level, is the global dimension of Hollywood blockbusters, as well as some other genres such as Asian horror films or Spaghetti Westerns that have acquired a global character and reached specific pockets of audience beyond their respective domestic markets. The second implied level of meaning is the new crop of films called "global films," termed as such because they lose their local embeddedness as texts and cultural products, and propagate the prowess of technique directed toward a vague universality. Films such as Zhang Yimou's enormously popular *Ying xiong/Hero* (2002), or Ang Lee's *Wo hu cang long/ Crouching Tiger, Hidden Dragon* (2000) became successful not because of cultural specificity but because they deploy and universalize the popular elements of the blockbuster. The era of globalization is marked by such products in other spheres as well. Tim Parks and Pankaj Mishra, for example, decry the rise of the "global novel" that escapes cultural particularity to present "homogenizing and depoliticizing" effects of narratives (Parks, 2010; Mishra, 2013). Both in the case of blockbusters and these global products, the use of *global* implies a shift toward homogenization, making it a difficult conceptual candidate to stand in for or replace *world cinema*.

The global dimension of cinema in Andrew's mapping connotes the interconnected nature of traffic, production, and distribution networks. For the first time, it is possible to say that a global community is immersed in the same film, creating a new boundary-less environment. The features of entropy and networks that suggest uncharted exchanges, influences, and the reception of films characterize this circulation traffic (Andrew, 2010a). International film festivals, the rapid transfers of films across the web, smart phones, and pirate channels transcend the traditional restricted channels of film traffic. The global is thus characterized by an experience of instantaneity in cinema that, chaotic as it may be, supplies a burst of energy hereto unseen in cinema.

In this environment, films and cinemas seek the attention of wider audiences, participating in an entropic energy. A cinephile or student today simply knows of more films and filmmakers than ever before. It is possible for students to know "the names of cineastes from Senegal, Mali and Burkina Faso whose work is funded in Europe and who expect to be screened on several continents" (Andrew, 2010a: vii). This suggests another dimension of the global that invokes a mode of address. That is, certain films address global audiences well beyond their immediate context, aspire to be part of the flow of global cinema, and draw attention from academic and critical circles. Speaking of such modes of address, however, Andrew implies a subtle system of exclusion in his conception of global cinema. Analyzing the (non)place or invisibility of Nollywood in global cinema, for example, he argues that Nollywood is an "anti-global phenomenon of stupendous proportions," since it has not participated in the global system of cinema or demanded attention in terms of circulation or analysis from Western academic film studies

(Andrew, 2010a: viii). Conceived in this manner, *global cinema* remains applicable only to global art cinema, films that circulate at film festivals and other art house film venues. As such, it excludes various other, oftentimes stronger currents in cinema such as Bollywood, Nollywood, or popular cinemas in different parts of the world. These currents similarly command a broader audience, and while they do get the attention of film scholars around the world, they tend to remain outside of the gambit of Eurocentric film studies.

A just and relevant conception of world cinema cannot be exclusionary, cannot privilege one discourse over the other, and yet has to provide pathways that allow us to see how films travel. It must account for the uneven and differentiated diversity of all cinemas in the world, not just art cinema. A systemic view of world cinema has to include Hollywood blockbusters, Asian horror films, and films that circulate in film festivals, as much as it has to include Bollywood and Nollywood as well as small, minor, diasporic, and other cinemas. The key here is that while we accept the totality of a system we must focus on mapping the relations between the elements in this system.

Hollywood is not world cinema

Hollywood rarely misses a chance to assert its claim on world cinema and it continues to be a dominant force around the world. In her opening monologue at the 71st Academy Awards in 1999, host Whoopi Goldberg remarked, "Tonight we gather to honor Hollywood's best, which is also the world's best. People came from all over the world to make movies, and those movies are seen all over the world." With its lofty claim that the best of Hollywood is also the best of world cinema, the most glamorous and coveted awards ceremony, the Oscars, is one of the most visible and uncritical celebrations of the global mastery of both Hollywood's product and its address. Major trade publications in the US continually report international revenues for its blockbusters, a sign of its innate confidence in dominating the world markets.[4] Undeniably, Hollywood is seen as the most significant force in the world for the quantity of box office tickets sold, gross box office profit, and the massive global distribution of its movies.[5]

Often, the global success of Hollywood is attributed not only to the financial power of the industry whose film budgets run to several hundred millions and which owns between forty to ninety percent of movies shown around the world, but to the narrative transparency of its storytelling. Studying the influence of Hollywood's aesthetic and narrative style on generations of filmmakers and viewers, David Bordwell famously asserted that to go beyond Hollywood, one must go through it; world cinema, therefore, denotes the global reach of Hollywood (Bordwell, 1985). His central thesis, that the classical Hollywood narrative style forms an aesthetic and narrative center against which other filmmakers and cinemas must negotiate their place, remains influential as a testament to its imperial power. Even in studies such as *Global Hollywood*, which approach Hollywood's hegemony critically and dissect in a nuanced and thorough manner the various material and cultural factors that contribute to Hollywood's global power, from the geographical relocation of cultural production to its relationship to world markets, the claim of Hollywood on world cinema is indisputable (Miller et al., 2001).

The technological, financial, and aesthetic prowess of Hollywood make it very difficult to formulate a conception of world cinema in which Hollywood does not stand as the dominant center. However, such a reductive view reduces other cinemas of the world to a relatively inferior, negative space. As Lúcia Nagib has argued, this perspective encourages the idea of world cinema as a "restrictive and negative" concept, defining *world cinema* as all cinema that is not Hollywood, existing at best on the periphery (2006: 30). While this view reinforces the notion that Hollywood is the center of world cinema, it is oblivious to the independence and power of other cinemas, some growing with distinct aesthetic and narrative identities of their own, staking significant space for themselves in world cinema. Nagib herself points to an example of Japanese cinema, which was prominent in the late 1930s and then in the mid-1950s in the number of films it produced, before it was surpassed by India in the 1970s (2006: 31). Challenging the singularity of Hollywood's dominance, these two cinemas claim a prominent berth in world cinema not merely for their strong production numbers but also for their influence and reach. Hollywood's power compels us to assess every other cinema in relation to its dominating presence, thus reducing other cinemas to the margins of the Hollywood-drawn world.

If Hollywood dominated world production and distribution for decades with its sheer glamour, publicity, and reach, other cinemas developed outside of its gambit, leading to a healthy diversity that has become impressively rich and complex. The most encouraging feature of the current picture of world cinema is the diversity and inexhaustible richness that flourishes despite the financial power and visibility of Hollywood. In smaller countries like Slovenia or larger markets like South Korea, Japan, and India, domestic cinema thrives in the face of Hollywood's presence and local producers have established themselves as leading players. In recent years, even the trade publications have routinely observed how various national film industries have been collecting a larger share of revenues against Hollywood blockbusters.[6] In 2013, examples of home-grown films outperforming the Hollywood fare such as *Man of Steel* and *World War Z* abound: *Chennai Express* (Rohit Shetty) in India, *Gam-si-ja-deul/Cold Eyes* (Ui-seok Jo, Byung-seo Kim) in South Korea, *Xiao shi dai/Tiny Times* (Guo Jingming) in China, *Kaze tachinu/The Wind Rises* (Hayao Miyazaki) in Japan, *Nosotros los Nobles/The Noble Family* (Gary Alazraki) in Mexico, *Foosball* (Juan José Campanella) in Argentina, *Legenda No. 17/Legend No. 17* (Nikolay Lebedev) in Russia, and many more. These local productions crushed their Hollywood counterparts at the box office in their respective countries, and were dubbed by the *Hollywood Reporter* as "the studios' new box office pain" (2013). By no means does this displace Global Hollywood as a dominant player in international markets, but it does force us to recognize a rising profile of other film industries and regional markets that stand alongside and on equal footing with Hollywood.

Judging the worth of cinemas based merely on box office figures and financial investment is misleading in understanding the role of cinema around the world. With different scales of budgets, technologies, labor, and aesthetic commitments, films continue to be produced in different parts of the world, and hardly any country is spared in the emerging picture of world cinema. These films flourish in varying degree of visibility, attempting to break the familiar territories of their audiences. All cinemas create their own spheres and participate in the current picture of world cinema. A systematic study of diverse and plural cinemas is possible only after bracketing the presence and power of Hollywood, and examining connections and intersections between Hollywood films and films made elsewhere.

The sheer power of Hollywood has also helped shape a certain sense of militancy to the notion of world cinema, perceived as everything that is not made in the image of Hollywood and that does not share its goals. This "oppositional, agile, low budget" cinema that "comes from a de-centered space of social, political and artistic discourse" forms one conception of world cinema, which has advantages in mobilizing certain artistic and political stances while also offering an antidote to the overwhelming power of Hollywood

(Chanan, 2011). However, while Hollywood cannot be equated to world cinema despite its own claims, it also cannot be written out of the larger map simply in the service of antagonism. Such a view provides an incomplete image of world cinema in which the power of Hollywood goes unquestioned and its relative strength remains unchallenged. Cinemas do not grow in isolation from each other, but form their identities in a system of relationships, where the powerful and the powerless occupy distinct yet fluid spaces. Thus, in a broadly systemic view of world cinema, Hollywood is one factor always inter-related to others, one component among many others.

Polycentric, polymorphic, and polyvalent world cinema

Many film scholars have made significant contributions to the development of a theo-retical framework for world cinema: Dudley Andrew, Lúcia Nagib, Stephanie Dennison and Song Hwee Lim, Nataša Ďurovičova, Rosalind Galt and Karl Schoonover, Shohini Chaudhuri, and Paul Cooke, among others.[7] Equally valuable insights have come from film scholars such as Paul Willemen, Michael Chanan, Dina Iordanova, David Martin-Jones, and Vincenz Hediger.[8] Their work underscores the importance of world cinema in contemporary film studies and presents us with a comprehensive and complex picture marked by two major themes. One, world cinema is a matter of *topography*, a way of defining and mapping the contours of the field and relationships among different ele-ments; and two, world cinema is a matter of *orientation*, perspective, or awareness of one's situatedness in the study of world cinema. "Any study of world cinema," Andrew says, "should put students inside unfamiliar conditions of viewing," implying an ever-expanding field outside of one's familiar world (2006: 19). He proposes an atlas—a col-lection of maps, each drawn with specific features. Maps, by definition, provide a place for each element and establish coordinates with other elements. The global dimension of films that we encounter is best grasped, Andrew contends, by "examining the overriding factors, then zero in on specific 'cinema sites'"—to navigate "the world of *world cinema*" (2006: 19). Considering world cinema as a part of a large system, Andrew's maps overlap with other models developed in film studies, together offering a comprehensive topogra-phy of and orientation in world cinema. To grasp the ever-changing complexity and the layered nature of this topography, we propose an approach to world cinema that anchors us positively in multiple loci and maps its numerous elements, as well as their intercon-nectedness and relationships of meaning.

Building on Andrew's approach, we propose three levels of approaching world cinema: *polycentric*, which includes multiple centers of activity and influence; *polymorphic*, which maps the relationships between different forms of cinema (transnational, diasporic, national cinema), each seen as a different manifestation of world cinema; and *polyvalent*, which focuses on multiple interpretations of films that are possible within the vast plurality of cultural perspectives. The unfamiliar worlds of films are unfamiliar to everyone in differ-ent ways, each interpreted differently from one's own ecosystem and inherently related to it. A *polyvalent* view allows for a multiplicity of orientations, without prioritizing any. These levels are by no means mutually exclusive, but rather provide different paths to understanding and approaching world cinema, and together account for its dynamic and heuristic networks. The specific films and cinemas we study may be simultaneously part of a polycentric system, situated in a specific center of power and activity, while they may also invoke national or transnational configurations. While polycentric perspective is a matter of topography (identifying different spheres as centers), a polymorphic perspective

acknowledges the current topographies of film studies (national, transnational, etc.) but urges their re-orientation to the totality of world cinema.

Beyond insisting on polyphonic voices destabilizing the hegemony of the West-centric approaches, we also have to emphasize the political significance of creating an egalitarian perspective where various constituents can register their voices. The radical insights of Jacques Rancière about the political dimension of aesthetics are of particular relevance for our project of "re-mapping" the current contours of world cinema. In Rancière's work, the operative principle of our shared experience of the world is what he calls "the distribution of the sensible/*partage du sensible*" (2004). This distribution consists of formal properties, laws, hierarchies embodied in the state or the established order of knowledge. It provides conditions of possibility for thought and perception, for what becomes visible and invisible, audible and inaudible, thinkable and unthinkable by our senses. Our experience of the world, the sensible, is thus structured through various regimes that delimit forms of inclusion and exclusion. Politics, for Rancière, is not a simple activist or oppositional gesture, but an assertion of voices excluded from these regimes that redistribute and reconfigure the sensible. The aim of aesthetic practice, of which cinema is part, is to achieve an egalitarian promise of the universal political axiom "we are all equal." To the extent that the distribution of the sensible partitions knowledge and the senses, it cannot advance equality. Therefore, politics allows people, ordinary people who have been excluded from distribution, to assert equality through aesthetic experience. That is, politics, rather than exercise of power, is assigning a visible and audible space to a particular object or sphere of experience. Rancière charts a path for all artistic expression to cause disruption in the order of the distribution of the sensible toward its redistribution.

The aim of cinema, argues Rancière in his *Intervals of Cinema* (2014), is not to provide an ideological critique, or to put representational analysis in service of finding deeper networks of meaning. Cinema needs to address the gaps/intervals that keep it away from achieving its goal of equality that is found in each moment a cinephile is immersed in the experience of films. Pedagogy, film theory, or any other meta-discourses structure knowledge from a vantage point of privilege. Therefore, breaking hierarchies in practice is for Rancière the first imperative in redistributing the sensible. The wide gulf between the elite corridors of knowledge and the experience of billions must be erased to approach the political dimension of experiencing cinema.

Rancière notes that writing on cinema faces two contradictory positions: to find words for the problems of cinema, its articulations and its gaps, and to value the experience of the cinephile, for whom a film is a "spectacle of shadows" and "residue of presences" that stay with us for a long time (2014: 8). The two positions are worlds apart. It is not a question of bridging the gap, but being acutely aware of the two contradictory dimensions of the sensible in which cinema operates. Decentering the existing hegemony is to redistribute the sensible, and to recognize the political dimension of that gesture. World cinema reaches out to us from various corners of the world, making it impossible to find a single heartbeat that sums up its expanse. For Francesco Casetti, the new realm of what he calls "expanded cinema" (new technologies, forms of production, modes of viewing) offers an arena of the global distribution of the sensible, where the new state of things breaks down the orderly sensorium and allows cinema to be accessible in various forms and on multiple levels, pointing to the egalitarian promise Rancière aspires to (2015: 125–127). Similarly, Kenneth W. Harrow turns to Rancière to institute a "metapolitics" where African cinema and Nollywood no longer negotiate their own positions vis-à-vis the colonialist subject, but put forward their own arguments, whose presence in the discourse is essential to the redistribution of the sensible (2013: 35). These subjects are not positioned in the antagonistic staging of resistance of earlier times, but move freely in a space of their own choosing, causing disruption to the existing order of things.

We introduce this dimension as a gesture that sets up a politics of the decentering project. The proposed five centers mark out spaces of conjunctive community for world cinema. Refusing hierarchy, the five centers and the polymorphic formations of different loci gesture toward an egalitarian politics of cinema, where theory and concepts reorient themselves to the central space of the spectators of world cinema, billions of whom redistribute the sensible each and every day.

Polycentric world cinema

Once Hollywood is displaced from its singular dominant place, world cinema appears to be made of multiple realms where production, visibility, and influence of various cinemas assume significant positions. As Lúcia Nagib et al. have suggested in their work, world cinema is a *polycentric* formation, defying the idea of a single center—most frequently Hollywood or European art cinema (Nagib et al., 2012). Building on this concept, we see world cinema as a field of cinematic power centers, each significant from its own position. Along with Hollywood's financial, distributive, and narrative power, Indian cinema and Bollywood, Asian cinemas (Japanese, Chinese, Hong Kong, Taiwanese, and South Korean cinema), European cinema, and Nigerian cinema or Nollywood present other cinematic centers. In terms of production and influence, these power centers present a collective snapshot of world cinema as it has emerged since the 1980s, and possess the following features: (1) a high level of cinematic activity; (2) the formation of their own spheres of influence, within and outside of their borders; and (3) a tradition of indigenous perspectives and scholarship on their cinemas. The map of world cinema seen through these centers effectively de-centers prevalent conceptions of this phenomenon. It allows for power to be seen from different loci in the world, each independent in some sense and each forming its own world of influence, while participating in the larger conception of world cinema. Power among them is not equal, and their differentiated status speaks to a number of factors such as financial power, aesthetic influence, cultural reach, technological dissemination, and a range of complex influences of political and social histories.

In terms of production numbers, Indian cinema leads with 1,966 films produced in 2015; video-films of Nollywood claim second place with well over 1,000 titles a year, and Hollywood is third with over 800 films. Japan, China, South Korea, Hong Kong, and other Asian countries produce over 1,100 films, and the European Union nations together produce over 1,500 films a year. Cinematic powers exert their presence with numbers, partly addressing their own audiences but in many ways widening their influence well beyond their borders and proximate regions. In distribution alone, Indian cinema, Bollywood in particular, covers large territories from West Asia to South East Asia, with a greater share now taken by diasporic audiences in North America, Africa, and Far East Asia. Asian cinema holds sway over this part of the world, but also has a significant influence on other cinemas, including Hollywood and European cinema. European cinema, in its complex diversity, makes a large contribution to the "global art cinema" valued by cinephiles in the West, along with a variety of domestic markets charting their own territories of influence. Nollywood asserts its presence not only through numbers, its unique aesthetic, and circulation, but also through its complex influence on African cinema in general. These power centers may be overwhelmed by Hollywood in the sheer strength of its capital, technology, and distribution networks, but in their own spheres they constitute a substantive part of world cinema.

Mapping world cinema through these five centers does not and should not eclipse their internal diversity and complexity. Just as Hollywood films merely form a larger monolith of the cinematic landscape in the US, overshadowing rich traditions of independent, documentary, and experimental film movements, each of these centers contains layers of complexity in their makeup. Indian cinema's projection of its strength on the global stage is always measured in terms of the formidable glare of Bollywood, but Indian cinema is rich with multiple language cinemas, from Bengali and Marathi cinema to Tamil and Karnataka film industries, which should not be equated with Bollywood or with mainstream Hindi cinema. Asian cinema contains within it multiple national traditions, engaged in a dynamic to present a collective profile to itself and to the world. Similarly, European cinema contains a vast diversity of national and regional cinematic traditions while projecting a collective identity.

Though these centers exert their own spheres of influence, and may be considered independent in some aspects, they are not isolated, evident in how they affect each other's growth or achievements. Adapting Moretti's world-systems model, Andrew says that an accurate model to describe spheres of influence for various components of world cinema is that of "waves," or how some specific development in one cinema has repercussions not only in adjacent cultures but also in different corners of the world. His celebrated example of how the French New Wave "rolled around the world" affecting the "cinema cultures of Britain, Japan, Cuba, Brazil, Yugoslavia and Taiwan" clearly points to the systemic influences of one cinema upon the other (Andrew, 2006: 22). Similar claims can be made regarding the influence of Hong Kong cinema on Hollywood, Hollywood on Bollywood, or European cinema's clout on art cinemas around the world. These influences are a corrective to traditional tendencies in classifying national cinemas, where each national cinema is seen as a rather isolated phenomenon, escaping the dialectical influences in its growth. As we discuss in the introduction, the centers do not provide an exhaustive account of the landscape of world cinema, and specific cases may be included, such as Latin American cinema or Russian cinema, to extend our map of world cinema beyond the five centers.

In various ways, these centers of influence have received sustained attention in Anglo-American film studies, and the studies devoted to each of them are rich and diverse. It is important to note, however, that each of these power centers have developed their own perspectives on their cinemas that tend to be ignored or obscured.[9] Growing scholarship on these centers attempts to both negotiate its place in relation to Western film theory and philosophy, and to find anchors in their own cultural traditions for understanding cinematic experience. Recognition of perspectives grounded in their own cultural contexts is an imperative for all scholars who respect the multiplicity of world cinema. Culturally and historically germane debates not only speak for the embedded cinematic traditions, but also raise healthy questions regarding determinism or hegemony of certain theoretical models and the need for cross-cultural understanding.

In her incisive and timely critique of film theory in the age of globalization, Masha Salazkina argues that while the dynamics of border crossing have redefined our objects of study, they have not informed our "experience of intellectual and theoretical process" that dictates our methodologies (2015: 332). Despite the rapidly growing amount of scholarship on previously ignored geopolitical regions, "theory" is still largely presumed to be a universal framework. If we accept that film culture is a global phenomenon, we also need to think about it globally and pay attention to "what kind of discourses have emerged elsewhere to conceptualize cinematic experience" (Salazkina, 2015: 337). A serious obstacle in this endeavor is that an extensive account of various traditions remains beyond our reach, partly due to what Salazkina describes as "the crisis of translation": the fact that translated contemporary works in film and media studies from outside of the disciplinary metropole are "far and few between" (2015: 340). To remedy this problem is an extensive and long-term task, but ours is a decisive and systematic gesture toward the effort to uncover various geopolitical vantage points that burst open our analytical tools and categories.

Polymorphic world cinema

The complexity of world cinema cannot be grasped at once, but in smaller steps and through different methodologies. When cinema morphs itself into world cinema in the late 1980s, the existing coordinates of studying various cinemas had to be reexamined. Film studies had already put in place different models for understanding a variety of frameworks through which to examine various cinemas. Each of these now has to be seen as part of a large system of world cinema. Our polymorphic model of world cinema utilizes the current models as pathways to map world cinema. We cannot consider national cinema such as that of Mexico, for example, in isolation from others, as propagating a vision that is separate and independent from other cinemas. Various forces such as international finance, festival circulation, and cross-national reception influence the identity of Mexican cinema. Many of its directors, from Alfonso Cuarón and Alejandro González Iñárritu to Guillermo del Toro and Rodrigo García are working outside of their national film industry, pointing not only to the reconfiguration of Mexican national cinema but also of Hollywood (over the last twenty years, eleven winners of the Best Director Academy Award have been from outside of the US). Similarly, Abbas Kiarostami (Iran), Wong Kar-wai (Hong Kong), and Bong Joon-ho (South Korea), while often showcased as representatives of their respective countries at international film festivals, are seen as "global art house" directors. Thus, traditional categories of analysis, from national to transnational cinemas, from small to minor or diasporic and postcolonial cinemas, far from being obsolete, need to be recognized in their fluidity and with a renewed configuration in the systemic construction of world cinema.

Various directions have emerged in demonstrating the interdependence of cinemas. Miriam Hansen steadfastly refutes the dominant model of how "the classical" cinema influenced other cinemas, shaping them into layers of affiliations and similarities (2010). Instead, she advocates a model that allows cinemas to affect each other horizontally, as if participating in the same system. The question for Hansen is "how particular film practices can be productively understood as *responding* . . . to the set of technological, economic, social, and perceptual transformations associated with the term modernity" (2010: 294). Her notion of cinema as "vernacular modernism" conceives of it as a heterotopic practice that "brings into play the impact of capitalist-industrial modernization and other aspects of modernity" (2010: 295). The dominant model of Hollywood interacted with vernacular modernisms around the world, forging affiliations of their own that were inflected by a larger culture. Hansen illustrates this through the example of films in China and Japan that were in continuous negotiations with Hollywood's globalizing vernacular, blending this vernacular with their own forms and interactions.

The illustrative aspect of Hansen's argument has persisted in other directions as well. For Andrew, cinemas develop their blended identities through waves of influence that travel not only to its proximate regions but also to the far corners of the cinematic world. He refines this concept by adapting the term of "*décalage*," a phased "discrepancy in space and deferral or jump in time" (Andrew, 2010b: 60). The earlier image of waves is here seen through differential phases in which films affect each other through space, but where their impact is also registered in a series of temporal slippages and delays. Of course, this transfer hardly takes place systematically in a systemic world. Andrew outlines five phases of these transformations and exchanges (national, cosmopolitan, the federated, world, and global cinema), where the fourth phase of world cinema is most prominently exemplified by the work of Zhang Yimou and his Fifth Generation peers, who immersed themselves in Chinese painting and literature, "soaked up the classic Chinese, Soviet, and Hollywood films," and the modernist works of Resnais, Tarkovsky, and Scorsese, and blended these influences with their own narrative style (Andrew, 2010b: 79). In contrast, Hou Hsiao-hsien's work is marked by an entirely different system of exchanges, Andrew points out, as his style develops largely away from Japanese and European influences and is derived primarily from Taiwan's own neorealist literary traditions. While he helps shape the Taiwanese New Wave in the 1980s through distinctly local material, Hou Hsiao-hsien also becomes a global celebrity and encourages young Taiwanese filmmakers to adapt to regional and global influences (Andrew, 2010b: 80).

Paul Willemen's "comparative studies approach" further advances the systemic inter-connectedness proposed by Hansen and Andrew (2005). Willemen rejects the universalism implied in the prevailing notions of world cinema that cloud the specificities of different cinemas. Equally important, cinemas need not be defined by the interest of those perched in the West. His comparative studies approach, instead, proposes that a common factor affecting all cinemas in the world is their encounter with the forces of capitalism. Willemen's aim is to find spaces for multiple voices, even as some of them do not register on the decibel level available to Western cinema. This model, he believes, would allow national cinemas to express specific manifestations of their own uneven patterns that are responding to conditions similar to other cinemas. Arguing that cinemas are facing a common force of (global) capital, his model of comparative cinema reveals the hierarchies and uneven developments that are at the forefront of globalization. Similar attempts to think of world cinema as part of a larger totality of world cultures has come from Fredric Jameson (2009) in his proposition of a "geopolitical" approach to cinema, where he advances the thesis that cinemas around world are shaped by the uneven forces of globalization. In his view, various cinemas struggle to acquire visibility in the same system of globalization; some of them succeed, while others remain relegated to a peripheral status. Thus, various components of world cinema are in a state of uneven development in a process that is symptomatic of the effects of globalization.

To return again to a visual metaphor, if peaks and spikes represented the polycentric view, then a polymorphic view of world cinema is captured as a geological formation, with crests and crevices, multiple layers, and interconnected surfaces. Add to it the dimension of time, and we get a dynamic polymorphism that shows how cinematic developments are connected, revealing temporal loops and slippages.

Polyvalent world cinema

For the third level of world cinema, two points of theoretical departure are important. First, Andrew bookends his atlas of world cinema with the pedagogical need to place the students of world cinema "inside unfamiliar conditions of viewing" rather than to conveniently translate for them all things foreign. "World Cinema should let us *know the territory differently*, whatever territory it is that a film comes from or concerns" (Andrew, 2006: 28). This experience of displacement always begins with watching specific films. When we encounter the worlds outside of one's own, we take the first step toward world cinema. Such an encounter with a film initiates a process of exploration and mapping where both the viewer's orientation and a film's place in the world reveal themselves.

The concept of polyvalence is about an understanding of how each film is perceived differently in different parts of the world, the fact that "every film is a foreign film, foreign to some audience somewhere" (Egoyan & Balfour, 2004: 21). Borrowed from the sciences as well as humanities and arts, *polyvalence* suggests multiple uses of the same object, the ability of things to be deployed differently in different contexts. If one of the founding premises of world cinema is that films are seen outside of their own cultural borders, then we must recognize that they are interpreted from different vantage points. Thus, de-centering Hollywood's hegemony in the conception of world cinema also means that the privileging of interpretations from Western observers must yield to the multitude of perspectives from elsewhere, and that every film and every viewer, no matter how global their claim, embodies a specific geopolitical orientation.

The unique context of multiple perspectives explains, for example, why *Slumdog Millionaire* (Danny Boyle, 2008) was widely acclaimed in the West as a triumphant adaptation of Bollywood conventions, while it failed to gain any traction in India, where it was negatively received both for its Orientalism and failed appropriation of Bollywood cinema. Polyvalence explains why American audiences found palatable the Hong Kong blockbuster *Yi dai zong shi/The Grandmaster* (Wong Kar-wai, 2013) only after it was re-edited and re-appropriated by its American distributor, the Weinstein Company, which stripped the film of its historical complexity and foregrounded a love story and the stylized aesthetic of kung fu action.[10] Further, it explains how global entertainment spectacle *Avatar* (James Cameron, 2009) was appropriated differently as a political film in various countries. As Yosefa Loshitzky explains, the film was seen as subversive and was removed from screens across China; seen by Bolivia's president Evo Morales as a resistance to capitalism and defense of nature; read in Britain as the story of European destruction of the Americas; and appropriated by Palestinians as an allegory of their grass-roots resistance to Israel's occupation of their land and natural resources (Loshitzky, 2012). These examples show that films mean something different to different viewers, and while the global world in which they circulate today suggests simultaneity of place and time, we are in fact all situated differently.

Dennison and Hwee Lim already posed a problem of world cinema as a problem of perspective:

> To situate World Cinema as a theoretical problem is to question not just what world cinema is but also to/for whom it is a problem, in what contexts, how and why; to interrogate to what purposes does it serve, under what kinds of mechanisms of power does it operate, and what audiences does it seek to address or perhaps empower.
>
> (2006: 9)

They point out that the conception of world cinema that has emerged in film studies serves only the interests of the Western academy and indeed Western viewer. Though it appears that the discourse on world cinema is dominant in the Western academy, multiple voices exist elsewhere that urge us to redraw the familiar map, turn it on its head.

In a recent volume that defines world cinema from the perspective of the "cinema of periphery," Iordanova's group project offers a paradigm that challenges entrenched canons of both film historiography and perspectives in film studies, aiming to "unveil and acknowledge a vibrant multitude of creative voices and forms of expression that originate and dwell well beyond and outside of commonly celebrated cultural hubs" (Iordanova, Martin-Jones, & Vidal, 2010: 3). It offers a discursive space to cinematic texts and traditions obscured in dominant histories—from the Scottish-Gaelic cinema to Australian Aboriginal cinema and the cinema of Québec—not to position them against the global power of Hollywood, but rather to change perspective and investigate how the world cinema landscape changes when these radically marginal voices are put center stage.

Thus, polyvalence is about seeing the world from the perspective of the periphery to displace the relationship between the center and periphery in world cinema, and to acknowledge that "there are multiple possible avenues to an artistic status quo" (Iordanova et al., 2010: 2). Given both the dominance of Western academic discourse in film studies and the difficulty of finding access to or scholarship on some of these cinemas, the task of allowing full articulation for these polyphonic voices appears to be a monumentally difficult task. But as Iordanova argues in the same volume, consistent efforts would eventually reveal "the suppressed treasure trove of cinematic content of peripheral cinema" (2010: 25). Polyvalent perspective recognizes that such efforts are an essential part of world cinema.

Since the first and primary encounter of a viewer with world cinema is through individual films, it is crucial to examine films to find the contours and the scope of the world they represent. Andrew calls for examining the film *as* map—cognitive map—while placing the film *on* the map, addressing the question of "How does a fictional universe from another part of the world orient its viewers to their global situation?" (Andrew, 2006: 16). Following Jameson's important formulation of "cognitive mapping," this activity becomes synonymous with establishing the film's coordinates in the map of world cinema, but is also about locating the orientation that is inscribed in the film itself. Approaching a film, one finds a figurative representation of the totality of world cinema, how the film projects its cultural borders (national, diasporic, small cinemas) and defines its scope (in identities, ideologies, etc.). Cognitive mapping is thus a double process whereby a film simultaneously exhibits its relation to world cinema and is also an embedded map of the world itself. Both steps begin with a polyvalent view, an awareness of how the viewers, and a given film, are situated in a specific context.

What world cinema is: from watching films to mapping cinema

All attempts at studying world cinema begin by watching films. Conceptual maps and theoretical models become necessary when the film is to be placed on a map to understand its geo-cultural coordinates. This process is at the heart of new world cinema, and it values both the fundamental encounter with films and the conceptual maps that guide us in understanding them.

In the Coen brothers' short film *World Cinema* (2007) made for the anthology *Chacun son cinéma/To Each His Own Cinema* (2007) a rancher type named Dan walks into a theater in the middle of nowhere playing two cinema classics: Jean Renoir's *Le règle de jeu/The Rules of the Game* (1939) and Nuri Bilge Ceylan's *Iklimler/Climates* (2006). Since he has never heard of either of the features, a helpful ticket clerk, Dimitri, guides his choice and assures him that both are masterpieces in their own right, and yes, they do include "the words up there to help follow the story along" (i.e. subtitles). Exasperated at the thought of watching a film with subtitles, Dan proceeds to inquire if there is nudity or livestock in either of the films. He finally decides to see *Climates*, and ends up wowed, confused but visibly enchanted by something profoundly unfamiliar. He may have no knowledge of Turkish cinema, no context in which to place and understand Ceylan's work, and may ultimately be deprived of the discussion he is clearly eager to have about the film with Dimitri (since his shift is over). Nevertheless, he connects with the film, relates to it and understands it on some level, asking the new ticket clerk to "tell Dimitri that the guy in the hat enjoyed the hell out of *Climates*," adding, "there's a helluva lot of truth in it."

In Wim Wenders's short film from the same anthology, titled *War in Peace*, a small village in Congo is screening films. A worn-out chalkboard outside displays the show times for three films from different parts of the world, all action films: *Shi mian mai fu/House of Flying Daggers* (2004) by Zhang Yimou, *Black Hawk Down* (2001) by Ridley Scott, and *Xi yang tian shi/So Close* (2002) by Corey Yuen. A small generator supplies power to the mud-covered stone building where an audience of mostly children is watching *Black Hawk Down*. The faces of children and a few men are shown in close-ups as they listen to the sounds of war and watch the spectacular images of violence in a Hollywood film. They appear strained, scared, and withdrawn; the images of war in the midst of a lived experience of war seem too much to bear. The children begin to leave the film theater, and soon a group of them are seen dancing in silhouette against the colors of twilight that grace the African skies. Wenders ends the film with captions on the persistence of violence in Congo, both current and historical.

In our third example, *The First Movie* (2009) by Mark Cousins, the filmmaker takes a collection of films and film cameras to Goptapa, a small village in the northern Iraqi Kurdish region. The children there have never before seen a film. As Cousins sets up an outdoor screen, they gather together to watch films, including Astrid Henning-Jensen's *Palle alene i verden/Palle Alone in the World* (1949), Mohammad Ali-Talebi's *Chakmeh/The Boot* (1993), and Steven Spielberg's *ET the Extra-Terrestrial* (1982). Initial bemusement quickly turns to excitement and unbound curiosity. Confronting the world of images entirely different from their own, children in Goptapa place cinema in the intermediate space between reality and imagination. Intrigued by it, they see cinema as a medium that is a part of, and expands, their world.

The three examples present three different locations where viewers embedded in their own cultures watch films from outside their own familiar contexts. The Coen brothers' film is simultaneously an admiring and humorous take on a cowboy-rancher watching art cinema, a nod to the remotely located theaters that screen films without an eye to the box office, and a fruitful commentary on how cinema is absorbed by the multitude of viewers. Dan deciphers films from his own vantage point, curious about the possible links to his own world but open to the experiences they bring. He is the first candidate for world cinema, making the most of what is available to him. Wim Wenders's film, with its mixed ambitions to comment on the Congo war and place cinema at the heart of the village life, brings forth the connect and disconnect between film images and the lived realities of the spaces in which films are seen. Children in this Congolese village (women are at home and men are at war!) cannot stomach the images of war since they brush painfully against their daily and personal experiences. The distant world of films is all too close to them. In Mark Cousins's film, the harshness of living conditions is softened and enriched by the encounters with cinema, and films open up as yet-unexplored worlds of imagination.

Even as they occupy different spaces, contexts, and experiences, at the heart of all three shorts lays a wide-eyed curiosity about films from different parts of the world.

In this way, these films draw out a kind of a microcosm of world cinema, where encounters with films open up worlds other than one's own. It is impossible to grasp their plurality except to begin somewhere and recognize that the merging paths of world cinema are intricately connected, and that world cinema looks different from different vantage points around the world. From the perspective of international film festivals, films by Abbas Kiarostami, Wong Kar-wai, Tsai Ming-liang, Carlos Reygadas, Béla Tarr, Mira Nair, Clair Denis, Atom Egoyan, and Lars von Trier are obvious candidates of world cinema. Scholars like Adrian Martin emphasize filmmakers who make outstanding contributions to cinematic form but remain relatively invisible: for him, Raúl Ruiz, Peter Tscherkassky, Philippe Grandrieux, Hou Hsiao-hsien, and Philippe Garrel all come to constitute "a kind of underground art cinema" (Martin, 2007). In yet another sphere of small and minor cinema studies, films by Veiko Õunpuu, Jan Cvitkovič, Aktan Abdykalykov, Sarah Maldoror, Álvaro Brechner, Oscar Godoy, and Athina Rachel Tsangari struggle to break out of the limited exposure they get at regional film festivals. Beyond these circles of recognition, what do we make of *cinepanettone* in Italy, *cine piquetero* in Argentina, or the internationalist cinema that is militant and experimental? And how does one accommodate the films from Palestine or regional cinemas of India? What about cinemas from the settler societies and Roma communities? And how do we approach Nollywood cinema, a powerful film industry which nevertheless struggles to gain visibility beyond its borders? Rarely discussed, these cinemas nevertheless bear an indelible stamp of world cinema.

World cinema is not just a gesture of including these cinematic voices but the process of identifying the factors and forces that either gain, or prevent them from gaining, visibility. If the concept of world cinema is accepted as an open territory where the issue of uneven visibility and power dynamic between its various components is put center stage and becomes key to our understanding of the territory, then it is possible to consider the totality as an opportunity to carefully map and study the relationships between them and consider in a comparative sense their relative visibility. If we maintain the basic tenet of world cinema that films are to be seen in cultural contexts outside of their own, then the spheres of visibility are fluid for different films. Each form of cinema, from European art cinema to minor or peripheral cinema, is caught in this politics of visibility where its capacity to reach wider audiences is a result of intervening forces of economics and institutional and state power. Each of these cinemas needs to be granted a perspective to conceive of world cinema from its own vantage point, while mapping its relations of power to the larger spheres of influence.

The "online abundance" that Iordanova (2014) writes about, the newly emerging films that can be accessed thanks to the fast-growing online dissemination system of films and clips, makes such a project all the more urgent and feasible. Particularly important is the extent to which this instant and abundant accessibility (issues of piracy notwithstanding) facilitates comparisons, juxtapositions, and aesthetic investigations of cinematic influences that were until now the privileged preserve of film scholars and historians. For Iordanova, even more exciting than the plethora of films is the new public sphere that has opened up outside of the academic circles to study world cinema, and we share her call to students and scholars to make use of the available resources: "There is now no excuse for ignorance of other cinemas or traditions or films. Comparative work is made easier, especially for projects that concern peripheral interactions" (Iordanova, 2014: 50). The emerging community of cinephiles in the US and Western and Eastern Europe, and in other countries, including South Africa, Turkey, and India, provide for another front in exploring world cinema. Whether it is online forums, blogs, websites, or cultures formed around streaming services, a continually expanding sphere has emerged, neatly chronicled by Jonathan Rosenbaum and Adrian Martin in their *Movie Mutations: The Changing Face of World Cinephilia*, where they note a "mysterious phenomenon of . . . global synchronicity" and cinephilia fueled by the easy access as much as by the development of shared film cultures. They observe that in these situations we "open ourselves to the world in ways that will be vital and generative," giving rise not only to new communities of cinephiles but also to new worlds of cinema and bodies of knowledge surrounding them (Rosenbaum & Martin, 2008: 61).

This emerging and already very vital realm of global cinephilia has transcended much of the contentious theoretical issues regarding Eurocentrism or the problematic dominance of Hollywood in world cinema. Online communities thrive on discovery, and their enthusiasm, unchecked at times, is clearly infectious. What used to be impromptu or planned discussion groups in film societies or cafés, and later university classrooms, has moved online with greater intensity and greater worldly character than ever before. Considered alongside the cautious, deliberate, and methodical discourse of the academic world, the persistent gap between these two realms seems surprising if not discouraging. For a true recognition of world cinema with global dimensions, these two worlds need to come together in a more fluid and less restrictive system of exchange. Surely filmmakers and film viewers, as well as film students, would welcome such a synergy of voices that already defines and energizes world cinema.

In his panoramic and layered account of the history of cinema, presented in a fifteen-chapter documentary *The Story of Film: An Odyssey* (2011), Mark Cousins continuously alludes to the fluid and dynamic aspect of cinema, as if to demonstrate emphatically that national and aesthetic boundaries never existed for the practitioners of cinema. He de-centers the power of Hollywood and sets out to demonstrate how cinema grows organically through ideas, images, motifs, and artistic impulses. Profits may be the engines of moneymakers, but for filmmakers the many worlds of images grow in tandem with each other. From one film to another and from one director to another, Cousins shows that cinema does not grow on the agenda of power or on the dictates of the market but on the artistic exchanges, the riffs, and the meta-connections that filmmakers make from one film to another. This account of cinema as an energetic medium of images across cultures, without the preset properties ascribed to it, is at the center of what world cinema is. It is a medium with very porous boundaries, if any. This is true for Gypsy filmmakers as it is for the sub-Saharan practitioners. It is true for amateur filmmakers in Eastern Europe as it is for aspiring professionals in Latin America. The multiple worlds of the variety of film practices and cultures must be brought closer to the world of scholarship, and Mark Cousins's account of world cinema certainly comes a step closer to this goal.

Notes

1 The two metaphors of the tree and of the wave are then adopted by Dudley Andrew in his seminal approach to world cinema, "An Atlas of World Cinema," in Stephanie Dennison and Song Hwee Lim (eds), *Remapping World Cinema*. New York, NY: Wallflower Press, 2006, pp. 19–29.
2 For a more extended discussion of this issue, see Aijaz Ahmed (2010), "'Show Me the Zulu Proust:' Some Thoughts on World Literature," *Revista Brasileira de Literatura Comparada* 17, pp. 11–45; and David Damrosch (2009), "Frames of World Literature," *Grenzen der Literatur: Zu Begriff und Phänomen des Literarischen*. Berlin/New York, NY: Walter de Gruyter, pp. 494–515.

3 See, for example, A.O. Scott, "What is a Foreign Movie Now?" *New York Times*, November 14, 2004, www.nytimes.com/2004/11/14/movies/14WORLD.html; Carrie Rickey, "Americans are Seeing Fewer and Fewer Foreign Films," Philly.com, May 9, 2010, http://articles.philly.com/2010-05-09/entertainment/24959939_1_foreign-language-films-american-film-foreign-films; A.O. Scott, "A Golden Age for Foreign Films, Mostly Unseen," *New York Times*, January 26, 2011, www.nytimes.com/2011/01/30/movies/awardsseason/30scott.html?_r=1&ref=movies; Jon Henley, "Foreign Cinema is Expanding Our Horizons," *The Guardian*, March 31, 2011, www.theguardian.com/film/2011/mar/31/foreign-film-festival-expand-horizons; and Jason Bailey, "Why Do Foreign Films have to be Dumbed Down for American Audiences," *Flavorwire*, August 20, 2013, http://flavorwire.com/410720/why-do-foreign-films-have-to-be-dumbed-down-for-american-audiences/

4 See, for example, "International Box Office," *Variety*, http://variety.com/v/film/international/; "International Box Office," *Screen Daily*, www.screendaily.com/box-office/international-box-office; or "Worldwide Box Office Grosses," *Box Office Guru*, December 26, 2013, www.boxofficeguru.com/intl.htm

5 This is explored more in depth in Chapter 3 on production practices. Of thirty-one surveyed countries, twenty-four see more than fifty percent of their box office admission for a U.S. movie. Of twenty top films worldwide by gross box office, all of them are at least partly Hollywood produced.

6 See, for example, a discussion of this phenomenon in the case of Korean cinema in Lee Hyo-won, "Korea Box Office 2013," *Hollywood Reporter*, December 26, 2013, www.hollywoodreporter.com/gallery/korea-box-office-2013-top-667379

7 See, for example, Dudley Andrew, "An Atlas of World Cinema," in Stephanie Dennison and Song Hwee Lim (eds), *Remapping World Cinema*, New York, NY: Wallflower Press, 2006, pp. 19–30; Lúcia Nagib, Chris Perriam, and Rajinder Dudrah (eds), *Theorizing World Cinema*, New York, NY: I.B. Tauris, 2012; Nataša Ďurovičová and Kathleen Newman (eds), *World Cinemas, Transnational Perspectives*, New York, NY: Routledge, 2010; Rosalind Galt and Karl Schoonover (eds), *Global Art Cinema: New Theories and Histories*, London: Oxford University Press, 2010; Shohini Chaudhuri, *Contemporary World Cinema: Europe, the Middle East, East Asia and South Asia*, Edinburgh University Press, 2005; and Paul Cooke (ed), *World Cinema's Dialogues with Hollywood*, Palgrave Macmillan, 2007.

8 Paul Willemen, "For a Comparative Film Studies," *Inter-Asia Cultural Studies* 6(1), 2005, pp. 98–112; Michael Chanan, "Who's for World Cinema?" A Paper for "The Wild Things of World Cinema," King's College, London, Postgrad Conference, 2011; David Martin-Jones, *Deleuze and World Cinemas*, New York: Continuum, 2011; Dina Iordanova, David Martin-Jones, and Belén Vidal, *Cinema at the Periphery*, Wayne State University Press, 2010; and Vincenz Hediger, "What Do We Know When We Know Where Something Is? World Cinema and the Question of Spatial Ordering," *Screening the Past*, www.screeningthepast.com/2013/10/what-do-we-know-when-we-know-where-something-is-world-cinema-and-the-question-of-spatial-ordering/

9 See, for example, Saer Maty Ba and Will Higbee (eds), *De-Westernizing Film Studies*, New York, NY: Routledge, 2012; or George Semsel (ed), *Chinese Film Theory: A Guide to the New Era*, New York, NY: Praeger, 1990.

10 A similar controversy about re-appropriation for American audiences surrounds Bong Joon-ho's *Snowpiercer* (2013), also distributed by the Weinstein Company.

Bibliography

Andrew, Dudley. (2006). "An Atlas of World Cinema." In Stephanie Dennison & Song Hwee Lim (eds), *Remapping World Cinema*. New York, NY: Wallflower Press, pp. 19–30.

Andrew, Dudley. (2010a). "Foreword." In Rosalind Galt & Karl Schoonover (eds), *Global Art Cinema: New Theories and Histories*. London: Oxford University Press, pp. v–xi.

Andrew, Dudley. (2010b). "Time Zones and Jetlag: The Flows and Phases of World Cinema." In Nataša Ďurovičova & Kathleen Newman (eds), *World Cinema, Transnational Perspectives*. New York, NY: Routledge, pp. 59–89.

Apter, Emily. (2013). *Against World Literature: On the Politics of Untranslatability*. London: Verso.

Bordwell, David. (1985). *The Classical Hollywood Cinema: Film Style and Mode of Production to 1960*. New York, NY: Columbia University Press.

Brenez, Nicole & Donal Foreman. (2012). "L'art le plus politique: Nicole Brenez with Donal Foreman." Interview by Donal Foreman, translated by Youna Kwak. *The Brooklyn Rail: Critical Perspectives on Arts, Politics, and Culture.* Available at: www.brooklynrail.org/2012/04/film/lart-le-plus-politiquenicole-brenez-with-donal-foreman

Casetti, Francesco. (2015). *The Lumiere Galaxy: Seven Key Words for the Cinema to Come.* New York, NY: Columbia University Press.

Chanan, Michael. (2011). "Who's For 'World Cinema'?" A Paper For "The Wild Things of World Cinema," Film Studies, King's College London, Graduate Student Conference, May 13. Available at: www.mchanan.com/wp-content/uploads/2010/08/Reflections-on-World-Cinema.pdf

Damrosch, David. (2003). *What Is World Literature?* Princeton, NJ: Princeton University Press.

Damrosch, David & Gayatri Chakravorty Spivak. (2011). "Comparative Literature/World Literature: A Discussion." *Comparative Literature Studies* 48(4), pp. 455–485.

Değirmenci, Koray. (2010). "Homegrown Sounds of Istanbul: World Music, Place, and Authenticity." *Turkish Studies* 11(2), pp. 251–268.

Dennison, Stephanie & Song Hwee Lim. (2006). "Situating World Cinema as a Theoretical Problem." In Stephanie Dennison & Song Hwee Lim (eds), *Remapping World Cinema: Identity, Culture and Politics in Film.* New York, NY: Wallflower Press, pp. 1–18.

de Turégano, Teresa Hoefert. (2012). "Transnational Cinematic Flows: World Cinema as World Music." *Film Studies for Free.* Available at: http://cmsw.mit.edu/mit2/Abstracts/wcwmart2.pdf. Accessed June 10, 2014.

Egoyan, Atom & Ian Balfour. (2004). "Introduction." *In Subtitles: On the Foreignness of Film.* Cambridge, MA: MIT Press, pp. 21–32.

Galt, Rosalind & Schoonover, Karl (eds). (2010a). "Introduction: The Impurity of Art Cinema." In *Global Art Cinema: New Theories and Histories.* London: Oxford University Press, pp. 3–27.

Galt, Rosalind & Schoonover, Karl (eds). (2010b). *Global Art Cinema: New Theories and Histories.* London: Oxford University Press.

Hansen, Miriam. (2010). "Vernacular Modernism: Tracking Cinema on a Global Scale." In Nataša Ďurovičova & Kathleen Newman (eds), *World Cinema, Transnational Perspectives.* New York, NY: Routledge, pp. 287–314.

Harrow, Kenneth W. (2013). *Trash: African Cinema from Below.* Bloomington, IN: Indiana University Press.

Hollywood Reporter. (2013). "Studios' New Box Office Pain: Homegrown Films are Beating Tentpoles Overseas." Available at: www.hollywoodreporter.com/gallery/studios-new-box-office-pain-606636#4-russia-legend-no-17. Accessed June 21, 2014.

Iordanova, Dina. (2014). "Instant, Abundant, and Ubiquitous: Cinema Moves Online." *Cineaste* 49(1), pp. 46–51.

Iordanova, Dina, David Martin-Jones, & Belén Vidal (eds). (2010). *Cinema at the Periphery.* Detroit, MI: Wayne State University Press.

Jameson, Fredric. (2009). *The Geopolitical Aesthetic: Cinema and Space in the World System.* Bloomington, IN: Indiana University Press.

Loshitzky, Yosefa. (2012). "Popular Cinema as Popular Resistance: *Avatar* in the Palestinian Imagi(nation)." *Third Text* 26(2), pp. 151–163.

Martin, Adrian. (2007). "Conversation Between Adrian Martin and Miradas de Cine." *Cinemascope* 7 (January–April). Available at: www.cinemascope.it/Issue%207/Articoli_n7/Articoli_n7_05/Adrian_Martin.pdf. Accessed June 10, 2014.

McLuhan, Marshall. (1994). *Understanding Media: The Extensions of Man.* Cambridge, MA: MIT Press, reprint edition.

Miller, Toby, Nitin Govil, John McMurria & Richard Mawell. (2001). *Global Hollywood.* London: BFI Publishing.

Mishra, Pankaj. (2013). "Beyond the Global Novel." *Financial Times,* September 27. Available at: www.ft.com/content/6e00ad86-26a2-11e3-9dc0-00144feab7de. Accessed June 10, 2014.

Moretti, Franco. (2000). "Conjectures on World Literature." *New Left Review* 1, pp. 54–68.

Nagib, Lúcia. (2006). "Toward a Positive Definition of World Cinema." In Stephanie Dennison & Song Hwee Lim (eds), *Remapping World Cinema: Identity, Culture and Politics in Film*. New York, NY: Wallflower Press, pp. 30–37.

Nagib, Lúcia, Chris Perriam, & Rajinder Dudrah (eds). (2012). *Theorizing World Cinema*. New York, NY: I.B. Tauris.

Parks, Tim. (2010). "The Dull New Global Novel." *New York Review of Books*, February 9. Available at: www.nybooks.com/daily/2010/02/09/the-dull-new-global-novel. Accessed June 12, 2014.

Rancière, Jacques. (2004). *The Politics of Aesthetics*. Trans. Gabriel Rockhill. New York, NY: Continuum.

Rancière, Jacques. (2014). *The Intervals of Cinema*. Trans. John Howe. New York, NY: Verso.

Rosenbaum, Jonathan & Adrian Martin (eds). (2008). *Movie Mutations: The Changing Face of World Cinephilia*. London: BFI Film Classics.

Ross, Kristin. (1993). "The World Literature and Cultural Studies." *Critical Inquiry* 19(4), pp. 666–676.

Salazkina, Masha. (2015). "Introduction: Film Theory in the Age of Neoliberal Globalization." *Framework: The Journal of Cinema and Media* 56(2), pp. 325–349.

Spivak, Gayatri Chakravorty. (2003). *Death of a Discipline*. New York, NY: Columbia University Press.

Willemen, Paul. (2005). "For a Comparative Film Studies." *Inter-Asia Cultural Studies* 6(1), pp. 98–112.

2 Watching world cinema

Figure 2.1 In Atom Egoyan's *Artaud Double Bill* (2007), two friends, Anna and Nicole, watch films in different theaters and share their experience through their smart phones

Atom Egoyan's short film *Artaud Double Bill* from the anthology *Chacun son cinéma/ To Each His Own Cinema* (2007) has become one of the most eloquent and provocative articulations of the fast-changing state of film exhibition and viewership in our times. In it, two friends, Anna and Nicole, plan to meet each other at the movies but somehow end up in different theaters watching different films: Anna is in a theater showing Jean-Luc Godard's *Vivre sa vie/My Life to Live* (1962), and Nicole is watching Egoyan's own film, *The Adjuster* (1991). As they realize their mistake, they begin chatting on their smart phones to connect to each other as well as to share their film experience in both text and images from the films. This initially simple set-up—two friends, two different films, historical time periods, two different theaters, two different screen technologies—soon develops into a complex and multiplying network that establishes significant connections and parallels between otherwise separate and seemingly incompatible locations, films, screen technologies, and viewing experiences.[1] As they watch the films—and film within a film—and their experiences merge, the events in both films merge as well and begin to comment on each other.

As Francesco Casetti (2011) observes in his incisive analysis of the film, in three minutes we watch several layers of our film experience opened up: different sets of spectators from different times and locations, different reactions to the same images, different phases of cinema history, and different screen technologies, all referencing each other in complex ways. *Artaud Double Bill* is about how cinema lives in theaters and on mobile phone screens as much as it is about spectatorship in transition. New technologies have dramatically reoriented our relationship to screens as we begin to watch films outside of film theaters, in our living rooms, on computers, laptops, tablets, and mobile phones. The final punctuation of Egoyan's short on the word "death" could well represent the announcement of the death of cinema as we know it, and the end of film viewership in theaters. But it is also a statement on the current transportability, mobility, and fluidity of cinema, on the new technologies that instantly capture and send images, ready to be shared and viewed on similar portable screens. Egoyan's film shows eloquently how films and screens on which they are viewed have become elastic, malleable, and ready to be relocated from film theaters.

The passage of films from large screens to hand-held, mobile ones has gone through a number of transitions. The story of cinematic exhibition is by no means a linear story in which older forms of viewing, particularly theatrical viewing, are being eclipsed and replaced by newer technologies and modes of viewing. At this moment in history, all forms of exhibition co-exist differently in various parts of the world. Films are being watched everywhere: in our living rooms, airplanes, trains, and classrooms, at office desks and vacation spots, on picnic benches, and yes, very much still in theaters. The multiple modes of watching point to the rich diversity of viewing practices around the world, some anchored in the traditions of cinema, some in cultural habits, and others in new technologies. Egoyan's short film merely hints at these changes in motion. Far from implying the "death" of film in a theater, however, it is pointing to a radical and ongoing transformation in ways of watching as the space and function of a movie theater are relocated and dispersed across multiple social and personal spaces. Experiencing and enjoying both the theatrical screen and their mobile screens, Anna and Nicole suggest a *simultaneity* that defines the ways in which different forms of film viewing co-exist and interact with each other.

Watching films in theaters

Since the early days of cinema, theatrical viewing has been the most dominant form of film experience. It is a tradition that has defined not only our interaction with film, but also our understanding and theorizing of cinema. Darkness, stationary seats, larger-than-life images projected on a screen, an invisible projection, a sound system, a complete separation from the external world, have been primary physical features defining the viewing experience. Theories of identification in cinema, the impressions of reality, and the impact of representations on our psyche have all been based on these features. The once-inseparable relationship between theatrical viewing and our perception of film is now going through a transformation with the relocation of cinema.

In addition to defining our film experience, theaters have functioned as important social sites. Movie theater buildings are significant landmarks in many neighborhoods, small towns, and cities. They are vital centers of the cultural geography of entertainment, proud architectural landmarks offering distinct marquees, large billboards, and seating comfort. When describing the act of film viewing, Roland Barthes (1980) states that one goes to a movie theater with two bodies, as it were: one engaged with the image on the screen and the other with the surroundings that include the theater, its location, the act of

a

b1

b2

c

d

Figures 2.2a–2.2d (a) Singapore's iconic Capitol Theater under renovation to be reclaimed as the city's main site for cinema entertainment. Image courtesy of Realimage/ Alamy Stock Photo

(b) The Thamada Cinema in Yangon, Myanmar, one of the more luxurious mid-century movie theaters left in Southeast Asia, which still draws capacity crowds. Image courtesy of Phillip Jablon

(c) People watch *Lawrence of Arabia* (1962) at the Secret Cinema, London

(d) An open-air theater at Locarno Piazza during the Locarno Film Festival. Image courtesy of imageBROKER/Alamy Stock Photo

entering and finding a seat, the sounds and the smells, other viewers—the whole "situation." The movie theater thus becomes a site of experiencing collectivity, a place where a community recognizes itself. Indeed, as Janet Harbord argues in *Film Cultures* (2002), the context of film exhibition, where and how we watch movies, is one of the most important markers of film culture, a distinct signature of social life, structures, and hierarchies. In a similar fashion, Richard Maltby (2011) recognizes the context of film exhibition— besides production, institutions, and texts themselves—as an integral aspect of the history of cinema, explaining how film-going habits influence and are influenced by cultural and social fabric. Accounts of these habits tell us "the qualities of the experience of cinema attendance were place-specific and shaped by the continuities of life in the family, the workplace, the neighborhood and community" (Maltby, 2011: 9).

Recently, research on the history of film viewing has gathered wider attention in film studies, with numerous new projects taking shape. The HOMER Project (The History of Moviegoing, Exhibition, and Reception) established in 2004 by a group of international scholars promotes the understanding of the international phenomena of film-going, exhibition, and reception. It collects and shares new data on film-going and exhibition, disseminates new models of collaborative research, and supports publications of related research findings.[2] In line with their efforts, the 2007 conference The Glow in Their Eyes: Global Perspectives on Film Cultures, Film Exhibition and Cinema-going, which explored the richness and diversity of movie-going practices around the world to affirm that the movie theater is an extension of social life, remains vital to exhibition studies.[3] Inspired by this conference, a collection of film-going experiences collected by *Senses of Cinema* reveal a fascinating diversity of viewing practices from around the world.[4] The accounts reveal how, for example, going to a movie theater is a gendered activity in Korea, sharing the gendered trademarks of other social activities such as meeting with friends in a coffee shop; it is a woman's social world. In Buenos Aires, Argentina, cinema-going today entails a cultural practice that originates in the ambiguous and complex legacy of the 1990s, when a new generation of Argentine filmmakers and audiences were engaging with the new social reality of disappearing film theaters (due to privatization) and thriving independent cinema of resistance. In Chile, moviegoers today still cherish the memory of going to a theater as an important collective act of resistance during the military dictatorship of the 1970s and 1980s. In Japan, movie-going remains an expression of cultural mannerisms and respectable behavior, giving rise (especially after the Second World War) to what some call "the silent spectator." In India, watching films is a near-celebratory, intense social experience often taking up entire afternoons or evenings, from dressing up to meeting friends at the theater. Here, getting a ticket for a newly released or popular film is an achievement, often a matter of stiff competition. In Eastern Europe, theaters supported by the state before 1990 still boast of their value as crucial social sites, with small coffee bars attached to them where viewers can spend time chatting about films and other matters. On the African continent, despite the rise in theaters introduced by the Colonial Film Units in metropolitan centers, and the more recent consumerism and modernization that brought multiplexes, a special value is placed on theatrical spaces that continue to thrive in schools, small establishments, open-air spaces, and smaller theaters. These rich and enduring viewing practices around the world go through a slow but certain transformation with the rise of new technologies and changes in the fabric of everyday life, but the cultural space of theater remains vital to our social life.

The rise of the multiplex

Just as movie theaters survived the arrival of television in the 1940s, the introduction of VHS tapes in the 1980s, home viewing, and digital technologies further repositioned the place of theatrical viewing and the movie theater experience soon morphed into multiple different forms. The rise of the multiplex is deeply connected to socio-economic transformations, first occurring in the Western world and then spreading elsewhere. The factors of urban migration, the expansion of capital, and the increased consumerization of society in the 1970s changed the landscape in which theaters functioned. Movie theaters moved away from city centers into suburban malls, relocating and transforming the nature of urban activities. The multiplex, a site of multiple screens and other consumption activities, formed a unique alliance between the transformed urban space and the centrality of consumer life.

Janet Harbord (2002) sees the emergence of the multiplex as a response to a crisis in declining cinema attendance, exacerbated in the 1970s and 1980s by the inception of video, which redirected entertainment from public cinema sites toward the domestic space. The multiplex was thus defined in contrast to both home entertainment and former

Figure 2.3 A multiplex in a shopping center, Cinema City Mega Mall in Bucharest, Romania, which contains fourteen digital cinema halls, including the first 4Dx cinema in Romania with high-tech motion seats and special effects. Image courtesy of Tanase Sorin/Shutterstock

cinema culture (Harbord, 2002: 52). It distinguished itself from home entertainment by maximizing the corporeal, sensory affect of cinema. Besides an expanded menu of movies enabled by multiple screens, the investment in technology created the surround-sound, wide-screen exhibition that boasted comfortable seating with bouncy chairs and extra leg room, curved screens that reflect color and light back onto audiences, and improved THX sound. The show-and-tell quality of multiplexes was also an attempt, as Charles Acland (2003) explains, to connect cinema-going to other forms of consumption, repositioning film not as a singular cultural object but as one commodity among many. The high-end video arcades, cafés and bars, merchandising outlets, party rooms, and video displays of coming attractions all come to constitute part of a multiplex where film is merely one component in a chain of associated consumer products (Acland, 2003: 196–228). The multiplex provides a context for the extension of the life of a film in other media, as well as an extension of a spatial experience that can be purchased and taken home.

Once a moviegoer encounters the veritable connective lounge of a multiplex, bringing local and global culture together, the specificity of a local experience of viewing is lost. Cinema-going is no longer a locally defined activity, but a globally marked act of consumption. One no longer comes to a theater to interact with the distinctness of a film object but rather to immerse oneself in the festive environment of consumerism. Multiplexes are on the rise in different parts of the world, including in poorer countries where the riches experienced in spaces of consumption are surrounded by the devastatingly destructive effects of globalization. Here, multiplexes are objects in an undifferentiated landscape where films that attract attention are positioned alongside other objects offered by global consumerism. An inescapable result of this marriage between film and consumer culture is the aggressive positioning and reach of Hollywood blockbusters through multiplexes, where blockbusters sell themselves along with commercial brands, seamlessly attaching a variety of commodities to filmic texts. What began with *Star Wars: Episode IV – A New Hope* (1977), which showered viewers with commodities from a filmic text before and after the film's release, has only gathered strength with franchises such as *The Avengers* (2012), *Transformers* (2007), *Warcraft* (2016), and others. This means that the spaces of multiplexes become inhospitable for the existence of films that are not dressed up as consumer products, making the circulation of independent or alternative films, or any films made outside of Hollywood, further specialized and pushed into the margins.

With the consolidation of consumer culture and the domination of film imports from Hollywood, the multiplex wave is an international one, developing in urban centers across North America, Latin America, Europe, and Asia. The growth in film theaters and multiplexes has been quite rapid around the world in recent years. In the UK, since their first emergence in Milton Keynes in 1985, the growth of multiplexes has continued, giving a much-needed elixir to the British film industry (Hoad, 2010). India has seen a twelve percent yearly increase in multiplexes, and China, which has around 40,000 multiplexes, has seen an exponential growth in the number of theaters and multiplexes, adding 5,077 new cinema screens in 2013 alone. At the end of 2016 the Asia-Pacific region dominates in the number of screens (66,350), followed by the US/Canada (43,531), Europe (41,840), and Latin America (12,197).

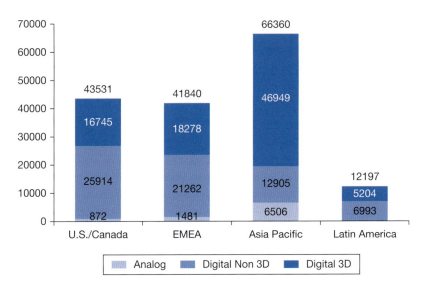

Figure 2.4 Cinema screens by format and region, 2016. Source: HIS Markit, MPAA Theatrical Market
  Statistics 2016; author's chart

Art house cinemas

Facing a whirlwind of multiplex expansion across the world, alternative sites of viewing persist, if on a different scale. In the US, Europe, India, and Asia, single-screen theaters attempt to claim spaces for diverse independent and non-commercial fare. As the multiplex expands, "the art-house increasingly takes on the appearance of a rare species, endangered and in need of protection" (Harbord, 2002: 50). Given the dominance of capital that multiplexes exhibit, single-screen (in some cases, dual- or triple-screen) theaters are facing the threat of extinction, a development that diminishes screening potential for numerous films. In the US, the number of theaters has expanded over the last decade, but among them less than 300 are art house cinemas.[5] In a gesture of small relief, some multiplexes are setting aside some screens for independent and world cinema. David Bordwell (2012a) refers to these as "smart house cinemas," and notes that there may be as many as 500 such theaters in the country, allowing the multiplexes to support the concept of art house cinemas while other screens bring in the requisite profit.

While multiplexes are owned by large exhibitor chains, most art house cinemas claim local ownership. Two notable chains in the US that own art house cinemas, Landmark Theaters (fifty theaters, 229 screens, and twenty-one markets) and Sundance Cinemas (six markets) own only a fraction of art cinemas in the country.[6] In 2006, the Sundance Institute initiated the Art House Project, which led to Art House Convergence (AHC), whose mission was to support the quality, growth, and sustainability of community-based and mission-driven art house cinemas in North America. AHC has evolved into a leading national resource for the support of independent or foreign film and the promotion of film culture. Today it includes larger distributors such as Fox Feature and Fox Searchlight, as well as theaters like the not-for-profit Jacob Burns Film Center in New York City. The movement represented by AHC is as much about nurturing a film experience and culture that distinguishes itself from the commercial one represented by multiplexes as it is about preserving the theater as an architectural site. Martin McCaffery, who runs Capri Theater in Montgomery, Alabama (the first theater to bring the works of Spike Lee and Ang Lee to Alabama, and still the only one to support foreign films as well as regional filmmakers), describes the difference between watching a movie at the Capri Theater and going to the nearby multiplex as "the difference between going to a restaurant and going to McDonalds," emphasizing the cultural value of the cinematic experience offered by an art house theater (quoted in Meyer, 2011). The value of this experience transcends the alternative film offerings and involves the site of the theater itself, which is often a historic building near the town center. A website *Cinema Treasures* (which has also been published as a book), run by Ross Melnick, is dedicated to such architecturally significant movie theaters and the preservation of the movie- going experience. Melnick's collection of theaters, referred to as the "architecture of fantasy," includes a list of over 23,000 theaters from 150 countries with constant updates. In the UK, *The Guardian* website calls them "bricks and mortar" cinemas housed in older, memorable buildings with their own flair and frequented by particular communities. In a tribute to these sites, it asked local viewers to profile their theaters (*The Guardian*, 2014).

Support for international films and art house cinemas is equally strong in Europe and in Asia. Important in Ireland and Scotland, for example, are the Irish Film Institute in

Figure 2.5 The Bryn Mawr Film Institute in Philadelphia. Image courtesy of Buck Sleuman

Dublin, Queen's Film Theater in Belfast, Kino in Cork, New Picture House Cinema in St Andrews, Scotland, and Sterling Theater in Scotland. London claims a number of theaters inspired by the South Bank screening rooms of the British Film Institute (BFI), including Ciné Lumière, the Prince Charles Theatre, and Curzon Cinemas (Eyles, 2014). Despite the prominence of multiplexes, Asian cities also feature impressive art house venues for independent and art films: the Edward Theatre in Bombay, La Scala Cinema in Bangkok, Cinecube and Arthouse Momo in Seoul, and Broadway Cinematheque and Olympian Cinema in Hong Kong, among many others. Just as the BFI launched the London Film Festival using the National Film Theater specifically built for the purpose, several cities around the world have relied on particular sites as venues for film festivals, making them central to the development of cinephile culture and world cinema. In fact, film festivals on a local and global scale have become a significant system of support for art house cinemas.

Figure 2.6a The Irish Film Institute in Dublin, Ireland

Figure 2.6b The Edward Theatre, a beautiful independent theater in Bombay, built in the 19th
century. Image courtesy of Dev Benegal

Figure 2.6c The Hyde Picture House in Leeds, England. Image courtesy of Tom Joy

Figure 2.6d The Traverse City Film Festival, co-founded by Michael Moore in 2005, revived the
decaying historic downtown State Theatre and evolved into one of the most important
U.S. festivals. Image courtesy of WENN/Alamy Stock Photo

Often an important event for a city, a film festival requires theatrical screens in a relatively centralized area. Therefore, cities have welcomed and supported film festivals for their value in reviving both cultural and economic capital. This has become particularly important for the cities in the West that have lost their profile after the suburban plight in the 1970s and 1980s; note, for example, the Traverse City Film Festival in Michigan, co-founded in 2005 by Michael Moore, which has evolved into the largest festival in the Midwest.

Support for such theaters has come from the state as well from independent funding organizations and film communities. The European Union's (EU) MEDIA Programme started in 1990 with a mission to protect and support single-screen movie theaters against the threatening economic and cultural influence of Hollywood (Oster, 2005). In India, the Film Finance Corporation, a state-sponsored body established to promote the production of art cinema, also began supporting the construction of art house cinemas in the cities, a task that has since gone to the independent exhibitors or local organizations in many cities (Prasad, 2001: 128). The combination of state support and private capital continues to provide funding for the construction of art house cinemas in many cities around the world.

Film societies, cine clubs, touring theaters

Before the struggle for the visibility of art house cinemas in a sea of multiplexes began, a strong tradition of film societies or cine clubs provided some of the most dependable opportunities for film lovers. They first emerged and thrived in Paris in the 1920s with café screenings, where they had an instrumental role in the creation of a buzzing, modernist cultural sphere. Collective experience generated by cine cafés led to the creation of the first film journals such as *Cahiers du cinéma*, the creative energy of which led to the remarkable symbiosis between filmmakers and theoreticians that fueled the French New Wave and offered a lasting imprint on world cinema. In the US, the first such important film society was Amos Vogel's Cinema 16, established in 1947. Vogel also created (with Richard Roud) the New York Film Festival in 1962, which found its home at the Film Society of Lincoln Center, a nucleus of New York City's cinephile culture. Although they are now a relatively thin presence in many countries, film societies have had a substantial role in cultivating a taste for world cinema. The International Federation of Film Societies, a network founded at the Cannes Film Festival in 1947, has continued the work of promoting international cinema on many continents, from Latin America to Asia. In Africa, some countries have no theaters but film societies still circulate films among clubs formed by local cinema aficionados. Tunisia boasts more film societies than film theaters; movie lovers pay membership to a film society, which brings films that are in circulation in various countries. In addition, institutions like Alliance Française have had an equally impressive reach in Eastern Europe, Africa, and Asia, supporting screenings and local film festivals. The venues for all these efforts are usually multipurpose media rooms or small theaters made available for weekly screenings. We can say that contemporary film festivals owe their genesis to the strength and tradition of such film societies.

An extension of the phenomenon of film societies, in the US as in many other countries, is a "micro-cinema movement," a form of a cine club revolving around makeshift theaters that establish residence in alternative spaces such as church basements, cafés, bars, or health clubs (Alvin, 2007). They show films with no marketing campaigns and no budgets, and since they rely on different systems of support, these cinemas are able to show truly alternative, adventurous works, going well beyond the usual independent and art house fare.

Various cultures have adopted inventive ways of watching films suitable for their own conditions, keeping theatrical culture alive even as technologies and lifestyles have gone through major transformations. In the US and also in Canada and Australia, wide-open spaces and automobile culture introduced the drive-in theater, a distinct and cherished object of the cultural landscape. The touring theaters of India, an impressive number of which still survive in the Western state of Maharashtra as they do elsewhere in the country, accommodate the needs of villagers to watch films.

a

b

Figures 2.7a & 2.7b Traveling tent cinemas in India. Images courtesy of Dev Benegal

These theaters, quite prominent in Asia, Latin America, and Africa, move from one village to another, screening films under a tent after dusk using a projector mounted on a van. In the desert areas of Western Asia, Bedouins, refugees, and other residents use similar set-ups in tents to project films and even to organize film festivals, such as the Sahara Film Festival in Algeria, now in its eleventh edition and attended by thousands of Sahrawi refugees, alongside international stars, directors, and cinephiles (Culshaw, 2008).

In Eastern Europe, the era of post-Second World War Soviet influence brought 16mm projectors to nearly every village. The socialist period in Hungary, Poland, and Romania, among other countries, secured a theater in each village, now vanishing due to the rapid rise of urban theaters and multiplexes. In Romania alone, the number of film theaters has declined considerably since 1990; two-thirds of its seventy theaters are in its two major cities, Bucharest and Cluj-Napoca (Dobroiu, 2014). In light of this decline, Cristian Mungiu took his Palme d'Or-winning film *4 luni, 3 saptamâni si 2 zile/4 Months, 3 Weeks, and 2 Days* (2007) to rural areas in a "caravan," a traveling show that screened films in school halls and other venues.[7] He found this venture so valuable that he repeated it with a package of Romanian and regional films. In 2011, another organization took a similar film caravan across Romania, Bulgaria, and other neighboring countries, carrying regional films with them. Similar in spirit and passion for theatrical viewing, Tilda Swinton and Mark Cousins embarked on a unique project called A Pilgrimage, a mobile cinema tour that brought cinema to the Scottish Highlands in 2009 and involved crowds pulling a trailer along the Highlands that unpacked into an 80-seat cinema.[8] Such examples affirm the idea that even in the days of mobile technologies, the integral relationship between cinema and theater still holds precious value for moviegoers, who go to great lengths to create and re-create the conditions of theatrical viewing.

Figure 2.7c The Sahara International Film Festival. Image courtesy of Andy Isaacson, andyisaacson.net

Figure 2.8 A Pilgrimage, a film festival organized by Mark Cousins and Tilda Swinton, depicted in Teal Greyhavens' documentary *Cinema is Everywhere* (2011)

Mobile media: VHS, VCD, DVD

Theaters have long used celluloid film projection systems for screening films, either in 16mm, 35mm, or 70mm. Looking back at the traditional formats from the vantage point of technologies such as VHS tapes, VCDs, DVDs, and Blu-ray, the greatest strength of celluloid for disseminating cinema across cultural borders was universal compatibility between a film format and projection system. A 16mm or 35mm film could be played anywhere in the world, a feature that was a great boon to the mobility of the film medium. On the other hand, VHS, DVD, and other digital systems have established zones and regions for films, making them compatible only with select equipment for playback. Although there are solutions to these problems, the universal compatibility of celluloid is hardly matched by these changes.

When Japanese electronics manufacturers introduced into the market an electromagnetic tape that could hold visual and audio information in the 1980s, a revolution in world cinema was underway. In subsequent years and decades, mobile media have gone through several phases of transformation, adapting to market competition and technological innovation. As a result, multiple formats came into existence in different parts of the world, driven by market competition and compatibility among technologies. Film viewing created a complex map of diverse practices. In the West and elsewhere, the popularity of VHS tapes gave rise to video rental and sales stores, changing the landscape of film viewing. DVD offered a more durable physical media and a better-quality image than VHS. The ease and cost of these technologies did not necessarily encourage transport and travel of films across regional borders. Various markets established different region codes and video encoding standards: NTSC prevailed in North America, and PAL and SECAM became common in Europe, parts of Asia, and East African countries.

DVDs were produced with signatures of multiple regions, increasing the compatibility of physical media with viewing technologies: there are six different region codes (R1 in the U.S. territories and Canada; R2 in Europe, Japan, and the Middle East; R3 in Taiwan, Korea, Hong Kong, etc.).

These changes brought cinema to viewers at a lower cost, but the cost of these technologies was still out of reach for audiences with lesser means. In Africa, Asia, and elsewhere, the technology of video CD or VCD appeared in 1993: a VHS tape on a CD, without the ability to move from scene to scene, and without any menus. Less cumbersome than a VHS and cheaper than a DVD, it was embraced as the preferred physical medium for film. In Africa, the entire industry of Nigerian film industry, now known as Nollywood, emerged on the strength of VCD, the popularity of which persists today, making Nigeria's large audience one of the most reliant on inexpensive media. Bollywood as well benefited from the inexpensive transportability of VCD, allowing it to enter the living rooms of the poor, and taking films to remote areas throughout the continent and beyond to Africa and East Asia. Nearly unknown to consumers in the West, VCDs reshaped world cinema elsewhere.

Current DVD manufacturing has maintained regional differences in coding, and while this incompatibility is seen as a rather artificial obstacle, it is an obstacle nevertheless. Multipurpose DVD players are expensive in the US, while they are more common and affordable in other parts of the world where DVDs are often produced with multi-region coding that allows them to be played anywhere. Region codes exist in part to control the rights and income from distribution in different territories. This system of film distribution allows less cross-border transfer, which in turn hinders the dissemination of world cinema. The success of Bollywood films (most of which are produced on multi-region DVDs) in various countries in Asia and Africa, for example, can be partly attributed to their cross-border transferability. It was only after the arrival of computers with increasingly sophisticated software that these media could be converted across various formats and transported across borders, which also became a major impetus behind piracy. For films of world cinema, the universality of format is an essential feature, and one that was already in existence with celluloid film.

Today, DVD remains a stable physical technology, making films of world cinema accessible to ordinary viewers. A subsequent innovation is that of an electronic file which can be transferred on the Internet through streaming services or user exchanges. If a sophisticated electronic file makes possible digital projection in theaters, DVD remains a technology that can bring quality images far superior to VHS and VCD to home viewers. Cinephiles can purchase them from outlets that distribute important titles in world cinema such as Criterion Collection, Kino Lorber, Cohen Media Group or Janus Films. Criterion, long cherished by cinephiles, has invested in meticulously produced DVD releases, with high-quality sound, images, and extra features. Its focus on publishing original critical essays as well as including critical commentaries on DVDs does much to cultivate cinephilia and scholarship on world cinema. Film Movement continues to acquire important film titles of world cinema for distribution in the US and maintains a steady schedule of screenings in micro-cinema settings in major cities. In the UK, Eureka! Entertainment's The Masters of Cinema Series, along with Curzon Artificial Eye, maintain a stellar record in producing high-quality DVDs. Studio Kanal in Germany, ARTE in France, Mongrel Media in Canada, and Eastern Eye/Madman in Australia and New Zealand all keep up the distribution of specialized catalogues of world cinema titles.

In focus 2.1   Piracy

With the low costs and portability of the VHS, VCD, and DVD formats, piracy instantly became an issue that only intensified with the arrival of computers, hard drives, software, and the Internet. The increasing ease with which recorded media can be copied and distributed makes the mechanical reproduction of films a scourge of the industry. Nearly thirty years later, with intense debates and regulations, piracy remains a controversial issue in world cinema. Major studios in the US alone are said to lose $6.1 billion each year to piracy, while the losses to the film industry worldwide are expected to be over $18.2 billion, a figure estimated in 2005. Sixty-two percent of the loss comes from copying physical media and thirty-eight percent from Internet piracy. China and Russia have the highest rate of piracy at ninety-three and eighty-one percent.[9] While the accuracy of these figures is difficult to verify, they do reveal data that presents a major loss to both major production companies that aim for large profits, and small independent producers and directors for whom piracy is not merely a matter of cutting into the profits but a matter of survival. Courts and law enforcement agencies in every country are fighting piracy, and yet it is a vexing problem for everyone in financial, legal, and moral terms. Each creative work is a result of specific and specialized labor, expert talents and skills, and a significant amount of financial investment. Artists and producers have been protected by copyright laws, prohibiting anyone from making copies without authorization, which may or may not involve financial compensation. For the supporters of small and independent producers and directors as well as for large production companies, anti-piracy or copyright laws provide the necessary protection to survive and to continue producing films.

The debates on piracy are marked by polarized terms, as Ramon Lobato observes in his extensive account of this complex issue (2012: 69–92). Identifying six levels of piracy, Lobato demonstrates that there are some substantially positive and unavoidably useful aspects of piracy. The first aspect of piracy represents the dominant view from the Motion Picture Association of America and its global component, Motion Pictures Association, where piracy is considered *theft*, a deliberate stealing of the product from artists and producers. Since piracy presents a major financial loss, stringent laws and other instruments in trade arrangements with various governments around the world are used to protect against such theft. This is the most vocal position on piracy, powered by the financial and institutional muscle wielded by Hollywood. It is a polarizing view that does not take the multiple layers of the function of piracy in different parts of the world into account.

The second level of piracy as a *free enterprise* presents the view that the equipment manufacturers that allow for duplication as well as those that copy content without permission enable the growth of a horizontal economy. Lower prices and wider availability of products allows for larger money flow; therefore, piracy is a strategy that contributes to the production of more activity and hence is desirable in certain contexts. In many ways, this activity can be seen in the deliberate collusion between the manufacturers and equipment vendors in Nigeria, who were mainly responsible for propelling the video-based industry of filmmaking in the country. The development of an "informal" or "shadow" economy in Nigeria is a prime example of how the

(continued)

(continued)

attractions of a global culture, the rapid movement of money and goods (video-films) and a deeper absorption into a secondary level of organized networks have produced one of the most complicated phenomena in piracy. Brian Larkin argues that piracy is key to the Nigerian film industry and to its economy, generating revenues for all participants in the region, although this activity remains hidden to the formal networks (2008: 217–241). So integral is the presence of piracy that even the producers who decry piracy participate in it. The growth of these enterprises connects Nigeria to networks of piracy in other countries where films from Bollywood and Hollywood are duplicated, subtitled, and re-packaged. What is more, it brings the Nigerian and African consumer into the cultural environment of globalization by making available the most recent films from abroad. Aligned with this view, Ravi Sundaram sees everyday piracy in India's electronic culture as part of "recycled modernity," a practice not defined by non-legality or resistance, but rather one that is "everyday in its imaginary, pirate in its practice, and mobile in its innovation," crucial to the articulation of everyday consumption and mobility vis-à-vis the state (1999: 62). This results in a deep ambivalence regarding piracy, framing it in terms that are neither oppositional nor ideological.

The third level of piracy, coming from a liberal perspective in the US, frames piracy within the issue of *free speech*. Arguing against iron-clad restrictions on copyright material, this strand of the piracy debate suggests that writers, scholars, practitioners, educators, DJs, animators, and software developers are entitled to use copyrighted material to create works that function as meta-products, as commentaries that allow consumers to express perspectives on films, television shows, and other media. This is essentially an anti-corporate stance, epitomized by the Electronic Frontier Foundation and Creative Commons, where the former advocates an open defense of creative work on copyrighted materials while the latter depends on limited permissions for non-profit, pedagogical, or scholarly purposes. Important contributions in this area have been achieved by Peter Decherney, who won an exemption to the Digital Millennium Copyright Act (DMCA)—which places many limits on the use of digital technology—for educators who use digital multimedia works for teaching, research, and publication. As Decherney (2007) argues, the fair use of film technology such as 35mm film, 16mm film, and video recording has been instrumental in the development of media studies, and the DMCA, with its prohibition on making or using clips, is a significant step backward in academic rights. In film studies, as in many other areas, this perspective has also allowed for the creation of an entirely new range of works by scholars. It is now possible for film critics, scholars, and cinephiles to create video essays or mash-ups of films, providing critical commentary on existing films. In effect, video essays can illustrate relations between films, illuminating techniques and subtleties as substantially as written research essays. Film scholar Catherine Grant's project *Audiovisualcy* marks an important milestone in the development of creative visual studies, establishing connections between written film studies and an emerging body of work on audiovisual film studies.[10] Pioneers in the video-essay genre and its most vocal proponents and practitioners, Cristina Álvarez López and Adrian Martin have opened up a sophisticated discourse on the genre and its significance for film studies.[11] The Society for Cinema and Media Studies boasts a new journal called *[In]Transition* based on video essays and digital scholarship.[12] Exciting projects such as these, crucial to the developments of new directions in film studies, are made possible both by the accessibility of films on DVDs and a new relaxation of copyright restrictions for scholarly purposes.

Lobato's fourth explanation of piracy revolves around a theoretical framework of *authorship*, expanding the notion of ownership and public domain. The idea of film genre, for example, particularly in the work of Steve Neale, has emerged as a concept where the audience constructs and shares the framework of connotations; without sharing, the concept of genre would not exist (Lobato, 2012: 80). Peter Decherney makes a similar case in regard to the copyright of works in the public domain. Copyright laws that have been shrinking the public domain, he argues, have serious implications for Hollywood and other cultural industries whose creativity has historically depended on access to the growing public domain. Examples such as Disney's *Snow White* in the 1930s, the many adaptations of Lewis Carroll's *Alice's Adventures in Wonderland*, and numerous others show that "filmmakers have consistently used public domain works to anchor artistic and technological innovation" (Decherney, 2011).

The fifth level of piracy belongs to the notion of piracy as *resistance*. Considering copyright laws as deliberately developed tools of power, particularly in the hands of those who have the means to enforce them, this perspective decries their control over creative processes. Lobato attributes the relevance of this idea to the domination of Hollywood in terms of forcing others to follow its dictates (Lobato, 2012: 81). Hollywood itself copies content willy-nilly from all sources. In the case of Quentin Tarantino's *Kill Bill* (2003–2004), it was difficult for anyone to hold Hollywood accountable for its clear dependence on Asian films.

The sixth level of piracy as *access* to films becomes key for world cinema in a number of ways. Possibly the most nuanced of all arguments, this is simultaneously a position of postcolonial resistance, a banal activity that is part of everyday life (not directed at any power), and a technique of dissemination that simply allows cultural products to reach further shores where there are no other structures for distribution or dissemination. Echoing the notion of pirate modernity, Lobato says that these pirate networks "provide the material routes for an alternative technological modernity" (2012: 84). On equally strong ground, he also supports Lawrence Liang's defense of piracy based on an "access to knowledge" paradigm, suggesting that access to works through piracy generates knowledge, creativity, and productivity (Liang, 2005). This sort of piracy is motivated primarily by the desire to see the works, rather than by economic reasons.

The modes of piracy include the copies of physical media but also the transfers of electronic files. The European Commission reported in 2014 that 68 percent of the viewers in ten countries watched their films by downloading or streaming, and about 34 percent did so each week.[13] Such downloading, peer-to-peer transfers, and use of BitTorrent have increased in intensity in countries outside of Western Europe (Lithuania, Romania, Poland) and formed an informal network that has become a stronger mode of distribution than official streaming services. The sharp differences in watching patterns suggests as much about the unevenness in economies and purchasing powers as it does about the ethical and legal problems in piracy and downloading. It is a vexing

(continued)

(continued)

problem for world cinema, and an uneasy choice between the desire to seek films outside of one's own circuits of access and the consideration of moral bases for doing so.

It is impossible to defend piracy on moral or financial terms. But the strict "all or nothing" logic of enforcement that sees piracy as a theft is equally indefensible. Piracy is an act of dissemination and desire. Though controversial, the rapid transfer of films to eager viewers of world cinema would be impossible without the complex networks of piracy. As we note frequently in this book, an entire generation of filmmakers in different parts of the world has grown up watching and being inspired by films of world cinema that were accessible only through pirate channels. Jia Zhangke, one of the key filmmakers of the Sixth Generation of Chinese cinema, has spoken on various occasions about the important role of pirated films, otherwise banned in China, in encouraging a subterranean strain of resistance against rules and restrictions, and offering film education and exposure for the new generation of Chinese filmmakers like himself.[14] Though morally complex, ambiguous, and multifaceted in its numerous manifestations and implications, piracy undoubtedly plays a role in promoting world cinema.

Home viewing, streaming, video on demand, and mobile screens

Home viewing

Mapping out a major transition in film viewing from theaters and multiplexes to living rooms, Barbara Klinger (2006) explains that new technologies made watching films a part of the everyday life of a family, but they also cultivated cinephile identities; renting, owning, and collecting films added an entirely new dimension to the film experience. Anne Friedberg (2000), analyzing the topography and the *mise-en-scène* of the new domestic screens and technologies, suggests that this was not only a new kind of cinema but "the end of cinema". Decades after its arrival, television performed a mediatory role in the transition of cinema from the exclusively theatrical mode of viewing to the multiplicity of new platforms, with smaller and more portable screens than ever before.

The unprecedented growth in cable and satellite television in the US and elsewhere in the 1980s altered the landscape of viewing. Many countries, including those in Asia and Latin America, moved quickly to direct-broadcast satellite that escaped the messy infrastructure of landline cables. Utilizing a new generation of communication satellites owned by major corporate behemoths like News Corporation, Telstra, Foxtel, and DirecTV, television expanded its grip and became a twenty-four-hour transporter of images to billions of homes, and the broadcasting of movies became a staple of television. Subscription and pay-TV channels emerged in the 1990s, allowing viewers to choose the kinds of films they could watch. In India and Korea, it became possible to watch Hollywood films alongside the domestic product. Diasporic populations across the world, from the UK, Australia, and the US, among others, were able to watch films from their home countries. All of this suddenly put the viewer in the place of the curator of her own viewing schedule. Indeed, if the idea was to watch films from South Korea or India in the US or in Europe, one could easily be preoccupied around the clock, inhabiting numerous time zones. Importantly, the implosion of choice made room for films outside of the mainstream, and many television channels opened up marginal, and in some cases not so marginal, space for non-mainstream films. Australia boasts a World Movies channel that is the "home of international and independent movies," and Channel Four in the UK and Rialto in New Zealand both emphasize their programming of "foreign films." While most of television grew formulaic, with Western, particularly U.S.-based, programming and franchises dominating other countries, it became possible to find some openings here and there to watch films outside of your own country on television.

The next wave of changes in watching films further transformed the spaces and screens in which they circulated. Physical media such as VHS, VCD, and DVD had already moved cinema out of theaters, and television had anchored it firmly in the living rooms. With the arrival of the Internet in the late 1980s, the choices of what, how, and when we could watch content, as well as the range of consumer electronic devices available, from computers, laptops, high-definition television sets and smart phones to portable players and video game consoles, further widened. The increased capacity of broadband signals makes the task of carrying images highly efficient, creating a perpetually connected society. Indeed, this timely convergence of the Internet infrastructure, technological devices, and the availability of images effectively deterritorializes the living room. Cinema moves online, ushering in a phase of streaming images, mobile media, and on-demand culture (Iordanova & Cunningham, 2012; Iordanova, 2013; Tryon, 2013a; Dixon, 2013). The viewer in the West becomes immersed in an entropic field of bewildering choices on every front, with theater no longer the central space for watching films.

Prominent companies such as Netflix, Amazon, and Apple have assumed enormous power as supranational corporations that serve as streaming services as well as retail giants making aggressive strides in Europe and in the urban centers of Asia, Latin America, and Africa. Other services such as Curzon on Demand, Blinkbox, Film4oD, *The Guardian*'s Screening Room (for world cinema) and LoveFilm (which has become Amazon Prime Instant Video) in the UK attempt to hold on to their own territories. The added power of satellite networks such as HBO, Star TV, Fox, and Showtime assures dominance by the U.S. players in this area. Even YouTube, for all its universalist claims, is an American company with the goal and potential to generate revenues through streaming images.

Technologies of reception for streaming images have also changed. The static *mise-en-scène* of television in the living space has become more fluid by moving onto the spaces of laptops, tablets, and smart phones. The Blackberry smart phone in Anna's hands in *Artaud Double Bill* was introduced in 2003, Apple introduced its iPhone in 2007, and Samsung came out with the Samsung Galaxy smart phone in 2009. Since then a plethora of devices have been introduced all over the world, most of them capable of streaming several hours of video content. The number of smart phone users worldwide reached over two billion in 2016, a number that is expected to jump to six billion by 2020 (Boxall, 2015), radically widening and transforming the landscape of streaming options. With television moving onto the Internet, the relationship between powerful content providers (Netflix, Amazon Instant Video, Hulu, YouTube), cable TV, and broadband service providers is therefore in constant friction and negotiation.[15] The velocity of these changes not only renders the printed word and its records obsolete but also continuously reshapes the media landscape.

While the changes in the West are euphoric and radical, they are by no means universal, even though critical and scholarly debates surrounding them often assume this universality. If the modes of watching were relatively similar across the world before the 1980s, the rapid introduction of new technologies created a markedly uneven state of watching films in different parts of the globe. It is important to recognize the dominance of technologies in the West against the scarcity of resources in other parts of the world, and the fact that it is Western capital and neoliberal trade policies that govern patterns of technological penetration. Talk of streaming movies and the digital delivery of images carries the force of utopian vision, but for the moment at least, these developments need to be absorbed patiently and carefully, with the recognition that things are in flux and it will take time to sort out the contradictory status of technological penetration and impact. In the meantime, the Western cinema viewer, at least, stands at an interesting threshold between the choices of the present and the promises of the future.

Netflix and the culture of streaming films

Netflix arrived in 1997, when DVDs were being rented out to viewers through neighborhood stores across the US such as Blockbuster, Empire, and Movies Unlimited. Gauging the efficiency and convenience of making DVDs available through mail-order service, Netflix utilized the potential of the Internet to allow viewers to make their choice of films. After consolidating these services from its inception, the company began streaming films and TV shows directly to personal computers in 2007. Over the next few years, Netflix integrated its software with hardware manufacturers of Blu-ray players, the Xbox 360, TV set-up boxes, and computer operating systems, further widening its appeal. With the introduction of streaming, the 6.3-million subscriber base in 2005 skyrocketed to over eighty million members globally in just under a decade, and a company that began as a DVD mail-order subscription service has contributed to the slow elimination of physical media (La Monica, 2016).

Netflix began its international expansion in Canada in 2010, adding the Caribbean, Latin America, the UK, Ireland, Sweden, Denmark, Norway, Finland, and the Netherlands, then expanding its services to other parts of Europe, Australia, Indonesia, and Saudi Arabia. By 2016, Netflix had added 130 more international markets, including large ones like India and Russia, with China as the only major market where it does not operate. As a measure of its staggering dominance, more than thirty percent of all Internet traffic in the US is attributed to Netflix on any given weeknight, and in 2017 Netflix members from around the world broke the record by streaming 250 million hours of video on a single day (Spangler, 2015; Roettgers, 2017). Netflix makes no attempt to hide its global ambitions, forecasting that its international revenues will surpass its U.S. revenue by 2020 (Williams, 2016). So powerful is the juggernaut of streaming services led by Netflix, followed by Hulu, Amazon Instant Video, and Apple iTunes, that revenues from streaming and downloads are expected to overtake box office revenues in 2017 (Thompson, 2015).

Over the next few years, the streaming industry is expected to grow. Netflix benefits from being the first entrant in the field, re-writing the practices of DVD rentals and overpowering competitors. Along with Hulu, Amazon Instant Video, Apple iTunes, and other companies (Vimeo, Sling TV, Crackle), Netflix is positioned to exploit the advantages of an efficient broadband network and the consumer habits of purchasing increasing amounts of content from within the confines of domestic spaces. Each of these companies brings a distinct feature of its own to the marketplace. With Amazon, the viewers have a single dealer that sells DVDs, including from third-party dealers in the country and abroad, and the tested abilities of one of the most efficient web services. Apple iTunes combines music and other downloadable products while focusing on new releases, often obtaining exclusive rights to online film release. Their brand recognition is synonymous with a broad palette of film viewing in the country, and they have helped shape a robust streaming culture that presents more than just an alternative to theatrical viewing.

Much of this growth goes beyond the world of film. Since 2011, both Netflix and Amazon have aggressively entered into the business of producing original programming (including films), beginning with Netflix's enormously successful *House of Cards* in 2013. Vastly boosting the size and importance of their original programming roster, Netflix and Amazon have also asserted their dominant position in the world of film distribution, causing earthquakes in the landscape of film festival markets by outbidding the studios: in 2015, Netflix made a splash by acquiring Cary Fukunaga's *Beasts of No Nation* for $12 million, and in 2016, twelve high-profile acquisitions (including *Manchester by the Sea*, *Tallulah*, and *Weiner Dog*) were made between the two companies at Sundance, stirring intense debates about the effect of these high-spending giants on the film industry eco-system (Lyttelton, 2016). Their presence, in fact, reaches to the heart of how we under-stand and define cinema, as both established directors such as Woody Allen, Spike Lee, Jim Jarmusch, and younger filmmakers such as Nate Parker and Cary Fukunaga have not only turned to Internet companies for distribution but also to produce content for them (for example, Woody Allen's Amazon series *Crisis in Six Scenes*).

The long tail

The massive engines of growth in streaming options beg the question for viewers of world cinema: where is the place for films from outside of the country where revenues are driven by Hollywood films, streamed television shows, and originally-produced con-tent? According to Chris Anderson, a writer at the *Economist* and a former chief edi-tor of *Wired* magazine, the answer to this question of access in a blockbuster-oriented economy can be found in the logic of what he calls "the long tail," a new model for media and entertainment industries (Anderson, 2008). Anderson notes that hit-driven economies where companies stocked up on major, popular titles with an eye on revenues are diminishing. Instead, thanks to the benefits offered by an expansive "shelf-space" of Internet-based retailers, there are abundant supplies for all kinds of interests, niche tastes, and specialty-driven palettes, allowing for various interests to thrive. This explains why Netflix, Amazon Instant Video, and iTunes can offer a diverse and expansive catalogue of films that caters to even very specific tastes. Anderson illustrates this with specific examples, where Netflix marketed an obscure documentary on allegations of pedophilia, *Capturing the Friedmans* (2003), and pulled similar success for *Daughter from Danang* (2002), a documentary on children of U.S. soldiers and Vietnamese women.

Discussions on streaming films and distribution/availability of films on the Internet have benefited from Anderson's insights on how companies work to make available rela-tively rare content outside of the gambit of the older, more established logic of box office returns. Dina Iordanova and the project Dynamics of World Cinema at St Andrews University argue that the logic of the long tail allows films from "smaller countries, film festivals, diasporic channels" to be disseminated beyond niche markets (Iordanova, 2008). Obvious beneficiaries of this new model of distribution are not only the companies who discover that the slowly accumulated profits on a large selection of products account for a healthy gain in revenue, thriving "like a blue whale, growing fat by eating millions of tiny shrimp" (Wu, 2006), but also the viewer who sees an expanded menu of available films.

Benefits for the producers, on the other hand, are unclear, since their gains come from relatively small "clicks" or "views" at the end of the long tail.

It is clear that the logic of the long tail contributes to the expanded spaces of the Internet that abolish the limits of physical stores and transportation. Among other things, and despite the fact that companies like Netflix have been reducing their film catalogue and focusing their efforts and resources on original programming, these expanded spaces and the logic of the long tail allow for a number of smaller and niche outlets that offer films not available through Amazon or Netflix to flourish. In the US, curated sites such as MUBI (branded as Netflix for independent cinema), Tribeca Shortlist, FilmStruck, and Shudder address the distinctive tastes of classic, art house, independent, or genre-based cinemas. The complete Criterion Collection is available on FilmStruck, a subscription streaming video service. Other sites offer a wider selection or become portals for managing access to niche streaming sites. Vimeo, FestivalScope, and MovieSaints exist alongside the major retailers of streaming films. Among these "boutique services" MUBI and Filmatique are particularly effective in establishing Internet-based communities that nurture specific tastes, slowly expanding their base of support and their presence in other countries; MUBI is set to launch in China, beating rivals such as Netflix to become the first known U.S. streaming platform in the Chinese market (Wiseman, 2016). These specialty sites find their footing in tandem with a continually expanding menu of mid-level sites such as Vudu, HBOGo, and SnagFilms. That these sites can construct viable business models and satisfy the viewers of world cinema is a testament to overcoming what Anderson calls "the tyranny of locality," where only a few theaters in a city dominate the screening space and circumscribe film choices (2008: 17).

The expanded market also gave rise to a host of sites for diasporic audiences. Bollywood films are streamed on sites such as ErosNow, BigFlix, and BoxTV, while Nollywood films are streamed across a number of Internet-based channels such as Ibaka TV and Iroko TV. Expansion continues in this area as a number of streaming sites emerge in an exceedingly competitive field. It should be noted that the argument about the long tail also applies to the wider choices of content that is available across the Internet. Television shows, both current and syndicated, occupy much of the streaming spectrum. World cinema viewers find spaces in the midst of this range as well, in cross-border flows of the Internet streaming channels. Channels such as MUBI can be accessed outside the US, adding an important and essential cross-border dimension to streaming services, much like satellite television did over three decades ago.

YouTube

Among the many streaming options, a giant that occupies the central space in the cross-border, transnational flow of images is YouTube. Without a parallel, YouTube has not only transformed the landscape for streaming images but has radically altered filmmaking practices, spectatorship, and the nature of visual culture. Established in 2005, the web-based video-sharing platform has become the fastest growing site in web history, with over a billion users. Seventy percent of its traffic comes from outside the US, and its local versions are available in eighty-eight countries (Statistic Brain, 2016). Allowing any user to upload videos and anyone with a stable Internet connection to stream these images, YouTube has become a cultural phenomenon and part of everyday activities. Its direct relevance for cinema comes from the space it creates and preserves for films. Apart from

Table 2.1 Smart phones, Internet speeds, and streaming services, 2016. Source: Pew Research Center

Smart phones, Internet speeds, and streaming services 2016

Source: Pew Research Center

Region	Number of smart phones	Average Internet speeds	Streaming services
US	65% of population— approx. 207 million people (2016)	31 Mb/s (2016)	Netflix, Hulu, Amazon, HBOGo, etc.
Europe	Approx. 60% of population Germany: 60% France: 50% UK: 68% Spain: 71% Italy: 60%	17 Mb/s (2016)	BBC iPlayer, Blinkbox, Canal+, FastpassTV, ivi.ru, Mail.ru, megogo. net, Netflix, Redbox Instant, RTÉ Player, Screenclick, Sky Now, TV Stream/Omelet.ru, TvMuse, Wuaki.tv
Asia	Hong Kong: 87% Malaysia: 63% South Korea: 88% China: 58% Japan: 49%	17–30 Mb/s (2016)	BIGFlix, BoxTV, ErosNow, First Media GO, Genflix, Indopia, Jiaflix, Mela, M1905, Niconico, Project Glue, Spuul, UseeTV, Viki, Youku Tudou
India	33%	3.5 Mb/s (2016)	BIGFlix, BoxTV, ErosNOW, Indopia, Mela, Spuul
Nigeria	30%	4.7 Mb/s (2016)	Naijapals, movies.lovenollywood.com, OnlineNigeria, NigeriaScreen

movie streaming channels in the US, the site offers a massive selection of films from the vaults of archives elsewhere. It has curated channels for streaming films, utilizing fully the availability of films that are in the public domain. It allows filmmakers to set up their own channels and viewers to curate their own, giving unprecedented control to everyone over streaming images. It shows new films, short films, experimental films, archival footage, documentary footage, film trailers, and film festival footage. It offers subscription channels, some of which are geared toward film viewing. It is a revenue generator from commercials on its site as well as through partner programs with companies from several countries. YouTube can boast of being a universal platform that appeals to the largest spectrum of interests around the world.

With its approach to partial or complete video, YouTube has ushered in an era of fragmented viewing, allowing viewers to create and watch images on thousands of mobile devices around the globe. Spontaneous, multi-user, diverse in its address, democratic in its accessibility, the platform has challenged film theory and its assumptions about authorship, textuality, narrative, aesthetics, and spectatorship, and film studies are still trying to grasp its full impact and potential (Lovink & Niederer, 2008; Snickars & Vondreau, 2009). For viewers, YouTube is an empowering platform that enables them to engage in media production and digital culture in ways never before possible. The platform has not only opened new possibilities for aspiring or established filmmakers, but entire film industries such as Nollywood, struggling to gain visibility through traditional channels and networks of film distribution and exhibition, rely on YouTube to make their films accessible worldwide.

In fact, for Nollywood, YouTube has proved to be a truly globalizing presence. More than any other medium or technological device, YouTube has transformed cinema into video form.

Despite its vast archive and reach, YouTube keeps a close watch on copyright issues for posted videos, scanning over 100 years of video every day (Statistic Brain, 2016) and removing any films, clips, or fan videos that involve copyright infringement. Strict penalties are imposed for such infringements. Much of what one sees on YouTube is either approved for streaming by companies who hold copyright or falls within public domain and archival usage. There is no doubt, however, that "online material related to silent cinema, animation, documentary, historical, scientific and industrial film and newsreels gets richer all the time" (Iordanova, 2013). The boon for archival or research projects enabled by YouTube is a gift to film scholars, but the restrictions on copyrighted material and slower Internet speeds in different parts of the world still present a limit to YouTube's full utility as a global medium for watching films.

In focus 2.2   Translation, subtitles, dubbing

The celebrated cross-border traffic of films faces a paradoxical situation: while the visual language of cinema is universally accessible, understanding film is conditioned upon the role of subtitles and translation. An encounter with films outside of one's own context requires facility in reading subtitles. The first and indispensable tool to help the viewers overcome the linguistic, as well as extra-linguistic and cultural, barriers, subtitles provide a necessary if partial entry into the world of film. They can make the original accessible, but they can also obscure and spoil it. Film studies have slowly turned their attention to the role of translation, subtitles, and dubbing, now made urgent with the rise of world cinema (Egoyan & Balfour, 2004; Đurovičova, 2010; Nornes, 2008; Fong & Au, 2009). Though subtitling is necessary for a film's wider reach, the cost of subtitling can be prohibitive for a filmmaker with a limited budget. The introduction of electronic subtitling and time coding, as well as the support of film festivals in this endeavor, has eased the process and improved the precision and visual quality of subtitles. When a DVD is released with multiple language subtitle options, it clearly indicates that the film is ready to move beyond its own linguistic context.

The complex dynamic of globalization has accelerated and expanded the traffic of films, but it has also made it more complicated. As Abé Mark Nornes argues in his extensive study on subtitling, *Cinema Babel* (2008), the global circulation of the moving image has a profound and contradictory effect on translation practices. More films are subjected to translation than ever before, creating a huge need for translation services, a vast network of professionals and expanded opportunities, but those practices become increasingly implicated in the darker side of the global system that depends on the exploitation of cheap labor, rationalization, homogenization, and a ruthless search for new markets.

Perhaps the most paradigmatic manifestation of this system, Nornes argues, is the advent of powerful translation companies involved in the production of made-to-order language tracks that rely on the so called "genesis file." Widely embraced for its convenience and the speed of service, Nornes compares the genesis file to "translation clearinghouses modeled on the one-stop, take-no-prisoners approach of Wal-Mart"

(Nornes, 2008: 234). It is worth quoting his description of the process at length to relate the aptness of the analogy:

> The genesis file is essentially an English language scenario/spotting list—a compilation of all dialogue is annotated with precise timings of all the subtitles. The translation house maintains relationships with translators across the planet, enabling clients to choose their target languages from a menu. Upon completion of the genesis file, the company sends the computer file to its translators as an email attachment. These translators simultaneously open the genesis file and substitute each line of dialogue with a translated subtitle in their own language. After the substitutions are complete, the new files are sent back to the translation house by email, where they are converted into discrete subtitle tracks on a single DVD, or any format from theatrical release, to television broadcast, to the World Wide Web. It is as simple as that. (2008: 234).

The irony of this dominant and seemingly efficient practice is that the genesis file, the master file, is always in the English language, regardless of the original language of the film, so that subtitles for texts from non-English-speaking countries are not just translations, but translations of translations. Often, translators (who work under short deadlines and low wages) have no access to the source text, no ability to adapt the timing of subtitles to the target language, and sometimes no video component of the text to be translated. Translators in the second or third languages—away from English—have the options to correct or improve upon the English translations, but most are reported not to indulge in the exercise (Pedersen, 2006). This practice may present a triumph for the production and distribution companies, saving costs and standardizing and accelerating film dissemination, but it is a great injustice to viewers, filmmakers, and their works' integrity, and undoubtedly disturbing to translators who take their job seriously. Among other problematic aspects, it also underscores the power dynamic of the global pecking order, where less dominant languages are considerably disadvantaged, while English assumes a surreptitious influence over defining world cinema. Nornes contends that the very name of the master file, "genesis," holds within it a "neo-imperial translation project positioning English as the source of all meaning" (2008: 235). Efficiency and profit take over the meaning of films and deem inconsequential the gestures of artists who labor over nuanced expressions in their films. It is merely one of the tragic features of globalization, where genuine discourse and artistic integrity are superseded by bottom-line-driven motives.

The imperial presence of English is also evident in the conditions that most film festivals place on the submission of films—a considerable change since the earlier years of the international film trade. Although festivals have been an international phenomenon since their beginning, and thus by definition sites of linguistic border-crossing, they also functioned as important platforms for national cinemas; language difference was an element that marked the film's national identity and asserted the specificity of national culture. As Ďurovičova explains, in the 1920s and 1930s it was an interest of every film-producing country to protect its own industry and national culture from outside intrusions and competition, and elements related to film translation were made

(continued)

(continued)

at a political level, with the aim of simultaneously controlling their specific culture and expanding it through international film trade (Đurovičova, 2010: 90-98). Thus, when in 1929 the Italian government ruled to dub all imported films in order to protect their national space, yet benefit from the imports' benefits, "they involved themselves in a discursive strategy of appropriation-via-translation" (Đurovičova, 2010: 95). Along the lines of this political strategy, the Venice Film Festival asserted itself since its beginning in 1932 "as a *translatio*-free zone, refusing to accept any versions or any translated films, whether dubbed or subtitled" (Đurovičova, 2010: 98). In fact, in the early years of festivals, subtitling was not part of the regulations and films were submitted in their original version. By the 1960s, most festivals required that films be submitted with subtitles in the host country's language. In recent decades, however, the electronic subtitling and digitization of the audiovisual industry has not only profoundly affected the subtitling practice, but asserts English as the primary language. Regardless of the festival's host country, English subtitles are required for the film to be considered by the programmers; Berlinale, for example, requires even German-language films to be submitted with English subtitles. The eminent global identity of even regional and national film festivals means that they have to succumb to the dominance of English language, a lingua franca that stamps the film's global availability and accessibility. And yet, the intricately contradictory nature of globalized traffic in film also allows filmmakers to take their films to film festivals and reach broader audiences, and the compromises in translations usually take second seat to this cherished goal.

For viewers, most of whom remain distant from the awareness of the hegemony and the vicissitudes of the genesis file, technological changes in subtitling have been a boon for film viewing. Perks such as BitTorrent downloads of film subtitles and DVDs with multiple subtitle tracks make the viewers' participation in global film culture seemingly effortless and instantaneous. While DVDs still contain regional specifications that curtail the flow of films and determine the language options available, the technology has also oriented itself toward a rather efficient erasure of any marks of foreignness, particularly when it comes to blockbusters with a global ambition. Đurovičova explains this process as one of "localization," a work of transcoding that includes all legible aspects of translation (language, operating system, scripts, icons, etc.) so that the viewers in any country can navigate through the DVD without ever being confronted with signs that the film is "not from here" (Đurovičova, 2010: 111–113). This is common for blockbusters with simultaneous global release, such as *The Lord of the Rings*, DVD editions of which are released in numerous versions, reformatted into all region zones, translated into over twenty languages, and offer supplemental material available to language-specific communities.

A different translation practice—dubbing—provides another dimension to the global traffic of film. A commonly used and common-sense method for children's films, the practice is much more controversial when applied to other films. Often sneered at, even provoking angry reactions (Jean Renoir famously said that if cinema existed in the Middle Ages, dubbers would be burnt as witches), and seen as despicable and as far inferior to subtitling, dubbing exists for several reasons. One, it can be a political and protectionist gesture, as was the case in many European countries in the 1930s, which mandated dubbing to protect the linguistic integrity of the native soil and block out foreign sound. In a reverse strategy, dubbing can be banned to protect the domestic film industry and preserve the gap between imports and regional product. Second, it addresses more effectively the problem of literacy and the burden of reading; while subtitling assumes a certain level of cultural capital from the viewer, dubbing, although more costly, makes sense in contexts where literacy is a major factor in film reception (between the two world wars, illiteracy rates in some European countries were often higher than thirty percent). And finally, dubbing is often preferred because it is a naturalized convention, an established film viewing habit that offers an instant comfort zone for the audience, while also being affordable in countries with larger markets. To accommodate these, Hollywood takes its films to nearly all non-English-speaking countries in a dubbed form (Crookes, 2011). Hollywood itself has a rather impenetrable, rarely broken, English-only wall when it comes to a mainstream product (Ang Lee's *Crouching Tiger, Hidden Dragon* broke this wall in 2002). Germany and Italy have large and systematic dubbing markets, and France, Spain, Turkey, Hungary, and Hong Kong also dub foreign films. The same is true in case of Iran, China, and Russian-speaking countries. The multilingual cultures of India see Hollywood blockbusters such as *Titanic* (James Cameron, 1996) and *Avatar* (James Cameron, 2009) translated in three to four languages including Hindi, the language of popular Indian cinema. *Slumdog Millionaire* (Danny Boyle, 2008) was released simultaneously in subtitled and dubbed forms, but the latter, called *Slumdog Crorepati*, outshone the original version. Martial arts films from East Asia have been popular in most parts of the world in their dubbed versions, often with compromised soundtracks.

Perhaps the most critical problem with both dubbing and subtitling has to do with the transformation of meaning involved in the process of translation; transferring meaning in film involves not just language and its complex nuances but acting, rhythm, timing, force, and so on. In the concluding paragraphs of his book, Nornes declares that the act of translation is a complex one, carrying numerous cultural, industrial, and ideological pressures, that "in an age when no film is complete until it crosses the frontier of language, it is the translator who has the last word. Global cinema is translator's cinema" (Nornes, 2008: 243). The difficulties and merits of both subtitling and dubbing are problems of translation, spawning all sorts of theoretical and practical issues. When native speakers watch a film in their own language, subtitled in another, they experience instantly the inaccuracies and failures of translations in conveying the nuances and cultural inflexions. Most accustomed to such failures are diasporic audiences, and watching a film with them provides instant lessons in the complexities of meaning transfer across space and time. If Walter Benjamin's succinct observation that "all translation is only a somewhat provisional way of coming to terms with the foreignness of languages" (1923: 75) holds true for subtitling of films, then subtitles are mere invitations into the world of cinema. They are not an end in themselves. We are impacted and experience films despite the difficulty of subtitles; the multitude of languages and cultures in which cinema takes form would be inaccessible without subtitles, despite their transient and problematic nature. Watching world cinema is to immerse oneself in and experience different worlds, and subtitles are a necessary layer of this experience. But the paradox of subtitles is also a paradox of watching world cinema. They bring you closer to a world that is inherently distant, strange, and inaccessible, and yet, by bringing it closer and making it more familiar they reveal not that world but only its untranslatability.

Digital projection in theaters

In the wake of an imploding revolution in the transmission and reception of images, the movie theater is undergoing profound changes as well. In the span of a few years, film industries across the world, from the US to China, India, and Korea have moved away from the tradition of celluloid to digital film and digital projection in theaters. Instead of celluloid reels, a projectionist receives a digital hard drive with a specific code to be activated and screened on a digital projector. With a majority of cinema screens having already converted to digital, combined with the majority of productions now being shot with high-end digital cameras, the need for 35mm film stock is evaporating rapidly.

Fujifilm stopped the production of 35mm film stock in 2013, while Kodak, emerging from bankruptcy and selling off its still photography and printing business, is currently the only company still producing celluloid stock. Kodak's support for 35mm film stock is fueled by cinematographers and filmmakers who remain devoted to celluloid—such as J.J. Abrams, whose *Star Trek Into Darkness* (2013) was shot on film, and Christopher Nolan, the most vocal defender of the superiority of celluloid—but also by some markets, such as Latin America and Eastern Europe, whose digital conversion rate is much slower due to cost.

David Bordwell outlines some of the major features of these tectonic changes in his digital book, *Pandora's Digital Box: Films, Files and Digital Movies* (2012b), in which he chronicles a massive shift in projection systems. These changes make projection booths versatile devices not simply for film projection but for beaming concerts and major events anywhere in the world. The quality of images for 1.3K, 2K, and 4K digital systems is progressively better with higher resolution and greater fidelity to the aspect ratio of the filmic image. For viewers, digital projection affirms two things. The quality of the image improves or remains steady as the frequent scratches to the film prints caused by transportation and physical touch are minimized. With the exhibition industry already investing millions in this change, theaters retain the exclusivity of theatrical quality and experience, remaining the mainstay for screenings, at least for their initial runs.

The speed and the range of this digital revolution are breathtakingly daunting and often challenging for the exhibition industry. In 2007, there were only 5,158 digital cinemas in the world, and 107,832 screens using 35mm celluloid. In 2012, there were 35,087 screens using 35mm, while digital cinemas of various kinds (digital 2-D, 3-D, and E-cinema) had expanded to 94,818 (Hancock, 2013). Over two-thirds of China's theaters were already digital in 2013, and all theaters in South Korea have digital projection. The EU has undertaken the conversion task with equal urgency: by 2013, at the peak of the conversion process, digital screens in France were at 92 percent and 93 percent in the UK.

Modifying projection systems to digital cinema is an expensive proposition, and while multiplexes have the resources and financial strength to undertake this transition, many small-town theaters have found it very difficult to raise funds on their own, and face extinction as a result. In Europe, the EU provides funds for conversion, while in China financial imperative and competition are driving the investment. The wave of changes taking place in all regions underscores the importance of theaters to the industry. Along with the possibilities of watching films in other formats and venues, it is theater that remains central to a broader conception of cinema. Theatrical screenings also remain key for film festivals, which continue to grow in number, from small

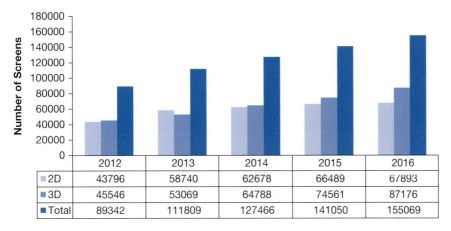

	2012	2013	2014	2015	2016
■ 2D	43796	58740	62678	66489	67893
■ 3D	45546	53069	64788	74561	87176
■ Total	89342	111809	127466	141050	155069

Figure 2.9 The worldwide number of digital and 3D screens, 2016. Source: FOCUS 2017, Marché du Film, Festival de Cannes

towns and cities to major cultural centers. Theater is still the space from which films are launched, even in parts of the world where video on demand (VoD) and online streaming has taken a strong hold. In the second edition of *The Business of Media Distribution*, Jeff Ulin, a former executive at Lucasfilm and Paramount, addresses digital delivery and many other factors that upset traditional models of distribution, and asserts the importance of the theatrical window despite new trends such as streaming and day-and-date release: "I don't see the theatrical window changing much for the time being. It is still the event that brands a property for decades of downstream consumption" (Tryon, 2013b). This sentiment certainly rings true if we look at the buzziest summer releases. Bong Joon-ho's *Snowpiercer* (2013), for example, a Korean blockbuster distributed by Radius in the US, used the benefits of both the limited-platform theatrical and wide VoD release. An unusual distribution strategy that would spell failure only a few years ago, the film was offered on VoD platforms only two weeks after its very successful limited theatrical release. The film had impressive theatrical earnings in its opening weekends, and skyrocketed to the No. 1 spot on iTunes and other digital platforms immediately after launching, making it the widest multi-platform release ever (Kohn, 2014). This case showed that theatrical and VoD platforms, rather than being mutually exclusive, co-exist and enhance each other, suggesting simultaneity of various kinds of screens and forms of watching.

We have indeed come very far from Susan Sontag's observation that "to see a great film only on television is not to have really seen that film" (1996). Justified, understandable, and still relevant as this position may be for many critics and filmmakers, watching films on 6in, 8in, or 10in screens has become too ubiquitous to dismiss. It is not merely that we live in a screen culture, where cinema is only one element among many—screens are everywhere, and we watch everything, anywhere and anytime—but the assumed hierarchy between different screens still evident in Sontag's statement, the privileged and exclusive status assigned to the large theatrical screen, is now obliterated. This, Friedberg explains, presents a major shift in our thinking:

Now, a variety of screens—long and wide and square, large and small, composed of grains, composed of pixels—compete for our attention without any arguments about hegemony . . . our assumptions about "spectatorship" have lost their theoretical pinions as screens have changed, as have our relations to them.

(Friedberg, 2000: 450)

The digital technology and the transformation of the screen, as Friedberg points out, have not only changed our watching habits but redefined the very nature of the moving image and our relation to it.

In the 1950s, Hollywood responded to the arrival of television by making its spectacles larger and more visceral, introducing new technologies such as CinemaScope and 3-D, as if to dare the medium of television to compete with it. Today, smaller and variable-size screens and their pervasiveness are eliciting a response of their own, although it is too early to predict the outcome of these transformations. What we can say with confidence is that rather than contributing to the demise of the cinematic and theatrical, new technologies are not mutually exclusive but co-exist and feed off each other to create new forms of expression. Noted directors like Terrence Malick, Lars von Trier, Kim Ki-duk, or Xavier Dolan embrace and integrate technological changes into their work while remaining profoundly devoted to the cinematic. Films such as *The Tree of Life* (Terrence Malick, 2011), *Melancholia* (Lars von Trier, 2011), *Arirang* (Kim Ki-duk, 2011) and *Mommy* (Xavier Dolan, 2014) all rely on digital technology only to retrieve the power of the analog cinematic image and its life on a large screen.

At the moment, while smart phones and tablets are ubiquitous, the experience of cinema still remains well-defined for most spectators in terms of semi-formal viewing situations, and the theater remains a primal space for experiencing moving images. Film viewing has expanded well beyond the four walls of a movie theater, and beyond the physical conditions that define it, yet we tend to create theater-like conditions of viewing, if possible, and modify the environment to resemble the one of the movie theater. This is obviously the case with the concept of home theater, which implies a "real cinema experience" at a private home, but it is also the case with smaller screens like tablets or smart phones. Minor modifications of our environment, such as drawing the screen closer and raising the sound on our headphones to minimize the background noise, are an essential part of what Francesco Casetti describes as "filmic experience" which, while altered and relocated from the material conditions of the theater, still survives:

Relocation emphasizes the role of experience. A given medium is defined by a specific type of watching, listening, attention, and sensibility. Therefore, it is not the permanence of its physical aspect but rather the permanence of its way of seeing, hearing, and sensing that assures its continuity. A medium survives as long as the form of experience that characterizes it survives.

(Casetti, 2012: 15)

Casetti explains that when the physical and technological space of cinema changes, when film goes through a radical process of relocation (from theaters to multiplexes, television, DVD, tablets, smart phones, virtual spaces, etc.), it risks losing its identity and specificity. Despite this, the filmic experience survives. New platforms are still delivery tools for film, we reinstate theatrical conditions of viewing regardless of where we watch films, and we still watch films in theaters. Further, despite the emergence of an incredible variety of extra-filmic and extra-theatrical practices, "it is also true that these new practices are promptly reinserted within the context of a theater, thus renewing the traits of the filmic experience" (Casetti, 2011: 9).

Let us return to Anna, Nicole, and their screens in *Artaud Double Bill*. Anna and Nicole are in a theater, our primary and most enduring site for watching films. Their smart phone screens are capable of breaking the isolation of the theatrical experience: capturing the film, they are watching and transmitting it to each other. In this instance alone, the singularity of the theatrical experience is broken and the space of the theater converges with spaces and practices outside and beyond it. Anna and Nicole only hint at the new ways of watching, the possibilities and implications of breaking our intimate, exclusive relationship with a theatrical screen. One can imagine both of them streaming films on their smart phones today, when films are part of the larger environment where both the screens and the viewers are only two elements among many. Egoyan's *Artaud Double Bill* is an effective example of our current transformation of the filmic experience and the relocation of cinema, but it is also an affirmation of the centrality of the film theater, where "more than elsewhere, a film is an event" that recuperates the sense of an experience (Casetti, 2012: 12). The convergence of technologies and cultures across borders places the film viewer in an enviable position to experience the moment that is unlike any other in cinema's history, both bewildering and amusing. As we watch and engage with world cinema, we also live through its most significant transition yet. In this transition, the theater is re-drawn yet retains its important position.

Activity 2.1

Below are some of the films that feature film-watching and theater as a central theme:

Cinema Paradiso (1988), Giuseppe Tornatore

Splendor (1989), Ettore Scola

The Adopted Son (1998), Aktan Arym Kubat

Good Bye, Dragon Inn (2003), Tsai Ming-liang

Fantasma (2006), Lisandro Alonso

Chacun son cinéma/To Each His Own Cinema (2007)

Road, Movie (2009), Dev Benegal

A Useful Life (2010), Federico Veiroj

Cinema is Everywhere (2011), Teal Greyhavens

Choose two films from different countries and different cultural contexts, and consider how the theater, and the experience of watching in a theater, features in different narratives.

Activity 2.2

In an anthology film produced for the 60th anniversary of the Cannes Film Festival, *Chacun son cinéma*, renowned world cinema auteurs pay tribute to cinema. For many of them, the theater is an essential part of their cinephilia. Choose at least three shorts where theater plays a key role and explore the connection between the director's vision of cinema and watching films in a theater.

Activity 2.3

Side by Side (2012), directed by Christopher Kenneally and produced by Justin Szlasa and Keanu Reeves, is a documentary that investigates the history and the process of both 35mm film and digital film. Through interviews with cinematographers and directors such as David Fincher, Steven Soderbergh, James Cameron, Christopher Nolan, and many others, arguments emerge both in defense of the celluloid and digital film. Consider these arguments "side by side" and formulate your own informed position on the issue.

Activity 2.4

For the occasion of the 70th Venice International Film Festival, the festival created a special project *Venezia 70—Future Reloaded*, where seventy directors from around the world reflect on the future of cinema in sixty- to ninety-second shorts. Watch the shorts and discuss how they bring together the past and the future of cinema.

Activity 2.5

The "In focus 2.2" section of this chapter discusses the issue of subtitles and dubbing. Pick a DVD of a foreign blockbuster film, such as Wong Kar-wai's *The Grandmaster* (2013), and examine its language options. How many and which language/subtitle options does the DVD offer? Watch sections of the film in both the subtitled and dubbed version, and compare the two. Which did you prefer, and why? What are the advantages/disadvantages of both the subtitled and dubbed versions?

Notes

1 Both Anna and Nicole are viewers of a multiple set of images. They not only experience each other's films, but in Godard's film, the protagonist, Nana, is also in a theater watching Carl Dreyer's *La passion de Jeanne d'Arc* (1928); and in *The Adjuster*, a film Nicole is watching, the protagonist Hera is also sitting in a cinema.

2 For more information on the HOMER Project and its activities, see its website at http://sb.dhpress. org/digitalhomer/about

3 See the conference site at: www.ecrea.eu/events/about/id/18. Accessed June 7, 2014.

4 The following accounts are based on personal recollections, conversations, and the symposium conducted by the journal, *Senses of Cinema*. Arthur Knight, Clara Pafort-Overduin, and Deb Verhoeven, "Senses of Cinema-Going: Brief Reports on Going to the Movies Around the World," *Senses of Cinema* 58. Available at: www.sensesofcinema.com/2011/feature-articles/senses-of-cinema-going-brief-reports-on-going-to-the-movies-around-the-world

5 For a discussion of art cinemas in the US, see David Bordwell, "Pandora's Box, Art House, Smart House," January 30, 2012. Available at: www.davidbordwell.net/blog/2012/01/30/pandoras-digital-box-art-house-smart-house. Bordwell here notes: "In the whole market, art houses are a blip. Figures are hard to come by, but Jack Foley, head of domestic distribution for Focus Features, estimates that there are about 250 core art house screens. In addition, other venues present art house product on an occasional basis or as part of cultural center programming."

6 See the Landmark Theaters and Sundance Cinemas websites. Available at: www.landmarktheatres. com/AboutLandmark/aboutindex.htm and www.sundancecinemas.com

7 See Richard Porton, "Not Just an Abortion Film: An Interview with Cristian Mungiu," *Cineaste* (March 28, 2008). Available at: www.cineaste.com/articles/not-just-an-abortion-film.htm. The DVD edition of the film also contains a short documentary on the film caravan.

8 For the accounts of this adventure see, for example, Severin Carrell, "Box Office Draw: Highland Film Fans Feel Pulling Power of Tilda Swinton," *The Guardian* (August 2, 2009), www.theguardian. com/film/2009/aug/02/tilda-swinton-mobile-cinema; or Nick James, "Tug of Love: A Cinema Pilgrimage," *BFI Film Forever* (April 23, 2014), www.bfi.org.uk/news-opinion/sight-sound-magazine/comment/tug-love-cinema-pilgrimage

9 These figures are derived from research conducted by the Motion Picture Association and the international firm LEK. See "The Cost of Movie Piracy," prepared by LEK, 2005, https://archive.org/details/MpaaPiracyReort. Accessed June 8, 2014

10 Audiovisualcy is an online forum for creative and critical video essays about films, moving image studies, and film theory, which establishes important connections between written film studies and an emerging body of work on audiovisual film studies. See Audiovisualcy: An Online Forum for Videographic Film Studies, available at http://vimeo.com/groups/audiovisualcy.

11 The work of Cristina Álvarez López and Adrian Martin appears in *Mubi's Notebook* (https://mubi.com/notebook/posts/author/269) and the *Audiovisual Essay* (http://reframe.sussex.ac.uk/audiovisualessay/) as part of a media studies research project. Their work uses simple digital editing tools to reshape existing footage with written or spoken text, creating new approaches to film criticism. In October 2016, Birkbeck Institute for the Moving Images organized a showcase of their video-essay practice: www.eventbrite.co.uk/e/adrian-martin-cristina-alvarez-lopez-the-audiovisual-essay-tickets-27189763314

12 Media Commons: A Digital Scholarly Network, Society for Cinema Studies, "Announcing [In]Transition," http://mediacommons.futureofthebook.org/content/announcing-intransition. Accessed June 8, 2014. Also see Jaimie Baron, "The Image as Direct Quotation: Identity, Transformation, and the Case for Fair Use," *Frames Cinema Journal*, http://framescinemajournal.com/article/the-image-as-direct-quotation

13 See European Commission, *A Profile of Current and Future Audience: Final Report*, EU, 2014. Available at www.eubusiness.com/topics/media/audience-profile; http://bookshop.europa.eu/is-bin/INTER-SHOP.enfinity/WFS/EU-Bookshop-Site/en_GB/-/EUR/ViewPublication-Start?PublicationKey=NC0414085. Accessed June 12, 2015.

14 References to Jia Zhangke's view on piracy can be found, for example, in his manifesto on independent cinema, "The Age of Amateur Cinema Will Return," at *Generate Films*, http://dgeneratefilms. com/critical-essays/jia-zhangke-the-age-of-amateur-cinema-will-return; Evan Osnos' "The Long

Shot," *New Yorker* (May 11, 2009), available at www.newyorker.com/magazine/2009/05/11/the-long-shot; or Walter Salles's documentary *Jia Zhangke: A Guy from Fenyang* (2016).

15 The friction between content providers and cable television has only increased with the introduction of devices such as Google Chromecast, which enables streaming from sources such as Netflix and YouTube on a Google Chrome browser, or Aereo, an Internet service company using antennae-like devices to allow you to broadcast and record shows on a cloud-based digital video recorder.

Bibliography

Acland, Charles R. (2003). *Screen Traffic: Movies, Multiplexes, and Global Culture*. Durham, NC: Duke University Press.

Alvin, Rebecca M. (2007). "Cinemas of the Future." *Cineaste* 32(3). Available at: www.cineaste.com/articles/cinemas-of-the-future.htm. Accessed September 5, 2016.

Anderson, Chris. (2008). *The Long Tail: Why the Future of Business is Selling Less of More*. New York, NY: Hyperion.

Barthes, Roland. (1980). "Upon Leaving the Movie Theater." In Theresa Hak Kyung Cha (ed), *Apparatus*. Trans. Bertrand Augst and Susan White. New York, NY: Tanam Press, pp. 1–7.

Benjamin, Walter. (1923). "The Task of the Translator." First printed as an introduction to the translation of Baudelaire's *Tableaux parisiens*. Translated by Harry Zohn. In *Illuminations: Walter Benjamin Essays and Reflections*. New York, NY: Schocken Books, 1968, pp. 69–82.

Bordwell. David. (2012a). "Pandora's Box, Art House, Smart House." David Bordwell's Observations on Film Art. Blog (January 30). Available at: www.davidbordwell.net/blog/2012/01/30/pandoras-digital-box-art-house-smart-house. Accessed June 15, 2014.

Bordwell, David. (2012b). *Pandora's Digital Box: Films, Files and Digital Movies*. Madison, WI: The Irvington Way Institute Press. Available at: www.davidbordwell.net/books/pandora.php. Accessed September 21, 2016.

Boxall, Andy. (2015). "The Number of Smartphones Users in the World is Expected to Reach a Giant 6.1 Billion by 2020." *Digital Trends* (June 3). Available at: www.digitaltrends.com/mobile/smartphone-users-number-6-1-billion-by-2020. Accessed October 5, 2016.

Casetti, Francesco. (2011). "Back from the Motherland: The Film Theater in the PostMedia Age." *Screen* 52(1), pp. 1–12.

Casetti, Francesco. (2012). "The Relocation of Cinema." *NECSUS: European Journal of Media Studies*. Available at: www.necsus-ejms.org/the-relocation-of-cinema. Accessed October 5, 2016.

Crookes, David. (2011). "How to Dub a Film." *The Independent* (October 4). Available at: www.independent.co.uk/arts-entertainment/films/features/how-to-dub-a-film-2365083.html. Accessed November 11, 2015.

Culshaw, Peter. (2008). "Sahara Film Festival: Desert Blues." *The Telegraph* (May 30). Available at: www.telegraph.co.uk/culture/film/starsandstories/3673756/Sahara-Film-Festival-desert-blues.html. Accessed June 4, 2014.

Decherney, Peter. (2007). "From Fair Use to Exemption." *Cinema Journal* 46(2), pp. 120–127.

Decherney, Peter. (2011). "Will Copyright Stifle Hollywood." *New York Times* (October 4). Available at: www.nytimes.com/2011/10/05/opinion/keep-works-in-the-public-domain-public.html?_r=2&ref=opinion. Accessed October 6, 2015.

Dixon, Wheeler Winston. (2013). *Streaming: Movies, Media and Instant Access*. Lexington, KY: University Press of Kentucky.

Dobroiu, Stefan. (2014). "Total Number of Romanian Screens Decreases to 260." *Cineuropa* (January 31). Available at: http://cineuropa.org/nw.aspx?t=newsdetail&l=en&did=251794. Accessed October 3, 2016.

Đurovičova, Nataša. (2010). "Vector, Flow, Zone: Towards a History of Cinematic *Translatio*." In Nataša Đurovičova & Kathleen Newman (eds), *World Cinema, Transnational Perspectives*. New York, NY: Routledge, pp. 90–121.

Egoyan, Atom & Ian Balfour (eds). (2004). *Subtitles: On the Foreignness of Film*. Cambridge, MA: MIT Press.

Eyles, Allen. (2014). "Cinemas and Cinemagoing: Art House and Repertory." *Screenonline*, British Film Institute (June 7). Available at: www.screenonline.org.uk/film/cinemas/sect5.html. Accessed October 5, 2016.

Fong, Gilbert C. F. & Kenneth K. L. Au (eds). (2009). *Dubbing and Subtitling in a World Context*. Hong Kong: Chinese University of Hong Kong.

Friedberg, Anne. (2000). "The End of Cinema: Multimedia and Technological Change." In Christine Gledhill, Anne Friedberg & Rajinder Kumar Dudrag (eds), *Reinventing Film Studies*. Bloomsbury Academic, pp. 439–452.

The Guardian cine-files. (2014). Available at: www.guardian.co.uk/film/series/cine-files. Accessed October 3, 2016.

Hancock, David. (2013). "Technology Moves to the Forefront in Cinema as Digital Overtakes Film." *IHS Technology Digest* (February 3). Available at: https://technology.ihs.com/421048/technology-moves-to-the-forefront-in-cinema-as-digital-overtakes-film. Accessed June 6, 2015.

Harbord, Janet. (2002). *Film Cultures*. New York, NY: Sage Publications.

Klinger, Barbara. (2006). *Beyond the Multiplex: Cinema, New Technologies, and the Home*. Berkeley, CA: University of California Press.

Hoad, Phil. (2010). "How Multiplex Cinemas Saved the British Film Industry 25 Years Ago." *The Guardian* (November 11). Available at: www.theguardian.com/film/2010/nov/11/multiplex-cinemas-the-point-milton-keynes. Accessed June 7, 2014.

Iordanova, Dina. (2008). *Budding Channels of Peripheral Cinema: The Long Tail of Global Film Circulation. Blurb on Demand*. Dynamics of World Cinema Internet-enabled Dissemination. Available at: www.st-andrews.ac.uk/worldcinema/index.php/strands/internet

Iordanova, Dina. (2013). "Instant, Abundant and Ubiquitous: Cinema Moves Online." *Cineaste* 39(1), pp. 46–50.

Iordanova, Dina & Stuart Cunningham (eds). (2012). *Digital Disruption: Cinema Moves On-Line*. St Andrews: St Andrews Film Studies.

Kohn, Eric. (2014). "*Snowpiercer* is Coming to VoD Early. Here's Why." *IndieWire* (July 16). Available at: www.indiewire.com/article/snowpiercer-is-coming-to-vod-early-heres-why-20140707. Accessed August 14, 2015.

La Monica, Paul R. (2016). "Will Netflix Top 75 Million Subscribers? It Better." *CNN Money* (January 18). Available at: http://money.cnn.com/2016/01/18/investing/netflix-earnings-preview-subscribers. Accessed October 6, 2016.

Larkin, Brian. (2008). "Degraded Images, Distorted Sounds: Nigerian Video and the Infrastructure of Piracy." In *Signal and Noise: Media, Infrastructure, and Urban Culture in Nigeria*. Durham, NC: Duke University Press, pp. 217-241.

Liang, Lawrence. (2005). "Porous Legalities and Avenues of Participation." In *Sarai Reader* 5. Delhi: Sarai.

Lovink, Geert & Sabine Niederer (eds). (2008). *Video Vortex Reader*. Amsterdam: Institute of Network Cultures.

Lobato, Ramon. (2012). *Shadow Economies of Cinema: Mapping Informal Film Distribution*. London: Palgrave Macmillan.

Lyttelton, Oliver. (2016). "Disruptors: How Netflix & Amazon Are Creating Greater Tumult in the Independent Film Industry." IndieWire (February 9). Available at: www.indiewire.com/2016/02/disruptors-how-netflix-amazon-are-creating-greater-tumult-in-the-independent-film-industry-272596. Accessed October 7, 2016.

Maltby, Richard. (2011). "New Cinema Histories." In Richard Maltby, Daniel Biltereyst and Phylippe Meers (eds), *Explorations in New Cinema History: Approaches and Case Studies*. Malden, MA: Wiley Blackwell.

Meyer, Elizabeth. (2011). "Art House Theater: Where Film Lovers Go Local." Independent Lens Blog (October 25). Available at: www.slideshare.net/ElizabethMeyer10/art-house-theaters-where-film-lovers-go-local-pbs. Accessed September 5, 2016.

Nornes, Abé Mark. (2008). *Cinema Babel: Translating Global Cinema*. Minneapolis, MN: University of Minnesota Press.

Oster, Silva. (2005). "Cinema on Life Support." *DW: Made for Minds* (July 18). Available at: www.dw.de/dw/article/0,,1648991,00.html. Accessed October 5, 2016.

Prasad, Madhava. (2001). *The Ideology of Hindi Film: A Historical Construction*. New York, NY: Oxford University Press.

Pedersen, Jan. (2006). "The Emergent Scandinavian Subtitling Norm." Conference paper, Stockholm University. DiVA: Digitala Vetenskapliga Arkivet. Available at: www.diva-portal.org/smash/record.jsf?pid=diva2:179287. Accessed September 10, 2015.

Roettgers, Janko. (2017). "Netflix's Latest Streaming Record: Members Viewed 250 Million Hours of Video on a Single Day in January." *Variety* (March 16). Available at: http://variety.com/2017/digital/news/netflix-250-million-hours-1202010393. Accessed March 20, 2017.

Sontag, Susan. (1996). "The Decay of Cinema." *New York Times* (February 25). Available at: http://partners.nytimes.com/books/00/03/12/specials/sontag-cinema.html. Accessed July 5, 2015.

Snickars, Pelle & Patrick Vondreau (eds). (2009). *The YouTube Reader*. Stockholm: National Library of Sweden.

Spangler, Todd. (2015). "Netflix Bandwidth Usage Climbs to Nearly 37% of Internet Traffic at Peak Hours." *Variety* (May 28). Available at: http://variety.com/2015/digital/news/netflix-bandwidth-usage-internet-traffic-1201507187. Accessed October 6, 2016.

Statistic Brain. (2016). "YouTube Company Statistics." Statistic Brain (September 1). Available at: www.statisticbrain.com/youtube-statistics. Accessed October 10, 2016.

Sundaram, Ravi. (1999). "Recycling Modernity: Pirate Electronic Cultures in India." *Third Text* 13(47), pp. 59–65.

Thompson, Anne. (2015). "Streaming Set to Overtake DVD Revenues and Box Office Take." *IndieWire* (June 4). Available at: www.indiewire.com/2015/06/streaming-set-to-overtake-dvd-revenues-and-box-office-take-187316. Accessed October 6, 2016.

Tryon, Chuck. (2013a). *On-Demand Culture: Digital Delivery and the Future of Movies*. New Brunswick, NJ: Rutgers University Press.

Tryon, Chuck. (2013b). "Theatrical Is Still the Event That Brands a Property for Downstream Consumption: *The Business of Media Distribution* Author Jeff Ulin." *Filmmaker Magazine* (November 25). Available at: http://filmmakermagazine.com/77361-theatrical-is-still-the-event-that-brands-a-property-for-decades-of-downstream-consumption-the-business-of-media-distribution-author-jeff-ulin/?utm_source=twitterfeed&utm_medium=twitter&utm_campaign=Feed%3A+FM_Blog+%28Filmmaker+Magazine+RSS+Feed%29#.U6Bni17VtZi. Accessed June 10, 2015.

Williams, Trey. (2016). "Netflix International Operations Could Surpass U.S. Business in Revenue by 2020." *MarketWatch* (August 23). Available at: www.marketwatch.com/story/netflixs-international-business-could-surpass-revenue-in-the-us-by-2020-2016-08-23. Accessed Oct 6, 2016.

Wiseman, Andreas. (2016). "MUBI China to Launch Following $50m Investment." *Screen Daily* (January 13). Available at: www.screendaily.com/5098849.article?utm_source=newsletter&utm_medium=email&utm _campaign=Newsletter82. Accessed October 10, 2016.

Wu, Tim. (2006). "The Wrong Tail." *Slate* (July 21). Available at: www.slate.com/articles/arts/books/2006/07/the_wrong_tail.single.html. Accessed October 19, 2016.*Figures 2.2a–2.2d*(d) An open-air theater at Locarno Piazza during the Locarno Film Festival. Image courtesy of imageBROKER/Alamy Stock Photo.

3   Film production and finance

Producing films is a daunting task, made more so by the varied conditions available to filmmakers in different parts of the world. There are different national, regional, and international systems of finance, legal conditions, and market incentives. Ideas, plans, and scripts are not always realized into productions, and even when films do get made, what counts as success is very relative—a success in one context or country can be considered a miserable failure in another. Whatever the context, however, some form of funding has to be secured before production can begin.

Unevenness in the availability of capital and resources around the world results in radical differences in filmmaking environments and production practices. If a major Hollywood film today requires an average budget of $140 million, an average European production costs about €6 million, while an average Nigerian video-film is produced for $40,000—figures that are hardly comparable. Despite vastly different conditions, expectations, and challenges, films are being made everywhere, and the number of films made around the world increases each year. As filmmaking transforms from a relatively isolated collection of national film industries to interactive, interdependent, and transnational structures, new contours have emerged in filmmaking practices. Although no substantial comparative analysis of these diverse conditions and patterns has been produced in film studies, the state of globalization and the flow of transnational capital provide some common ground that allows us to compare production practices across different nations and regions.

The following account of film production models is not exhaustive, but focused on our proposed cinematic power centers. Production practices in Hollywood are radically different from those in other parts of the world, as they are shaped entirely by the principles of free-market capitalism, and they generate resources that are out of reach for any other industry. While the principles of free-market capitalism are guided by the steady rhetoric of removing the state from everyday life and keeping it out of Hollywood film production, nearly all industries outside of Hollywood receive some form of state support. As the forces of capital trammel over state support in many countries, some less than others, finance from governments or government-supported bodies continues to play a key role in filmmaking. Nigeria's prolific industry may be an exception, but its informal economy defies comparison to the free enterprise of Hollywood.

With the purpose of finding some links among dispersed and complex practices, we highlight five different paradigms of production. First, Hollywood's intervention in film production outside of the US is rendered effective by its capital resources and its attractive market that assures exposure and financial returns. Second, the European Union (EU) provides a unique transnational state structure along with private capital. Third, Asia offers a different and unique configuration, where strong national industries—China, Japan,

Hong Kong, and Korea—serve as agencies toward an informal transnational production structure. Here, regional identity and an environment of co-production is not based on a formal state structure (as in the case of the EU) but is rather spurred by both globalization as well as a long history of regional relationships and collaboration between Asian countries. Fourth, the Indian model of production is transitioning from an informal economy of private money to formal industry structures that aim to resemble similar ones elsewhere. The small but significant support of the state, even after the economic liberalization of the 1990s, remains important for this country, which boasts the transnational powerhouse of Bollywood. Fifth, we look at the informal economy of Nollywood, Nigeria's powerful video-film industry that continues its prolific production and has become a major force in the region's economy and cultural influence.

Filmmakers elsewhere in the world, outside these five contexts, continue to make films that do not necessarily use or fall within these structures. There are other examples of national film industries and transnational collaborations, such as in Latin America or Africa, that bear resemblances to these structures yet require accounts of their own. Filmmakers often seek capital on their own, outside of these structures; there is an increasing trend of production support through international film festivals, as well as regional collaborations such as Ibero-America, which invites collaboration between Spain and Latin American countries. Though not exhaustive, we hope that the following accounts offer a snapshot of the complex diversity that characterizes current production models in world cinema.

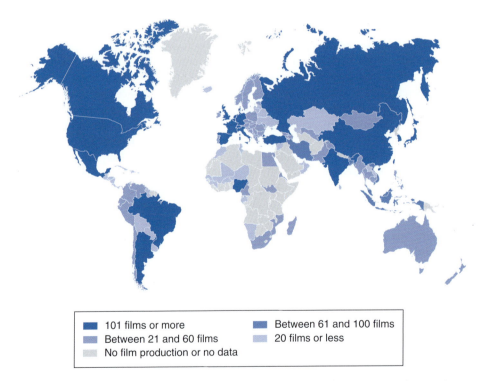

Figure 3.1 Concentration of film production. Source: UNESCO Institute for Statistics, http://uis. unesco.org, extracted June 2017

Hollywood's interventions

Hollywood exerts enormous influence over the production and circulation of films from different parts of the globe. One of the case studies illustrating such an influence is the controversy that erupted surrounding *Yi dai zong shi/The Grandmaster* (2013), a film based on the life of a major figure in Chinese martial arts, Ip Man, made by Hong Kong film director and noted festival auteur Wong Kar-wai. In the US, the film is distributed by the Weinstein Company, known for bringing recognition, patronage, and commercial success to a number of "foreign films." Allegedly, Harvey Weinstein compelled the director to re-edit the film and produce a more linear narrative with expository title cards to suit the tastes of American audiences. The charge was promptly denied by the company itself, even as the idea of Wong Kar-wai re-editing his own films was quite common for those familiar with the director's work. Many critics defended the edits of Wong Kar-wai for the North American market, based on his prevalent reputation as a director who tends to experiment frequently with the final edits of his films for different markets (Bordwell, 2013). Several versions of the film began circulating; while the more complex version existed for Asian and European territories, the one released in the US foregrounded a love story and the stylized aesthetic of kung fu action, stripping the film of much of its historical complexity.

Accusations among cinephiles and critics persisted, fueled by similar reports regarding Weinstein's habits of tampering with filmmakers' work, a trend that had gained him the legendary title of "Harvey Scissorhands." Around the same time, Bong Joon-ho, the famed Korean director, faced twenty-minute cuts to his film, *Snowpiercer* (2013) in order to make the film more accessible to the broader public, including, as Harvey Weinstein explained, "to audiences in Iowa . . . and Oklahoma" (quoted in Shaw-Williams, 2013). And in September 2013, Weinstein moved the release date of Olivier Dahan's *Grace of Monaco* (2013), slated to open the 2014 Cannes Film Festival, to modify the filmmaker's version of the film. This gesture resulted in an angry public response by Dahan, who called the re-edit "catastrophic," violating his artistic integrity to suit the tastes of the market: "It's got hardly anything to do with the film. It's only about the money, the release strategy, millions of dollars . . ." (quoted in Child, 2013). In some ways, this state of affairs is quite ordinary, and one can easily come across more tales of intervention into artistic processes by those who hold the reins, or the money, in their hands. Financiers defend such interventions as necessary to ensure the commercial viability of certain titles, even as they challenge the artistic integrity of filmmakers.

Harvey Weinstein, while credited with supporting film productions outside of Hollywood, has earned a reputation for putting commercial viability above all other considerations. His major triumph in distributing *Cinema Paradiso* (1988), by Giuseppe Tornatore, a flop that became a global hit after Weinstein's re-edit, set the tone for future successes with other "foreign films" in the US. The gross for *Cinema Paradiso* was $12.3 million, a figure that far surpassed the film's production costs. Under his leadership, Miramax built an enormous influence, acquiring and distributing films not only in the US but also in other markets, including Asia and Europe. Among the ten top-grossing foreign-language films in the US, Miramax claims five spots, wielding considerable influence over others (Box Office Mojo, 2016). Its noted acquisitions include Krzysztof Kieślowski's Three Colors Trilogy, *Blue* (1993), *White* (1994), and *Red* (1994); Chen Kaige's *Ba wang bie ji/Farewell My Concubine* (1993); Stephen Chow's *Siu Lam juk kau/Shaolin Soccer* (2001); Jean-Pierre Jeunet's *Amélie* (2001); Fernando Meirelles's *Cidade de Deus/City of God* (2002), and Michel Hazanavicius's *The Artist* (2011), a film that broke out of the "foreign-language feature" category at the Academy Awards and won the Oscar for best film.

Weinstein's reputation for tinkering with the edits of foreign films points to something else: an aggressive attempt by U.S. distributors and producers to define the concept of world cinema, shaping it in their own image. Hollywood's financial muscle is on clear display with blockbusters crowding up multiplexes in far corners of the globe, but its interests in financing filmmakers in other countries only to appropriate their work suggests domination by other means. The role of Weinstein as a distributor thus takes on a new meaning when his company ends up serving as the principal financial backer of the film. With an uncanny skill to identify potentially profitable and critically acclaimed productions, his role has also extended to that of a producer—as was the case with Lasse Hallström's *Chocolat* (2000)—and his clout, skills, and financial investment into film production not only influence access to the market and publicity efforts, but also shape the aesthetics and narrative of these films in important ways.

The power of market imperatives on the distribution of world cinema presents a dilemma both for filmmakers whose work is distributed in the US and for audiences who receive them. Discussing the controversy surrounding the re-edit of Wong Kar-wai's *The Grandmaster*, Jason Bailey asks, "Why do foreign films have to be dumbed down for American audiences?" (Bailey, 2013). In his detailed study of Harvey Weinstein and Miramax, Peter Biskind calls this process the "Miramaxization" of films, whereby they are tailored for maximum appeal to the mass market and the potential for a box office bonanza, a process that compromises the artistic independence of filmmakers (Biskind, 2004: 193). Paul McDonald draws parallels between Miramax's foreign film distribution tactics with its successful U.S. independent film distribution, terming the phenomenon the "Indiewoodization" of foreign-language films (McDonald, 2009). *The Guardian*'s Phil Hoad attributes this trend to the success of *Cinema Paradiso* (1988), which gave rise to "the postcard art house" movie that would dominate the map of world cinema for decades, blocking out the diversity of world cinema practices. He defines them as "glossy, streamlined foreign-language films—bottled classics with a life-affirming tang and a little twist of another culture" (Hoad, 2013).

Table 3.1 Top-grossing foreign films in the US (source: Box Office Mojo).

Top-grossing foreign films

Rank	Title	Country	Lifetime Gross (millions)	Year
1	Crouching Tiger, Hidden Dragon	Taiwan	$128	2000
2	Life Is Beautiful	Italy	$57.5	1997
3	Hero	China	$53.7	2002
4	Instructions Not Included	Mexico	$44.5	2013
5	Pan's Labyrinth	Mexico	$37.6	2006
6	Amélie	France	$33.3	2001
7	Jet Li's Fearless	China	$24.6	2006
8	Il Postino	Italy	$21.8	1994
9	Like Water for Chocolate	Mexico	$21.7	1992
10	La Cage aux Folles	France	$20.4	1978

In the 1990s, other film companies, distributors, and producers moved into the field, strengthening the trend initiated by the Weinstein Company, with a deeper impact on world cinema. Most major studios established "specialty divisions" dedicated to the distribution and financing of foreign films. Thus, Fine Line Features distributed Julio Medem's *Los amantes del Circulo Polar/Lovers of the Arctic Circle* (1998), Lars von Trier's *Dancer in the Dark* (2000), and Joshua Martson's *Maria Full of Grace* (2004). Focus Features bought the rights to Eric Rohmer's *Conte d'automne/Autumn Tale* (1998), Emir Kusturica's *Crna mačka, beli macor/Black Cat, White Cat* (1998), Jean-Pierre and Luc Dardenne's *Rosetta* (1999), and Mira Nair's *Monsoon Wedding* (2001). Fox Searchlight got Bernardo Bertolucci's *The Dreamers* (2003), and Deepa Mehta's *Water* (2005). New Line Cinema bought Guillermo del Toro's *Pan's Labyrinth* (2006), Orion Classics bought Pedro Almodovar's *Mujeres al borde de un ataque de nervios/Women on the Edge of a Nervous Breakdown* (1988), and Sony Pictures Classics distributed Zhang Yimou's *Shi mian mai fu/House of Flying Daggers* (2004), Michael Haneke's *Das weiße Band/The White Ribbon* (2009), and Asghar Farhadi's *Jodaeiye Nader az Simin/A Separation* (2011). As Hoad says, these films "narrowed tastes and reduced discoveries," and "encouraged more filmmakers outside the US to frame their stories commercially in the hope of distribution" (Hoad, 2013). If there is a concern regarding the concept of world cinema being churned into a uniform marketing brand, homogenizing the diversity of films, it arises from this development of the power of the US to shape the world in its own image.

Along with bigger companies, "boutique" distributors in the US have emerged who continue to bring different kinds of films to audiences, released on a number of platforms including DVDs and digital downloads. Among these, Kino Lorber, Film Movement, Amplify, Drafthouse, Strand Releasing, IFC Films, Vertical Entertainment, and Zeitgeist Films solicit films at festivals to bring them to world cinema audiences. They purchase distribution rights in the range of €20,000 to €60,000, a pittance in comparison to larger titles that other distributors acquire, but this sum meets a sizeable chunk of the production budget for films from abroad, providing some relief while also opening them to audiences beyond their borders.

Overall, Hollywood's role in shaping the conception of world cinema for its domestic and international markets suggests a hegemonic, restrictive influence. The advantages of U.S. distributors are unparalleled in world cinema, and they include the ability to spread overheads and costs over a large number of films, leverage over pricing and advertising efforts, bargaining power over exhibitors, a worldwide distribution network already in place for the blockbusters, and worldwide administrative and logistical support (Jäckel, 2003: 93). Given these benefits, most directors and producers prefer American investment in their projects, "despite vociferous protests against Hollywood domination and loss of creative control" (Jäckel, 2003: 54). Films circulating in world cinema aspire to penetrate the global mainstream but Hollywood's influence suggests a narrowly circumscribed taste and reduced discovery. As a result, a limited number of films produced around the world gain visibility and receive patronage, with Hollywood's version of world cinema circulating already-established names and film-producing countries. In support of its financial goals, Hollywood thus significantly cultivates the taste and defines the scope of world cinema.

European production models

The proximity of nation states in Europe has historically encouraged a collective identity for European national cinemas. Europe had already begun the process of forming a financial union since the 1970s, but it is only with the formation of the European Union in the early 1990s that a formal transnational body was established that supported cultural production in its member states. While the history of support and financing before this transformative development is complex, all the efforts to organize stable structures of support have been formalized over the past three decades. Europe has emerged as a political and financial union of twenty-eight countries with an attempt to sustain itself as an economic force on the world stage. With a population of 743 million, it offers a market larger than the US and is a formidable part of the world economy.

Filmmaking is a process that involves many players and phases, a kind of a "value chain" that sees the film from its conception to reception (Finney, 2010: 11). It begins with a development phase that involves a concept, idea, script, and assembling a team of director, scriptwriter, cinematographer, editor, actors, and various other on- and off-camera participants. A well-conceived idea seeks sources of financing in the hope that a film production is launched with adequate resources. Followed by shooting and post-production activities (editing, sound, lab support) films depend on distributors to reach the exhibition sector. An extensive publicity campaign is essential at this point to expose audiences to the coming attraction of the film's release, often determining in important ways the film's popular and critical reception. Apart from the creative phase that shapes the conception of the film, the most crucial, and often the most arduous and challenging phase is that of securing financing.

The filmmaking process is supported by two sources of funding: private (banks, sales of distribution rights, broadcaster's funding, co-production finance, and other investments) and public (government grants, loans, lines of credit, tax concessions, material support in terms of transportation, locations, logistics, incentives-awards for productions that promote national culture; Jäckel, 2003: 41-52). The combination of public and private funds, observed in nearly all neoliberal economies outside the US, has entirely replaced the total state funding prevalent before the 1980s particularly in Eastern European countries. Even in the US, where this model is absent, various state governments have begun offering incentives to production companies to highlight the visibility of state resources and to generate revenue for local economies. Raising money for film production is much like starting a business, with a range of complex options available to filmmakers, where a distinction can be made between finance and investment (Finney, 2010: 62). Financing comes in the form of a loan, to be returned with reasonable interest as soon as the film collects box office returns. Investment, on the other hand, is different in the sense that funders seek a share of the profits made from a film after it has garnered minimal returns at the box office.

Forms of private funding

Among private financiers, there are five main levels: corporate finance (private companies, banks and completion guarantors such as the European Investment Bank and the European Commission); equity finance (broadcasters such as Canal + in France, ARTE in Germany/France, media groups such as Bertelsmann in Germany, Vivendi in France, Bonnier AB in Sweden, and BBC in the UK); distributors that bring in money from pre-sales; co-production finance; and other sources of sponsorships (Jäckel, 2003: 44). Nationally based institutions encourage local producers with expectations that capital outside the country will join in the spirit of co-production. Transnational organizations deliberately set out to achieve collaborations among the EU members, and in some countries like France, the Netherlands, and Italy broadcasters are legally required to invest in film production. With this, they diversify their programming and broaden viewership across national borders. Enforcing the idea of unity strongly promoted by the EU, multilateral co-production and co-financing are becoming commonplace, and co-productions remain one of the major features of European cinema, even as the term itself cannot explain fully the scope of what happens in specific cases. Co-productions have been a boon especially to producers from smaller countries, which lack stronger and richer sources of finance available to their counterparts. The ultimate goal of these structures is to achieve seamless collaboration on a regional European level.

While these are distinct financial entities, their larger motive is to set up a series of activities for the European audiovisual industry, a common rubric of support in Europe that includes film production, exhibition, and archiving. The initial announcement of the European Investment Bank (EIB) for €1 billion, distributed across all activities involving film, provides a stable support structure for film production activities. As a unified entity, Europe wants to build up all systems and structures to project a common culture. Further, as the statement by the EIB clearly indicates, this allows Europe to face challenges and compete with Hollywood in a competitive global economy. Viviane Reding of the European Commission summarized the sentiment in Cannes in 2001: "I cannot accept the fact that American films account for 75 percent of box-office takings in Europe while the EU produces more films than the United States. I will not sit back and watch our young artistic talents and audiovisual entrepreneurs disappear across the Atlantic" (EIB Press Release, 2001). Private banks in many European countries have joined this effort with their own initiatives for film funding, creating a broad European network for film production financing.

Public funding and state support

Outside the US, the state provides support for a diverse range of cultural production including film, in part to strengthen national industries against competition from the outside, especially from Hollywood, and to protect artists from dependence on the market. In former socialist countries, the idea of state support has gone hand in hand with the central role of education (rather than entertainment) accorded to film by the state. Moreover, film, whose international circulation brings potential for recognition, becomes a vital currency for economically isolated nations. Countries like the former Yugoslavia or Romania established central film studios and constructed a network of theaters. The models of state support were redesigned in most European countries after 1989, and formerly socialist countries in Eastern and South Europe joined in the process.

Two major organizations have played a key role in shaping public funding in Europe since the 1980s: Eurimages and MEDIA Programme. Eurimages (the European Cinema Support Fund) was set up in 1988 by the Council of Europe to support the co-production of feature, animation and documentary films, and its membership has expanded from ten participating countries to thirty-seven members. The UK joined in 1992 but withdrew in 2011, and British producers have continued to protest since, urging to rejoin Eurimages to safeguard official ties with Europe, a call that is especially significant after Brexit (Macnab, 2016). In recent years, many smaller countries such as Cyprus and Estonia joined in, whose small markets make co-production support a necessity. Eurimages' initial funding of about €8 million has grown to the current annual budget of €25 million, and since 1989 the fund has supported close to two thousand European co-productions for approximately

€530 million (Eurimages, 2016). Jäckel notes that "the Eurimages board pays particular attention to projects originating in member states with low cinematographic production levels and to co-productions that bring together co-producers from states with high and low production levels" (2003: 77). Eurimages funding, available in the form of soft loans (co-production support) or subsidies (theatrical distribution, exhibition, and digital equipment for cinema theaters) is meant to encourage cooperation between established professionals in different countries. The allocation of co-production funds is based on a point system where points are awarded based on a certain "European character," outlined in the European Convention of Cinematographic Production.

The expansion of the EU to include the countries of Eastern Europe invited a complex diversification of film production. Smaller countries such as Romania, Slovenia, Croatia, and Montenegro found the support and cooperation of Eurimages essential as they moved from socialist to competitive free-market economies. Each nation has its own funding institution that takes charge of funds allocation: the Ministry of Culture in Poland; the Motion Picture Foundation in Hungary; the Film Fund for the Development of Czech Cinema, and the National Film Center in Bulgaria. Television financing remains an important factor in these countries. In Slovenia, for example, the Slovenian Film Center provides film funding together with RTV Slovenia.

For Eastern European countries, the inequity among European member states in political and economic terms weighs heavily on the conditions of co-production. Questioning the stated fairness of Eurimages' support of these countries, Dina Iordanova points out that the requirement of including cross-cultural content to construct European character in films often results in artificial insertions into narratives, producing a merely decorative mix of all things European derogatorily termed "Europudding" (Iordanova, 1999). Second, the Eurimages fund replaced the more effective and targeted mechanisms of funding Eastern European films (such as the French initiative Fonds ECO), complicating the opportunities for filmmakers outside of Western Europe. Instead of the more specifically-designated earlier establishments, Eastern European filmmakers have to compete for funding along with their formidable peers in Western Europe, which means the funding for Eastern European countries became sporadic and selective after the 1990s, focusing on established auteurs such as István Szabó, Jan Svěrák, or Goran Paskaljević, and narrowing the range for new filmmakers. Third, to acquire funding from Eurimages, filmmakers are required to have fifty percent of their financing secured in their own country. Since this level of support is difficult to garner in smaller countries, many filmmakers prefer to migrate to the West to become eligible for funds in a new host country (Iordanova, 1999: 56). This situation explains a paradox for the mission of Eurimages and the EU more generally: while their aim is to achieve parity through collaboration, the national context of films, which should not be a factor in a pan-European institution, ends up playing a determining role.

The EU launched a larger initiative, MEDIA Programme, in 1987 to promote an image of a unified Europe, counter the dominance of American cultural imports, and respond to changes in technology and institutions shaped by globalization. For the past three decades, the program has undergone several transformations, resembling the models of planned economies that set out objectives with specified budgets. Its continued success has allowed it to expand and support a broader range of activities beyond production, such as Media Salles (1992), which focuses on exhibition; SCRIPT (the European Script Fund); EFDO (the European Film Distribution Office); MEDIA Mundus, which promotes cooperation with countries outside of the EU; and BABEL (Broadcasting Across the Barriers of European Languages). In its broader conception of audiovisual media, its focus has included training, workshops, support for film festivals, and the European Film Academy (1988), which holds an annual award ceremony for Best European Film. In addition, in a rare and remarkable move on the world stage, MEDIA Programme has boosted the profile of the short film form on the world stage through supporting the production and exhibition of such films. MEDIA Programme has built a transnational infrastructure with no parallel in the world. For a filmmaker, this presents an impressive array of options to produce and market films within and outside Europe.

Since January 2014, under the new name of Creative Europe, MEDIA Programme has broadened the support for film by making it an integral part of the creative economy of the region. With a budget of €1.46 billion to be used over the next seven years, the program will "provide a boost for the cultural and creative sectors, which are a major source of jobs and growth," creating a healthier environment for film production by supporting the growth of all areas that contribute to the film industry: technology and software development, creative writing, trans-media projects, screenwriting, photography, acting, animation, and literature, among others (European Commission, 2014). This makes Europe a leader in global shifts and policy imperatives to re-think culture as an economic engine to promote the growth of local-sector jobs and to bring attention to aspiring filmmakers from neglected regions.

Table 3.2 Number of feature films produced in the EU in 2016 (including documentary features and major co-productions). Source: FOCUS, Marché du Film, 2017.

Country	Films produced in 2016
1 Spain	241
2 France	224
3 Italy	217
4 Germany	213
5 UK	141
6 Czech Republic	72
7 Netherlands	60
8 Belgium	54
9 Denmark	54
10 Poland	48
11 Sweden	47
12 Romania	42
13 Finland	40
14 Austria	37
15 Greece	29
16 Ireland	25
17 Portugal	23
18 Bulgaria	22
19 Hungary	18
20 Slovakia	18
21 Estonia	17
22 Latvia	17
23 Slovenia	16
24 Lithuania	12
25 Croatia	10
26 Cyprus	2
Total EU	1,699

The achievements of Eurimages and MEDIA underscore the EU's commitment to cultivate and maintain a high level of integrity for its cultural production in the age of globalization. The dispute between the US and Europe regarding the GATT (General Agreement on Tariffs and Trade) is a good indication of the risks involved in framing culture in economic terms. As the GATT comes up for its twenty-year renewal, the US insists that films be among the products included in the free trade across the Atlantic. France, spearheading the defense on behalf of Europe, has held its ground on "cultural exception" that would exempt all cultural products, including film, from such a trade deal. According to journalist Agnès C. Poirier, "the US considers cinema and the arts as entertainment industries making profits; Europe considers culture as the product of ideas that go beyond a strict commercial value" (2013). Joining the fray, renowned European filmmakers including Luc and Jean-Pierre Dardenne, Costa-Gavras, Michael Haneke, Joachim Lafosse, Béla Tarr, and scores of others signed a petition declaring that "culture is at the very heart of European identity and ideals," and therefore the cultural exception is non-negotiable (Petition of European Filmmakers, 2013). Such conflicts, not exclusive to Europe, are the hallmark of frictions created by neoliberal policies like free trade that, for all their talk of free cross-border traffic, endanger the diversity of cultural and regional identity and manifest in filmmaking.

Asian production models

The institutional structures developed by the EU, even in the midst of new neoliberal economic policies, present a distinct phase hitherto unknown in world cinema. Through a combination of private and public funding structures, Europe has made important strides in reconciling the slow but certain dissolution of national cinemas and the increased role of transnational co-productions. Unlike Europe, Asia does not have a formal geopolitical collective such as the EU or other formal institutions, at least not on the scale established in Europe, but it exhibits a similar process of transformation from national to transnational cinema configurations. A global economic system has positioned Asia as a powerful economic region. Seen by the West as a key market entity for its future growth, Asia has also developed a regional Asian identity that serves as a counterforce to the influences of the global economy. Production models in Asia show an intermediate phase between the models of national cinemas (the cinemas of China, Japan, Korea, and Hong Kong) and the regionalization of Asian film industries. We will focus here on a brief background of the sustaining agency of national cinemas and their movement toward transnational co-production and regionalization, the dynamic of which is crucial to our study of Asian cinema as one of the world cinema centers.

China

China offers one of the most impressive examples of measured state control over the domestic film industry, controlled liberalization in investment policies toward growth in all sectors of the industry, and a steady rise to dominance in the global markets.

The Tiananmen Square events of 1989 began the impressive process of transformation from the state-centered socialist economy to a restricted yet radical phase of market capitalism. In the 1980s, filmmakers as well as studios benefited substantially from the state subsidies, which sustained much of the production of this period. A number of film studios had expanded three-fold in the early 1980s, low box office returns did not create

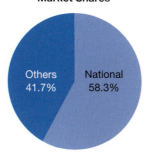

People's Republic of China Statistics, 2016
Market Shares

Others
41.7%

National
58.3%

Population	1 379.0 million
GDP Per Capita	8 261 USD
Gross Box Office	6.60 bn USD
Admissions	1.37 billion

Figure 3.2 People's Republic of China information chart, 2016. Source: FOCUS 2016, Marché du Film, 2017

the pressure that other industries faced, and all creative expression in China adopted skillful paths of self-censorship, making the best of the rather porous confines of "the velvet prison" (Pickowicz, 2011). Although the metaphor of the "velvet prison" in many ways recalls the old socialist bureaucracies in Eastern Europe that maintained tight control over the filmmaking process, it was also "a strategic retreat of the state" from the film industry, enabling filmmakers to produce high-quality art films under controlled pressure (Pickowicz, 2011: 316).

The post-Tiananmen Square period marks a sea change in the Chinese economic system, re-orienting it domestically and internationally to a globalized reality and launching it as a major global economic force. Capital flows have been liberalized and investors from China, Taiwan, and Hong Kong (then still not under Chinese control) have supported productions to boost regional collaboration. The film industry, monitored by the State Administration of Radio, Film and Television (SARFT) consists of a number of state-supported platforms. The largest of them, China Film Group (CFG), dispenses enormous resources to all areas of films, from script development, distribution, and digital cinema construction and conversion to advertising. CFG is a powerful mechanism to exercise state control, procedures for which are meticulously laid out for filmmakers to follow (Yeh & Williams, 2008).

During the period of film marketization, China has diversified local production while raising its cultural and economic profile in world cinema. Despite continued regulations, it has increased imports to create more breathing room for domestic cinema, encouraged the construction of new movie theaters across the country, and promoted the production of films through state support and private capital from within the region. Along with broader liberalization of economic policies since the 1990s, China has also encouraged foreign investment in film production. The Film Market Entry Rules formulated in 2003 allow foreign investors to incorporate a film production company and enter into a co-production agreement through such ventures. As a result, a number of Hollywood producers have entered the Chinese market, and studios such as Disney, Warner Bros.,

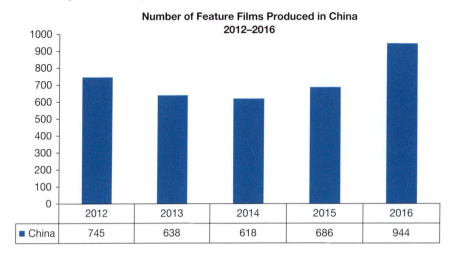

Figure 3.3 Number of Chinese feature films produced, 2012–2016. Source: FOCUS 2017

and Paramount have launched co-production projects with their Chinese counterparts. These projects may provide an opening to filmmakers to make inroads into Chinese tastes for world cinema.

China became a member of the World Trade Organization (WTO) in 2001, setting it on course to relax a number of its policies in the film industry. The first noticeable change brought about by this move was to allow twenty films from abroad into the country's market. With this agreement, the domestic market faced fierce competition from foreign films, but it also allowed the planners to expand the market, build new theaters, and encourage national studios to produce both blockbusters and more experimental films, still limited by censorship standards. In a continuous negotiation with the US, China increased its foreign-import quota to thirty-four in 2012, and Huaxia Film Distribution has been allowed to join in to import films. Most of these films, if not all of them, are mainstream imports from the West, dominated by Hollywood blockbusters. The increase of revenue share for foreign distributors to twenty-five percent offers itself as an attractive proposition for markets abroad since China's audience and market have been growing steadily at an impressive rate: the box office total of $3 billion in 2013 jumped to $6.78 billion in 2015 (Brzeski, 2015), new screens are being built every day, and China's market is expected to exceed the U.S. market by 2018. For these reasons, the U.S. industry is obsessed with China as a key territorial prospect for growth.

All this does not bode well for domestic or foreign imports that are not blockbusters. Art cinema, or films made in smaller producing countries, find no place in China's booming market, as they find it impossible to fulfill two major goals of the national film industry: provide a large box office return or achieve success comparable to that of renowned local filmmakers. While the quota for alternative product may increase in the coming years, China remains an elusive market for world cinema, except for the strong role of regional film festivals that support art cinema. Despite the fact that local filmmakers find it difficult to match the success of Hollywood productions—according to *Variety*, more than 70 percent of the Chinese movies shown in theaters lose money—the support of the state has allowed the film industry to diversify in regional and international markets (Lau, 2014).

Thus, a shift in the long-term trend of Hollywood domination can be observed since 2013, when seven out of ten top-grossing films were domestic productions, contributing to 71 percent of total annual box office revenues. Even the American movie that made it into the Chinese top ten, *Iron Man 3*, is technically considered an American–Chinese co-production, with an alternate Chinese version. This Hollywood down trend, largely attributed to the lack of variety in remakes, sequels, and reboots, already presents a concern to the U.S. studios, who depend on Chinese box office returns to break even (Trendacosta, 2014).

Hong Kong

Hong Kong Statistics, 2016
Market Shares

National 18.1%

Others 81.9%

Population	7.4 million
GDP Per Capita	42 963 USD
Gross Box Office	251.2 M USD
Admissions	28.3 million

Figure 3.4 Hong Kong information chart. Source: FOCUS 2017, Marché du Film

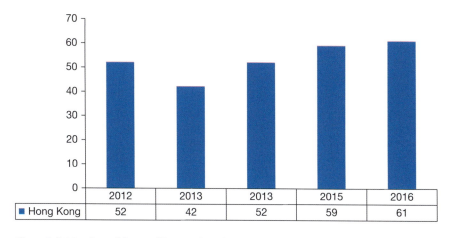

	2012	2013	2013	2015	2016
■ Hong Kong	52	42	52	59	61

Figure 3.5 Number of feature films produced in Hong Kong, 2012–2016. Source: FOCUS 2017

For decades, the Hong Kong film industry was one of the most robust and high-profile in the world, boasting not only a strong domestic industry but also the most widely exported product of popular action films epitomized in the works of Bruce Lee and Jackie Chan. After kung fu and action film dominated the 1970s, the cinema of Hong Kong went through a transformative phase in the 1980s with the New Wave, introducing a transformative aesthetic and refined narratives that turned away from martial arts films (Bordwell, 2008). In this decade, big studios such as Shaw Brothers closed and production shifted into the hands of an independent production house system. A new generation of formidable filmmakers who were often trained in the West—Clara Law, Stanley Kwan, Gordon Chan, Mabel Cheung, and others—took over. Their experiments, although supported by set-ups outside studios, were in many ways enabled by the surplus generated by studio-funded films, and sprawling distribution networks that included East Asia regions, as well as diasporic networks. Boasting a strong popular cinema as well as the New Wave's art cinema, the Hong Kong film industry became a regional powerhouse during this period, sustained a major rise in production, and captured broad audiences in Taiwan, Korea, Japan, and other Asian countries.

Given its international visibility, stable studio structure, massive revenue potential (one of the largest in the world) and a continuous output of narratives with a potential for festival and foreign exhibition acclaim, Hong Kong cinema started attracting investors from Taiwan, Japan, and other Asian countries. The local triad structures—criminal organizations in Hong Kong, Taiwan, and other places—controlled the money flow, seeing it as a money-laundering device but also a reliable source of income (Bordwell, 2008: 45). Attendance at movie theaters continued to swell in the 1980s and early 1990s, both in Hong Kong and abroad. However, this "golden age" of Hong Kong filmmaking, with John Woo, Ringo Lam, and Tsui Hark leading the charge, began a decline in the mid-1990s, and the affiliation with Mainland China precipitated a major transformation in the industry. The number of productions decreased from 238 in 1993 to merely forty films per year since 1999 (Hoad, 2011). This decline, which made the Hong Kong industry less powerful than it had been for decades, is sometimes seen as a natural consequence of overproduction during the golden age, but it also had to do with the first wave of digital piracy, the Asian economic crisis of 1997, and the shrinking market thereafter.

Hong Kong witnessed a major transformation in 1997, when the territory switched control from the UK to the People's Republic of China. Hong Kong gained status as a Special Administrative Region, acquiring a dual identity of its allegiance to the mainland while allowing it a separate identity. Since then the Hong Kong film industry has lost its independent status in world cinema and is marked by a conflict-ridden relationship with Mainland China. Films made in Hong Kong are subject to Chinese censorship pressures while the much larger and economically and politically powerful Chinese film industry uses Hong Kong talent as part of its labor.

Somewhat easing the tension between Mainland China and Hong Kong, the Mainland and Hong Kong Closer Economic Partnership Agreement (CEPA) was signed in 2003, with an objective to strengthen trade and investment cooperation between Hong Kong and Mainland China. The agreement opened the door to the vast mainland market, eased restrictions on Hong Kong films, removed the global import quota for such films, and contributed to a steady rise in Hong Kong–China co-productions. But such co-productions, crucial as they are to the sustainability of Hong Kong cinema, are still dominated by rules that favor China. For example, one-third of the crew members must come from the mainland, and the narratives need to be connected to broader Chinese contexts (Pang, 2007). Such conditions are feared to have a negative effect on the development of Hong Kong cinema, coopting it entirely into Chinese cinema and erasing its local identity. According to Chu Yiu-wai, "It is now an open secret that Hong Kong directors have to self-censor their work in order to enter the mainland market," and in this shift toward "becoming Chinese," only a few established directors, such as Johnnie To, chose to remain local (Chu, 2010: 138).

Despite this identity crisis, Hong Kong has been able to maintain its visibility if not freedom in world cinema. The Hong Kong International Film Festival, long an influential agent in forging Asian identity, remains one of the most important festivals in world cinema. Affiliating itself with the Hong Kong International Film Festival Society, it generates substantial support for Asian filmmakers: in 2013, it funded Apichatpong Weerasethakul from Thailand, Wang Bing from China, and Naomi Kawase from Japan, among others (HAF Report, 2013). The Hong Kong Trade Development Council promotes production on several levels, particularly supporting smaller projects. By plugging into the emerging influence of film festivals and strategic efforts in creative industries, it has established two bodies: FILMART, which promotes multi-media production including film; and the Hong Kong Asia Financing Forum, or HAF, based on Rotterdam's CineMart, a co-production forum that allows various participants to establish co-production ventures (HAF Report, 2013).

As these initiatives and projects garner broader exposure and connect to a larger regional and international circuit of filmmaking, Hong Kong may not retain its influence as a center of production and a filmmaking hub with distinct roots in local culture, but it certainly retains its position in the promotion of regional cinema through the production and exhibition of regional films. With an industry caught in the transformations brought about by a nexus of global and postcolonial forces, Hong Kong's local cinema thrives, but its identity is more soluble than it has ever been before.

Japan

Japan has enjoyed a healthy film industry for decades, and a high visibility in the Asian region and in the West. Its economic stability, sustained audience interest and continuous modes of innovation have resulted in a film industry that presents itself as a major player in the region. Japan enjoyed its own "golden age" in the 1960s with hefty national film production and wide international recognition for its films, particularly through major film auteurs such as Akira Kurosawa, Kenji Mizoguchi, Hiroshi Inagaki, and Nagisa Oshima. While the visibility of Japanese cinema suffered after the collapse of the studio system in the 1970s, it rebounded in the 1980s with the rise of independent filmmaking, which led to many small-scale film import and distribution companies, and the spectacular success of anime. This spotlight began to dim as the imports of foreign films, particularly from the US, UK, and other Western countries increased their share.

The Motion Picture Association of Japan reports that the decline turned around in 2004 as the share of domestic films began to rise (reaching 53 percent in 2006), and it has continued to rise ever since. Attendance jumped to 170 million for the first time since 1983 and the box office revenue went up to ¥210 billion ($2 billion). The Japanese film industry now claims a larger share of the market compared to its imports of foreign films, 60.6 percent to 39.4 percent respectively (MPPJ, 2013). When it comes to imports, Hollywood dominates, with blockbusters generating most of the revenues. Major U.S. studios have their own Japanese ancillaries, such as Warner Entertainment Japan and 20th Century Fox Japan. Other than the Hollywood fare, Japanese audiences find diversity in Asian productions such as those from China and Hong Kong, with a strong investment in and relationship with the latter. The national film industry in Japan, however, provides strong competition to Hollywood films. In 2012, for example, Pixar's *Monsters University* made $90 million while a Japanese production, Hayao Miyazaki's *The Wind Rises*, made nearly $150 million (Schilling, 2013).

The Japanese film industry attributes this success to its well-developed "alliance" model that integrates production, distribution, and exhibition. The three major producers, Shochiku, Toei, and Toho, control the largest share of the market through an innovative alliance structure. Aligning themselves with television networks, publicity and promotion agencies, and exhibition networks, these companies reduce all other costs of inter-agency transactions, reaching a balanced coordination to achieve their success. Daring and stable in their strategic hold over the entertainment industry at large, their integrated model assures security for the market. Independent film production companies thrive as well, though at a much lesser degree than the majors. They rely on co-production deals to finance their films, independent distributors to exhibit them, and festivals in the region, particularly the Tokyo International Film Festival and Busan Film Festival, which have been able, with varying degrees of difficulty, to generate funding for co-productions. Although the state plays an important role in the film industry, its dominance is far less pronounced than in China, and filmmakers have been able to produce films with investments of market capital (foreign and national). UniJapan (the Japan Association for International Promotion of the Moving Image) provides a combined platform for film festivals and other promotional activities for the distribution of Japanese films abroad. The organization is now taking the lead in international co-productions (Blair, 2012).

**Japan Statistics 2016
Market Shares**

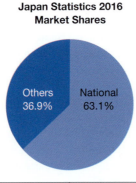

Population	126.8 million
GDP Per Capita	37 304 USD
Gross Box Office	2.17 bn USD
Admissions	180.2 billion

Figure 3.6 Japan information chart. Source: FOCUS 2017

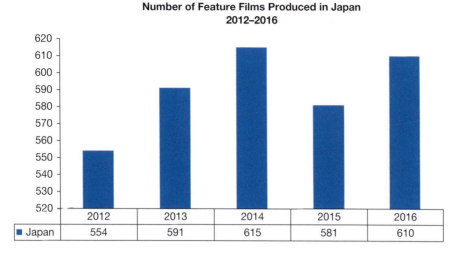

Number of Feature Films Produced in Japan
2012–2016

	2012	2013	2014	2015	2016
▪ Japan	554	591	615	581	610

Figure 3.7 Number of Japanese films produced, 2012–2016. Source: FOCUS 2017

Japan holds a distinct advantage among Asian countries with the genre of anime, in demand all over the world. Anime is the country's most significant export, cultivating audiences around the world. Over the years, its strength has expanded from film to television and DVD markets, with additional revenues from merchandizing and other related ventures. With increasing sophistication in technique and narrative, it continues to be a signature export in recent decades and an important contribution to world cinema. Studio Ghibli, a major force in innovation co-founded by Miyazaki, often single-handedly moves the needle in revenue for the Japanese film industry. In 2001 and 2002, the market sales of anime were saved by *Spirited Away*, while in 2004 *Howl's Moving Castle* achieved a similar feat (JETRO, 2005). Nearly 60 percent of anime shown around the world is from Japan, and it is widely mimicked elsewhere. The Disney Group, itself an animation powerhouse, has set up a "content purchase" division in its Japanese organization, demonstrating a humbling consent to anime's dominance.

Japan stands out as an independently successful example in Asian cinema, and it remains a prototypical national model with a sustained and powerful presence on the world cinema stage. Nevertheless, it is intricately linked to other countries, particularly China and Korea, through a complex web of colonial and postcolonial relations. The idea of pan-Asian cinema, and the increasing role of globalized networks in launching co-productions that tend to erase historical restrictions, have prevailed in the region.

South Korea

Now a strong presence in the region and elsewhere, South Korean cinema (North Korean cinema remains invisible due to the country's isolation) has gone through a number of crises due to economic and film policies, political turmoil, strict state regulation, and censorship that caused the film industry to stagnate. A low-key domestic film industry since its beginning, it acquired a higher profile in the late 1980s and a spectacular global presence in the 1990s. The late 1980s mark a significant transformation in Korea, when massive demonstrations by student activists, laborers, and the urban middle class resulted in a transfer of power that led to more open and creative cultural production in South Korea.

South Korea Statistics 2016
Market Shares

Population	50.8 million
GDP Per Capita	27 633 USD
Gross Box Office	1.45 bn USD
Admissions	217 billion

Figure 3.8 South Korea information chart, 2016. Source: FOCUS 2017

It was not until a major revision to the Motion Picture Law was introduced in 1984 that regulations were again relaxed, foreign film importation liberalized, and doors opened to independent production, which allowed a new generation of filmmakers to enter the film industry. South Korean cinema began to increase productivity, encourage the creativity of a new generation of filmmakers, and assert itself as a competitive regional and global player. The burgeoning film industry gained international recognition, and domestic film production companies increased from twenty-five to ninety-eight between 1985 and 1989 (Paquet, 2010: 48).

Film production in Korea after the 1980s was supported by the private capital of Korean business conglomerates or *chaebols* that entered the video business, first producing videocassettes and recorders and eventually financing filmmaking. Samsung, SKC, Daewoo, Hyundai, and later Orion and others, became involved in the film industry, starting film production projects of their own. *Chaebols* completely transformed the structure of the industry, introducing a vertically integrated system that had them involved in every stage of the business: financing, production, distribution, and exhibition, as well as international sales. These heavyweights brought capital, the ability to stand up to and compete with the branch offices of the U.S. major studios, and a muscle that was needed to support Korean cinema's growth in the coming years. The second generation of conglomerates (CJ, Orion, and Lotte) also contributed to a considerable increase in screens; today they own multiplex chains nationwide, occupying eighty percent of the market. Their involvement in the industry continued until the economic crisis of 1997, which brought financial instability to the market, making investment unstable with currency fluctuations and the ongoing competition from foreign companies. Many of the *chaebols* divested from the business, and with budgets upended and investment in foreign imports becoming more expensive, the industry began to shift toward less expensive films.

Two events are notable in the phenomenon of Korean cinema's rapid rise from a low-profile industry to a regional and global powerhouse. First, because of the close economic and political proximity of South Korea and the US, imported films increased manyfold, from 25 in 1984 to 264 in 1989. Moreover, an agreement between South Korea and the US allowed the latter to operate local offices for its major studios, and the very presence of these companies—20th Century Fox, Warner Bros., Columbia TriStar, Disney—transformed everything from nationwide distribution to financing structures and limited space for domestic product. Sensing Hollywood's aggression, the Korean film industry reacted strongly to the limits placed on the growth of its own cinema. Its strong protest led to a greater investment in the industry and relatively stricter regulations on foreign players. The second moment of transformation comes with Korea's membership in the WTO and the advent of globalization. In an effort to promote Korean cultural capital on the global stage, the state launched the *Hallyu* program, promoting cultural production in all spheres including film. The burst of activity in cultural production also aligned with the discovery of new talents and new structures of financing and distribution to propel the industry to its strongest phase.

In the era of globalization and market deregulation, the South Korean government took a proactive role, considering film business as one of the most profitable economic activities, and its cultural policy has continually supported the film sector. In 1999, the Korean government established the Korean Film Council (KOFIC), which has played a significant role in stimulating and protecting the domestic industry. The KOFIC helps it by promoting South Korean cinema home and abroad, providing grants and funding, and supporting art house theaters and independent productions. Abroad, the KOFIC sponsors and organizes film festivals, publishes English-language books, and supports the release and screening of Korean productions. With its Film Development Fund, established in 2007, the KOFIC is able to successfully steer domestic film production. It attempts to support the production of short films in particular, a feature it shares with its European counterparts. South Korea's two major film festivals (among many others), Busan and Jeonju, provide the most recent platforms for the launch of Korean cinema. The KOFIC has been central for festivals as well, underscoring the importance of well-managed state support to fuel an industry. Despite a slowdown in the mid-2000s, the Korean film industry has emerged as a strong contributor to regional and world cinemas; most of the major filmmakers from the late-1990s continue to work and produce quality films today.

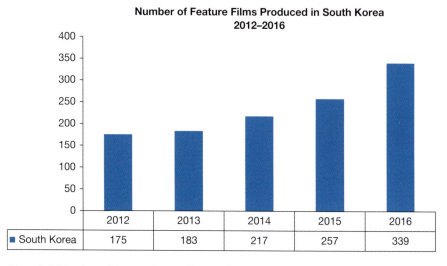

Figure 3.9 Number of Korean feature films produced, 2012–2016. Source: FOCUS 2017

Like few other cinemas around the world, Korean cinema—in no small part thanks to high-quality domestic blockbusters—claims almost 60 percent of the market share for domestic films despite the fierce competition with foreign films, a notable feat in itself.

The cultural and geographic proximity of Asian industries produced a consistent history of co-production. Japanese and Taiwanese capital and Hong Kong's talent led to a series of impressive co-production efforts. Some component of each of these national cinemas was always engaged in constructing a shared regional film industry. The political events in each of these countries (China in 1989; Korea in 1985; Hong Kong in 1997) and the tidal waves of globalization in the 1990s mark a major transition in Asian cinema. The period after the 1990s witnessed intense efforts in co-production, pan-Asian cinema, and regional blockbusters. From that point on onwards, Asian cinema grew in collective strength to affirm regional and cultural identities, and to develop a defensive front against the Western dominance. During this period, the national cinemas in Asia have come together not only in their regional strength but in their immensely powerful global profile.

Indian production models

Although it is the largest film industry in the world in terms of its prodigious output (around 1,000 feature films per year) as well as its audience (an annual audience of over three billion at home and millions more overseas), film production in India has been rather chaotic, its structures lacking established formal practices. Films are produced in more than twenty languages, with Hindi, the national language, dominating in terms of influence and visibility. Despite the importance of the local industry, India lacks a national support scheme, and private capital runs most of the industry, with its paths difficult to track. The Indian film industry creates a subterranean economy of its own, generating money that is not taxed or accounted for in any institutions. Such practices have given rise to continuous speculations about the film industry creating what is known as "the black market," with its insidious mechanisms feeding an underground culture that also supports, and is supported by, organized crime. And yet, films have been produced with remarkable

Population	1 310 million
GDP Per Capita	1 719 USD
Gross Box Office	1.5 bn USD
Admissions	2.02 billion

Figure 3.10 India information chart, 2016. Source: FOCUS 2017

alacrity, with an average of two to three released daily in a country of more than a billion people. Cities and their cultures dominate film production. Bombay-Mumbai leads the charge, positioning itself as the capital of filmmaking in the country, giving a recent boost to "Bollywood cinema," as it has been known for the past three decades. Chennai (formerly Madras), with Tamil films, has a larger share of films among other cities, though Kolkata (Calcutta) and Trivandrum are also large film production centers.

Most notable shifts in production practices started during the 1990s, when the economy began shaking off the old profile of a socialist and isolated entity. Broad-scale policies of economic liberalization allowed private capital to flow more freely, shaping corporatization of Indian society and positioning its plunge into the global market. India's rise as a global economic power began around this time, making its economy competitive in a number of ways. The government, realizing the moribund nature of the film industry, and recognizing its powerful potential to contribute to the overall economy, began the process of granting the status of "industry" to film in 1998–2000 (Puntambekar, 2013: 2). The business and industry at large responded to this gesture and stepped in to formalize structures of finance, production, and distribution. Major businesses such as Reliance Group created Reliance Big Entertainment, which entered the field to give it a structure and respectability. Over the years, it also developed enough muscle to become a major player in the global entertainment industry, spreading its reach to production in Hollywood, new media, and distribution in different parts of the world.

In her study of transformations of the Indian film industry, Tejaswini Ganti says that since the 1990s "filmmakers and business leaders have rationalized the production, distribution, and exhibition process, most commonly referred to as the 'corporatization' of the industry" (Ganti, 2012: 5). Corporate players have seized control of these processes to bring them in line with the models in existence elsewhere in the world. This is a major transformation, still underway in many quarters of the economy. Information and data are being gathered for the first time in a systematic way to track production flows and audience reception figures. Ganti maintains that these changes in the integration of the industry come hand in hand with what she calls its "gentrification," the process of legitimization of the Hindi film industry by the middle classes and the elite. Families and groups that have controlled film continue to exert control, insulating themselves and filmmakers from the rest of society, a tendency also visible in films themselves, which increasingly display "wealthy protagonists and the near complete erasure of the working class, urban poor, and rural dwellers once prominent as protagonists/heroes in Hindi films" (Ganti, 2012: 4). Additionally, filmmaking activity has expanded into entertainment fields such as television, music, magazines, and related industries that cash in on films. The increasing presence of multiplexes in the cities has also allowed the film industry to bank on strategic marketing efforts, reducing uncertainty in the business. The earlier rhetoric of the state that asserted cinema as an instrument of social change has shifted to cinema as an economic engine, an entertainment industry with a multi-billion revenue potential.

Along with Reliance Big Entertainment, UTV Motion Pictures, Sahara One, Eros Entertainment, Yash Raj Films, and PVR Pictures, several others have emerged as significant production houses. Fully realizing the potential for investment amid reliable structures of the industry, international, mostly Western corporations have moved into the arena, a process that began soon after the recognition of the "industry" status for film (Puntambekar, 2013: 60). Companies such as Merrill Lynch, Goldman Sachs, and Citigroup have invested in the film and TV economy, and investment from media companies abroad has continued to flow in. Reliance has partnered with

DreamWorks in the US, Yash Raj Films and UTV partner with Disney, and Ramesh Sippy Entertainment with Warner Bros., to name just a few examples. Many of these main players have assumed global reach in distribution as well. UTV, Reliance, and Eros International distribute films in U.S. and U.K. multiplexes, marking the recent global dominance of the Indian film industry. Indian films are now regularly released in U.S. multiplexes, some with the muscle to play for several weeks at a time, a feat that no other foreign cinema has been able to accomplish. The economic reforms of the 1990s transformed a socialist economy into one oriented toward global neoliberal currents. A large part of the population migrated to Western countries, acquiring wealth and stability in business and technology enterprises. Already a significant presence for decades, the Indian diaspora has wielded considerable influence over India through its financial power, making substantial investments in the national economy, specifically its film industry. India's diaspora, one of the largest in the world, has shaped film production from the 1990s, supporting the emergence of Bollywood as a cultural commodity with film as its strongest agent.

The glare of the film industry marketed as "Bollywood" tends to mask the vast diversity of India's multiple-language cinemas, and has eclipsed the presence of quality cinema, often called "the parallel cinema," produced in India for decades. The government has taken steps to combat this imbalance since the 1960s. In 1975, two earlier institutions, the Film Finance Corporation and the Film Export Corporation, were combined into the National Film Development Corporation (NFDC), with an explicit mission to co-produce quality films. The organization has become a reassuring presence for independent filmmakers and co-production activities. In the 1960s, the Film Finance Corporation helped start the Indian New Wave, which made meaningful films that won wide approval from the literate middle class. In the 1980s, the NFDC continued this effort, co-financing and supporting productions so they could raise more money, and also expanded in the exhibition and import of films. Over the past twenty years, it has become a competent organization that holds workshops for scriptwriters, nurtures filmmakers, represents Indian cinema abroad at film festivals, and supports art house theaters.

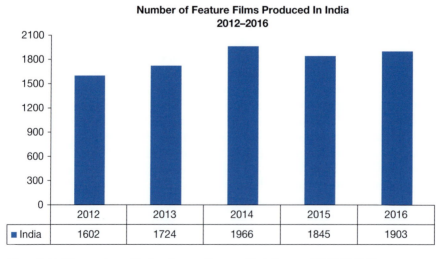

Number of Feature Films Produced In India 2012–2016

	2012	2013	2014	2015	2016
■ India	1602	1724	1966	1845	1903

Figure 3.11 The number of Indian feature films certified. Source: FOCUS 2017

State support for film production in India, as in other countries, is meant to guard the local industry against the purely commercial aims of the dominant cinema. It also protects the multiple-language cinemas that thrive in India. Contemporary Indian cinema has a higher global profile because of the commodity glare of Bollywood. In fact, behind Bollywood's shiny façade exists one of the most complex, rich, and sturdy industries in the world, which includes multiple-language and independent cinema.

Nigerian cinema/Nollywood

Africa is a large, fragmented market with an underdeveloped production industry and unreliable statistics. While notable cinema production exists only in a few countries— Egypt, Morocco, and South Africa—there is an alternative video-format production trend that has not only dominated the region, but also asserted itself as one of the largest film producers in the world. With nearly 1,000–1,200 video-films produced each year, over 75 percent of them in local languages, Nigerian cinema has become the second-largest filmmaking industry in the world (behind Bollywood and followed by Hollywood). Commonly dubbed "Nollywood," a term that is both honorific and pejorative, it is recognized mainly for its prolific production and unique cultural identity, akin to that of Bollywood. Produced in video in multiple languages—Igbo, Yoruba, Hausa, Bini, and English—phenomenally popular Nigerian films are made in different urban centers of the country, led by sprawling Lagos, which produces more than fifty video-films per week. Unique in its distribution model and entirely bypassing theatrical distribution (the only two or three surviving theaters in Lagos show Western films), Nollywood's video-films are seen mostly in households across the continent and, in recent years, in diasporic communities around the world. It is an industry asserting itself on the world stage almost solely based on numbers and a distinctive form of production-distribution processes. The industry now generates $590 million annually, is the country's second-largest employer, and has contributed significantly to Nigeria's present status as Africa's largest economy (Moudio, 2013).

The rise of the video-film industry in Nigeria is closely connected to political, social, and economic crises in the country caused by the collapse of the economy in the late 1980s, the exclusion of Nigeria and Africa from the process of globalization, and an indelible loyalty to cultural traditions. Nigerian video-films exhibit an integrated response to these three factors. As the domestic economy collapsed, TV collapsed with it, and filmmakers felt an urgent need to use whatever means available to represent their culture on film. Those who had worked in the Yoruba traveling theater tradition joined unemployed theater artists and others to start the production of videos, and the business community, particularly dealers of video recorders and players, began financing this practice (Haynes, 2002). The government of Nigeria made a loan fund of $200 million available to the industry, which until today remains in the hands of equipment merchants and sellers in Lagos. Video-films are produced on miniscule budgets, from $20,000 to $70,000, shot in a matter of days in available locations around the city, usually finished within a month, and become profitable within two or three weeks of their release. Released on VCDs or DVDs, most movies sell more than 20,000 units, and the most successful ones sell over 200,000.

The production of video-films in Nigeria proceeds at a frenetic pace. A producer, generally an entrepreneur in the street markets of Lagos dealing with sales of home video equipment, summons a director to make a film. The crews are assembled by combing through the available local talent. Scripts are prepared in advance but subject to improvisations and conditions on the production sets. Video-films are shot on location, with natural light or makeshift lighting equipment; power generators are a necessity since the supply of electricity is erratic. Sound recording is poor and relies on the control of the shooting environment, including negotiating with the noise of generators.

An air of informality permeates all areas of the Nollywood industry, making the most vivid imprint on the production set/location. The crew stays together as a community, with local catering and general banter providing glue for their interactions. In an industry that displays such a high rate of production, competition among filmmakers is tough, and fame based on their earlier successes is an essential condition to launch more projects. As revenues accumulate, the quality of production is improving, from digital cameras to sophisticated editing equipment and digital effects, resulting in more formalized facets of production. Distribution of films is equally chaotic and informal, but the results are impressive. Since video-films are distributed on mobile media—VCDs, DVDs—the cost of reproduction is low and the speed of dissemination quite rapid. A vast network of distribution exists among vendors of video equipment, distributors-manufacturers of VCDs and DVDs, and corner shops that sell video-films. There are a few video parlors, small rooms that are used as makeshift screening facilities, but their popularity is outweighed by home viewing, generally in family settings. The vendors of video equipment and cassettes still control a large share of the distribution network. Terms often used in a broader global context—*production system, distribution network*—thus have entirely different connotations in Nollywood. Charting the rise of the "informal economies of cinema" around the world, Ramon Lobato credits the "unique distribution model" for the success of the Nigerian video-film industry (Lobato, 2012: 55-67). The informal channels, first honed with the piracy of Bollywood and Hollywood films, have become refined, forming a complex network that combines the distribution of original and pirated copies of video-films. When video-films change hands, there is little if any formal revenue sharing. Somehow the money reaches the producers, although the industry itself thrives on the dispersed reach of video-films.

A very complex phenomenon in this process is the role of piracy. If piracy troubles other parts of film industries, in Nollywood it is a central engine of the distribution system. The paradox of piracy complicates the production and distribution of Nollywood video-films. On the one hand, piracy is a major drain on the revenue-earning potential of video-films; Nollywood insiders estimate that up to fifty percent of the industry's profits are currently being lost to this endemic corruption. Improved video compression technology only adds fuel to the piracy fire, allowing five to twenty films to be squeezed onto one disc and sold for $4, when a legitimate Nollywood DVD sells from $7 to $10. All filmmakers, particularly successful ones, have become increasingly vocal against the epidemic of piracy. On the other hand, the struggle for visibility is so high that producers willingly resort to piracy networks to distribute their films. Additionally, since many television networks in the region also depend on Nollywood video-films, original or pirated, wider exposure brings rewards to producers and directors. These informal distribution networks, of which pirated products form a part, are impossible to track but are in many ways dependable in their own ability to generate revenues. The Nigerian Copyright Commission, whose birth in the late 1980s coincided with the rise of Nollywood, has introduced many measures to police the copyright infringements and step in line with global intellectual property policies. The challenges are daunting, however, and legal scholars have only recently begun to grapple with the complexity of the Nigeria-specific context within the broader discourse of intellectual property (Oguamanam, 2011).

Despite these contentious issues, the industry is the second-largest employer after the government, and although it is an informal economy without traceable institutions or structures, its vibrancy is evident both in its economic growth and its cultural influence. The fact that a gross domestic product growth rate is attributed largely to the popularity of the Nigerian film industry is a feat that speaks for itself, and raises questions about the exclusion of Nigeria from the discussions of global production models (Moudio, 2013). The informal distribution processes of Nollywood provide some of the reasons "why Nigeria has been overlooked as one of the giants of global film culture" (Lobato, 2012: 59). There are few, if any, similarities with structures at work in other parts of the world. The "radically horizontal" model of distribution with the near-central place of piracy defies any attempt to collect data or formulate systematic conclusions. It is imperative to acknowledge, however, that many film cultures and industries are grappling with major issues that have always defined Nollywood, and as such offer important lessons. The use of direct-to-mobile media that is the backbone of the Nollywood film industry is now shaping much of the relocation of cinema from theaters to mobile devices elsewhere, and the issue of piracy so central to Nollywood is becoming an important feature of the dissemination of world cinema. For both reasons, the phenomenon of the Nollywood film industry, unique as it is in its own context, can help us better understand the broader emerging issues of contemporary cinema.

Other models of production

Co-production funds

One of the recurrent features of the dominant production practices map discussed in this chapter is a certain transition from the national model of production to transnational or regional production practices. An exhaustive account of such practices would reveal that regional production and co-production are fast becoming a standard everywhere in the world. Even outside of the dominant case studies explained here, we can find numerous other instances that align with this trend in various degrees and different manifestations. The Nordic countries—Denmark, Finland, Iceland, Norway, and Sweden—for example established an organization called Nordisk Film and TV Fund in 1990, to support financing for feature, animated, short, and documentary films, assist filmmakers in distribution and dubbing, and promote a "Nordic" identity.

The case of Latin America also provides an important example of such developments, where local producers are increasingly looking to make films elsewhere in the region. In Latin America, the national cinema model certainly remains relevant, with each national industry carving its own space in film production and with national agencies and funds playing an important role in national film production and support: National Film and TV Agency Ancine in Brazil, the National Institute of Cinema and Audiovisual Arts in Argentina, the Mexican Film Institute in Mexico, and the Arts and Audiovisual Industry Council in Chile, among others. Despite the impact of these institutions on the national film industries, Latin American countries in the post-1990s period have increasingly adopted a regional collaboration model.

In 1998, the Conference of Cinematographic Authorities of Ibero-America established a co-production fund called Programa Ibermedia, directly modeled on the EU's MEDIA Programme. Led by Spain with a significant investment of its own, Ibermedia includes other Spanish- and Portuguese-speaking nations that have greater geographical and cultural proximity. Originally including seven members, Ibermedia now has over twenty members including Argentina, Bolivia, Brazil, Chile, Colombia, Cuba, the Dominican Republic, Ecuador, Guatemala, Mexico, Panama, Peru, Portugal, Puerto Rico, Spain,

Uruguay, and Venezuela. Each country contributes to the fund that supports filmmaking in Spanish- and Portuguese-speaking cultures. The goals are to promote the integration of Latin American companies into audiovisual transnational networks, support co-production projects of independent Latin American producers, increase promotion and distribution of Latin American films, and promote training and the exchange of professionals in the Latin American audiovisual industry (Falicov, 2007). The program's goal is to create a Latin American audiovisual identity through collaborative production of films and other media. To date, the fund has dispensed $78 million that went to 500 films and numerous other projects, including financial aid to media companies. The organization aims to distribute films within the Latin American market and make the regional industry competitive in the global market (Falicov, 2007: 21). Interestingly, some of its productions are plagued by similar problems as those of Eurimages or MEDIA Programme in Europe, in that the promotion of cross-cultural content through co-production has the tendency to dilute the integrity of films, giving rise to absurd hybrids.

Since the launch of Ibermedia, other co-production funds, many of them bilateral in nature, have emerged that foster regional collaboration in Latin America. In 2016, for example, Argentina and Chile established a bilateral co-production fund, modeled on an already-existing Argentina–Brazil co-production fund. Funds such as these are crucial to a stronger positioning of national film industries in the competitive world cinema market (Hopewell, 2016).

Film festivals' production funds

Along with various co-production models, international film festival financing has also assumed a greater role in the production of world cinema. Since the 1990s, festivals have ceased to function as mere exhibition and distribution platforms, and have been directly involved in the production and co-production of films through the increasing importance of the specialized monetary funds designed to support new, formally innovative filmmakers and local film industries: the Cannes Cinefondation, the World Cinema Fund in Berlin, the Asian Project Market (APM) of Busan, the Balkan fund of Thessaloniki, CineMart of Rotterdam, FILMART of Hong Kong, and many others. These establishments have varying degrees of involvement in the production process. Some function more as service and finance hubs, such as FILMART, which is actually run by the Hong Kong Trade and Development Council and is part of a larger network of global co-production (partnered with the Hubert Bals Fund (HBF) and the APM), while others, such as the HBF, are much more closely involved in both the production and marketing of their product. All of them, however, assume an important role in the production of world cinema.

One of the earliest and most influential is the HBF, established in 1988 by the Rotterdam Film Festival, which has so far funded over 1,000 projects by independent filmmakers from Asia, the Middle East, Eastern Europe, Africa and Latin America, and supported training workshops in Ethiopia, Vietnam, and Costa Rica. In 2013, the HBF had about €500,000 at its disposal, offering individual grants of up to €10,000 for script and project development and €20,000 for post-production. Each year, the Rotterdam Film Festival then screens a large part of what it calls the year's "harvest" of completed films supported by the fund, which are screened either in competition or the main sections: Bright Future, Spectrum, or Signals. The HBF is also instrumental in distributing the funded films, either securing a third-party distributor or releasing a film on DVD under the festival's own label, Tiger Releases.

Individual production of films

So far, this chapter has focused on institutional or semi-formal models of filmmaking prevalent in world cinema after the late 1980s. The institutional structures outlined here suggest that filmmakers have a larger variety of formal mechanisms available to them than ever before. Nevertheless, filmmakers working anywhere in the world, including the five regions discussed here, face enormous hurdles in raising funds to materialize their visions. Very few filmmakers begin such a process with substantial resources readily available to them. Whether in Hollywood, Estonia, or the Philippines, a filmmaker must convince potential investors to invest in their project.

Recently, digital platforms and the idea of crowdfunding, a process in which artists turn directly to audiences to fund their work, have made it more possible for individual filmmakers to completely bypass the moneyed structures and traditional avenues of investment in raising money for their projects. Crowdfunding websites such as Kickstarter, Indiegogo, or Slated have become a standard for independent film production, bringing numerous creative projects to life, in many cases leading to critical acclaim and recognition. Kickstarter-funded documentary shorts such as *Sun Come Up* (Jennifer Redfearn, 2011) and *Incident in New Baghdad* (James Spione, 2011) have been nominated for Academy Awards. In 2016, nineteen Kickstarter films were programmed at the Tribeca Film Festival.

Filmmakers in small cinemas face more monumental tasks of raising money. More often than not, the narrative of how filmmakers raise money for their production is as fascinating as the narrative of the film itself. As we move away from the moneyed classes in Hollywood or elsewhere, resources become scarcer and film production a daunting task. Behind the rosy curtain of film releases, box office returns, and festival awards are numerous tales of filmmakers who struggle, wait years for their productions to materialize, or are simply forced to abandon a project that has been in the works for a long time. Particularly in the countries of West Asia and Latin America, or those countries that have remained weaker economic and political players (from Macedonia to Cuba to Saudi Arabia), filmmakers face Sisyphus-like tasks to raise funds and enable their narratives to see the light of day. Their challenges are profoundly different, in scale and specificity, from filmmakers who work in the US, Japan, Korea, or Hong Kong. No single source can supply them with the funds and no single regulation can clear up their bureaucratic hurdles. Under these circumstances, filmmakers who still manage to make films, take them to local film festivals, or bring them to audiences by other means have registered (relatively) small victories in the face of adversity.

The map of production in world cinema today is made up of sad and happy paradoxes. At one end we have Hollywood, with astronomic budgets for single films that often exceed the total annual budgets of many national film industries; at the other end are aspiring filmmakers who raise money through their own employment, borrow from relatives, max out credit cards, or turn to crowdfunding or any available resource in order to make films on miniscule budgets. Yet, as Hollywood techniques of production and marketing achieve a higher degree of sophistication and astronomical costs, new technologies of production and distribution have liberated filmmakers and made film production cheaper and more accessible than ever before. It is now possible for a filmmaker in Nigeria to use an inexpensive digital camera and make a film within two weeks. An aspiring student or amateur can now make her own film and put it on YouTube. Even in the days of despair and out-of-reach resources in the West, world cinema thus contains a multitude of stories of unique creative projects with the potential to garner attention and worldwide exposure.

Activity 3.1

Watch any three films from any part of the world and pay attention to the rolling credits at the end. Identify the sponsors who have funded the film. Identify locations where it was produced. Identify the nationality of major players (director of cinematography, screenwriter, etc.) and make a summary of the production patterns you observe.

Activity 3.2

Find a trade magazine from your own country, such as *Variety*, *The Hollywood Reporter*, and *Screen Daily*. Look for the most recent production activities. What films are being launched into production? What other industry news related to film production do you find interesting?

Activity 3.3

Identify a state-sponsored agency in your country that supports film production (for those in the US, you can identify three major studios), and explore how many and what kind of films they have funded in the last few years.

Activity 3.4

Identify two co-productions from each of the regions, including Latin America, discussed in this chapter. Which are the co-producing countries/companies? What are the funding resources? What kinds of films are being co-produced?

Further reading

Biskind, Peter. (2004). *Down and Dirty Pictures: Miramax, Sundance, And the Rise of Independent Film*. New York, NY: Simon and Schuster.

Cheuk, Pak Tong. (2008). *Hong Kong New Wave Cinema (1978–2000)*. Bristol, UK: Intellect.

Finney, Angus. (2010). *The International Film Business: A Market Guide Beyond Hollywood*. London: Routledge.

Finney, Angus. (2013). *Developing Feature Films in Europe: A Practical Guide*. London and New York, NY: Taylor and Francis.

Ganti, Tejaswini. (2012). *Producing Bollywood: Inside the Contemporary Hindi Film Industry*. Durham, NC: Duke University Press.

Lobato, Ramon. (2012). *Shadow Economies of Cinema: Mapping Informal Film Distribution*. London: Palgrave.

Louie, Kam (ed). (2010). *Hong Kong Culture: Word and Image*. Hong Kong: Hong Kong University Press.

Paquet, Darcy. (2010). *New Korean Cinema: Breaking the Waves*. London: Wallflower Press.
Pickowicz, Paul. (2011). *China on Film: A Century of Exploitation, Confrontation, and Controversy*. Lanham, MD: Rowman & Littlefield.
Puntambekar, Aswin. (2013). *From Bombay to Bollywood: The Making of a Global Film Industry*. New York, NY: New York University Press.
Wood, Mary P. (2007). *Contemporary European Cinema*. London: Hodder Arnold.

Bibliography

Bailey, Jason. (2013). "Why Do Foreign Films have to be Dumbed Down for American Audiences." *Flavorwire* (August 20). Available at: http://flavorwire.com/410720/why-do-foreign-films-have-to-be-dumbed-down-for-american-audiences. Accessed October 8, 2015.
Biskind, Peter. (2004). *Down and Dirty Pictures; Miramax, Sundance, And the Rise of Independent Film*. New York, NY: Simon and Schuster.
Blair, Gavin J. (2012). "Filmart 2012: Japanese Government to Fund International Co-Productions." *Hollywood Reporter* (March 20). Available at: www.hollywoodreporter.com/news/filmart-2012-japanese-government-fund-302061. Accessed October 16, 2016.
Bordwell, David. (2000). *Planet Hong Kong: Popular Cinema and the Art of Entertainment*. Cambridge, MA: Harvard University Press.
Bordwell, David. (2013). "*The Grandmaster*: Moving Forward, Turning Back." Blog entry in Observations on Film Art (September 23). Available at: www.davidbordwell.net/blog/2013/09/23/the-grandmaster-moving-forward-turning-back. Accessed November 3, 2015.
Box Office Mojo. (2016). "Total Grosses of Foreign Language Films, 1980–present." Box Office Mojo (October 9). Available at: www.boxofficemojo.com/genres/chart/?id=foreign.htm
Brzeski, Patrick. (2015). "China's Box Office Grows Astonishing 48% in 2015, Hits $6.78 Billion." *Hollywood Reporter* (December 31). Available at: www.hollywoodreporter.com/news/china-box-office-grows-astonishing-851629. Accessed June 30, 2016.
Cheuk, Pak Tong. (2008). *Hong Kong New Wave Cinema (1978–2000)*. Bristol, UK: Intellect.
Child, Ben. (2013). "*Grace of Monaco* Director Calls Harvey Weinstein Re-edit a 'Pile of Shit.'" *The Guardian* (October 21). Available at: www.theguardian.com/film/2013/oct/21/grace-monaco-director-harvey-weinstein. Accessed October 10, 2016.
Chu, Yiu-wai. (2010). "One Country Two Cultures? Post-1997 Hong Kong Cinema and Co-Productions." In Kam Louie (ed), *Hong Kong Culture: Word and Image*. Hong Kong: Hong Kong University Press.
Eurimages. (2016). "Co-production Funding History." Eurimages. Available at: www.coe.int/t/dg4/eurimages/History/Coproduction/default_en.asp. Accessed November 2, 2016.
European Investment Bank. (2001). "€1 billion for European Film and Audiovisual Industry: Two European Union Initiatives." Press release (May 18). Available at: www.eib.org/about/press/2001/2001-030-eur-1-billion-for-european-film-and-audiovisual-industry.htm. Accessed March 3, 2017.
European Commission. (2014). "Creative Europe." The European Commission. Available at: http://ec.europa.eu/culture/creative-europe/index_en.htm. Accessed March 2, 2017.
Falicov, Tamara L. (2007). "Programa Ibermedia: Co-Production and the Cultural Politics of Constructing an Ibero-American Audiovisual Space." *Spectator* 27(2). Hyung-Sook Lee (ed), *Special Issue: Hybrid Media, Ambivalent Feelings*, pp. 21–30.
Finney, Angus. (2010). *The International Film Business: A Market Guide Beyond Hollywood*. New York, NY: Routledge.
Ganti, Tejaswini. (2012). *Producing Bollywood: Inside the Contemporary Hindi Film Industry*. Durham, NC: Duke University Press.
HAF 2013 Report. "Hong Kong Convention and Exhibition Center." Available at: www.haf.org.hk/haf/report2013.htm. Accessed December 11, 2016.
Haynes, Jonathan. (2002). "Devaluation and Video Boom: Economics and Thematics." In Jane I. Guyer, LaRay Denzer, & Adigun Agbaje (eds), *Money Struggles and City Life: Devaluation in Ibadan and Other Urban Centers in Southern Nigeria, 1986–1996*. Portsmouth, NH: Heinemann.

Hoad, Phil. (2011). "Back in Action: The Fall and Rise of Hong Kong film." *The Guardian* (September 13). Available at: www.theguardian.com/film/filmblog/2011/sep/13/hong-kong-film-week-action

Hoad, Phil. (2013). "*Cinema Paradiso* and the Rise of the Postcard Arthouse Movie." *The Guardian* (December 5). Available at: www.theguardian.com/film/2013/dec/05/cinema-paradiso-postcard-arthouse-movie-us. Accessed October 9, 2015.

Hopewell, John. (2016). "Cannes: Argentina, Chile Launch Bilateral Co-Prod Fund." *Variety* (May 23). Available at: http://variety.com/2016/film/global/cannes-argentina-chile-bilateral-co-prod-fund-1201780928. Accessed October 16, 2016.

Iordanova, Dina. (1999). "East Europe's Cinema Industries Since 1989, Financing Structure and Studios." *The Public* 6, pp. 45–60.

Jäckel, Anne. (2003). *European Film Industries*. London: BFI Publishing.

JETRO Japan Economic Monthly. (2005). "Japan Animation Industry Trends." Available at: www. jetro.go.jp/ext_images/en/reports/market/pdf/2005_35_r.pdf. Accessed October 16, 2016.

Lau, Shirley. (2014). "FilMart: China Industry Shows Signs of Bubble." *Variety* (April 1). Available at: http://variety.com/2014/biz/news/filmart-china-industry-shows-signs-of-bubble-1201150916. Accessed Dec 11, 2016.

Lobato, Ramon. (2012). *Shadow Economies of Cinema: Mapping Informal Film Distribution*. London: Palgrave.

Macnab, Geoffrey. (2016). "Could the UK Rejoin Eurimages After Brexit." *Screen Daily* (June 30). Available at: www.screendaily.com/territories/uk-ireland/could-the-uk-rejoin-eurimages-following-brexit/5106300.article. Accessed October 10, 2016.

McDonald, Paul. (2009). "Miramax, *Life is Beautiful*, and the Indiewoodization of the Foreign-Language Film Market in the USA." *New Review of Film and Television Studies* 7(4), pp. 353–375.

MPPJ (Motion Picture Producers of Japan). (2013). "Statistics of Film Industry in Japan, 1955–2013." Available at: www.eiren.org/statistics_e/index.html. Accessed July 3, 2016.

Moudio, Rebecca. (2013). "Nigeria's Film Industry: A Potential Gold Mine?" *Africa Renewal Magazine* (May 24). Available at: www.un.org/africarenewal/magazine/may-2013/nigeria%E2%80%99s-film-industry-potential-gold-mine. Accessed July 10, 2016.

Oguamanam, Chidi. (2011). "Beyond Nollywood and Piracy: In Search of an IP Policy for Nigeria." *NIALS Journal of Intellectual Property Maiden Edition*, pp. 3–37.

Pang, Laikwan. (2007). "Postcolonial Hong Kong Cinema: Utilitarianism and (Trans) local." *Postcolonial Studies* 10(4), pp. 413–430.

Paquet, Darcy. (2010). *New Korean Cinema: Breaking the Waves*. London: Wallflower Press.

Petition of European Filmmakers. (2013). "The Cultural Exception is Non-Negotiable." April 25. Available at: www.lapetition.be/petition.php/the-cultural-exception-is-non-negotiable/12826. Accessed October 10, 2016.

Pickowicz, Paul G. (2011). "Velvet Prisons and the Political Economy of Chinese Filmmaking in the 1980s and Early 1990s." In *China on Film: A Century of Exploitation, Confrontation and Controversy*. Lanham, MD: Rowman & Littlefield Publishers, pp. 301–329.

Poirier, Agnès C. (2013). "Why France is gearing up for a culture war with the United States." *The Guardian* (June 7). Available at: www.theguardian.com/commentisfree/2013/jun/07/france-culture-war-united-states. Accessed October 10, 2016.

Puntambekar, Aswin. (2013). *From Bombay to Bollywood: The Making of a Global Film Industry*. New York, NY: New York University Press.

Schilling, Mark. (2013). "Why Hollywood Movies are Plummeting at Japan Box Office." *Variety* (October 23). Available at: https://variety.com/2013/biz/news/japan-hollywood-no-longer-dominates-box-office-1200752940. Accessed July 10, 2016.

Shaw-Williams, Hannah. (2013). "Weinstein Cuts *Snowpiercer* by 20 Minutes for US Release." ScreenRant (June 8). Available at: http://screenrant.com/snowpiercer-deleted-scenes-us-theatrical-cut-version. Accessed Oct 10, 2016.

Trendacosta, Katharine. (2014). "Will a New Report on China's American Film Fatigue Change Hollywood? IO9 (June 11). Available at: http://io9.com/will-a-new-report-on-chinas-american-film-fatigue-chang-1589162148. Accessed Oct 10, 2016.

Yeh, Emilie Yueh-yu & Darrell Davis Williams. (2008). "Renationalizing China's Film Industry: Case Study on the China Film Group and Film Marketization." *Journal of Chinese Cinemas* 2(1), pp. 37–51.

4 Film festivals and world cinema

Contemporary world cinema is unthinkable without the influence, reach, and diversity of film festivals. Once a limited but impactful province of state power display, film festivals have become a key force in the film business, and a central platform for the exhibition and distribution of international cinema—indeed any cinema not bound into Hollywood's network. All levels of film cultures, from local and regional to international, have witnessed an incredible proliferation of film festivals since the 1980s, and they have become one of the biggest growth industries. While there is no reliable count, some accounts suggest there are nearly 10,000 festivals in all corners of the globe (Follows, 2013). From global demands to local needs, film festivals fulfill a variety of functions that may seem mutually exclusive: they are vehicles for geopolitical agendas but also promote cinephilia and the art of cinema; they are important marketplaces with business purposes, but they also focus on programming and cultivating audiences; they are media events endowing films with cultural and economic capital, and they are tourist events playing a key role in cities' marketing and branding. Their uniqueness and power lies in blending different functions seamlessly, making them an integral part of the festival phenomenon.

Because film festivals present an almost impossibly complex convergence site for various functions, they offer fruitful grounds on which to investigate contemporary world cinema networks. Their breadth and depth is so profound that they now command an entire field: film festival studies. Rarely celebratory in their focus, festival studies chart the history of film festivals at all levels, critique their hegemonic role in shaping production practices, and examine their role in shaping cultural identities. Since the discourse of film festivals is deeply intertwined with the practices of watching, production, and exhibition, with the formation of cinematic power centers, and indeed, with the very conceptual frame of world cinema, the study of film festivals is an essential component of any attempt to map world cinema. While it is important to acknowledge the complicated web of functions performed by them, of particular interest for our context is the crucial role that festivals play in the production of knowledge that guides our understanding of national and, more recently, world cinema. That is, this chapter explores the ways in which festivals are not only exhibition and distribution platforms, but play an active role in *shaping* the very landscape of world cinema, and by implication our understanding of it.

The genesis of film festivals can be outlined in three phases: in their first, post-Second World War phase, festivals were funded by the state, served as important vehicles for national identity, and were largely motivated by political and ideological interests; in their second phase (in the 1960s), festivals asserted themselves as independent from a nation-state in an attempt to extricate themselves from political and commercial interests, and reinvented themselves as sites that provide support to and nurture cinema as high art; in their third, globalized phase (since the 1980s), festivals proliferate around the globe, diversify in their function, and form a complex global festival network. This phase is the most instrumental to the formation of world cinema as outlined in this book, and is therefore the primary focus of the chapter.

Figures 4.1a & 4.1b Official posters for the first Venice Film Festival in 1932 and Cannes Film Festival in 1939. Photo © AGIP/Bridgeman Images and poster by Jean Gabriel Domergue/De Agostini Picture Library/Bridgeman Images

Film festivals and national cinema

A film festival is a European phenomenon, established just before the Second World War. In their initial phase, festivals were driven mainly by geopolitical agendas, and were used as platforms for European national cinemas. The first organized on a regular basis was the Venice Film Festival, established as part of the Venice Biennale arts festival in 1932.

While it was welcomed by cinephiles and the international film community, it soon became clear that the festival's role was not only to revive the glory of Italian cinema after its decline in the 1920s; it was used by Mussolini's government, along with other institutions (such as the Fascist Youth Cinema Club, journal *Bianco e nero*, and Cinecittà film studio), as a powerful ideological instrument to legitimize the fascist nation-state and help consolidate the goals of the fascist regime (Wong, 2011: 38). This became evident as the awards began to favor the countries of the fascist alliance, particularly in 1938 when the festival's main prize, the Mussolini Cup, was awarded to Leni Riefenstahl's *Olympia* (1938) and Goffredo Alessandrini's *Luciano Serra, Pilot* (1938), produced by Mussolini's son Vittorio—despite the fact that France was tipped to win the festival with Jean Renoir's *La Grande Illusion / The Great Illusion* (1937) (de Valck, 2007: 48).

It was this clear display of political prejudice toward Hitler and Mussolini's regime that angered American, British, and French participants and led them to join forces in the establishment of the Cannes Film Festival, which was scheduled to take place in September 1939 but was postponed until 1946 due to the outbreak of war.

The first Cannes festival became "one of the most festive immediate post-war events," with gala events, parties, and receptions organized alongside the film program, and a highlight was the screening of the anti-fascist *Roma città aperta / Rome, Open City* (1946) by Roberto Rossellini (de Valck, 2007: 49).

The primacy of geopolitical agendas continued in the post-war era, with the Cold War playing a key role in the formation of new festivals. The Locarno and Karlovy Vary festivals, started in 1946 just days before the opening of Cannes, also owe their existence to political controversy. Karlovy Vary, although first conceived as a bridge between East and West (presenting entries both from the domestic industry and the US, France, the UK, and Sweden), was remodeled following the consolidation of communist power in 1948 as a showcase for a socialist film production from the Eastern Bloc, awarding a variety of prizes to movies from communist countries. Similarly, the Berlin Film Festival, or the Berlinale, founded in 1951, played a significant role in the Cold War cinematic conflict. Certainly welcomed as a much-needed opportunity to revive Germany's rich cinema traditions, it was used as a strategic tactic by the US in the Cold War, a powerful example to the communist East of democratic and capitalist values. This was evident both in its representation (it excluded movies from communist countries while allowing the US and UK to submit more entries than other invited countries) and in its use of border theaters as primary venues (de Valck, 2007: 52). Thus, if Venice and Cannes could still claim the attractive location and tourism as their key motivating factors, the political and ideological function of the Berlin Film Festival was clearly center stage.[1]

The importance of geopolitical factors during the first festival phase is integrally connected, de Valck argues, to the formation of festivals as showcases for national cinema and a statement of national identity—a particularly important move in the post-war era when the European nations were struggling to rebuild their national identities and recover from the devastating effects of the conflict (2007: 56). Comparable to international competitions such as the Olympic Games or Nobel prizes, film festivals were part of the project of modernity in which European nations used culture and cinema in particular to affirm their national distinction and heritage. Additionally, the Europe-based festival network served as a consolidated response of the weakened European film industry to the American domination of the film market.

American cinema had flooded the European market since the end of the First World War, and the first European festivals positioned themselves against this hegemony to protect and offer exposure to their films, even as they relied on the powerful presence of American films and their stars to increase their own popularity. Not coincidentally, therefore, many festivals first emerge as national entities, primarily showcasing films from their own countries and thus controlling their national image, even as they promote global connections.[2]

Interestingly, the development of film festivals' cultural and political sphere grows in tandem with the critical and academic sphere. That is, as festivals played an important role in shaping national identity and promoting geopolitical agendas, they also helped shape the very concept of national cinema and dominant approaches to the study of it. It is no accident that the showcasing of national cinema that defined the first phase of the festivals ran parallel to the dominant paradigms that guided most studies of European national cinemas, where films produced in a particular country were seen as reflecting something essential about this country as a nation. Thus, German Expressionist cinema of the 1920s was examined as a reflection of the chaos of the Weimar Republic and the symptom of a troubled German soul; the Italian historical super-spectacles of the 1910s and 1920s were seen as a projection of the Roman imperial dream that haunts the Italian psyche up to the Second World War; and post-war Japanese cinema and its "presentational aesthetic" was connected to the transcendental approach to life manifested in Japanese architecture, the tea ceremony, or haiku poetry.

Film festivals and art cinema

The global change that characterized the 1960s, radically transforming social relationships as well as the geopolitical and cinematic maps of the world, also profoundly affected film festival history. The famous events of 1968—student movements in Berkeley, Berlin, Rio de Janeiro, Tokyo, Bangkok, and Mexico that all participated in a global revolt against capitalism, colonialism, and imperialism—had significant social and political consequences that also echoed in the world of the arts and cinema specifically. Especially in France, cinema played an important role in the riots as the young filmmakers who would go on to form the French New Wave (Godard, Truffaut, and Louis Malle) protested against the dismissal of Henri Langlois, the head of the *Cinémathèque Française*. They attacked the Cannes Film Festival as an institution that supported commercial and political interest rather than film as art and young auteurs, and demanded its reorganization.

These events not only led to significant changes in the functioning of the Cannes festival, but also contributed to a global reconsideration of the role of film festivals. First, a new selection procedure was instituted, where various national governments and national committees were no longer responsible for selecting entries. This role now went to the festival director, who became "the embodiment of the festival's image in the international film festival [IFF] circuit," and was free to select films outside the influence of national film bodies, according to artistic considerations (de Valck, 2007: 63). Second, the more noncompetitive and open parallel events outside of the main competition emerged, such as Director's Fortnight, which showcased young directors and new, innovative approaches to film. Not only Cannes but all other festivals followed this reorganization. Berlin established the Young Film Forum, a platform for progressive cinema and young experimental directors that would give visibility to filmmakers such as Theo Angelopoulos, Mrinal Sen, Chantal Akerman, and Aki Kaurismäki, and introduce Asian cinema to European audiences. Locarno began promoting breaks with established models, became one of the first festivals to screen Chinese films, and pioneered Iranian and Korean cinema on European screens (Wong, 2011: 46–48). Rather than serving as a showcase of national cinema, the primary role assigned to the institution of film festivals

Figure 4.2 Jean-Luc Godard, Francois Truffaut, and Roman Polanski at the 1968 strike at the Cannes Film Festival. Image courtesy of Sipa Press/REX/Shutterstock

in this phase was to promote cinema as high art and the director as auteur. Film festivals in the 1960s became devoted to art cinema on an international scale, with it serving as a kind of a lingua franca of international cinema.

The 1950s and 1960s are also decades that see a considerable expansion in the festival network in terms of both location and cinematic interests. The first American festival begins in San Francisco in 1957, and many new festivals emerge within Europe itself: Moscow (1959) in Russia, San Sebastian (1953) in Spain, Viennale in Austria (1960), Cork (1956) in Ireland, and London in the UK (1956), among others. While the festival circuit is still dominated by Europe, new festivals begin to emerge beyond Europe that offer an important alternative to its art-cinema-dominated festival circuit: Cartagena (1968), the oldest festival in Latin America; the IFF of India (1952) in Goa; the Indonesian Film Festival (1955) in Jakarta; Carthage (1966) in Tunisia; Sydney (1954) in Australia; and Golden Horse (1962) in Taipei, Taiwan. As such festivals emerge on a global scale, they expand their programming beyond the art cinema sphere offered by European film festivals, showcasing popular and regional cinema.

Film festivals and world cinema

The most important moment for our context of world cinema is the 1980s, when festivals spread over the entire globe, diversify, and become institutionalized, forming an international film festival network. The older European festivals lose their exclusivity as festivals become a truly global phenomenon with transnational networks and circuits. This development results in an entirely new landscape of world cinema, whose imaginary and real movement through the festival network comes to reflect and shape global film production.

Among various other functions, their incredible proliferation and diversification make the institution of the film festival the most spectacular platform for the release of all kinds of film, with different festivals performing different functions and carving out spaces for a diverse spectrum of cinemas and film cultures. Importantly for our context, this phase of the global spread of festivals has a deep impact on the concept of world cinema, as festival programming becomes marked not only by the recognition of new auteurs but also an interest in unfamiliar cinematic cultures. De Valck describes this phase as "the age of programmers," when programming combines cinephilia with political awareness and an urge for new discoveries, offering exposure to as-yet unseen cinemas (2007: 174). New festivals begin searching for new discoveries, new auteurs, and new national cinemas to distinguish themselves in the growing and increasingly competitive festival circuit. This urge for new discoveries, however, was not an internal development; rather, it was intensely embedded within the larger cultural changes and revolutionary movements since the 1960s that swept through Europe, the Soviet bloc, the US, and Latin America. A whole series of novel new waves flooded the international film circuit in the 1970s: Czechoslovakia, Poland, Yugoslavia, Brazil, Cuba, Argentina, Japan, and Russia, followed by the 1980s new waves from Taiwan, West Africa, Spain, Ireland, Iran, New Zealand, and China. These movements all brought a combination of controversial subject matter, formal innovation, and socio-political messages, finding eager audiences at the new, regional, and thematic film festivals.

The Pesaro Film Festival in Italy, established in 1965, for example, distinguished itself as a festival supporting alternative film movements—films from Eastern Europe, Japan, Africa, and the Arab countries—using the format of roundtable discussions rather than juries and competition, while still offering international exposure. It was also the first festival to offer exposure to the new Latin American cinema movement, organizing retrospectives of the Brazilian Cinema Novo and Cuban cinema, and featuring screenings of revolutionary films such as Argentina's *La hora de los hornos/Hour of the Furnaces* (Octavio Getino and Fernando Solanas, 1968), Bolivia's *Yawar Mallku/Blood of the Condor* and *El coraje del pueblo/Courage of the People* (Jorge Sanjinés, 1969 and 1971), the Cuban *Memorias del subdesarrollo/Memories of Underdevelopment* (Tomás Gutiérrez Alea, 1968), and *Lucía* (Humberto Solás, 1968). Pesaro was instrumental to these films, many of which remained long unavailable in the US, as well as to the concurrent development of Third Cinema movements and discourses surrounding them. Similarly, Rotterdam, which had to distinguish itself both from the cultural center of Amsterdam at home and the global map, concentrated on idiosyncratic new talent, particularly from Asia, plus independent and experimental cinema, and video and media art.

Another significant development in the 1980s is a prolific spread of smaller, regional, and thematic film festivals that add new dimensions to the festival network in terms of issues, aesthetic, and audiences. Wong argues that the most visible changes in the festival world during this period come from smaller, specifically oriented, festivals around the world (2011: 52). These specialized or thematic festivals focus on particular subject matters, political issues (human rights; women's rights; lesbian, gay, bisexual, and transgender (LGBT) topics; or ecology), or thematic and generic distinctions (festivals devoted to musicals, food, animation, documentaries, shorts, or ethnography). While they are small, not as influential as A-list and major regional festivals, and cater to particular issues and audiences, they nevertheless constitute an important part of the festival network and are integrally "connected to other festivals in terms of the circulation of films, texts, and film knowledge" (Wong, 2011: 52). If, for A-list festivals, the globalization of film festivals led to bigger competition, an emphasis on world premieres, and festival prizes, these smaller festivals emerged with different goals and dedication. Some focus on the creation of specialized knowledge (such as the Pordenone Film Festival created in 1982—the most important silent film festival—which became key to the rediscovery, preservation, and study of early cinema), others on regional specialization or particular subjects or political issues. Often, these festivals tend to be oriented toward audiences rather than formal competitions and markets. Most American film festivals—New York, Philadelphia, Chicago, San Francisco, or Telluride, among others—that proliferate during this era are audience-oriented and also serve as important launching pads for U.S. distribution.

The emphasis on consistent programming, specialization, and new discoveries during the era of global proliferation of festivals allowed new events to carve out a niche and acquire a competitive position in the global festival and cinematic map. However, while this urge for discovery is often sincere and benefits both the festival and the filmmakers it supports, it is important to recognize that it also carries with it a hierarchy of powers and the colonial tendency to explore new territories that significantly affects and shapes the discourse of world cinema (Wong, 2011: 179). While this structure of hierarchy can be read on several levels, and it is important to acknowledge them as equally important, we highlight those that more directly concern our central question of festivals as agents in the creation of the sphere of world cinema.[3]

Global networks

One of the aspects of festivals that accompanies the process of globalization and increasingly transnational influences is their redefined position in the global network of the festival circuit and a conscious attempt to nurture a global identity and connections. Festivals leave their single affiliation with the cities and aim to become world cinema festivals, both in their programming and general profile. According to Wong,

> The very internationalist flow of film festivals makes it necessary that they maintain global networks, from the more formal arrangements of FIAPF [the International Federation of Film Producers Association], to the informal but very real festival calendar that all international festivals respect with caution, to consultancies and friendships among programmers and critics.

(2011: 60)

While major festivals like Cannes, Venice, Berlin, San Sebastian, or Toronto have their own national contexts and are closely aligned with their host cities and communities, they also begin to participate in global flows and seek to showcase new cinemas from around the world.

The Tehran Film Festival, started in 1972 under the repressive Shah regime, transformed itself into the Fajr IFF in 1982, and while it was extremely important to Iranian cinematic culture, local audiences, and filmmakers, it also screened international cinema, including works from Angelopoulos, Ozu, and Tarkovsky. The Fespaco film festival (1969), Hong Kong IFF (1977), and Havana Film Festival (1979) have all served as showcases for their national cinemas while fostering distinct patterns of global connection within a larger system. As Liz Czach's work on the Toronto festival has shown, this festival (which began in 1976) has been a promoter of Canadian cinema since the beginning and has a key role in the shaping of Canadian national cinema, but also has deep transnational roots. It positions Canadian films on the international stage, serves as a center for North American distribution, and is promoted as one of the leading launching pads for international cinema (Czach, 2004: 80). Even Sundance, which began in 1978 as a festival dedicated to promoting American independent cinema, and is perhaps the most American of festivals, has oriented itself globally, adding the World Cinema Competition section and an international audience prize.

To explain this local/global functioning of the festivals, festival scholars turn to the global network and system theories that have become popular since the 1990s. These scholars explain how festivals function as a system, a network in which local elements are linked to global structures marked by heterogeneity and plurality.[4] This does not mean, however, that power is equally distributed within new heterogeneous flows, and unequal geopolitical power relations between film festivals all but disappear when festivals start undergoing the spatial reconfiguration in the 1980s and 1990s. Julian Stringer argues that the festival circuit is "a metaphor for the geographically uneven development that characterizes the world of international film culture," and the issues of unequal global cultural exchange and power are both pervasive and multifaceted (Stringer, 2011: 137). The "A festivals" have always been more powerful, both in economic foundation, cultural production, and star power. Cannes stands at the top, followed by Venice, Berlin, and other, older European festivals. Films that premiere or are awarded here gain more visibility, and as they continue their festival rounds other festivals add Cannes or Venice logos and prizes to their own promotional material for the film, affirming the festival hierarchy.

This results in a rather arbitrary and "unproblematic presentation of the cream of various national cinemas at top festivals in the West on the one hand, and, on the other hand, the second-rate selections that are left for the newer festivals in Third World countries," with smaller film festivals assuming a subordinate position in the global arena of the international film festival circuit (de Valck, 2007: 71). Thus, significant regional film festivals such as Fespaco, the most important cultural event in Africa, or the Thessaloniki IFF, a central launching pad for Balkan cinema, are often passed over for important premieres that prefer to choose more prestigious Western festivals. In his case study of the Thessaloniki IFF, Dimitris Kerkinos notes:

> As there are not many festivals which focus on the Balkan region, the major difficulty in presenting Balkan films comes from the producers' and sales agents' wish to participate in "A Festivals," such as Rotterdam, Berlin, Cannes, Karlovy Vary, Locarno, Venice, and San Sebastian (listed chronologically). As these festivals want their films to be premieres, the most interesting films prefer to wait to be selected by them rather than to apply to TIFF's Balkan Survey section.
>
> (2009: 174)

In this competition, B festivals, important as they are in their own right, clearly lose against A festivals, reinforcing their subordinate position in the hierarchy of the festival network.

Philip Cheah, a critic who regularly reviews Asian festivals, echoes this sentiment precisely, arguing that film festival is now a post-colonial arena, marked by the matrix of power that culture is trapped in (Cheah, 2011). He questions the excitement of the media in the Philippines, Singapore, Thailand, and Indonesia when a local film gets selected in Cannes, despite the fact that there are many prominent festivals in Central Asia, with over thirty of them in Seoul alone. The fact that an Asian film being selected at a prominent Asian film festival is not considered as significant points to what Cheah describes as "the legacy of colonialism and imperialism" in the mapping of world cinema, where if the film does not exist in the Western frame of reference, it simply does not deserve attention. Rather than the culture, film festivals are interested in "the cultural power" and they express this cultural power by "mapping the world, by interpreting and insisting what they think are cultural trends" (Cheah, 2011).

Another manifestation of this power dynamic is that while all festivals are in the business of making new discoveries, what matters is not the discovery itself but how it gets made and who acknowledges it. It is interesting that "discoveries" have always been located at smaller local and regional festivals. Hong Kong has been the main stage for Chinese filmmakers (Wong Kar-wai, Jia Zhangke), Fajr for Iranian filmmakers, and Transylvania for Romanian filmmakers, and smaller festivals such as Locarno have given exposure to Iranian cinema much before its appearance at Cannes. It is also these smaller regional film festivals that are known for sections that promote directors' first work: Rotterdam's Tiger Awards, for example, was founded to promote a director's first or second work, and has a reputation for discovering Asian cinema; Pesaro is dedicated to new cinema; and Locarno has a first-film competition (Wong, 2011: 92). However, these festivals have functioned merely as a springboard, dependent on scouting programmers from Cannes or Berlin who have the power to acknowledge and promote these discoveries and therefore mark them as such. As Wong argues at length, the top-tier festivals and their showcases continue to be the measure of success, and the infrastructure they have built over the years consolidates the significance of certain films and auteurs who may have been discovered elsewhere or whose works are then picked up by other festivals (2011: 92).

A festival film? Producing the genre of world cinema

The most written-about manifestation of this global inequality concerns the generic label of "festival films." The concept of the "festival film" has appeared against the assumption that festivals are open and all-inclusive platforms for world cinema, and implies a clear delimitation of the kind of films that appeal to the festival sphere. Scholars, critics, and programmers who study festivals have been pointing to a consistency and a pattern in this body of work, films with their own set of thematic and stylistic rules, made to appeal to the international festival sphere. One of the first elaborations of this phenomenon can be found in the 2008 review of the Rotterdam Film Festival (IFFR) by James Quandt, a director of programming at the Cinematheque Ontario in Toronto since 1990, who describes an emergence of an international art house festival formula, varied yet adhering to an established set of aesthetic elements:

> *Adagio* rhythms and oblique narrative; a tone of quietude and reticence, an aura of unexplained or unearned anguish; attenuated takes, long tracking or panning shots, often of depopulated landscapes; prolonged hand-held follow shots of solo people walking; slow dollies to a window or open-door framing nature; a materialist sound design; and a preponderance of Tarkovskian imagery.
>
> (2009: 76)

More recently, Cindy Wong devoted a book chapter to the discussion and definition of the genre of "festival films." Acknowledging the difficulty and limitations of any attempt at defining a phenomenon that is in constant flux, she describes a similar set of aesthetic features pointed out by Quandt. According to Wong, festival films are defined as much by what they are *not*—these films are not geared toward mass audiences, and therefore they do not follow the conventions of commercial cinema—as they are defined by certain characteristics very much tied to art cinema conventions: "their seriousness/minimalism in vision and sound; their open and demanding narrative structures; their intertextuality (including their use of 'stars'); and finally, their subject matter, including controversy as well as freedom" (2011: 68). And contradictory to this established set of characteristics is a search for novelty, for discovery that challenges yet confirms the meaning of festival films. Whether we agree with the specificities of these definitions, their larger point is certainly worth noting: once a so-called discovery becomes established by a major festival, this recognition will then almost always include the process of canonization where specific film styles also influence and shape further discoveries, forming expectation and frameworks within which to read and understand a certain group of films.

An important element of this conceptual framework that determines the strategy of inclusion and exclusion, the politics of recognition, is the notion of national allegory, the simultaneous ability of a film to project national specificity on the one hand and universality on the other. The process of how a text gets read in a global context was already the basic concern of Jameson's "Third World Literature in the Era of Multinational Capitalism," where he suggests that the national identity of a smaller nation is a product of their positioning in relation to the First World and its dominant discourse; a response to the gaze of the outside world, rather than some internal reflection (Jameson, 1986). In his later work, he expands this notion to his theory of national cinema, where national cinemas are reduced to the essential features ascribed to them from the outside (Jameson, 2004). Jameson considers films produced by small nations as part of a generalization that groups them together, as national allegories overtly couched in psychic or existential problems, and in a style that somehow bears the preconceived cultural specificity to the outside viewer. The issue, therefore, is not so much individual filmmakers and their auteurist signature, but the very conceptual and discursive practices that assign to the filmmakers the "national burden" of capturing the essence of national cinema if they are to be offered a visible spot on the map of world cinema.

Among other things, this points to the persistence of the notion of the national, so often dismissed and deemed as outdated and inadequate in accounting for the complexity of the transnational networks that define contemporary world cinema. As Elsaesser has shown in his study of contemporary European cinema, *national* all but disappears; rather, it returns as one of the two major strategies with which festivals profile their programming and market new cinemas. In other words, *national* has come back as a form of branding, a marketing tool, signifying the local—maybe reinventing the national—for external, global use. With a tendency toward self-ethnography, the films' signifiers are not essentialist assertions of national identity but "have developed formulas that can accommodate various and even contradictory signifiers of nationhood . . . in order to relaunch a region or national stereotypes, or to reflect the image that (one assumes) that other has of oneself" (Elsaesser, 2005: 71). The national has thus become a second-order signifier, a floating designation that hovers uncertainly over the films' identity, but whose meaning is something that is continuously appropriated and re-appropriated by the festivals for clever marketing purposes.

The rise of specific national cinemas and auteurs at specific historical points is thus always connected to the interaction of forces that make a certain new cinema attractive because it is already familiar and readable on certain levels, and the paradigms of both a festival film and national allegory seem to play an important role in this process. As Wong describes, Japanese cinema was "discovered" by Venice when it screened *Rashomon* in 1951. While the film may have seemed new in its narrative strategy of narrating the same event from different points of view, it was a fairly classical text in many other ways (compared to Ozu, for example), falling into the familiar paradigms of art cinema as well as offering the timeless, exotic, and mythical image of Japan. As a result, Cannes and Venice invited Japan to submit films throughout the 1950s and 1960s, with Kurosawa and Mizoguchi becoming prominent auteurs for these festivals (from 1952 to 1955, all of Venice's Japanese entries were Mizoguchi's; Wong, 2011: 92). In the same vein, Indian cinema in the 1950s is dominated by Satyajit Ray while Hindi popular cinema (a genre that tends to evade the national allegory paradigm) never breaks into the festival circuit. The canonization of China's Fifth Generation at Western film festivals can be seen as a consequence of a similar process, as the European orientation, exotic culturalism, and political position against the Cultural Revolution made this group of films particularly attractive for critically engaged Western audiences.

This process of genrefication, so deeply embedded in the discovery and innovation paradigm, seems to undermine or at best exist in constant tension with one of the most important guiding principles embraced by most festivals: thematic and aesthetic novelty. As Wong says, "festivals have been ideologically constructed as free spaces where films of all subject matters are welcome," breaking the walls of censorship (real or implicit) in Hollywood and national cinemas (2011: 90). One can easily trace, for example, the controversial package of sex and violence that has long dominated Cannes' official selection, from Oshima's *In the Realm of the Senses* in 1976 to Claire Denis' *Trouble Every Day* in 2001, von Trier's *Antichrist* in 2009, Leos Carax's *Holy Motors* in 2011, and Abdellatif Kechiche's *Blue is the Warmest Color* in 2012. While festivals proclaim themselves as "zones that champion freedom," this freedom is already a result of a pre-fixed expectation about certain national cinema. For example, Park Chan-wook, famous for his *Vengeance trilogy*, and Kim Ki-duk, whose films have included very graphic scenes of genital mutilation, are two renowned auteurs whose presence on the festival circuit almost single-handedly shaped and defined the discourse of violence in South Korean cinema. Similarly, it was the international success of Pedro Almodóvar's "auteur's cinema," his representations of homosexuality/transsexuality that draw on styles and themes characteristic of both popular and underground cinema, which subsequently identified these qualities as part of the discourse on diversity that still serves as the main location of Spanishness in Spanish cinema. Festivals may be freer to show controversial and extreme movies, but such themes and aesthetics also constitute critical elements of the festival genre and the canon of films against which new entries will be measured.

Many filmmakers have vocally complained about pre-set expectations that drive the festival programming of world cinema.[5] Such sentiment can even be found in the review of the 2013 IFFR, which perhaps more than any other A-list festival has been strongly associated with innovation, new talent, sophisticated audiences, and cinephilia, embodied best in its Exploding Cinema section. Despite this status, *Variety* critic Jay Weissberg laments:

> Perhaps the biggest problem of IFFR is that they are convinced that their conception of cinema has resulted in broadening the horizons of the medium, but those horizons have essentially been reduced to something very specific: an art house cinema characterized by pale story lines, hand-held camera work and the conception of the superiority of youth culture . . . A broader range of contemporary cinema should be

offered that goes beyond navel gazing, the aestheticization of Third World poverty, prostitution and misconduct of teenagers.

(quoted in Wolfs, 2013)

That premiere-heavy and expansion-driven festivals such as Rotterdam, Berlin, or Sundance nurture a specific kind of festival film, attempting to replicate the past successes and create a brand (a strategy not unlike Hollywood's modus operandi) is a frequent observation by festival scholars, critics, and programmers, who concede that such festivals "do just as much harm as good to the world of cinema," creating a rather hermetic system that is resistant to change and thus does not respond adequately to the reality of a rapidly changing film world (Peranson, 2009: 33).

The problem of genre production that shapes the discourse of world cinema is further compounded by the festivals' expansion into the very film production process. As discussed in Chapter 3, since the 1990s festivals have ceased to function as mere exhibition and distribution platforms, and have been directly involved in the production and co-production of films through the increasing importance of the specialized monetary funds designed to support new, formally innovative filmmakers and local film industries: the Cannes Cinefondation, World Cinema Fund in Berlin, Asian Project Market of Busan, Balkan fund of Thessaloniki, CineMart of Rotterdam, FILMART of Hong Kong, and many others. These establishments have varying degrees of involvement in the production process, but all of them assume an important role in shaping the landscape of world cinema. One of the most influential funds, the Hubert Bals Fund (HBF), has played a big role in financing and distributing projects by independent filmmakers all over the world.

An impressive number of careers of prominent world cinema auteurs today were jump-started and affected by the ripple effect of this influential fund: Sergei Loznitsa (Belarus), Carlos Reygadas (Mexico), Nuri Bilge Ceylan (Turkey), Dominga Sotomayor

HUBERT BALS FUND

Figure 4.3 The logo for the Hubert Bals Fund; 2014 was the fund's silver jubilee. Image courtesy of International Film Festival Rotterdam

(Chile), Aditya Assarat (Thailand), and Marie Ka (Senegal), to name just a few. Looking beyond the programming and evaluation of finished products, with these funds many festivals demand a say in which films are artistically interesting before they are made, make narrative and artistic suggestions, and thus exert direct and indirect influence on film production as they help a film transition from local economies to the global market. The HBF catalogue, for example, makes quite clear that the desired entries "should be original, authentic and rooted in the culture of the applicant's country." They foreground authenticity and originality so crucial to the festival's identity, but frame it in the familiar dynamic of the festival film genre: a combination of local flavor, universal appeal, and international style. Thus, valuable as these funds are, they often end up influencing the kind of film that is made, a development that adds another layer of meaning to the label "festival film" as these films are not only predominantly "produced *for* the festival circuit, but also partially *by* (and with the cultural approval of) the festival circuit" (de Valck, 2007: 181). Discoveries, therefore, can be understood not as an act of mere exposure but an act of creation.

In focus 4.1   Discovering Iranian cinema

A closer look at the emergence and evolution of national cinema waves often reveals how the "discovery" that takes place within the international festival circuit shapes specific categories of national cinema and influences the process of production, visual look, and narrative tendencies of a national cinema. In an engaging analysis of Iranian cinema on the festival circuit, Azadeh Farahmand argues that the aesthetic and narrative evolution of what has come to be known as Iranian cinema since the 1960s has little to do with some essential characteristics or common traits of national cinema. Rather, it has to be understood as an institutional formation shaped by its exhibition context (Farahmand, 2010).

This is an important argument to be made for Iranian cinema in particular, which is widely recognized as one of the most distinctive, innovative, and exciting national cinemas in the world. With the phenomenal success and festival exposure in the late 1990s of established masters like Abbas Kiarostami, Dariush Mehrjui, and Mohsen Makhmalbaf, as well as newcomers such as Majid Majidi, Abolfazl Jalili, Samira Makhmalbaf, Jafar Panahi, and Bahman Ghobadi, Iranian cinema became all the rage. By the mid-1990s, hardly any major festival took place without including Iranian films in its line-up, and new festivals emerged exclusively devoted to showcasing Iranian cinema.

In 1997, Kiarostami's *T'am e guilass/A Taste of Cherry* became the first Iranian film to win the Palme d'Or, and soon everyone referred to this unprecedented appearance of Iranian films in the festival circuit as New Iranian Cinema.

If much critical and scholarly work that surrounds the phenomenon focuses on aesthetic analysis to define the thriving national cinema, Farahmand shows how this phenomenon masks a complex picture of the thriving film culture industry in Iran and is strongly aligned with specific tastes and expectations of the global festival community. That is, the phenomenon of the Iranian festival film has less to do with internal characteristics of Iranian national cinema and more to do with a serendipitous alignment

(continued)

(continued)

Figure 4.4 Abbas Kiarostami receives the Palme d'Or for his *Taste of Cherry* in 1997. Image
courtesy of Michel Gangne/AFP/Getty

Figure 4.5 The London Iranian Film Festival, an annual festival that presents Iranian cinema in
the UK

between the aims of the domestic film industry and those of an international festival circuit eager to champion a new discovery.

The first Iranian wave of the 1970s was very much a homegrown phenomenon, a result of several factors that began brewing in the late 1950s: "The growing middle class embraced cinema as a medium of intellectual engagement, cultural conversation, and social criticism . . . Topics such as poverty, corruption, personal revenge, and government bureaucracy were discussed in literature, theater, poetry, and cinema" (Farahmand, 2010: 270). But it was the elaborate orchestration of the Tehran IFF (1972), positioned as a cultural bridge between the East and West, that provided a platform to this cinema, and the international reaction to these films that "genre-fied" the first new wave. A group of political protest films, such as Dariush Mehrjui's *Gaav/Cow* (1969), and his second feature *Postchi/The Postman* (1972), after receiving major attention at Venice and Cannes respectively, were immediately situated as Third World allegories, with its director cast as a rising auteur. Farahmand contends that it was not only the collective showcasing of these Iranian films at the high-profile Tehran festival that helped define the canon and frame it as Iran's new homegrown cinematic movement, but also the favorable conditions in the international festival world, which were able to appropriate this national film movement within the already familiar and then-popular framework of Third Cinema as well as other national new waves of the 1960s (2010: 272).

It is no coincidence then that in the context of the 1979 revolution and the hostage crisis, the political films and revolutionary ideas that dominated in the 1970s gave way to films that offered a humane view of the people and culture of Iran. These films feature gentle and simple stories about children and women, couched in a simple realist aesthetic that blurs the distinction between fiction and documentary: *Badkonake sefid/ The White Balloon* (Jafar Panahi, 1995), *Ayneh/The Mirror* (Jafar Panahi, 1997), *Rang-e khoda/The Color of Paradise* (Majid Majidi, 1999), *Sib/The Apple* (Samira Makhmalbaf, 1998), among others. Farahmand points out that while the 1970s films were received by international audiences as political allegories framed in the context of Third Cinema, the festival films of the 1990s were interpreted within a framework that focused "on simplicity, poetry, humanism, and philosophical themes" (2010: 275). These characteristics became generic qualities that filmmakers, agents, programmers, critics, and academics highlighted and passed along, reinforcing a process that folded these features back into local production trends and the texture of subsequent films.

The advent of a more repressive Ahmadinejad regime in 2005 that replaced the liberal cultural atmosphere of the reformist Khatami era and tightened the government's control of the film industry led to a more subdued representation of Iranian films on the festival circuit, and raised further questions about the legacy of Iranian cinema. A thinner representation of Iranian films in the festival circuit during the post-Khatami era was seen as a reflection of both the new regime and the fact that the novelty of Iranian cinema on the festival circuit had worn out—a symptom of a national cinema trapped in a web of national and international politics, and of dependence on the festival circuit for financing and distribution that limits the thematic and formal experimentation of filmmakers in order to appeal to the needs of the market.

(continued)

(continued)

The long-standing transnational circulation and absorption of Iranian cinema on the international festival stage has contributed to a diversification and a breakthrough of Iranian cinema beyond festival art cinema into global mainstream cultural production. The impressive success and critical acclaim of Asghar Farhadi on the global stage is a particularly strong case in point. Farhadi's films, such as *Darbareye Elly/About Elly* (2009), *Jodaeiye Nader az Simin/A Separation* (2011), *Le passé/The Past* (2013), and *Forushande/The Salesman* (2016), paint a complex microcosm of modern Iran in a highly mobile, global framework. They are nuanced portraits of the layered relations among Iranian classes, genders, and social groups that deftly navigate and question the legitimacy of the Islamic Republic. However, they transcend cultural specificity with a recognizable style of psychological filmmaking, middle-class characters, and narratives that could be set anywhere. When in 2012 *A Separation* won the Academy Award for Best Foreign Language Film, "the event marked an institutional acceptance of an Iranian film as part of a mainstream global cinema" (Atwood, 2015: 33), presenting a kind of peak of the global circulation of Iranian's art cinema, but also opening doors to the recognition of a more diverse body of films as well as heterogeneous scholarly approaches to Iranian cinema that move away from the familiar "art-house cinema as national cinema" frameworks (Atwood & Decherney, 2015).

It is perhaps precisely this breaking-through of Iranian cinema into a mainstream global cinema that opened doors to films such as *A Girl Walks Home Alone at Night* (2014), a genre-bending and boundary-breaking black-and-white film by a California-based Iranian American filmmaker Ana Lily Amirpour that sits all but comfortably within the canonized category of Iranian festival films. Causing a powerful splash after its 2014 premiere at the Sundance Film Festival, Amirpour's debut film features the Girl, a lonely and silent young heroine in a traditional black veil, a vampire who roams the night streets of Bad City, a fictional district on the outskirts of a city that could be either Tehran or Detroit. Her bloody adventures are a defiant expression of female desire and agency that draws and redraws the lines of gender politics and social justice. Seen as one of the most important discoveries of 2014, the film, publicized simply as an "Iranian vampire film" is a thematically, stylistically, and discursively layered film that masterfully repurposes the fabric of a culturally specific context and sexual politics into a uniquely quilted, trans-cultural, and trans-generic product. It urges us to adopt its vampire-like hunger for a new and expanded understanding of the diverse and heterogeneous body of work, as well as the (local and global) forces that make up Iranian cinema and shape its circulation in the global film culture.

In focus 4.2   The creation of the Romanian New Wave

The festival context plays a similarly determining role in the "discovery" of the Romanian New Wave, which became the talk of the festival circuit in the early 2000s with a young generation of filmmakers for whom the 1989 revolution proved a formative event. Building on the wider success and exposure of Eastern European cinema after the breakdown of the communist bloc in Eastern Europe in the 1990s, Romanian films transitioned from the local Romanian festival in Transylvania and regional festivals in Sarajevo and Thessaloniki to larger European festivals like London, Locarno, Rotterdam, and finally Cannes. In 2001 and 2002, Christi Puiu's *Marfa si banii/Stuff and Dough* and Cristian Mungiu's *Occident* competed in the Director's Fortnight at Cannes. In 2005, Puiu's second feature, *Moartea domnului Lăzărescu/The Death of Mr. Lazarescu,* won the prize at Cannes' *Un Certain Regard* section, followed by many more prizes around the world, a development that is generally seen as a defining leap for Romanian cinema, propelling the wave— justifiably so, as the wave seemed unstoppable and only growing in force. In 2006, Corneliu Porumboiu won the Camera d'Or best-first-feature award for *A fost sau n-a fost?/12:08 East of Bucharest*. In 2007, Cristian Nemescu's posthumous *California Dreamin'* won the prize in the *Un Certain Regard* section, and Mungiu's *4 luni, 3 saptamâni si 2 zile/4 Months, 3 Weeks, 2 Days* won the Palme d'Or, a first for a Romanian film.

Figure 4.6 Cristian Mungiu wins the Palme d'Or for *4 Months, 3 Weeks, 2 Days* at the 2007 Cannes Film Festival. Image courtesy of Romaniello/Venturelli/REX/ Shutterstock

(continued)

(continued)

In *The New York Times'* first comprehensive review of this movement, "New Wave on the Black Sea," A. O. Scott observes that "the Romanian new wave has arrived" (Scott, 2008).

He asserts that this cannot possibly be a mere "serendipitous convergence of a bunch of idiosyncratic talents" since there is so much overlap and continuity found in this cinema (Scott, 2008). Interestingly, the filmmakers themselves resisted this designation and insisted in several interviews that there is no such thing as a Romanian New Wave or Romanian film industry, that they are just a few individuals who happened to have made films around the same time, who happened to have gained recognition at the same time. Mungiu in particular articulated the awareness of this process of discovery and its creation, noting in a press conference in Bucharest, "If I had presented the same film in 2002, the likelihood that I would have received Palme d'Or would have been almost nil . . . I capitalized on the growing sympathy for Romanian cinema" (Romania News Watch, 2007).

The recognition of this discovery went hand in hand with the recognition of a stylistic and thematic coherence in this group of films, the process of genrefication that falls rather squarely within the paradigms of national allegory and the festival film genre. A.O. Scott describes the following characteristics of Romanian cinema: "a penchant for long takes and fixed camera positions; a taste for plain lighting and everyday décor; a preference for stories set amid ordinary life," narratives confined on a single day and focused on a single action, with "a palpable impulse to tell the truth" (Scott, 2008). In the same sentence, he points to the affinity of this minimalist and neo-neorealist style with other contemporary European auteurs such as the Dardenne brothers. Thematically, as Wong observes, these films emerge from and respond to the same political and social milieu, presenting stories of the traumas of the Ceausescu era and confusions of the Euro consumerist present at the moment when the audience is eager to hear them. They seem to create a mythic Romania, where pre-1989 always evokes a very oppressive communist regime, while the post-1989 country has become "a lackluster dystopia with a government that seems to have inherited many of the old communist ways of running things" (Wong, 2011: 96).

The process of genrefication determines not only the framework within which to interpret this body of work but also the readings and reception of individual films. For example, Cristian Mungiu's *4 Months*, a suspenseful story of an illegal abortion set in the last days of Ceausescu's regime, is situated firmly within the discourse on the Romanian New Wave: focus on a single act that is completed by the end of the narrative, Mungiu's austere camerawork, long takes, very controlled camera movements, drab lighting, consistent focus on minute details and routines of the pre-1989 Romanian life, the quotidian tyranny of life under Ceausescu. The film thus readily offers itself as a national allegory, while its "issue oriented" narrative of illegal abortion also has a more general and universal appeal that can easily be appropriated within a broader discourse on abortion.[6] On the other hand, many crucial aspects of the film are masked or erased by this framework, such as the film's emphasis on the all-consuming aspects of economics and a fundamentally capitalist logic that sustains the power of a communist regime. *4 Months*, after all, eschews moral arguments surrounding abortion and focuses primarily on the issues of economic transaction, using its visual and narrative economy to depict a society under Ceausescu's communist policies that is guided by profoundly capitalist impulses—rather than standing in opposition to them.

If, on the one hand, the austere aesthetic that jump-started New Romanian Cinema (somber narratives, minute attention to *mise-en-scène*, long takes) can be seen as a logical reaction to the loud didacticism, symbolism, and histrionics of pre-1989 Romanian cinema, its rootedness in the festival discourse on Romanian cinema created a specific set of expectations against which to measure and judge other Romanian films. So profound was the influence of this aesthetic prescription that many critics have divided Romanian cinema into two major "eras," BC and AC—before Christi and after Christi—and every film that did not fit into this aesthetic prerogative invited the question, "What does this film have to do with Romanian cinema?" (Filimon, 2014). Moreover, while the process of genrefication was crucial to the discovery of Romanian cinema on the festival circuit and its international acclaim, it did not contribute to its success at home or the growth of the Romanian film industry, creating a rather haunting specter for the new generation of Romanian filmmakers. Applauded as it was by film festivals and academia, the movement did not achieve any commercial success with Romanian audiences, and the very films that were festival successes had rather appalling box office figures in Romania. In 2010, domestic films assumed a mere 2.5 percent share of the market. Commenting on this dangerous rift, Monica Filimon notes, "Once the awards fade away, these films may estrange even the small public they have managed to cultivate in their native country," and Phil Hoad of the *Guardian* echoes, "The rift between the Romanian new wave and its home audience could end up hurting the global profile of the industry, if the movement runs to seed" (Filimon, 2014; Hoad, 2013).

The implications of the commercial failure of New Romanian Cinema are not lost on the young generation of Romanian filmmakers, many of who seem to be addressing the very rift created by the process of genrefication, embracing approaches to form and plot that defy the aesthetics and expectations of the New Romanian Cinema. As Filimon observes, many films showcased at the 2006 "Making Waves" retrospective in New York indicate "a turn toward a more self-referential, polymorphous, whimsical cinema" which is less an instrument of moral reflection and investigation into the reality of the social world, and more "a commentary on cinema as a practice" (Filimon, 2014). This cinema walks the line much more aggressively between commercial and art cinema to capture wider and more diverse audiences, and calls attention to the need for a small film industry to move beyond a short-lived festival spotlight if it is to remain sustainable, to develop a solid infrastructure and a coherent strategy that promotes both production and distribution, commercial and art cinema, new and experienced filmmakers alike.

Digital delivery and the creation of global film culture

We cannot underestimate the role that film festivals have recently played in shaping global film culture by taking advantage of online distribution platforms and social media, and reimagining their traditional distribution and exhibition practices. Festivals are traditionally conceived as singular events, relying on exclusive access to new films prior to their the-atrical, DVD, or online release. In the age of digital revolution, however, many festi-vals, both smaller ones associated with independent filmmaking—Sundance, Slumdance, Tribeca, South by Southwest—and historically older A-list festivals like Venice or Berlin, have begun collaborating with digital platforms, and have rebranded themselves as dis-tributors, streaming selected films on various online platforms like Netflix and iTunes or on-demand services (Tryon, 2013).

The Sundance Film Festival, long associated with the nurturing and discovery of indie films, rebranded itself and expanded independent film distribution by placing its current and past titles on various digital platforms (iTunes, Amazon, Netflix) and the festival's own distribution platform, Sundance Now. South by Southwest, perhaps most known for launching the careers of filmmakers associated with the Mumblecore movement, started offering on-demand services (the Independent Film Channel) for films currently playing at the festival. Even the world's oldest international film festivals such as Venice, Berlin, and Cannes, whose exclusivity and specific geographic embed-dedness are crucial elements of their identity, have aligned themselves with new mod-els that have significant implications for how we understand a festival film and world cinema. In 2012, for example, the world's oldest film festival, Venice, has partnered with Ridley Scott's production company and YouTube to create an online film festival called Your Film Festival, conceived as a global competition where aspiring filmmakers could submit their short films, and ten finalists chosen by YouTube users were then screened in Venice.

A pioneer in digital delivery, Tribeca has become "one of the most visible partici-pants in the reinvention of festivals as online events shaped by digital delivery and social media tools" (Tryon, 2013: 169). Starting in 2007, Tribeca launched a series of online initiatives that opened up the festival to larger audiences and allowed its presence to remain alive and vital well beyond the actual festival event: the creation of virtual attendance through a "Festival Streaming Room," where select feature and short films are available for streaming; a live feed of the red-carpet area, award shows, panels, and other special events in real time; the Filmmaker Feed, a social media tool that connects viewers to the filmmaker and the festival beyond what the event can offer; and offer-ing select films on a variety of video-on-demand platforms as well as iTunes, Amazon, and Vudu.

By embracing these new models, festivals have rebranded themselves from exclu-sive events taking place in specific locations to a global media phenomenon, opening themselves up to much wider and diverse audiences. More importantly, they have redefined the traditional window system of distribution, where a successful festival run serves as a preamble for theatrical run and DVD release. By distributing films online during the festival itself, often skipping a theatrical screening altogether, they have altered the cultural value often associated with festival films, and cultivated entirely new markets and audiences for those same films. Through online participation, fes-tivals have not only become available to wider audiences, but also increased oppor-tunities for filmmakers' participation; in doing so, they are further untethering their connection with the city and the nation to become a truly global phenomenon. This development confirms their new role in world cinema, where films are seen beyond and outside of rigid frameworks placed upon them by various—geographic, industrial, cultural—constraints.

The importance of smaller and regional film festivals: the Sarajevo Film Festival

In his account of the festival ecosystem, Mark Peranson (2009) distinguishes between "business festivals" and "audience festivals". The business model is exemplified by major festivals with markets (Cannes, Berlin, Venice, Toronto, Sundance, etc.), which are characterized by high budgets, corporate sponsorship, large staffs, and a focus on premieres and major competitions. Audience festivals (most festivals in a city near you—Vancouver, Philadelphia, Buenos Aires), on the other hand, are characterized by low budgets and depend on attendance revenue, and have limited sponsorship, no production funds, small staffs, little business presence, and minor competitions. While Peranson's is merely a conceptual model, and many festivals in fact combine elements of both types, it does effectively call attention to a power dynamic and hierarchies in the festival network. Adding to the power of the business festivals is not only their central and powerful positioning in this ecosystem, but the critical and media attention that is paid to them.

Certainly, one cannot deny that the heavyweights are the most important festivals in the world, and paying attention to them is key to understanding the forces that shape world cinema. Simultaneously, however, taking this hierarchy for granted does not provide an understanding of the ways in which smaller "audience" festivals function and make an impact. These festivals may not register when we apply to them the categories that define the giants: the presence of sales agents, distributors, funds, and vast international media. However, they have a unique, no less significant, presence in the festival network, with their own interplay between the business/audience dynamic that requires a different understanding of what is commonly considered "small" or "large." They may be small compared to Cannes, but large within their own regional context; they may be insignificant as business festivals compared to Toronto, for example, but they function as key business platforms for secondary or tertiary film production markets and perform a significant cultural function for the involved communities.

Numerous festivals, small, thematic, or regional, could be discussed as examples here. We will focus on one such festival, the Sarajevo Film Festival (SFF), initially a tiny singular event that has evolved into the most important platform for the cinema of Southeastern Europe. The festival was born in October 1993 during the long and terrifying siege of Sarajevo, when most of the city was destroyed and left with no food, water, electricity, or medicine, let alone projectors and screens. Haris Pašović, a theater and film director from Sarajevo who was determined to keep alive the cultural pulse of the city (he had directed a production of *Waiting for Godot* in Sarajevo with Susan Sontag that same year), petitioned the international community and wrote letters to filmmakers such as Wim Wenders and festival programmers such as Mark Cousins to help him obtain the films. Hoping to get about ten films and gather thirty people to watch them, he ended up receiving about 200 films from around the world, VHS copies of which were smuggled into the city with great difficulty. Kenneth Turan, describing the event in its intrepid infancy, explains how film cassettes were smuggled in, workers were paid in cigarettes, flour, and cooking oil, and car engines were rigged to run the few available projectors (Turan, 2002).

The festival was held in the Bosnian Cultural Center, where thirty-seven films (some in 35 mm, but many on VHS) from 15 countries were presented, with full attendance every night. Without concern for picture or sound quality, with a "take what you can get" approach that did not discriminate among films and had no formal schedule, submission procedure, competition sections, glamour, or parties—only a bunch of films and a determination to watch them—the event attracted 15,000 people who risked their lives navigating shelling and sniping to make it to the screenings and see films like Francis Ford Coppola's *Dracula* (1992) or Paul Verhoeven's *Basic Instinct* (1992). Mirsad Purivatra, the current festival director, recalls:

> It was a war cinema, one hundred seats and a video beam projector, but in spite of the war, in spite of the shelling, it was packed every night we had a showing. The audience reception of films was completely different here. Sharon Stone in *Basic Instinct*, no big comment. But there was a dinner scene in the film that got two minutes of applause.
>
> (quoted in Turan, 2002: 97)

In a letter printed in the festival's program, published in the Sarajevo daily *Oslobođjenje*, Pašović said,

> Sarajevo is the city in which the world of the 20th century, the world in which we were born and brought up, has died. In other places the dying is taking place. Here we live beyond the end of the world.[7]

Following this line of thought, Pašović called the event "Beyond the End of the World," encapsulating the spirit of the culturally rich, cosmopolitan city whose longing for art and cinema proved stronger than the destruction of the war, and whose citizens showed that fighting for culture is inseparable from fighting for life. The SFF was thus inaugurated as a unique cultural event.

In 1997, the festival gained a more formal structure and its sponsorship expanded from humanitarian groups to corporate backing by Renault and Swissair, among others. Attendance and the number of films more than doubled, and the Bosnian government issued a postage stamp to commemorate the festival. In 2001, the European Film Association granted the SFF the ability to nominate shorts from the Europe's Best Short Film competition, and the winning film from that year's competition, Danis Tanović's *Ničija zemlja/No Man's Land*, went on to win the Academy Award for Best Foreign Language Film.

Figure 4.7 "Beyond the End of the World," the first edition of the SFF, in 1993

Figure 4.8 The Sarajevo Open Air Theater, boasting 2,500 seats

Since its inception, the SFF has established itself as the most important focal point for networking and showcasing the cinema of the region, recognized by the FIAPF as a Competitive Specialized Festival. It has recharged the regional production that was curtailed by the war, and its regional competition programs (open to Albania, Austria, Bosnia and Herzegovina, Bulgaria, Croatia, Greece, Hungary, Macedonia, Romania, Serbia and Montenegro, Slovenia, and Turkey), comprised of narrative, documentary, and shorts competitions, remain the centerpiece of the festival. Some of its sections include New Currents, a showcase of first or second features; Panorama, a selection of international fiction, many of them shown in an outdoor atrium of a fire station; Panorama Documentaries, which are accompanied by their directors; and Open Air, a hugely popular mainstream and art house nightly screening which tends to pack 2,500 viewers into an outdoor space.

Quite a rarity for such a festival, there is also a children's program (more than 35,000 kids are bussed in from all over Bosnia and Herzegovina for screenings) and a group of films for teens. The festival has also launched programs that make it an important catalyst and platform for initiatives such as the formation of national film funds in the region, and engagements of TV companies in film production: Cinelink (modeled on Rotterdam's Cinemart, and launched jointly by the SFF and Rotterdam's HBF), a network of cooperation that pairs producers and investors with directors and screenwriters; and the Talent Campus, modeled on Berlin's, which helps train young filmmakers in directing, screenwriting, and acting.

The festival has expanded from 15,000 viewers and thirty-seven films in its first edition to more than 100,000 viewers and over 200 films. Yet, even as it has morphed into the most exclusive showcase of Balkan cinema, it is still marked by its geopolitical stamp, with signs of the war still quite visible in the city itself. Sarajevo's history not only makes up an important part of the SFF event, but is consciously used as part of its identity and self-understanding. The 2009 promotional literature, for example, states:

> This year's edition of the SFF marks a small jubilee . . . It's a short time for a European festival, but a long way for us, who started it all in a city under siege . . . We aspired to create a festival that would celebrate life through the celebration of film, promote regional cinematography, affirm young and novel film expression, and establish a platform for the exchange of experience and resources in this part of the world.
>
> (Jockims, 2012)

Among other things, this statement foregrounds the cultural significance that regional festivals often carry, beyond increasing tourist dollars and attracting investors for its films. As Iordanova points out, festivals such as this one, while they vary in function, degree of visibility, and access to resources, and tend to be marginalized in relation to the big festivals in the festival galaxy, are significant not only as exhibition and networking platforms for regional cinema but play a key role in national identity formation, conflict negotiation, community building, and cultural diplomacy. In the space of the festival,

> organizers and audiences form a community, an actual one, that congregates face-to-face for the purpose of fostering an 'imagined community' that comes live in the act of watching a film and imagining distant human beings becoming part of one's own experience.
>
> (Iordanova, 2010: 13)

The festival event can thus be seen as a political act that mediates national and transnational identities in a new way.

The SFF is certainly one of the elements that shapes Balkan film culture and resonates with the wider social and political identity of the region. On the most basic level, as people are intensely aware of the negative associations attached to the term "Balkan," the festival, as a symbol of transnational modern culture, becomes a way of battling the stigma of the Balkans and earning Sarajevo a spot in the cosmopolitan map. But it is also a concrete step toward regional community building and cultural diplomacy. In this context, it is significant to see how the interplay between film culture and social/political identity as reflected in the festival has evolved. For example, the early years of the festival were noteworthy for films from Croatia, Slovenia, and Macedonia, while no films came from Serbia, despite the fact that the directors and films that were international favorites at the time (Emir Kusturica, Srđjan Dragojević, Goran Paskaljević) were Serbian. Sarajevo-born Emir Kusturica—a cultural hero before the war who fled the city during the war and renounced his Bosniak roots—went unmentioned despite his international acclaim and visibility. However, the 2009 Sarajevo Award for Best Film went to Serbian director Vladimir Perišić's *Obični ljudi/Ordinary People*, and the 2010 Best Film award to another Serbian film, Nikola Ležaić's *Tilva Roš*. These were the first Serbian films to win the award in the festival's history, a change that reflects how the promotion of film culture shapes the collective regional identity, but also how this collective identity is reflected outside of its own boundaries. Similarly, the festival's Regional Forum, which encourages co-productions and the usage of new technologies in marketing, and its Talent Campus, which uses this strategy in training young talent, were started with a premise that a strong regional profile should go hand in hand with transnational cooperation and conscious positioning within the European film industry.

In this sense, the festival's global visibility and international status is as important as its regional status, and has been strongly nurtured by the SFF. The festival's focus on international cinema has been its most notable element since the beginning, an important move for a city full of cinephilia but limited distribution. One of the biggest highlights of the festival is the "Tribute to . . ." section, a retrospective of a renowned director who is invited to and participates in the festival. The subjects of past tributes include Béla Tarr, Alexander Payne, Alfonso Cuarón, Carlos Reygadas, Mike Leigh, Abel Ferrara, and Todd Haynes. Alongside this focus on international cinema is the presence of A-list Hollywood stars at the festival, certainly one of the strongest factors in attracting international press to an event that tends to be overlooked by mainstream media. Even in its first edition, the festival organizers tried to fly in stars Vanessa Redgrave, Jeremy Irons, and Daniel Day-Lewis (the United Nations refused permission to do it), and today the notable figures who have attended the festival and are considered "the friends of Sarajevo" include Mike Leigh, Bono of U2, John Malkovich, Willem Dafoe, Steve Buscemi, Morgan Freeman, Jeremy Irons, Michael Moore, Mickey Rourke, Angelina Jolie, and Brad Pitt.

An important benchmark in this area was the appearance of Angelina Jolie and Brad Pitt at the 2011 SFF, which was more than just a red-carpet event, since the festival heavily promoted Jolie's directorial debut *In the Land of Blood and Honey*, a film about the war in Bosnia that gained considerable international attention.

Figure 4.9 Bono arrives at the 6th SFF; he is pictured here with Mirsad Purivatra, the festival organizer. Image courtesy of Elma Okić/REX/Shutterstock

Figure 4.10 Angelina Jolie and Brad Pitt at the 2011 SFF. Image courtesy of Danilo Krstanović/
            Reuters

The SFF is only one example of the impact of smaller and regional film festivals and their expanding presence in a broader sphere, despite the burgeoning (self)importance of the mega-festivals discussed earlier. As the most powerful festivals like Cannes, Berlin, and Venice assert themselves as the center of the festival galaxy, attracting most publicity, making the most of the expanded media, and driven by a constant need to expand, smaller regional markets are just as significant in maintaining the balance of this galaxy, and should be evaluated in their own right. As Iordanova points out, rather than running in competition or conflict with the festival behemoths, these festivals constitute a dispersed yet "parallel circuit" that takes place outside the group of large competitive festivals, although in co-existence with it (Iordanova, 2010: 31). Part of the project of the *Film Festival Yearbook* volumes that Iordanova edits is precisely to map the history, presence, and impact of such festivals, and the current editions present a considerable achievement in developing a systematic approach to even the most marginalized parts of the festival circuit, from indigenous and diasporic to human rights film festivals around the world. The Film Festival Research Network, founded by Marijke de Valck and Skadi Loist, is another effort in connecting the various aspects of festival research and fostering interdisciplinary exchange between academics and professionals that leads to a better understanding of this complex phenomenon.

The increasing spread and influence of such festivals underscores our argument that world cinema does not consist of only the visible centers, that it is indeed a polycentric, varied, and interconnected phenomenon. Dispersed and numerous as they are, the small, regional, and thematic festivals nevertheless constitute a networked system where a small film from an unknown director that would otherwise not be seen beyond its immediate context gets exposure, is picked up by other festivals, and gains the possibility of more global visibility. With the decline of art house cinemas, such festivals assume an increasingly significant role in building reputation, audiences, and a market for excellent films that escape the major festivals. Iordanova argues that the value of the festival chain cannot be ignored, not least because for many films and many directors, this is where the film's journey both begins and ends: "In this respect, festivals are no substitute for something else. Screening the film at festivals is not a means of getting the film to real exhibition; it *is* the real exhibition" (Iordanova, 2009: 24). Further, as the smaller festivals are plugged into circuits created by larger festivals, they provide capillary forms of dissemination for world cinema titles that circulate at larger festivals. And finally, such festivals bring attention to the polyvalence of world cinema, insofar as they provide a context-specific, culturally situated perspective on world cinema. As festivals such as the SFF showcase and give visibility to smaller or regional cinemas in a larger, world cinema context, they not only develop a localized and diverse perspective on world cinema, but provide an important counterbalance to cinemas with higher visibility and a global profile.

The net effect of thousands of such film festivals, appearing in nearly every major cultural center around the world, is to bring world cinema to wider audiences, forming a networked traffic of films each year, while creating exhibition and network platforms for local filmmakers. To say that these capillary forms of festival circuits and events are crucial to the survival of world cinema is an understatement. As occasional events, they remain outside of the reach of theatrical statistics. In terms of revenue, they are hardly attractive for filmmakers. But in terms of cultural and cinematic effect, their contribution to world cinema remains priceless.

Activity 4.1

There are quite a few films whose main theme is the phenomenon of film festivals. In *Room 666* (1982), director Wim Wenders sets up a static camera in his hotel room at the Cannes Film Festival and interviews other directors about the future of cinema. In *Heart of the Festival: Gilles Jacob Cannes Collection* (2005), long-time Cannes director Gilles Jacob peers behind the curtains of the king of all film festivals. *Cannes Man* (1996) by Richard Martini is a comedic take on this same festival. And in *Guest* (2010), director José Luis Guerin documents his experience during a year of touring the festival circuit. Watch at least two of such films. What aspect of the film festival do they focus on—the glamour, the business, or the films? How are these aspects interrelated? What do they say about the culture of film festivals?

Activity 4.2

One of the highlights of the Karlovy Vary IFF is the official trailer, a commissioned short usually starring a cinematic icon (John Malkovich, Jude Law, Helen Mirren, etc.) revealed during the opening ceremony. Most of these shorts are available on YouTube (for example http://www.youtube.com/watch?v=5fNTli9bvRM). Watch a few shorts and consider how the festival uses the format of short film and celebrity presence for a global promotion of this regional festival.

Activity 4.3

Visit the website of one A-list international film festival (such as Berlin, Venice, Toronto) and a smaller, regional film festival, perhaps one connected to your city/ region. Look at their mission statement/philosophy. What differences do you find in the way they describe, promote, and identify themselves?

Activity 4.4

Find out if there is a film festival in your home town or city organized on an annual basis. What kind of a film festival is it? Examine its most recent program. Where do the films come from? Can you recognize any of the filmmakers represented?

Notes

1   It is also during this time of the first proliferation and growth of film festivals that the International Federation of Film Societies (IFFS) was set up in order to coordinate the various interests and legitimize festivals as a diverse yet unified entity. The IFFS, set up in 1947 in Cannes, established both the hierarchy of festivals (granting higher status to "A-category" festivals—Cannes, Venice, Karlovy Vary, and Berlin, at first) and the festival calendar, which determined the position of a particular festival in relation to other events.

2   While this connection between festivals, national identity, and geopolitical agendas has changed through time, it is still very much a part of festivals' dynamic. Festivals have always offered fertile ground for diplomatic disputes and conflicts, with nations trying to prevent screenings of unflattering films or exerting their powers to foreground their visions. For the 1951 Cannes Film Festival, the USSR boycotted a Czech production, *Four in a Jeep*; in 1953, the US protested against the Japanese entry *Children of Hiroshima*; in 1956, the German government blocked the screening of Alain Resnais' *Night and Fog*, to offer just a few examples. Such diplomatic disputes continue to be a regular feature of A-list festivals in particular, since they attract more media visibility. In 2010, for example, Cannes was brimming with political controversies surrounding the following films: Rachid Bouchareb's *Outside the Law*, about the Algerian war for independence, caused an uproar; the screening of Sabina Guzzanti's provocative documentary on Berlusconi's ties to organized crime, *Draquila*, enraged the Italian Minister of Culture, which boycotted the festival; and more controversy surrounded the jailed filmmakers Jafar Panahi and Roman Polanski, both subjects of petitions seeking their freedom.

3   For example, one could explore festivals' relationship with Hollywood, where the international nature of programming must be balanced with Hollywood glamour, and where Hollywood can negotiate publicity and presence around the festival cycle. Or we could discuss international relationships, where festivals must grapple with political relations, boycotts, and censorship; or the latest developments in technology that force festivals to negotiate their traditional reliance on physical space and place with an online presence and digital conversion.

4   Particularly influential are Bruno Latour and his Actor Network theory, Luhmann's theory of "autopoiesis," or Manuel Castells's concept of "space of flows." See, for example, Bruno Latour, "On Recalling ANT," in John Law and John Hassard (eds), *Actor Network Theory and After*, Oxford: Blackwell Publishers, 1999, pp. 15–29; Niklas Luhmann, *Essays on Self-Reference*, New York, NY: Columbia University Press, 1990; and Manuel Castells, *The Rise of the Network Society*, Cambridge: Blackwell Publishers, 2002.

5   For example, in a letter to Cannes via *Time* in 1997, Malaysian filmmaker Mansor Bin Puteh complained: "Why are the same filmmakers from Asia getting recognition from Cannes? The answer is that they are making the types of films that are liked in Cannes. Basically, there are only five types of

films: those that deal with poverty or illiteracy, homosexuality and incest, anti-government sentiments, anti-colonialism, and historical epics. Asian filmmakers must make one of those types in order to win recognition at Cannes. China and Iran, which are rich in history and tradition, must surely have other interesting stories they could put on screen. Cannes has destroyed the very essence of cinema and made the medium one for forcing filmmakers to scream propaganda for them."

6   This dual appeal of the film was efficiently evoked by the nickname or appellation the film received almost as soon as it showed it Cannes: "that Romanian abortion movie." As in, "have you seen that Romanian abortion movie?"

7   See the letter translated in its entirety in Daniel Hjorth and Monika Kostera (eds), *Entrepreneurship and the Experience Economy*, Copenhagen Business School Press, 2007, pp. 81–82.

Further reading

Biskind, Peter. (2004). *Down and Dirty Pictures: Miramax, Sundance, and the Rise of Independent Film.* New York, NY: Simon & Schuster.

Dayan, Daniel. (2000). "Looking for Sundance: The Social Construction of a Film Festival." In Ib Bondebjerg (ed), *Moving Images, Culture, and the Mind.* London: University of Luton Press, pp. 43–52.

de Valck, Marijke & Malte Hagener (eds). (2005). *Cinephilia: Movies, Love and Memory.* Amsterdam: Amsterdam University Press.

Iordanova, Dina & Ruby Cheung (eds). (2010). *Film Festival Yearbook 2: Film Festivals and Imagined Communities.* St Andrews: St Andrews University Press.

Iordanova, Dina & Ruby Cheung (eds). (2011). *Film Festival Yearbook 3: Film Festivals and East Asia.* St Andrews: St Andrews University Press.

Iordanova, Dina & Ragan Rhyne (eds). (2009). *Film Festival Yearbook 1: The Festival Circuit.* St Andrews: St Andrews University Press.

Iordanova, Dina & Leshu Torchin (eds). (2012). *Film Festival Yearbook 4: Film Festivals and Activism.* St Andrews: St Andrews University Press.

Marlow-Mann, Alex (ed). (2013). *Film Festival Yearbook 5: Archival Film Festivals.* St Andrews: St Andrews University Press.

Porton, Richard (ed). (2009). *Dekalog 3: On Film Festivals.* New York, NY: Wallflower Press.

Rouff, Jeffrey (ed). (2012). *Coming Soon to a Festival Near You: Programming Film Festivals.* St Andrews: St Andrews Film Studies.

Bibliography

Atwood, Blake. (2015). "Re/Form: New Forms in Cinema and Media in Post-Khatami Iran." In Peter Decherney & Blake Atwood (eds), *Iranian Cinema in a Global Context: Policy, Politics, and Form.* New York, NY: Routledge, pp. 33–61.

Cheah, Philip. (2011). "My Travel in the Post-Colonial Film Festival World." *BigOfeature*, blog entry (November 16). Available at: http://asiapacificfilms.tv/host-philip-cheah-blog-my-travels-in-the-post-colonial-film-festival-world. Accessed October 29, 2016.

Czach, Liz. (2004). "Film Festivals, Programming, and the Building of a National Cinema." *Moving Image* 4(1), pp. 76–88.

Decherney, Peter & Blake Atwood (eds). (2015). *Iranian Cinema in a Global Context: Policy, Politics, and Form.* New York, NY: Routledge.

de Valck, Marijke. (2007). *Film Festivals: From European Geopolitics to Global Cinephilia.* Amsterdam: Amsterdam University Press.

Elsaesser, Thomas. (2005). *European Cinema: Face to Face with Hollywood.* Amsterdam: Amsterdam University Press.

Farahmand, Azadeh. (2010). "Disentangling the International Festival Circuit: Genre and Iranian Cinema." In Rosalind Galt & Karl Schoonover (eds), *Global Art Cinema.* New York, NY: Oxford University Press, pp. 263–278.

Filimon, Monica. (2014). "Beyond New Romanian Cinema: Old Traps and New Beginnings." *Cineaste* 39(2).

Follows, Steven. (2013). "How Many Festivals Are There in the World?" *Stephen Follows Film Data and Education Blog* (August 19). Available at: http://stephenfollows.com/film-festivals-pt1-the-truths-behind-film-festivals. Accessed June 18, 2014.

Hoad, Phil. (2013). "Romania's New Wave Could Dry Up If It Doesn't Get Home Support." *The Guardian* (March 12). Available at: www.theguardian.com/film/filmblog/2013/mar/12/romanian-new-wave-after-hollywood. Accessed October 13, 2016.

Iordanova, Dina. (2009). "The Film Festival Circuit." In Dina Iordanova & Ragan Rhyne (eds), *Film Festival Yearbook 1: The Festival Circuit*. St Andrews: St Andrews Film Studies, pp. 23–39.

Iordanova, Dina. (2010). "Mediating Diaspora: Film Festivals and Imagined Communities." In Dina Iordanova & Ruby Cheung (eds), *Film Festival Yearbook 2: Film Festivals and Imagined Communities*. St Andrews: St Andrews Film Studies, pp. 12–45.

Jameson, Fredric. (1986). "Third World Literature in the Era of Multinational Capitalism." *Social Text* 15, pp. 65–89.

Jameson, Fredric. (2004). "Thoughts on Balkan Cinema." In Atom Egoyan & Ian Balfour (eds), *Subtitles: On the Foreignness of Film*. Cambridge, MA: MIT Press, pp. 231–258.

Jockims, Trevor Laurence. (2012). "Why a War During a Film Festival: A History of the Sarajevo Film Festival." *KinoKultura*. Available at: www.kinokultura.com/specials/14/jockims.shtml. Accessed June 16, 2015.

Kerkinos, Dimitris. (2009). "Programming Balkan Films at the Thessaloniki International Film Festival." In Dina Iordanova & Ragan Rhyne (eds), *Film Festival Yearbook 1: The Festival Circuit*. St Andrews: St Andrews Film Studies, pp. 168–179.

Peranson, Mark. (2009). "Two Models of Film Festivals." In Richard Porton (ed), *Dekalog 3: On Film Festivals*. New York, NY: Wallflower Press, pp. 23–38.

Quandt, James. (2009). "'The Sandwich Process': Simon Field Talks About Polemics and Poetry at Film Festivals." In Richard Porton (ed), *Dekalog 3: On Film Festivals*. New York, NY: Wallflower, pp. 76–77.

Romania News Watch. (2007). "Growing Sympathy for Romania Secured Cannes Prize: Director." *Romania News Watch* (May 31). Available at: www.romanianewswatch.com/2007/05/growing-sympathy-for-romania-secured.html. Accessed July 6, 2014.

Scott, A.O. (2008). "New Wave on the Black Sea." *New York Times* (Jan 20). Available at: www.nytimes.com/2008/01/20/magazine/20Romanian-t.html. Accessed Oct 25, 2016.

Stringer, Julian. (2011). "Global Cities and the International Film Festival Economy." In Mark Shiel &Tony Fitzmaurice (eds), *Cinema and the City: Film and Urban Societies in a Global Context*. Oxford: Blackwell, pp. 134–144.

Tryon, Chuck. (2013). *On Demand Culture: Digital Delivery and the Future of Movies*. New Brunswick, NJ: Rutgers University Press.

Turan, Kenneth. (2002). "Sarajevo." In *Sundance to Sarajevo: Film Festivals and the World They Made*. Los Angeles, CA: University of California Press, pp. 89–108.

Wolfs, Karin. (2013). "Directors Make Too Many Festival Films: Where is the IFFR?" *De Film Krant* (February 2013). Available at: www.filmkrant.nl/TS_februari_2013. Accessed October 20, 2016.

Wong, Cindy Hing-Yuk. (2011). *Film Festivals: Culture, People, and Power on the Global Screen*. New Brunswick, NJ: Rutgers University Press.

5   Indian cinema and Bollywood

For nearly four decades, Indian cinema has been a strong presence on the world stage largely due to the strength of its numbers alone. With a nearly consistent annual output of over 1,000 films, India remains the most prolific film-producing country in the world, also claiming the largest film audience. The impressive numbers have constituted their own logic, so much so that the idea of Indian cinema often begins and ends with the mention of its massive output. In critical and scholarly circles in the West, little attention was paid to its films in the past, with the exception of masters such as Satyajit Ray and Mrinal Sen. In many ways, the strength in numbers fits the "Western vision of India's fecundity," continuing the colonialist imagination of India as peculiar in its prodigious output of everything, from its hidden wealth to its insurmountable social problems (Govil, 2010: 108). The discourses of globalization, from the size of its markets to the attractiveness of global capital, only confirm the perception of India as a prolific producer and a consumer with one of the fastest-growing markets in the world. The Indian film industry proudly recognizes this visibility based on the strength of its numbers as a reliable marker of its distinction on a world stage.

The issue of size, however, is complicated and misleading. Indian cinema is indeed prolific, but its international presence has been dominated by its recent moniker of "Bollywood." Though Bollywood gives the film industry a spectacular global presence, it happens to be a small component of the industry, masking the rich diversity not only of other strands of Hindi cinema—long a culturally dominant form with nationwide distribution—but also cinemas emerging from multiple languages. Cinemas of multiple languages contribute to the share of total production, including Tamil cinema (from Tamil Nadu), Telugu (Andhra Pradesh), Kannada (Karnataka), Malayalam (Kerala), Bengali (West Bengal), and Marathi (Maharashtra). For a long time, Hindi cinema eclipsed the diversity, richness, and multiplicity of Indian cinema, only extending this influence in the age of globalization under the banner of Bollywood at home and abroad. In recent decades, Bollywood has been forcefully and mistakenly equated with the Indian film industry, entirely masking the profile of Indian cinema. For this reason, understanding the place and complexity of Indian cinema must begin with a clarification of its nomenclature, a delineation of the shifting connotations of Bollywood.

Bollywood: what is in a name?

Tejaswini Ganti remarks that "-ollywood" has become a very generative and productive morpheme to refer to the centers of media production (Ganti, 2012a). The morpheme has generated a number of copycat names all over the world, as each cinematic formation aspires to the level of power and glamour of Hollywood. The Nigerian film industry embraces *Nollywood* in a similar vein, as an aspirational term, vying for visibility and prominence, and to some extent claiming it in its own limited sphere. For Bollywood, which comprises only twenty percent of India's total annual film production, its aspirations are to be measured in terms of output, glamour, and influence. In an Indian cultural context, where words themselves have the power of summoning what they represent, the very invocation of the term contains the capacity to align itself with Hollywood.

The Bollywood film industry is centered in Bombay, the West Coast city of India, which shares geographical kinship with Los Angeles, the famed West Coast city that is the locus of Hollywood. The exact genesis of the term is rather unclear. The Oxford English Dictionary recognized *Bollywood* as a term in 2001, calling it a "blend of Bombay and Hollywood." In scholarly discourse, Ashish Rajadhyaksha traces it back to journalists in Bombay who used it in light-hearted jest, in comparison with the film industry based in Calcutta's Tollygunge area called Tollywood, or in the Madras-based industry called Mollywood (2003: 29). Madhava Prasad locates the etymology to 1932, when a film professional's correspondence invoked Tollywood, which was named as a center of production aspiring to its original model (Prasad, 2003). Neither imitative-derivate in its character nor a counter-point to Hollywood, *Bollywood*, for Prasad, is an empty signifier, with a shifting and open meaning for different interests in Indian cinema.

Though immensely popular over the last few decades, the term "Bollywood" has been simultaneously embraced, celebrated, critiqued, vilified, and employed by different sectors of the discourse. In the Indian popular press, *Bollywood* is a construct on a par with Hollywood, competing with its Western counterpart in gossip and glamour. It is embraced by the industry but often rejected by some of its greatest players such as Shah Rukh Khan and Amitabh Bachchan for the pejorative reputation it brings in the canon of global cinema. One of the most well-known actors of the alternative or "new wave" cinema in India, Om Puri, who has acted in Bollywood as well as international co-productions, sees it as a derogatory term that the industry should "recognize as an insult and not use it" (Press Trust of India, 2007). Nearly three decades after its global emergence, *Bollywood* circulates with different meanings: as a critical category in scholarly work, a term of choice in the popular press, a commodity in the global marketplace, and a strong discursive force shaping Indian cinema. Though in some ways the triumph of *Bollywood* as a term over other terms represents a triumph of its "global sweep" and "national coding," its widespread use has eclipsed Indian cinema itself, giving way to a nebulous realm where its meaning slips from caricature to ridicule (Mishra, 2006). As we will show, while Bollywood is in fact a very recent creation (emerging in the 1990s), it is frequently misunderstood to stand in for Indian cinema as a whole. It is therefore crucial to understand Bollywood as a distinct phenomenon that shapes and influences, yet does not encompass Indian cinema in its entirety.

An account of Bollywood's influence and place in Indian and world cinema can be based on Rajadhyaksha's seminal argument that Indian cinema itself has been "Bollywoodized," overshadowed and influenced by a recent discursive construction in the neoliberal economic age of globalization (2003). Extending this insight, we propose that the process of "Bollywoodization" can be best understood in three phases.

In the **first phase**, Bollywood cinema, a peculiar form of the dominant Hindi language/mainstream Indian cinema, emerges in the early 1990s as a *cultural industry* due to various factors at home and abroad. In a fortuitous moment for cinema, the cultural and economic patronage of the NRI (the Non-resident Indian) diasporic communities, which were not only affluent but maintained an active connection to the homeland and helped fuel its economy, gave a powerful boost to the industry. The support and involvement of Indians abroad was the single most powerful force that shaped Bollywood in the 1990s, complemented by India's adoption of liberal economic policies in 1992 that opened up its state-controlled economy to global capital. The Hindi film industry responded by framing its narratives with Indians living abroad, mapping their desires onto cinematic narratives that charted a new space for the affluence, conflicts, and experiences of the diaspora. Aditya Chopra's *Dilwale Dulhania Le Jayenge/ Heartthrobs Will Win the Brides* (1995) is credited with breaking ground in this respect as one of the major box office successes at home and abroad, followed by numerous other films. These were stories of love among the young that moved from one global metropolitan setting to another, and protagonists who remained Indian despite their foreign experiences (Dudrah, 2002: 29). This representation of Indians living abroad was markedly different from the earlier paradigms in which male characters living abroad were portrayed as villainous, morally corrupt, and lacking the traditionally held Indian values of honesty and loyalty. The change was palpable and deliberate, reflecting Indian cinema's vigorous response to global changes in economy, culture, and identity.

The success of these films was merely one major aspect of the phenomenon. Rajadhyaksha points out that the industry found it necessary to "convert all this hoopla into a stable market that would guarantee their next product an audience" (2003: 27). These narratives had a strong appeal for the global diaspora spread across the world, and the technological sophistication in production values powered with star personas only added to their appeal. The Bollywood film industry's shrewd moves created a cultural ethos around these films, giving rise to a culture industry, "from websites to chat shows . . . advertising, soap operas to music video, niche marketing of various products, satellite channels, journalism, the Indipop 'remix' audio cassette and CD industry" (Rajadhyaksha, 2003: 30). In effect, Bollywood, now a libidinal product of the desires of diasporic Indians, had separated itself from Indian cinema.

The **second phase** is marked by the *marketing of Bollywood abroad*, embedding it as a commodity on several levels, both as a film industry and as the consumer products attached to it. Brand Bollywood was born, which "was not the content of cinema—as constituted by film narrative—but a certain kind of allure produced by a characteristic visual excess brought in by spectacle, choreography, costume and music" (Raghavendra, 2012: 31). Bollywood burst out of films and into all places of commodity and culture. The "Indian Summer of 2002" in London was a momentous occasion for this transformation. Department store Selfridge's went through a "Bollywood makeover," stocking shelves with Indian fashion and furniture, accessories, and music. Andrew Lloyd Webber produced a musical called *Bombay Dreams* with A.R. Rahman, the well-known film music composer. On UK television Channel 4 launched Bollywood programming. A new high-budget film, *Devdas* (Sanjay Leela Bhansali, 2002), a much-publicized remake of 1936 and 1955 versions, was released a month later. A series of other events followed in public venues, museums, theaters, and shopping malls, turning Bollywood into a cultural event. It was a triumph of the commodification of Bollywood, with the full cooperation of the industry itself. It was also a moment when Bollywood and, by association, Indian cinema entered its world cinema phase as a center of power and influence, shaping a larger perception of Indian cinema as well as of India itself.

With its entry onto the stage of publicity and mediascape, Bollywood becomes prominent in the imagination of Western popular culture. When pop stars such as Selena

Gomez, Madonna, Iggy Azalea, and Shakira inflect their performances with Indian ico-nography, its immediate frame of reference is Bollywood iconography. Very few have seen films from Bollywood, but nearly everyone is familiar with Bollywood dance sequences. Baz Luhrmann's nod to Bollywood's global presence in *Moulin Rouge!* (2001) allowed it to emerge as a harbinger of Bollywood cinema's growing visibility in the West. Terry Zwigoff inserted a song from a 1965 Hindi film, *Gumnaam*, at the beginning of his film *Ghost World* (2000). Danny Boyle plugged into the Bollywood culture by inserting a song-and-dance sequence, with little relationship to the narrative, at the end of *Slumdog Millionaire* (2008).

Befitting the consumer culture's appetite for new commodities, the creation of Bollywood as a cultural shorthand for all things Indian was as expansive as it was trans-formative, a success emblematic of the powerful alignment between the culture industry and globalization. Bollywood became not only the name of a film industry shaped by the desires of Indians abroad, but also a new shiny commodity that subsumed all Indian cul-tural production. In effect, Bollywood replaced the Kama Sutra as long-time orientalist shorthand for India. From that point on, every Indian film was a Bollywood film and all aspects of Indian culture had some connection to Bollywood culture. The examples are numerous. Ritesh Batra's *The Lunchbox* (2014), a film that carries hardly any elements of a Bollywood film, was recognized only as a "Bollywood anomaly" (Harris, 2014). Irrfan Khan, whose rich portfolio includes few Bollywood films, and who is known in the US for his distinctly non-Bollywood roles in Mira Nair's *The Namesake* (2006) or Ang Lee's *Life of Pi* (2012), among many others, is still referred to as a "Bollywood" actor (Shattuck, 2012). In this sense, the naming of all things Indian as Bollywood lends it an orientalist inflection, a packed emblem that ignores the complexity of what is left out.

Bollywood's "otherness," however, remained prominent even as the category of world cinema expanded in the 1990s. Bollywood film itself remained inaccessible, a distant object from a different world, its presence felt without accessing the films them-selves. Kaushik Bhaumik detects the entry of Bollywood into world cinema as occurring "through diverse cultural registers, not all pertaining to film" (Bhaumik, 2006: 192). It was accepted as a "genre" of world cinema, akin to thrillers or martial arts films from other parts of the world. From music to its colorful panoply of costumes, fashions, dances, stars, and scattered but persistent references to its caricatured iconography, Bollywood's pres-ence in world cinema remained "spectral." In effect, Bollywood entered world cinema as a culture of images and commodities, announcing a two-fold relation. Bollywood's commodification portrays an idea of "unchanging essence that distinguishes it from Hollywood," while it also "signals a certain reflexivity, becoming a cinema of itself as it were, recognizing its own unique position in the world, the contrastive pleasures and values that it represents vis-à-vis Hollywood" (Prasad, 2008: 50). Thus, in asserting its exclusive position, its "otherness" in world cinema, Bollywood ironically achieved what it set out to do—it became more than cinema, a cultural force with global ambitions akin to Hollywood.

The **third phase** is marked by a kind of return of Bollywood commodity produc-tion back home to shape Indian culture and identity: *the Bollywoodization of Indian cinema and culture.*

In his map of this transformation, Rajadhyaksha identifies two levels of influence brought about by Bollywood on Indian culture: the reconceptualization of the nation as one tuned in to the desires of the diaspora, and the transformation of the domestic film industry now shaped by the ambitions of Bollywood abroad (2003: 30–38). The two levels, though not separate, offer a composite lens into Indian cinema after Bollywoodization, with each layer intricately woven into the other to influence that vision.

In tracking the genealogy of the process, Rajadhyaksha notes the ability of the Indian film industry to "assemble a national market, even devising a narrative mode" as an unparalleled event in the history of world cinema (2003: 33). Cinema's role in opening and shaping a terrain for national identity worked on several levels, including providing a meta-language for the articulation of national ideology, constructing staples of national fictions, and reproducing the "state form" in narratives (Prasad, 1998; Virdi, 2003). Bollywood's accomplishments abroad were remarkable. It was able to produce a combination of culturally authentic cinema, bringing to its narratives a charge of a nativist, nostalgic, culturally authentic image of culture at home, with a globally laced discourse on romance, family, and community lives abroad. The indigenous view of Indian culture developed abroad began to influence the narratives of the Indian nation, fulfilling the aims of statist enterprise toward the film industry. Bollywood propelled India into a new terrain of the global nation, shaped by Indians abroad and not contained by its territorial identity. The new phase of Indian modernity is located in the sphere of "modernity at large," as Arjun Appadurai maps it in his diagnosis of post-national formations in the age of globalization (Appadurai, 1996). Bollywood was now more than just cinema. As a cultural product projected onto and produced by the economy of goods, images, dominant television content, the radio and music industry, websites, and cyber-cultures returned home to shape Indian culture.

In 1998, the state, steeped in policies of economic liberalization, granted cinema the status of an industry for the first time since independence in 1947. In 2000, it positioned banks to make funds available to the industry, set capital flows in motion, and instituted organizational changes and international exchanges. The state took full command of constructing Bollywood on two levels: first by promoting and supporting films closer to the political ideology of the ruling party (the Bharatiya Janata Party, or BJP, from 1999 until 2004, and again since 2014), offering an image of India as a nation bereft of conflicts, but well-poised to coopt the affluent diasporic communities; and second, through the censor board, which reinforces this ideology by controlling the content of films. The political campaign of the BJP heralded an image of Indians abroad energized by Bollywood in its "India shining" campaign, with the dual strategy of portraying economic prosperity rooted in the party's ideology of essentialist Hinduism and communal identity (Therwath, 2010). The family-centered narratives with their "all-happy-in-the-end" romances, or what Monika Mehta calls "good cinema," have had the effect of nullifying the struggles of class inequality that figured in films before Bollywood (Mehta, 2005: 142). Through a series of maneuvers to grant certificates to family films that affirm its image of a nation as well as brazenly intervening in the affairs of the censor board, the state continues its influence over the film industry. The spheres of economics, industry, and culture converged within this narrative as India moved onto the stage of globalization.

Along with the transformation of the conception of the nation and the relationship among various components of industry and culture, the process of Bollywoodization was realized in its most immediate form for the viewer in the films themselves. On the other side of these changes, Bollywood, recharged with film narratives of Indians abroad, returns home to transform mainstream Hindi cinema, "Bollywoodizing" it. In a peculiar instance of this phase, Vidhu Vinod Chopra's film *Parineeta* (2005), based on a 1914 Bengali novel, inserts a song-and-dance sequence by Rekha, a guest star, imitating the song sequence from Baz Luhrmann's *Moulin Rouge!* It is a reciprocal if imitative cue-in to the export of Bollywood now absorbed at home. The overall scope of these transformations is wide, varied, and complex. Though changes in narrative cinematic style can be palpable in any cinema over time, we will later trace some broad shifts in Hindi cinema in its "Bollywoodized" phase that revolve around the representation of the family, the figure of the foreigner, and the roles of language and foreign land/spaces.

Bollywoodization marks a significant phase in Indian cinema, and its widespread orientalizing and globalizing signature abroad make way for its entry into new world cinema. The discursive influence of Bollywood clouds the perception of Indian cinema in general, making it necessary to distinguish it from all the films that emerge on the world stage, from the rich cinema of Indian diasporic filmmakers (Mira Nair, Gurinder Chadha, and Deepa Mehta, among others) to films that are increasingly gaining currency at film festivals and among audiences abroad, such as Ashutosh Gowariker's *Lagaan: Once Upon a Time in India* (2001) or Rithesh Batra's *The Lunchbox* (2013). Thus, when we say "Bollywood films," we do not mean any film from India, but films that belong to a specific transition in Indian cinema after the 1990s. Mainstream Hindi cinema, cinemas in various languages, and independent cinema remain vibrant in India, with various degrees of immersion in world cinema. The importance of Indian cinema as one of the five centers of world cinema requires that we extricate it from Bollywood, which despite its large imprint, is a misnomer for its diversity as well as its long-standing global presence.

Indian cinema's spheres of influence

One of the unique features of Indian cinema's long-standing worldwide presence is that it has found durable support in its diasporic audiences. What is more, Indian cinema's cultural influences shaped the cinemas and cultures from the Caribbean and Turkey to Fiji. Indian films traveled to several countries from Africa to East Asia, blending with and shaping diverse cultures, arts, and musical traditions of different regions. Rarely recognized in film studies, Indian cinema has long created an alternative to Hollywood's global presence, flourishing in the same environment where Hollywood and Asian films circulated. In their account of Indian cinema's global reach, Dimitris Eleftheriotis and Dina Iordanova make a strong claim that "the high visibility of the recent scholarship around diasporic cultural production and distribution has overshadowed other, equally viable and important, forms of international circulation of images" (2006: 79). Often, they observe, the efforts of Bollywood scholarship quickly move to the recent diaspora-driven circulation of films abroad. Disproportionate growth in scholarship in the pre- and post-Bollywood phases has produced mixed results, whereby scholars often fail to distinguish between the two phases.

When we speak of the influence of Indian cinema, we need to distinguish between two diasporas. The "old diaspora" was created in non-Western countries by indentured labor exported to the Caribbean, Fiji, Guyana, South Africa, and elsewhere (Mishra, 2002: 235). Indian cinema traveled abroad in disorganized, random channels, either in bilateral exchanges created between states or through informal uncharted attempts. For these early immigrants, cinema was a central part of their everyday lives, with continued support through the scant circuits of distribution until videotapes arrived in the mid-1980s. The new diaspora is a creation of large-scale migration during globalization as businessmen and women, professionals, and intellectuals migrated in large numbers to the US, the UK, Europe, Australia, and New Zealand. In marked contrast to the old diaspora, the new diaspora is economically stronger. Mobile and active in its host countries as well as in

India, this diaspora maintains active contact with the homeland and its purchasing power makes it a force in the country. Their cultural, economic relationship to the homeland shapes the relationships of the two diasporas to Indian cinema. Although the discourse on the new diaspora is more pronounced because of the visibility of Bollywood on the global stage and its active relationship to the culture and economy of the homeland, it is important to emphasize that the two diasporas are very different, that their engagement with Indian cinema constitutes two different historical levels, and that the role of the old diaspora underscores the long-standing global influence of Indian cinema in place much before its recent Bollywood phase.

Influence of Indian cinema on non-Indian audiences

It is a singular and unique achievement for a popular national cinema to influence such a wide expanse of the world population. "Long before I had encountered any living Indian, I was well acquainted with Indian films," says Bulgarian film scholar Dina Iordanova (2006: 114). Brian Larkin speaks of his encounter with a friend in Nigeria who says, "As soon as I knew film, I knew *Mother India*" (2012). These are common tales from people who lived in non-Western countries from the 1950s through the 1980s, but their record remains scattered, except in the case of Africa, where Brian Larkin and Laura Fair researched travels and reception patterns of Indian films over decades. Responding to the paucity of information, Eleftheriotis and Iordanova propose a New Historicist notion of an anecdote as an index of contextual richness, considering anecdotal evidence as a necessary step in opening up a comparative approach to studying the influence of Indian cinema abroad (2006). Their account of testimonials of film professionals, academic scholars, novelists, and diplomats from around the world presents a mosaic of transnational exchanges and concludes that Indian cinema was widely accepted and admired by audiences from Africa to Asia because its narratives created worlds close to their own, while the distinctive features of music and dance created fluid hybrid cultures across a broad spectrum of cultural and social diversity. Indian cinema both shaped and keyed into collective modes

Figure 5.1 Raj Kapoor and Nargis in the iconic Indian film *Awaara* (1951)

of viewing and identifying with films, creating a culture of images, motifs, and music that moved generations.

Among the narratives of Indian cinema abroad, Raj Kapoor's 1951 film *Awaara/Wanderer* is so well known that it established itself as part of the everyday folklore for film viewers abroad and in India. It reached nearly every country in Asia, Africa, and the regions flanking these continents. The film was dubbed in several languages and played in theaters for decades all across Asian and African countries. The status of the film and its director and star, Raj Kapoor, is legendary. It was the "most popular film among domestic and foreign movies in Soviet theaters; its 63.7 million viewers were the largest audience of the decade for a single film," reports Sudha Rajagopalan in her account of Indian films in Soviet cinemas (2009: 2). Raj Kapoor and his co-star Nargis were treated as major celebrities and dignitaries in the country, the press gushed over Kapoor's charm and artistic skills, and generations of Soviet parents named their sons after him. In Turkey, the film had immense appeal among elite and mainstream audiences, who found its emotional engagement and music close to their cultural sensibilities, and compared it with their own cinema (Gurata, 2010). The film was re-released in cinemas and on television and remade several times by Turkish filmmakers. From Egypt, Iran, Iraq, Afghanistan, Pakistan, to Indonesia, Singapore, and Sub-Saharan African countries, *Awaara* was a perpetual popular hit. It influenced many filmmakers in these countries, including China's Jia Zhangke, who credits *Awara* for inspiring his own art. The film's theme song, "Awaara hoon," became an anthem for young people across the globe, adapted into many languages and recorded by musicians from various countries. It remains popular even today, from Turkey to China, where it was said to be a favorite of Mao Zedong.

Awaara is a rich case study in the enduring popularity of Indian cinema abroad, dispersed in terms of its effects and embraced by audiences as they adapted its elements into their own cultural contexts. It set the trend of Indian films traveling to distant parts of the world, and identifiable features of Indian films developed a stable appeal across diverse cultures: familiar star personas who were glamorous but not distant from their world; heuristic-hybrid energies of music and dance; and narratives of struggle that simultaneously created spaces of identification for audiences with diverse cultural backgrounds and maintained distance from their alternatives in the West.

After *Awaara*, Indian films continued to gain worldwide currency: *Aan* (1953), *Shree 420* (1955), *Mother India* (1957), *Lajwanti* (1958), *Sangam* (1964), *Zanjeer* (1973), *Deewaar* (1975), *Sholay* (1975), *Amar Akbar Anthony* (1977), *Disco Dancer* (1982), and *Mard* (1985), among several others. In the wake of Raj Kapoor, other Indian film stars gained widespread popularity: Dilip Kumar, Nimmi, and Madhubala became household names in East Africa. "From the melodramatic heydays of Raj Kapoor and Dev Anand to the flash and fights of Amitabh Bachchan, and Dharmendra," Tanzanians preferred Indian actors to Western or Asian actors (Fair, 2010: 92). In Nigeria, Indian film stars were given "Hausa" nicknames, and in the Soviet Union, Mithun Chakraborty, Dharmendra, and Anil Kapoor won over audiences because they were "real men" who could arouse emotions, be attentive to elders, and "combine ostentation and glamour with modesty, restraint and empathy" (Rajgopalan, 2009). In the age of Bollywood, the appeal of film stars abroad continues but it is now fueled by marketing campaigns and the use of technology. Shah Rukh Khan has become the face of Bollywood among diasporic audiences as well as for anyone slightly familiar with Bollywood's glamour. No film actor has come close to generating as much interest, even commanding an international academic conference focused on his image. The new stars are part of the global mainstream cinema, integral to its mechanisms of popularity and glamour, while the earlier stars banked on their screen personas and the spaces of identification their films provided for the audiences.

Song and dance remain an enduring feature of popular Hindi cinema, leading to the mistaken identity of Indian cinema as musicals. The peculiar quality of Indian film songs that stay with the viewers beyond the screening event is a keystone of Indian cinema's popularity abroad. For cultures around the world, the songs and music blended across cultures and musical traditions, creating some of the most intriguing hybrid musical forms. Even a cursory look at the genres it affected around the world—*taarab* music in coastal Tanzania and Mombasa, Indonesian/Javanese *danghut*, Trinidadian *chutney*, Greek *indo-prepi*, the *bandiri* music of Hausa in Nigeria, *Čoček* music of Romani tradition in the Balkans, the Bulgarian folk wedding music called *chalga*—speaks of a heuristic, generative potential of film music in far corners of the world. As viewers were exposed to films from the West and Asia, their affection for Indian cinema was facilitated by the songs and the versatility of musical forms they generated in these regions. The reception of Indian films in various cultures created cross-cultural energies of friction, controversies, and absorption. In Greece, audiences in the 1950s and 1960s found Indian actresses to be graceful and demure while Hausa viewers saw in them a promiscuous sexuality (Larkin, 2004: 104). Where sexuality and expressions of emotions in public spaces were restricted under cultural codes, the eroticism of dances proved provocative to local cultural norms. In Kenya and Tanzania, sexuality on screen was an inspiration for viewers, especially women who could vicariously explore it along with romance and marriage, while in Afghanistan and other countries in Asia, the sexuality of dance sequences created both tensions with the moral codes of the censors and space for male audiences to encounter sexual expression in public, where it is culturally prohibited (Fuglesang, 1994). The circulation of images on videotapes and portable media has only increased the popularity of films fueled by dance and sexuality. Juxtaposed against its more graphic manifestations in Western films, the appeal of sexuality in Indian films, expressed in a broad spectrum of poise, eroticism, and the provocative dimensions of dance, offered an alternative that opened up a significant space for Indian films in diverse cultures.

Importantly, Indian cinema made these forays with lasting impact in the presence of Hollywood films and in the context of the images and narratives from the West. Reflecting on this phenomenon, Vasudevan notes that diverse audiences found deep resonance in the peculiar features of Indian film narratives (2000: 121). He identifies these features as: dramas and conflicts of kinship relations; melodramatic narratives that approached conflicts in moral rather than psychological terms; and sufficient room for coincidences or forces of fate in their plots, accompanied by exotic, amusing, and attractive elements of spectacle, action, dance, and songs. The visual style of the films was simplified in a manner similar to the classical Hollywood continuity style, though these techniques were adapted to fit a world that was chaotic and unpredictable, yet immensely visual.

Indian films traveled outside the geography of Western cultures to countries that were until recently termed the Third World, or even those of the Global South. For these "societies of transition," Indian film narratives provided both a cultural process of interpreting social conflicts and an alternative framework to imagine a world outside of Hollywood's sphere of influence, negating its modernity. Melodrama was the dominant agency of Indian films during these decades, offering a narrative path of transformation from older structures of powers and modes of production to their newer forms. Serving in the transition from the colonial to postcolonial social structures, melodrama was the drama of capitalist modernization. In the case of Africa, both on the east and west coastal regions, Indian films could travel "because they became a foil against which postcolonial identity can be fashioned, critiqued, and debated" (Larkin, 2008: 218). The poor-class protagonists facing "villainous landlords, overbearing patriarchs, meddlesome in-laws, and corrupt police and politicians" were part of the narratives of Indian films that offered a way to face modernity by defending traditional values (Fair, 2009: 66). They addressed the Third World modernist dilemma of how to incorporate technological and scientific development into society without the hollow mimicry of Western individualism, consumer capitalism, and moral bankruptcy. Creating a universe of their own, a kind of parallel modernity outside of Hollywood's modernity, these films mobilized desire in their narrative embodiments of the central conflicts and enabled the audience to incorporate an imagining of another culture into their own lives.

The circulation of Indian cinema flourished in the same environment where Hollywood maintained its presence. The audiences found its ethos and aesthetic as a resistance and alternative to the West and its popular culture; Indian cinema was not only distant from the West's values but also from its colonizing cultural power. As a cinema with a peculiar popular aesthetic deeply embedded in its own cultural contexts, it opened up spaces of identification for communities, creating friction, hybridity, and synergy across the global sphere. For those willing to notice, there are other narratives of influence in world cinema besides the loud and aggressive power of Hollywood's narrative, and being attuned to those is a necessary act in understanding the dynamic of world cinema.

Indian cinema and the diaspora

While India has the largest domestic film audience in the world, it also claims the largest diaspora in the world, over sixteen million on all continents. The dominant role that films play in the lives of Indians can hardly be overstated. From its stars to songs, from images to narratives and public visibility, cinema dominates the cultural sphere in India. The intensity and intimacy with which the audience forms a relationship with Indian films accompanied Indians when they left their homeland. The creation of Bollywood abroad is a unique result of the diasporic involvement of Indians, and in that sense theirs is an outsized role compared to the involvement of any other diasporas influencing the film industry at home.

All diasporas must negotiate their identities between the host cultures and the cultures of the homeland, and all diasporic identities are produced in discourses of history and culture. For older Indian diasporas spread across the world, their connection to the homeland was enlivened by the cultures and memories invoked in Indian cinema. For them, the identification with Indian film created a culture-specific imagined community, offering alternative ties of belonging, a longing for an imagined home that could not be realized in the host country. For diasporas spread across the world, placed on a lower social ladder, Indian films offered a realm of identification for their own aspirations while also keeping alive memories of religions, customs, and songs. The new diaspora approaches Indian cinema from a different social position and purpose. This diaspora is engaged in the social mobility offered by globalization. Indian cinema for them serves not only as a means to connect to their homeland, but they also use it as a medium to actively shape their vision of India. Bollywood cinema, together with upper-class Indians, is engaged with constructing a vision of India that remains hermetic in relation to host cultures. As a result, Bollywood's participation in world cinema is often seen as an *effect* of a globalized commodity marketplace of images, rather than as a medium that negotiates its place with other cultures.

Although Bollywood does not address the frictions or relationships of diasporic communities with their host cultures, Indian diasporic filmmakers have taken up this task. Diasporic filmmakers use the motives and narratives of Bombay cinema to work through their hybrid relationships with their host cultures. Films such as Mira Nair's *Mississippi Masala* (1991), Srinivas Krishna's *Masala* (1992), Gurinder Chadha's *Bhaji on the Beach* (1993), Udayan Prasad's *My Son the Fanatic* (1997), and Anurag Mehta's *American Chai* (2001), invoke the lexicon of Bollywood films in a manner that serves as a meta-commentary on Bollywood. Diasporic filmmakers' work, which we discuss in a different chapter, is a distinct component of world cinema and markedly different from the fantasy films of Bollywood, which are projections of diasporic lives by the Bombay film industry. Diasporic cinema thus addresses different subject positions and places from where their identities are imagined and can speak, projecting a diasporic imaginary in a style markedly different from Bollywood. Therefore, conflating all cinemas of Indian filmmakers into Bollywood misplaces a complex variety of representations.

Bollywood's diasporic cultures

One of the integral features of Indian immigrant life abroad, nearly as essential as finding spices and meal ingredients, is the habit of watching films. In fact, in most Indian communities the activities of movie watching and grocery shopping go hand in hand, and are nurtured by the same outfits. The entire network of distribution of Bollywood movies came to existence in the 1980s as screenings in movie theaters declined and were replaced by home viewing enabled by the VHS technology. As a parallel network of distribution, along with theatrical screenings, TV, and satellite channels, grocery stores created an immensely powerful culture of renting and buying, which included associated merchandise such as photographs, cassettes, and movie posters. In intensity and scope, it is a unique phenomenon not easily observed in other immigrant communities.

Recognizing the purchasing power of relatively affluent Indian communities in Western countries, media companies increased their investments to offer a panoply of satellite and cable TV channels in the mid-1990s. Targeted to niche markets of immigrants, such offerings included continuous streaming of Bollywood films, and channels that broadcast film songs, along with other attractions such as cricket games. Until Netflix turned to streaming and producing its own shows, its collection of Bollywood films was one of the most impressive available for viewers in the US. Indian audiences have always considered films to be an integral part of everyday experience, especially music, whose tunes and lyrics play a powerful role in and outside of films themselves. On an average, a young Indian can instantly recall hundreds of songs, whose presence increased with the availability of cassettes, CDs, and later smart phones, with Bollywood songs as the most popular choice of ringtones.

The characterization of near-exclusive spaces for the Indian community to watch films is a long-standing feature of viewing situations for Bollywood films. The importance of spaces such as living rooms, theaters, and multiplexes for the diasporic experience is foregrounded in the ethnographic studies by Marie Gillespie in South Asian families in the Southall section of London in 1989. For these families, watching Indian films was a response "to the social and cultural marginalization of minorities," offering spaces of respite in a culture that had excluded them (Gillespie, 1989: 228). It created an empowering situation, where relationships with the broader culture outside the community were negotiated. Younger generations, firmly placed in the Westernized cultures around them, developed a more sophisticated, playful, and critical position in relation to Bollywood images and regard it with both love and disdain. Bollywood presents a different media-scape for these generations, offering them positions from which to critique the culture while also selectively participating in it; they may be savvy and skeptical about the fantasy offered by the films, and perhaps not even care about the narrative, but they watch it for the special dress designs, the stars, or the music.

Recognizable figures of public life, Bollywood stars have a pervasive presence in media culture, which allows films to exist as super-textual entities playing into and upping their effect. As a perfect testimony to this, the last two decades or so have witnessed the emergence of "Hindi cinema entertainment shows." In these massive cultural events, major Bollywood film stars along with a strong contingent of secondary stars, including musicians, comedians, and dancers, entertain an audience of mostly Indian origins. Short skits, comedy sketches, fireworks, and spectacularly staged dances fill the event. The troupe travels to different cities and countries, invigorating the community it visits. To consider this a mere publicity tour for a specific film (as such an event is perceived in the West) is misleading; in Bollywood, such an extra-textual spectacle exists on its own, expanding its lifespan on the web and YouTube, and making film somewhat incidental to its success.

One such event on a larger scale is held under the aegis of the "International Indian Film Academy," a marketing outfit that gives awards to Bollywood films. The awards have been held in many countries, including the UK, the Netherlands, Singapore, Dubai, and Canada. At a recent event in the US, Kevin Spacey and John Travolta won the adulation of the audience and millions on social media for wearing Indian clothes and dancing to Bollywood tunes. This event, along with the entertainment spectacles by the Bollywood industry, stands alongside a series of film festivals, from Los Angeles and Toronto to Melbourne and Paris that, for the most part, scrupulously avoid the Bollywood fare, and allow the communities to watch films outside of the mainstream, including India's multiple-languages cinema.

Bollywood's presence on the web is, as yet, an untold and developing story. Writing on the topic of "Bollyweb," Ananda Mitra features a sub-heading, "Search for Bollywood on the Web and See What Happens!" (2008). His is hardly an overstatement as Bollywood occupies a sizeable amount of space on the web. YouTube has become a major depository of film songs, film clips, old films, clips from news and entertainment shows, fan videos, mash-ups, and nostalgic fare of images of theaters and costumes. A number of online portals stream films and sell everything closely or remotely related to Bollywood, from desktop wallpapers to celebrity news and images, consumer products, and songs. This sort of fan-driven culture has a devotional quality to it, building strong online communities in pursuit of the admired figures. A large, active, and enthusiastic audience in India with access to inexpensive Internet technology enables many savvy investors to cash in on the explosive interaction between web-based technology, social media forms, and Bollywood.

Song and dance, the principal features of mainstream Indian cinema, occupy significant space in the cultural life of Indians living abroad. Circulating well beyond their exhibition context, their independent existence floats across all cultural spaces. Film songs are heard on public-address systems at wedding ceremonies, parties, restaurants, and religious gatherings. Some key film songs have become religious songs while some religious *bhajans* have made a smooth transition to cinema, adding to their wider dissemination.

A famous recent example of this is Rani Mukherjee in *Kuch Kuch Hota Hai* (1998) singing "Om Jai Jagdish Hare," a song that asserts her inner Indian core despite her life abroad. Bhajans such as "Vaishnav Jan to ene kahiye," one of the favorites of Mahatma Gandhi's, became a staple in scores of films. Similarly, *qawwali*, a Sufi devotional song form, has been adapted by cinema and secularized in the process. Religious cultures and film have transposed themselves onto each other in the area of songs and music. Religion in cinema is the "living religion of here and now" where rituals are picked up from films, and films and production activities begin with invocation of religion, mostly loosely defined notions of Hinduism (Dwyer, 2006: 161).

If songs are the pervasive links to film culture, dance becomes its performative component, adapting to the vernacular modernities of different communities. One of the remarkable features of the new life of Bollywood cinema is its expansion into all sorts of ancillary activities, and the emergence of Bollywood dance clubs, popular in the UK, Australia, and many other countries, is a prominent aspect of this development. Younger generations cling to Bollywood as the most identifiable marker of their parents' homeland and act out their identities on the space of the dance floor. The performative aspect of Bollywood dance, which deploys bodies in spaces invoked by cinema, provides moments of fantasies while allowing for the "inscription of locality onto bodies" (Appadurai, 1996: 179). When younger generations want to connect to Indian culture, Bollywood song and dance become a medium through which they can perform their relationship to India by providing a local inflection to popular film dances. One of the most well-known examples comes from the film *Devdas* (2002), whose song-and-dance sequences performed by two of the most glamorous Bollywood stars (Aishwarya Rai and Madhuri Dixit) can be seen enacted and performed by young people from Trinidad to London. When diasporic communities perform dances, they subscribe unwittingly or otherwise to the orientalist perceptions of India and Bollywood, obscuring the line between what is considered an authentic expression of one's culture and its performance in a discursive context. Since Western and Indian performative spaces merge on the dance floors, such spaces have also become key for the performance of queer identities, utilizing the cultural context of same-sex relationships in films to engage queer desires. Bollywood films produce what Dudrah calls "haptic urban ethnoscapes" where desires are played out in urban spaces as tactile responses to film images. In his close readings of such venues, he shows how diasporic communities deploy desires on the larger canvas of the cinematic image display (Dudrah, 2010).

The emergence of dance clubs in key metropolitan centers in the West is matched by their expanded presence in Indian cities. The neoliberal economy of the early 1990s freed up a constrained and repressed body, generating interest among West-oriented young people who already longed for the social life afforded by dance clubs. The dance form of Bhangra, long an ethnically specific marker of Northern Punjabi culture, proliferated in Bollywood blockbusters of the 1990s, modified and appropriated into an expression of joy. In Britain of the 1980s and 1990s, Bhangra took its own shape, blended with cross-cultural beats, and elevated itself into one of the most popular dance forms in clubs. Bhangra's alliance with Bollywood, increasingly adapted and popularized as a generic dance in films, added to this energy. The trajectory of Bhangra from a distinctively ethnic dance form to an eclectic, hybrid one performed in spaces across continents and blended into other musical genres speaks to a transformation of Bollywood's cultures from modernity to postmodernity. Unique among such blends is "basement Bhangra" popularized by DJ Rekha Malhotra in New York City, where hip-hop dance music is layered with a sonic and visual collage of film clips and Bollywood classics to create a party space where diasporic identities are performed. Such spaces have become important for community building in the post-9/11 climate in the US, particularly to combat the racist appropriation and stereotypes of people of South Asian origin.

Indian cinema after Bollywoodization

Bollywood has given Indian cinema its global profile since the 1990s, while influencing Indian cinema at home. We identify four broad thematic and stylistic directions in the trajectory of Indian cinema triggered by its Bollywood phase. First, Bollywood itself moves beyond its diasporic phase to brazen global ambitions, expanding from family films to spectacles, franchises, and blockbusters. Second, the mainstream Hindi cinema at home, now "Bollywoodized," adapts to make the most of Bollywood's glamour, capital, star power, and reach. Empowered by the neoliberal flows of financing and the spaces opened up by Bollywood, filmmakers at home compete with current streams of popular cinema. Third, the cinemas of multiple languages, a unique feature of India's multicultural heritage, reinvest their energies into bold ventures and experiments to move beyond their local and regional spaces. The fourth direction, a relatively smaller but energetic part of Indian cinema that is raising its profile in festival circuits and international audiences, may be termed as "the cinema of new social realism." Films by the directors in this group, closest to the category of independent cinema, are situated in the growing idiom of realism in world cinema, working both with dominant conventions in Indian cinema and aligning themselves with the world cinema trends.

From family dramas to blockbusters

The dominant narrative(s) of Hindi cinema

The main narrative model of Indian cinema in its post-independence, postcolonial phase remains that of a family-oriented romance, with multiple ingredients woven into it. Since Indian cinema is intricately tied to the economic and power structures around it, the "feudal family romance" model served as a mediatory form that allowed Indian society to manage its transformations from the pre-capitalist to modernist phase (Prasad, 1998: 67). To achieve this, cinema negotiated with realism and melodrama to address the conflict between modernist institutions of the state and emergent forms of capitalist development. Unlike the Hollywood structure of linearity, the narratives of Indian cinema develop a complex visual and aesthetic mode of address. The linear realistic narrative stays in place despite other, potentially distracting levels (song-and-dance sequences, comedic scenes). In this aesthetic universe, the melodramatic mode maps the struggles between the old and emergent forces, where individual will and emotions are resisted through the tropes of moral absolutes. This unique combination of narrative and aesthetic strategies gave Indian cinema its adaptability over decades, capable of responding to and amending changing conditions.

In a similar model, Vasudevan (2011) traces the strength of Indian cinema to the social film that took shape in the 1950s. He notes that melodrama invoked the real through *mise-en-scène* that included social spaces (such as life on the street) and by making the middle-class subject move through the institutional structures of modernity. Far from disavowing the real, narratives allowed multiple paths for individual desires to navigate through the social. Both Prasad and Vasudevan show how a certain visual economy of framing and spacing allows the social film to position the spectator in relation to a world of both family and the nation, both melodrama and realism. The social film went through transformations in the subsequent decades and continued in three different tracks in the 1970s. The middle-class cinema of Gulzar (*Aandhi/The Storm*, 1975; *Mere Apne/My Dear Ones*, 1971), Basu Chatterjee (*Rajnigandha/Tuberose*, 1974*)*, Hrishikesh Mukherjee (*Guddi*, 1971*)*, and Basu Bhattacharya (*Anubhav/Experience*, 1971) foregrounds the narratives of protagonists who are unlikely to challenge the state legitimacy and turn their attention to quotidian issues. The second strand, known as the "new" cinema of India, encapsulates developmental realism that challenges feudal values and structures. Films such as Shyam Benegal's *Ankur/The Seedling* (1974), *Nishant/Night's End* (1975), and *Manthan/Churning* (1976) construct developmental realism that allows the middle-class-citizen subject to work through a transformation from a feudal to a modernist state, while taking into account the vast majorities of outcasts. The third strand came in the populist cinema of a rebellious anti-hero, who had detached himself from the soft compassion of Raj Kapoor, one of his predecessors, to fashion an aggressive plebian protagonist giving voice to vast audiences in the country. These narratives used the symbolic economy of a supersized persona of Amitabh Bachchan in tandem with the narratives of a subaltern subject to mobilize the populist sentiment in favor of social reform. The star persona elevated to the level of a supra-textual existence allowed these narratives to become fantasy structures to work though discontent in society. Bachchan's key films—to this date some of the most memorable films for Indian audiences—*Zanjeer* (1973), *Deewaar* (1975), *Sholay* (1975), and *Don (1978)* shaped a career that was in full force until the 1980s.

Bollywood family films after the 1990s such as *Dilwale Dulhania Le Jayenge* (1995) and *Kabhi Alvida Naa Kehna* (2006) keep the tenets of the feudal family narrative but adapt it to a new climate of global identity. The former's protagonists are Raj and Simran, NRIs living in London who are in love. Simran was raised by a strict and conservative father, while Raj's father is more liberal. Simran's father brings her back to India, keeping his promise of marriage to his close friend's son, but when faced with the developing

Figure 5.2 Simran (Kajol) and Raj's (Shah Rukh Khan) romance through Europe in *Dilwale Dulhania Le Jayenge* (1995) by Aditya Chopra

Figure 5.3 Sam (Amitabh Bachchan) and his son Rishi (Abishek Bachchan) in the family drama *Kabhi Alvida Naa Kehna* (2006) by Karan Johar

relationship and love between Simran and Raj, he eventually gives in. In this reconciliation, his earlier "feudal" power is transformed into an adaptive stance of a father who is willing to straddle two cultures and generations. In *Kabhi Alvida Naa Kehna*, a widowed father flirts with younger women, witnesses the break-up of his son's marriage, and has to accept his son's divorce on his deathbed.

Families go through a series of cultural clashes but leave behind an imprint of a traditional yet tolerant heritage for the successive generations. In these films, the agency of the family's transformation and adaptability has moved from a mother to a father, who is seen as an arbiter of navigating national identity in the global arena (Vasudevan, 2011: 362–380). The narratives now become vehicles to confront the realities of cross-cultural adaptations through the melodramatic mode, while affirming the lasting value of tradition.

As Bollywood films address the diasporic spectator in order to assure a sustained patronage for itself, they raise ambitions to move beyond diasporic audiences and place national identity on a broader geo-political landscape. Karan Johar's *My Name is Khan* (2010), an expensive production with lavish investment by 20th Century Fox, inserts itself into post-9/11 global politics. A Muslim-Indian man (played by Shah Rukh Khan) with Asperger's syndrome is detained as a terrorist suspect in the charged post-9/11 atmosphere in the US. His efforts to meet the U.S. President to get himself exonerated come to fruition but only after revealing cracks in cultural and social perceptions. The film abandons the song-and-dance sequences in search of a broader appeal, but the realism of terrorism is eclipsed first by a romance in Khan's personal life, and by a melodramatic flair in the second part of the film when he proves himself to be a Samaritan to a hurricane-hit African American community in Georgia. The deft combination of melodrama and realism found impressive appeal among Indian diasporic audiences—the film was the highest-grossing Bollywood film overseas upon its release—but this very same formula was also the reason for the film's failed attempt to attract a wider international audience.

Bollywood's confidence in moving to new territories is evident in its ability to create spectacles. Both diasporic and domestic audiences swoon over its "quest of global distinction" (Ganti, 2012b). Bollywood is no longer tethered to the state, which welcomes the transformation of the nation as an art form to the nation as a brand. Two spectacles underscore Bollywood's sense of self-branding: Farah Khan's *Om Shanti Om* (2007) and the *Dhoom/The Blast* trilogy (2004, 2006, and 2013), both of which project Bollywood's reach into competitive markets of Hollywood blockbusters. *Om Shanti Om* is a quintessential Bollywood spectacle that pays tribute to and pokes fun of the Bollywood film industry. It is a story of a minor actor in the 1970s, Om, who dreams of becoming a star and has his eyes set on the leading lady, Shanti. As he gets involved in an altercation between the film producer and his object of desire, he dies in a car accident. Thirty years later, he is reborn/reincarnated as a successful Bollywood star but still pines for his love from past life. The tagline of the film ("For some dreams, one lifetime is not enough!") is enacted through a series of excessive spectacles and melodramatic flourishes, with over forty Bollywood movie stars appearing in the course of the film. The film uses Bollywood itself as a brand placement within the film, creating a perpetual circle of commodified star personas seamlessly sliding between films, commercials, and other popular media. In this film, Bollywood's endorsement of itself and its brand-making process is a perfect emblem of cinema's power exceeding that of the state.

Dhoom is the largest film franchise from Bollywood, featuring two Bombay cops who pursue criminals in each of the three films. The first of the trilogy is set among gangs in the city, the second moves from Bombay to the Namibian desert to Rio de Janeiro, while the third is set in the city of Chicago. Fast-paced and action-packed, with requisite elements of dance, sexuality, and comedy, the films feature one major star, Abhishek Bachchan, and co-stars with rising power: John Abraham, Hrithik Roshan, and Aamir Khan. The films have gained increasing popularity over the years: *Dhoom 3* became the highest-grossing Bollywood film of all time in international markets, playing in 4,000 theaters in India and on 700 screens abroad (Chute, 2013). It is also Bollywood's most successful merchandise platform, having established partnerships with clothing companies, playing cards, video and computer games, sports and biking products, electronic gadgets, and a range of other products. On its heels, another successful franchise, *Krrish* (2006), directed by Rakesh Roshan, has shaped its own merchandising boom, expanding the industry in India. These spectacles are melodramatic fantasies, with Bollywood's own ingredients of song, dance, and star power propelling them to higher revenues. Their technical and technological sophistication definitively brings Bollywood into blockbuster territory, with an urge to continuously break earlier thresholds set by the industry.

Hindi mainstream cinema after Bollywood

An industry shaken, shaped by, and deeply dependent on Bollywood's cultural capital has grown in different directions. A new group of filmmakers, some of them trained at the Film and Television Institute of India, some outsiders, with others arriving from cinemas of other languages, have produced a variety of styles that breathe energy into the industry. Rajkumar Hirani, Ram Gopal Varma, Vidhu Vinod Chopra, Anurag Basu, and Mani Ratnam produce films with a range of distance from the heterogeneous, multi-pronged narratives of Hindi cinema.

Indian cinema witnessed the emergence of genres that crystalize social concerns related to action, crime, and gangster politics. These genre forms construct narratives embedded in the diagnosis of the social realm, laced with aesthetic styles far more diverse than previously seen in Indian cinema. If the previous phase in Hindi cinema was given to generating fantasies, dreams, and distractions, new mainstream Hindi cinema inches closer to the reality of the social and political life of the nation, confronting these issues without barring the entertainment appeal. The India that emerges in this phase is an "asymmetric nation," caught between the torrents of globalization and an immediate awareness of its own schisms, from corruption and crime to anxiety about the nation's relationship with the global (Raghavendra, 2014: 225). While Bollywood extends the nation into the sphere of the global, mainstream cinema at home turns its attention on the expansive grip of capital, from street corruption that creates a maze of moralities to the merging of politics and the corporate sector.

The Indian crime genre develops in many shades after the 1990s, mapping a spatial configuration of Bombay onto gangster narratives. As the underworld becomes visible, the "dreamscape of urban modernity and desire" disintegrates the city into a site of ruin, reminding us that "consumption comes at a price" (Mazumdar, 2007: 195). Gangster-crime films made in this phase of Bollywood provide a panoramic attempt by the industry to come to grips with this crisis both through an intense dramatization of crime and a slow, if uneven, re-working of the narrative form. Ram Gopal Varma's *Satya* (1998), *Company* (2002), and *Sarkar* (2005); Vidhu Vinod Chopra's *Parinda* (1989); Vishal Bhardwaj's *Maqbool* (2003) and *Kaminey/The Scoundrels* (2009); Madhur Bhandarkar's *Page 3* (2005); Mani Ratnam's *Guru* (2007); Mahesh Manjrekar's *Vaastav/The Reality* (1999); and Apporva Lakhia's *Shootout at Lokhandwala* (2007), among others, interrogate levels of crime in the city while offering a broad panorama of its post-1990s disintegration. Anurag Kashyap's crime spectacular *Gangs of Wasseypur* (2012) moves to the rural northeast to focus on a vicious backdrop that festered while the country was subjected to fantasies and dreams. Its gritty realism returns to the theme of crime as the corrupt foundation of society even as the nation moves to a broader horizon of the global. The downward trajectory of a gangster mob in spaces inhabited by the underclass of India's global city is mapped in Kanu Behl's *Titli/Butterfly* (2014). A loner in the midst of a family of petty criminals that barely holds itself together, the protagonist Titli attempts to shake off his ties to his corrupt family and invest in a mall parking garage that is being built in the Delhi suburbs. The narrative sets him on a path of hopeless redemption through a fierce backdrop of brutal, abject violence, unrelenting in its downward spiral. The setting of rising malls, towering housing, and corporate structures intruding on the skyline crystalizes Titli and his family's troubles: there is no respite in the onslaught of advancing forces of new capital.

Corruption at all levels moves to the center of narrative concerns in many films. In Rakesh Omprakash Mehra's *Rang De Basanti/Let It Show Saffron* (2006), a young British woman comes to India to make a film on the revolutionaries of the freedom struggle. She meets four young men who are slowly transformed into contemporary revolutionaries until they realize that the government is corrupt, inept, and negligent. The discovery about new India against the backdrop of the freedom fighters' vision provokes a crisis and confrontation with the government. The film was a blockbuster when it was released, and is still considered a landmark film on state corruption. A number of other films focusing on corruption steered Bollywood into the contemporary political moment: Dibakar Banerjee's comedy *Khosla Ka Ghosla/Khosla's Nest* (2006), Ram Gopal Varma's *Sarkar Raj* (2008) and *Rann/Battle* (2010), Prakash Jha's *Rajneeti/Politics* (2010), and Raj Kumar Gupta's *No One Killed Jessica* (2011) provide a window into Bollywood's interest in corruption in everyday life and the institutions.

In the midst of these changes, Bollywood finds the star persona of Aamir Khan shaping a number of new directions. He was already a star of considerable popular appeal when his 2001 film *Lagaan: Once Upon a Time in India*, directed by Ashutosh Gowariker, received large international acclaim and global recognition. A story set during the British colonial occupation of India, it offers a singular narrative of a small group of villagers led by Bhuvan (Khan) who win a cricket match against the occupiers, symbolizing a common man's victory over the powerful, a favored trope of Indian cinema. The film retains some of the elements of Bollywood narrative: song and dance, melodrama, and the spectacular unraveling of exotic landscape and culture. The popularity of the film among non-diasporic audiences and its Oscar nomination were in synch with the Academy's preference for simpler narratives that highlight cultural specificity while avoiding political or social complexities. For Indian cinema, it was a groundbreaking success, and for Khan, it opened a new terrain that enabled him to use his star persona at home.

Since then, Khan has straddled a path of Bollywood blockbusters such as *Rang De Basanti* (2006), *Fanaa* (2006), *3 Idiots* (2009), *Dhoom 3* (2013), and *PK* (2014). In 2007, Aamir Khan co-directed *Taare Zameen Par/Like Stars on Earth*, a patient but skillful narrative attempt to reshape social perception on dyslexia and elementary education. Along with the critique of higher education in *3 Idiots*, this film cemented Khan's role as a socially conscious film star. The role of film stars in politics is not new, but in mainstream Indian cinema Khan stands out as something of an exception, using his Bollywood visibility for constructing a strong social voice, even as this voice strategically avoids too much friction and thus still serves the interests of the industry. He produced Anusha Rizvi's *Peepli Live* (2010), dramatizing the crisis in the lives of Indian farmers as they resorted to suicide in the wake of dire economic and environmental conditions. The film is unique in contemporary Indian cinema for its deliberate disclosure of the realism of farmers' lives, the crass appetite of the media for sensationalism, and the deep-rooted callousness among politicians. As he uses films to find a different voice within Bollywood, Aamir Khan has amplified his role in television as well, a stark departure from the dominant trend in the industry, where star personas have entirely given into the commercial apparatus.

In focus 5.1   Rajkumar Hirani and Ram Gopal Varma: mavericks transform the mainstream

The arrival of capital and new talent diversified and revitalized Hindi mainstream cinema, with a new generation of filmmakers who utilized the power of mainstream genre spectacle, but shaped it into new modes of representation. Rajkumar Hirani and Ram Gopal Varma are exemplary in this regard as auteurs of popular cinema that breaks from the simple fantasy structures of the earlier films and enters into new modes of social realism.

Rajkumar Hirani has consistently used the ingredients of mainstream cinema for mild pedagogical social aims. In the immensely popular *Lage Raho Munna Bhai/Go On, Munna Bhai* (2006), a sequel to his *Munna Bhai MBBS* (2003), the protagonist Munna Bhai ("little brother," an affectionate term for the son in a family) is a street thug working the streets of Bombay, smitten with the voice of Janhavi, a radio DJ. He uses his gangster skills and connections to win a radio quiz on Gandhi, eliciting an interview with Janhavi during which he pretends to be a Gandhi scholar. As he carries the role forward, he visits a library to study Gandhi, who appears to him as a supernatural figure, an apparition to offer advice and knowledge. Transformed by the experience, Munna

(continued)

(continued)

Bhai advocates honesty, non-violence, and the ethics of social concern. Instead of practicing *dadagiri* (small-time, strong-arm gangsterism), the film proposes a Gandhi-inspired *gandhi-giri*—using Gandhi-like tactics to deal with conflicts. Though the film is a romantic comedy, often trivializing street violence, it effectively invokes the importance of the figure of Gandhi for the younger generation.

After utilizing the star power of Sunjay Dutt in the *Munna Bhai* films, Hirani successfully employs Aamir Khan in his next two blockbusters. In *3 Idiots* (2009), about a prankster who proves himself successful in medical school, overshadowing his peers and rebelling against the head of the institution, Hirani mocks the rote styles of educational systems in India to suggest that they need to be liberated from entrenched outmodedness and adopt creativity-driven styles of learning. Hirani's recent film *PK* (2014) is a religious satire, a story about an extraterrestrial, PK, who comes to Earth on a research mission. Stranded in Rajasthan, he struggles to understand India's dizzying religious landscape, make sense of his own life, and return to his celestial home. The simplicity of his purpose is overshadowed by the pretentions of religious rituals, and the more PK tries to understand the logic that drives them, the more he exposes the contradictory aspects of organized religion in the lives of Indians. The followers of the nationalist Hindu party considered the film to be a betrayal of Hinduism, although it spoofs the blind faith of all religions. Aggravated further by the identity of its Muslim lead star, the controversy took an ugly turn with violent protests in many parts of the country. The populist appeal of the film, however, overcame the loud and violent protests against it; *PK* emerged as the highest-grossing Indian film of all time, and was among the top ten highest earners in the US in its opening weekend.

In Hirani's films, the individual protagonist is poised to resist institutions but without the presumed support of the traditional family structures. The protagonists of his films, particularly of *3 Idiots* and *PK*, are loners, their backgrounds hidden, their outward thrust motivated by a pure sense of purpose to restore the ethical basis of national identity. The films' song-and-dance sequences are woven into the narrative, with no presence of the dream-fantasy sequences prevalent in traditional Bollywood narratives.

Figure 5.4 PK (Aamir Khan) lands on Earth in Rajkumar Hirani's *PK* (2014)

Sub-plots are nearly absent, and dedicated to enhancing the central character's moral purpose. While all have the element of romance, romance itself is undermined in favor of the socially-minded focus of the narrative. Hirani thus utilizes Bollywood ingredients to bring the glare of publicity to narratives that attempt to win popular appeal at home and abroad and stir up social issues. His films stand at the threshold of recovering national identity from its state of contamination by corruption, stagnancy, and orthodoxy.

Ram Gopal Varma is known as the maverick filmmaker of the new mainstream Hindi cinema. His three-decades-long career is varied and uneven but full of experimental verve and innovative spirit. Already a successful director in Telugu cinema, he made a transition to the mainstream Hindi cinema with his breakthrough film *Satya* (1998), released during the era of economic liberalization. *Satya* unfolds an increasingly realistic landscape of a city infested with crime and exploitative politics, putting in place a visual and narrative idiom markedly different from traditional Bollywood. Satya is a migrant who arrives in the city and is immediately thrown into the underworld through a gangster he meets in a prison. His nameless character, his willing embrace of violence in the city, and lack of warmth is a sharp departure from the migrant in Raj Kapoor's *Shree 420* (1955) or *Awaara*, where crime is borne out of reluctance. Set in the lower-class neighborhoods of Bombay, the film moves through its slums, crowded streets, manic traffic, congested spaces, and gang violence with a relentless, gritty realism that exposes the city's brutal conditions. It is a portrait of Bombay without its glamour and glitz, commodity and commerce, and the spectacular cityscape along the coastline is visible only in the background from the rocks in the distance where the poor sit. While the narrative has a subtext of a love story, the romance takes shape in the claustrophobic spaces inhabited by ordinary citizens, and there are no allusions to the song-and-dance fantasy spaces commonplace in Bollywood. *Satya* thus presents a significant break from Bollywood, taking a turn toward "narrative integration, character-driven, point of view storytelling and even, occasionally, the elimination of the 'distractive' features of song, dance, and comedy sequences" (Vasudevan, 2013: 204).

Varma's critique of social realities takes a forceful turn in *Company* (2002) and *Sarkar* (2005), where he focuses his lens on the power-broker class of the city. In *Company*, the gang violence expands from the marginal, survival economy of the streets to the corrupt intrigues of capitalism, broadening the criminal cartel from Bombay to Hong Kong, Switzerland, and Kenya. In *Sarkar*, Varma moves from a narrative based on an international gangster to a local political leader who governs an underworld of terror by extortion and corruption that reaches deep into the circuits of power. Often compared to Francis Ford Coppola's *The Godfather* (1972) and Martin Scorsese's *Goodfellas* (1990), these films mark a break from Bollywood as much as they open up a new phase of Indian cinema by igniting a gangster genre within it. Varma's commitment to establishing a new cinematic space in Bollywood is evident in his production company, RGV Factory, whose aim is to recruit new talent and bring mainstream Hindi cinema into alliance with Hollywood and Asian cinema. The company produced Varma's horror film *Bhoot* (2003), Sriram Raghavan's *Ek Hasina Thi/Once Was a Beautiful Woman* (2004), anthology film *Darna Zaroori Hai/You Will Get Scared* (2006), and several others before giving in to the marketing and distribution model of Bollywood. Varma's attempts to find a niche within Bollywood and offer a different kind of mainstream film makes him a notable departure from, although still a part of, the Bollywood machine.

Cinemas of multiple languages

It is a great irony and a politically fraught feature of Indian cinema that only a fraction of its cinema gains visibility in the larger landscape of world cinema. Although the map of world cinema now includes a variety of positions and approaches such as "small cinemas," "cinemas of periphery," or "minor cinemas" that restore the voices of different manifestations and localities, little attention has been paid to the cinemas that developed asymmetrically within various national cinemas, concealing the multiplicity of formations under a single representative category. India offers an unparalleled complexity of this kind in world cinema. While Hindi cinema has dominated the country's film culture for decades, films have been produced in over two-dozen Indian languages, with some language cinemas making sizeable contributions. The largest film industry in India comes from the Tamil language (287 films produced in 2014) with Chennai (Tamil Nadu) as the capital of production, followed by films in other languages: Telugu (255; Hyderabad), Malayalam (150; Thiruvananthapuram-Kerala), and Kannada (150; Bengaluru-Karnataka), among others. All these industries are located in southern India, while the Marathi film industry is centered in the western city of Bombay, and the Bengali film industry in Kolkata (Calcutta).

There are several issues in considering these cinemas as an integral part of Indian cinema. Cinemas of India have often been called "regional" cinemas, a label that misleads and masks the identity of these traditions. As we rethink the relationships between the local, the national, and the global, it is no longer useful to think in terms of "regional" cinemas of India; rather, these are *cinemas of multiple languages*. The terminology of "regions" suggests a politically viable but practically defunct concept for several reasons. First, in the transformed landscape of the post-1990s cinemas, the emerging practices of production in the country are not limited to geographic boundaries of states or regions, but are spread across the country. Bhojpuri cinema stands as a good example of this trend. Arising from a fluid dialect of the Hindi language, Bhojpuri cinema emerged from eastern Uttar Pradesh and Bihar in the 1960s, but now claims production, distribution, and support across a wide swath of the country. It is a prominent cultural production for migrants across India and from the Caribbean to East Asia, posing a number of questions on popular culture, identity, the nation, and the global migrant identity (Tripathy, 2007). It is one of the many emerging realms of production, encouraged by the availability of digital technology of production and distribution.

Second, as the idea of the nation itself has expanded beyond traditional borders into the global sphere, it is hard to think of regional identities as isolated from the fluidity of relationships across larger territories, beyond cultural and linguistic borders. Tamil cinema, with its own reach across regional and national borders, offers a useful paradigm of such language cinema. It boasts a rich cultural heritage and influence, with its production output often outpacing Hindi cinema. The Tamil language is at the heart of the culture, with its own sense of ethno-nationalism that marks a space of difference from the pan-Indian identity presumed by the mainstream cinema. Along with the power of language, Selvaraj Velayutham notes, "Tamil cinema is always about Tamlians" (2008: 8). Embedded in a national culture, Tamil cinema has had an ambiguous, simultaneously collaborative and antagonistic relationship with the dominant Hindi cinema. This binary relationship has experienced a reorientation in the past few decades, influencing its own diaspora abroad, while consistently exchanging and influencing other-language films, including mainstream Hindi cinema. Thus, Tamil cinema exists as an "assemblage" where identities are de-territorialized across a dynamically dispersed space of cinema, technologies, exhibition cultures, politics, and identity (Devdas and Velayutham, 2012). It is part of the imagined worlds across geographical boundaries, in a broader field of other cinemas.

The third reason to opt for a model of multiple-language instead of regional cinemas is the remarkable permeability of films and directors from one realm to another. As films are dubbed, remade, then brought back to the region, they become part of the larger fabric of cinema in India, while directors work in multiple languages and in Hindi mainstream cinema. Hindi film producers keep a watchful eye on successful films in local regions, only to remake them into national blockbusters. This sort of transfer, a feature of Indian cinema for decades, has accelerated since the late 1990s. Director Siddique, for example, made *Bodyguard* in 2010 in Malayalam, and the film was remade in the Telugu, Tamil, Kannada, and Hindi languages. Sreenu Vaitla's Telugu film *Ready* (2008) was remade with the same title in Hindi in 2011. Tamil film *Singam* (Hari, 2010) was subsequently dubbed in Telugu (*Yamudu*, 2010), remade in Kannada as *Kempe Gowda* (2011), in Hindi as *Singham* (2011), and in Bengali as *Shotru* (2011). While such remakes are often motivated by considerations of box office success, films in India add another layer of intrigue to the notion of remakes by remaking Hollywood and East Asian films. Tamil film *Ghajini* (A.R. Murugadoss, 2005) is both inspired by and a remake of Christopher Nolan's *Memento* (2000), adapting select elements of it and adding music and romance to the narrative. Successful with Tamil audiences, the film was remade in Hindi in 2008 by the same director with Aamir Khan in the lead. It was a sensational blockbuster at the box office, expanding its commercial influence into video games as well. It is clear that in the midst of remakes and dubs, there is now an increasing trend in the rise of multilingual films that further erase borders between cinemas.

The diversity of multiple-language cinemas in India offers instructive lessons for world cinema, as similar multiplicities can be found in the regions of Asia, Europe, South America, or Africa. It is vital to maintain the emphasis on the specificities of various cinemas, but such specificities are embedded in a relationship of exchange with other contexts, which transform the character and discourse of each cinema. To think of world cinema after the 1980s is to think of a widening expansion of such spheres that exist in relationships of difference and mutual identities. It is to move beyond binary relationships between regional, national, and world cinema. In India, the shape of the new "global nation" constituted by Bollywood's expansive profile and its complicit partnership with the state makes it even more necessary to weave in the role played by the cinemas of multiple languages in the shaping of national identity.

In focus 5.2   Mani Ratnam: negotiating the local and the national

We discussed the example of Ram Gopal Varma in his successful transition from Tamil to Hindi mainstream cinema. While such movements have always been part of Indian cinema, the main feature of the recent movement of directors from the local to a national level concerns their ability to translate and position their own local identity into the national context. Tamil director Mani Ratnam's work presents some of the fundamental dilemmas in this dual movement that involves marking a specific identity and broadening its horizons on a wider sphere, of speaking the local and the national in the same interlocution.

(continued)

(continued)

In a career that spans three decades, Mani Ratnam has made films in Tamil, Malayalam, Kannada, and Telugu, and several of his films have been remade and dubbed in other languages. His national breakthrough came in 1987 with the release of *Nayakan/The Hero*, first made in Tamil and later dubbed in Hindi as *Velu Nayakan*. Ostensibly based on Francis Ford Coppola's *The Godfather* (1972), the film was energized by a memorable performance by Kamal Haasan, one of the leading actors of Tamil cinema. It is a narrative of an orphan child from Tamil Nadu who moves to Bombay's Tamil community and rises to power in the city's world of crime. A story of a singular figure whose integrity and loyalty to his own people mark him as a hero to Tamilians on a broader stage, *Nayakan* spoke of class issues, the nation's ability to absorb its diversity, and the criminal life of the migrants in a major city. The film played up what had been a feature of many Tamil films of the past, the anti-national and anti-North feelings. The film's patchwork of Hollywood conventions, combined with a character-centered, evenly-paced, tense narrative, allowed Ratnam to make a regional film in a national context.

The film's strong ethnic emphasis was eclipsed by his subsequent films, *Roja/Rose* (1992), the first of Ratnam's "terror trilogy" that included *Bombay* (1994) and *Dil Se/ From the Heart* (1998). *Roja* is the most intriguing film in the trilogy, offering lessons on several levels, from the relationship between the local and the national to the changes in narrative form and contingencies of translation. An intense debate among scholars followed its reception, inviting criticism as well as appreciation for its innovative narrative (Bharucha, 1994; Chakravarthy & Pandian, 1994; Niranjana, 1994). At the center of the film's narrative is Roja, a village girl who accepts a proposition to marry a technocratic Tamil man from Chennai.

After their wedding, she accompanies him to the picturesque border state of Kashmir, where he works as a cryptologist for the army. When he is kidnapped by Muslim separatists, she works ceaselessly to secure his release, going through many difficulties; speaking only Tamil, the army officials and the authorities (who speak only

Figure 5.5 Roja (Madhoo) and her husband Rishi (Arvind Swamy) in Mani Ratnam's *Roja* (1992)

Hindi) are dismissive of her "Madrasi," a North Indian dismissal of a minor language in the south.

Roja is a gendered embodiment of the Tamil nation inserted into the national scene where her husband, a captive of the militants, negotiates religion and the nation with his kidnappers. The difference of language and identity that marks Roja's place in the discourse of the nation becomes pivotal in Ratnam's film, a difference that is only present in the original Tamil version. When the film was released to national audiences, it was dubbed in Hindi, erasing its central dynamic of locating Tamil identity in a pan-Indian context. The Hindi-dubbed version also engages in other absurdities by replacing Tamil Nadu with Uttar Pradesh, a northern state, as well as replacing the conflict-ridden Kashmir, which could not be accessed for filming, with other locales. Commenting on these displacements, Vasudevan notes, "The gap between the physical and narrative referent exposes the crevasse between a desired emotional fullness-of romance, of the nation-state in its ideal form—and its realization" (2011: 223).

The realism of images presented on a tableau attractive for the visual pleasure of a "tourist" also frames a narrative of conflict in the challenge of Muslim terrorists to the nation-state. The much-touted realism of the film is in service of modernity through the eyes of the country's rising middle class. Ratnam deploys the familiar elements of the dominant narrative form of Hindi cinema (melodrama, song and dance), oriented toward restoring the nation-state as it is toward locating a regional identity within it. It has a dynamic similar to the one in the family dramas, where an individual finds a distinct space within the family and the social sphere is here deployed to represent the Tamil identity within the modern Indian nation.

Roja advocates assertive identity for the Indian nation-state while its reductive depiction of the Muslims in the narrative also suggests the alignment of national identity with that of Hindu identity, a recasting of the secular into the local mainstream. Its foregrounding of a narrow patriotism positioned against the militancy of the rebels leaves no room for a broader, cosmopolitan vision of the nation. It makes an important contribution, however, to a new narrative form that foregrounds realism while still utilizing melodramatic and popular cultural elements of song and dance, and inscribes local identity into the larger national one.

Other examples of language cinemas

Tamil cinema

Aadukalam/Arena (Vetrimaran, 2011); and *Aaranya Kaandam/Jungle Saga* (Thiagarajan Kumararaja, 2011).

Marathi cinema

Deool/The Temple, *Valu*, and *Vihir* (Umesh Vinayak Kulkarni, 2011, 2008, and 2009); *Gabhricha Paus/The Damned Rain* (Satish Manwar, 2009); *Court* (Chaitanya Tamhane, 2014); *Fandry* (Nagraj Manjule, 2013); *Shwaas/The Breath* (Sandeep Sawant, 2004); and *Dombivli Fast* (Nishikant Kamat, 2005).

Bengali cinema

Byomkesh Bakshi, *Abar Byomkesh*, and *Byomkesh Phire Elo* (Anjan Dutt, 2010, 2012, and 2014); *Swet Patharer Thala/The Marble Plate* (Tapan Sinha, 1992); *Ushnatar Janye* and *Arekti Premer Golpo/Just Another Love Story* (Kaushik Ganguly, 2003 and 2010); *Chitrangada/The Crowning Wish* (Rituparno Ghosh, 2012); *Autograph* (Srijit Mukherji, 2010); *Antaheen/The Endless Wait* and *Aparakito Tumi/You, the Undefeated* (Aniruddha Roy Chowdhury, 2009 and 2012); and *Asha Jaoar Majhe/Labour of Love* (Aditya Vikram Sengupta, 2014).

Malayalam cinema

Adaminte Makan Abu/Abu, Son of Adam (Salim Ahamed, 2011); *Drishyam/The Sight* (Jeethu Joseph, 2013); and *Kutty Srank/The Sailor of Hearts* (Shaji N. Karun, 2009).

Assamese cinema

Pokhi/And the River Flows, *Konikar Ramdhenu/Ride on the Rainbow*, and *Baandhon/The Waves of Silence* (Jahnu Barua, 1999, 2002, and 2012); and *Haladhar/The Yeoman* (Sanjeev Hazarika, 1992).

The cinema of new social realism

After the 1990s, a smaller but energetic segment of the film industry took a turn away from the dominant conventions to produce films that were accessible to home audiences, and found appeal at international film festivals. Three factors contributed to this development. First, the neoliberal policies that brought capital to the Bombay film industry also opened up avenues to other filmmakers, diversifying the industry. Second, a new generation of filmmakers exposed to widely available films from around the world entered the industry and were energized by the scope of world cinema. Third, the expansion and availability of new technologies of production, distribution, and exhibition opened up opportunities for producers and filmmakers to launch their productions. To some extent, Bollywood's global profile helped the circulation of these films abroad as well. This strand of Indian cinema is hard to define in terms of category. Still utilizing partial or full state funding from the National Film Development Corporation, or NFDC (together with international co-production or private capital), it is markedly different from the social film supported by the state in the 1960s and 1970s, as well as from the blend of realism in the mainstream Hindi cinema practiced by filmmakers like Ram Gopal Varma. This cinema also demonstrates greater fluidity between the cinemas of multiple languages and films that are produced on the periphery of the mainstream cinema industry in Bombay.

The most influential figure in this strand is Anurag Kashyap, a filmmaker whose oeuvre continues to expand in several directions. Kashyap wrote the screenplay of Ram Gopal Varma's influential *Satya* in 1998, building a career as a writer and contributing to many films including Mani Ratnam's *Yuva*, Deepa Mehta's *Water* (2005), and Vikramaditya's *Udaan* (2010). He has produced nearly a dozen feature films and several short films in a brief time span, while also serving as a film producer, cultivating a generation of filmmakers who have shaped this strand of Indian cinema. Kashyap's open antagonism toward the spectacle-intensive Bollywood, and his affinity to sensational cinema styles in the West and Far East, advocacy of new filmmakers, active support for the short film form, and keen visibility in high-profile film festivals place him at a vanguard of new Indian cinema.

Kashyap's first feature-directorial effort, *Paanch/Five* (2000), uses the backdrop of the city of Bombay to weave a narrative about a band that gets involved in crime and violence, unraveling a world of media dominance, corruption, and a diminishing value of human life. The film defies an easy analysis in its "expressionistic tapestry of urban life," and with a narrative that struggles to "articulate something that has not yet been captured within the Bombay film industry" (Mazumdar, 2007: 200–202). Kashyap's next venture, *Black Friday* (2007), creates a semi-fictional account of activities behind the 1993 Bombay bombings that shook the city into riots and bloodshed. With a thriller pace that rapidly blends real footage with filmed versions of the background, the film constructs a realist document that subtly hides its own bias against the terrorists. Kashyap's slow evolution into a director who values the economy of narrative and invests in the visual quality of his films comes to maturity in *That Girl in Yellow Boots* (2010). Playing up a subdued but ever-present trope of Anglo-Indians struggling on the margins of culture, the film is a character study of a British girl searching for her Indian father in Bombay. Her troubled, confused relationships become understated plots against the spaces of the city inscribed by sex, morality, and its marginal inhabitants.

Kashyap's most widely known effort to date, his five-and-a-half-hour-long *Gangs of Wasseypur* (2012) was popular at home and received a healthy reception at film festivals and theatrical releases in the West. It is an ambitious production that did much to attract critics and admirers to Kashyap, establishing him as an emphatic practitioner of realism. The crime narrative of *Gangs of Wasseypur* was released in two parts, spanning a seventy-year rivalry between families and clans in the rural coal-mining area of Eastern India. In a fast-paced, panoramic, graphic, dramatic, and violent narrative, the film goes through generations of family members charged with a thirst for revenge and domination of the region.

Figure 5.6 Faizal (Nawazuddin Siddiqui) transforms into a ruthless gang lord in *Gangs of Wasseypur – Part 2* (2012) by Anurag Kashyap

The script attempts to keep some semblance of plots, relationships, and events but the visual spectacle of violence and occasional sex move to the foreground, nearly dismantling the narrative. Its complete embrace of violence, graphic in a manner previously unseen in Indian cinema, made it popular among audiences and raised Kashyap's profile. The film represents a threshold in several respects. It confirms him as a bold practitioner of visual techniques associated with the action films of Quentin Tarantino, Martin Scorsese, and Francis Ford Coppola, as well as masters of crime-action direction in Asian cinema, such as John Woo and Johnnie To. The film distances itself from the excesses of Bollywood and mainstream Hindi cinema. When music is used, it is integrated into the setting. Filmed in gritty, dusty, rural environments, which reveal the traditional housing styles as much as the random pathways between them, *Gangs of Wasseypur* marks a departure for Indian cinema in its invocation of a new, sensory realism that anchors the spectator's vision in the claim of "authenticity," exposing real locations in distant parts of India.

Kashyap aims for the visceral pleasure in graphic violence admired by his audiences abroad, but in the process roots the images in an Indian landscape, the rough, dusty spaces, in a radical departure from the glossy and cleaned-up country of the mainstream cinema and its Bollywood appendage.

Aligned with the increasing trends of realism in world cinema, the assertive indexicality of his images constructs what Lúcia Nagib (2011) calls the "ethics of realism" in world cinema, making representation a consequence of choices in the mode of production and address of film. Kashyap's films, nearly all of them explorations of the material conditions of the setting and its people, pursue cultural realism rather than commercial realism of an established idiom. The camera rarely takes distance from the settings, maintaining an interrogative, almost frenetic eye into the spaces of living and action. His realism creates its own milieu, responsive to the transformation in the world rather than to the conventions etched in cinema.

As a writer of his own films, Kashyap anchors his images in the vernaculars of the places and regions of the country. According to Amitava Kumar (2012), the idiomatic descriptions of emotions and situations in *Gangs of Wasseypur* assert the dialects of the people even as the film's flashy violence demonstrates an "irresponsible profligacy" of its own. The script restlessly enacts the Wittgenstein idea of "forms of life" in the specificity of phrases,

Figure 5.7 Gritty, dusty, rural environments in *Gangs of Wasseypur – Part 2*

accents, and expressions, as when a butcher tells the policeman: "This is Wasseypur. Here even a pigeon flies with only one wing, and with the other it tries to protect its honor." Even smart phone ringtones are suggestive of the acerbic taunts relevant to the situations; when family members are hiding from possible assault, a ringtone sings a Bollywood song in Hindi, "I am a villain, not a hero." In films such as *Black Friday* (2004), *Gulaal* (2009), and *Ugly* (2013), Kashyap uses lived-language, a sharp departure from the linguistic dominance in mainstream cinema where northern dialects of Hindi and Urdu have prevailed for decades, underscoring the inherent class bias of the vision propagated by films. The dimension of realism is enhanced through language as well as his choice of settings and actors.

Framing his narrative and rapid-fire violence in the realism of images and language also positions Kashyap to launch a mild but caustic attack on mainstream film culture. There are numerous references to Bollywood films, actors, and characters, none too reverent but all meant to reinforce the impression that everyone in the country carries films in their heads and in their lives. In one instance, a gang leader, a Don-like figure, outlasts everyone because he does not "watch Bollywood movies." He says everyone "is trying to become a hero of his imaginary film . . . as long as there are movies in this country, people will continue to be fooled." He tells his son that he cannot do serious gang work if he watches films (in this case, it is particularly caustic since the son wants to watch the popular *Dilwale Dulhania Le Jayenge!*). Kashyap's double-edged film both parodies Bollywood and acknowledges the necessity of its support for success.

Kashyap also actively supports the production of short films, including anthology films such as *Bombay Talkies* (2013), and *India-is* (2012), a significant gesture in the country that has been codified by the hegemonic mainstream cinema. Proclaiming that "short films will redefine Indian cinema," he has encouraged other young filmmakers to produce such films, allowing for bolder experimentation and creating spaces within the sphere of Bollywood mode of production (Kashyap, 2013).

Many other directors have continued to work in the same strain of filmmaking: Vikramaditya Motwane with *Udaan/Flight* (2010); Shlok Sharma with *Haraamkhor/Bastard* (2015); Neeraj Ghaywan with *Masaan/Fly Away Solo* (2015), winner of the Fipresci prize in the *Un Certain Regard* section at Cannes; and Bikas Mishra with *Chauranga/Four Colours* (2014). Refusing to take a step back from launching a social critique of conditions in different parts of India, these films aim to cultivate spectatorship within the country, but mostly rely on film festivals at home and abroad, as well as partial state funding and co-production arrangements for sustenance.

In focus 5.3   New and bold currents in Indian cinema: *Liar's Dice* (2014), *Asha Jaoar Majhe/Labor of Love* (2014), and *Qissa: The Tale of a Lonely Ghost* (2013)

Some recently released films that have achieved broader circulation are great examples of the diversity of visual styles. Among them is Geethu Mohandas's debut feature, *Liar's Dice* (2014), a treatise on silent pain borne by the residents of a snowy northern region, where men are forced to leave their families to find work in the cities' bustling new economy. Worried because she has not heard from her husband, the film's

(continued)

(continued)

protagonist Kamla leaves home to find him, accompanied by her five-year-old daughter and her pet lamb. On her way, she meets Nawazuddin, an escapee from a border guard unit who is making a trek to the city. A complicated journey of a married woman and a mysterious, abrasive man comes to a head against the backdrop of rising construction in the outskirts of New Delhi where Kamla's husband, among scores of migrant workers, went to satisfy the ambitions of an expansive corporate economy with cheap labor. *Liar's Dice* is a meticulously-paced narrative that maintains fidelity to its location (Kashyap collaborator Rajeev Ravi is the cinematographer) and reveals the anxiety of a search with each successive step. Unfolding on the same terrain of corporate destruction as Kanu Behl's *Titli*, violence in Mohandas's film is silent yet deeply felt. The address of its imaginary is no longer the nation but its expanded borders onto the global, and the spaces of incursion by capital on people's lives.

Aditya Vikram Sengupta's *Labor of Love* (2014), unique in its visual construction and narrative rhythm, foretells another transition in new Indian cinema. The film, whose original Bengali title *Asha Jaoar Majhe (In the Midst of Coming and Going)* was changed for film festivals and eventually for domestic release, is constructed in two sequences that depict a working day in the life of a young couple in the city of Kolkata. In the

Figures 5.8 & 5.9 In *Labor of Love*, the staircase to the young couple's apartment marks their separation as well as their bond

background of labor protests highlighted by radio news announcing the dire conditions for employment in the city, Sengupta first tracks the day of the husband at home, who has returned from his night shift; he rests, eats his meals, and shops for the next day's meal while his wife works. During the night, they switch roles; she comes home in the evening, prepares meals, washes clothes, and readies to return to work just as her husband's night shift is coming to an end.

The camera maintains a lyrical, slow movement on objects, characters, and spaces, mostly in a calculated rhythm of pans. Natural light and the rough surfaces of everyday life fill the frame, and the passing of time is viscerally felt. A brief moment of their face-to-face meeting in the morning shifts to a magical realist scene, in part an ode to their married life, and in part a nod to a silver lining of their oppressive existence.

The film's deliberate attempt to locate it in the "slow cinema" movement identifies it with the politically charged work of Tsai Ming-liang, Béla Tarr, and Wong Kar-wai. The film does justice to both its titles; it is a meditation on time that separates the couple, and a pungent critique of "labor" that constitutes a relationship. The notion of labor also works to underscore the alienation of the two characters, the prototypes of thousands of others fortunate to find employment and willing to pay a heavy cost to keep it.

Much like Tsai Ming-liang, who draws a contrast between levels of cultural and social disintegration in a globalized world, and Béla Tarr, who uses cinematic movement to draw out the revolutionary strength of the image, Sengupta's film intercepts the established codes of image and narrative in Indian cinema, especially in its afflicted phase after the 1990s. Dialogue is absent, as if unable to add to the complexity of the image. His use of songs (from popular Bengali films and light classical Indian music) interspersed throughout the film anchors the characters' lives in the ethos of the working class. It is a lyrical exercise to bend the arc of melodramatic narrative in Indian cinema by shifting its pathos to new political and artistic aims. Sengupta's film is an uncompromising attempt to align Indian cinema with different currents in world cinema without orientalist and imitative tendencies.

Figure 5.10 The young married couple's rare meeting in a dream-like scene in *Labor of Love*

(continued)

(continued)

Anup Singh's *Qissa: The Tale of a Lonely Ghost* (2013) marks another bold departure for Indian cinema. A graduate of the Film and Television Institute of India, Singh assembles a co-production with the state support of the NFDC, Germany's Heimat Film, Augustus Film of the Netherlands, and France's Ciné-Sud Promotion. Made in the Punjabi language with an Indian cast, *Qissa* is set in the period of India's partition, centered on a family led by a patriarchal figure named Umber, who longs for a son to affirm his identity in the tradition of families led by men. When his wife gives birth to their fourth girl, he refuses to accept it and raises her as his son.

His insistence and tradition silence his wife and the secret stays away from their daughters. As he forces his girl-raised-as-a-son to marry a girl, the wounds of gender conflicts precipitate the crisis. After his death, the second half of the narrative shifts its focus on his return as a ghost, still haunting his traumatized daughter. Married, the women hide from the society that would reject them but find a certain comfort in the discovery and freedom of their own sexualities.

Singh uses the figure of the ghost to work through the traumas caused to his family. His ghostly presence signifies his patriarchal presence, the unshakeable power of tradition, and a condemnation of the practice of gender preference with a desire to break it. These scenes, oscillating between the real and the impressionistic, are neither abstract nor magical-realist but rather suggest a cinematic figuration, a composite capable of showing the inescapable cruelty inflicted by patriarchal culture on women. It is a piercing, exemplary critique of the grip of orthodoxy and its struggles to come to terms with the changing conditions of life. With clever shifts in realist connotations, the film is very clear in its narrative premise of exposing the blind spots of patriarchy that strictly circumscribes women's sexuality.

These films underscore a cinematic turn that marks a departure both from the mainstream Hindi cinema and Bollywood, without mimicking the general grid of the festival films yet opening up to diverse currents in world cinema. Their most remarkable achievement is to shift the narrative to its political and social dimension in a film culture that is otherwise dominated by commercially oriented images. For decades, as

Figure 5.11 In Anup Singh's *Qissa: The Tale of a Lonely Ghost* (2013), father Umber (Irrfan Khan) teaches his daughter Kanwar (Tillotama Shome) the skills of manliness

Figures 5.12 & 5.13 Neeli (Rasika Dugal) and Kanwar discovering each other as women in Anup Singh's *Qissa*

Bhaumik (2006) observes, Indian film remained hermetically sealed in vestiges of its own peculiarity, or it was reduced to genre cinema that crossed borders based on its distinct, in this case, exotic appeal. These films show that Indian cinema can transcend these limitations, and circulate to broader audiences outside the country without being subsumed by the generic category of Bollywood.

Indian theoretical perspectives

Film scholarship in Indian cinema has grown vigorously over the past three decades. Except for some older works, most of it is in English and imminently accessible to outsiders. Nearly all Indian film scholars are very much part of Western film studies, but within India a number of journals and newspapers, and web journalism, have added to a healthy growth of books in the field. Though there has been an interest in Bollywood among Indian scholars outside the country, increasing attention to historical and critical works on other aspects of cinema comes from within the country. In short, scholarship in Indian cinema is marked by its versatility in adapting different approaches to the study of cinema.

Discussions on specific theories of image and representation in an Indian context have remained a concern among scholars focused on the mainstream Hindi cinema. On the one hand, academic scholars looked down upon commercial cinema, dismissed for its spectacles, disaggregated narratives, song–and–dance sequences, interruptions to the narrative flow, and kitsch-generating abilities. The preference of critical and theoretical discourse was to focus on the intellectually challenging "new wave cinema" of the 1960s and 1970s. On the other hand, the effort to decipher the powerful appeal of peculiarities of mainstream popular cinema required film scholars to turn to the specificity of cultural-historical contexts to understand its aesthetics and forms of storytelling. Audiences in the West carried the same puzzle in their minds for decades, dismissing Indian films as generic, carnival-like displays of dances, unrealistic settings, and exotic colors. Indian cinema remained isolated from the stream of world cinema for decades because of its perceived inaccessibility, while the Bollywood phase in the 1990s that made it popular among diasporic audiences and expanded its broad market appeal reduced it to orientalist exoticization, making it an odd genre in world cinema. Generic use of the term "Bollywood" distanced the spectator of world cinema from Indian cinema, except for some exceptions that reached wider audiences.

Theories of Indian cinema, a complex, divergent, and dispersed discourse itself, are focused on understanding the aesthetics of mainstream cinema. There is no agreement among scholars on which aesthetic approach or tradition explains the construction of visuals and narrative of this cinema but it is possible to summarize some of their major precepts: the idea of looking, the very conception of what is seen on the screen; the importance of affects in encounters with the cinematic image; and the forms of storytelling and lively eclecticism of traditions.

Looking, frontality, and framing

The act of seeing is central to cinema; going to a theater involves an attempt to watch something on the screen, an effort of purpose. The act of *Darsana* (Sanskrit) in such an encounter involves seeing and looking, a "willful and tangible act" of exchange of sight, of a relationship (Lutgendorf, 2006). Here the viewer is in a reciprocal relationship with the image, entirely aware that what is seen on the screen also sees the viewer. The image has a field of authority that also situates the viewer, a relationship quite different from the perspective in the West that places a viewer in an isolated position to possess the image in the process of identification. *Darsana* is different from the notion of the gaze, which is not a reciprocal relationship. The notion of *Darsana* is commonplace in everyday life as in seeing deities or making an effort to see an important, revered public figure, including film stars.

The encounter of *Darsana* leads to an aesthetic of "frontality," positioning the object in an image for a sustained relationship with the viewer. When images are arranged frontally in relation to the audience, they solicit the viewer and allow for an exchange of looks between the screen and the audience, which is not commonly found in the Western cinematic grammar. It defines a different mode of address in cinema. Though the gesture of seeing by the image is present only vicariously, the animated incarnation of the image on the screen assumes a posture toward the viewer, materialized in a number of ways on the screen (Lutgendorf, 2006: 233). The actors face the camera, express emotions with their eyes, as if to acknowledge the gesture of being seen. A common feature of image construction in cinema, frontality is a signifying act, the appearance of which lingers,

Figures 5.14–5.16 Frontality from *Hum Aapke Hain Koun* (1994), where the frontal positioning of the image constructs a decorative *mise-en-scène* and invites an exchange of looks between the screen and the audience

assuming a communion of sights with the viewer. This also creates space in a cinematic frame where action is limited to 180 degrees, as in a theatrical proscenium.

In further examining the implications of this aesthetic, Vasudevan (2001) proposes that framing in cinema occurs in an iconic and tableau mode. Using the ideas of Roland

Barthes, he identifies iconic framing as fixing the meaning of the image by associating it with some context or creating a mythic dimension for that image, while tableau framing shows composition that gives "an illustrative summary" of a situation, embedded in the narrative (2001: 105). Both modes are presented in the 180-degree space in front of the camera, creating a spatial pause in the narrative. Contrasting this arrangement with the codes of continuity editing, Vasudevan observes that the viewer identifies with the specific relationships in tableau and framing, limiting them to universal reception as it happens in classical Hollywood films.

When Prasad takes up the dominant narrative form of the feudal family film, he suggests that the ingenuity of Hindi cinema was to transform a cultural form of *Darśana* into an authoritative presence on the screen that exercised symbolic dominance over the viewers (1998: 30). Viewers' domination by the power of the spectacle on the screen in which the aristocrats assumed authority suggested the ideological power of the aesthetic of Hindi cinema. The kind of power afforded to the Western viewer as a voyeur is replaced by the direct address of the feudal presence, explaining in part the power that films have on audiences. These modes of frontality and framing are very much present in mainstream films, even as they blend with the conventions of continuity editing.

Aesthetics of affect

One of the ways to understand the immense popularity of Hindi films is to suggest that as a popular art form, it borrows from the earlier traditions of the arts, particularly the great text of the Nātyaśāstra, a treatise on drama. In his essay "Is There an Indian Way of Filmmaking?" Philip Lutgendorf points out that the main presentational tenets of the Nātyaśāstra continued to be practiced in Sanskrit theater, then in the Parsi theater in nineteenth century and later in commercial film (2006: 235). The inclusion of songs and dances thus became integral to films, unlike in the West, where these elements are received either within generic norms of a musical or seen as an element that interrupts a narrative flow. Words and speech become important, as suggested by the popularity of "dialogs," unique rhetorical pieces of conversation in the script. The "rasa" theory of affect says that the performance on the screen is aimed at evoking an affective feeling in the viewer, a compendium of emotions and a response to these emotions savored in the context of the "rasa" theory. The experience of cinema occurs not merely on the visual level but also engages the senses of hearing, listening, and savoring the moment in which they are absorbed. Lutgendorf explains that the multiple shifts and turns observed in watching Hindi films, a mix of forms such as comedy, romance, and adventure, and rapid transitions in locales, are meant to provide a range of affective options to a viewer who seeks it from the experience of watching (2006: 238). Narratives move along to evoke affect and may appear disjointed and disruptive.

Forms of narrative/storytelling

As we discussed, the dominant Hindi cinema utilizes a disaggregative, disruptive narrative that proceeds in multiple directions, unlike the dominant narrative form in Hollywood that aims to maintain narrative coherence in its address. Its motifs and images appear recurrent, while its emphasis on family relations remains stable even through its transformative phases. Film scholars adapt multiple ways to explain this feature of narratives, often pointing to the grand epics of Hindu culture, the *Ramayana* and *Mahabharata*, as a cultural framework used by films for their narrative structures. Featuring a heterogeneity of plots and progressions, these epics are indeed great examples of intertextual trajectories, discontinuities, and multiple sub-narratives that characterize popular Indian cinema. The effect of encountering such structures may be distracting to a viewer outside the cultural context, but for viewers of Hindi cinema it is a common and expected feature of storytelling.

The risk in accepting the Hindi film narratives as continuous with the ancient, premodern epics is to assume that there is an unchanging cultural essence in all film narratives, untainted by modernity. Hindi film narrative accentuated by the aesthetics of frontality appears to belong to a pre-modern phase, thus returning the discourse to orientalist culture unable to accept modernity. Other approaches to the heterogeneous narrative structure offer a different view, more in tune with the reality of how film narrative has continued through its transformations. In a well-known analysis of *Andaz* (Mehboob Khan, 1949), Vasudevan demonstrates that Indian cinema had already moved into modernity by deploying the conventions of classical Hollywood narrative, along with frontal address. He argues that in the narratives of Indian cinema, both conventions are present, though not "systematically deployed" (2001: 106). Though the aesthetic conventions outlined here are still observed in Hindi films, the trajectory that Vasudevan observes in films of the 1950s has continued to a complex phase of maturity that assimilates and uses eclectic features from various sources. Amartya Sen (2005) offers an example of Satyajit Ray, for decades India's most well-known filmmaker, as a filmmaker who has achieved a synthesis of heterodox Indian traditions with the modernist premise to underscore the malleable, adaptive nature of cultural production in the country. The narrative forms of Indian cinema have also come from the storytelling traditions of *qissa* traditions of Sufi-Muslim culture and *dastan* traditions of Persian cultures. These forms too developed as multiple strands of narratives, growing on several levels, presenting heterogeneous forms of narrative to listeners. Increasing complexity in the trajectory of Indian cinema displays a challenging diversity of storytelling forms, offering a heuristically rich model with which to approach the study of Indian cinema.

Activity 5.1

Consult the UNESCO Institute for Statistics website (www.uis.unesco.org/culture/Pages/movie-statistics.aspx) to find out as much information as you can about the feature film production in India in the past year. Is India still the largest film producer? How does it compare to other industries? Then use Box Office Mojo or Box Office Guru to identify the top-grossing films produced in India last year. How do they compare in revenue with films released in previous years?

Activity 5.2

Watch a recent Bollywood film available on a streaming service or your local theater. What distinct features can you observe in the film? For example, how does the film depict family in relation to the family structures and values in your own environment? How does it use language, which languages are spoken, and is there a prevalent use of English? Does it use foreign locations?

Activity 5.3

Choose a popular Hindi mainstream film from before the Bollywood phase, such as *Shree 420* (Raj Kapoor, 1955), *Awaara* (Raj Kapoor, 1951), *Sholay* (Ramesh Sippy, 1975), *Deewar* (Yash Chopra, 1975), or *Pyaasa* (Guru Dutt, 1957). Compare it with a post-1990s Bollywood film, such as *Swades* (Ashutosh Gowariker, 2004), *Rang De Basanti* (Rakesh Omprakash Mehra, 2006), *Veer Zaara* (Yash Chopra, 2004), *3 Idiots* (Rajkumar Hirani, 2009), or *Devdas* (Sanjay Leela Bhansali, 2002). Compare and identify both stylistic and thematic features: the place of song and dance, choreography, the use of English language, and foreign locations.

Activity 5.4

Watch any two remakes that Bollywood has made of Hollywood films, plus the original versions: *Bang Bang* (2014) and *Knight and Day* (2010); *Sangharsh* (1999) and *The Silence of the Lambs* (1991); *We Are Family* (2010) and *Stepmom* (1998); *Partner* (2007) and *Hitch* (2005); *Kaante* (2002) and *Reservoir Dogs* (1992). What can you say about the nature of the adaptation? How do the protagonists and their stories compare? Can you identify different underlying values, assumptions, or cultural codes?

Activity 5.5

One of the most enduring examples of the transformation of Hindi popular cinema is the story of Devdas, which has been adapted and reinvented many times. The most prominent version, by Bimal Roy in 1955, was remade by Sanjay Leela Bhansali in 2002, and again by Anurag Kashyap in 2009 as *Dev.D*. Compare the most recent versions: *Devdas* (2002) and *Dev.D* (2009). How do the two films address differently their contemporary social realities? What transformations are depicted in regard to family ties, relationships, or sexuality? In what ways are the characters constructed differently? Can you identify in what ways *Dev.D* breaks the conventions of mainstream Hindi cinema?

Bibliography

Appadurai, Arjun. (1996). *Modernity at Large: Cultural Dimensions of Globalization*. Minneapolis, MN: University of Minnesota Press.

Bharucha, Rustom. (1994). "On the Border of Fascism: Manufacture of Consent in *Roja*," *Economic and Political Weekly* 29(23), pp. 1389–1395.

Bhaumik, Kaushik. (2006). "Consuming Bollywood in the Global Age: The Case of an 'Unfine' World Cinema." In Stephanie Dennison & Song Hwee Lim (eds), *Remapping World Cinema: Identity, Culture and Politics in Film*. London: Wallflower Press, pp. 188-198.

Chakravarthy, Venkatesh & M.S.S. Pandian. (1994). "More on *Roja*." *Economic and Political Weekly* 29(11), pp. 642–644.

Chute, David. (2013). "Film Review: *Dhoom 3*." *Variety* (December 21). Available at: http://variety. com/2013/film/reviews/film-review-dhoom-3-1200983530/ Accessed July 20, 2015.

Devdas, Vijay & Selvaraj Velayutham. (2012). "Cinema in Motion: Tracking Tamil Cinema's Assemblage." In Anjali Gera Roy & Chua Beng Huat (eds), *Travels of Bollywood Cinema: From Bombay to LA*. New Delhi: Oxford University Press, pp. 164–182.

Dudrah, Rajinder Kumar. (2002). "Vilayati Bollywood: Popular Hindi Cinema-Going and Diasporic South Asian Identity in Birmingham (UK)." *Javnost–The Public* 9(1), pp. 19–36.

Dudrah, Rajinder Kumar. (2010). "Haptic Urban Ethnoscapes: Representation, Diasporic Media and Urban Cultural Landscapes." *Journal of Media Practice* 11(1), pp. 31–46.

Dwyer, Rachel. (2006). *Filming the Gods: Religion and Indian Cinema*. New York, NY: Routledge.

Eleftheriotis, Dimitris & Dina Iordanova. (2006). "Introduction: Indian Cinema in the World." *South Asian Popular Culture* 4(2), pp. 79–82.

Fair, Laura. (2009). "Making Love in the Indian Ocean: Hindi Film, Zanzibari Audiences, and the Construction of Romance in the 1950s and 1960s." In Jennifer Cole & Lynn M. Thomas (eds), *Love in Africa*. Chicago, IL: University of Chicago Press, pp. 58–82.

Fair, Laura. (2010). "'They Stole the Show!': Indian Films in Coastal Tanzania, 1950s–1960s." *Journal of African Media Studies* 2(1), pp. 91–106.

Fuglesang, Minou. (1994). *Veils and Videos: Female Youth Culture on the Kenyan Coast*. Stockholm: Stockholm University.

Ganti, Tejaswini. (2012a). *Producing Bollywood: Inside the Contemporary Hindi Film Industry*. Durham, NC: Duke University Press.

Ganti, Tejaswini. (2012b). "No Longer a Frivolous Singing and Dancing Nation of Movie-Makers: The Hindi Film Industry and Its Quest for Global Distinction." *Visual Anthropology* 25, pp. 340–365.

Gillespie, Marie. (1989). "Technology and Tradition: Audio-visual Culture Among South Asian Families in West London." *Cultural Studies* 3(2), pp. 226–239.

Govil, Nitin. (2010). "Size Matters." *BioScope* 1(2), pp. 105–109.

Gurata, Ahmet. (2010). "'The Road to Vagrancy:' Translation and Reception of Indian Cinema in Turkey." *BioScope* 1(1), pp. 67–90.

Harris, Gardiner. (2014). "An Indian Appetizer, Subtly Spiced: 'The Lunchbox,' a Bollywood Anomaly, Comes to America." *New York Times* (February 21). Available at: www.nytimes.com/2014/02/23/ movies/the-lunchbox-a-bollywood-anomaly-comes-to-america.html?_r=0. Accessed July 1, 2015.

Iordanova, Dina, et al. (2006). "Indian Cinema's Global Reach: Historiography Through Testimonies." *South Asian Popular Culture* 4(2), pp. 113–140.

Kashyap, Anurag. (2013). "Short Films Will Redefine Indian Cinema: Interview." *Times of India* (June 7). Available at: http://timesofindia.indiatimes.com/entertainment/hindi/bollywood/news/Short-films-will-redefine-Indian-cinema-future-Anurag-Kashyap/articleshow/20456885.cms. Accessed June 15, 2015.

Kumar, Amitava. (2012). "Bullet Points from a Hit-Man." *Tehelka* (June 16). Available at: http://archive. tehelka.com/story_main53.asp?filename=hub160612AMITAVA.asp. Accessed June 15, 2015.

Larkin, Brian. (2004). "Bandiri Music, Globalization, and Urban Experience in Nigeria." *Social Text* 22(4), pp. 91–112.

Larkin, Brian. (2008). "Itineraries of Indian Cinema: African Videos, Bollywood, and Global Media." In Rajinder Dudrah & Jigna Desai (eds), *The Bollywood Reader*. Maidenhead: Open University Press, pp. 216–229.

Larkin, Brian. (2012). "Bollywood Comes to Nigeria." *Samar: South Asian Magazine for Action and Reflection* 8. Available at: www.samarmagazine.org/archive/articles/21. Accessed June 12, 2015.

Lutgendorf, Philip. (2006). "Is There an Indian Way of Filmmaking?" *International Journal of Hindu Studies* 10(3), pp. 227–256.

Mazumdar, Ranjani. (2007). *Bombay Cinema: An Archive of the City*. Minneapolis, MN: University of Minnesota Press.

Mehta, Monika. (2005). "Globalizing Bombay Cinema: Reproducing the Indian State and Family." *Cultural Dynamics* 17(2), pp. 135–154.

Mishra, Vijay. (2002). *Bombay Cinema: Temples of Desire*. New York, NY: Routledge.

Mishra, Vijay. (2006). *Bollywood Cinema: A Critical Genealogy*. Wellington: Victoria University of Wellington, Asian Studies Institute.

Mitra, Ananda. (2008). "Bollyweb: Search for Bollywood on the Web and See What Happens!" In Anandam P. Kavoori & Aswin Punathambekar (eds), *Global Bollywood*. New York, NY: New York University Press, pp. 268–281.

Nagib, Lúcia (ed). (2011). *World Cinema and Ethics of Realism*. New York, NY: Continuum International Publishing Group.

Niranjana, Tejaswini. (1994). "Integrating Whose Nation." *Economic and Political Weekly* 29(3), pp. 79–82.

Prasad, Madhava. (1998). *Ideology of Hindi Film: A Historical Construction*. Delhi: Oxford University Press.

Prasad, Madhava. (2003). "This Thing Called Bollywood." *India-Seminar* (May 3). Available at: www.india-seminar.com/2003/525/525%20madhava%20prasad.htm. Accessed June 12, 2015.

Prasad, Madhava. (2008). "Surviving Bollywood." In Anandam P. Kavoori & Aswin Punathambekar (eds), *Global Bollywood*. New York, NY: New York University Press, pp. 41–51.

Press Trust of India. (2007). "Calling Us Bollywood is Derogatory: Naseeruddin, Om." *News 18* (July 3). Available at: http://ibnlive.in.com/news/calling-us-bollywood-is-derogatory-naseeruddin-om/43941-8.html. Accessed June 11, 2015.

Raghavendra, M.K. (2012). "Mainstream Hindi Cinema and Brand Bollywood: The Transformation of a Cultural Artifact." In Anjali Gera Roy (ed), *The Magic of Bollywood: At Home and Abroad*. Los Angeles, CA: Sage Publications.

Raghavendra, M.K. (2014). *The Politics of Hindi Cinema in the New Millennium: Bollywood and the Anglophone Indian Nation*. New York, NY: Oxford University Press.

Rajadhyaksha, Ashish. (2003). "The 'Bollywoodization' of the Indian Cinema: Cultural Nationalism in a Global Arena." *Inter-Asia Cultural Studies* 4(1), pp. 25–39.

Rajagopalan, Sudha. (2009). *Indian Films in Soviet Cinemas: The Culture of Movie-going After Stalin*. Bloomington, IN: Indiana University Press.

Sen, Amartya. (2005). *The Argumentative Indian: Writings on Indian History, Culture, and Identity*. New York, NY: Farrar, Strauss and Giroux.

Shattuck, Kathryn. (2012). "Bollywood Hero, American Everyman." *New York Times* (February 24). Available at: www.nytimes.com/2012/02/26/movies/irrfan-khan-bollywood-hero-american-everyman.html?pagewanted=all. Accessed June 5, 2015.

Therwath, Ingrid. (2010). "'Shining Indians': Diaspora and Exemplarity in Bollywood." *South Asia Multidisciplinary Academic Journal* 4. Available at: http://samaj.revues.org/3000. Accessed May 1, 2015

Tripathy, Ratnakar. (2007). "Bhojpuri Cinema: Regional Resonances in the Hindi Heartland." *South Asian Popular Culture* 5(2), pp. 145–165.

Vasudevan, Ravi. (2000). "The Cultural Politics of Address in a 'Transitional' Cinema." In Christine Gledhill & Linda Williams (eds), *Reinventing Film Studies*. Oxford: Oxford University Press, pp. 98–129.

Vasudevan, Ravi. (2001). "Shifting Codes, Dissolving Identities: The Hindi Social Film of the 1950s as Popular Culture." In Ravi Vasudevan (ed), *Making Meaning in Indian Cinema*. New Delhi: Oxford University Press, pp. 99–121.

Vasudevan, Ravi. (2011). *The Melodramatic Public: Film Form and Spectatorship in Indian Cinema*. New York, NY: Palgrave MacMillan.

Vasudevan, Ravi. (2013). "Notes on the Contemporary Film Experience: Bollywood, Genre Diversity, and Video Circuits." In Ravi Sundaram (ed), *No Limits: Media Studies from India*. New Delhi: Oxford University Press, pp. 199-223.

Velayutham, Selvaraj (ed). (2008). *Tamil Cinema: The Cultural Politics of India's Other Film Industry*. New York, NY: Routledge.

Virdi Jyotika. (2003). *The Cinematic Imagination: Indian Film as Social History*. New Brunswick, NJ: Rutgers University Press.

6   African cinema and Nollywood

Nollywood, the video-film industry from Nigeria, emerged on the scene in the early 1990s, when film industries around the world were going through major transformations of economy, production, and ideology. Since then, a spate of newspaper and magazine articles, photo essays, and documentaries have come out on this youngest film industry in world cinema, which express mostly curiosity about this film phenomenon defined by low budgets, spontaneous and improvised acting, poor production quality, and unfathomable production rates. For film studies Nollywood is an oddity, rather anachronistic in its emergence. For the press, it remains a novelty. As geopolitical and economic transformations were reshaping other cinemas, new technologies were redefining filmmaking and viewing, and the idea of national cinema was thrown into question, Nollywood's unique form of production, distribution, and appeal pushed for a reassessment of these transformations and concepts in significant ways. Nearly two-and-a-half decades later, it is necessary to realign our compass and redraw the world cinema map to include this distinct industry. Current models based on proposed canons of transnationalism, festival cinema, and global art cinema cannot accommodate Nollywood. It lacks the glamour, visibility, and gravitas of current models. It does not have recognized auteurs and it does not boast a track record of film history and archives for its legitimation. Nevertheless, Nollywood has a life of its own, away from Western film studies, claiming substantial scholarship with vigorous debates on its place in African cinema, its continually refined production practices, and its undeniable presence in the discourse on world cinema (Haynes, 2010).

Nollywood's profligacy puts it on par with the most powerful centers of production around the world. It is second only to Bollywood, with Hollywood trailing behind it. The film industry is already one of the largest components of Nigeria's economy, which in turn has become the largest among all African countries (Friedman, 2014). Growing in strength in terms of employment, popularity, and visibility, video-films from Nigeria have become one of its largest exports. While international film festivals have largely ignored the phenomenon that presents an uneasy fit with the usual festival fare, this situation is also changing as we speak. In its recent 2016 edition, the Toronto International Film Festival focused on Lagos in its "City to City Spotlight" program, in what is to date the highest-profile festival exposure of the industry (TIFF, 2016).

To pay attention to Nollywood is to consider the nexus of the art cinema from Francophone countries, popular in the Western academy and film festivals, and the video-films from Nigeria, popular in the country and the continent. Nollywood challenges the conception of world cinema as a totalitarian enterprise (Hollywood), as a selective mode (art house and film festivals), and as a contrarian model (a militant conception of Third Cinema).

Its invisibility in the broader landscape of film studies, its immense popularity among African and diasporic audiences, and its adoption of technological formats at the moment of its insertion in the emergent forms of cinema present both significant challenges and valuable insights to the theoretical conception of world cinema.

Nollywood: what is in a name?

In his essay "'Nollywood': What's in a Name?" Jonathan Haynes (2007) admits that despite a host of connotations associated with the name "Nollywood," it is here to stay. It is a preferred term for journalists who revel in its currency, and has been embraced by the industry and scholars. For practitioners vying to acquire Hollywood's visibility and glamour, it is an aspirational term akin to Bollywood, shaped into a marketing brand in the era of globalization. Nevertheless, it is hardly a term everyone agrees on, not least because its name masks its internal diversity. *Nollywood* refers to three broad industries, characterized by their ethnicities and languages. Kannywood, of the Hausa culture in the north and based in the city of Kano, has its own industry developed in deep affiliation with Islam. It is distinct from the two industries in the south around Lagos: Yoruba (Yoruwood) and Igbo (Igbowood) video-films, which are both inflected by different traditions. Other emergent and smaller industries based on ethnicities and languages also belong to the industry: Edowood (Edo films), Urhobowood (Urhobo films), and Wafiwood (Warri pidgin-English films).

Nollywood's identity is deeply associated with the city of Lagos, its main production center. A city transitioning to modernity, with a considerable history of colonialism and dictatorships, Lagos is a center of commerce, a hub of an informal economy, and an intersection of the complex class relations animating it. The contradictions, dramas, and diversity of the city are embedded in the video-films of Nollywood; the city writes itself onto the films as much as the films mediate their relationship to it. In many ways, Nollywood is much like Lagos, the "postcolonial incredible," a composite image of contrasts and disorders that holds its distinct identity and defies any externally imposed logic (Adesokan, 2011a). In the north, the city of Kano in the Hausa culture was equally central to the development and identity of this cinema. Placed in the Islamic culture's codes of morality and ethos, cinema brought by the colonialists grew in tandem with the cultural topography of Kano, its contrasts deeply woven into the fabric of cinema. Nollywood's identity is closely tied to the modernist evolution of these cities.

By adapting the morpheme, Nollywood aligns itself with Hollywood and Bollywood in the same moment of the neoliberal economies of globalization. Alessandro Jedlowski (2011) shows how the genealogy of Nollywood begins with a nod to its aspirational posture, but quickly asserts the difference from the two other giant industries. For him, the features that construct the brand of Nollywood include the insistently small-screen production, deploying video-film to project the country's movement from tradition, corruption, poverty, and class divisions to modernity, and its increasing regional and global profile. If there is a process of "Nollywoodization" of the Nigerian video industry, it is characterized by contradictory forces. Its aspirations to compete as a global brand with broader geographic reach within Africa and the world stand side by side with Nollywood's struggles to overcome colonial vestiges and the grip of superstition, a contradiction that is only exacerbated by Nollywood's increasingly global profile.

Despite its widely accepted use, the term "Nollywood" remains pejorative in many circles. An industry based on videos produced on shoestring budgets, circulated on pirated media, and based on an imitative posture invites scorn from intellectual circles within Africa and abroad. Films focused on occult, voodoo practices and supernatural motifs are seen as marks of low, pre-modern culture. The poor quality and unique style of images does not invite easy comparison to the kind of cinema that has developed elsewhere, including in some parts of Africa. For many African countries, Nollywood represents a cultural regression. Its video format and raw aesthetics prompt passionate attacks from the country's artists, who deem the lowbrow culture produced by a cottage industry, however prolific, as undeserving of space in the intellectual discourse. Ola Balogun, a pioneering Nigerian filmmaker who worked with celluloid before the arrival of video-films, describes the industry as a debased art form with "childishly conceived, amateur-ishly written, and thoroughly predictable" productions (quoted in Okome, 2010: 34). In his keynote address to the Panafrican Film and Television Festival of Ouagadougou (FESPACO) in 2013, Nigerian Nobel Prize winner Wole Soyinka criticized Nollywood for its exaggerative quality, superficiality, and lack of reflective capacity (Soyinka, 2013). Video artist Zina Saro-Wiwa (2008) defends the industry vigorously, but admits that Nollywood's quality is a "scandal for a nation that has produced some of the world's greatest writers and whose oral culture is so rich." Despite criticism, Nollywood carves its own paradigm, detached from the dominant perceptions of acceptability. Its numerical strength invites attention, but its unique forms and cultures challenge the canonical conceptions of African and world cinema.

Away from the binaries of high and low cultures, scholars of Nollywood cinema approach video-films as the country's most popular expression, as genuine products of the popular imagination. For Manthia Diawara, Nollywood is a "repository of new social imaginary in Africa, a new purveyor of habitus . . . and a mirror of our fantasies of escape from economic and social problems" (2010: 177). Onookome Okome calls it a "vernacular of the poor" that "draws its own map of social and cultural programs and narrative possibilities" (2010: 37). Jonathan Haynes argues that "videos are to be read as responses to the anxieties of contemporary West African life" (2010: 107). Aboubakar Sanogo, introducing a special In Focus section of *Cinema Journal* on African cinema and Nollywood, asserts that studying African cinema and Nollywood underscores the "radical contingency of the legacy" of film and media studies by "displacing the gaze" on the disciplinary objects to broaden the terrain of inquiry (2015: 119). They all point to a broadening consensus that Nollywood cannot and should not be ignored, or merely treated as a curious yet not-worthy-of-study phenomenon.

African cinema and Nollywood

Nollywood's transition to world cinema is negotiated through its relationship with African cinema, which itself remains an elusive ideological object in film studies. For decades, the continent has served as a generic territory of exotic locales to film romantic or historical Hollywood films. The practice is pervasive, from the early Tarzan films and Bob Hope comic adventures to the more recent *Out of Africa* (1985), *Blood Diamond* (2006), and *The Last King of Scotland* (2006). What we dubiously consider *African films* are films made by notable directors whose work is distributed at film festivals and in metropolitan art house cinemas. The very notion of "African cinema" has preoccupied scholars against the prevailing perception that African cinema does not have an identity of its own. Since most films that circulate and gain recognition at film festivals or elsewhere are Francophone films, the issue puts more pressure on the problem of understanding the video-film industry of Nollywood, much of which is in English and local languages, as well as the emergent practices of video-films in Ghana, Senegal, Cameroon, and Morocco.

In his analysis of new African cinema, Diawara (2010) discusses an important transition in African cinema in the 1980s. Since Ousmane Sembène's *Black Girl* (1966) and other works influenced by him (Sarah Maldoror's *Sambizanga*, 1972; or Souleymane Cissé's *Baara/Work*, 1978) that formed the backbone of the militant Third Cinema movement, we have witnessed a division of African cinema into two different strands: experimental or "*art et essai* cinema" on the one hand, and popular cinema on the other (Diawara, 2010: 138). The art cinema new wave caters to festivals and audiences outside Africa. It is largely supported by French capital and showcased at European film festivals and the FESPACO. Distant from the militancy of the Third Cinema movement, these films (for example, Souleymane Cissé's *Yeelen/Brightness*, 1987, or Idrissa Ouedraogo's *Tilaï/The Law*, 1990) are less political, more contemplative of local traditions, experiment with film language, and are characterized by beautiful images, carefully composed frames, and good editing. They come to form a school of their own, charting new paths for African filmmakers who gain international visibility. This new wave cinema, however, is caught in a bind. As a cinema that is sustained and showcased solely by film festivals and their capital (the Hubert Bals Fund of the International Film Festival of Rotterdam, for example, is known for its commitment to African filmmakers), its programming under the homogenizing umbrella of African cinema tends to mask the diversity of its films, thus producing a ceaseless search and questioning of the phenomenon of "authenticity" in the cinema of the African continent (Diawara, 1992: 35–50).

The populist strand of cinema, on the other hand, which includes genre cinema such as Westerns, comedy, and melodrama, "concerns itself with winning back African spectators from Hollywood movies" (Diawara, 2010: 138). Directors of African popular cinema such as Mansour Sora Wade, Moussa Sène Absa, Zola Maseko, and Boubakar Diallo appeal to spectators with narrative films that "deploy African ingredients and spices within old genres" (Diawara, 2010: 143). Nollywood video-films constitute an important part of African popular cinema, and their sheer expanse makes it increasingly difficult to ignore their presence and impact, even for festivals that look down on the phenomenon due to its lack of high aesthetic qualities.

The FESPACO's policy of accepting only 35 mm films blocked Nollywood for years until the policy was revised in 2015 (Obenson, 2013). Occasionally accorded space at film festivals under the guise of organized workshops related to African film industries, Nollywood is relegated to the "workshopping culture" that often includes screening one or two introductory documentaries on Nollywood, accompanied by a panel of academics and filmmakers who discuss the industry (Haynes, 2011: 79). If a Nollywood director is included, well-known names such as Tunde Kelani or Kunle Afolayan are often preferred, listed as "video-makers" to mark their difference from Francophone "filmmakers" such as Idrissa Ouedraogo. These conundrums are not limited to Nollywood's place in African cinema, but are aimed at the heart of African cinema's identity as an art-based, vanguard cinema admired abroad yet received at home as "calabash films" (anthropological stereotypes of Africa) or "embassy films" (since they are mostly screened in foreign embassies on the continent).

The gap between African filmmakers' popularity abroad and domestic preferences is glaring. Internationally-renowned African films find little appeal with African audiences who (when it comes to foreign films) prefer to watch Hollywood films, Indian cinema, and popular Asian cinema. Cities in Africa made the construction of movie theaters part of their push toward modernity, but were it not for the FESPACO and other film festivals emerging in metropolitan areas, it would be nearly impossible to find works of noted African directors in these cities. In sharp contrast, video-films are extremely popular in Nigeria as well as many African countries. South Africa's Africa Magic satellite service has a channel for each of Nollywood's components—Yoruba, Hausa, and Igbo films. Nollywood films dominate the service and its awards event, the Africa Viewers' Choice Awards. Among diasporic audiences, video-films have been distributed in stores across the US and UK, a practice reminiscent of the circulation of Indian cinema abroad, although their reach is outside of statistical data.

Nollywood's appeal to African audiences far exceeds the appeal of Africa's own film-makers. Nollywood's popularity in the continent has created "pan-Africanism" that has eluded the FESPACO for decades. As John C. McCall (2007) stresses, this common identity cannot be simply presumed because of the wide popularity of video-film products, and it raises for the first time a condition of common cinematic experience for African viewers. Measured against Francophone cinema, it is important to see how Nollywood's popular appeal and its strength in creating an alternative discourse of images and production realign the conception of pan-African identity. It is also a question of considering popular cinema's place on the map of world cinema, determining its relationship to its broader system.

Understanding Nollywood

Nigeria's transition from a poor participant in African cinema to a leading video-film producer is a story of the failure of infrastructural and state support for filmmaking, and the triumph of the entrepreneurial, commodity-driven economy galvanized by filmmakers. Before the implementation of the Structural Adjustment Program (SAP), the small film industry in Nigeria was, along with Ghana, a leader in Anglophone production. Until the mid-1980s, filmmakers in Nollywood produced films in 16 mm and reversal film format, with partial, erratic support from the state and with some American funding. Resources that were already scarce dwindled completely with the SAP imposed by the International Monetary Fund (IMF) on Nigeria and several African countries in 1986. According to Gary Kafer (2014), "While the intent was to liquidate the country's external debts and introduce the 'developing nation' into the global market economy, the SAP's neoliberal strategies brought about a new era of neocolonialism." Devaluing the Nigerian currency Naira and privatizing state-owned enterprises, the SAP negatively impacted vulnerable social groups and intensified a serious decline in the economy.

Other factors converged in the period of the SAP imposition that all provided impetus for the emerging video-film industry in the 1990s. These factors include the large number of personnel trained in and working for the Nigerian Television Authority looking for employment in the aftermath of cuts, the widespread availability of inexpensive VCR technology, the strengthening of an already rampant economy of foreign film piracy on the streets of Lagos, withering state support, and the oil economy that created a wide economic rift between classes. Nollywood's moment of emergence is commonly traced to Kenneth Nnebue, a director influenced by the Yoruba theater who was also an electronic equipment dealer in Lagos. In 1992, he co-wrote and produced a video-film called *Living in Bondage* in the Igbo language with English subtitles. This tale of a man's sacrifice of his wife to a cult to get rich, only to be haunted by her ghost, was a huge hit with viewers at home and announced the beginning of the boom of inexpensive video-films made as rapidly as they were sold and watched by millions.

In tracing the emergence of Nollywood in the early 1990s, it is important to note the period preceding it, specifically the Yoruba traveling theater's connections to cinema, seen as the "most auspicious single factor in the evolution of the indigenous cinema in Nigeria" (Adesanya, 2000: 38). The first film in this tradition, *Ajani Ogun* (1976) by Ola Balogun, was a major theatrical success, building tracks between theater and cinema and fostering collaboration between the two media. Blending traditional forms with the issues of the contemporary moment in Nigeria, Yoruba cinema raised the hopes of many, including Wole Soyinka (1979), for whom a Yoruba theater-cinema confluence was a bright spot in the future of national culture because it did not yield to the aesthetic principles of the West, yet showed alternative ways of gaining appeal beyond the arts of intellectuals. Yoruba theater artists began making video-films in the late 1980s, merging the two into what would become a popular art of video-films. Like popular arts in Africa that were "syncretic, concerned with social change and associated with the masses," video-film adapted these goals to produce a popular form that was simultaneously entertaining, performative, and engaging (Barber, 1987: 23).

Production of video-films

The arrival of video-films in the markets of Lagos disproved the notion that once, "Africans consumed cinema but could not make it" (Haynes, 2011: 68). Films are made with a video camera, first using videotape, then mini-DV, and later digital formats. Minimal lighting kits are used for location shooting, with domestic interiors, Lagos neighborhoods, and rural areas as favored locales.

There is little control over sound recording and environmental noise often interrupts filming. Most of the shooting takes place in continuous, often minimal sessions that last over a few days or weeks. Budgets are small, averaging $25,000 and rarely exceeding $50,000. Scripts are weak and often improvised and all sorts of efforts are made to keep costs down.

Figure 6.1 On the set of a Nollywood production. Source: *Nollywood*, Al Jazeera World

The heritage of theatrical tradition leaves its mark on acting and the actors' careers. In Nollywood's early days, it was important to sign known actors in order to increase the chances of attracting investments for future projects. A sense of community is forged among actors, and recently a star system has developed that assumes transnational dimensions (Tsika, 2015).

In their flourishing production, video-films utilize talents, techniques, and content from a range of media to create genuinely different films. Improvisation emerges as a characteristic of video-films, from scriptwriting and acting to editing. If borrowing from all sorts of "foreign" sources has been a hallmark of African popular culture, Nigerian video-films

a

b

Figures 6.2a & 6.2b A Nollywood market with Nollywood DVDs. Source: *Nollywood*, Al Jazeera World

too borrow elements from any source possible, including Hollywood, Western television, and Asian and Indian cinemas. Once borrowed, these elements are absorbed into local contexts. Scholars frequently refer to the idea of "bricolage" in this context, situating Nollywood films as prime examples of appropriation, modification, and adaptation of cultures and cinemas around them (Barber, 1987: 23). The spectator of Nollywood films, despite regional diversity, is positioned to navigate a culture of hybrid products and thus, the global exchange of images.

Films are edited on home-video equipment, as no major editing facilities exist. Videotapes and video compact discs (VCDs) dominated the industry in the 1990s, but these were quickly converted to DVD formats. Copies of video-films flood the marketplace, making piracy an unavoidable aspect of the industry.

Broadcast television cuts into the profits of DVDs, while also disseminating the name of the director. Igbo businessmen control the trade and finance of the video-films. Many directors launch their own productions, hoping they will be able to attract finance for their next productions. Video-film production coincided with computers and other digital technologies. Since there are no large companies controlling the production and dissemination of films, a vast "visual vernacular" of posters, photography, and other images has become commonplace all over the country and the region (Larkin, 2008: 174). Much like Hollywood, Bollywood, and Asian cinema a culture of glamour has emerged around Nollywood, with images, publications, websites, and award ceremonies making up a sizeable popular culture surrounding the industry.

Spectatorship

Prodigiously produced video-films have led to unique viewing practices in the country that have transformed gender and social roles in the newly formed public sphere. In his extensive history of cinema-going practices in Nigeria, Brian Larkin notes that cinema theaters remapped the sociality of cultural space, blending the material presence of cinema (its architecture, images, and sounds) with the "immateriality" of experiences. Watching was not merely an activity of passive spectatorship or one act of consumption among many; it was a sensual activity charged with a moral dimension that led to transformations in the social relations of gender, class, and individuality (Larkin, 2002: 322). This affective, moral economy of cinema was reconfigured once again with the arrival of video-films. On the one hand, the influence of theater traditions remains strong and theatrical releases still play a role. For filmmakers in the Yoruba tradition, theatrical exhibition means continuing their performative tradition of presenting arts to the community. Opening films in theaters before releasing them on the video-film format has the twin effect of reducing piracy in the first weeks and collecting revenues while the video-films are new. The practice of theatrical release continues in the northern Hausa culture where producers arrange screenings in cinema halls across the region, and where the tradition of drama clubs and theaters prove beneficial for the circulation of video-films. In the north, as well as in other rural areas of Nigeria (and elsewhere in Africa), viewers watch films in traveling theaters, known as *majigi* (magic), a leftover from the colonial era.

Besides theaters, new public spaces have emerged in Lagos and other parts of Igbo and Yoruba cultures, constituted through what is termed "street audiences" (Okome, 2007a: 6). As video-films are screened on street corners and in video parlors, viewers gather around to watch them.

a

b

Figures 6.3a & 6.3b Among the unique viewing practices that Nollywood has given rise to are "street audiences," with viewers gathering on city street corners to watch films. Source: *Nollywood Babylon* (2008), Ben Addelman and Samir Mallal, DVD still

They stand at street corners and extemporaneous, informal spaces, recreating the absorption of cultural forms rooted in popular culture traditions but redeployed in urban terrain. These spaces designate fluid traffic, as viewers absorb parts of the video, conduct a conversation, and move on to other spaces in the city. Okome observes that these street-corner publics are becoming integral to the visual topography of the city, particularly in the evening hours when traffic is more intense. Another common viewing space, video parlors, simple settings with some chairs and a television set, are located in small houses or buildings. Such spaces reinsert video-films into once-popular forms of performance and theater and also align with the larger sites of Nollywood circulation.

Mostly, however, video-film viewing takes place in the domestic environment. The space of the home is so central to the aesthetic of video-films that it becomes a key setting for its dramas, creating a realm of identification for the viewers. Home viewing offers security in socially turbulent times, as images create an environment of safety and entertainment at the same time. For women and children home is a particularly comforting and secure zone for watching films. This practice opens a domestic living space to the outside world, and enables participation from a distance. In a culture that allows women only limited and strictly circumscribed mobility, domestic viewing forms a space of particular significance. In the northern Islamic Hausa culture, where religious prohibition of images creates a negative conception for cinema, home viewing, particularly for women (who are not allowed to watch films in public), offers safe spaces to encounter an image culture. Thus, watching cinema at home is not merely a matter of entertainment but also of acquiring a distinct moral freedom and position (Larkin, 2008: 225). Moreover, this encounter with images in a domestic space has much wider implications for women's public expressions and subjectivity, as they adapt and appropriate the films' fashions, gestures, and images into their own presence in the public sphere.

Distribution on a local level and the wide dissemination of images to be consumed on television sets is the most distinctive feature of Nollywood, producing a unique kind of spectatorship that in turn has shaped the structure of Nollywood narratives. Adejunmobi (2015a) suggests that the conditions of television viewing, defined by interruptions and an episodic and fragmented nature, existing in a continuous, prolonged flow, significantly affect the narrative structure of video-films and signify a "televisual turn" of African film. Video-films such as Kenneth Nnebue's *Glamour Girls* (1994) are made of episodic narratives, integrating the practice of interrupted viewings into their narrative strategy. Video-films in Nollywood display a penchant for producing sequels, creating narrative continuity of a single story over several episodes. As VCDs and DVDs of films broadcast on television immediately flood the market, they allow spectators to remain immersed in a familiar narrative universe, and in the process create their own "publics," groups of spectators who share this viewing experience. Adejunmobi's thesis casts light on video-films not merely as a habit of watching films but also as a form of sociality, generating unique forms of viewing to suit the structures of everyday lives. Thus, Nollywood's revolution is not merely in adapting video-films as an alternative form of production, but also in shaping emergent forms of spectatorship in world cinema.

In the midst of the widespread dissemination of video-films, it should be noted that Nigerians also have an appetite for foreign films. In Hausa culture, Indian cinema is as pervasive as Nollywood. In the Yoruba and Igbo cultures in the south, Hollywood and Asian films add to the images available through an informal, pirate economy. As cities like Lagos continue to grow and the Nigerian state adopts the neoliberal private economy, shopping centers and multiplexes provide new venues for watching films, with very different social and cultural implications than home viewing. Television is part of the formal economy, a reminder of state-level institutions that propagate state vision, while the video industry works outside the realm of the state and its institutions. State control exists through the process of censorship (the Nigeria Film and Video Censors Board, or NFVCB) but as Paul Ugor (2007) argues, there is an internal dynamic in the industry shaped by market forces. Watching video-films as a spontaneous, informal, and private activity is not so much positioned against the state as it presents a different stage of media development that coincides with the vast changes in the global economy. Video-films connect the local and the global outside of the national, an entirely unique configuration in comparison to other cinema industries around the world.

Ethnicity and languages

A country of 150 million, Nigeria is the most populous country in Africa. It has two religions: Christianity with increasing Pentecostal influence in the south, and Islam in the north. With 250 local languages and diverse ethnicities, Nigeria is the most diverse linguistic place on the continent. Most video-film production is organized around ethnicities—Yoruba, Hausa, and Igbo—and produced in languages such as Edo, Urhobo, Itsekeri, Efik, and Nupe, among others (Haynes & Okome, 1998). One of the main features of the constellation of ethnic cinemas in Nollywood is that it takes over the function of state institutions, making production horizontal and its structures informal.

Each of these ethnic strands is embedded in specific cultural traditions even as they all function as part of the country's popular culture. The most prolific and dominant are Yoruba films from the south, generally addressed to Yoruba audiences. Their deep connection and traditional folk format make the narratives didactic and pedagogical, with an emphasis on oral forms. Their melodramas are steeped in traditional spirituality, invocations of ghosts, and other spiritual phenomena. Narratives in Hausa video-films have three predominant features: romance, Islam-influenced values and situations, and song-and-dance sequences. Dramatic forms dominate Igbo films and involve domestic intrigue, magic, deities, and spirits, with stories that address conflicts between the community and the individual, traditional and urban life, the occult, and modernity. Films are set in Lagos, and often use English or pidgin English. The Yoruba and Hausa video industries are the strongest in their reach and ethnic imprint while the Igbo and other industries are smaller in comparison. The differences in themes and narrative forms are strikingly clear on one level, even as they address similar issues faced by Nigerians. Those differences tend to be the sharpest between the northern Hausa culture and the southern Yoruba and Igbo cultures, in part because of their different histories and religious beliefs. Hausa viewers in the north, with their Islamic identity and affinity for Indian films, find little appeal in the video-films from the south, driven by a Christian ethos and different ethnic histories (Adamu, 2007: 87).

Differences in ethnicities embedded in video-films are further complicated by the use of specific languages, including English. Yoruba video-films are rarely addressed to non-Yoruba speakers and the same can be said about Hausa in the north. Both ethnicities also spread outside Nigeria in West Africa, which helps their dissemination. Igbo businessmen recognized the market appeal of English-language production and quickly adapted to making films in English, rapidly increasing the pace of English-language film production (Adejunmobi, 2004: 104). English-language films travel outside the country to the diaspora through streaming services in the West. Considerable efforts are being made to subtitle these films, while to some extent dubbing continues in part of the industry (Hamilton & Daramola, 2012). Since the Yoruba and Hausa languages are shared with some countries in Africa, films still travel in their original languages, but dubbing and subtitling in French is quite prevalent in order to facilitate circulation in Francophone African countries. Françoise Ugochukwu (2013) reports that in Cameroon and Gabon, Nigerian video-films are dubbed in French and distributed as "African movies." The effort also gets considerable support from the French government, and Paris now holds an annual Nollywood film festival. Linguistic diversity in the films, Nigerians' desire to take their films abroad, and ethnic divisions in the industry complicate the picture of film production and dissemination. What is certain is that for an informal industry, Nollywood grows with a steady pace and with increasing sophistication in techniques and production values.

Postcolony and the spectral

Nollywood is a product of a complex dialectic between external and internal forces—the history of colonialism, the global economy, local arts traditions, religious diversity, economic and social conditions—the context of which provides useful pathways to understand the particularity of Nollywood's aesthetics, narrative forms, and its popularity in the continent. To open up a historical, political, and theoretical context for Africa, Cameroonian scholar Achille Mbembe (2001) proposes a framework of "postcolony" that radically revises the traditional understanding of postcolonial subjectivity in Africa. Mindful of the persistent alterity that marks the Western discourse on Africa, and questioning its implications for postcolonial identity politics and "third worldism" that relegate the region to a marginal position of difference, the notion of postcolony examines Africa from within its own crucible. Africa, Mbembe says, is characterized by multiple, non-convergent, non-linear trajectories, all of which make up the complexity of its political, cultural, and lived experience (2001: 15–16). With neocolonial struggles and the negation of its subjectivity internalized, Africa develops a set of institutions, political machinery, regimes of violence, material practices, signs, figures, and visual imagery, structuring a new common sense that gives some internal coherence to otherwise "chaotically pluralistic" societies (Mbembe, 2001: 16). In the postcolony, the powers and institutions produce the "banality of power," the grotesque, and the obscene through corruption, violence, scarcity, hideous displays of wealth, and exercise of banal forms of repression (Mbembe, 1992: 4). While the grotesque in Mikhail Bakhtin's works is the means of resistance and parody of power, in Mbembe's formulation the perspective is shifted; the functions of resistance and critique are internalized in the state and its authority figures, which use the grotesque and the obscene to extend their power. Once these impulses are domesticated, the "popular culture borrows the ideological repertoire of officialdom," and the official world mimics popular vulgarity in its procedures and practices (Mbembe, 1992: 10). The reversal of the position of resistance and domination creates a society in which there are no dominant and dominated but a perverse energy in the shared discourse of power between the plebian society and the powerful. The dualism between the powerful and the powerless is thus replaced with the shared aesthetics of power that govern the subjectivities of both.

Though by the 1980s colonial powers had left Africa, a new global power was unleashed on the continent in the form of the SAP by the IMF and the World Bank, this time in the form of economic disruption and realignments. The promises and devastation caused by the reforms imposed by a neoliberal economy collided with the realities of postcolony all over Africa. The violence of structural reforms, the wide rift in the population's poverty, and the onslaught of the global market and capital created dislocations and discontinuities in African societies. In Comaroff and Comaroff's view, the confluence of these factors created "occult economies" in the region, a series of practices energized by the magical and inscrutable mechanisms of economic exchanges, which replaced realistic, material structures (1999: 28). The occult and magical dimension of these practices, "the spectral," aligned with the materiality that occupied people's everyday life. The forces at work—excessive deregulation, the rise of the market as the master terrain for gauging and building wealth, the invisibility of capital's flows—met an economy of casinos, pyramid schemes, gambling, and similar financial scams. One of the most notorious examples were the so-called "Nigerian 419" email scams, where the scammers offer large amounts of money in exchange for helping them transfer wealth "trapped" in central banks due to war or government restrictions. Occult economies include a visual culture of spectral attractions in the market of commodities on television, film, advertising, and other media. Satanic practices, the rise of religious iconography and narratives, tourism of zombie and monster sites, and television shows on sorcery and witchcraft are all part of occult economies, operational through the media and visual culture technologies. Once marginal or part of the disappearing traditions, these practices successfully coopted the technologies and networks of neoliberal economies. They define the social and cultural discourse of power while also shaping the broader aesthetic framework in which video-films develop.

Comaroff and Comaroff's extensive thesis on the occult economy explains how magical narratives and imagery offer imagined solutions and reconciliations in times of uncertainty and insecurity, social disruptions, and frustrations (1999: 279). In an age of abundance on a global scale, wealth and wellbeing are promised to be within reach but remain forever elusive. When ghosts and spirits appear in video-films, they are mimicking major signifiers of global capitalism while keeping the viewers enchanted by the imagined figures that offer solutions to daily dilemmas. In different ways, this phenomenon can also be observed elsewhere, including Western television and film, where the rising popularity of zombie, vampire, and supernatural world narratives shift the terrain of realism to the magical realm. Here, ghosts and spirit figures are no longer otherworldly phenomena but spectral figures that address the enigmas of everyday life (Peeren & Pilar Blanco, 2010). For Laura Mulvey (2005), the appearance of such figures is one effect of the anxiety surrounding new technologies, as well as part of a broader response to epistemic cultural transitions. For Tom Gunning (1995), the phenomenon can be traced to spirit photography at modernism's dawn, where the phantom images of death and spirits defied the indexical basis of photography, presenting images that were attractive because they were impossible to fathom.

The spectral in African video-films belongs to a related but different register of anxiety regarding current transformations. In both African and Western contexts, the spectral is a result of ruptures, shifts, and difficulties in the contemporary moment. While in the West it emerges as a manifestation of the anxiety about new technologies, connoting the instability of the self and the impossibility of the real, in Africa the spectral is imbued with a palimpsest of local traditions and the global conditions weighing on them. It is less a clash between the modern and the postmodern but one between the pre-modern and the modern, a result of severe contradictions between promise and reality framed within a fragile and unstable social and institutional infrastructure (Garritano, 2012). Helplessness in the face of the daunting powers of global wealth and an air of prosperity are best confronted within different worlds where magic, the occult, and the mystical offer respite and solutions.

Commodity and religious imaginary

The postcolony adapts the mechanisms of the occult economy, while employing the apparatus of video-film to produce what Mbembe (2004) calls "the aesthetics of superfluity." Since commodities are ubiquitous and capital consumes everything from tradition to politics, there emerges a "world of gratifications and fleeting pleasures," sensuality pervading objects, wealth, and the image. In the regime of overflowing but distant value in an ever-expanding sphere of commodities, two distinct imaginaries mediate the spectator's relationship with social conditions, the "*imaginaire of consumption*" and the "*religious imaginaire*" (Mbembe, 2002). They work on corporeal and symbolic levels, in the realm of bio-power and the spectral, shaping the functions of power from the body to social mechanisms while forming the discourse on Nollywood video-films.

It is an understatement to say that images of commodities dominate Nollywood video-films; their omnipresence is the first evidence of the local gazing at the global. Since scarcity is the norm in Africa, commodities do not circulate with the same intensity as in other parts of the world. For the postcolony to maintain its authority, though, the desire for commodities must still be mobilized. That is, the consumer culture must create desire despite a lack of access to material goods. It is here that film, television, advertising, and other market instruments are essential in creating fantasies that stimulate the powers of imagination to desire unattainable objects. Commodities are thus not simply for consumption, but "they organize desires and provoke fantasies," possessing spectral power and evoking the objects' fetishistic nature (Mbembe, 2004: 401). They are rarely used to critique global consumerism. Rather, their glamorous appeal is brought into the tactile vicinity of the viewer in the comfort of the living room. Green-Simms notes that one such object, the Mercedes-Benz car, appears ubiquitously in video-films, signifying social status, individual mobility, wealth, and fantasy (2010: 211). The car appears as the ultimate fetish of this projected life. If for Francophone, militant filmmakers in Africa, from Sembène to Djibril Diop Mambéty, the car was a symbol of colonialism, an object of parody, critique, and distance, in Nollywood the Mercedes appears as a reward and a fetish, enhancing the powers of its owner to participate in consumer society, even as it simultaneously signifies declining morality, corruption of power, and misplaced wealth. The *mise-en-scène* of video-films is filled with consumer goods: luxurious mansions, embroidered robes, cell phones, designer sunglasses, exercise equipment, large television sets, and other items that can be acquired only by surplus income. The camera often lingers on commodities at home, and when it does move out of these domestic confines, it blocks off the material conditions in the environment. If there are images of cities, such as Lagos or Accra (in Ghana), they are presented from long views, obscuring the reality and specificity of their social pulse.

Religious imaginary manifests itself in Nollywood's activation of religion, a potent force in Africans' lives that is integral to shaping the epistemic framework in the age of neoliberal capitalism and occult economy. Religion and the powers of the state become a mediatory force operating between the material and the spiritual world. The power of religion finds a particular ally in the Pentecostal religion of the south and elsewhere in Africa, including Ghana (Meyer, 1998). Their alliance with the image-making prowess of the modern technology of video-film, a broad affinity with media institutions, and the processes of politics make for one of the most illuminating chapters in the era of occult economies and globalization. The work of religious imaginary operates on a different cultural and social level in the Islam-dominated northern Hausa culture, but in the south, it is an aesthetic resource, a force that integrates and mobilizes the technologies and the anxieties of the moment to forge a new form of mediated religion.

Following Mbembe's notion of the postcolony and Comaroff and Comaroff's thesis on occult economies, the most valuable insights in this area come from Birgit Meyer, who has done extensive work on the new public sphere created by the intersection of Ghanaian videos and Pentecostalism (1998; 2002; 2006a; 2006b; 2010). The rise of religious influence, she explains, was enabled by a vacuum created by the absence of state power after the neoliberal economy emerged in the mid-1980s. The new conditions have created a new public sphere, uniting the populace into a nearly singular community whose identity is rooted in a shared aesthetic formation where religion, the state, and the media create a world of believing, sharing, and using images motivated by religion. It is an experience in people's daily lives where video-films acquire a style, a whole discourse of signification that becomes their signature influence on spectators.

For Pentecostalists, cinema and video-film are sacred spaces that reveal the invisible forces of the occult, the ghosts, and spirits, much like the spaces of temples. Here, the *mise-en-scène* appears as a revelation of the invisible real. The camera is meant to throw light on the "powers of darkness." The interlocutors of this act, the Pentecostalists, appear to be modernist by casting aside the fearful, hidden fears of other faiths (Meyer, 2006b: 432). The powers of the religion are exercised through the camera, bringing forth the divine and its opponents. Pervasive and mesmerizing in their presence, the imagery created and operated by religious discourse invites viewers to map their desires onto a world of possibilities. Pentecostal influence on video-films achieves many goals: it imparts moral lessons about the experience of life, alleviates the insecurities of daily life, assumes authority in the public realm, extends faith in religion, and harnesses new forms of vision to shed light on what remains outside the realm of experience of the real. Contrary to the impression that the mediatory role of religion and the media makes African culture "pre-modern," this is in fact a modernist cultural turn, where religion coopts and mobilizes the machinery of projecting images, adjusting to new means of extending its powers. In his discussion of "modernity at large," Arjun Appadurai explains that some cultures blur the line between realistic and fictional landscapes and construct "imagined worlds that are chimerical, aesthetic, even fantastic objects, particularly if assessed by the criteria of some other perspective, some other imagined world" (1996: 35). To accord the particular mediascape of religion and Nollywood a distinct status of its own, without reducing it to the caricature of "another world," is to understand the polycentric aesthetics of world cinema. Modernity in the southern video-films is thus the dialectic of the local and the global, transformed into the local idiom of religion, power, and iconography.

In the northern Islamic Hausa culture, religion and video operate in a different dynamic. Uncompromisingly rooted in local culture, they negotiate traditions and social roles in their own context. Hausa audiences support the entire industry on their own, and prefer their films to either the southern video-films or films from other parts of Africa (Adamu, 2007: 87). Muslims in the north view southern culture and its video-films in particular as participants in the westernization of Africa, as signs of backwardness, so they use their own video-films to showcase their moral superiority. Narratives often introduce an Islamic scholar who struggles against the occult, and they ridicule magicians, ghost figures, and other signs of the occult. Particularly troublesome for Islam is the influence of Indian films in the north, with their songs and dance routines and rather progressive social roles. Since many Hindi songs and dances come from Hindu tradition, their influence is considered a matter of cultural contamination, and Hausa producers are often accused of "corruption of culture and religion" by showing, for instance, women without head coverings or wearing Western clothes (Ibrahim, 2013: 70). The internal tensions within Islam are about values of modernity while the struggles with the southern neighbors are over the notions of identity, Christian hegemony, and unabashed hints of paganism. Despite the tensions and debates over values, video-films are enormously popular within the region, subordinating all other forms of life.

The tensions between northern and southern traditions are certainly reflected in video-films. Hausa video-films seek a different form of modernity than their southern counterparts in a complex dynamic between the influences of Indian cinema, Islam, and the overpowering presence of the Christian-Pentecostal dominated south. But both northern and southern parts of Nigeria were caught in the same maelstrom in the 1990s, and video-films in both regions took upon the task of alleviating insecurities created by these harsh conditions and contradictions. They both reify the cultural traditions and make room for religion to adapt to the image, and both do it through melodramatic form and shared aesthetic features.

Narrative form and aesthetics

In aligning Nollywood video-films with African popular culture, Okome identifies different genres. Utilizing cities like Lagos, the city video-films (for example, Chris Obi Rapu's *Living in Bondage*, 1992/1993) use the figure of the city as an ordering system in the narrative (2007b: 3). Set in a space where the alienation of the characters is at its most intense, where the flood of capital and its elusive presence are inscribed into the lives of the residents, these films construct the effects of an occult economy and the alienation of the city as twin forces that always work together. Another popularized and lucrative genre of video-films is comedy, where humor may be used in subversive rhetoric to critique the ills of modern society and its grip on everyday life (for example, Kingsley Ogoro's *Osuofia in London*, 2003). Focused on entertainment and the occult, these genres often come under criticism for lacking an overt political edge that, in most critical defenses of Nollywood, is to be recuperated through readings of films and their popularity among audiences. Haynes (2006) pushes against this charge by pointing out three genres that target the powers of the state, the rich, and the powerful in society. These genres are distinguished in various ways through narratives that critique the autocracy of traditional rulers (*Saworoide/Brass Bells*, 1999; *Ti Oluwa Ni Ile*, 1993), crime thrillers that portray vigilante groups and other miscreants as cleansers of society (Lancelot Imasuem's *Issakaba*, *I–IV*, 2001/2002), and melodramas that involve the powerful and the rich only to ridicule their lives and maneuvers (Kenneth Nnebue's *True Confession*, 1995; Teco Benson's *State of Emergency*, 2004). The occult makes its presence in these genres to punish the powerful, but with milder tones than it does in the occult video-film itself.

Films set abroad comprise another Nollywood genre, with features that set them apart from films set exclusively in the country. Films in this genre are recent, following the success of *Osuofia in London* in 2003 and Tade Ogidan's *Dangerous Twins* in 2004. In his explorations of Nollywood's imagination of the foreign, Haynes discovers that films set abroad in diverse locations show a tunnel vision that reveals little interest in cultures or people abroad, a lack of knowledge about foreign settings and their customs, and the use of locations abroad for adventures or self-discovery (2013: 73). In films such as *Goodbye New York* (Tchidi Chikere, 2004), or *London Forever* (Chico Ejiro, 2004), sequences about shopping, tourism, the introduction of a foreign lover, and encounters with African communities to seek some help are frequent. Perhaps the most intriguing aspect of this genre is a lack of the occult, which Haynes attributes to several possible factors, including the push against the occult narratives by the censor board, exhaustion with tired formulas, or even the presence of functioning state apparatuses abroad. As much as Nollywood video-films are entrenched into the occult at home, these narratives exhibit their extraordinary adaptability to different conditions of experience. We do not observe this tendency in Bollywood, for example, which sticks to a narrative formula even when set abroad.

By far the most popular and dominant narrative form of Nollywood video-films is melodrama. Melodrama's abilities to dramatize social, political, and moral conflicts in personal terms find an unlimited reservoir in the nexus of postcolony, popular culture, religion, and commodity culture. Economic shock, social strife, and values of the old and the new are channeled effectively in melodrama, which can offer both moral solutions and dependable pleasure. Different religious contexts in the north and the south offer specific inflections and different orientations of the genre, but in both cases melodrama is the fulcrum of imaginative expression in popular culture. The excessive and fantastic qualities of melodrama take on a peculiar form in video-films of the south, characterized by decorative and ornate costumes, palatial houses with lavish interiors, and consumer goods, all of which provide a setting for the lives of the powerful, the elite, pastors, businessmen, and politicians (Larkin, 2008: 183). The supernatural and spectral images of otherworldly figures populate dramas of financial, sexual, and moral corruption, erasing any referents to reality. The routine of people's daily life is largely non-existent, and if it is present, it is only in the form of emblematic figures of economic depravity, a surplus of wealth, and religious discourse. In their unique variation in Nollywood, melodramas heighten the range of emotional responses of the spectator to elicit shocks and exaggerated emotions. Though it is a common feature of melodramas to incite an emotional response through a series of narrative devices such as coincidence, implausibility, unexpected events, and disruptive resolutions to minor conflicts, the particular inflection in Nollywood video-films is characterized by outrageous infractions on many possible fronts. In what Larkin terms "aesthetics of outrage," the intensity of responses brought about by transgressions in ethical, sexual, and moral spheres produces revulsion that agitates the spectator's sensory apparatus (2008: 172). In a related concept of "aesthetic of exhortation," Adesokan (2011b: 81) describes an aesthetic and rhetorical relationship of these narratives with the spectator, whereby the melodramatic form joins with a didactic stance in order to subsume all conflicts to morality. Both suggest an aesthetic construction in which transgressions of all kinds are embedded in a narrative with a rhetorical posture aimed at provoking a reaction that itself transcends recognized codes.

In the north, as we have seen, video-films develop in a culture already familiar with Indian films, adapting to and negotiating the Islamic culture and its mores. If southern video-films are in the grips of a transnational evangelical Pentecostalism, manipulating its local cultures to its own ends, northern video-films are caught between the influence of Indian films and Islam (Larkin, 2008: 194). In Hausa culture, traditions of popular literature (the Onishta market literature and *soyayya* love stories) merged with the romance narratives of Indian films, replacing the aesthetics of outrage with romantic tales inspired by Indian cinema. For Abdalla Uba Adamu (2007), a scholar of Hausa video-films, three kinds of conflicts in Indian films find appeal in Hausa narratives: the love triangle, forced marriage, and song-and-dance routines. Love triangles posit tensions of possible moral transgression, forced marriage challenges the notions of freedom and love, and song-and-dance sequences allow settings to imagine alternative realities away from the realism of the narratives. If the severity of the economic rift in metropolitan centers such as Lagos is felt in southern video-films, the shock and the crises of the economy are still felt in the north, but the region tends to be more culturally isolated because of its affinity with Islam.

Both regions use melodramas to imagine solutions to their current dilemmas through their own cultural traditions. For students of Nollywood cinema, the two industries are quite distinct, each oriented toward different audiences and different realms of influence. Spectral iconography and transgressive aesthetics bring more of the attention surrounding Nollywood to southern video-films, aligning them with the occult economies and the postcolony. Both are two distinct modes of Nollywood, however, demanding berths in world cinema and calling for a conception of popular cinema in the midst of the canonizing influences of African art/festival cinema.

In focus 6.1   *Living in Bondage* (Chris Obi Rapu, 1992/1993)

A Nollywood "classic," *Living in Bondage* prefigures both the industry it sets in motion and its aesthetic and generic preoccupations, especially the occult dimension. The film, about a man who joins a secret cult and kills his wife to gain wealth, only to become haunted by her ghost, defines "the essential core of the Nollywood film text: violence, juju, magic, blood sacrifice, prostitution and religion" (Okome, 2013: 147). For this reason alone, it is a seminal film and an essential first step in understanding Nollywood. The film's protagonist, Andy Okeke, is a city worker in Lagos in the early 1990s, dreaming of a better life. Driven to achieve his goal, he finds a role model in his friend Paulo, who is devoted to expensive cars and the display of wealth, ignoring his wife's resistance to the life of wealth and greed.

Soon, Paulo introduces him to a secret cult whose leader sells human body parts, a phenomenon described in Nigeria as "blood money." To join the group, he is asked to fulfill a ritual of sacrificing someone close to him. After his failed attempt to present a prostitute for the sacrifice ritual, he turns to his wife, who agrees. However, the ritual turns her into a possessed, mesmerized figure as she dies in a hospital. Soon after, Andy becomes rich, and as he prepares for his second marriage, the ghost of his first wife appears to him in the midst of the wedding ceremony. The marriage cannot take place and his new bride runs away. In the second part of the film, Andy's troubles take a number of twists and turns, and the ghost of his first wife keeps appearing at moments of his infractions, making him helpless and dependent on the cult that destroyed his life. He is haunted by his first wife's spirit, and his friends and lovers suffer brutal deaths. Andy roams the streets of Lagos, then is saved by a born-again Christian woman whose church restores his life and the social position he occupied at the beginning of the film.

Living in Bondage is an archetypal film of the occult economy, given its themes of greed, human sacrifice for financial gain, magical appearance of wealth, lack of morality, and magical solutions. The city of Lagos is central as a site where characters experience frustrations and despair in reaction to its promised wealth and prosperous economy. In this "simple tale of moral transgression" and its consequences, the ethical essence and moral center is located in the recurring spectral figure of Andy's wife, who warns against a loss of control over material conditions, and offers a quick lesson on and solutions to moral transgressions and the danger of temptations. Audiences relished a tale that transformed the drudgery of everyday life into melodramatic tensions between evil and moral beings, and blood money and its powers to invite haunting ghosts. The film foresaw the prominent genres of Nollywood, from the occult genre and city film to hallelujah film (Okome, 2013).

As a founding Nollywood video-film, these narrative features are articulated in a popular language that integrates the domestic, marital sphere with the wider social context. It is also important to note the deeper trajectories embedded in the narrative. As in many other Nollywood productions, the narrative does not return to the triumph of its protagonist, and rests on traditional values that are positioned against the temptations of wealth and greed. The film rejects an encounter with the world of money while flirting with and critiquing the occult in African tradition. *Living in Bondage* is an inward-looking narrative, but the condition of *bondage* is not

Figures 6.4a & 6.4b A seminal Nollywood film, Chris Obi Rapu's *Living in Bondage* (1992/1993)

generated by the traditions of Africa. Rather, the films posit *bondage* as a powerful interlacing of money and greed represented by the glittery, high-rise landscape of Lagos and the entrenched occult culture.

The New Nollywood

Nollywood's aesthetic qualities and its cottage industry-like production systems assigned it a peripheral status at best, and invited complete neglect at worst. "New Nollywood" has emerged since the early 2000s as a product of the international gaze upon the industry, a desire for respectability, and a movement attempting to break away from the "old" Nollywood. The trend remains limited to southern English-language video-films, not including Hausa- and Yoruba-language productions.

The exponential growth of the industry including the challenges faced by an informal economy and piracy threatened profits for a large number of video-films. New technologies of distribution, such as satellite television networks from M-Net and other companies, forced video-films to compete for airtime, making an additional dent in the profit margins of producers. In the meantime, the NFVCB attempted to formalize the notoriously informal structure of production and business. While these factors did not result in an alternative business structure, they did force the industry to explore other options. Nollywood also witnessed the rise of a middle class in the country and on the continent, a relatively affluent diaspora abroad, and greater curiosity and receptivity from audiences abroad. Shopping malls and multiplexes expanded in Lagos, Abuja, Enugu, and Port Harcourt, screening Hollywood blockbusters but also offering screening opportunities for homegrown productions. Streaming services such as iROKOtv and iBAKATV emerged abroad, with subscription plans for Nollywood films. Nollywood also found an entirely new avenue to distribute its fare abroad through YouTube. These new services did not increase the revenue but they did brighten the prospects of a new chapter for the industry.

Sensing the shifting winds in business, technology, and distribution systems, a group of directors began an effort to alter the course and quality of Nollywood with streamlined narratives, better image quality (often with 35 mm), expanded locations, and a technical finesse never before seen in video-films. Their films are made for theatrical distribution and directors deliberately use 35 mm to prevent piracy, at least until the end of theatrical run. They are also broadcast on streaming channels in Europe, the US, and Asia. New Nollywood directors, some with diasporic roots, are not only better known abroad but are given the lauded status of auteurs: Kunle Afolayan (*Irapada*, 2007; *Araromire/ The Figurine*, 2009; *Phone Swap*, 2012; *October 1*, 2014), Tunde Kelani (*Arugba*, 2008; *Thunderbolt: Magun*, 2000), Jeta Amata (*The Amazing Grace, 2006*), Mahmood Ali-Balogun (*Tango with Me*, 2010), Stephanie Okereke (*Through the Looking Glass*, 2007), Obi Emelonye (*The Mirror Boy*, 2011; *Last Flight to Abuja*, 2012). Kunle Afolayan and Tunde Kelani remain the vanguard of this phase, propagating their fame and work abroad. Already well known in Nigeria for his family name of actors and directors, Jeta Amata started his career in video-films. After making a new Nollywood film, *Inale* (2010), he moved subsequent films abroad, some featuring major stars (*The Amazing Grace* with Nick Moran and *Black Gold: Struggle for the Niger Delta* with Tom Sizemore).

The New Nollywood opens up bold avenues for the industry that has been fueled by informal structures, but as significant as this is, it represents only a sliver of production that still remains a self-financed, popular industry with the dominant aesthetics trends outlined earlier. Financial support abroad is not strong enough to effect major transformations. While reception at regional film festivals has been increasing, for much of world cinema Nollywood remains an industry whose shape, functioning, and aesthetics are marginal, or too commercial to be considered auteur cinema. While New Nollywood directors have demonstrated that it is possible to produce quality films and participate in a broader economy of images, Nollywood retains its character as a cinema formulated and energized by popular culture.

In focus 6.2   New Nollywood auteurs: Tunde Kelani, Kunle Afolayan, and Obi Emelonye

Tunde Kelani: When California Newsreel, the most prominent distributor of African cinema in the US, acquired Tunde Kelani's video-film *Thunderbolt: Magun* (2000), it marked an important change in the conception of African cinema in the West. It was a clear sign that Nollywood had arrived in the zone of international film viewers and scholarship. Steve Smith's introduction to the film begins with a background to Nollywood's video-films, and blurbs on its website include comments from Brian Larkin stating that "Kelani, one of Nigeria's best-known directors, has brought the technical quality of African cinema to Nigerian video" (California Newsreel, 2000).

Thunderbolt: *Magun* is an engaging narrative that captures many of Nollywood's themes, while it also achieves breakthroughs in representing the politics of ethnicity, sexuality, and the grip of the occult tradition. The film narrates the story of a couple—an Igbo woman, Ngozi, and a Yoruba man, Yinka—married in spite of the conflict between their tribes. He works as a construction engineer in a nearby city, and she works as a school teacher in a rural area. Yinka starts suspecting that his wife is unfaithful while he is away because "Igbos are not trustworthy." That Ngozi has inherited large sums of money from her grandmother and become financially independent only adds to his suspicions. While Ngozi is distressed by the accusation, she struggles to make the marriage work, loves her husband, and believes in the harmony between tribes. The first half of the story is a reworking of the Othello narrative with classic melodrama elements, and the second part incorporates a supernatural dimension. A ghost-like figure appears to Ngozi in the market to warn her of impending danger, and we soon learn that Yinka has placed a curse of *magun* on her, later described as "African AIDS." On the one hand, anyone having sex with her would die in miserable and shocking conditions, and on the other hand, if she does not have sex within nine weeks, she will die. Ngozi's treatment by a herbalist forms an intriguing sub-narrative in the film about traditional African medicine. The herbalist, charging a high price to treat her, informs her that for the final phase of treatment, she must have sex with a man other than her husband. She is shocked by the suggestion but agrees to having sex with her Yoruba admirer, Dimeji, who is rescued from near-death by the herbalist and his fellow practitioners. Ngozi and Dimeji are reconciled to live happily thereafter, her inherited wealth is safe, her husband realizes his evil ways, and the tribes are reconciled.

Kelani discloses the lives of ordinary Nigerians stricken with jealousy, envy, and greed, their reliance on traditional, occultist treatments, and ways of reconciling tribal rivalries through closer understanding between people. Its low-key melodrama makes room for an intimate depiction of the characters. Ngozi and Yinka's lives are quite prosperous; owning spacious houses, Ngozi can afford another apartment in the rural area where she works, and they have a maid to look after their child. Audiences watch how the lives of the rich are caught in the same problems as their own, while also enjoying the modes of punishment meted out to them that provide a sense of justice. The film's protagonist is a modern African woman, educated and employed, and the narrative is focused on her agony during painful treatment, her husband's lack of faith, her loyalty despite the men who pursue her, and her firm resolve not to transfer discontent and anger to the tribes.

(continued)

(continued)

a

b

Figures 6.5a & 6.5b One of Nigeria's best-known auteurs, Tunde Kelani, shows the interweaving of ethnicity, sexuality, and the occult tradition in *Thunderbolt: Magun* (2000)

A progressive film in this regard, it simultaneously uses the locus of a woman to impart a public lesson on AIDS, and the prohibitions and threats surrounding sex are stigmas that mostly burden her, not him. The moral lessons regarding sexuality and other conflicts are enunciated in a typically didactic fashion: the vice-principal of Ngozi's school gives a pedagogical lecture to describe the affliction by saying, "If I were a doctor, I'd name *magun* 'Instant Terminator AIDS.' Better still, 'Thunderbolt AIDS.'" At the end of the film, Ngozi offers a moral statement on tribal harmony, "There are only good people and bad people. These are the two tribes. You are a good man, and that's all I want in my life." Adesokan calls such didacticism a main feature of Nollywood's "aesthetics of exhortation" (2011b: 97). In its intended moral lessons, in connecting the narrative to its social, pedagogical contexts, Tunde Kelani's film makes for a classic example of Nollywood's aesthetic and narrative style. Unlike African cinema's modes of colonial critique, Kelani situates these goals in the practice of popular storytelling, turning his attention to the aspirations and concerns of the community.

As one of Nollywood's most prominent directors, Kelani has an impressive portfolio of video-films. A principal Yoruba cameraman from the celluloid era of Nigerian cinema in the 1970s and 1980s, Kelani and his productions have roots in the theatrical traditions. His production company, Mainframe Productions, is a widely recognized brand in Nollywood, known for its prolific presence and consistent quality, and he is among the most sought-after Nollywood figures at film festivals and international conferences. If *Living in Bondage* established the viability and popularity of video-films, Kelani's productions moved video-films closer to conventional cinema, maintaining precise control over the image and deploying allegorical narratives to construct a critique of traditions and politics.

Kunle Afolayan: In an effort to place Nollywood scholarship within the field of film studies, the notion of a "Nollywood auteur" has gained increasing importance. Nnebue and Kelani's consistent productions and commitments to high-quality video-film have elevated their status and provided greater visibility to the industry. The New Nollywood phase has made the task easier, with films that have a technical finesse and narrative sophistication and directors who have attained the status of accomplished Nollywood auteurs. Among such directors, Kunle Afolayan stands out as the most important figure, referred to as the "Scorsese of Lagos" in a prominent *New York Times Magazine* profile (Rice, 2012).

His first film, *Irapada/Redemption* (2007) puts motherhood and family relationships in a diverse community at the center of a melodramatic narrative. The protagonist, Dewunni, played by Afolayan himself, goes through a series of crises, from his foster mother's death and memories of his biological mother to his wife's difficulties in childbirth. His path to redemption uncovers a complex undercurrent of communal relationships and negotiation of one's identity in the context of Yoruba traditions. Afolayan's second film, *Araromire/The Figurine* (2009), is an ambitious production that broke significant ground for Nollywood.

In distribution alone, the film became a flashpoint for evaluating Nollywood's global profile. It was screened to wide critical acclaim in the very last hour of the 2009

(continued)

(continued)

a

b

Figures 6.6a & 6.6b The film that broke significant ground for Nollywood, Kunle Afolayan's
Araromire/The Figurine (2009)

Rotterdam Film Festival. At the FESPACO in 2011 it was showcased in the little-known
video section (McCain, 2011). *The Figurine* has since been used as the subject of many
educational studies, and an entire scholarly volume on the film, *Auteuring Nollywood:
Critical Perspectives on The Figurine*, was published in 2014. As the most vocal of
Nollywood's advocates on the international scene, Afolayan has continued to make
popular films and appear at various film festivals. In a first of its kind, his pan-African

thriller *The CEO* (2016) premiered on board an Air France flight from Lagos to Paris, complete with a red-carpet show at the check-in counter.

Technically sophisticated and deeply rooted in storytelling traditions, Afolayan's films maintain a wide appeal in the increasingly popular New Nollywood idiom. His light-hearted comedy *Phone Swap* (2012), widely popular among the upper-middle class in Africa, resembles a product placement commercial for BlackBerry smart phones. It is a romance tale woven around Akin, a Yoruba businessman, and Mary, an Igbo designer with modest ambitions and a modest income.

These two strangers find themselves in a clumsy encounter at the airport, and each ends up with a BlackBerry that belongs to the other. Compelled to continue their separate journeys, they are forced to enter each other's lives, to adjust to lives outside of their comfort zones defined by class, tradition, and cultures. The principal focus of the narrative is to reconcile two individuals across familiar divides in Nigeria, now made more complicated by the rise of the business class and the necessity of smart phones. Through a predictable narrative with a refreshing absence of occult, spiritual elements, Afolayan brings together the worlds of tradition and modernity, city and the country, fate and pragmatism. The images have the crisp quality of commercials and the development of narrative in two different spaces allows for a skillful deployment of cross-cutting actions.

Obi Emelonye: Two other films from the New Nollywood phase are important because of the transition they demonstrate, moving away from the earlier phase of occult-centered narratives into the realm of social dramas. Written, produced, and directed by Obi Emelonye, a UK-based Nigerian filmmaker, *The Mirror Boy* (2011) became one of the highest-selling Nollywood films, and the longest-running movie by any African in U.K. cinemas. Starring Genevieve Nnaji, one of the best-known and bankable Nigerian stars, the film tells a story of single mother Teema and her young son Tijani, who return to Gambia on a short break to escape racial discrimination in British society. Upon their arrival, the young boy sees an apparition—another boy, smiling at him in a mirror and vanishing. This ghost-like figure lures in Tijani, setting in

Figure 6.7 Phone Swap (2012) by Kunle Afolayan made it to the big screen with theatrical releases in Ghana and Nigeria

(continued)

(continued)

motion a chain of events that cause him to get lost in a forbidding forest. The mother, panic stricken, sets out to find her son, who is continually drawn to a mysterious environment of magical appearances and spirits.

On this thriller-like journey, a London-based Nigerian boy eventually finds his dual, hybrid identity that brings him closer to the world and the mystery of the father he has never seen. A familiar narrative premise to audiences accustomed to Nollywood film is here framed within the perspective and identity issues of second-generation Nigerians living abroad. Despite its relatively low budget, the film boasts

a

b

Figures 6.8a & 6.8b In one of the highest-selling Nollywood films, Obi Emelonye's *Mirror Boy* (2011), a young boy, Tijani, is lured by a ghost-like apparition and gets lost in a forest

high production values, and its elevated status is a good example of New Nollywood's attempt to construct a crossover identity to appeal to wider audiences and arouse international curiosity.

Emelonye departs from this context in his big-budget, polished spectacle, *Last Flight to Abuja* (2012). Set up as a suspense-filled disaster film about a mid-flight malfunction on a Nigerian commercial airplane, the film was a box office hit in Nigeria, shown across West Africa and London and dubbed "the Nigerian blockbuster." Through non-linear sequencing, Emelonye presents a collage of characters—young lovers, an elderly couple, a corporate party, a sportsman on the path to success—each with his or her own professional and emotional baggage, whose stories intertwine and whose relationships are both questioned and strengthened by the mid-air crisis. The film generated a great deal of publicity before its release, partly because of its star-studded cast, and partly because its London premiere coincided with the fateful crash of Dana Air flight 992 from Abuja, which killed everyone on board. Shocked by the coincidence, Emelonye decided to use the movie to flag aviation safety issues in Nigeria, turning it into an advocacy film and donating some of the film's profits to an airplane crash victims fund.

Nollywood's sphere of influence

While the economy of Nigeria is isolated from direct participation in globalization, Nollywood exerts great influence beyond Nigeria's borders, which may be seen broadly in four areas: the popularity and appeal of Nollywood videos in Africa; its close relationship with and influence over other industries in the region that, despite their own distinctiveness, continue to grow in Nollywood's shadow; Nollywood's popularity among Nigerian and African diasporic audiences; and the influence of Nollywood's mode of production and aesthetics on other, similar film trends. These accounts are largely limited to southern video-films in the English language and the few Yoruba films that can travel thanks to subtitles.

Nollywood, Africa, and African cinema

Assessing Nollywood's influence on the African continent, Haynes (2011: 71) terms it a "juggernaut," while Krings and Okome describe it as "the most visible form of cultural machine on the African continent" (2013: 1). The industry is supported by an enthusiastic population of the most populous country in Africa that makes up one-fourth of sub-Saharan Africa. Its theatrical and folk traditions are strong, and the two religions in Nigeria that wield a huge influence over the video industry are not contained within the country but reach larger populations in Africa. Claims of Nollywood forging a new "pan-Africanism" are based on the deep-seated popularity of the videos across the continent. Part of Nollywood's appeal comes from its low cost and ease of transportability across borders. New DVD formats that can accommodate five or six videos at a time, the capacity of satellite and cable television channels, and the possibility of digital copies, all contribute to the cultural power of Nollywood. In many parts of Africa, this unchecked proliferation is seen as cultural imperialism, an intrusion that stifles creative powers of their own industries, and several countries—including Ghana, the Republic of Congo, and Tanzania—have put protectionist measures in place against the glut of video-films that arrive across their borders (*The Economist*, 2010). The charge is unique since it comes against an informal economy hardly supported by the state and in cultures where piracy has been prevalent throughout the age of digital technologies.

Nollywood's main appeal comes from its place in African popular cultural forms. Despite cultural and linguistic differences, people in Africa recognize their own struggles in video-films, which constitute what Adejunmobi calls a "phenomenological proximity," a shared world of images, motifs, and stories that offer a certainty of narrative trajectories by tapping into the imaginaries of the occult and consumption (2010: 110). The poor audio-visual quality of films, rather than an impediment, functions as a draw, positioned in proximity to people's everyday lives frustrated with scant resources; audiences find a certain kind of "home grown" familiarity in the raw quality of the images. Unlike the imported images and sounds, including those from the former colonizers, Nollywood images are claimed as their own, made by Africans about African lives, and met with pride across the continent (Adejunmobi, 2010). Since popular culture circulates in Africa as an improvised form, with gaps to be filled and meanings to be invested, the aesthetic of video-films presents no obstacles to their circulation in the continent (Barber, 1987). Similarly, the exaggerative, melodramatic mode of video-films that favors gestures and other non-verbal elements easily crosses linguistic barriers. Nollywood is at the center of popular culture that includes the iconography and traditions of African life while generating its own, widely imitated fashion and the world of stardom. The influence of Nollywood, variously termed "Africanity," "African-ness," or "pan-Africanism," speaks for a common identity of the continent.

Nollywood is caught in the paradox of being the most popular cinema in Africa, yet its appeal remains limited within Africa. Responding to its internal appeal, Diawara describes Nollywood as a "repository of a new social imaginary in Africa," its video screen a "mirror of Africa" (2000: 171). Though video-films address the dislocations of cultures and identities in Africa, a kind of "Afro-pessimism" prevails, where films are unable to escape their hermetic world, invent new forms, or improve upon their features. For Diawara, Nollywood is confined to the cultural frame of magic and witchcraft, not relying on modernity and enlightenment tradition to form its image of the nation. However, a wider view suggests that Nollywood is not merely judged on the quality of its films or its aesthetics and raw production values, but that it is, as Carmela Garritano (2014) puts it, a "worldly creative practice" that consistently announces its locus in the world. According to this view, Nollywood's place within African cinema is not limited to its capacity to generate its own cultural forms, but points to the ability to "foreground, translate, fragment, and disrupt realities and imaginaries originating elsewhere, and in the process place these forms and processes in the service of one's own making" (Mbembe & Nuttal, 2004: 348). Certainly part of multiple vernacular modernities, it nevertheless demands to be seen in relation to the world. Nollywood's deftness in integrating local traditions to frame the anxieties of the contemporary moment, its endurance in adapting different cultural motifs and images, its cultivation of the star system, and its export of a mode of production at a crucial moment of cinema's technological transformation, all confirm its worldliness.

As a dominant force shaping Afro-modernity, Nollywood's relationship to African cinema is not laced with antagonism or opposition, but is an element that shapes African cinema in general. We have to reject a single conceptualization of African cinema as auteurist cinema supported by European film festivals and production funds and consider its various elements, including art cinema, diasporic cinema, and Nollywood. Nollywood may offer a different kind of production, distribution, and aesthetic model, which poses many questions for African cinema, but as the largest and most popular cinema it offers a central path through which to access contemporary African cinema and examine its mark on world cinema.

Nollywood and video-film industries within Africa

Ghana

In addition to its larger cultural influence in Africa, Nollywood's oversized glow eclipses and poses a threat to other vital video-film industries in the region. Most notable among them is the industry from Ghana, often named "Ghallywood" (also "Ghanawood" or "Gollywood"). Ghana's video-film industry, which emerged in the 1980s (preceding Nollywood), is a remarkably vibrant industry that adds to the complexity of the African film landscape and even contests some of Nollywood's claims on influence (Adjei, 2014). The Ghanaian industry, along with other industries on the continent, resists "Nollywoodization" or "Nigerianization" with the incessant flood of video-films and dominance of its actors and producers. Meanwhile, Nollywood is wary of losing its dominance, particularly as it attempts to reform the informal industry (Aveh, 2014; Adeyemi, 2009). Despite frequent friction, the two industries collaborate in a number of areas, from controlling piracy to launching transnational co-productions that address common motifs of tradition and religion. The two industries have developed alongside each other, with near-parallel histories and overlapping discourses. Both share the economic, cultural, religious, and social contexts of Africa, and both seek to define themselves as distinct film industries. Nollywood, a composite of several industries, shares the English-language, popular-culture tradition, and influences of Pentecostal beliefs and practices with the Ghanaian video industry. In discursive and cultural contexts, the Ghanaian industry is often discussed alongside Nigerian video-films. Nollywood scholars often shift in their references and analyses between Nigerian and Ghanaian video-films, underscoring the shared influences and trends in aesthetics (Garritano, 2013).

Yet, despite their similarities and nearly parallel growth in film forms and cultural influences, the Ghanaian industry deserves its own berth and specificity as a minor cinema in Africa. Garritano's profile of the industry distinguishes it from Nollywood by pointing to some features that resist the direct influence of Nollywood. Observing that in Ghana the term "movie" is used more widely than "video-film," Garritano (2013) notes that producers and directors were focused on making "professional" movies from 1992 until 2000, shifting their plots from poverty to individualism and wealth and aiming for superior production values. Made by directors who were trained in film schools, these films constructed grand global fantasies about commodities and power: Socrate Safo's *Ghost Tears* (1992), Nick Narh Teye's *Jennifer: So Lovely, So Deadly* (1998), and Veronica Quarshie's *A Stab in the Dark* (1998), to name a few. The genre suggested a clean break from Ghana's video-films and, more importantly, it opened up a new form to push against the influence of Nollywood. The genre of "sakawa" movies emerged about Nigerian 419 Internet scams that expressed discontent toward corruption but also desire for wealth, captivating audiences by allowing them to visualize Internet magic. Garritano's account of Ghanaian movies shows how the industry developed a specific form of the local, separating itself from and resisting Nollywood's incursion from piracy to production. By carving out a minor cinema that seeks its own "worldliness," circumscribing the local in the field of transnational influences (including a relationship with Nollywood), Garritano shows how it is possible to maintain a local identity despite the overpowering shadow of Nollywood.

Tanzania

Tanzania's industry is a typical microcosm of Nollywood's influence and the synergy generated in the host cultures. Mathias Krings (2010) discusses multiple ways in which Tanzania reacted to Nollywood's influence. Immensely popular in Tanzania, Nollywood video-films reached their peak popularity between 2003 and 2006, overshadowing local production. Within a span of few years, Tanzanians absorbed Nollywood video-films into their local traditions, making their own industry more popular than the West African imports. Tanzania now boasts its own "Bongowood" industry based in Dar es Salaam, though it looks to its major influence for inspiration, with films about gender relations and the occult economy holding the broadest appeal. Made in Kiswahili, the local flavor and accessibility of films such as Mtitu Game's *Dar 2 Lagos* (2006) contribute to their wide appeal in Tanzania. These local productions become "bloody bricolages" by blending ethnic motifs of horror, the occult, and witchcraft with Nollywood's penchant for dramas of moral conflicts and religious imagery, as well as Hollywood's techniques of generating fear through soundtracks and framing (Böhme, 2013).

Nollywood video-films find seamless alliance with the local traditions of storytelling and performance in Tanzania. Krings describes how the tradition of narration, a "local variety of dubbing" that first gathered strength in the 1980s video parlors of Uganda, was adapted by Tanzanians' video-films following their local folk traditions (Krings, 2013: 306). With performers translating and interpreting the narratives, often interjecting their own perspectives, the storytellers transformed the cinematic form into a local hybrid, and thus created an entirely new form presented in these video parlors. Tanzanian appropriation of Nollywood film into a local idiom demonstrates both the popularity of Nollywood and the nimble flexibility of Tanzanian culture to mold it into local traditions.

Nollywood in the global diaspora

Unlike the cinema of India/Bollywood, Nollywood's video-film industry did not receive a boost from the infusion of large capital supported by its diaspora; nor did it become part of the spectacularization of culture in the global commodity market. Nollywood's entry into the global sphere of circulation has charted an unconventional path. While shunned by film festivals and global institutional networks, Nollywood has created viewership and markets through informal networks of piracy enabled by new technologies. In addition, Nollywood films travel through streaming sites, satellite channels, fan sites, and the Internet. Streaming sites such as iROKOtv, iBAKATV, Buni TV, Dobox, and Sparrow Station, and apps such as NollyLand, contribute to the easy accessibility and ubiquitous presence of Nollywood. Since 2005, YouTube has been an unwitting ally in distributing Nollywood's films, thus challenging and diminishing YouTube's role in monitoring content for copyright reasons.

Despite piracy, streaming services, and YouTube, the appeal of video-films remains limited to the global African diaspora. In Adesokan's words, video-films have a unique place in world cinema in that they are not easily *readable by*, but are intensely *present in*, the world (2009: 402). Because of its global popularity, African diasporic audiences warmly embrace the product from the home continent. For a geographically diverse African diaspora in the UK, France, Belgium, and the Caribbean, the video-films offer spaces for negotiating and maintaining identity, as well as enlivening and strengthening their relationship to home (Ugochukwu, 2011). As is the case with African audiences, the

video-films construct the proximity of experience for diasporic viewers as well, where constitutive values of what is good, bad, desirable, and corrupt are shared. Nollywood's appeal to diasporic audiences in varied cultural contexts offers a common thread rarely offered by any other African cultural sphere.

Nollywood video-films animate a discourse of identification by offering racial and political identification for people of African origins already positioned in the ambivalent world of "the Black Atlantic" experience. Where the relationship of Africans to their host cultures is marked by racial tensions, Nollywood provides a reliable respite and a substantive ground for "authenticity" and identity. For some African Americans in the US, Nollywood video-films offer an "African modernity" closer to their aspirations and resistant to the persistent caricatures of race in Western image culture and commerce (Haynes, 2010). Nollywood may not offer much to those who seek "Afrocentricity" and images of cultural dignity, but its uncanny ability to respond to the anxieties of the global age with addictive melodramas holds a wide appeal.

The influence of Nollywood's production style

The influence of Nollywood's style of production is observed most immediately in Africa itself, where a variety of film forms are produced on video with small budgets, deeply energized by local, cultural, and political issues (Petry, 2015). In Egypt, Yousry Nasrallah, already a director who combines personal narratives with political issues, took part in an anthology ("Tamantashar Yom/*Eighteen Days*) on the events of the Arab Spring. In Burkina Faso, filmmaker Boubacar Diallo shifted his focus to low-budget films for their artistic license and independence by remaking films in popular genres and the local idiom (Petry, 2015: 266). These instances point toward an increasing consolidation of production and distribution practices in the global south, but at the margins of major film industries. In mapping film production practices in Europe, Jedlowski (2013) identifies a group of filmmakers from Nigeria producing diasporic films. Their production companies competed with and collaborated with the industry at home, while each pursued a different strategy to produce and market their films. A number of directors are part of this account of "Nollywood abroad": in the Netherlands, Tony Dele Akinyemi and Leonard Ajayi-Odekhiran produced Dapo Junior (2000), *Holland Heat* (2002), and *From Amsterdam with Love* (2003); in Germany, Isaac Izoya's Ehizoya Golden Entertainment produced *Zero Your Mind* (2003), *Love in Berlin* . . . *The Meeting Point* (2007), and *Run But Can't Hide I & II* (2008); in Belgium, John Osas Omoregie's company ANAABEL produced *Igho Ebube Ebo* (2003), *Desperate Heart* (2007), *Mama Why Me? I & II* (2008), *The Immigrant Eyes* (2010), and *Amazing World* (2010). Among the most successful of these is Obi Emelonye, whose company Basic Input produced *Good Friends* (2000) and eventually *The Mirror Boy* (2011) and *Last Flight to Abuja* (2012). These filmmakers began their careers with small-budget productions and affordable technologies, but these quickly grew into technically refined works in recent years. Produced as entertaining narratives with commercial appeal, their narratives explore the "in-between-ness" of diasporic identity, moving Nollywood to the immigrant communities in the West.

Nollywood's most important export is its mode of production. Quite simply, Nollywood style is defined by films that are produced on video by local producers on shoestring budgets using affordable technology, with improvised scripts and acting, and are shot on available locations and distributed through informal networks including YouTube. It is Nollywood's imprint on cinema to combine video technology with an

informal and undisciplined aesthetic, and while this style might be maligned as inferior and illegitimate cinema, it is also one that insists on developing outside of the established conventions and institutions, taking full advantages of avenues opened by globalized technologies, the economy, and the media, while also refuting mainstream cinematic conventions (Geiger, 2012). The practices of Nollywood have taken hold in other parts of the world, where various cinemas have created subterranean networks even before the arrival of the Internet. In various parts of India, for example, new forms of cinema have emerged that use digital video and circulate on VCDs, much like Nollywood (Vasudevan, 2013: 216). In the US and UK, a similar development is part of a transformation in independent cinema often referred to as the "DIY movement." While a new generation of filmmakers from Nigeria are shaping the DIY movement in the diaspora, in the West DIY filmmaking is an act of resistance against financial and distribution controls, facilitated by the new technologies. As Claudia Hoffman argues, the Nollywood style of production "derives a political contribution from its independence from colonial, postcolonial, and neocolonial power structures in terms of production and distribution" (2011: 228).

On a larger scale, it is necessary to recognize Nollywood's significant contribution to cinema even before the arrival of Internet and digital technologies started questioning the specificity of cinema, television, and video. Specifically, this has to do with the relationship between Nollywood and the so-called "amateur" cinema in the West, and its significance for national identity (Czach, 2014). Positioned against the professional economy and practices, amateur films establish an archive of culture, demonstrate influences outside of the recognized institutions of cinema, and play a role in shaping ideas of the nation. These are "vernacular" discourses that develop either outside the spheres of dominant practices or in relationships of resistance to them, and can be seen as part of a heterogeneous discourses on minor cinemas and minor transnational practices around the world. They can include short films and video, queer cinema, or any other cinema that recognizes its marginal identity and consciously maintains a position outside the major cinematic languages (White, 2008; Khoo, 2014). Minor cinema adapts the aesthetics, narratives, and production within major cinemas but carves out its own path and politics. With distinct achievements to its credit and its place as a minor transnational cinema, Nollywood should be an important part of these discussions.

Nollywood and world cinema

To recognize Nollywood's place in world cinema, we need a framework that opens up the current canons and established structures of African or other regional/national cinemas. As one of Nollywood's strongest proponents and scholars, Haynes has argued that to understand it, one should not view Nollywood from the outside, as an exotic curiosity, but rather one must pay attention to how the world looks to Nollywood, the kind of address it develops in its encounter with the world. He sees in Nollywood a consistent narrative of the effects of globalization, with its peculiarities firmly connected to the conditions that gave rise to it (Haynes, 2000). A new approach must recognize Nollywood not as an anomaly on the world stage, but as a component that requires a redrawing of relationships in the larger system of world cinema. If world cinema is conceived of in terms of "global art cinema," Nollywood appears too isolated, an "antiglobal phenomenon of stupendous proportions," one that offers rich anthropological material but is not meant for outside viewers (Andrew, 2010: vii). The conception of world cinema as art cinema of instantaneous global transfer across the globe, where Nollywood is merely an

oddity in the category of folk culture, sets up a problematic dichotomy of high and low that denies a systemic view of cinema where all components have dynamic if uneven relationships to each other.

To begin with, Nollywood disrupts the model of African cinema. Long known for its fiercely liberationist stance until the 1980s and its position as *cinéma engagé*, African cinema touted the works of filmmakers such as Med Hondo, Sarah Maldoor, Haile Gerima, Djibril Diop Mambéty, Cheick Oumar Sissoko, and Ousmane Sembène, who emphasized oppositionality and postcolonial critique. It was an exemplary mode of Third Cinema, aligned with similar movements in other regions, particularly the global south. According to Harrow (2011), the originary impulse to see African cinema in its agitprop mode has been eclipsed by the new developments in African films, most notably in Nollywood. African cinema is now a palimpsestic cinema that molds the older motives of critique and rebellion into newer forms of popular culture. Nollywood maintains the militant mode of African cinema in its popular narratives marked by an aesthetic of hybridity, imminently sensitive to the dynamic between the local and the global contexts.

In their mapping of subsequent transformations in Third Cinema, Shohat and Stam (2012) observe multiple emerging discourses, each of which absorbs the specificity of political conditions and aesthetic forms around it while responding to influences outside their traditional borders. The conditions of postcoloniality and the effects of neocolonialism are part of the forces that make these new cultural expressions hybrid and dynamic. Hybridity, a discourse marked by contamination, exchanges, reciprocity, and syncretism, is at times forced by colonial relations while at other times it is an adaptation to the postcolonial, post-nationalistic environment. These different cinema movements, they point out, are also *chronotopic*, developing in multiple epochs of their cultural and historic contexts, even as they exist simultaneously in a shared space. Along with hybridity and polymorphic temporal markers, the new forms of Third Cinema share a strategic recuperation of the marginal, aligning themselves with the weak, the despised, the imperfect, and the "trashy," in their resistance to the dominant. As such, Third Cinema evokes what Stam (2003) terms an "aesthetics of garbage," a reworking of the contextual factors to carve out a position from which to examine the world. Quite distinct from similar concerns in philosophy and the avant-garde, where the practice of incorporating detritus constitutes an activity of critique that looks at the world from the privileged, narrowly defined lens of modernism, the "aesthetics of garbage" in Third Cinema is an aesthetic device, a subversive tool that becomes a political instrument, reconfiguring garbage and trash—an ingredient in everyday life that is outcast from the social sphere—into a metaphor, a charged locus for the examination of politics and culture. From dead bodies to trash piles, from the sheer materiality of poverty to the crudeness of everyday struggles, garbage is used in these films as a site from which to launch a critique of power, and as a way to redeem the value of worthless objects. According to Stam (2003), the "aesthetics of garbage" re-positions the posture of militancy in Third Cinema, cultivates the trait of turning strategic weakness into tactical strength, and appropriates an existing discourse for its own ends.

Several Third Cinema movements in Latin America and elsewhere offer a view of such an "aesthetics of garbage" strategy. In his political manifesto for the Brazilian Cinema Novo movement in the 1960s and 1970s, Glauber Rocha (a key figure of Cinema Novo) advocates a subversion of the "tyranny of technique" and commercialism in Hollywood and European art cinema. He invites filmmakers of all stripes to use cinema as a consciousness-raising tool, to create an anti-imperialist and anti-capitalist critique from a position of violence. Using the "aesthetics of hunger," the filmmakers should make "sad, ugly . . . desperate films" to make

the public aware of their desperate condition and urge them to participate in the struggle for national liberation. Similarly, in his conception of "imperfect cinema," Cuban director Julio García Espinosa defended filmmaking as popular art made by the people, as opposed to mass art handed down to them for consumption (MacKenzie, 2014). These films valued accessibility over technical sophistication, enjoyment and lucidity over high-culture neuroses, and they responded to the "waste" created by consumerism and commercial cinema. In Africa, Ousmane Sembène proposed that a true African cinema could emerge only by adapting a strategy of making films by "*mégotage*" (as opposed to montage) or building with cigarette butts, by all means necessary and despite the difficulties. Similar tendencies abound in other parts of world cinema: Teshome Gabriel's (2005) reworking of Third Cinema as cinema of "nomadic aesthetics," and Kobena Mercer's (2005) "diaspora aesthetics" justify cinemas that represent marginal positions, providing a perspective of the dispossessed. These movements defend aesthetic styles that may seem crude in comparison with the glossy aesthetics of dominant cinemas, but such a raw aesthetic becomes a deliberate representational strategy of turning "trash" into powerful political critique. Trash here is both a material object produced by the excesses of wealth, and an allegorical position from which to view society as a whole.

In his study of contemporary African cinema, Harrow (2013) deploys the aesthetics of trash as both an objective and figurative template. African cinema, he observes, has been haunted by trash, employed in films such as Ousmane Sembène's *Black Girl* (1966) or Cheikh Oumar Sissoko's *Nyamanton* (1986) to motivate change and mobilize desire. In these films, trash is located in the hybrid formations of consumer excess and depravity. Harrow deploys contemporary cultural theory and philosophy to situate the politics of trash in various perspectives, from the genesis of power in modern societies to issues of marginality and migrants whose cultures remain hidden from the global lens. Nollywood as well is situated within this template, with its visual excess and baroque aesthetics. Justifiably, trash in Harrow's work is not another maligned stereotype for Africa but the advancement of a critical position firmly situated in other debates outlined in this chapter and elsewhere in studies of Africa and Nollywood. One can trace a trajectory of Third Cinema's aesthetics of trash transformed in Nollywood into an aesthetic rooted in popular culture. Nollywood is a cinema that articulates its opposition without the explicit political stance of Third Cinema, positioning its critique in the forms of pleasure generated in the most intimate spaces of everyday life.

Questions of pleasure in popular culture make consumption an urgently political issue. The terrain and conditions of this pleasure are different from those of folk cultures navigated by anthropology. Produced in the realm of commodity production, the pleasure of popular culture has little to do with folk art, but is rather a historically-specific response to the aesthetic appropriation of consumption, mobilized in the space between the local and the global. When we consider multiple levels of pleasures generated by Nollywood video-films, a pleasure that oscillates "between mimesis and fantasy, proximity and distance, desire and revulsion," we must pay attention to the political aspect of watching video-films (Garritano, 2013: 248). To recall Fredric Jameson's (1977) thesis on reading popular culture, attending to moments and figures of pleasure in video-films is to be alert to their capacity to allegorize political response, to make visible the critiques and conflicts in their narratives and aesthetics. It is one thing to dismiss Nollywood for "poor quality." However, as Jameson argues, the so-called "bad qualities" in a film are precisely what is good about it, in that they reveal the ideologies submerged in films.

The popular and pleasure in world cinema and Nollywood

Together with many other popular cinemas, Nollywood shares the experience of being excluded from the attention of film studies. Consider mainstream Hindi films, which languished on the sidelines for decades as "nightmarishly lengthy, second-rate copies of Hollywood trash, to be dismissed with patronizing amusement or facetious quips" (Thomas, 1985: 117). Even those inside scholarly circles in India considered these films embarrassingly odd compared to the art cinema of Satyajit Ray or Mrinal Sen. In Italy, holiday movies known as *cinepanettone*, while very popular during holiday season, are regarded as a despised genre of Italian cinema. Both Italian film scholars and viewers point out the genre's superficiality, banality, vulgarity, repetitive plot lines, the clownish buffoonery of its characters, and the immature stereotypes of men, women, and foreign cultures as a source of embarrassment that tarnishes the reputation of Italian cinema (O'Leary, 2014: 261). In Turkey, the immensely popular film genre Yeşilçam cinema invites disdain for its pastiche forms and its unhindered ability (helped by lack of copy right regulations) to mimic Hollywood's iconography. Its tradition of subverting, modifying, domesticating, and translating the idiom of Hollywood and other global genres to construct its own "carnivalesque" appeal does not sit well with the highly regarded achievements of Turkey's art cinema directors such as Yılmaz Güney, Nuri Bilge Ceylan, or Fatih Akin.

Academic studies of these popular cinemas that take their role in world cinema seriously are relatively few and recent, and are perhaps most strongly represented in Bollywood studies, which have made important inroads into the world cinema discursive sphere. Rosie Thomas (1985), for example, vigorously defends Bollywood's place on the basis of its complex appeal and pleasure for large audiences, which, she says, is "ruthlessly discriminating" in its reception of the films. Alan O'Leary (2014) makes a consistent case for approaching *cinepanettone* as an index of Italian national cinema since its appeal to audiences discloses complex patterns of reception that allow for a construction of a community and a feeling of home for its audiences. For him too the element of spectatorial pleasure provides access to understanding the popularity of this cinema. Similarly, in Turkey, popular cinema constructs a "global pastiche of aesthetics, and a performative play with gender, technology and nationalism," orienting national identity as a critique of discourses in the global stream of culture (Harris, 2008: 88). Each of these genres has been excluded from the diversity of world cinema, and each of them forms a different trajectory into world cinema. In Bollywood, Indian cinema allowed itself to be marketed abroad, popularizing itself on orientalist terms. Its popularity is less subversive than assertive of its national-diasporic identity. *Cinepanettone* retreats into a sphere of pleasure entirely isolated from the art cinema discourse as much as it is a carnivalesque embrace of low culture. Yeşilçam cinema in Turkey inscribes the global onto the local identities and projects the local back into the global sphere on its own terms. Nollywood too borrows from cinemas around the world including Indian cinema, but transforms rejection, isolation, and abjection into popular narrative forms that tap into local desire.

A common feature among these examples of popular cinema is pleasure in the popular realm, generating carnivalesque appeal in its subversion of the powers inscribed upon it. Approaching such films through the established notions of good taste misses the emphasis on their efforts to subvert aesthetic and political norms. The disorienting narrative structure and song-and-dance sequences in Indian popular cinema, the perceived excess and vulgarity of *cinepanettone* in Italy, the cheap generic tropes in Turkish Yeşilçam cinema, may appear foreign and unworthy to viewers for whom the "high value" of art cinema is the norm of artistic merit, but they are aimed at creating pleasure in popular culture and subverting norms of decency touted by the official culture. Their grotesque realism and the unabashed embrace of the carnivalesque is a powerful force in mobilizing popular desire and constructing a sense of community. Among such filmic strands that mobilize popular pleasure and allegorize collective concerns and resistances, Nollywood stands as a paradigmatic example, whose global visibility should not only shed light on its unique features and position, but also bring attention to the significant role of other popular cinemas.

In focus 6.3   *Bamako* (2006): a *mise-en-scène* of Nollywood, African cinema, and world cinema

Abderrahmane Sissako's film *Bamako* (2006) is one of the richest and most ambitious films of recent world cinema, offering an inexhaustible resource for a variety of disciplines from political science and comparative literature to film studies. Importantly for our context, *Bamako* reveals itself as a rich pedagogical case, a fine site for mapping the configurations of Nollywood, African cinema, and world cinema.

In Sissako's film, the courtyard of a married couple (Chaka and Melé)—Sissako plays on the word "*la cour*," which is both a court of justice and a courtyard—becomes a setting for a fictional trial, where the plaintiffs are Africans holding the IMF and the World Bank accountable for the ruinous policies of the SAP that wrought havoc across the continent in the mid-1980s. Allegations are made by African lawyers, and powerful testimonies are mounted by ordinary Africans who testify patiently, angrily, and eloquently to the cruel consequences of debt servicing and privatization, which include mass migration, loss of control over natural resources and infrastructure, political corruption, and a declining standard of living.

As the trial unfolds, the quotidian lives of Africans continue separately from and intertwined with the trial: women dyeing cloth, people reading and chatting, a bride dressing up for her wedding, children playing, and Chaka caring for his sick daughter. Sissako's observational poetics peel away layers of African life without drawing pedantic connections between them, each layer occupying a place of its own. He juxtaposes the discursive nature of the trial against the materiality and informality of everyday movements, gestures, sounds, and sights in the courtyard. Sissako further opens the space of the narrative to interjections of elements from a broader landscape of African lives: refugees attempting to escape through the Sahara, images of dispassionate young people outside the compound, feigning their weak interest in the proceedings, and Chaka attending a religious sermon. In the midst of the emerging tableau of subnarratives he inserts a short film within a film, a mock-spaghetti western called *Death in Timbuktu*, which is broadcast on television to the eager eyes of children and families seeking relief from the tedium of the trial and everyday life.

Sissako's trial becomes a case for seeking popular justice, where those affected by global capitalism seek direct intervention on their own turf. While the militancy of the trial, its overt political commitment, and its emphasis on realism invoke Third Cinema

a

b

Figures 6.9a & 6.9b In Abderrahmane Sissako's *Bamako* (2006), a married couple's courtyard
becomes a court where African people are suing the World Bank and
IMF over the policies that had devastating effects on the African
continent

(continued)

(continued)

aesthetics, its lyricism and fragmented narrative are aligned with the Second, art cinema aesthetic, with a nod to the First, mainstream cinema through the genre of the Western (Gabara, 2010). In testifying to the strength of the film to speak for Africa, Alison J. Murray Levine argues that it is to be approached as a *mise-en-scène de la parole*, revealing the "performative role of cinema in the modern world" (2012: 153). In her view, the space of the courtyard emerges as a theater for collective voices and performances, where the act of speaking takes precedence. In a world where Africans can hardly hear themselves speak, *Bamako* stages articulate, elaborate witness testimonies mixed with gaps, silences, and expressions that defy language.

One of the most complex of such interjections comes from the griot (storyteller), Zegue Bamba, as he gets up from his seat and moves forward to the podium to deliver his lyrical, searing speech, a "cry from the heart" as he calls it. His body is charged with the spirit of his words, his eyes closed, his face immersed in the depths of his feeling. The courtyard attendees listen as if spellbound, intently focused on his words. Sissako does not translate Bamba's speech, allowing it to stand as direct yet inaccessible performance. When Bamba is denied the opportunity to speak, he says, "My words won't remain within me." Sissako has staged in the courtyard the complex interplay of discourses that characterize Africa. There is the imposing and intrusive presence of world economic powers, a compliant African bureaucracy, the African lawyer advocating a singular position on behalf of collective voices, the testimonies of Africans who articulate their suffering, and the griot who insists on speaking his own language, defying compliance with authority and claiming the validity of his realities.

It is as if Sissako has staged Murray Levine's concept of *mise-en-scène de la parole*, which points to the co-existence of multiple languages in the same space, and

Figure 6.10 The griot Zegue Bamba offering his powerful testimony on his own terms, in his own language, compelling everyone to listen despite the impossibility of understanding him

stands as an allegorical model for comparative literature and world cinema. For Gayatri Spivak, Sissako's staging, his *mise-en-scène* of multiple languages in the "world court" where the woes of Africa find voice (particularly against the hegemonic French in which the trial is conducted), and their ultimate non-translatability, present a model for the comparative study of languages and world literature. She calls for studying "the very moves of languaging," posing *Bamako* as a "teaching text" that demonstrates the incommensurability of languages (2009: 612).

Extending this view, we propose that Sissako's film also presents a pedagogical model for the study of world cinema, where translation is simultaneously a necessary and impossible task. Bamba's speech is one of the most striking moments in the film, an utterance that demands attention, a discourse that insists on its own difference. His performative moment, with the image and the words incommensurable, ruptures the standard relationship between the two; words are not sayable yet they are perceived, and images are not visible yet they can be heard. According to Harrow,

> The sentence and image are joined, sentence-image, flowing in Bambara speech, griot and audience, from the naked image of a pain being recorded, a demand being heard, and finally, a broader world of interpretation aching to be admitted to the circle of those who understand.
>
> (2013: 192–193)

Harrow's use of philosopher Jacques Rancière's (2007) concept of "sentence-image" focuses on how the gap between the word and the image opens up space for under-standing the politics of cinema's potential. By providing this key moment as an allegorical instance of claiming the right to speak where voices have lost their place, Sissako's film demands a re-orientation to the neglected elements of African and world cinema. We locate Nollywood among the voices that demand to be heard, claiming their space among the multiplicity of discourses.

Alongside the *mise-en-scène de la parole*, Sissako presents various cinematic strands and their relationships within world cinema: the documentary mode of the courtyard proceedings, the Nollywood-like drama among the characters, the melodra-matic position of Melé's singing performances. His short film insert, *Death in Timbuktu*, forms the most salient nexus of Sissako's constellation of African cinemas.

The film within a film, a parody of an Italian spaghetti western—itself a remake of Hollywood's Western—the film invokes the "Cassava Western," an African adaptation of the global genre that constitutes a powerful and problematic grip on the imaginary of African audiences (Jaji, 2014). Sissako's 16 mm film is screened on television (an inter-medial gesture recognizing a televisual turn in Africa), interrupted by crosscuts of the audience watching in a dark room. In the film, Danny Glover's character—a vigilante cowboy—is defending an African town where cowboys kill senselessly and indis-criminately. The simultaneous effectiveness and absurdity of violence in an imported lexicon of Western dominance is powerfully positioned against the pretense and for-mality of the courtyard proceedings. At the same time, as Tsitsi Jaji (2014) argues, it invites comparisons with it, as the callous, dismissive reactions of the cowboys under-score the continuity between the screen violence and the barbarity of Western policies

(continued)

(continued)

a

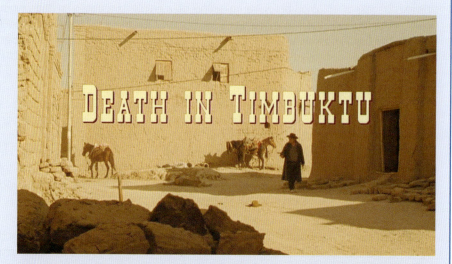

b

Figures 6.11a & 6.11b A film within a film, a spaghetti western called *Death in Timbuktu*, featuring Zeka Laplaine and Jean-Henri Roger as cowboys, establishes a link between economic and cultural colonization

toward Africa. In the words of the African lawyer in a trial: "Even in our imagination, we are raped." The global powers cause as much harm in Africa through their cultural dominance as they do through financial strangleholds.

Death in Timbuktu stages a further twist on a Western trope through the casting of independent filmmakers in the cowboy roles: Zeka Laplaine of Congo, Jean-Henri Roger of France, Elia Suleiman of Palestine, and Sissako himself as Dramane (the usual alter ego name he uses in his films). By casting them as cowboys who "shoot" on screen, Sissako produces a sharp commentary on their roles as independent film-makers. They not only expose the cultural colonization of Africa, how Africa is "shot" on screen, but their screen violence is also an attack on the conventions of cinema, as well as the power relations they are trapped in as filmmakers. Danny Glover's role as a savior of the African town extends to his role off-screen, both as one of the producers of *Bamako* and a film artist-activist with a considerable contribution toward larger pan-African solidarity. That such a savior must come from a successful actor in mainstream Western film is an indictment of Africa's dependence on Western patronage, but it is also a display of this patronage's limitations, made evident by the considerable gap between the fictional, on-screen power of Danny Glover the Cowboy, and the less tangible, off-screen power of Danny Glover the Producer. The insertion of *Death in Timbuktu* into the trial allows Sissako to map competing currents in African cinema, while also mapping African cinema in relation to the West.

Bamako constructs a richly varied tapestry of languages and images, layering them to provoke questions on politics, globalization, and cinema. The film consistently points to the world outside of the frame, each articulation of the image leading to a formation in world cinema, each cinematic trope mapping its own relation to the global situation. *Bamako* can thus be seen as a *mise-en-scène* of Nollywood, African cinema, and world cinema. Here, the *mise-en-scène* is not constituted by empirical elements in an image, but as Adrian Martin suggests, it should be seen as a frame of reference and activities that constitutes cinema's *dispositif*, staging discursive components into an image (2014: 197). *Bamako* directs our attention to the components that constitute the *mise-en-scène* of Third Cinema, Second Cinema, Nollywood, and Africa's dependence on Western representation of the continent, and its ability to approximate these images for critique. Through the staging of the trial, which speaks for the grip that Western dominance holds over African cinema in general, Sissako inserts juxtapositions and interjections to make up a map of African cinema, its role in the continent and its relationship with world cinema.

As a stage for learning, *Bamako* offers a number of places for immersion. Zegue Bamba, like Nollywood, finds his distinct voice and affirms a right to be heard, even though he cannot be understood. He speaks to the panel of judges but his remarks, delivered with eyes shut, are projected to a much broader stage, to his fellow Africans affected by neoliberal economic aggression. In *Bamako*, cinema lives through a television screen, and filmmakers play roles out of their place as cowboys in a Western, laying bare the ironies of their vocation. And everyday life affected by the financial powers continues undisturbed, although it exists on the margins with death hovering just around the corner and desperation silencing the victims. The film provides a view of African cinema as a silent interplay of multiple enunciations (although influenced by Francophone patronage), all within our register of notice. Sissako's Africa is addressed to an audience outside of Africa, harboring the desire to be heard. The multiplicity it presents cannot be reduced to simple propositions. But its invitation to the urgency of paying attention is indispensable.

African theoretical perspectives

The strangeness of Nollywood disappears once placed in its context and seen in a systematic relationship with other elements of world cinema. Nollywood demands both a wider lens to see beyond the discourse of art cinema and festival films, and a shift of perspective to understand how a cinema so distinct and rooted in local conditions achieves such a strong global profile and wide popular support.

Since the 1980s, Diawara has argued that the ingenuity of African cinema remained out of the European film critics' vision because their own framework was imposed on a cinema with its own aesthetic forms. While Nollywood remains absent in his earlier studies, Diawara's (2010) later accounts include emerging currents of "new popular African cinema" where he returns to the question of authenticity. His new categories elude Nollywood as well but in his separate account of video-films in Nigeria he provides a central framework for the specificity of African aesthetics that undergirds most popular African cinema, including Nollywood. This distinct theoretical profile includes the influence of storytelling traditions (exemplified strongly by Sembène, the founder-advocate for an indigenous approach to cinema); theories of image and spectatorship in popular African cinema, informed by Senegalese philosopher-poet Léopold Sédar Senghor's mask/face concept; and Nollywood's reflexivity in aligning itself with narrative rationalities of the West, forging a palimpsestic aesthetic of the local response to a global influence.

The context of African oral tradition is seen as fundamental for the study of African cinema (Cham, 1996; Dovey, 2012). The most important figure in this tradition is the griot, who preserves and performs narratives in the community, and whose techniques of storytelling and performance style influence, consciously or unconsciously, filmmakers' sensibilities. Immersed in the culture and placed at the heart of the community, griots' narratives are laced with gestures, stories, and musical interludes, integrated organically with the life of the community. The presence of a storyteller and the function of storytelling inform many elements of African films, from the *mise-en-scène* to the role of other art forms in cinema, including dance, song, and the slowly unfolding pace of everyday lives. Griots' persona and storytelling are key elements, for example, of Sembène's cinematic style and his status as a father of African cinema. In his effort to highlight African cinema's independence from its Western caricatures, Sembène constructed images of Africans through carefully drawn three-dimensional characters, emphasizing their humanity, and placing spectators inside a community rather than as outsiders watching a spectacle produced for their pleasure and consumption. African cinema's search for its own identity is thus part of its project of deconstructing the Western iconography of Africa. Nollywood's lineage with Yoruba theater keeps the storytelling tradition alive in its video-films while adapting its didacticism to its aesthetics of shock and exhortation, where the realism of the image is superseded by the emergence of the occult- and commodity-informed aesthetic. Though Nollywood does not pursue a conscious relationship to Sembène's film practice, both are firmly rooted in the aesthetic of storytelling traditions.

In his re-evaluation of African cinema, although not alluding directly to Nollywood, Diawara proposes the emergence of a "popular African cinema," a notion that proposes an authentic African cinema that "meets spectators where they are," contrasted with art cinema nurtured by experimental approaches, foreign funding, and film festival circuits (2010). He observes that filmmakers such as Moustapha Alasanne (*Le retour d'un aventurier*, 1966), Kwaw Ansah (*Love Brewed in an African Pot*, 1981), and Souleymane Cissé (*Finyé*, 1982) attempt to subvert Western genres by infusing them with elements of African popular culture, particularly religious beliefs, folklore, superstitions, and the terrain of everyday life (2010: 162–174). Locating the popularity of these films in their imagery and narrative, rather than in reception and audience appeal, Diawara discloses an aesthetic element, a genesis of the image that provides a distinct signature for African film and Nollywood. That is, these films construct a unique relationship between the spectator and the image, based on the concept of mask/face, a concept articulated in Senghor's theory of *Négritude* aesthetics (Senghor, 1993).

According to Senghor (1993), each image/face carries the spirit of the ancestor and a deep connection to the past. Each mask/face is a thus a vessel of another presence, a trace of the past that can be "summoned to life." A filmmaker charges a close-up with the possessive powers of a mask that inspires intense affect or identification. Thus, a spectator of African film discovers a relationship to the Other through an identification with the image. Drawing from Senghor, Diawara suggests that the viewer perceives the ancestry of African life-force in the image, with an innate identification with the Other. To encounter an image is to face the mask, to find a trace of an ancestor, a life-force that connects us to "a world of ancestors, and relating us to the world of film" (Diawara, 2010: 151). Rather than positioned outside, perceiving a vanishing point in the image as in the Renaissance painting (in the Western epistemology), the viewer becomes an integral part of the world of the image, a world to which she belongs but that also reflects the Other.

Films that invoke contexts of origins, relying on motifs, images, and performances of popular culture, follow Senghor's urge for preserving *Négritude*. When discussing Nollywood, Diawara says, "It is as if Senghor's theories of identification and his concept of mask/face were made for Nollywood films" (2010: 178). Characters are charged with a spirituality that can determine their fates and spectators approach these images to affirm the meaning of their own lives, their own predicaments. Diawara's characterization of Nollywood video-films' mobility, their aspirations against pessimism, toward a life without corruption and with happiness and wealth, remains an influential marker of this paradigm. The spectator's mobility is embedded in and inspired by the relationship to the image, with redemption, wealth, and prosperity both projected onto and emanating from the screen. Says Diawara: "[W]e begin to see Juju and Christianity as mere facades and narrative enablers of the desire to move from . . . his/her present situation for a new location" in career and social strata and from local to the global (2010: 179). Diawara's application of Senghor's concept of face/mask and identification in Nollywood confirms the long-standing argument made by scholars like Okome, Haynes, Larkin, Adejunmobi, and Garritano that Nollywood's immersion and embrace of Africa's traditions of popular arts gives it a distinct cinematic identity.

Nollywood's ingenuity arises from another distinct feature of the adaptability of local, African traditions to larger spheres of influence from outside of Africa. Nollywood's aesthetic represents a palimpsest on several levels: in its adaptation of African popular arts, the identification and mobility promised by its narratives, and its positioning vis-à-vis Hollywood, Indian cinema, telenovelas, and other strands of world cultures. Nollywood features a hybrid portrait, rooted at home in an authentic *Négritude* aesthetic but at play with other forces in the world. Nollywood negotiates its influences far away from the ambit of African cinema, engaging with the world far less systematically but closer to its aspirations to provide a view from below.

The adherence of old Nollywood to the local, home-grown features comes under strain as it starts engaging with wider audiences and better production values, a strain particularly visible in the New Nollywood, which becomes a new site of aesthetic and ideological tension. Films of New Nollywood emerge from the aspirations of the new middle class, the increasing influence of a neoliberal economy at home, and global aspirations for acceptability and circulation. Nollywood confronted modernity in its first phase, but in a gesture that was stuck at the level of aspiration. Characters did not get the rewards for their aspirations and when they did, it was always a sign of corruption or evil motives. In contrast, there is a careful embrace of Western modernity in New Nollywood, along with an attempt to distance itself both from this modernity and from the perpetual influence of the occult and spirit-laden narratives. It is difficult to predict the future trajectory of Nollywood, but currently it seems to be in a "middle phase" of simultaneously distancing itself from and embracing both the Western model of rationality and the traditional African model of occult, animism, and the spiritual (Okoye, 2014).

Two examples productively illustrate Nollywood's adaptability to the changed circumstances where it moves away from the older paradigms and accepts Western modernity in its narratives, less to mock it or use it for subversion and more to question its complete domination. In Emelonye's aforementioned film about an airline disaster, *The Last Flight to Abuja* (2012), the only death in the airline crash turns out to be a corrupt IT official, hinting more at poetic justice than deliberate punishment from otherworldly spirits. Later, the only passenger who does not get on board at the inexplicable urging of his young daughter turns to her after the event with gratitude for keeping him alive. It is unclear what makes the child keep her father off the flight, but it definitely invokes the otherworldly spirits, irrevocably present in old Nollywood but merely hinted at here.

Nollywood's slow but certain transition to modernity is also at play in Kunle Afolayan's film *Araromire/The Figurine* (2009). The film has become exemplary for many reasons, from inaugurating the auteur phase in Nollywood and challenging the cultural and aesthetic assumption of old Nollywood to its subtle but firm questioning of alternative epistemologies for narratives. In the film, Sola, a working-class man with a poor work ethic, finds a dusty figurine while in a forest with his friend Femi. Soon after the discovery, his life improves; material wealth, marital bliss, and a professional life arrive at his doorstep, also blessing Femi. The figurine, supposedly endowed with the power to enforce a seven-year blessing on its owners, begins to show a declining influence after seven years. Sola denies that the spiritual presence of the figurine affected his rise and downfall, but his wife Mona begins to suspect as much and attempts to destroy the possessed object. The narrative involves Femi's desires for Mona and a tale of suspense as he attempts to get closer to her and eliminate Sola from their lives. The changing fortunes of the character, the narrative suggests, may be pure coincidence, or the result of occult machinations of a figurine whose tale goes back to 1908. Denying a clear resolution, Afolayan ends the film with a question: "Who do you believe?"

Afolayan's film fits perfectly in the older paradigm of the occult narrative, where wealth is a limited blessing of powers one cannot see, and individual fortunes are at the mercy of forces that were commonplace nearly a century ago. Its narrative is filmed as a melodrama, dwelling on the devious desires of a jilted man, Femi, making the most of the foolish beliefs of others, exploiting them for his own gains. The tension between Sola, a firm unbeliever in the power of the occult, and Mona, a pregnant woman deeply sensitive to what she knows of the occult through her studies, is palpable in the film. While Afolayan questions the dominance of occult narrative, reducing it to a coincidence in a rational world where such things may provide order to a chaotic world, his narrative nevertheless expends a considerable amount of energy to allow the viewer to map its progression, demonstrating its continuing grip on the imagination on Nollywood. For Adejunmobi, "*The Figurine* represents the first major attempt in recent Nigerian filmmaking to call into question the reflexive privileging of occult economies or violations in the moral economy" to account for the fortunes of characters (2015b: 38).

The three elements in the evolution of image in video-films—embedding griot-driven storytelling with linear narratives addressed to a community of spectators; foregrounding the face/mask through the image to invoke the spectator's relation to the primal, ancestral Other in African popular culture; and the ambiguous turn toward accommodating

Western rationality and aesthetic—demonstrate the significance and shifts in the indigenous theoretical perspectives of one of the largest film industries in the world. They also explain African cinema's posture toward the world, beginning with a claim to an independent, local aesthetic to a hybrid approach that desires accessibility. Nollywood's aesthetic is palimpsestic as it presents layers of traditions and positions in relation to cinemas elsewhere. That it has been able to do this without any help from foreign funding and with powerful support of its audiences is a testament to its independence from other forces in Africa and world cinema.

Activity 6.1

Search for a Nollywood Hausa video-film on YouTube. Which features of the film make an impression on you? What can you say about the narrative, cinematography, décor, acting, and presence/absence of songs? How do they compare to the cinematic standards we are used to? Can you identify what you would call a film's "vision" (against a common accusation that these films are made so fast, so cheaply, and under such commercial pressure that they do not realize a specific vision)?

Activity 6.2

Tunde Kelani is considered one of the auteurs of New Nollywood. After watching at least one of his films, discuss how the film straddles the commercial and art house elements. What are the distinct imprints of the director?

Activity 6.3

Watch Kunle Afolayan's *Araromire/The Figurine*, and discuss how the film engages the question of modernity, the relationship between the traditional and the modern. What does the film's ending—the question "what do you think"—signify? What kind of a challenge does it pose to the spectator?

Activity 6.4

Think of a Hollywood film or a television show that features a theme of the occult or the spectral (such as *American Horror Story*, *The X-Files*, or *True Detective*). How does the use of the occult compare to the role of the occult in Nollywood?

Bibliography

Aboubakar, Sanogo. (2015). "Introduction to In Focus: Studying African Cinema and Media Today." *Cinema Journal* 54(2), pp. 114–119.

Adamu, Abdalla Uba. (2007). "Currying Favor: Eastern Media Influences and the Hausa Video Film." *Film International* 5(4), pp. 80–92.

Adejunmobi, Moradewun. (2004). *Vernacular Palaver: Imaginations of the Local and Non-Native Languages in West Africa*. Bristol: Multilingual Matters.

Adejunmobi, Moradewun. (2010). "Charting Nollywood's Appeal Locally and Globally." *African Literatures Today* 28, pp. 106–121.

Adejunmobi, Moradewun. (2015a). "African Film's Televisual Turn." *Cinema Journal* 43(2), pp. 120–125.

Adejunmobi, Moradewun. (2015b). "Neoliberal Rationalities in Old and New Nollywood." *African Studies Review* 58(3), pp. 31–53.

Adesanya, Afolabi. (2000). "From Film to Video." In Jonathan Hayes (ed), *Nigerian Video Films: Revised and Expanded Edition*. Athens, OH: Ohio University Center for International Studies, pp. 37–48.

Adesokan, Akin. (2009). "Excess Luggage: Nigerian Films and the World of Immigrants." In Isidore Okpewho & Nkiru Nzegwu (eds), *The New African Diaspora*. Bloomington, IN: Indiana University Press, pp. 401–422.

Adesokan, Akin. (2011a). "Anticipating Nollywood-Lagos Circa 1996." *Social Dynamics* 37(1), pp. 96–97.

Adesokan, Akin. (2011b). *Postcolonial Artists and Global Aesthetics*. Bloomington, IN: Indiana University Press.

Adeyemi, Taiwo. (2009). "Cultural Nationalism: The 'Nollywoodization' of Nigerian Cinema." *Journal of Performing Arts* 4(1), pp. 21–32.

Adjei, Mawuli. (2014). "The Video-Movie Industry in Ghana: Evolution and the Search for Identity." *Research on Humanities and Social Sciences* 4(17), pp. 61–68.

Andrew, Dudley. (2010). "Foreword." In Rosalind Galt & Karl Schoonover (eds), *Global Art Cinema: New Theories and Histories*. London: Oxford University Press, pp. v–xi.

Appadurai, Arjun. (1996). *Modernity at Large: Cultural Dimensions of Globalization*. Minneapolis, MN: University of Minnesota Press.

Aveh, Africanus. (2014). "The Nigerianization of Ghanaian Eyes." *Journal of African Cinemas* 6(1), pp. 109–122.

Barber, Karin. (1987). "Popular Arts in Africa." *African Studies Review* 30(3), pp. 1–78.

Böhme, Claudia. (2013). "Bloody Bricolages: Traces of Nollywood in Tanzanian Video Films." In Matthias Krings & Onookome Okome (eds), *Global Nollywood: The Transnational Dimensions of African Video Film Industry*. Bloomington, IN: Indiana University Press, pp. 327–346.

California Newsreel. "*Thunderbolt* (2000)." *California Newsreel*. Available at: http://newsreel.org/video/ THUNDERBOLT

Cham, Mbye. (1996). "Introduction." In Imruh Bakari & Mbye Cham (eds), *African Experiences of Cinema*. London: BFI, pp. 1–14.

Comaroff, Jean & John L. Comaroff. (1999). "Occult Economies and the Violence of Abstraction: Notes from the South African Postcolony." *American Ethnologist* 26(2), pp. 279–303.

Czach, Liz. (2014). "Home Movies and Amateur Film as National Cinema." In Laura Rascaroli, Gwenda Young, & Barry Monahan (eds), *Amateur Filmmaking: The Home Movie, the Archive, the Web*. New York, NY: Bloomsbury Academic, pp. 27–37.

Diawara, Manthia. (1992). *African Cinema: Politics and Culture*. Bloomington, IN: Indiana University Press.

Diawara, Manthia. (2000). *In Search of Africa*. Boston, MA: Harvard University Press.

Diawara, Manthia. (2010). *African Film: New Forms of Aesthetics and Politics*. Munich: Prestel.

Dovey, Lindiwe. (2012). "Storytelling in Contemporary African Fiction Film and Video." In Lina Khatib (ed), *Storytelling in World Cinema: Forms, Vol. 1*. New York, NY: Columbia University Press, pp. 89–103.

The Economist. (2010). "Nollywood: Lights, Camera, Africa." December 10. Available at: www.econo mist.com/node/17723124. Accessed November 11, 2016.

Friedman, Uri. (2014). "How Nigeria Became Africa's Largest Economy Overnight." *The Atlantic* (April 7). Available at: www.theatlantic.com/international/archive/2014/04/how-nigeria-became-africas-largest-economy-overnight/360288. Accessed October 6, 2016.

Gabara, Rachel. (2010). "Abderrahmane Sissako: Second and Third Cinema in the First Person." In Rosalind Galt & Karl Schoonover (eds), *Global Art Cinema: New Theories and Histories*. New York, NY: Oxford University Press, pp. 320–333.

Gabriel, Teshome. (2005). "Thoughts on Nomadic Aesthetics and the Black Independent Cinema: Traces of a Journey." Available at: http://teshomegabriel.net. Accessed October 10, 2016.

Garritano, Carmela. (2012). "Blood Money, Big Men and Zombies: Understanding Africa's Occult Narratives in the Context of Neoliberal Capitalism." *Manycinemas* 3, pp. 50–65.

Garritano, Carmela. (2013). *African Video Movies and Global Desires: A Ghanaian History*. Athens, OH: Ohio University Research in International Studies.

Garritano, Carmela. (2014). "Nollywood: An Archive of Africa's Worldliness." *Black Camera* 5(2), pp. 44–52.

Geiger, Jeffrey. (2012). "Nollywood Style: Nigerian Movies and Shifting Perceptions of Worth." *Film International* 10(6), pp. 58–72.

Green-Simms, Lindsay. (2010). "The Return of the Mercedes: From Ousmane Sembène to Kenneth Nnebue." In Mahir Saul & Ralph A. Austen (eds), *Viewing African Cinema in the Twenty-First Century: Art Films and the Nollywood Video Revolution*. Athens, OH: Ohio University Press, pp. 205–229.

Gunning, Tom. (1995). "Phantom Images and Modern Manifestations: Spirit Photography, Magic Theater, Trick Films, and Photography's Uncanny." In Patrice Petro (ed), *Fugitive Images: From Photography to Video*. Bloomington, IN: Indiana University Press, pp. 42–71.

Hamilton, Kunle & Yomi Daramola. (2012). *Nollywood and the Challenge of Movie Subtitles: Assessing Problems of Subtitling in Nigerian Home Video Industry and Showing the Way Forward*. Saarbrücken, Germany: LAP Lambert Academic Publishing.

Harris, Sarah. (2008). "Turkish Popular Cinema: National Claims, Transnational Flows." *International Journal of the Humanities* 6(3), pp. 77–88.

Harrow, Kenneth. (2011). "Toward a New Paradigm of African Cinema." *Critical Interventions* 5(1), pp. 218–236.

Harrow, Kenneth. (2013). *Trash: African Cinema from Below*. Bloomington, IN: Indiana University Press.

Haynes, Jonathan. (2000). "Introduction: Nigerian Video Films." In Jonathan Haynes (ed), *Nigerian Video Films, Revised and Expanded Edition*. Athens, OH: Ohio University Center for International Studies, pp. 1–36.

Haynes, Jonathan. (2006). "Political Critique in Nigerian Video Films." *African Affairs* 105(421), pp. 511–533.

Haynes, Jonathan. (2007a). "'Nollywood': What's in a Name?" *Film International* 5(4), pp. 106–108.

Haynes, Jonathan. (2007b). "Video Boom: Nigeria and Ghana." *Postcolonial Text* 3(2), pp. 1–10.

Haynes, Jonathan. (2010). "A Literature Review: Nigerian and Ghanaian Videos." *Journal of African Cultural Studies* 22(1), pp. 105–120.

Haynes, Jonathan. (2011). "African Cinema and Nollywood: Contradictions." *Situations: Project of the Radical Imagination* 4(1), pp. 67–90.

Haynes, Jonathan. (2013). "The Nollywood Diaspora: A Nigerian Video Genre." In Matthias Krings & Onookome Okome (eds), *Global Nollywood: The Transnational Dimensions of an African Video Film Industry*. Bloomington, IN: Indiana University Press, pp. 73–99.

Haynes, Jonathan & Onookome Okome. (1998). "Evolving Popular Media: Nigerian Video Film." *Research in African Literatures* 29(3), pp. 106–128.

Hoffmann, Claudia. (2011). "Nollywood in Transit: The Globalization of Nigerian Video Culture." In Sandra Ponzanesi & Marguerite Waller (eds), *Postcolonial Cinema Studies*. New York, NY: Routledge, pp. 218–232.

Ibrahim, Muhammad Muhsin. (2013). "Hausa Film: Compatible or Incompatible with Islam." *Performing Islam* 2(2), pp. 165–179.

Jaji, Tsitsi. (2014). "Cassava Westerns: Ways of Watching Abderrahmane Sissako." *Black Camera* 6(1), pp. 154–177.

Jameson, Fredric. (1977). "Class and Allegory in Contemporary Mass Culture: *Dog Day Afternoon* as a Political Film." *College English* 38(8), pp. 843–859.

Jedlowski, Alessandro. (2011). "When the Nigerian Video Film Industry Became 'Nollywood': Naming, Branding and the Videos' Transnational Mobility." *Estudos Afro-Asiátcos* 33(1/2/3), pp. 225–251.

Jedlowski, Alessandro. (2013). "Exporting Nollywood: Nigerian Video Filmmaking in Europe." In P. Szczepanik & P. Vonderau (eds), *Behind the Screen: European Contributions to Production Studies.* New York, NY: Palgrave Macmillan, pp. 171–185.

Kafer, Gary. (2014). "Introduction to Nollywood Cinema." *NollywoodArcadia.* Available at: http://nol lywood.arcadia.edu/introduction. Accessed June 13, 2014.

Khoo, Olivia. (2014). "The Minor Transnationalism of Queer Asian Cinema: Female Authorship and the Short Film Format." *Camera Obscura* 29(1), pp. 33–57.

Krings, Matthias. (2010). "Nollywood Goes East: The Localization of Nigerian Video Films in Tanzania." In Mahir Saul & Ralph A. Austen (eds), *Viewing African Cinema in the Twenty-First Century: Art Film and the Nollywood Video Revolution.* Athens, OH: Ohio University Press, pp. 74–91.

Krings, Matthias. (2013). "*Karishika* with Kiswahili Flavor: A Nollywood Film Retold by a Tanzanian Video Narrator." In Matthias Krings & Onookome Okome (eds), *Global Nollywood: The Transnational Dimensions of African Video Film Industry.* Bloomington, IN: Indiana University Press, pp. 306–327.

Krings, Matthias & Onookome Okome. (2013). "Nollywood and Its Diaspora: An Introduction." In Matthias Krings & Onookome Okome (eds), *Global Nollywood: The Transnational Dimensions of an African Video Film Industry.* Bloomington, IN: Indiana University Press, pp. 1–22.

Larkin, Brian. (2002). "The Materiality of Cinema Theaters in Northern Nigeria." In Faye D. Ginsburg, Lila Abu-Lughod, & Brian Larkin (eds), *Media Worlds: Anthropology on New Terrain.* Berkeley, CA: University of California Press, pp. 319–336.

Larkin, Brian. (2008). *Signal and Noise: Media, Infrastructure, and Urban Culture in Nigeria.* Durham, NC: Duke University Press.

MacKenzie, Scott (ed). (2014). *Film Manifestos and Global Cinema Cultures.* Berkeley, CA: University of California Press.

Martin, Adrian. (2014). *Mise-En-Scène and Film Style: From Classical Hollywood to New Media Art.* London: Palgrave McMillan.

Mbembe, Achille. (1992). "Provisional Notes on the Postcolony." *Africa: Journal of the International African Institute* 62(1) (1992), pp. 3–37.

Mbembe, Achille. (2001). *On the Postcolony.* Berkeley, CA: University of California Press.

Mbembe, Achille. (2002). "African Modes of Self-Writing." *Public Culture* 14(1), pp. 239–273.

Mbembe, Achille. (2004). "Aesthetics of Superfluity." *Public Culture* 16(3), pp. 373–405.

Mbembe, Achille & Sarah Nuttal. (2004). "Writing the World From an African Metropolis." *Public Culture* 16(3), pp. 347–372.

McCain, Carmen. (2011). "FESPACO: Politics of video and Afolayan's *The Figurine*." A Tunanina . . . Blog (March 13). Available at: http://carmenmccain.com/2011/03/13/fespaco-politics-of-video-and-afolayans-the-figurine. Accessed July 21, 2016.

McCall, John C. (2007). "The Pan-Africanism We Have: Nollywood's Invention of Africa." *Film International* 5(4), pp. 92–96.

Mercer, Kobena. (2005). "Diaspora Aesthetics and Visual Culture." In Harry Justin Elam & Kennell Jackson (eds), *Black Cultural Traffic: Crossroads in Global Performance and Popular Culture.* Ann Arbor, MI: University of Michigan Press, pp. 141–161.

Meyer, Birgit. (1998). "The Power of Money, Politics, Occult Practices." *African Studies Review* 41(3), pp. 15–37.

Meyer, Birgit. (2002). "Pentecostalism, Prosperity, and Popular Cinema in Ghanaian Cinema." *Culture and Religion* 3(1), pp. 67–87.

Meyer, Birgit. (2006a). "Impossible Representations, Pentecostalism, Vision and Video Technology in Ghana." In Birgit Meyer & Annelies Moors (eds), *Religion, Media, and the Public Sphere.* Bloomington, IN: Indiana University Press, pp. 290–312.

Meyer, Birgit. (2006b). "Religious Revelation, Secrecy, and the Limits of Representation." *Anthropological Theory* 6(4), pp. 431–453.

Meyer, Birgit. (2010). "From Imagined Communities to Aesthetic Formations: Religious Mediations, Sensational Forms, and Style of Binding." In Birgit Meyer (ed), *Aesthetic Formations: Media, Religion, and the Senses*. London: Palgrave Macmillan, pp. 1–28.

Mulvey, Laura. (2005). *Death 24x a Second: Stillness and the Moving Image*. London: Reaktion Books.

Murray Levine, Alison J. (2012). "Words on Trial: Oral Performance in Abderrahmane Sissako's *Bamako*." *Studies in French Cinema* 12(2), pp. 151–167.

Obenson, Tambay A. (2013). "FESPACO 2013: Festival Announces Significant Changes for Next Edition (2015)." *IndieWire* (March 3). Available at: http://blogs.indiewire.com/shadowandact/fespaco-2013-festival-announces-significant-changes-for-next-edition-2015. Accessed July 22, 2016.

Okome, Onookome. (2007a). "Nollywood: Spectatorship, Audience and the Sites of Consumption." *Postcolonial Text* 3(2), pp. 1–21.

Okome, Onookome. (2007b). "West African Cinema: Africa at the Movies." *Postcolonial Text* 3(2), pp. 1–17.

Okome, Onookome. (2010). "Nollywood and its Critics." In Mahir Saul & Ralph A. Austen (eds), *Viewing African Cinema in the Twenty-First Century: Art Films and the Nollywood Video Revolution*. Athens, OH: Ohio University Press, pp. 26–41.

Okome, Onookome. (2013). "A Nollywood Classic: *Living in Bondage* (Kenneth Nnebue, 1992/1993)." In Lizelle Bisschoff & David Murphy (eds), *Africa's Lost Classics: New Histories of African Cinema*. London: Legenda, pp. 145–153.

Okoye, Chukwuma. (2014). "Animist Order and the Ghost of Modernity in Kunle Afolayan's *The Figurine*." In Adeshina Afolayan (ed), *Auteuring Nollywood: Critical Perspectives on The Figurine*. Ibadan: University Press PLC, pp. 118–134.

O'Leary, Alan. (2014). "Italian National Cinema: The Cinepanettone." In Peter Bondanella (ed), *The Italian Cinema Book*. London: Palgrave Macmillan, pp. 261–267.

Peeren, Esther & Maria del Pilar Blanco. (2010). "Introduction." In Esther Peeren & Maria del Pilar Blanco (ed), *Popular Ghosts: The Haunted Spaces of Everyday Culture*. New York, NY: Bloomsbury Academic, pp. ix–xxiv.

Petty, Sheila. (2015). "Digital Video Films as 'Independent' African Cinema." In Doris Baltruschat & Mary P. Erickson (eds), *Independent Filmmaking Around the Globe*. Toronto: University of Toronto, pp. 255–269.

Rancière, Jacques. (2007). "Sentence, Image, History." In *The Future of the Image*. Trans. G. Elliott. New York, NY: Verso, pp. 33–67.

Rice, Andrew. (2012). "A Scorsese in Lagos: The Making of Nigeria's Film Industry." *New York Times Magazine* (February 23). Available at: www.nytimes.com/2012/02/26/magazine/nollywood-movies.html. Accessed November 16, 2016.

Saro-Wiwa, Zina. (2008). "No Going Back." Zina Saro Wiwa Blog. Available at: www.zinasarowiwa.com/wp-content/uploads/2013/03/NO-GOING-BACK-NOLLYWOOD-ESSAY.pdf. Accessed November 3, 2016.

Senghor, Léopold Sédar. (1993). "Negritude: A Humanism of the Twentieth Century." In P. Williams & E. Chrisman (eds), *Colonial Discourse and Postcolonial Theory*. London: Longman, pp. 27–35.

Shohat, Ella & Robert Stam. (2012). "Narrativising Visual Culture: Towards a Polycentric Aesthetics." In Nicholas Mirzoeff (ed), *The Visual Culture Reader*. New York, NY: Routledge, pp. 27–49.

Soyinka, Wole. (1979). "Theatre and the Emergence of the Nigerian Film Industry." In Alfred E. Opubor & Onuora E. Nwuneli (eds), *The Development and Growth of the Film Industry in Nigeria*. Lagos: Third Press International, pp. 97–104.

Soyinka, Wole. (2013). "A Name is More Than the Tyranny of Taste." *IndieWire* (February 27). Available at: www.indiewire.com/2013/02/fespaco-2013-read-the-transcript-of-wole-soyinkas-epic-keynote-address-speech-137942. Accessed November 3, 2016.

Spivak, Gayatri. (2009). "Rethinking Comparativism." *New Literary History* 40(3), pp. 609–626.

Stam, Robert. (2003). "Beyond Third Cinema: The Aesthetics of Hybridity." In Anthony R. Guneratne & Wimal Dissanayake (eds), *Rethinking Third Cinema*. New York, NY: Routledge, pp. 31–48.

Thomas, Rosie. (1985). "Indian Cinema: Pleasures and Popularity." *Screen* 26(3/4), pp. 116–131.

TIFF (Toronto International Film Festival). (2016). "Lagos, Nigeria, in City to City Spotlight at 41st Toronto International Film Festival." April 26. Available at: www.tiff.net/the-review/lagos-nigeria-in-city-to-city-spotlight-at-41st-toronto-international-film. Accessed November 2, 2016.

Tsika, Noah A. (2015). *Nollywood Stars: Media and Migration in West Africa and the Diaspora*. Bloomington: IN: Indiana University Press.

Ugochukwu, Françoise. (2011). "Nollywood: Nigerians' Umbilical Cord." *African Renaissance* 8(2), pp. 59–75.

Ugochukwu, Françoise. (2013). "Nollywood Across Languages: Issues in Dubbing and Subtitling." *Journal of Intercultural Communication* 33. Available at: www.immi.se/intercultural/nr33/ugochukwu.html. Accessed Nov 10, 2016.

Ugor, Paul. (2007). "Censorship and the Content of Nigerian Home Video Films." *Postcolonial Text* 3(1), pp. 1–22.

Vasudevan, Ravi. (2013). "Notes on Contemporary Film Experience: 'Bollywood,' Genre Diversity, and Video Circuits." In Ravi Sundaram (ed), *No Limits: Media Studies from India*. New Delhi: Oxford University Press, pp. 199–223.

White, Patricia. (2008). "Lesbian Minor Cinema." *Screen* 49(4), pp. 410–425.

7 Asian cinema

Multiple cinemas of Asian countries—China, Hong Kong, Japan, Taiwan, Korea, and other East Asian countries—are often discussed in film studies under the rubric of "Asian cinema." Their collective strength in production volume is significant, totaling nearly 1,500 films a year, making Asia the third largest film industry in the world after Indian cinema and Nollywood. But numbers alone hardly sum up its role in world cinema, as Asian cinema has emerged since the 1980s as one of the strongest film industries and a major force in shaping contemporary world cinema. Traditionally, but not topographically, Asian cinema is a regional cinema. Within the region, a complex transnational dynamic works across shared economic, political, and cultural histories, constructing a paradigm of collectivity. At the same time, Asian cinema engages with various conditions and currents in world cinema. Thus, more than the sum of national cinemas of the region, Asian cinema has a dual identity, as it constructs an exemplary collective dynamism within the region while interacting with and influencing other components of world cinema.

The first two centers of world cinema in our polycentric framework emerge from specific national contexts. Indian cinema, along with its recent incarnation in Bollywood, is a national cinema first, which assumed transnational and global dimensions after the 1980s. Nigeria's Nollywood, too, is rooted in its national traditions, and exerts enormous influence over the production and cultures in Africa and other parts of the world. Unlike these two centers and despite strong traditions of national cinemas in the region, Asian cinema is an example of systemic complexity and offers one of the strongest cases for a comparative framework. Each national cinema within the region participates in the process of forging a transnational-regional identity, projecting a collective character of Asian cinema into the larger system of world cinema.

The conception of Asian cinema emerges at a crucial moment for new world cinema, in the post-1980s era of globalization, neoliberal economic policies, and greater global circulation of images and technologies. Asian cinema is a product of the regionalization of Asia, with three major factors dominating the landscape of globalization since the 1980s. These factors are: (a) the geopolitical emergence of Asia as an economic-cultural power and concurrent appropriation of Asia as a market by the West; (b) the increasing power of the film festivals in the region that shape and promote a collective identity for these cinemas; and (c) the hegemonic influence of Western film studies and responses to it within the region. Asian cinema is continually shaped by the forces in the West, as well as the need to define its identity in the era of globalization.

Asia, regionalization, and Asian cinema

The genealogy of Asian cinema is closely connected with the changing ideas about Asia itself. While our main concern is with the emergent sphere of Asian cinema since globalization in the late 1980s, a brief background on earlier conceptions of Asia and Asian cinema will allow us to put the current state of affairs into a proper context. Asia and Asian cinema remain fluid, shifting concepts. According to Presenjit Duara's distinction between a region and regionalization, a region is an area of unplanned or evolutionary interaction, while regionalization is a "more active, often ideologically driven political process of creating a region" (2010: 963). Asian cinema, too, is hardly a cinema of the region or an aggregate of cinemas in a geographic area, but rather a discursive construct shaped by economic, industrial, and academic perspectives, all of which have taken on specific roles in shaping the current concept in film studies. It is important to identify the three historic periods of the notion of Asia—that of the region before and after the Second World War, the Cold War, and globalization—which, we will see, are closely connected to and influence the changing notions of Asian cinema.

In his incisive study of modern China, Wang Hui asserts, "historically speaking, the idea of Asia is not Asian, but rather European" (2011: 12). Pointing to the fact that the concept of Asia has been shaped by the West since the Homeric epics and the writings of Hegel and Marx, he echoes Edward Said's influential argument in *Orientalism* that European modernity constructed an Orient in its vision of the East so as to affirm its own identity, mapping it onto the geographic space of Asia that became both a site of fear of the Other and a space for its colonial fantasies. Said (1979; 1993) argues that the unequal relationship between Europe and the East continued throughout the colonial period until the mid-twentieth century, shaping perceptions of Asia for centuries and masking the diversity and specificity of its nations.

Against this history, Asian imaginaries have been produced in response to the dominance of the West. The Second World War brought forth a different role for Asia, exposing the imperial global ambitions of Japan and reminding the world of the long-festering imperialization within the region. This period witnessed the earliest form of "pan-Asianism, absorbed into Japanese imperialism" (Duara, 2010: 973). In Duara's account, multiple cultural and intellectual visions of pan-Asian identity were advocated by various thinkers, from Japanese imperialists (Okakura Tenshin) and a community based on Buddhism (Zhang Taiyan) to rational, worldly society (Rabindranath Tagore) (2010: 969). Just as the West shaped the ideas of Asia as an imaginary construct imposed on diverse cultures, Asian intellectuals themselves formulated a concept of Asia in the spirit of collective imaginary that resists being defined by foreign powers.

The post-war era was marked by decolonization and deimperialization in many parts of the region, creating the possibility of a new dynamic among Asian nations. During the Cold War period, the political polarization between the two superpowers divided the nations of Asia along ideological lines, forging partial regional alliances on economic and political fronts, yet maintaining the nations as dominant players.

Globalization in the 1980s further changed the ideological alignments, with free-market economies and neoliberal trade policies dominating the geopolitical spheres and cultural domains. While the West propagated the dominant utopian view that globalization was to bring equal growth and exchange shared across the globe, the rest of the world experienced gross inequalities that affected all aspects of life and effectively continued the practices of colonialism under a different guise. The dominance of global capital, with its center of gravity positioned firmly in the West, created threats for national identities and cultures that had strived for independence in the post-Cold War era of decolonization. Faced with these threats, many nations realigned in regional configurations partly to acquire their own distinct identity and partly to forge a front against new forms of global capital dominance. Thus, regional integration emerges as an essential aspect of globalization, and regional identities are formed through various tracks, from inter-state migration to political alliances, from economic interests to cultural exchanges. However, regionalization itself is a complex engine. Effective regionalization requires the agency of the nation-states to facilitate inter-state migration of capital, labor, and foreign relations. But the process of adapting to global capitalism also requires a fluid nation with permeable borders to participate in regional exchanges. Asian transnationalism and a new regional identity emerge as results of these contradictory forces.

The identity of Asia as a region is thus the result of two competing forces: appropriation of the West and an internal desire for its own collective identity. It is as much an imagined region as it is a strategic reality, a new form of transnationalism that attempts to reconfigure national and global relations. It is molded both by the West, which sees Asia as a market and a territory for its ambitions, and by the internal desire to cultivate Asian identity in the face of the homogenizing forces of globalization. Cinema, like other forms of popular culture, takes center stage to shape and critique Asian identity (Huat, 2014).

The genealogy of Asian cinema is inseparable from the geopolitical forces outlined above: (a) the imperialist view of Asian cinema propagated by Japan; (b) the national cinema model prevalent during the Cold War and shaped by the Western film studies; and (c) cinema of regionalization that has emerged since globalization in the 1980s (Lee, 2011). The earliest record of Asian cinema, as Abe Mark Nornes notes, comes from a programmatic statement in Ichikawa Sai's 1941 book, *The Creation and Construction of Asian Cinema*. Here, Ichikawa provides profiles of industries in the region, offering a snapshot of Asian cinema, but also proposing a policy in which Japan and China take a leading role and where countries collaborate with each other to consolidate a regional industry (Nornes, 2013: 180). Though materialized to some extent, the Second World War and the ensuing Cold War period interrupted Ichikawa's imperialist vision of Asian cinema as an industry. They created an uneven collection of national cinemas of the region, with Japanese, Chinese, and Hong Kong cinemas attracting the most attention. The notion of regional Asian cinema remained dormant during the Cold War period, as the model of Asian cinema as a collection of national cinemas gained currency.

Throughout the 1980s, realignments in old power relations, globalization, and neo-liberal policies swept through the region. Vast political transformations within China, Korea, Taiwan, and other Asian countries changed their internal policies. China turned to liberalization under the leadership of Deng Xiaoping. South Korea opted for democratic elections in 1988. And trade policies, economic liberalism, and the growth of global consumer markets created the "dragon economies" of Hong Kong, Singapore, South Korea, and Taiwan. With the added muscle of Japan and India's fast-expanding economic power, these changes made Asia a significant global economic force and positioned it as the epicenter of global economic activities in what is often referred to as "the Asian Century." The new economic and political climate created conditions that were ripe for greater cross-border exchanges in the region, forging a new phase of regional dynamism in the world.

The emergence of Asian cinema as a film market

The Asian film industry emerged as a lucrative economic market for the Western film industry. The expanding middle class and their new resources contributed to the rise of new modes of consumerism, multiplexes, malls, and the marketing of Western commodities, images, and popular culture. The expansion of the entertainment economy went hand in hand with the rise of commodity cultures and distinct currents of popular culture developed in the region. Cinema is but one component of these transformations. The proximity of nations and shared cultural spheres made it possible for cinema, television, and popular culture to expand beyond the boundaries of each nation, forging a distinct cultural identity for Asia.

For the West, globalization meant the expansion of its economic potential and the creation of a large global market for its products. Sensing the changing winds in the Asian cultural sphere, Western economies (including Hollywood) moved in quickly to establish their presence, combining an economic appetite with the discovery of a new aesthetic potential. Hollywood film imports increased substantially in the region, and Hollywood began to see Asia as a principal economic engine for its future growth, the centerpiece for marketing and distribution—a drive that still persists today. From the 1950s through the 1970s, Hollywood earned thirty percent of its revenue overseas. This figure has increased to two-thirds since the 1980s, mostly due to Asia (Klein, 2003). The distribution of Hollywood films in Hong Kong, South Korea, China, and other countries increased to such an extent that revenue figures from these countries now occupy a prominent place in Hollywood reports.

Hollywood utilized the already popular achievements of Asian cinema for its own global market ambitions. It turned its attention to established stars and formulas of Asian cinema, such as Jackie Chan and Hong Kong martial arts films. It started recruiting stars like Chan and John Woo for its own lucrative productions: Chan became a bankable star in Hollywood with *Rush Hour* (1998, 2001, and 2007), while John Woo's films *Face-Off* (1997), *Mission Impossible II* (2000), *Windtalkers* (2002), and *Paycheck* (2003) sealed Hollywood profiles for both. With the financial and marketing power of Hollywood, Asian directors and actors like Ringo Lam, Tsui Hark, and Chow Yun-fat acquired global profiles and an enduring appeal in Western Asia, Europe, Africa, and Latin America.

Hollywood's marketing machinery increased the power of action films but it also injected Asian cinema into the Hollywood mainstream. Forever hungry to appropriate new ideas and expand markets, Hollywood's appetite to make Asian cinema part of its own fare, and its aggressive recruitment of well-known national cinema talent, has no parallel in world cinema. Hollywood has rarely taken interest in appropriating, for example, Indian or African cinema on such a scale, which makes the relationship between Asian cinema and Hollywood unique. Miramax and New Line Cinema took the lead in recruiting Hong Kong action cinema stars and courting art cinema auteurs. With Quentin Tarantino as his "trendspotter," Harvey Weinstein of Miramax launched aggressive efforts to acquire and distribute Asian films to Western viewers (Dombrowski, 2008). When New Line Cinema released Jackie Chan's *Rumble in the Bronx* (1995), Asian films had become a recognizable commodity for American audiences, encouraging a series of productions by Miramax and others. The release of Ang Lee's *Crouching Tiger, Hidden Dragon* (2000) nearly integrated Asian cinema into mainstream Hollywood, while changing the logic of foreign-language film distribution in the US. Christina Klein argues that this aggressive integration of Asian cinema into Hollywood created a "global cinema" that effectively obliterated cultural and stylistic specificity of films in an attempt to capture a global appeal. The similarities of Miramax-produced films such as Zhang Yimou's *Hero* (2002) and Quentin Tarantino's *Kill Bill, Vol. 1 and 2* (2003, 2004) serve as merely one example of this stylistic integration which, when powered by Hollywood's marketing muscle, makes national film industries "little more than a branch of the global" (Klein, 2004a). Hollywood's master lesson in global marketing of a culturally specific product can be seen in Zhang Yimou's latest big-budget period epic, *The Great Wall* (2017), an American–Chinese co-production starring Matt Damon. Here, Yimou deploys a narrative deeply rooted in the Chinese culture, combining it with the power of a Hollywood star to position it as a global blockbuster.

Hollywood has kept a keen eye on local successes in Asian cinema, particularly Korean and Chinese cinema. Park Chan-wook made an English language debut with *Stoker* (2013), starring Nicole Kidman and Mia Wasikowska, after achieving immense popularity with his *Oldeuboi/Oldboy* (2003). Similarly, Kim Jee-woon made *The Last Stand* (2013) after the success of his Korean productions, *Janghwa, Hongryeon/A Tale of Two Sisters* (2003) and *Ang-ma-reul bo-at-da/I Saw the Devil* (2010). And Bong Joon-ho's reputation as a blockbuster director of the Korean hits *Gwoemul/The Host* (2006) and *Salinui chueok/Memories of Murder* (2003) made him a perfect candidate to direct a big budget sci-fi film, *Snowpiercer* (2013), starring Tilda Swinton and Chris Evans. After the economic liberalization and decolonization of Hong Kong, China, with its rapidly expanding circuits of multiplexes and large audiences, also appeared to be a fertile and irresistible market for Hollywood's global ambitions and box office growth. The appeal to Chinese audiences becomes such a strong prerogative for Hollywood that it is rare for any recent Hollywood blockbuster not to make references to China or address Chinese viewers in some way. Whether it is scenes involving the Chinese space station in *Gravity* (2013), references to the Chinese space program in *The Martian* (2015), or the central role of the Chinese General Shang (Tzi Ma) in the narrative of *Arrival* (2016), Hollywood includes visible nods to the fastest-growing film market in the world, and acknowledges the key role of Asia in its global reach.

As Hollywood's presence and reach expanded, the domestic film industries in Asia moved to strengthen their own industries and create a regional identity. The emergence of local cultural waves in particular created a strong front against the homogenizing forces of globalization. The case of South Korea is exemplary in this regard as it moved swiftly in the mid-1980s to remove protectionist trade barriers, increase access to foreign capital, ease censorship restrictions, and create exhibition policies that benefited local productions. According to Klein, one of the first responses to Hollywood's influence was to copy Hollywood's formulas and appropriate its cinematic style to the South Korean cultural context. To many detractors, such mimicry is a display of the aesthetic and cultural dominance of the Western behemoth and a surrender of Korean cultural authenticity—a critique that led to an accusatory dubbing of the practice as the "Copywood" industry. On the other hand, a growing debate suggests that Korean blockbusters adopt a Hollywood formula only to make it uniquely their own, offering "a localized response to globalization" and creating important conditions for charting "the emotional landscape of national identity" (Ok, 2009; Klein, 2004b).

Produced with increased sophistication in production values and marketing strategies, Korean blockbusters combine local cultural elements with the dominant influence of Hollywood, and their uniqueness comes not merely in positioning national identity against the West, but also in imbuing production and narratives with regional, Asian elements to forge a unique regional identity. Mutual influences of individual cultures from Japan to Korea have been uneven from time to time, but the shared space of regional culture provides an identity in which Asian cinema thrives. Thus, Asian identity is transnational while it also represents a constellation of different national identities, defying the notion of a homogenous cultural space and giving rise to a cultural formation with distinctly local and regional roots.

Asian cinema and film festivals

A European creation, film festivals became a global phenomenon after the 1980s, and their boom coincided with the boom of Asian cinema. In the 1980s, Asia developed its own film festivals, which have played a crucial role in contributing to the most rapidly-developing regional film industry. These festivals forge a visible place for Asian cinema at European film festivals and promote the notion of Asian cinema as a realm of studies. In a region that is diverse, multilingual, complex, and historically intertwined with strong traditions of national film industries, these festivals are central to shaping the idea of Asian cinema for the region and for the world.

The first initiative to define and promote Asian cinema comes from the oldest film festival in the region, the Hong Kong International Film Festival (HKIFF). The HKIFF started in 1977, in the late stages of the British colonial government, as a gathering of local cinephiles and a cultural event for the residents. Its initial programming emphasized the art cinema model of major film festivals in the West, combined with the screening of Asian films. It evolved quickly into a larger venture, focusing on local cinema and films from Indonesia, South Korea, Thailand, and Sri Lanka, with films from Asian countries acquiring a broader berth at the festival by the late 1980s. The festival allowed regional filmmakers from Hong Kong, Taiwan, and China to form stronger bonds and to appeal to both local and Western audiences as representatives of regional Asian cinema (Teo, 2009). Over the years, the festival became a place to discover key works of Hong Kong cinema, and also a space for the encounter between major films from the West and regional cinema. This is consistent with the regional role of Hong Kong as a mediating space between the Eastern and Western worlds, and as a hub of economic activity, the festival also became a space for the encounter between major films. Throughout the 1980s, the HKIFF remained the most prestigious film festival showcasing Asian films; it was the first, for example, to show Zhang Yimou's *Huang tu di/Yellow Earth* outside of China in 1985.

The festival remained stable through the political transformations in 1997 and in subsequent years, expanding beyond distribution into the production of film by establishing a co-production financing platform, the Hong Kong–Asia Film Financing Forum. The establishment of the Asian Film Award in 2007 underscored the importance of delineating Asian cinema within the global network of film festivals, and recognized the regional industries' visibility on the world stage that was enabled by the festival's cultural capital. Throughout the changes in political and cultural climates and the emergent politics of global and regional film festivals, the HKIFF has remained a "unique node of the local and the global," a feature embedded in the aims of other film festivals in the region, most notably the Pusan International Film Festival (PIFF, or BIFF after *Pusan* was changed to *Busan*), for which it remains a model (Wong, 2015).

The HKIFF's central value to Asian cinema came in its ability to provide space for films made by filmmakers in the region who would not have otherwise received any exposure. Films screened at the festival, says Cindy Hing-Yuk Wong (2015), constructed a realm for films larger than any single nation-state, presenting a forum for the perspective of the local audiences and filmmakers. The festival took up a pedagogical function for Asian cinema in the early years and later its archival projects shaped long-term strength for the cinema of the region. As it cultivated local audiences, the festival was also a key venue for Western critics and filmmakers to discover Asian cinema.

As the Korean film industry gained prominence, the city of Pusan established the PIFF in 1996, now known as the fastest-growing film festival in Asia and one of the top ten in the world. Though it kept Korean cinema at the center of its interests, the PIFF advanced a "regionalization strategy" to conceptualize a regional identity for Asian cinema and to actively build up regional networks (Ahn, 2012: 2). Employing a complex model of promoting the creative economy of the city, showcasing Korean national cinema, and serving as a platform for Asian films of note, the PIFF became an Asian hub for films and festival culture in the region. Since its inception, the PIFF has established a number of mechanisms to promote the production of Asian cinema: an Asian Film Academy for the training of filmmakers; the Pusan Promotion Plan (PPP), which later became the Asian Project Market, to support the investment in Asian films; the Asian Film Market, an extensive platform for supporting all areas of film production; the Asian Cinema Fund, to support independent film production; and the Asian Film Commission Network, to advance cooperation between national industries to sustain Asian cinema. After nearly two decades, the festival became a key locus for maintaining the notion of Asian cinema both as an industry and a site for pedagogical purposes.

In her wide-ranging study of the PIFF, Soojeong Ahn (2012) argues that the PIFF's work in conceptualizing and manipulating regional identity for a cinema is its distinctive achievement, not found in other film festivals. Although regionalization was its mission, the PIFF belonged to the Korean film industry, offering prime space for films from that country and with it a sense of competition between Korean and Hong Kong cinema. Yet the merit of the festival, argues Ahn, is in negotiating the tensions and contradictions between national, regional, and global interests. In this sense, the PIFF worked in tandem with the geopolitical and cultural forces in the region that also shaped the identity of Asia as a region in the period of globalization.

Korea launched the official entry into globalization called *Saegaehwa*, marking a sharp break from the restrictive policies of the past. The period also gave rise to *Hallyu*, the Korean New Wave, which exploded in all parts of cultural production, gripping the nation and the region with cultural expressions. The exponential rise in cinephilia in the country (known in Korea as "cine-mania"), according to Soyoung Kim (2005), contributed to the cultural role of film festivals in shaping identity on multiple levels, and film festivals became venues for large-scale public expressions of cinephilia as they expanded and diversified. Some focused on culture, gender, and activism (such as a women's film festival in Seoul), some were sponsored by the corporate sector (Samsung Nices Short Film Festival), and national festivals such as the PIFF were shaped by collaborations between the state and the corporate world. The commitment to the processes of regional identity made the PIFF a major force in Asian cinema, increasing its value for transnational transactions across commercial, national, and cultural levels.

The crucial role of film festivals to work simultaneously on economic and cultural aspects, and as venues to promote the art of cinema, makes them unique in raising the multiple (commercial and aesthetic) profiles of Asian cinema at the very moment when Asia became an economic and commercial force. Film festivals in the region shared the goal of showcasing Asian cinema as they negotiated the tensions among themselves on national levels, while also bringing films from the West to their own viewers. Their desire to develop a counter-weight to the Western festivals and to nurture a notion of Asian cinema provided dual stability to film festivals in Asia. Their prominence and contributions to the study of film festivals is further evidence that Asian cinema is no longer on the periphery but a marker of the decentered territory of world cinema. Dina Iordanova (2011) calls the rise of Asian cinema festivals the "most exciting development in world cinema over the past two decades," while Joshua Neves (2012: 231) terms their activity as "world building" that takes place on its own ground.

Asian cinema as a scholarly discourse

The concept of Asian cinema, says Mitsuhiro Yoshimoto, is a "relatively recent invention in film studies in the US" (2010: 452). Before the emergence of Asian cinema in the 1980s, films from Asia were approached under the umbrella of either the auteur cinema (Akira Kurosawa, Nagisa Oshima, Yasujiro Ozu, or Satyajit Ray) or national cinema model (China, Japan), fitting the geopolitical model of world relations.

Interest in Japanese cinema in the West, according to Yoshimoto, gained currency during and after the Second World War as a way to discover clues to national character, a necessary ingredient to influence policies and propaganda. Film studies and Western culture took note of Japanese cinema when Kurosawa's *Rashomon* (1950) won the Grand Prix at the Venice Film Festival in 1951. As film studies turned its attention to an auteur from the East with distinct aesthetic and cultural context, it had discovered the Other of Western cinema. Yoshimoto proposes that the establishment of film studies as a discipline was itself based on the discovery of cinema of the East, particularly Japanese cinema, as "the polar opposite of Hollywood as the standard" (2010: 453). The two mainstays of academic film studies in the West, auteurism and national cinema, were predicated on aiming at directors and films that affirmed cultural particularity because they were different than the conventions, iconography, and style of Hollywood. The first feature was meant to capture directors as "transmitters of their culture," while the second was aimed at establishing a "national essence" in a group of films. Applying these concepts to films from Asia perpetuated the Western notions of the East as its dyadic other.

The genesis of Asian cinema as a scholarly discourse in the post-1990s landscape of world cinema coincides with the acceptance of Hollywood's global dominance. Fredric Jameson argues that the moment is crystalized in the publication of the book *The Classical Hollywood Cinema*, authored by David Bordwell, Janet Staiger, and Kristin Thompson in 1985, which famously asserted a universal dominance of the classical Hollywood style and simultaneous demise of various stylistic and formal experimentations in cinemas two decades earlier (1998: 62). The pronouncement was timely in establishing the formal and political dominance of Hollywood along with its economic hegemony in relation to other cinemas. Thus, the globalization of the institutional model of film studies recreated the climate in which the diversity of cinemas came to be measured in Hollywood's shadow. Asian cinema, too, came to be defined by the regulative notion of classical Hollywood cinema.

The recognition of Asian cinema as a realm of study in the early 1990s surpassed and served as a corrective to earlier, essentializing tendencies in the approach to films from the region. The increased visibility of Asian films at European film festivals and Asian film festivals' own efforts at providing a platform for its cinema contributed to a more complex idea of Asian cinema, and studies of Asian films urged for theoretical rigor in cross-cultural analysis and exposed limitations of theoretical models in vastly different contexts. Efforts at defining Asian cinema as an alternative mode compared to Hollywood were replaced by a recognition of "the polycentric imagining of the world," where no single center monopolizes either the production or the methods by which cinematic meaning is created (Yoshimoto, 2010: 454). We will delineate some of the main features of the emergent discourse that defines Asian cinema as a key formation in world cinema that brackets earlier ideologically-based assumptions and frameworks.

Asian cinema, geography, and critical regionalism

When Stephen Teo asks, "Where does Asia begin and where does it end?" he points to the ambivalent status of Asia, confounded by the competing conceptions and meanings surrounding this term (2013: 2). There is the Asia-Pacific, South Asia, South East Asia, East Asia, and West Asia, known in the West under its colonialist euphemism of "the Middle East." In film studies, too, there are many areas of Asian cinema: East Asian cinema, South Asian cinema, and a large, slippery notion of Asian cinema with multiple versions informed by geographic areas. In popular usage and journalistic discourses, Asian cinema contains a broad spectrum of cinemas. The Busan IFF includes the films of South Asia as well as East Asia, from India and Sri Lanka to Malaysia and Japan. The festival's list of the top one hundred Asian films released on the occasion of its 20th anniversary includes films from the Western edge of Asia: Iran, Kazakhstan, Kuwait, and Turkmenistan. Edited volumes on Asian cinema include Turkish, Indian, and Iranian cinemas (Eleftheriotis & Needham, 2006; Ciecko, 2006). Including Indian cinema in his account of Asian cinema, Teo (2013) develops a complex theory of shared aesthetic parameters of cinemas from India to Taiwan, demonstrating how these cinemas influence each other in narrative and other realms. For Eleftheriotis (2006), Turkish cinema, because of its geographic and cultural location on the margins of two continents, also constitutes a part of Asian cinema, offering an exemplary model for conceptualizing the wide reach and diversity of Asian cinema. In her introduction to an anthology on Asian cinema, Anne Tereska Ciecko (2006: 12–31) presents Asian cinema as a collection of interacting multiple voices, positions, and popularities in cinemas from India and Bangladesh to Malaysia and Taiwan. The emerging studies of "Australasian cinema" flesh out the intricate relationship between Asian and Australian cinemas' shared diasporic histories, transfers, and exchanges (Khoo, Small, & Yue, 2008).

Each of these configurations of Asian cinema provides different insights, and all point to the fact that Asia is not a geographic region with strict boundaries but a fluid notion, used strategically for specific purposes in scholarly studies. Given this complexity, it is important to map the contours and circumscribe the discourse on Asian cinema. Our model of Asian cinema, for example, does not cover Indian cinema, although film festivals often include it in their profile of Asian cinema. In our polycentric framework, the cinemas of India deserve their own berth due to their distinct, strong profile, and their own sphere of influence and transnational trajectories. Asian cinema is conceived of as cinema of East Asia not as a matter of convenience or random choice, but because the current scholarship on Asian cinema and its process of regionalization focuses on nations (Japan, South Korea, China, Hong Kong, and Taiwan) that share a cultural and political history that is more closely related than to India, Turkey, or Iran.

Second, as the emphasis on East Asian cinemas as Asian cinema suggests, the process of regionalization is always a historically specific one. Regionalization is a response to pressures and re-orientations brought about by globalization. In this new landscape, there are different layers of relationships between the local, national, regional, and global. At the same time, globalization opens up a larger sphere of relationships for the local, without necessarily mediating through the national. To address this dilemma when it comes to the issue of "many Asias," Gayatri Spivak (2007) deploys the concept of "critical regionalism" that allows us to connect and re-territorialize the local within broader patterns of collectivity away from the national framework. The region, for Spivak, is not an aggregate of nation-states, not a stable or limited place, but rather a cumulative effect of the interplay among various manifestations of the region, always in a plural form. Spivak speaks of critical regionalism as a strategic cultural approach that conceives of a region in its relationship with the global, where the local is intertwined in specific configuration with the global, bypassing national and postcolonial contexts. Films produced during globalization carry a particular burden of connecting the local into the global, and in that sense they enrich regional and world cinema. James Tweedie's *Age of New Waves* (2013) is the clearest example of this method, as he maps new waves in Asia, Europe, and elsewhere in a borderless, de-centered world, where each stylistic modulation imbricates the local filmmaking into a wider sphere of similar currents elsewhere.

A notable strategy in Spivak's conception of critical regionalism arises out of the recognition that conditions of postcolonial experience are not necessarily bound by geographical proximity, as in a region. The local may be inscribed large in global postcoloniality. Such a step, she states, recognizes "other Asias," aligned and realigned from different positions to address specific questions of relations and alliances (Spivak, 2007). In this schema, then, all the variable configurations of Asian cinema that exist in film studies, including of Turkish, Iranian, Indian, and Australasian cinema, are the recognition of multiple critical regionalisms. Our conception of East Asian cinema as Asian cinema is one such configuration of Asian cinema, aligned with the dominant model in the current discourse on Asian cinema.

Inter-Asian and trans-Asian cinemas

The regionalization process in Asian cinema is, in the nomenclature of film studies, a process of transnationalism. Through exchange, interaction, collaboration, traversal of national boundaries, competition, and symbiotic energies, cinemas in Asia exhibit signs of a breakdown of the old order, in which cinemas were seen in their national contexts as markers of relatively stable identities. The new configurations compel new theoretical vocabularies, understanding, and practices of transnational cinemas. In their influential effort to theorize transnational cinemas, Will Higbee and Song Hwee Lim (2010) set parameters of "critical transnationalism" in film studies by defining it in a more specific sense, not as a general category for all films that involve transnational factors. Transnationalism in film is a specific product of globalization, the waning influence of national cinemas, and neoliberal policies of free trade. *Transnational* cinema is not a substitute for *world* cinema, but a specific alignment of texts, cultures, and practices of production and circulation. Various alignments in Asian cinemas after the 1990s suggest this form of critical transnationalism. Transnational trajectories in Asian cinemas operate internally across national cinemas and also develop transnational configurations with other parts of world cinema.

We identify two levels of transnationalism in Asian cinemas: *inter-Asian* and *trans-Asian* cinemas. Mutual influences of the Korean and Hong Kong cinemas, for example, constitute an inter-Asian relationship, while Korean or Hong Kong cinemas' global reach and interactions with other cinemas outside of Asia signal a trans-Asian cinema. It should be clear that these divisions are by no means straightforward and are deployed in order to offer some pedagogical clarity in the complexity of the transnational dynamic within Asian cinema. In fact, the two terms, *inter-Asian* and *trans-Asian*, are often used in Asian cinema scholarship interchangeably and with mixed meanings.[1] The practice of transnationalism hardly comes with neat categories. Cinema of one nation may exist in a transnational relationship with other Asian national cinemas as well as with other cinemas of the world. Interconnections can exist in the areas of finance, production, narrative movements, trans-cultural contexts, circulation, and reception, and are too varied to be mapped within a single and clear category. Thus, while it is impossible to demarcate the lines between how a film ceases to be engaged in "inter-Asian" relationships and becomes involved in a "trans-Asian," global context, the two methodological categories should elucidate two different conditions and realms of influence.

Koichi Iwabuchi (2014: 46) observes that the Euro-American West must overcome the long-standing disposition of "not-listening" to Asia and other parts of the world by ignoring the regionally rooted dynamics of other cinemas. Cinemas in East Asia are thriving as industries, the currents of cultural transfers are impressively intricate and manifold, and scholarly discourse insists on re-orienting perspectives to the internal regional dynamics. In tracking the influences and growths of cinemas in different parts of the world, Dudley Andrew (2013) turns to the metaphor of "roots" to study how cinemas are traced to their national histories and contexts before they are engaged in relationships with other cinemas to form "waves." The nature of "inter-Asian" cinemas is also illustrated by the model of interconnected rhizomatic lines, made of various currents flowing from national cinemas to their neighbors with whom they share time and space. A conceptual term for such a design is proposed by Chris Berry (2013) who, following Gilles Deleuze and Felix Guattari, calls Asian cinemas an "assemblage." A multiplicity of interconnected influences, an amorphous formation of changing configurations, Asian cinemas emerge as a particular constellation of discourses that draw together, stake out, and occupy a certain territory. They are unpredictable and without a systematic organization, but in their dynamic form they reveal myriad ways in which various components of Asian cinema construct a collectivity. If rhizomatic relations between different parts of Asian cinemas are pathways, then the assemblage of Asian cinema is a dynamic formation. Rather than "unified region or coherent culture," dynamism and historicity are at the heart of such configurations of inter-Asian cinemas (Berry, 2013: 469). While approaching the uniquely transnational assemblage of Asian cinema, a crucial example presents itself in the case of Chinese cinema. Sheldon Hsiao-peng Lu (1997: 3) contends that the very notion of transnational cinema applies most fittingly to Chinese cinemas, particularly in their post-1990s transnationalism. Lu's transnational constellation of "Chinese-language cinemas" includes the cinemas of Chinese-speaking countries—cinemas of Taiwan, Hong Kong, Singapore, and Mainland China—which share a common language and dialect variations. We maintain that such a mapping between various components of Asian cinemas may still be categorized as inter-Asian, which in this case may be inter-Asian Chinese cinemas.

Inter-Asian cinema is shaped in the larger milieu of transfers and transnational productions in popular culture including music, pop art, and television dramas, and a wide-ranging circulation of commodities. Popular culture waves from Korea, Japan, and Hong Kong move beyond national borders and influence consumers from neighboring countries. In recent years, influences such as anime and K-pop have moved beyond the region to great appeal in distant corners of the world, but their first and most forceful appeal is cultivated in the inter-Asian region, where cultural contexts, proximity, and market integration of cultural production work as fuels to the regionalization of popular culture and the media (Otmazgin & Ben-Ari, 2013: 4). Private capital and entrepreneurism, the middle-class consumerism that started flourishing in the region after the seismic changes of the 1990s, and an active role of the nation-state in removing restrictions on trans-border flows all created fertile conditions within which the inter-Asian cultural sphere would thrive. We look at the influences of the Korean Wave, *Hallyu*, and the Japanese cultural influence from anime to television dramas as two exemplary, although by no means exceptional, paradigms of inter-Asian cultural space (the influence of Taiwanese television dramas or Hong Kong's popular cultures form similar currents for the transnational Asian cultural sphere). We then trace the regional/inter-Asian trajectories from Korean-, Japanese-, and Chinese-language cinemas. Numerous connections among various discourses of Asian cinema exist, from independent cinemas to trans/digital media convergence across borders and technologies. The task of mapping inter-Asian connections is thus necessarily incomplete, uneven, and unjust to all the tensions, conflicts, and fissures. Such a task, however partial, is essential only to underscore the unique constellation of East Asian cinemas in the larger landscape of world cinema. The concept of "inter-Asia" suggests a formation away from transnational currents in world cinema or the influence of the West, and hence quite exemplary among all the constellations in world cinema.

The category of trans-Asian, on the other hand, is about tracing the unique features of Asian cinema's engagement with the rest of the world. Action, martial arts, and horror films from Asia have influenced cinema and audiences around the world. Unlike the cinemas of India and Nollywood, Asian cinema is also fully engaged with the discourses of global art cinema. This dual engagement with popular and art cinemas from various parts of the world illustrates the full range of influences of Asian cinema on world cinema.

Inter-Asian cultural sphere

The inter-Asian configuration of Asian cinema takes place within the shared cultural spheres created in popular culture, music, fashion, and television. Cinema circulates within Asia under the influence of and interacting with the traffic of cultural products across borders, creating a regional transnational traffic. Asian cultural and cinematic traffic is quite unique in this respect. The influence of these cultural products goes well beyond regional borders, but its principle nourishment and circulation is imminently Asian. We discuss two examples of cultural influences in Asia: the Korean Wave or *Hallyu* unleashed in the region in the 1990s that became a significant cross-border cultural force, and Japanese popular culture that underscored Japan's renewed presence in the region through television programs and pop music. There are similarly significant popular culture influences from Hong Kong, Taiwan, and China, and the circulation of specific products from smaller countries such as Indonesia, Thailand, and Malaysia, all of which make a substantive contribution to the regionalization of Asia.

Korea's *Hallyu*

The term *Hallyu* (literally meaning "the flow of Korea") was coined by the Chinese media around 1998 to describe the growing fascination with and global popularity of South Korean culture among young people. *Hallyu* was initiated as an official policy by the Korean government in the mid-1990s. Promoting the policies of globalization, Korea started broadcasting television series in China, Japan, and South East Asia, and generally encouraged the expansion of the country's culture industry abroad in an attempt to increase its "soft power" and strengthen Korean influence and reputation in the region. *Hallyu* was driven by the success of K-pop and K-dramas across the

Asian region. The products of *Hallyu* include the exhibition and mimicry of Western lifestyles, and the display of material wealth in tension with traditional values of communal life, filial responsibility, disciplined work ethics, and empathy toward social minorities. It is thus a distinctly Korean product enmeshed in the regional culture and popularized by the inter-Asian markets.

Having gone through a difficult period during the 1980s, the Korean film industry's boom after the mid-1990s has to be seen against this larger cultural backdrop of the Korean Wave or *Hallyu*. As the state lifted several restrictions in 1996, and new capital led to increased production and new infrastructure, the Korean New Wave received a boost from the powerful regional cultural force of *Hallyu*. Within a short period, a cinema that was hardly noticeable on the international scene took off in the midst of economic booms and regionalization in Asia. Korean films circulate in the region along with its television dramas (for example, the Korean television drama *Winter Sonata* (2002), which was extremely popular in Japan, China, and other neighboring countries), pop music (such as the boy band HOT), and media celebrities. Add commodity products to the cultural productions and it is easy to see how the popularity of all things Korean, from handbags to comic books, video games, haircuts, and cuisine, shapes the East Asian cultural sphere.

In the new, global phase of the Korean Wave, termed *Hallyu 2.0*, digital technologies and social media have energized the sphere through fan cultures and adaptations of Korean styles not merely in Asia but elsewhere in the world (Lee & Nornes, 2015). As the recent success and fame of the Korean rapper PSY ("Gangnam Style") demonstrates, digital technologies are now the motivating force behind the growth of *Hallyu*, disseminating and engaging wider audiences around the globe, further empowered by the convergence of multimedia and telecommunications technologies that integrate the production, distribution, and consumption of *Hallyu 2.0*. If the regional sphere was the hallmark of *Hallyu*, then global influence has become the telling feature of *Hallyu 2.0*.

The embeddedness of Korean cinema within the larger cultural phenomenon of *Hallyu* shows that Korean cinema acquires the transnational character within Asia before its global profile. Describing the quintessential transnationalism of Korean cinema, Andrew observes that "no other cinema, perhaps that of Iran, has moved so directly from the local to the global, with scarcely an intermediate stage" (2013: 20). A shift in perspective from within Asia itself reveals a different picture—that Korean cinema's inter-Asian transnationalism, its regional embeddedness, precedes its global reputation. Korean cinema has engaged its East Asian neighbors in creating what Jungbong Choi terms a "transnational-Korean cinematrix" that shows how cinema grows outside of the rigid limits of films into cultural realms, power relations, and socio-cultural influences (Choi, 2012). It suggests the impossibility of considering Korean cinema as an isolated phenomenon separated from other cultural forces and their deep connections in the dynamism of inter-Asian identity.

Initiated by the Korean government, *Hallyu* has grown into a sphere of its own, a product of regional realignments on multiple fronts. Choi explains that the rise of Korea's influence in the inter-Asian sphere is a result of the waning influence of Japan after the end of Cold War, China's rise as a global economic power, and economic regionalization among East Asian countries accelerated by neoliberal movement of capital (Choi, 2010: 128). In the meantime, Korea's transition to compressed modernity, moving from an agrarian society to a high-tech information society in less than four decades, created conditions for Korea's rise in the region and a centerpiece of cultural influence. The popularity of *Hallyu* as an inter-Asian cultural sphere of influence affirms a postcolonial expression of modernity, setting in motion two forces: the regionalization of East Asian identity and a counter-position to the Western domination of the region. Its emergence provides a space for inter-Asian negotiation of modernities. Korean cinema stepped up to make the most of this new climate with removed protectionist measures and capital flow, using the power of a regional audience to expand into a transnational sphere. It opened up enthusiastically to transnational connections on multiple fronts, from co-productions with Asian neighbors and the exporting of actors to embedding transnational trajectories within their narratives.

Kawaii culture: Japan's (re-)entry into Asian regionalization

For a long period, Japan's position in Asian cinema remained ambivalent. After the Second World War, it became a rapidly modernized and technologically advanced economic power. Japan shared with other Asian nations a cultural environment, but its imperial legacy distanced it from the rest of East Asia. This tension placed Japan's identity "in the asymmetrical triad between 'Asia,' 'the West,' and 'Japan'" (Iwabuchi, 2002a: 7). As the economic and cultural power of its Asian neighbors increased after the economic liberalization in the 1990s, Japan began its "re-entry" into the Asian region.

Japan's cultural production in the 1990s provided the medium through which to develop inter-Asian collaboration. In the commodity circulation that has become a powerful force in the Asian regionalization, Japan has contributed with its cultural products, from television dramas, pop music, anime, manga, and theater to food and fashion, which all rapidly circulated and gained immense popularity in East and South East Asian countries. Aided and guided by state institutions, Japan reshaped its cultural policy to expand its soft power in the region and worldwide. Domestic industries were encouraged to produce export-oriented commodities and present a renewed, friendlier Japan in the region. A new program initiative called "Japan's 21st Century Vision," akin to the creative industries model in the West, focused on the production of culture and promotion of creativity in multiple areas, from technology to culture (Otmazgin, 2012).

There is a wide recognition of the Japanese "wave" in Asia since the 1990s and the "cool Japan" or "Kawaii" ("cute") culture that has swept across Asia like a tornado. Japanese television programs such as *Tokyo Love Story*, *Yamatonadeshiko*, *The 101st Proposal*, *All Under One Roof*, and *Long Vacation* are popular in all Asian countries. Japanese video games and manga comic books dominate East Asia's market, and Japanese animated characters, depicted on products in the markets in every Asian city, have created their own sub-cultural influences: Astro Boy, Sailor Moon, Lupin, Doraemon, Tiger Mask, Detective Conan, Hello Kitty, Ampan Man, and Pokémon, among others. *Pokémon Go*, a smartphone game released in 2016 that blends the real and digital worlds, has turned into an unprecedented craze not only in the region but throughout the world. Teenagers have adopted Japanese hairstyles and lifestyles, and Japanese pop music, or J-pop, is wildly popular across Asia, creating together with television dramas a shared cultural realm and identity with Hong Kong and Taiwan (Stevens, 2007; Mitsui & Hosokawa, 2001). Karaoke, the great Japanese invention that has done much to widen the popularity of all kinds of music genres, from Hindi film songs to pop songs from around the world, has become another powerful agent in Japan's popularity across cultural borders. Karaoke became a symbol of modernity in East Asian cultures from Korea to Thailand, contributing to a participatory sphere where popular music from the region and elsewhere in the world was absorbed across national divides (Zhou & Tarocco, 2007).

A number of perspectives are advanced to explain the popularity of Japanese culture in Asia, from cultural proximity to shared sensibilities. Iwabuchi speaks of the impact of "popular Asianism" in Japan that awakened Japanese responses to their own predicament in the moment of globalization. He finds an ideological nostalgia in Japan in its encounters with Hong Kong culture, where the Japanese attempted to locate a "different mode of non-Western mimetic modernity" (Iwabuchi, 2002b: 548). Each culture in Asia experiences a different modernity coming to its shores from another part of the region, animating the formation of Asia and Asian cinema. In the new media landscape, each medium feeds into the other. Radio and television shows promote other cultural products, affinities with celebrities work across different media spheres, social media circulate and promote products across borders, and the popularity of one product creates conditions for the acceptance of the other. Asia's experience of itself takes place under the broader influence of Western culture, capital, and globalization. A vexing issue for students of Asian cinema and media remains: Asian modernity is experienced not merely as a response to Western modernity but to the dynamic of inter-Asian exchanges that take place despite or outside of external influences. These intersecting influences from one nation to the other in the midst of global capital present one of the most dynamic sites through which to consider various modernities in the wake of transnational cultures and cinemas.

Categories of inter-Asian cinemas

Interactions and collaborations among various components of Asian cinema are evident across three main categories: inter-Asian co-productions, pan-Asian and anthology films, and blockbusters. Overlapping and complex in their relations, the categories provide a broad map of cinematic practices within Asia, and all of them involve transnational relations on some level of filmmaking. Inter-Asian co-production activities may be tracked from one national cinema to the other only to the extent that the national context provides one locus of orientation in this assemblage. Anthology films represent a level of collaboration embedded at all stages of film practice, from finance and production to narrative and intertextuality—a kind of unity in dispersion that allows a collective film to promote relationships within a region. Hailed explicitly as projects of regionalization, pan-Asian productions are meant to project an interactive, unified vision of Asian cinema, involving multiple nations in their production as well as narrative construction. And blockbusters from Korea, China, and Hong Kong suggest a regional synergy to elevate Asian cinema to a level of global engagement, new to the region since the 1990s.

Co-production

Co-productions are often the first step toward forming alliances and exchanges between different cinemas. Asian national cinemas enjoyed a long history of interaction before the tumultuous events of the late 1990s. Accounts of co-productions between Korean and other Asian producers in the 1970s and earlier phases, for example, suggest that Korean cinema was engaged in the process of "Asianization," working in shared areas within the region, and was deeply engaged with Hong Kong, Japan, and Taiwan until the 1970s (Lee, 2012; Shim & Yecies, 2012). Korean and Hong Kong filmmakers initiated Pan Asian Big Pictures, which charted networks of productions that strengthened regional collaborations. Efforts pursued by producers and national institutions in the region were notable but not comparable to the intense energy in co-productions after the 1990s.

Co-productions have four broad aims: broaden the appeal to audiences outside of national borders (particularly important for smaller Asian nations); increase return on investment to create conditions for survival and health for each cinema; secure regional turf against the dominance of Hollywood imports; and create a pan-Asian identity for the region to foster further exchanges and transfers for multiple cinemas. The financial crises of the late 1990s from Singapore to Korea created difficult conditions for cultural production in the region. The new climate resulted in a large influx of capital and cultural products including films from the West, requiring producers to resort to building defenses to protect regional industries. These conditions compelled filmmakers to resort to co-productions, creating in the process a shared signifier of "Asia" that sustained their industries.

Davis and Yeh point out the operations of different "clusters" for inter-Asian and pan-Asian productions (2007: 90). These clusters include companies that collaborate across national borders and aim for shared viewership: Hong Kong's Applause Pictures; South Korea's Sidus, Show East, and CJ Entertainment; Japan's Kadokawa; Singapore's Raintree Media-Corp; Taiwan's Arc Light Films; and Japan's Y2K and NHK, which focus on pan-Asian fare. The larger, cross-border Chinese-language cinema is aided by its own co-production companies: Media Asia, Jackie Chan's JCE Group, China Film Corp., and Shanghai Film Group. Capital that flows through these production companies often includes investment outside of Asia, while some producers and companies widen their co-production activities beyond this inter-Asian effort for global co-productions.

While Asia engages in co-productions without a formal regional institutional support (such as the one provided by the European Union and its media organizations), co-production is "a new mode of production, creating spaces for negotiating meanings and identities" (DeBoer, 2014: 2). Working across national and cultural boundaries is not an easy task, and it becomes particularly difficult when participating nations share tension-filled histories. Japan propagated its own vision of pan-Asian cinema before the Second World War, and had to renegotiate its relationship with Asian neighbors in the post-war era. Japan's relationship with Korea, for example, marred by colonial occupation, eased slowly through a number of mutual gestures. On the other hand, the contemporary moment positioned China strongly to the center due to its financial power and its large market. Co-productions awaken complex cross-cultural referential worlds that simultaneously provide a place for inter-cultural negotiations and create new regional opportunities for identity formation.

Hong Kong's inter-Asia connections

In some ways, Hong Kong has always been a regional cinema, engaged with countries in the region and exporting its films and popular culture to Asia and other parts of the world. In the changes that took place, particularly after 1997, Hong Kong took an active lead in regional production, this time as a strategy to construct a regional identity that would present a frontier against foreign influences and protect regional industries. Peter Chan, the founder of Hong Kong's Applause Pictures, is credited for advocating the notion of pan-Asian productions, predicting that co-productions would be the "future of Asian production" (quoted in DeBoer, 2014: 2). The company has made important strides in pan-Asian productions, with some notable achievements to its docket. Some of its co-productions include the Thai-language melodrama *Jan Dara* (Nonzee Nimibutr, 2001), Korean melodrama *Bomnaleun ganda/One Fine Spring Day* (Jin-ho Hur, 2001),

Hong Kong's horror drama *Gin gwai/The Eye* (Danny and Oxide Pang, 2002) and two sequels, *Gin gwai 2/The Eye 2* (2004) and *Gin gwai 10/The Eye 3* (2005). Applause also took the lead in producing notable pan-Asian anthology films, such as *San Geng/Three* (2002) and *San Geng Ti/Three . . . Extremes* (2004).

Hong Kong cinema's popular film genres, from comedy and martial arts to period drama and action films, have provided a shared regional cinema even before the events of the 1990s, and have been a major component of inter-Asian cinematic exchanges. Hong Kong–Korea interaction resulted in what Hyung-sook Lee calls a "Hong Kong Film Syndrome," a phase of acceptance and popularity of films that allowed Koreans to engage in resistance and negotiation to the challenges of local political circumstances (Lee, 2006). Films made by Ann Hui, John Woo, and Tsui Hark, and actors from Hong Kong cinema—Maggie Cheung, Brigitte Lin, Joey Wong, Chow Yun-fat, Andy Lau— provided the industry with an alternative, innovative model during the domestic industry crisis. Prominent roles for women created alternative perspectives on gender roles, and cultural proximity and shared experiences of colonialism intensified the appeal of Hong Kong cinema over Western films.

Hong Kong cinema went through a major transition after its realignment with Mainland China in 1997. Filmmakers adapted to the new realm of influences, from the pressures of censorship to the availability of funding and cheap labor, and access to a large audience. Hong Kong cinema's regional connections with Mainland China display a range of tensions and opportunities. As an illustration of the relationship of Hong Kong to Mainland China, Ruby Cheung discusses the case of *Tou ze/A Simple Life* (2012), directed by Ann Hui (2016: 1–3). In this low-budget co-production financed by Mainland China, Hui recruited Andy Lau, one of the most well-known Hong Kong actors, whose character, Roger, is a young master in love with an older maid and Chinese immigrant, Tao Jie. Widely applauded and successful, Cheung argues, the film should be taken as an example of transition to a new life for Hong Kong residents and their cinema. Andy Lau promoted the film as an advocate of Hong Kong cinema attempting to retain its independence and distinctiveness in the age of transition. New Hong Kong cinema and film culture after 1997 is a cinema of transition, negotiating its relationship with Mainland China, attempting to maintain its identity while also discovering its place in the larger Chinese cultural landscape.

Japan's inter-Asia connections

Japan became a self-appointed center for Asian collaborative projects in the 1990s, with a conscious goal to set grounds for the Japanese re-entry into Asia. Along with other projects, the most significant of these ventures was a series of six full-length feature films, *Asian Beat* (1991/1992), with directors from Hong Kong, Thailand, Taiwan, Malaysia, Singapore, and Japan, whose aim was to make Tokyo the center of regional collaborative and co-production ventures. All six films had a common link, a mandatory stipulation introduced by producer Hayashi Kaizô that all films include a Japanese character named "Tokio" (Masatoshi Nagase) traveling through Asia in search of the people who killed his parents. The narrative figure cleverly serves as a medium through which Japanese viewers encounter the lives of other Asians and see Asia through a different lens, as his persona is modified in each film according to the inflections of a particular culture, its place in the region, and its relationship with Japan. The manner in which each film adapts to the persona of Nagase, himself a transnational celebrity who starred in Jim Jarmusch's

Mystery Train (1989), left open a map of fissures and disjunctions in relationships between Japan and other Asian nations. His cross-border fame aligned fittingly with a narrative of mobility, providing "a nexus across which competing geometries of power intersect," and thus established new encounters across Asia's borders (DeBoer, 2008: 176). This made the collective project a paradigmatic case for the process of Japan's re-engagement with the region.

The phenomenal flow of pop culture products between Japan and Hong Kong in the 1990s encouraged many prominent Hong Kong directors to work on Japanese-financed films. Lam Ngai Kai's *Fuyajo/Sleepless Town* (1998) is a prototypical case of hybrid identities that crystalize the issues of transnational film production. A modern noir set in Japan, the film features a Chinese-Japanese gangster who becomes embroiled in gang war among various Chinese gangs. The rather meandering narrative intersperses diverse ethnic identities of gangs from Taiwan, Beijing, and Shanghai, which creates for an interesting hybrid neo-noir, deploying many of the classic noir elements, such as high-contrast lighting, skewed camera angles, a male narrator, and the femme fatale, imbued with Kai's own unique style. Invoking both the Japanese yakuza and Hong Kong action film genres, the film's hybrid identity was received rather uncomfortably by audiences. As one critic puts it, the film's hybridity, rather than resulting in productive creative tensions, leads to an "unplayful experiment in the consequence of co-production, uncertain parentage, dual natures, mixed origins" (Kreicer, 1998).

Shunji Iwai's film *Suwaroteiru/Swallowtail Butterfly* (1996) stands out as another example of Japanese co-production that embeds the dilemmas of Japan's interactions with the region. Set in the future Japan (against the background of an economic boom and strong yen currency) in Yentown, the slums that surround Tokyo, Osaka, and other large Japanese cities, it is a story of a teenage girl, Ageha (Butterfly), born in Japan to a Chinese prostitute, who lives on the margins with other immigrants and moves from one Yentown to another in order to make a fortune. Eventually she is taken in by a Chinese prostitute, Glico, and under her care Ageha starts a new life. One day, they find a Frank Sinatra cassette tape of "My Way," in which they discover coded messages to become rich via counterfeiting practices. Not able to accept the newfound riches in the mainstream of society, Glico becomes a singing star in nightclubs, while Ageha, after surviving a series of fateful encounters with yakuza gangsters and the immigration authorities, becomes an independent leader of a reunited group, transforming from a caterpillar to a butterfly. The film's story about foreigners moving from the margins to the mainstream of Japanese society taps into the debate surrounding the role of immigrants in the future, in the face of Japan's low birth rate and its deleterious impact on the economy and work force. The influx of foreigners gives rise both to new opportunities as well as paranoia about Japan's homogeneous identity. As Steven Shaviro (2004) notes, the film is not only multilingual and multi-ethnic, but it deploys a variety of techniques, making it a "celebration of movement and collage," blending the elements of documentary, thriller genre, fantasy, and music videos. The film's nod to multiple cultures including American pop culture reinforces the multiplicity of cultures that make up contemporary Japan and destabilizes the notion that Japanese cinema is positioned as the Other of the Western classical canon.

Pan-Asian cinema

According to Stephen Teo, after the Asian financial meltdown in 1997 the trend of pan-Asian production was initiated by the Pusan IFF and its PPP, which sought "to provide marketing momentum for Asian film projects, bringing together film financiers, producers, buyers from all over the world" (2008: 342). The intention was to get projects off the ground, and be popularized by Peter Chan's Applause Pictures, which launched various co-productions and anthology films. Particularly relevant for the Hong Kong film industry as a means to regain Asian markets in the China-dominated economy, pan-Asian films pose challenging questions about pan-Asian production as a market strategy on the one hand, and pan-Asian identity formation on the other.

In focus 7.1   Pan-Asianism in Chen Kaige's *Wu ji/The Promise* (2005) and Peter Chan's *Ru guo · Ai/Perhaps Love* (2005)

Hong Kong and China are the leaders in the production of pan-Asian projects. One of the most striking examples from China comes from the renowned Fifth Generation director Chen Kaige's *Wu ji/The Promise* (2005), a blockbuster that drew audiences in Asia and abroad. A lavish drama (at $30 million, it is supposed to be China's most expensive production) set in a fantastical China, the film constructs a romantic-adventure tale of three male leads pursuing a woman. General Guangming (Japanese actor Hiroyuki Sanada), slave Kunlun (South Korean actor Jang Dong-gun), and Duke Wuhuan (Hong Kong actor Nicholas Tse) pursue princess Quingchen (Cecilia Chung from Hong Kong). Kunlun's mission is not merely to defeat others, but to bring Quingchen to an earlier moment in her life when she can renegotiate the deal she made with goddess Manshen, who re-writes an earlier promise to make her happy without everlasting love.

The film's spectacular imagery shows little regard for the specificity of contexts as characters from different countries blend into a Chinese kingdom. Costumes are designed from blended imaginary contexts, rather than a specific historical period in China, Korea, or Japan. The romantic tale is constructed in the *wuxia* (martial arts) genre, maintaining a transcendental sensationalism.

Figure 7.1a Chen Kaige's pan-Asian production *The Promise* (2005), set in a fantastical China and featuring spectacular imagery, posits pan-Asianism as an economic imperative

(continued)

(continued)

Addressing the film's conception of pan-Asian identity, Teo describes it as "a contemporary example of non-culturally specific historical epic" that projects pan-Asianism as an economic imperative of marketing and transnationalism under the Chinese rubric (2008: 351). Pan-Asian identity depicted in this film is indicative of a pre-national phase of Asia, unified under ideological notions of common cultural traits such as barbarism. The unity imagined in the spectacle of pan-Asian cinema, Teo contends, is that of a region brought together for economic expediency and survival, combining elements that lack context and keeping an eye on commercial gains.

Another successful pan-Asian project comes from Peter Chan of Alliance Pictures, a strong advocate of the pan-Asian productions, who directed and produced a visually spectacular musical, *Ru guo · Ai/Perhaps Love*. The film, funded by Hong Kong's TVB and Malaysia's Astro Shaw, features inter-Asian casting: Ji Jin-hee from Korea (Monty, a chorus figure), Takeshi Kaneshiro from Japan (Lin Jian-dong, a Hong Kong actor-lead male star), Zhou Xun from China (Sun Na, a film star), and Jacky Cheung (Nie Wen, a film director) from Hong Kong. The film was choreographed by Farah Khan from India and filmed by Australia's Christopher Doyle and Hong Kong's Peter Pau. Filmed in Beijing and Shanghai, the film is about Mainland director Nie Wen, who decides to film a musical starring his Mainland girlfriend Sun Na and Hong Kong film star Lin Jian-dong. Unbeknownst to him, the two had a relationship ten years ago that Sun now refuses to acknowledge. The plot of the musical concerns two young lovers who are separated when the girl loses her memory. The musical within the film starts blending with the main narrative in a film-within-a-film structure, and Lin Jian-dong's rekindled passion gets Nie Wen's film production into trouble, as the film moves between contemporary Hong Kong and nostalgic Shanghai.

Most notable for its musical numbers, dances, and flamboyant visual spectacles that transition between two different cultures and time periods, *Perhaps Love*

Figure 7.1b Peter Chan's *Perhaps Love* (2005) blends the styles of Hong Kong and Chinese cinema with Bollywood and Hollywood musicals, constructing a transnational genre onto which various cultures can be inscribed

blends the styles of Hong Kong and Chinese cinema together with Bollywood style and Hollywood musicals, from Bob Fosse's *Sweet Charity* (1969) to Baz Luhrmann's *Moulin Rouge!* (2001).

As Teo points out, pan-Asianism here is broader than East Asia, combining elements of Hong Kong, Chinese cinema, Bollywood, and Hollywood into a transnational generic construction onto which various cultural inscriptions can be made. The film's oscillation between the past and the present, the struggles of memory and forgetting, nostalgia and identity renewal, crystalizes the quest for a pan-Asian identity. Teo concludes, "if *The Promise* is an allegory of globalization, *Perhaps Love* is a metaphor of its renewal" (2008: 352).

Pan-Asian productions gained considerable exposure and revenue outside of Asia. The appeal of the two films, blockbusters in their own right, was immense outside of Asia, and they gained popular success and critical acclaim in Europe and elsewhere. *The Promise*, for example, was nominated for eleven prizes at the 25th Hong Kong Awards, closed the Venice film festival in 2005, and was submitted as Hong Kong's official entry for the Oscars in 2006. As instances of successful pan-Asian productions, these films projected an inter-Asian identity to the rest of the world. Within the region, their success pointed to various dilemmas about the possibility of pan-Asian identity, constructing a shared identity that transcends national subject-positions. As Teo argues, cross-border transfers of resources and talent work on quite a different level from textual cross-references that signify on a cultural level. It is precisely this collection of cultural and national signifiers, a cultural unity constructed by shared iconography, that poses important questions. That is, pan-Asianism as an economic strategy and pan-Asianism as an identity proposition are not necessarily aligned and pose a different set of questions with different political ramifications. Erasing the distinctness of identity where "culture is at once transcended and becomes transcendental," Asian cinema is "an *ideal* that, like Hollywood, strives to be universal" but may not realize pan-Asianness as a viable identity (Teo, 2008: 355). The discourse of pan-Asian cinema fails to create a stable signifier for the region. The meaning of Asia remains in flux, moving between different modes of representation as national-ethnic identities are placed in a milieu different from their own.

Other examples of pan–Asian cinema

Zhang Yimou's *Hero* (2002) and *House of Flying Daggers* (2004); He Ping's *Warriors of Heaven and Earth* (2003); Tsui Hark's *Seven Swords* (2005) and *Zhì qu weihu shan/The Taking of Tiger Mountain* (2014); Jackie Chan's *The Myth* (2005); Jacob Cheung's *Mo gong/A Battle of Wits* (2006); and John Woo's *Jian yu/Reign of Assassins* (2010) and *Chi bi/Red Cliff* (2008).

Pan-Asian anthology films

Anthology films, made of multiple commissioned short films from different countries that share a common idea, theme, or genre, forge a number of connections among contexts, texts, and conditions of production. To produce an anthology film is to bring together a collection of filmmakers and production teams, each working in a different space, while allowing their contributions to become part of a feature-length project. As this format is enjoying its resurgence around the world since the mid-1980s, inter-Asian anthology films perform a prominent role in constructing regional dynamism between directors, production teams, and cinemas.

DeBoer provides an account of the role played by Japan's film industry in the 1990s, recognizing that anthology films were a "significant mode of production in the early to mid-1990s" (2014: 117). Two projects—a 1993 anthology film called *Southern Winds* (Mike De Leon of the Philippines, Shoji Kokami of Japan, Slamet Rahardjo of Indonesia, and Cherd Songsri of Thailand), and the series of six full-length feature films called *Asian Beat*, put Japan at the center of co-production in Asia. In Hong Kong, horror anthology films produced by Peter Chan (Applause Pictures) set the parameters for inter-Asian collective films: *San Geng/Three* (2002) included short films by Kim Jee-woon from Korea, Nonzee Nimibutr from Thailand, and Peter Chan from Hong Kong, while the second, *San Geng Ti/Three. . . Extremes* (2004), involved Fruit Chan from Hong Kong, Takashi Miike from Japan, and Chan-wook Park from Korea. Both films addressed horror, one of the popular genres of Asian cinema, with an aim to produce a pan-Asian collaboration that brings together directors from different Asian countries, mediating between national film industries and their regional and global markets. Short film contributions to these two anthology films, complex in their linguistic and cultural make-up, simultaneously construct an appeal to regional viewers through specific narrative and visual markers, and widen this appeal through a play with the horror genre—a feature that becomes a basic mark of pan-Asian projects (Lim, 2015).

Anthology films as collective productions are crucial for constructing a collective identity on many levels. A collection of films by different directors and from different contexts is bound to be uneven, but in their intertextual, collective identity, they project an internal dynamism different from other forms of co-production ventures. A producer coordinates production of multiple independent teams, maintaining some sense of coherence and diversity among films that share a common theme or a genre. Feature-length film is seen as a package where multiple short films are invariably viewed in the context of other films. If in some cases short films are released separately from the collective anthology film, or (as in case of Peter Chan's *Dumplings*) some short films are made into feature films, the intertextual association with a collective, inter-Asian project remains, contributing to a mode of production and circulation with undeniable advantages for the regional identity. In terms of the regional production of anthology films, Asia remains one of the most active producers in the world. Several projects have been completed, including: *Visitors* (2009), with contributions from Hong Sang-soo (Korea), Naomi Kawase (Japan), and Lav Diaz (the Philippines) on the difficulty of coping with the arrival of a neighbor/stranger; *Nan fang lai xin/Letters from the South* (2013), with shorts by Aditya Assarat (Thailand), Sun Koh (Singapore), Tan Chui Mui (Malaysia), Royston Tan (Singapore), Tsai Ming-liang (Taiwan), and Chao Te-Yin, also known as Midi Z (Malaysia), which reflect on diaspora directors' relationship with the Chinese homeland; *Breakfast, Lunch, Dinner* (2010), an anthology project by women directors from the region (Wang Jing from China, Anocha Suwichakornpong from Thailand, and Kaz Cai from Singapore) that reflects on women's subjectivity and regional identity.

Regional blockbusters

Blockbusters from Asia suggest a significant development in world cinema, beyond showing that box office giants are not the sole province of Hollywood. In fact, in recent years locally-made successful films from different parts of the world have presented a significant challenge to the dominance of Hollywood blockbusters in foreign markets. As Hollywood took note of the rising prominence of Asian blockbusters, it tried to jump on the bandwagon by importing talent from Asia to strengthen the appeal of its own block-buster formula. The financial investment and reach of blockbusters in Asia is dwarfed in comparison to Hollywood productions, but their inter-Asian influence is undenia-ble, from solidifying gains for local industries to providing alternative forms of popular films for their own audiences. Korean blockbusters remain dominant in their exemplary rejuvenation of Asian cinema, while Chinese blockbusters show an increasing power in attracting transnational talent and resources.

Korean blockbusters

We discussed the rise of blockbusters in Korea as a national response to Hollywood's dominance in Asian cinema. The success of *Swiri/Shiri*, directed by Je-gyu Kang, in 1999 was a tremendous cultural, economic, and industrial event. Already a record-breaker at the box office at home, the film was released in Japan, Hong Kong, Taiwan, and Singapore, earning a large share at the box office ($14 million in Japan alone), even out-grossing *Titanic* (no small feat, considering that *Titanic* was the highest earner worldwide) (Kim M., 2000). With a production budget of $5 million, much higher than most Korean films at the time, *Shiri* has crossed many thresholds and marked the beginning of a new, successful phase for the Korean film industry. It announced the birth of the Korean regional blockbuster, demonstrating to the West that it was possible to make films with box office success in mind, with high production values and narrative structures that engaged local audiences in large numbers by adapting the blockbuster action film formula of Hollywood to nationally specific issues. The significance of *Shiri* is such that "the his-tory of Korean cinema can be divided into before *Shiri* and after *Shiri*" (Kim J., 2004).

Dubbed by the local papers as "the small fish that sank *Titanic*," the film takes its name from a species of fish indigenous to the North and South Korean freshwater streams. The film is full of metaphors of fish, signifying the conditions of transfer between the two divided countries, and addressing rather directly the controversial topic of Korean reunification (Choong, 2005: 327). The film opens in 1992 at a training camp for agents in North Korea led by a military officer who believes in unifying the two Koreas. A par-ticularly talented female agent, Hui, is assigned to take out key political and military figures in South Korea. After years of covert missions, and after she has undergone plastic surgery and changed her identity (to Lee Myeong-hyeon), she resurfaces in South Korea, and falls in love with a South Korean intelligence officer, Ryu, who is assigned to track her down (not knowing her true identity). As Ryu and his partner Lee also get involved in prevent-ing a terrorist attack in Seoul planned by the North Korean terrorists (they want to steal a top-secret South Korean weapon, a liquid bomb called CTX, to blow up a stadium during a North versus South Korean soccer match), the personal becomes political and matters of the state blend with matters of the heart. Ryu foils the attempts to overthrow both the South and North governments, and Hui is killed by her lover at the climax of the film.

The narrative blends the elements of action thrillers and melodrama, visual spectacle and romance, to broaden the appeal of the film for audiences. Energetic, fluid, at times spasmodic camera movements and rapid cuts are interspersed with plush images of the prosperous consumer economy of South Korea, equipped with a rich urban landscape and technologies. Successfully combining the romantic plot with Hong Kong-style action, the film set the standard by which subsequent efforts would be measured.

a

b

Figures 7.2a & 7.2b Kang Je-gyu's *Shiri* (1999) announced the birth of Korean blockbuster. A North
        Korean female agent, Hui (Yunjin Kim), and her final confrontation with Ryu
        (Han Suk-kyu), a South Korean intelligence officer she is in love with

Shiri's success came from its versatility in adapting to foreign influences. The film's
narrative begins with a spectacular sequence in North Korea, witnessing Hui in thrilling
military maneuvers and displaying her superior skills. Thereafter, the narrative moves
from one crisis to another, punctuating the line of causality. All loose ends are tied up
in the end, culminating in a climax of mixed results for the leading man of the film, but
affirming the safety of the nation. An action film that relies on the familiarity with Hong
Kong gangster and action films, *Shiri* manages to blend a romantic tale into its fast-paced
narrative about conflict between the two nations. In a departure from the Cold War
master narrative, the film offers a more positive depiction of North Koreans, yet never
loses its focus on depicting its Northern neighbor as a cauldron of danger and despair,

while the cityscape of Seoul appears in its neoliberal grandeur cleansed of its past. In its appeal to large audiences it mustered, *Shiri* accomplishes a number of goals: mobilizing national sentiment against a volatile neighbor, asserting independence in charting its own history of resolving conflicts while safeguarding everyday life in modern Korea, and presenting a narrative of national identity against North Korean that remains, for the most part, an imagined invisibility. The most salient achievement of the film comes in forging a "compromise between foreign forms and local materials" (Kim S., 2006: 195). It offers a mode of resistance to Hollywood domination and manages to come up with a potent indigenous formula that would "de-Westernize the blockbuster" for many subsequent films and shape a contested terrain for the localization of a global trend (Berry, 2003: 220).

The success of Korean blockbusters is attributed not only to the revived film industry and economic boom, but also a rising nationalist sentiment, clearly tapped into in *Shiri* then further articulated by the blockbusters that followed. Park Chan-wook's action thriller *Kongdong gyeongbiguyok, JSA/Joint Security Area* (2000) involves an investigation of two North Korean soldiers in the Demilitarized Zone between the two Koreas, conducted by an officer from the Swiss military. Constructed through a series of flashbacks, the narrative hinges on the secretive bond and illicit friendship between the soldiers in the two countries. Presented as a mystery, the film points both to projected fears and hopes for reunification, and further normalizes the cinematic depiction of North Korea. After its spectacularly successful nationwide release, the film was sold to Japan, where it opened on 225 screens and stayed among the top ten films for many weeks. Another notable case of inter-Asian circulation of a Korean film is a romantic comedy, *Yeopgijeogin geunyeo/My Sassy Girl* (2001), directed by Kwak Jae-young, which became a blockbuster hit throughout the entire region, dominating the box office in Hong Kong, China, Taiwan, and Japan. It was remade in China and the US, and twice in India. There is an eleven-part adaptation for Japanese television, and plans for a sequel produced as a collaboration between China and Korea.

These films, along with many other hits such as Kim Yuong-jun's *Bicheonmu/Bichunmoo* (2000), Yang Yun-ho's *Libera Me* (2000), and Lee Si-myung's *2009: loseutu maemorijeu/2009: Lost Memories* (2000), transposed national issues and traumas onto a broader Asian scene. They adapted the techniques of Hollywood blockbusters, now aimed at national conflicts but with a wider regional appeal. Satellite networks and television channels have increased the circulation of Korean films in the region, riding on the popularity of *Hallyu*, which has created conditions for wide distribution through music and television dramas. The regional popularity of Korean blockbusters has only accelerated exports for all other Korean films, and Asia (with Japan and Thailand as top markets) remains their largest export market, increasing from 21 percent in 1998 to 72 percent in 2012 (Noh, 2013). The trend of blockbusters in the region occupies a critical space for a regional industry that attempts to establish its difference from global trends while also providing a regional counter-force to the global dominance of Hollywood blockbusters.

Chinese blockbusters

Mainland Chinese cinema courted the idea of big-picture (*dapian*) and epic films (*jupian*) based on historic events or biographies of major figures long before adapting blockbusters (Berry & Farquhar, 2006: 211). The breakthrough arrived with Ang Lee's *Wo hu cang long/Crouching Tiger, Hidden Dragon* (2000). Made with a budget of $15 million, the film was a major success for the Chinese film industry, earning $200 million worldwide.

It won accolades in the West, including Academy Awards and major profits in DVD sales. The film reactivated the martial arts genre and reanimated the long-lasting fame of Bruce Lee in the world's imagination, while for many it signified "an anti-imperialistic aesthetic of defiance" (Davis & Yeh, 2007: 25). Local Asian contexts in the film were dressed up in Hollywood's spectacular style with a narrative that maintained roots in the Chinese culture and language. The production and financing made a breakthrough as well, combining Edko Films from Hong Kong, Zoom Hunt International Productions in Taiwan, Asia Union Film and Entertainment in China, and state institutions in China. An exemplary instance of an art house film crossing over to achieve success in the mainstream, the film has been heralded for its achievements on many levels. For Asian cinema, it was a benchmark that harnessed local cultures and resources for global success, providing a major boost to its global profile despite its lack of success in China itself (Davis & Yeh, 2007: 27). In Olivia Khoo's view, it is important to note the inter-Asia credentials of *Crouching Tiger, Hidden Dragon*. The film "inscribes China's relationship to Asia" not only because it brings Ang Lee back to the Chinese culture and language after his transnational projects, but also points to a vision and imaginary space of Asia where a female hero challenges the patriarchy on her return from the diaspora (2007: 163). Lee finds in Asia the energy for his female warrior, which in itself is not uncommon to *wuxia*, but his film forms her representation in an Asian context, strengthening a regional imaginary. Khoo finds in this and other blockbusters from China (such as *The House of Flying Daggers* and *The Myth*) a national past now rejuvenated with inter-Asian connections, from casting to narratives.

The film announced the awakening of the Chinese film industry to the logic of the blockbuster. Made against the benchmark of this blockbuster aimed at the international market, Zhang Yimou's film *Ying xiong/Hero* (2002) was a culture-specific film that would appeal to audiences in and outside of Asia. Made with similar models of financing ($31 million), the film became China's most profitable film domestically and abroad. The assembly of talents was markedly transnational, with a cast from across

a

Stephen Chow's *Kung fu/Kung Fu Hustle* (2004), and Tsui Hark's *Qi jian/Seven Swords* (2005) among others. All films are rooted in the Asian vernacular of martial arts, a genre that continues with Wong Kar-wai's *Yi dai zong shi/The Grandmaster* (2013) and Hou Hsiao-hsien's *Nie yin niang/The Assassin* (2015). With roots in popular stories, folk legends, fiction, and television dramas, martial arts remain prominent in Chinese-language cultures of Asia.

The resilience of the genre in the region contributed to directors turning to blockbusters, and the star quality and recognition of some of the major actors have contributed to its popularity in the region.

Hong Kong blockbusters

In terms of the regional dynamic, the Hong Kong film industry has operated in the shadow of the strongest regional player. China's products not only dominate the markets in East Asia but also deploy East Asia as a hinterland to engage with Hollywood in the production of English-speaking films. This creates an unequal interdependence, with the Chinese film industry boasting definite economic and political advantage, and Japan and South Korea as powerful players as well. Despite the unequal power relations in the region and the fact that Hong Kong's industry has been coopted by China, Hong Kong films continue to be made in the local tradition and with an imprint of Hong Kong film culture.

Andrew Lau and Alan Mak's crime thriller *Mou gaan dou/Infernal Affairs* (2002) gave a boost to Hong Kong's film industry at a time when it was suffering from the post-1997 slump and Hollywood domination. The film surpassed the gains of *Titanic* in Hong Kong and earned twice the revenues of *The Promise*. The Media Asia Production Company inaugurated a successful franchise with the film, producing two sequels with sustained success. In the age of threats of piracy and foreign domination, and dwindling theater attendance, the film revived the industry and made its mark by giving Asia its third path-breaking blockbuster. *Infernal Affairs* was a unique effort in Hong Kong cinema in the careers of Lau and Mak; Lau had worked as a cinematographer with Shaw Brothers, acted in films by Wong Kar-wai and Ringo Lam, and made a series of films with Alan Mak in 2000 called *Young and Dangerous*, based on a comic book series. The film also recruited Tony Leung Chiu-wai, one of the most dependable stars of Chinese and Hong Kong art and commercial cinema, to play a police officer who lives as a member of a triad. With an aesthetic that represents a departure from earlier Hong Kong films, the film features a strict economy of movement and plot, without the flair for violence and action, and cinematography that avoids the flashiness of violence and excess. As a disciplined and restrained production, it revived the confidence of the local industry and rewrote the practice of gangster films of earlier decades. Davis and Yeh (2007: 31) suggest that as the former "perpetrators of excess," Lau and Mak were the perfect candidates to practice restraint.

The trilogy was consistent even if the commercial temptation has the forewarnings of lax production values and excess. The first film involves a conflict between the triad mole and an undercover police officer, with a climactic final confrontation that results in both of their deaths. Both the police officer and the mole appear morally equivalent, and the two perform their roles in a professional mode. The second film, *Infernal Affairs 2* (2003), is a prequel, borrowing from *The Godfather Part II* (1974) and depicting the lives of the two protagonists at an earlier age, igniting the narrative of nostalgia for Hong Kong. *Infernal Affairs 3* (2003) brings back the main stars, Tony Leung Chiu-wai and Andy Lau, and in a nod to Mainland China, actor Chen Daoming (from Yimou's *Hero*) as a gangster. Flashbacks of Andy Lau's character reveal psychological crises in his life, from psychosis to schizophrenia, compounding the issue of a breakdown of subjectivity and memory. The device allows the film to introduce an element of reconciliation between China and Hong Kong as tensions dissolve in an amicable resolution.

The film's title, *Wi jian dao* in Mandarin or *Mou Gan Dou* in Cantonese, refers to "continuous hell," signifying tales of moral struggles in a Buddhist framework and offering clues to a diagnosis of the Hong Kong society. The trilogy provides space for a nostalgic revival of Hong Kong's memory as it suggests how pressure of reconciliation may bring about a disorder of mind and action. It provides a tableau of trajectories and intersections to read Hong Kong cinema's place in relation to Mainland China, while both face pressures to articulate themselves while coming to terms with the fissures of the past (Lee V., 2009).

a

b

Figures 7.4a & 7.4b Andrew Lau and Alan Mak's crime thriller *Infernal Affairs* (2002) became a regional benchmark for a blockbuster. Serving as an inspiration for Martin Scorsese's *The Departed* (2006), it underscores the influence of Asian popular cinema on other cinemas including Hollywood

As a regional benchmark for a blockbuster, the *Infernal Affairs* trilogy appealed to the neighboring Asian countries and to Mainland China, suggesting the dominance of popular cinema in the region. It is notable that the three blockbuster benchmarks from the region involve talents that also have a strong presence in art house cinema. Combined with Johnnie To's polished flair for violence embedded in a calculated and precise *mise-en-scène*, the trilogy set a threshold of Hong Kong cinema's transformation in the regional industry. It was now possible to adapt to new circumstances, utilize all aspects of aesthetic capital, deploy collaborative financial resources, and construct a realm of cinema that would create a regional identity for itself, using local elements to acquire global presence and stature. That *Infernal Affairs* became an inspiration for Martin Scorsese's *The Departed* (2006) only underscores the capacity of regional cinema to exert influence on films elsewhere, and points to the fact that the waves of influence between Asia and the West flow in both art cinema and popular cinema.

The localism of inter-Asian cinema

While local traditions of film production existed before the 1990s, they are now re-inscribed into the global space of cultural flows as they successfully carry out the task of constructing an inter-Asian identity. This phenomenon of maintaining a local sphere that is fully aware of the globalized spaces around it is often referred to as a "glocal" sphere, a term borrowed from Japanese *dochakuka* (from *dochaku*, living on one's own land), based on the practices of adapting farming techniques to one's own land (Iwabuchi, 2002a: 93). The concept was then deployed by Japanese marketing practices in the 1980s to suggest multiple interactions between the global and local spheres of cultural production, and popularized by sociologist Roland Robertson (1995), who used the term "glocalization" in place of *globalization* to discuss the simultaneous presence of universalizing and particularizing elements.

In his attempt to grasp the plurality of cinemas within Mainland China, a perplexing problem on its own, Yingjin Zhang proposes that localism, or what he calls "locality," is a spatial category, where cinematic practices produce the space of the local and are shaped by the relationship between the local and the global. Describing cinematic discourses as being engaged in the "interplay between the production of space and the space of production," he proposes a spatial mapping that is necessarily "heterogeneous, conflictual and contested" (Zhang Y., 2010a: 137). The idea of the production of space overrides the notion of pre-given spatial categories such as the regional, national, or the global. Instead, space is constructed in and through discourses, and is thus both a product of representation in cinema and a discursive practice.

Viewed in this manner, we can conceive of localism as made of multiple localities, or what Zhang (2010a) calls "polylocalities." The local is always inescapably tied to the global, and the relationship between the two is not symmetrical; each space is connected to and affected by the global in a different configuration in the same map of polylocalities. Zhang concludes that an appropriate sense of locality is evident in a "place-based imagination," a discourse through which the local asserts itself in difference to polylocalities and writes its own voices into the global. This complex interaction produces an incredibly intricate and complex map of local activities within Asian cinema. It is impossible to discuss all of them here, but they should be seen as an important feature of a cinema that is constantly shaping and being shaped by the interaction among its various constituents.

Localism in Korean independent cinema

In her appraisal of the climate in which Asian cinema adapted to blockbusters, Soyoung Kim says, "The key issue that local blockbusters bring to the fore lies not so much in the actual amounts of real profit they generate as the investments they show in national cultural value" (2003: 11). Though blockbusters awaken regional energies to engage with the local and the global spheres, alternative, local discourses emerge within the same space, such as the feminist sphere mobilized on and by the Internet and digital technologies that include documentary production and other activist expressions. Short film production in the region as well serves as a counter-current to cinema with dominant international currency by emphasizing political positions and marking a discourse of what Olivia Khoo (2004) terms as "minor cinema" that attempts to transform mainstream practices. This form of "minor trans-nationalism" brings together networks of filmmakers through a variety of channels, where short films function as agile texts that circulate widely among regional audiences. Short films were central to independent film production in the early 1990s in Korea, though by the mid-2000s filmmakers opted for feature films by financing their own productions outside the mainstream circuits. Leesong Hee-il, an openly gay filmmaker, made *Huhoehaji anha/No Regret* (2006), widely regarded as the first film to handle an affair between a prostitute in a gay bar and a rich man. Zhang Lu, an ethnic Korean from China, works across both cultures to produce independent films, directing his own films (*Gyeonggye/Desert Dream*, 2007) and producing *Guedo/Life Track* (Jin Guang-hao, 2007). Independent film reached its peak in 2009 with several accomplished filmmakers such as Park Jung-bum, Jang Kun-jae, Jo Sung-hee, and Kim Kyung-mook, many of who have looked to the BIFF for support in launching their productions.

Rob Wilson observes that there is a resistance toward "transnational semiotics and Hollywood simulacra" in Korea, a trend perhaps most strongly exemplified by the career of the renowned Korean director Im Kwon-taek (2001: 308). Known as the father of New Korean Cinema, and the most internationally decorated Korean director in the 1980s, Im Kwon-taek is mostly known for commercial genre films in his earlier career. He turned to art cinema in the 1980s to explore sensitive historical and cultural identity issues, indicating a "turn inward toward affirming the local imaginary" where local subjects invoke global questions (Wilson, 2001: 309). His film *Sopyonje* (1993) was the most successful Korean film before globalization and liberalization in the industry. The narrative claims a local folk song tradition (*p'ansori*) that includes chants, lyrics, and spoken tales accompanied by drums. A reputed *p'ansori* singer, Yu-bong, wants to pass on the tradition to his son Tong-ho and his daughter Song-hwa. He believes that a *p'ansori* singer must identify with grief and suffering and hence must become blind, a belief that his son finds unacceptable, so he leaves home. Years later he returns in search of his father, and finds that he has passed away. His sister, criminally blinded by his father, has become an accomplished singer. Im Kwon-taek films the final union between Tong-ho and Song-hwa in an ecstatic burst suggestive of the heightened value of the surviving music as much as the intensity of *haan*, the intense sentiment of injustice, pain, and deep sorrow.

The film's intense nationalist sentiment is placed in a broader framework, in defense of the effort necessary to preserve the traditions. The film embodies the injurious

a

b

Figures 7.5a & 7.5b Im Kwon-taek's successful film *Sopyonje* (1993), about a *p'ansori* singer who wants
to pass a local folk song tradition to his children, engages the question of the
local Korean national identity, threatened both by the history of colonization and
globalization

values of patriarchy and injustice against women, a sentiment that is ultimately glossed
over and legitimized by the sentimentality of protecting the local traditions. Despite
the film's ambivalence toward the rigidity of traditions, its foregrounding of the local
against the global, dialectic between perceived orientalism, and stubborn refusal to
subscribe to the dominant cultural forms pervading the national space, invited intense
debates surrounding the film and produced "one of the most powerful nationalist discourses in Korea" (Kim K., 2001: 27). Invoking Buddhist and local traditions in his

films (*Mandala*, 1981; *Ch'ukje/Festival*, 1996; and *Chunhyangdyun/ Chunhyang*, 2000), Im engages with the question of local Korean identity at a moment when this identity has been threatened not only by a long history of colonization, but by its new guise under globalization.

Localism in Hong Kong

In Davis and Yeh's view, the "new localisms" of Asian cinema provide a level of vitality different from that of film festivals and blockbusters (2007). These projects attempt to differentiate themselves from the co-opting capacity of Hollywood. They bear complex markers of confluence between the local and the global and mobilize specific cultural contexts in addressing Asian audiences without reducing their export value.

The most salient example of impression of local contexts inscribed onto the sophistication of aesthetic techniques comes from the films of Hong Kong director Johnnie To. To, also known as To Kei-Fung, established Milkyway Image with Wai Ka-Fai in 1996 to create a consistent record of locally flavored films in several genres, from gangster films and comedies to action-adventure and ghost stories that have become the hallmark of local cinema. Trained in Hong Kong's television and studio system, To is a consummate visual artist, bringing an unusual and eclectic flair in *mise-en-scène* and editing to his popular films. His recent experimentation with style, *Hua li shang ban zu/Office* (2015), a 3D musical adapted from Sylvia Chang's hit stage play *Design for Living*, combines a uniquely stylized, theatrical corporate setting with a narrative as powerfully melodramatic as it is sharply critical of Hong Kong's financial sector and the aggression of capital wielded through authoritarian populism in the region. Milkyway Image resisted the temptation to go global, producing films that use older local traditions, from gangster films to supernatural concepts. The Closer Economic Partnership Agreement removed restrictions on distributing films into the Greater Chinese market, allowing Milkyway to produce locally flavored films. The company's local ties have only affirmed its independence from Hollywood models and from outsourcing its talent.

To's association with Milkyway and his status as its producer and chief executive did not impede his reputation as a stand-alone auteur, a stature clearly cemented by the HKIFF, which organized a retrospective of his work in 1999 and identified him as a major director in contemporary Hong Kong cinema. Johnnie To's auteur status is marked by incredible versatility and skillful navigation between different genres: *Cheung foh/The Mission* (1999) is a crime film that explores the ordinary mechanics of professionalism; *Fong juk/Exiled* (2006) is an action drama that lays bare the dynamic of a gang of hitmen assigned to target one among them; *Daai zek lou/Running on Karma* (2003), presented in a maze of fantasy visions and crises, is a genre mishmash framed in a Buddhist parable that examines the Buddhist precepts of karma; *Dai si gin/Breaking News* (2004) is an action film that serves as a critique of the unassuming confluence between the culture of violence and media spectacles, beginning with a spectacularly memorable seven-minute-long opening sequence that sets the tone for a virtuoso display of images and movements; and *Man jeuk/Sparrow* (2008), invoking Jacques Demy's *The Umbrellas of Cherbourg* (1964), is a lyrical and lighthearted comedy, leading the viewer through a maze of images strewn with sounds and silences, constructed in the graceful poetry of sensory pleasure.

To's films on the politics of triads, *Hak se wui/Election* (2005) and *Hak se wui wo wai kwai/Triad Election* (2006), give a glimpse of his stance toward Mainland China and the traditions of gangland Hong Kong. *Election* (2005) borrows from considerable research into the triad traditions and delivers a narrative in subdued action, punctuated by violent scenes. In *Triad Election* (2006), the intrigue continues with the added element of the passive police state. Davis and Yeh note that To's triad films are positioned against the state support of the *Infernal Affairs* trilogy, by locating triad politics outside of the state institutions, particularly the police, thereby exposing China's control as authoritarian at the end of *Triad Election* (2007: 49). To's films critique the forces of threats to Hong Kong traditions symbolized in the sites of triad activities, the neoliberal capitalism that attempts to usurp the traditions, and the authoritarianism lurking at the borders.

Johnnie To's mastery of filmmaking and his steadfast re-working of the earlier forms of gangster films and other genres have made him a favorite of the regional and international film festival circuits. In the West, he is regarded as a master of Hong Kong cinema, and his recognition in both popular and critical circles is just one proof of his

a

b

Figure 7.6 Johnnie To's films on the politics of the triads, *Election* (2005) and *Triad Election* (2006), expose the triads' activities and authoritarian control as threats to Hong Kong traditions

successful mediation between popular genre and art cinema (Teo, 2007). While his films share an affinity with the Western genres, his allegiance to Hong Kong cinema makes him a distinctive representative of localism in the age of globalization. He continues to work by engaging with the local idiom although his films have acquired global circulation. His international engagement in *Vengeance* (2009), for example, included a French pop star and actor, Johnny Hallyday, and actress Sylvie Testud, but the film is a Hong Kong action-crime adventure that presents a library of masterful compositions geometrical in their stillness as well as in their spatial mobility. Appealing simultaneously to popular tastes and aesthetic connoisseurs may be the strongest component of Johnnie To's worldly localism.

Localism in Mainland China

Chinese cinema presents one of the most perplexing configurations not merely for Asian cinema but also for the cartography of world cinema. It is at once a transnational, postnational, multilingual, diverse, and heterogeneous collection of cinematic practices that present intricate and interwoven relations among its components. As we indicated earlier, scholars advance the idea of "Chinese-language cinemas" to speak for the collective national cinemas of Mainland China, Taiwan, and Hong Kong. Others propose the notion of "sinophone" cinemas covering cultural, linguistic, and epistemological frameworks of cinemas in cultures in global diasporas as well as the immediate regional cinemas of Singapore, Indonesia, or Malaysia.[2]

The question of approaching the multiplicity of Chinese cinemas is hardly settled. In the midst of these debates, we want to emphasize that the regional character of Chinese cinemas is best grasped in its inter-Asian profile, since the discourses of Chinese cinema construct regional identity and influence. We will focus on three examples of localities in Chinese cinema: Chinese popular cinema led by the films of Feng Xiaogang; Zhang Yimou, a major director of the Fifth Generation, as an example of the mixed trajectory from the historic-mythic spectacles to the realist cinema; and the films of Jia Zhangke as signature attempts of the Sixth Generation filmmakers to inscribe the local into the global.

Localism of Chinese popular cinema

Along with post-1990s liberalization, television flourished in the midst of a broad expansion of online media. The domestic market represented a major transition for film production, which was set to exploit the synergy with other media. Gradually-intensifying energy in the media sector allowed film and television to flourish alongside each other, and television provided a reliable mode for circulating films, opening up several creative avenues from animation to television series. Three large categories of production existed in the early 1990s, driven by different objectives: state-subsidized and propagandist "main melody films" (*zhuxuanlü dianying*) that were promoting official ideology, art films (*yishu dianying*) that pursued aesthetics and prestige, and entertainment, or commercially-driven films (*shangye dianying*) which took up the largest share of the film production (Zhang Y., 2010b: 43). By the end of the 1990s, Zhang notes, as main melody films started recruiting art film directors and entertainment and art films moved closer to official ideology, the state strategically maneuvered this "new alliance of art, politics, and capital" to put the needs of the market (domestic and overseas) center stage (2010b: 45). The career of Feng Xiaogang, one the most important directors of popular cinema in China, points to these transitions but also presents a unique testament to his ability to increase the artistic prestige of commercial film, while maintaining popular appeal.

Feng Xiaogang worked in the early 1990s as a television scriptwriter, making comedy his forte. He wrote and directed *Beijing ren zai Niu Yue/A Native of Beijing in New York* (1992), a high-budget television series filmed on location, with Jian Wen, who was already a major film star. Feng formed a production company, Sweet Dreams, with his co-writer Wang Shu, a major writer in his own right. Sensing the coming force of market-driven media, the state installed a pedagogical function for cinema to instill Chinese values and insisted on narratives that would have relevance to the lives of Chinese people. The rapid and hectic changes introduced by the Ministry of Radio, Film, and Television and controlled by the Communist Party were in part a response to the onslaught of imports but also an attempt to maintain control over cultural production. Under these conditions, Feng and Wang's projects ran into trouble and were restricted. Their aim of social critique was no longer viable and they had to find an alternative.

Feng changed the tone by incorporating comedy into his film *Jiafang yifang/Party A, Party B*, also known as *The Dream Factory* (1997), moving to a different level of popular film called *hesui pian* or "celebration pictures" that cashed in on the upsurge in spending and available audiences. The film earned over $4 million, encouraging him and Beijing Film Company, Huayi Brothers, and China Film Group to produce several "New Year films" in China. These films emphasized little triumphs for common people, mocked privileged classes, and viewed America as a less-than-happy place. For the most part, they remain entertaining films without posing challenges to cultural policies. The phenomenon is not unlike the *cinepanettone* in Italy, except that Feng's films couched the critique of consumerist excesses so pervasive in Chinese society at the time. The mask of popular comedy appeal in these films evaded sharp questions from the censors, brought Feng into the mainstream, and launched him into a career of a dependable filmmaker of the Chinese New Year films.

Party A, Party B is about four friends who open a "dream factory" that offers people a way to fulfill their dreams. The film's Beijing-Northern dialect, its consistent lighthearted laughter, satire, and portrayal of the common man, appealed to audiences, cementing Feng's fame as the most important director of China's popular cinema. His subsequent New Year film, *A World Without Thieves* (2004), exposed the anxiety of the rising upper-middle class that had embraced the commercial commodity culture in the new era. A con couple who have taken the life of theft attempt to shake it off as they happen to meet a simple rural boy on a train. In the course of their encounter with him, they realize the futility of stealing. The film's focus on the embrace of high-price commodities and sacrifice of morals touched audiences. In his recent New Year films, *Fei cheng wu rao/If You Are the One* (2008) and its sequel, *If You Are the One, II* (2010), Feng zeroes in on online dating and courtship rituals among the Chinese middle class, ridiculing the empty values of changing times. The sequel begins with an elaborate divorce ceremony and the narrative proceeds to show comic romance between an old man and his young paramour. The backdrops are luxurious and the display of wealth and an upscale lifestyle is used to narrate a story of love that lacks depth.

As the new millennium dawned, China entered the global marketplace by joining the World Trade Organization. Internally, the industry went through an intense period of consolidation to combat blockbusters. Film became one of the official industries, open-ing it up for private investments and giving a boost to diverse productions. The Chinese industry stepped up to modernize its technology and polish its images to meet the slick and spectacular appeal of blockbusters. This was the time of enormous success for the Chinese film industry, exemplified by the production of films such as Zhang Yimou's *Hero* (2002) and *House of Flying Daggers* (2004), and Chen Kaige's *The Promise* (2005). The influx of capital, technology, and energy allowed Feng to enter the third phase in his career, as he continues to work adeptly in a variety of genres. In his disaster-spectacle *Tang shan da di zhen/Aftershock* (2010), China's first IMAX disaster film, Feng gave Chinese audiences an engaging narrative with dazzling computer-generated effects. Melodramatic to the core, the film centers on a mother who is asked to choose one of her twin children in the aftermath of an earthquake. She survives with her son while unbeknownst to her the daughter survives in a different part of the country. The narrative is book-ended by two earthquakes, in 1976 and 2008, emphasizing family bonds and perseverance as the forces that bond a nation together. The film ends up placing the agency of the nation in the hands of the mother, who ends up choosing a boy over the girl, an issue fraught with darker implications in a country with a one-child policy.

a

b

Figures 7.7a & 7.7b In China's first IMAX disaster film, Feng Xiaogang's *Aftershock* (2010), a mother is forced to choose one of her twin children in the aftermath of an earthquake. The emotionally charged images show the abandoned girl and mother after the earthquake

Feng took up the *wuxia* genre in his 2006 film *Ye yan/The Banquet*, which brought him international acclaim. The lavish production set in the tenth century successfully plugged into the international appeal of the *wuxia* spectacles. The film, loosely adapting elements of Hamlet and Macbeth, was released in the West under the title of *Legend of the Black Scorpion*, with the star power of Zhang Yi, Ge You, and Daniel Wu. Feng's attempts to gain audiences abroad, however, did not succeed as he was unable to make the specificity of humor and dialect work in a broader context. He recruited Donald Sutherland for his West-oriented film *Da wan/Big Shot's Funeral* (2001), but it is a weak effort to reflect on the incommensurability of languages and understanding between the East and West.

Feng's films remain far more popular within China than the works of Zhang Yimou or Chen Kaige, who made the most of the changing conditions in the industry and took up big-budget productions in the new millennium. Domestic films such as *Ren zai jiong tu/Lost in Thailand* (Zheng Xu, 2012), *Xi you: Xian mo pian/Journey to the West* (Stephen Chow and Chin-kin Kwok, 2013), *Xin hua lu fang/Breakup Buddies* (Hao Ning, 2014), and *Zhuo yao ji/Monster Hunt* (Raman Hui, 2015) have made major gains in the last few years. Although Hollywood relies ever so heavily on returns from China's box office, domestically-produced films such as these give it a strong competitive edge and often perform better than Hollywood productions. Because of its sheer size and high regional profile, China's domestic industry, insisting on its localism, is becoming one of the strongest in the world.

In focus 7.2 Between Fifth and Sixth Generation: Zhang Yimou and mediated realism in *Not One Less* (1999)

In Mainland China's vibrant filmmaking history, the most consequential period for Chinese cinema's radical turn and its participation in world cinema arrived in the early 1980s when Zhang Yimou, Chen Kaige, Tian Zhuangzhuang, Wu Ziniu, Li Shaohong, and others graduated from the Beijing Film Academy. State policies allowed them access to multiple, smaller production facilities such as the Xi'an and Guanxi film studios, while the expanding television industry opened more avenues for work. Their films gained fame at international film festivals and in scholarly circles. Since then, a retroactive, convenient, and simplifying chronology of "Fifth" and "Sixth" generations gained currency in identifying the various phases of film history in China that tend to hide the rich diversity and fissures within filmmaking generations. The Fifth Generation films—from Zhang Junzhao's *Yigho he Bage/One and Eight* (1983) and Wu Ziniu's *Diexue Heigu/Bloody Track Valley* (1984) to Tian Zhuangzhuang's *Lan feng zheng/The Blue Kite* (1993), Chen Kaige's *Huang tu di/Yellow Earth* (1984) and Zhang Yimou's *Hong gao liang/Red Sorghum* (1987)—come from filmmakers who stepped out after the Cultural Revolution in China, a turbulent and violent period that ushered in a period of reforms in the country. These filmmakers were widely influenced by Chinese history and culture, and were also exposed to Western influences.

(continued)

(continued)

They elevated Chinese cinema from within, steering aesthetic and narrative tendencies for decades. Their films reached film festival circuits and won awards while spurring an increase in scholarly interest in the West on the emerging waves of Chinese cinema. The rich contributions of these filmmakers are too complex and varied to be catalogued here. We focus on Zhang Yimou, as his career offers the most paradigmatic case of the Fifth Generation and the subsequent developments of localism in Chinese cinema.

Felicia Chan identifies three different phases in Zhang's career (2013: 263). The first phase is marked by the international recognition of his "red trilogy"—*Hong gao liang/Red Sorghum* (1987), *Judou/Ju Dou* (1990), and *Da hong deng long gao gao gua/Raise the Red Lantern* (1991)—which became emblematic of the Fifth Generation's radical contributions to Chinese cinema. In the second phase of his career, Zhang turns toward localism, developing a realist aesthetic with narratives set in the present: *Qiu Ju da guan si/The Story of Qiu Ju* (1992), *Yi ge dou bu neng shao/Not One Less* (1999), and *Xing fu shi guang/Happy Times* (2000). In the third phase, as the grip of the censors, state control, and sponsorship began to fade away, he turned to blockbusters with films such as *Ying xiong/Hero* (2002), *Shi mian mai fu/House of Flying Daggers* (2004), and *Jin ling shi san chai/Flowers of War* (2011). In these films, Zhang banks on his fame, deploying earlier aesthetic achievements with an eye on fame and box office success. In 2008, he also directed the Beijing Olympics opening ceremony, televised live to one of the largest global audiences for any Chinese television event. Although he remains most recognized for the lush visual displays of *Raise the Red Lantern*, or the special effects and action sequences of *Hero*, it is his realist films that develop most incisively the discourse of localism that speaks of the transitional moment in Chinese society as well as in his career.

During these phases, responses to Zhang's political and aesthetic choices have varied, moving from a revolutionary Fifth Generation filmmaker to being a "sellout" (Chan, 2013: 264). The most common perception of these transitions in Zhang's work suggest that he began his career as a Fifth Generation filmmaker by marking a break from the socialist realist aesthetic of the earlier generation, deploying a spectacular, opulent aesthetic to represent the past from the perspective of the present. Within the Chinese filmmaking context, his was a rebellious act. For the outside world, his "rural" films projected an ethnography of Chinese generations, framed in spectacular imagery, exotic colors, and movement, raising the scope of contemporary orientalist views in the West. Zhang's films won several awards at international film festivals and he became a darling of Western scholars interested in studying or teaching Chinese cinema in the post-Mao period. Combined with reports of censorship battles (*Raise the Red Lantern* was banned from domestic exhibition), Zhang's films were seen in the West as attempts at ambiguity that couched political messages in displaced, if exotic, historic spectacles. The specific contexts of the films' narratives were mythic and allowed for the reading of an additional layer of political subtleties.

Rey Chow complicates this notion by arguing that the Fifth Generation and Zhang practiced an "auto-ethnography," whereby the filmmakers set up an exhibition of their own cultures not merely to cater to Western tastes but to turn the orientalist gaze back on itself (1995: 55–57). The "self-gazing" staged by Zhang displays a modern anxiety beneath the images, searching for the conflicts of the Cultural Revolution in Chinese history. Quoting a Chinese critic who remarks that the film's settings and images were "alien" and "remote" to local viewers, Chow argues that Zhang is providing an incisive tool to audiences at home to gain a self-reflexive approach, to defamiliarize the mythic, primitive China (1995: 81). The aesthetic mode of Zhang's films creates a "split discourse that presents and questions what it presents simultaneously" (Zhang B., 1998). Much has been written, for example, about Zhang's visual articulation of female images and their representation of both visual spectacle and social repression. The spectacle of ethnographic detail in *Raise the Red Lantern*, about a student who becomes a concubine, the fourth mistress, cannot be easily dismissed as coopted orientalism. The patriarch in the film remains visible only by his symbolic presence, not his appearance. In one instance, as the protagonist Songlian (Gong Li) stares into the camera, she defies patriarchy, while the audience becomes the object of the gaze. Her gaze, emanating from the screen of "vivid colors and images" is "intense and discomforting," moving the spectator into a jolting consciousness of ethnic identity (Chow, 1995: 168).

If for the West these films work as repositories of their orientalist views, they perform entirely different roles in the Chinese context, where they become tools for self-examination. Chow launches an elaborate and complex argument on the logic of visuality adapted and translated through Western technologies of seeing to demonstrate that what is seen as mere orientalist exhibition of cultures is, in fact, a rich nexus of the local-global dialectic where the local inserts itself as a discourse of translating a culture onto a large landscape of globalization. In reviewing Chow's work, Benzi Zhang argues that the Fifth Generation films reveal a violence of translating the cultures onto the global landscape and insist on charting the modes of postcolonial survival (Zhang B., 1998). Combine this with Tweedie's thesis that the Fifth Generation films are not merely exhibitionist canvases of an older, mythic culture but they display narrative strategies of resistance, and we see that Zhang Yimou's work is not merely an exemplary celebration of filmmaking catering to Western audiences but a complex critique of Chinese identity, history, and memory for local audiences. The films achieve this through the deft use of protagonists, including women, who rebel against the archaic system. For example, the soldier in *Yellow Earth* collects folk songs, representing the state while he himself engages in a rebellion against the older customs that imprison women and rural people (Tweedie, 2013: 264).

After the success of his rural historical spectacles, Zhang turns his attention to the realist conditions of contemporary China while embodying the documentary ethos of the Sixth Generation. His *Not One Less* (1999) stands out as an excellent example of Zhang's commitment to critiquing local conditions while inflecting this critique with a broader awareness of change underway in contemporary Chinese society. The film itself has a checkered history of festival and domestic releases though it remains a fitting example of both Zhang's adaptability to new circumstances and his commitment to maintaining a dual gaze that invariably gives rise to conflicting interpretations at home and abroad.[3]

(continued)

(continued)

The film is set in a small school in an impoverished Chinese village of Hebei, where the only school teacher has to leave to attend to his sick mother. A shy thirteen-year-old girl with no education or experience, Wei Minzhi, gets the job as his substitute. She is warned that dropping out has been a trend and that she must not lose any children during his absence—given her inexperience, the task of "not one less" becomes her main responsibility. One day, a young pupil named Zhang Huike fails to show up, because his mother, poor, ill, and debt-ridden, has sent him to the city to find work. Determined not to lose him, and particularly inventive, Wei earns enough money with the children's help to go to the city and find Zhang. Wandering through the money-driven and alienating urban environment, and after several failed attempts at locating him, she manages to get the attention of a local television station. Her appeal and her story impresses the media and gains enormous empathy from its audience, the missing student is found, and the reporters accompany them back to the village, showering the school with supplies and gifts from the city folks. Zhang Yimou films the story in a realist style, documenting details and ways of living in the villages as much as the rote bureaucracies and cold lives of an urban environment.

Straightforwardly addressing the high drop-out rate in rural China and weaving this social issue into the film as extra-diegetic information, it was perceived by many critics as an infomercial or a propaganda statement on behalf of the state and its education reform, whose goal was to guarantee nine years of compulsory education to all children regardless of economic background. The film was received warmly both at home and in festival circuits (it won the Golden Lion at Venice in 1999), its local production and realist style regarded as a great example of Zhang's realist phase and a welcome departure from the perceived orientalism and exhibitionism of his early films. More than exemplifying the imposed dichotomy that separates the phases in Zhang's oeuvre, the film is a rich meditation on the dynamic of the local-global that characterizes contemporary China, both its economy and media-scape. Insofar as the realism of the film's rural setting moves to urban spaces owned by the media that have the capacity to pervade and transform everything they touch, the film is as much about the transformation of the local/country as it is about the transformation of the image (including Zhang's own films) in the multimedia global world.

This transformation underlies the film's main trajectory from a poor rural village to the mediatized world of the city. In order to earn money for the bus ride to the city, Wei and her students decide to move bricks in a factory near their school; moving one brick pays fifteen cents, so they calculate that to earn fifteen Yuan (the price of a bus ticket), they need to move one hundred bricks. This simple and measurable correspondence between labor and its value, although already out of balance, becomes completely abstracted and equivocal once we migrate to the city, where higher proportions of return/earnings on Wei's labor become glaringly clear, and where value is determined, Chow explains, not by physical labor but by the "mediatized image that arbitrates, that not only achieves her goal for her but also has the ability to make resources proliferate beyond her wildest imagination" (2003: 145). Both Chow and Tweedie's readings of the film stress that the new regime of the image is not only at the core of Zhang's critique of the Reform economy, but that it also informs Zhang's use of realism as a contact zone between the local and global. We cannot take its realism for granted, Tweedie argues, as the film both constructs a realist image of a specific place and reveals the fragility and transformation of this image as it becomes absorbed into a global market of commodified images (2013: 272). The media environment in which Wei becomes enmeshed is on the one hand a powerful tool to shed light on her story and her village, but the process of exposing it is also a process of ripping it out of its real-world context, turning it into a cliché, a stereotype, and a commodity fetish. This becomes a crucial aspect of the dilemma of localism: once the materially grounded, realist images that accompany Wei and her students' plight are absorbed into the new medium, it forever changes the nature of these image as well as the reality they are based upon.

a

b

Figures 7.8a & 7.8b Zhang Yimou's *Not One Less* (1999). The transformation of realism in the film's rural setting to a commodified, mediated realism of the urban media-scape

(continued)

(continued)

In this way, the return of Wei and Zhang Huike to the village with the entire television entourage cannot be read as a resolution of the narrative conflict, a typical happy ending, but signifies the process by which the globalized media industry transforms into its own idiom the nature of the local at a mere brush with it, as it is simultaneously a powerful way of disseminating it. Zhang's subtle trajectory from realism to mediated realism, Tweedie says, not only subverts our blind faith in the immediacy of realism but frames cinema as a medium no longer "capable of documenting the world with exceptional fidelity because reality itself has been refashioned after the cinematic image" (2013: 273).

Localism of the Sixth Generation

The events of 1989 at Tiananmen Square had a far-reaching impact on Chinese culture. A post-socialist era began, where socialism and capitalism embraced each other, while the country entered the global economy, with a vast scale of social and economic implications. For Chinese cinema, this was a period of drastic transformation. Throughout the 1980s, filmmakers of the Fifth Generation had altered the established aesthetic norms and shaken the orthodoxy in the industry. Their art cinema showed a new direction to filmmakers in the country, while gaining considerable reputation abroad. During the era of transformation (*zhuanxing*) in the 1990s, the planned, socialist economy gave way to a market economy and privatization. In Zhang Zhen's view, cinema was of crucial importance for the state during this period since, already carrying an ideological function, it now had added financial value for the state. Cinema stood as "the emblematic force field where convoluted and competing claims for 'transformation' collide" (2007: 3). Chinese cinema during this decade and since became a cinema of transformation, a process that expanded the realm of productions, creating multiple practices, forms, styles, and movements.

Domestic production flourished on a number of fronts while also opening borders for imports from Hollywood on a revenue-sharing basis. The domestic industry oriented itself to the market as it faced a slow breakdown of the stable studio system. Multiple modes of production emerged in the country as a result of this transformation, both as a manifestation and a critique of the changing conditions in post-Socialist China. Commercial cinema maintains its capacity to bring audiences to theaters and to provide a counterbalance to Hollywood. The Sixth Generation cinema emerges to articulate social conditions, economic divides, and cultural ruptures in the country. Alongside it, a robust documentary movement reinstates and reframes a faith in the truth content of the filmic image, and independent and underground cinemas emerge to create a front of resistance against efforts to suppress the voices of dissent and rebellion. This period also witnesses a broad-scale alliance between filmmakers and other media, including digital video, art, and photography. The divergent spaces of Chinese cinema are now deeply responsive to the availability of foreign and domestic capital, the legitimizing support of film festivals in the region and across the world, and the spaces of circulation-exhibition in and outside of the country.

Graduates of the Beijing Academy born in the 1960s, having grown up during the Cultural Revolution, began filmmaking in the 1990s and documenting the great transformation around them. Commonly referred to as "the urban generation," these filmmakers watched the transition to urban economy and large-scale expansion, as cities became the staging ground for the state to map its powers. It was the cities that displayed most glaringly the inequities, exploitation of labor under the brutal market ambitions, inter-state migration, and displacement of population. And it was the effects of these social changes that became the subject for this group of directors, who unblinkingly focus their camera on disability, homosexuality, alcoholism, migrant work, and the widening gap between the rich and poor.

Often, the binary comparison between this group of filmmakers and the Fifth Generation relies on this change of focus: if the "swath of Yellow Earth" is "etched in our minds as the quintessential image of the Fifth Generation," says Zhang Zhen, the equivalent symbolic image of the Sixth Generation would be "the ubiquity of the bulldozer, the building crane, and the debris of urban ruins" (2007: 3). Largely state-supported, spectacular historical images and sweeping allegorical, mythical narratives gave way to contemporary urban settings and the realities of everyday city life, shot with low budgets, on digital video, and financed outside of the state-owned studio system, often with international support. Ironically, even though their films are stubbornly grounded in and address contemporary China, their positioning against state support and ideology and their rebellious status in the industry made this group of filmmakers more dependent on the patronage of film festivals and overseas finance, including from Taiwan and Hong Kong. According to Zhang, "It is not an exaggeration to state that there would not have been an uninterrupted, sizable output of Sixth Generation films in the 1990s without the moral and financial support of international film festivals and arts foundations overseas" (2010b: 48). The overarching irony of this phenomenon must be the fact that films articulating most strongly the Chinese localism are financed by international sources.

In focus 7.3 Localism of the Sixth Generation: *Beijing Bastards, Beijing Bicycle,* and *Suzhou River*

Considered the earliest film of the Sixth Generation, *Beijing za zhong/Beijing Bastards* (Zhang Yuan, 1993) captures the preoccupation of this group of filmmakers with giving expression to urban angst and loss of locus in everyday life as greater forces of change overtake their goals. The film depicts the life of an alienated generation at the end of the century. The notion of "bastards" is focused on the youths that live on the margins of the city without parental patronage or any other support system. They are underground rockers, freelance painters, unemployed, summarized by one disaffected character in the film as "the kind of people who make a living by following their instincts and are all classified as social alien elements." Their embrace of crime, rape, and drugs broadens the pejorative meaning of the film's title. The central character is a struggling rock musician, Karzi (played by the rock star Cui Jian), searching for his pregnant girlfriend Mao Mao, who has left him. Other characters in the film include a painter, a bar owner, and a writer, all of whom find themselves stuck and alienated in

(continued)

(continued)

a world taken over by violence, crime, and drugs. While *Beijing Bastards* clearly positioned itself against the official attitude toward Western underground music so central to this film, the same depiction had an entirely different effect abroad, where "Western spectators were titillated to discover the existence of an underground rock culture in Beijing" (Reynaud, 2007: 269). When the film was broadcast on television in the UK in 1995, the audience stayed up "until midnight to watch an underground production," creating a special allure for films that had run into rough weather with Chinese authorities (Zhang Y., 2010b: 52).

As becomes characteristic for a number of subsequent films of the Sixth Generation, the city here becomes a staging ground for the struggles of globalization, and a central site of China's transformation. The megacity carves massive disjunctions into the spaces and lives of the people, exposing the divisive powers of market capitalism alongside the fractures it creates, all of this in full view of the visitors who consider the city to be a nerve center of prosperity. The city, as Zhang Yimou's *Not One Less* already showed, is also an embodiment of a massive image-making machine with a power to propel minor incidents into global phenomena. If the cities were vilified as centers of greed and commerce during Mao's China, and served as staging grounds for fantasies in commercial films, in the Sixth Generation films the cities become central spaces onto which the anxieties of modernism are mapped to expose its ruptures to the naked eye.

Filmed with a hand-held camera, the film brings out the rough and tumble of the marginalized generation in the country's capital. The spontaneous, energetic atmosphere of concerts is filmed in relatively vivid colors with abundant lights in the frame, while the lives of the protagonists are shot in grey tones and slower camera movements. Persistent rain lends an air of acute despair to the already squalid conditions in the city, a reflection of "the state of mind of young people in contemporary China. A state of mind that can be described as the global outcome of a bastardized contemporary culture" (Reynaud, 2007: 269). The film became a signature statement of the disintegrating urban life at home, a clear sign that the cinematic canvas was now ready for an extended treatment of the imminent present of China, no longer dwelling in the allegorical fantasies of the past.

Shiqi sui de dan che/Beijing Bicycle (2001) is directed by Wang Xiaoshuai, one of the leading Sixth Generation filmmakers, and is part of the "Tale of Three Cities" project by Taiwanese producers Peggy Chiao and Hsu Hsiao-ming. *Beijing Bicycle* is a deceptively simple portrait of children struggling in China's metropolis, where the survival of residents and migrants has become a major social issue. The film appealed to audiences at home and gained critical acclaim in the West, winning the Grand Jury Prize at the Berlin Film Festival. It is an eloquent statement on the simultaneously layered spaces constructed by the cities that become the nexus of the country's economic and social transitions. The narrative centers on Guei, a seventeen-year-old migrant worker who works as a delivery boy, struggling to earn enough to purchase his own mountain bike. After his work bicycle is stolen, Guei goes on a strenuous search for the bike that, it turns out, was sold at a flea market to an upper-class boy, Jian. The bike, while not crucial to his survival, as it is for Guei, has nevertheless become an important part of Jian's life—he uses it to affirm his status and impress girls and his friends. Both desperate to keep possession of the bicycle, Guei and Jian become involved in intense pursuit and competition, each chasing their own version of the Chinese dream.

Wang's portraits of Guei and Jian, and their different symbolic associations with the bicycle (it is work and survival for one, leisure and a status symbol for the other) as a foundation of their identities, suggest two levels of struggling classes in the city, migrant workers and an urban middle class, radically different yet aligned and united in their desire for the same commodity object and life in an urban jungle. The two young boys are positioned alongside each other, without implying any judgment on their status, but it is Guei who begins and ends the narrative as a protagonist of the suffering classes in China's global cities. He is the emblematic nexus of the local being threatened by and inscribed into the global. As Guei bikes through the city streets, he is one among hundreds, as the skyscrapers, bridges, and crowds make his navigation claustrophobic and impeded. The bicycle moves through the wide and modern streets of the city as well as through the narrow alleyways (*hutong*), two distinct structures representing China's transition. The *hutong* alleyways, a large network of labyrinthine lanes and quadrangles where the residents live, are now remapped by the expansion of modern buildings and high-rises of the capitol. Guei struggles in both parts of the city: in the new city, he is making a living on low wages, while in the *hutong*, he is fighting for his social survival. Wang reserves the spaces of the *hutong* for the final decisive fight between Guei and Jian and the destruction of the bike. It is here, a space left behind and about to be forgotten in the city's splendid development, that the migrant labor and the up-and-coming bourgeois class face their punishment. The two modes of spaces, the new metropolis and the old *hutong*, appear equally distressful and dystopian. If Beijing is a city locked in a tension between the local-global dynamic, the local is poised for defeat in the *hutong*, signifying both the sacrifice of migrant workers in their quest for survival and the liminal spaces assigned to them for that struggle.

The most eloquent statement of China's wounds in absorbing the shock of the transitional era comes in the final scene of the film. Beaten and bruised, Guei carries his broken and bent bicycle across a busy intersection. His body moves in slow motion, extending the time in which we can absorb the injustice of the moment. With bicyclists in their lane and cars in the middle of the road, China's mobility is mapped onto two registers of this figurative image. Guei is defeated but determined in his slow motion, while the speed of the reform is in the background, frozen momentarily by Guei's resolute gesture of carving out his own space in the city. Guei moves out of the frame in the final shot and we are left to accept the grim reality that a culture of speed, efficiency, and market socialism cannot be stopped, but neither can it defeat or erase Guei.

Gritty realism, the main feature of the Sixth Generation, remains prominent on the surface of the film but it is also rendered problematic. In its story of a young boy searching for a lost bicycle in a busy city that moves in its own impersonal logic, and in its portrait of the crowds, the film bears striking resemblance to the Italian neo-realist classic, *The Bicycle Thieves* (Vittorio De Sica, 1948). But while the film is firmly situated in the realist ethos of filmmaking, in its juxtaposition of the historical and contemporary

(continued)

(continued)

a

b

Figures 7.9a & 7.9b Beijing Bicycle (2001) by Wang Xiaoshuai: for both Guei (who represents a
struggling working class) and Jian (urban middle class), the bicycle presents
an important foundation for their identities. In the final scene, Guei carries
his bicycle in slow motion against the unstoppable flow of modernity

spaces of a Chinese city Wang suggests that realism for its own sake is insufficient
and has only limited value for fleshing out the paradoxes of modernity. Wang's film is
a hybrid text, as Richard Letteri (2007) observes, deploying realism to frame its larger
context but then rupturing its promise by blending it with other stylistic modes. Guei's
encounter with the city's modernity is as tragic as it is comic and even melodramatic,
resulting in narrative ambiguity that brackets its realistic posture. The final scene,
for example, when Guei awkwardly stops the traffic and thus impedes the relentless

movement forward into modernity, could be read as a critique of Guei's "backward" mentality and stubbornness. His determination to take possession of the bike, a commodity object that has now lost its function and acts as a literal and metaphorical burden on his shoulders (he can no longer ride it, and has to carry it, but he *owns* it), can be seen as both an act of surrender as well as resistance to the forces of capitalism. The lyrical nature and ambiguity of the last scene belies its realism by refusing to give agency either to the new working class or to modernity.

The simultaneous reliance on and doubt in the ability of the realist image to capture the pulse of a massive megacity is even more intensely articulated in Lou Ye's *Suzhou he/Suzhou River* (2000), one of the landmark films of the Sixth Generation that won the Tiger Award at the Rotterdam IFF. Since the film was presented there without permission, Lou was banned from making films for two years, in one instance out of many over the course of his career (Lim, 2010). Initially part of a television project (the unfinished *Chaoji chengshi/The Super City* anthology), and a German–Chinese co-production, it is a rare example of a film moving from television to mainstream and art cinema. It is a definitive statement in encapsulating the multiple dimensions of China's economic boom, from the agency of its youth to the role of the image in implicating the viewer in the transitional conditions of China's development.

The film revolves around a motorcycle courier in Shanghai who traffics in illegal goods; the motorcycle, like Wang's bicycle earlier, symbolizes the mobility of a new and powerless generation to connect the local to the global. The film is narrated by a videographer who records the events as he moves about in Shanghai, capturing through both direct witnessing and his lens the traffic, waste, and unstoppable flow of goods and detritus that fuels the economic boom in the city. While the film, like many others that emerge from this group, bases itself on a specific part of a megacity, it is concerned not merely with documenting it but, as Tweedie points out, with "the more abstract relationship between the city, the camera, and the spectator," constantly undermining the perspective of the viewer and the documentary mode in which it begins (2013: 179). For Lou, the images become the transitory medium to document the realities of the city and the young generation, foregrounding their ceaseless movement, flightiness, and paradoxes of the new digital technologies. "My camera doesn't lie," said Lou in an interview, a statement that may as well belong to the videographer in the film. But it is a statement that, rather than asserting faith in the documentary-style, observational mode, implicates and pulls the camera in a self-reflexive manner into "the same polluted waters and social milieu of the post-socialist Shanghai/China that it represents," and blends the observational mode with the videographer's own fantasies and desires (Hageman, 2009: 79). The choice of digital video as a recording medium for both the reality and fantasy elements of the film is suggestive of Lou's attempt to map the past and the present of the city in an idiom of the modern, juxtaposing the sewage, waste, and hard labor on the water with the glossy fantasies spun along its banks.

Revealing the gap between the old city being demolished and the new digital technology used to document this destruction,

(continued)

(continued)

a

b

Figures 7.10a & 7.10b In *Suzhou River* (2000), Lou Ye mixes documentation of the realities of the
megacity of Shanghai with the protagonist/videographer's desires and fantasies

> *Suzhou River* transforms the cinematic image into a medium that stutters when
> confronted with the remainder of the city . . . The Shanghai viewed in these stut-
> tering frames is out of joint with the medium used to represent it."
>
> (Hageman, 2009: 282)

It is a film that, like many of the Sixth Generation works, is committed to displaying as
well as reflecting on the ambiguities of the present and the images that represent it.

Just like *Beijing Bicycle*, this film too remaps a classic Western text, Alfred
Hitchcock's *Vertigo* (1958), onto the Chinese landscape of a city in rapid transition.

Figure 7.10c The object of desire in *Suzhou River*, which recalls the object of desire in Alfred Hitchcock's *Vertigo* (1958)

While *Vertigo* is set in a romantic and lush landscape of San Francisco and its art museums, Lou's film is set on the banks of a river marked by frantic, nervous, and disjointed lives.

We never see the illusions and dreams of an obsessed male protagonist but rather the hectic, fragmented, anxiety-ridden movements of a videographer whose focus turns to waste, sewage, and toiling labor. The illusory object of desire acquires in this film a frenetic rhythm of appearance. Lou has not only destabilized the structure of the subject's desire, fantasy, and gaze by dispersing it onto the fractured landscape of industrial and neoliberal growth, but he also paints a shivering portrait of a city and the lives condemned to perennially-shifting ground beneath their feet. Vertigo here is not only a minor handicap but a catatonic, fatal condition that shatters one's existence. If in *Vertigo* the agency rests with the main protagonist, Scottie, here the agency is possessed by a camera that is constantly on the move, in a hurry to capture the unstable, rapidly shifting, and disappearing landscape.

In focus 7.4   Interrogative localism in Jia Zhangke's *Still Life* (2006)

If the Sixth Generation has a vanguard and leading spokesman it is Jia Zhangke, the most well-known filmmaker among his peers, who has directed some of the key films of the generation and maintained the most consistent output. He may be the most widely discussed Chinese director in film studies in the West, and among cinephilic circles

(continued)

(continued)

around the world. Known as "the poet of globalization" (Mello, 2014), Jia has mapped a complex history of China's period of transformations, from the plight of Chinese people in the hinterland to the experience of migration and environmental changes.

Jia Zhangke became interested in making films after watching Chen Kaige's *Yellow Earth*, and later became a critic of Zhang Yimou and Chen Kaige (Zhang X., 2010: 74). Deeply influenced by self-conscious exposure to the works of Federico Fellini, Vittorio De Sica, Robert Bresson, Hou Hsiao-hsien, and Yasujiro Ozu, Jia honed his own talents in depicting the lives of people rooted in rural and urban spaces, whose conditions painted an overwhelming background canvas. Leaving behind the metaphysical and spectacular images of the Fifth Generation, Jia moves toward mapping the space of the transformative reality of ordinary lives, bringing cinema from the mythical echelons to the street level. Describing Jia's ethic in presenting reality, Zhang Xudong says,

> Rather than trying to capture a totality of "completeness" (*wanzhengxing*), Jia seeks to break its silence and to show the facial expressions of this giant economic entity often by making audible and visible what is muffled or blurred, or forgotten altogether.
>
> (2010: 78)

Always situating his films in the present, Jia foregrounds the lives of those who have been rendered immobile by economic and social forces. Jia's films, says Zhang, are best understood "as an attempt at cognitive mapping" of the reality of the true transformation of China's emerging spaces that stand between the transformation of the city and rural landscapes. Zhang calls these spaces "*xiancheng*" or country-level spaces (Zhang X., 2010: 76). Situated between the once-stable social and cultural structure of the rural area and cities leaping to modernity and power, *xiancheng* produces a different habitus, becoming a sphere of a working class stuck in transition. Life in these in-between spaces is made of a series of compromises between the desire of the people to survive and the scars of failures left by the unfulfilled promises of state power. Jia, himself a resident of one such *xiancheng* (the Fenyang province), moves through such spaces in China as a chronicler, pausing to document the lives of the unemployed youth, urban wanderers, migrant laborers, laid off state-workers, and artists practicing disappearing arts.

Jia Zhangke's *Sanxia haoren/Still Life* (2006) is one of the masterly works of Chinese and world cinema, a film made profoundly rich with its visual and aural language and its deft blending of cinematic techniques with a moral and political commitment to the spaces and conditions upon which the narrative unfolds. The setting is the Three Gorges Dam, the largest hydroelectric power plant in China and the largest water conservation project in the world. Set in Fengjie, a two-thousand-year-old city on the banks of the Yangtze River, the construction project was completed in 2012 and caused devastating destruction and displacement of over one million people, radically transforming one of China's most iconic landscapes of splendid natural beauty and deep-rooted presence in the country's poems, paintings, and collective and cultural memory. Its brutal dismantling, remapping, and displacement of its residents, laborers, and migrants are at the center of Jia's narrative. Han Sanming, a coal miner from

Shanxi, arrives in Fengjie in search of his wife and daughter, who left Shanxi more than fifteen years ago without a trace. Determined to find them among the distressed population of laborers and displaced residents, Han takes a job in one of the several demolition projects that mark the landscape—destroying, ironically, the very history and spaces that the protagonists are searching for. The film's other narrative thread revolves around Shen Hong, a nurse from Taiyuan who arrives in Fengjie to locate her estranged husband, well-off engineer Guo Bin, whom she wants to divorce. Her search also takes her through the debris and demolition, as well as the new and glamorous construction projects arising near the beautiful waters of the Yangtze River.

The two stories of search are based on Jia's documents of life in Fengjie, marked by displacement, uncertainty, and distress in the city on the verge of erasure and flooding. Barges in the river move equipment and material, and people living on the riverbanks occupy any spot they find, putting up torn pieces of cloth or other material to create a sense of privacy. The tenacity of life is evident in the details of their gestures, behaviors, and daily routines. Jia's earlier choice of long shots is enriched here with a series of medium and medium-long shots. The final meeting between Shen Hong and Guo Bin takes place in bright sunlight with the shimmering sight of water and concrete in the background, while the long take at the construction site is shot in gloomy rain as Han discovers the body of his friend buried in the rubble. These shots depict the materiality of the landscape, with equal dedication and focus placed on small objects—bottles, boxes, photographs—which may lack, as Tweedie suggests, the symbolic power of concrete structures and nature, but are nevertheless "as deeply imbricated in human relations as the river or the land," patiently and slowly etched into memory by Jia's camera before they disappear under the rubble (2013: 296). The narrative punctuated by chapters—Cigarettes, Liquor, Tea, and Toffee—uses four objects that assume a catalytic and connective function among the social relations of working classes. If we take into account the English iteration of the film title, *Still Life*, Jia's focus on four objects of quotidian currency underscores the moment of beholding the objects in an image of still life, a gesture quite potent against the impending erasure of history and community witnessed by the residents of Fengjie.

Jia's use of another catalyst throughout the film—that of currency/money—carries different significations. As Dai Jinhua points out, unlike the four "organic currencies," money has no human connection for the lower classes, yet it becomes an instrument in their hands for satire, critique, investment in their own dreams, and, more importantly, a kind of a figuration of polylocality (Dai, 2014). When his co-workers ask Han if he has seen Kuimen—the well-known part of the Three Gorges—on his journey, he appears puzzled, so they produce a Renminbi banknote featuring an image of Kuimen. Realizing it, Han takes another note out, this one with the image of Shanxi, Hukou Falls on the Yellow River. Each resident invests his distinct identity in the banknote, invoking memory and homesickness but also the power of currency to transform the spaces it represents. In the next sequence, Han holds a banknote with the iconic Kuimen on one side against the actual landscape with the rising levels of water evident in the background—a pristine yet highly ironic image, as the currency depicts the beauty soon to be destroyed by the very same currency.

(continued)

(continued)

Figure 7.11a Jia Zhangke's *Still Life* (2006): an image of the Three Gorges on a banknote is examined against the actual landscape with the visibly rising levels of water in the background

The irony only deepens when Han flips the banknote over to the other side that features Mao's image. In his juxtaposition of the currency of quotidian life with money, Jia invokes the classic role of money in the destruction of the particularity of objects, and lays bare the wide gap between the glossy promises of the state, commodity objects, and their destructive power.

As Jia displays the vast, capital-intensive transformation and destruction in Fengjie in a realist idiom, the soundscape formulates another moral and social-political level of signification (Ping, 2011). The film tracks nostalgic reflections on the lives of Han and Shen through old songs, memories, and burdens, as it also spreads an aural spectrum of life in Fengjie. An array of sounds, from minute to massive movements, register the materiality of lives, while the persistent beat of the hammers of construction workers fills the landscape as bodies move with disciplinary obedience. Jia positions the body, strong but bare, worn but willing, in the foreground, against the massive transformations in the environment. A boy singer's songs and screams are juxtaposed against the measured but grateful smiles of the audience, workers in their cramped residence are held in a tight frame as the sound of their chopsticks and bowls keep a rhythm. The soundscape in the film offers permanence to the disappearing life in Fengjie, as the diegetic sound of work and daily activities exists in the frame alongside the slightly exaggerated, non-diegetic sounds of hammers, cracks, and falling debris that are in discord with the image yet continuously haunt it (Bertozzi, 2012: 165). Along with a realist tone of the film, the deliberate sounds in the background, such as the water splashing against the boats, convey a lasting imprint of life that destabilizes the documentary quality of the narrative, interjecting it with surreal elements that transform contingency into permanent memory. Images filled with the sounds of the natural world, notes Philippa Lovatt (2012), arrest the flow and "resist the velocity" of the demolition work. In her account of the "spectral landscapes" of the film, Lovatt sees Jia's efforts to construct a landscape of textured, discursive spaces of forceful transformation of life with multiple tracks of embedded sounds as a gesture of "heteroglossia," offering multilevel resistance to the unitary power of the state.

Jia's *Still Life* is framed in the realism of the present and shaped in a methodical visual dexterity of the camera. Yet, it is the magic-realist or science fiction interjections in the film that illuminate the political import of the film for its locus in world cinema. Zhang argues that *Still Life* is an example of "geographic imagination," "the awareness of how lives in one place are affected by the unseen actions of distant strangers elsewhere" (Zhang Y., 2010b: 98). Jia expands the scope of the sphere of the global, defining it as boundless but powerful, able to affect and delineate the local in myriad ways. The trajectories are embedded in various scenes where the narrative departs from its realist ethic, illustrating how Jia is placing in the film a centrifugal force that connects the local to the global. In one such scene, as Han and Shen stare at the horizon, a flying saucer moves across the sky, disappears and appears again. In another instance, a building/structure that is unlike any in the area, a tower with uneven floors and frameless windows, appears in the background, and later in the narrative takes off like a rocket, with no connection to or response from anyone in the frame. And in the final scene a lone, silhouetted figure is balancing a tightrope between two buildings.

In a film ostensibly meant to frame a crisis in the lives in *xiancheng*, where the largest state-sponsored project is erecting a promise of prosperity for the nation, these non-realist elements pose puzzling questions. The injustices of the Three Gorges project are real, captured in painterly images with granular detail, but the promise, scope, and ambition of the state project exists in the realm of magic and science fiction. These surreal elements destabilize the pretense of this promise, as well as deliver an indictment of the inherited burden of realism in Chinese cinema, which remained in the shadow of a state-sponsored aesthetic. The unique blend of realism and science fiction of *Still Life* thus disengages itself from both the socialist realism façade of the Maoist aesthetic and pretensions to authenticity of the post-war art cinema. It exposes the brute reality of destruction and displacement caused by the hydropower project, suggesting that a modernization project embodied by the Three Gorges Dam "is a continuation of decades of grand promises rather than a transition to a new historical era" (Tweedie, 2013: 299), with the fantastical nature of these grand promises becoming commonplace and ordinary.

The realist aesthetic thus finds itself in a predicament, no longer capable of conveying the precocity or the promise in the region. In this film, the real is presented in a destabilizing juxtaposition between natural beauty and destruction. The science fictional elements mediate between the two, complicating the ability of either to convey the potency and magnitude of the situation. Caught between the "haunting sense of mystery in the area" and the "interplay of capital, labor, and nature," the film demonstrates the limits of representation (Zhang Y., 2010b: 98). *Still Life* is an imminent, self-reflexive statement on how the local articulates itself. The trajectories into the

(continued)

(continued)

b

c

Figures 7.11b & 7.11c The magic/realist interjections in the film that destabilize the promise of realism

"other world" of flying saucers and rocket-houses finally suggest a liminal world that locks the local into a global stratosphere, much like a grounded, specifically situated structure that is propelled into global space, unfathomable and strange yet an indelible part of the locality's new life. It is a test-parable of the deepest effects of globalization, whose powers reach the innermost spaces of regions and localities. The only option left, according to Jia's distressing *Still Life*, is to jolt the present with fantastical inter-ruptions in order to acquire the fullest possible awareness of the local articulation.

***

Still Life was produced after Jia completed *Shijie/The World* (2004), and both received state financing. Jia has become a world cinema auteur, a privileged group of filmmakers whose films are included in the canon, patronized by international film critics and film festivals. Still a maverick at home compared to the big-budget fame of Zhang Yimou, Jia is no longer part of the documentary-independent film movement that began in the late 1990s. His early films, the hometown trilogy consisting of *Xiao Wu/The Pickpocket* (1997), *Zhantai/Platform* (2002), and *Ren xiao yao/Unknown Pleasures* (2002), steadfastly developed a realist framework for depicting the hidden lives and spaces of mid-level cities in China, giving voice to the fast-vanishing present in a country under rapid transformation. The films were not released domestically, although they helped Jia gain fame abroad as an emerging auteur from China. This only contributed to the perception that the films were made for foreign audiences. Meanwhile, he became an inspiring figure for his peers, since these films were made outside the system with a decidedly different aesthetic (Jaffee, 2004).

The label of independent cinema produced without the blessing of the state drew currency abroad. The entrenched fetish of seeking voices raised against any oppressive system outside the West, combined with the realistic qualities of the images and the narratives, increased the appeal of Jia's and other Sixth Generation films. It is rather ironic that the films that articulate and speak to the conditions of localism within China are better known abroad and receive funding from abroad. Since their support comes from sources outside the country, filmmakers bracket out the audiences at home, and their realist depictions of local conditions tend to be received, problematically so, within the international conventions of art cinema realism that eagerly equates the mode with transparent authenticity, even as this very gesture also ensures further patronage from film festivals, critics, and funding agencies.

Inspired and guided by theoretical writings in Chinese cinema, Tweedie delineates this specific version of realism from the earlier modes as an attempt to rewrite the earlier codes of socialist realism while also carefully separating it from the raw, granular realism of documentary filmmakers such as Wu Wenguang or Wang Bing (2013). The realism of the Sixth Generation as well as Jia Zhangke's own poetic style capture the Chinese experience at the crucial nexus of the imposed modernity of globalization and the local yearning for a different modernity of its own. From this struggle emerges a cinema of "persistence and endurance" whose dedication is to record the "overabundance of details" that exceed the demands of a dramatic narrative (Tweedie, 2013: 301). Slow, methodically-rooted images in which on-screen time is but a fraction of the experiential and reflective pangs of the pain suffered in spaces marked as local allow films to link tracks with the outside world, while still maintaining their specificity. The cinema of "distended time and details," as Tweedie calls it, overloads "the viewer's capacity to perceive, categorize, order and forget," offering a relationship that demands questioning and reflection (2013: 236). In this respect, Jia Zhangke's skillful poetic realism creates positions from which the viewer can interrogate realism, not merely witness what it captures. The strength of Jia's blend of realism and poetic, magic-realist moments is precisely in that it moves beyond unraveling "the particularity of the world before the camera" to reflect on its operating system (Tweedie, 2013: 236). The experience of the local is opened to the outside world through a flow of images that communicate inertia and a static immobility in the interrogative mode.

Trans-Asian cinema

As is the case with other centers engaged with world cinema, Asia's connections and exchanges outside the region occur in the same uneven, multi-directional, and interactive patterns. First, Asian cinema faces the force of Hollywood, whose power to hegemonize and absorb the distinctly local-regional cultural products remains dominant. Domestic industries, caught in a whirlwind of Hollywood's incursions into its spheres, adapt, modify, and surrender to the iconic, stylistic, and narrative forces of the massive industry. Thus, while the task of mapping how a region makes its identity distinct necessarily passes through the thick shield of Hollywood's presence, a polycentric view softens the impact of Hollywood's claim. Significantly, Asian cinema is the only cinema that challenges Hollywood in the production of popular films with transnational appeal, while it also claims a powerful presence in the canon of global art cinema.

In his discussion of the relationship between Hollywood and other parts of world cinema, Tweedie explains that Hollywood's dominance in generating a master narrative of globalization comes from its ability to align its films with commodity production and control of the capital. Its version of new modernity turns out to be an ideological screen that masks other powerful currents of growth, exchanges, and advances in cinematic narratives and form. The alternative emerges from a different discourse in world cinema, attributed to "an insurgency devoted to the representation of the modern and the real" (Tweedie, 2013: 1–2). As young filmmakers experienced a "visual culture of accelerated modernization" in European and Asian cities, their experimentation with the film form created "new waves" of cinema across continents. Exchanges and movements of these new waves pose a powerful counterpart to Hollywood's global presence, aligning in concerns, styles, and substance to create an alternative vision of global modernity. Tweedie (2013) identifies the creative energies in cinemas of Taiwan, China, Hong Kong, Spain, Mexico, and Korea as part of this global art cinema movement. The conceptual ingenuity in moving beyond the rigid categories of national and transnational cinemas, while also providing a stream of linkages and mobility of forms, becomes a necessary foundation for global art cinema.

But when one takes a broader view, it becomes clear that equating art cinema with world cinema only limits the reach of the latter. Nollywood and parts of Indian cinema, for example, remain distant from the accelerated modernization experienced in the creative urban spaces that Tweedie speaks of. They remain outside the gambit of youth and consumer revolutions, offering instead a vastly different experience of modernity and modes of survival during globalization. Rather than experimenting with cinematic form within art cinema modes, their recourse has been to make cinema that appeals to large audiences, in the popular idiom rooted in folk and local traditions. While it is true that filmmakers from these cinemas have knocked on the doors of international film festivals with limited success, they can hardly claim to represent "waves" that register the pulses of modernities. For them, as we have discussed in earlier chapters, the notions of modernity and the real belong to different epistemological frameworks, and they require a different way of drawing the map of world cinema.

Asian cinema in particular assumes a distinct position on this map, insofar as its output of transnationally influential popular films is as powerful as its art cinema. Asian cinema's trans-Asian profile is thus made of both dimensions, popular and art cinema. Exchanges and interactions of Asian popular cinema with other cinemas of the world has produced one of the most impressive and extensive accounts in film history. The martial arts style and stars such as Bruce Lee, for example, have been extremely popular and influential in India and Africa for decades, and they offer a testimony to transnational influences in world cinema even before the 1980s. The tracks of influence after the 1980s, however, may be best traced by Asian cinema's encounter with Hollywood, its fierce competitor on the world stage. We discussed how Hollywood's marketing machine and its appetite for expanding markets for its films created a notion of "Asian cinema" in the 1980s and 1990s. Here, we focus on a different dimension of this encounter, the influence of Asian films on Hollywood itself.

Popular cinema, blockbusters, and Hollywood

One of Hollywood's inherent gifts is that it is enormously hospitable to immigrant artists and migrated ideas. Jackie Chan made films in the US in the 1980s, while Akira Kurosawa's *Shichinin no samurai/Seven Samurai* (1954) became an immediate template for its remake, *The Magnificent Seven* (John Sturges, 1960). As Hollywood moved to appropriate the marketplace of Asia in the 1990s, it faced entirely different circumstances from the previous decades, with a fast-growing economy and audience size in China, and the tempting market appeal of the action-film styles of Hong Kong, Korean, and Chinese filmmakers. Although its financial prowess and insatiable appetite for dominance allowed Hollywood to turn these factors into an advantage, the process of adaptation has meant that Hollywood changed from within in a number of ways—and this, more than an example of Hollywood's hegemony, is a testament to Asian cinema's influence on a global scale. As Christina Klein puts it, "Hollywood is becoming Asianized in diverse ways, while Asian film industries are in turn becoming Hollywoodized" (Klein, 2004c).

If, until now, the US has been the largest film market in terms of revenue (and India in terms of audience size), China is expected to become the largest market in terms of both revenue and audience size by 2018 (Knowledge at Wharton, 2016). This has all kinds of implications for Hollywood and China, but the net effect of a growing audience and revenue share is profoundly altering the way in which Hollywood films are made. Forever mindful of the Chinese viewer, Hollywood films include nods to their power in the forms of narrative references placed in blockbuster films. Alfonso Cuarón's *Gravity* (2013) strategically placed a Chinese space station in its opening scene. James Cameron will place Chinese elements in a sequel to *Avatar*. The producers of the *Red Dawn* (2012) remake changed the original Chinese attacking force into a North Korean one, a much safer geopolitical target. *The Martian* (2015) portrays a Chinese space agency in a positive light. The Chinese stars Donnie Yen and Jiang Wen were cast in the recent Star Wars film, *Rogue One: A Star Wars Story* (2016), a maneuver used earlier with *Iron Man 3* (2013), where one of the settings was moved to China and included the celebrity Fan Bingbing. The Chinese government assumes a key role in the narrative of *Arrival* (2016). Not unlike the venerated (mal)practice of product placement that unashamedly removes the line between narrative and commercial aims, courting the Chinese audience and film industry, including the censorship requirements by way of references, language use, casting, or settings, is expected to intensify in the coming years (Zeitchik & Landreth, 2012).

One of the most radical examples of adapting the films to woo Chinese audiences may be seen in case of a recent blockbuster, *Warcraft* (2016). The film had a rather meager performance in the domestic market ($24 million on the opening weekend) while earning $156 million on the opening weekend in China, offering a clear temptation to forgo profits at home to appease Chinese audiences, a likely indication of a major change in the way blockbusters are made (McFarland, 2016). Beyond casual references, such a turn in Hollywood includes drastic changes in narrative and style to adapt to the Chinese censors. As the *Guardian* critic states,

> If your movie features a Chinese villain, change his nationality. If your plot omits a scene in China, insert one—preferably with gleaming skyscrapers. If your production deal lacks a Chinese partner, find one. If Beijing's censors dislike certain scenes, cut them.
>
> (Carroll, 2013)

This transformation and adjustment to the Chinese market is only expected to intensify as the Chinese buy Hollywood studios or its shares. The purchase of AMC Entertainment by one of the biggest Chinese film corporations, Dalian Wanda Group, ensured an important amount of control over film production and distribution. Moreover, beyond buying Hollywood studios, China is establishing itself as the most powerful global entertainment force by investing on a grand scale in its own film production. Dalian Wanda Group, for example, invested $135 million into Zhang Yimou's *The Great Wall* (2017), expected to become the first Chinese global blockbuster on, or overtaking, the Hollywood scale.

Martial arts and wuxia style

Martial arts from Hong Kong and China may be the most successful form of action film genre around the world. Bruce Lee, one of the biggest action film icons of the twentieth century, contributed to the global popularity of martial arts films. His martial arts sequences infused with kinetic action profoundly influenced the genre of martial arts films and its stars. Jackie Chan had a successful career in Hong Kong before moving to Hollywood to launch one of the most illustrious hybrid careers on two continents. Chan harnessed the marketing machine by popularizing and refreshing the martial arts form already established by Bruce Lee. Audiences were no longer watching martial arts films from afar; they had become an integral part of their own fare.

When Ang Lee's *Crouching Tiger, Hidden Dragon* (2000) exploded on the global stage, it had imported the native *wuxia pian* (Chinese sword action film) into its global blockbuster formula. Hollywood alone has the power to take a local genre and use the prowess of its marketing machine to make it globally appealing. Bordwell notes that Hollywood had revitalized the *wuxia pian* by putting "the graceful body at the center of its *mise en scène*" (2007: 401). The kinetic and high-quality cinematography of *Crouching Tiger* created an alluring context for action films. Martial arts was no longer dependent on the glamour of a singular actor, as was the case with Bruce Lee, but it was reenergized by adding to it Hong Kong's reputation for action cinema. Hong Kong's leading action choreographer for Lee's films, Yuen Woo-ping, lent his talents to many Hollywood films, including the Wachowskis' *Matrix* trilogy (1999–2003), Quentin Tarantino's *Kill Bill* (2003, 2004), and Rob Minkoff's *The Forbidden Kingdom* (2008). There is no denying that this revitalization of *wuxia pian* from Bruce Lee to Ang Lee shows a transformation from the glamour of one star to the powerful image machine of Hollywood. *Crouching Tiger*, the most popular foreign-language film in the US, demonstrates the enormous prowess of Hollywood in lending Chinese visual culture a global profile. It stands out as a powerful instance of how Asian cinema becomes a focus of Hollywood's renewed global ambitions. In this sense, Hollywood can be seen as both the strongest purveyor and benefactor of cinematic diversity, as well as its biggest exploiter.

In the 1990s John Woo, one of Hong Kong's leading directors, became the first major Asian filmmaker to work in Hollywood. After a successful career as a Hong Kong action film director with films such as *Dip huet gaai tau/Bullet in the Head* (1990) and *Lat sau san taam/Hard Boiled* (1992), he made six films with major stars in Hollywood, including Jean-Claude Van Damme in *Hard Target* (1993), John Travolta in *Broken Arrow* (1996), Nicolas Cage and John Travolta in *Face/Off* (1997), Tom Cruise in *Mission Impossible II* (2000), Nicolas Cage in *Windtalkers* (2002), and Ben Affleck in *Paycheck* (2003). Woo had recharged the *wuxia pian* tradition of sword play into ballistic gun action where heroes are engaged in the ethics of friendships and rivalry placed within gang culture. The sensational attraction of his Hong Kong films was precisely his deployment of a dynamic within the Confucian ethics of friendship and loyalties, where the dramas of relationships among groups of leading men reveal a deeper cultural fabric of the society (Magnan-Park, 2007). In his American films, this ideology is transformed to fit into the individualistic ethic suited to the Western market, thus diluting a key feature of his cinematic style. After returning from Hollywood, Woo made *Chi bi/Red Cliff* (2008), a spectacular blockbuster and at the time the most expensive Chinese film ever made. Based on one of the classical novels, it plays out the dynamic of the turbulent period at the end of the Han Dynasty through relationships between men, the dogmatically stubborn prime minister of the north and a resourceful alliance in the south.

Among Hollywood's directors most influenced by the Asian style, Quentin Tarantino ranks the highest. He has built a career as a cinephile filmmaker, clearly demonstrating his taste for borrowing and blending genres from different parts of world cinema, including Japanese samurai films, Hong Kong's martial arts films, and Italian spaghetti westerns. His first feature, *Reservoir Dogs* (1992), owes much to Ringo Lam's 1987 film *Lung foo fong wan/City on Fire*. The two *Kill Bill* (2003, 2004) films are the fullest expression of his gratitude to the martial arts of Asian cinema and its great iconic heritage. Tarantino has served as a talent scout for Harvey Weinstein in Hong Kong, lent his name and efforts to promote Zhang Yimou's *Hero* in its theatrical and DVD release, and has openly admired the merits of films and filmmakers from Asian cinema for decades. In an illuminating study of the Asianization of Hollywood cinema, Leon Hunt calls Tarantino a "transnational gatekeeper" who acts as a catalyst in promoting and incorporating influences from Asian cinema (Hunt, 2008). Tarantino regularly places references and icons from Asian cinema in his films as a connoisseur of taste who not only pays homage to but has internalized Asian popular cinema.

Some critics may think of this as reckless borrowing and copying that dilutes his own creativity, but the persistent drive in Tarantino to borrow and blend the elements of Asian cinema into his own can be understood on different levels. First, Tarantino's career emerged and developed in an age of a new kind of cinephilia where viewers have easy access to films from distant corners of the world, facilitating their appreciation for citations and references from other cinemas. Tarantino, David Desser notes, simply provides a tonic for the impulse of this "video store" cinephilia, where the viewers find themselves comfortable in a field of intertextual references, and where the popularity of films such as *Reservoir Dogs* fuels a further discovery of Hong Kong cinema (2006: 208). Second, Tarantino is a product of and practitioner in the age of hip-hop, sampling, and dynamism in different forms of popular arts (Desser, 2003). An accomplished scriptwriter, Tarantino prides himself on making films that seamlessly mix, blend, and reference the works he admires, believing that the viewer's widened range is well suited for this style.

Tarantino is one of the more established cinephile auteurs shaping Hollywood in the shadow of Asian cinematic styles. The tendency to adapt wholesale the iconic and motion potential of Asian cinema became pervasive in the late 1980s and persists today. At one end, one could place French producer-director Luc Besson's efforts to incorporate talents from Asia. Besson co-wrote and co-produced *The Transporter* series (Corey Yuen and Louis Leterrier, 2002; Louis Leterrier, 2005; Olivier Megaton, 2008) and wrote and co-produced *Unleashed* (Louis Leterrier, 2005), featuring Jet Li and Shu Qi alongside Western stars like Jason Statham and Morgan Freeman. At the other end, we have a glut of Hollywood films that import Asian imagery, such as the *Rush Hour* series (Brett Ratner, 1998, 2001, and 2007), which made martial arts "cool" and complimentary to American masculinity. Hollywood dilutes and generalizes different styles (karate, judo, kung fu, taekwondo, aikido) into "martial arts," detaching itself from realism. "Martial arts" may be shorthand for invoking connections to the kinetics of Asian style, but in doing so it complicates a number of representational issues. Examples of this tendency abound in Hollywood, from the various iterations of *The Karate Kid* (the original, *Part II, Part III,* and *Next Karate Kid*—1984, 1986, 1989, and 1994 respectively—and a remake with Jackie Chan in 2010), all of which romanticize and generalize the notions of martial arts in the service of breaking new grounds of popularity. From *The Matrix* to the *Kung Fu Panda* series (2008, 2011, 2016), Hollywood remains ambivalent about representing Asia and absorbing its influences. It shows a level of absorption that simultaneously opens up domestic and global audiences to a different culture, and problematically frames this culture in sometimes subtle and sometimes overtly racist entanglements, engagements, and transformations.

Remakes

Remakes have been a regular staple of world cinema and Hollywood, both in art and commercial-popular film forms. But in the age of globalization, Hollywood finds in remakes a particularly dependable source of additional revenue, harnessing the memory and reputation of films made in other countries. Hollywood's engagement in transnational remakes fits its profile of a chauvinistic cannibal in the global industry. Jennifer Forrest and Leonard R. Koos observe that Hollywood has increased "vigorously its remaking activity, especially of foreign films" since the 1980s (2001: 3). Widely decried by the critics at the time for its ruthless "plundering of ready-made foreign products," the practice has continued until today. While there is little doubt about their observation that "remakes participate in American global colonization" (Forrest & Koos, 2001: 2), it is equally valid to see how the dearth of investment in its own creative resources has allowed Hollywood to transform itself, tilting a significant part of its efforts toward remaking foreign films. Remakes are so ubiquitous in the popular press and on websites/blogs that they cultivate a different level of popular cinephilia, expressed in obsessive accounts and lists that detect similarities and differences between them. Scholarship on the topic assumes a wide range, from empirical studies that conduct what Adrian Martin calls "a simple one-to-one exegesis" of films to studies of remakes as an important form of transnational cultural exchange (Martin, 2008a). Filmmakers and films never work in isolation; there is always an intertextual give-and-take among various films. Tarantino's practiced cinephilia is a form of remake itself, an intertextuality worked out on an intensely cross-contextual level. Remakes raise all kinds of important questions, from the issues of adaptation, translation, and hybridity to exchanges. They are caught in the complex logic of repetition, difference, and memory. They point out, among other things, the fetishistic desires in embracing remakes as lost objects that are repossessed again and again.

Embedded within these theoretical topographies, the remakes of foreign films, and Asian films in particular, pose important questions. The spectatorial and textual dynamic of remakes of Asian cinema are best understood through the lens of remakes as an industrial category. When Gary Xu asks, "Why has remaking East Asian films become such a popular trend at the turn of the millennium?" he points to the fact that Hollywood's interest in remaking films that have already gained success in Asian markets forms a major stream of its production for domestic and international audiences (2007: 155). Producers in Hollywood spot successful films in local Asian markets and harness their potential for larger markets by investing more in marketing and distribution. Sensing the temptations and possibility for profit in a lucrative global market that Hollywood offers in its remakes, producers in Asia are often eager to sell their rights to film products. Xu (2007) calls this an activity of "outsourcing" whereby the Asian markets are used as experiments for making higher-profile films.

Horror has continued to be a favorite for remakes in Hollywood. One of the most famous and successful examples here is Hideo Nakata's horror film *Ringu* (1998), remade by Gore Verbinski as *The Ring* (2002). Nakata's *Dark Water* (2005) was remade with the same title by Walter Salles in 2005; and Nakata also directed a sequel to *The Ring* in Hollywood, *The Ring Two* (2005). Takashi Shimizu made a television series called *Ju-on* in Japan, which he remade in Hollywood as *The Grudge* (2004). Kiyoshi Kurosawa's *Kairo* (2001) was remade as *Pulse* in 2006 by Jim Sonzero. Takashi Miike's *Chakushin ari* (2003) was remade as *One Missed Call* by Eric Valette in 2008. Other horror film remakes from Asia include *Shutter* (Masayuki Ochiai, 2008), a remake of a 2004 Thai horror film of the same name by Banjong Pisanthanakun and Parkpoom Wongpoom; Kim Jee-woon's *Janghwa, Hongryeon/A Tale of Two Sisters* (2003) which was remade as *The Uninvited* (2009) by Charles and Thomas Guard; and Danny and Oxide Pang's *Gin gwai/The Eye* (2002), remade as *The Eye* by David Moreau and Xavier Palud in 2008.

Films originating in Asia have specific cultural roots, gender roles, ghost figures, motifs of horror, and spatial and temporal coordinates. Horror has a unique tradition in Japanese cinema, dynamically intertwined with its own history and global engagements, including those with the US. Inflections on the genre from Korea, Hong Kong, and elsewhere in China are deeply motivated by a complex array of considerations that are out of reach for popular audiences in multiplexes in the US. When Hollywood remakes these films, the main intent is to capitalize on the strengths of the original, to tap into the core of their appeal and remake the narratives and images for audiences that have remote connection, if any, to the original contexts of films. All cultural references have to be "Americanized or else eliminated altogether" (Vandell, 2014: 53). *Ringu*'s remake was adapted in the U.S.-style aura, embodied by spacing and framing of the image, the subdued emphasis on movement of the narrative, and ambiguity in the characters that gives way to the dramatic imperatives of narrative movement, the familiar setting of the American suburban life, and explicitly positioned horror. The original *Ringu* was itself an adaptation of the Japanese novel *Ring*, which in turn draws on a Japanese folktale, thus forming a complex intertext, a web of connections and culturally-rooted meanings (Wee, 2011). When remade in Hollywood, the act of transnational remaking presents a new form of colonization that empties out the specificity of cultural contexts. The "foreignness" in Asian films is attractive to Hollywood only to the extent that it is amenable to changes and hospitable to its own ideology.

Although Hollywood's practice of remaking popular cinema from other countries is aimed at large gains at the box office, the exercise has brought uneven results. It has invited directors of the originals in their own countries and also summoned major figures at home for the task. The recent example of the remake of Korean director Park Chan-wook's *Oldeuboi/Oldboy* (2003) by Spike Lee in 2013 with Josh Brolin did not perform as expected. As Hollywood invests in films produced in Asia, often reserving the rights for remakes, in the process it transforms local industries and leaves the door open for making profits with remakes that often circulate easily in Asian markets. Hollywood's appetite shows how it is transforming itself while also dominating the world.

Trans-Asian art cinema: the adventures of film form

Each of the five centers entered into a new constellation of exchanges and influences after the 1980s, but none so vast and influential as the emergence of global art cinema. Once a realm of limited cinephilic circulation in film societies, cine clubs, and regional or international film festivals, art cinema formed a global sphere, aided by technological revolution and the rising influence of regional and international film festivals. A distinct global formation after the 1980s, art cinema nourishes the energy in academic scholarship, fuels the circuits of film festivals, cultivates legions of cinephiles, and attracts the elite economy of transnational sponsors. A major share of this energy in art cinema comes from Asian cinema, which presents an extraordinarily powerful front in the sphere that was once almost exclusively a province of European cinema.

In one way or another, cinema responded to the globally-pervasive conditions of economic development and the speed of cultural transfers across national borders. Asian filmmakers found that film language had to be experimented with to produce articulate responses at this nexus of the local and the global. Their sensibilities were shaped both in their own local traditions, from China to Japan and from Taiwan to Thailand, and in the experiments from Europe and elsewhere brought to their doorstep by new modes of circulation. Tweedie's masterful account of these changes describes the process as "an explosion of world cinema," and "an insurgency devoted to the representation of the modern and the real" (2013: 2). Developed in part as a counter-current to Hollywood's version of global cinema, and as a cinematic wave that was parallel to other similar waves around the world, art cinema incorporated a critique of the imposed modernity of globalization with an inquisitive urge to find alternative modes of expression.

An impressive variety of art cinemas from around the world circulate in a common global art cinema orbit, which often results in a problematic blending of their conditions, emergences, and allegiances. That is, art cinema from Asia blends with a galaxy of auteurs from other cinemas that populate the world of film festivals. For Fredric Jameson, for example, Tsai Ming-liang is a late modernist auteur in the company of directors such as Béla Tarr, Abbas Kiarostami, Victor Erice, Raúl Ruiz, Theo Angelopoulos, Manoel de Oliviera and others (2006: 1). For Thomas Elsaesser, a new generation of auteurs from different parts of the world are creative artists untethered from their national contexts, sharing more in common with each other than with their peers at home, all subscribing to a realist mode of

> quasi-documentary, ethnographic engagement with the slow rhythms of the everyday, with the lives of ordinary people, . . . the wasted desolation of the shanty towns and urban slums, or the ennui and anomie of the newly affluent Asian middle classes."
>
> (2009: 4)

Missing in these generalizations are both the recognition in their work of the vastly varied and locally situated responses to a shared condition, and the specific inflections of the notion of modernity that brings these auteurs and their films together.

The emergence of the directors of global art cinema is a local manifestation loyal to its specificity, defying the notion of a universal or transnational modernity. It is defined in "the tension between a drive toward speedy cosmopolitanism—and a will to regionalism, a desire to sit in one place and observe how the forces and traces of history sink deep there" (Martin, 2010). Asian cinema engaged in the differentiated spectrum of multiple modernities after the 1980s from its own loci, at times with a regional energy fueled by the Hong Kong and Pusan/Busan film festivals, and at times as trajectories from specific local spaces that link to the global discourse of art cinema. Global art cinemas thus emerge from the conditions that are both common (global capital) and differentiated by virtue of challenges, re-articulations, and disruptions that reveal their locally-rooted conditions.

The new waves in Asian cinema, according to Tweedie's map, are modeled after the French New Wave, a critical response to the hegemony of Western consumer culture and Hollywood film (2013). Two decades after the Second World War, new waves from Italy, Germany, Brazil, and Japan marked a period of revolutions in cinema that experimented with film form. Filmmakers of the French New Wave—Jean-Luc Godard, François Truffaut, Claude Chabrol, and Jacques Rivette—reinvented cinema, critiquing consumerism and Hollywood while also exploring the possibility of film language to articulate the experience of their generation. Though filmmakers in Asia and elsewhere tapped into the well of radical rebellion of the French New Wave, their variegated modernities, and consequently the language with which to address them, were firmly placed in the national contexts of their cinemas.

In Japan, a generation of filmmakers born in the 1950s and 1960s shaped the art cinema that became a regular feature of international film festivals: Takeshi Kitano, Shinji Aoyama, Shunji Iwai, Naomi Kawase, Hirokazu Koreeda, Ryōsuke Hashiguchi, Kiyoshi Kurosawa, Takashi Miike, Hideo Nakata, and Masayuki Suo. Aaron Gerow observes that their circulation and success abroad can be partially attributed to the changing perceptions of Japanese cinema and its context. The films of the 1950s and 1960s were received well because they were defined as "art films" that affirmed the universal humanist paradigm placed in an exotic, distant world. Meanwhile, contemporary Japanese cinema that circulates abroad is both popular genre cinema (such as gangster or horror films) and art cinema that distances itself from the universal humanism to explore internal tensions and identity crises in the face of encounters with the outside, minorities, and ethnic others (Gerow, 2002). These filmmakers follow an interrogative mode, breaking with Japanese cinematic conventions and storytelling modes. In Naomi Kawase's personal documentary narratives, she turns the lens on herself, placating the desire to know others, to submit herself to a quiet self-examination. Shinji Aoyama works in different genres, popular and art films, to tap into the political potential of experiences in globalization, either in its absence where hope has left a whole generation, or in its intense expressions in horror, violence, and withdrawal from life. The dominant style in recent Japanese cinema is that of "detachment," says Gerow, bending the film form in experimentation with compositions, editing, the excessive signification of the image, or in quiet distancing from the scene of action (2002: 4).

One of the most well-known art cinema directors from Japan, Takeshi Kitano, has been wooing festival juries and art house audiences around the world. He has charted a fascinating career as a television stand-up comic, a salesman, an author at home (where he is known as "Beat Takeshi"), and a quirky, accomplished film auteur abroad with a wide appeal beyond festival audiences. He began filmmaking in the 1970s, but his 1997 film *Hana-bi/Fireworks*, about a police detective (played by Kitano) forced to retire after a tragic accident, was a breakthrough domestically and on the international stage, winning the Golden Lion at Venice. The film's success abroad acknowledged implicitly that films gaining a reputation abroad were valuable to Japanese cinema. This marked the beginning of a new period after the astonishing success of Japanese cinema in the 1950s and 1960s. *Hana-bi* refines his earlier aesthetic, using deadpan acting and long, static shots, and focusing on creating a gestalt of the space, slowly filling in details. Critics widely cite the influence of Yasujiro Ozu on his work, recast in the volcanic violence that remains in meticulously shot sequences. The images are laced with the slow rhythm of quotidian details, while surprises come in the form of violent eruptions and emotional detours. The combination of the steady, quiet, painterly quality of filmic frames and the rapid, eruptive violence of gang culture was unique for Japanese cinema and an aesthetic novelty for the international audiences.

As in the case of Japan, the intense wave of cinephilia in Korea also energized a generation of filmmakers and audiences to use film as a central tool with which to question and represent their changing world. Korean art cinema is as strong at home as it is abroad, a formidable presence at regional and international film festivals. On both fronts, Korean cinema boasts an enduring following. Writing in *Film Comment*, Chuck Stephens notes that Korean cinema has gone through a "perpetual renaissance" over nearly two decades (2004: 36). The first new wave begins in the 1980s with Park Kwang-su, Kim Hong-joon, Jang Kil-soo, and others who belonged to an active cinephile group in Seoul. This wave emerges in a liberated climate, having left behind years of crippling censorship. The first impulse for these filmmakers was to stay rooted in realism; to depict the working classes, radicalized student population, urbanization, family and relationship breakdowns, and the moral and political fiber of the society (Standish, 1993). The second wave, known as the Korean New Wave or the New Korean Cinema, represents another surge of creative activity taking place in the transformation of the industry in response to Hollywood's distribution in the country, and buoyed by film festival support and international recognition. Filmmakers of this generation—Park Chan-wook, Lee Chong-dong, Kim Ki-duk, Hong Sang-soo, Bong Joon-ho, and Im Sang-soo—are notable representatives of art cinema from South Korea, and each of them has developed a distinct profile since the mid-1990s. Park Chan-wook had already broken new ground with *JSA: Joint Security Area* in 2000, followed by *Boksuneun naui geot/Sympathy for Mr. Vengeance* (2002), a slow-brewing kidnapping-revenge drama with a chilling grip on the narrative. The second film in the trilogy, *Oldeuboi/Oldboy* (2003), garnered enormous praise and popularity abroad, and by the time he made a third installment, *Chinjeolhan geumjassi/Sympathy for Lady Vengeance* (2005), Korean cinema's turn to violence was entrenched in the public mind. The most eclectic director in this group, Kim Ki-duk, has worked on the edge of provocation and obsessive focus on autobiographical threads. Wildly popular in many parts of the world, he is a "toast of European festival circuit" (Rayns, 2004: 51). His films range from narratives of sexual perversions and narcissistic obsessions in *Seom/The Isle* (2000) or *Nappeun Namja/Bad Guy* (2001), and a sexual-spiritual meditation set in a Buddhist monastery in *Bom yeoreum gaeul gyeoul geurigo bom/ Spring, Summer, Fall, Winter . . . and Spring* (2003), to a psychosexual crime drama in *Pieta* (2012). His profoundly personal, digitally filmed exercise in *Arirang* (2011), which won *Un Certain Regard* at Cannes, is a stunningly indulgent but gripping documentary of his self-imposed exile to reflect on the ethics and responsibilities as a filmmaker.

In focus 7.5 Trans-Asian art cinema: Hong Sang-soo and Hou Hsiao-hsien

A director who perhaps most lucidly represents the zeitgeist of Korean cinema is Hong Sang-soo. He emerged onto the Korean film stage in 1995 with his debut feature *Dajiga umule pajinnal/The Day a Pig Fell Into the Well*, and has since made sixteen features, all of which were shown and many honoured at international film festivals: *Geuk jang jeon/Tale of Cinema* (2005), *Bam gua nat/Night and Day* (2008), *Hahaha* (2010), and *Ok-hui-ui yeonghwa/Oki's Movie* (2010), to name only a few. A filmmaker of simple style and reflectively slow pace, a poet of unhurried memory, and a probing artist of the everyday, he has produced an impressive and prolific body of work with one of the most distinctive styles in contemporary art cinema. Devoid of big drama but offering a complex yet playful canvas onto which he charts the relationship between the personal, artistic, and political, Hong's films center on characters, mostly urban intellectuals and young artists who, in Richard Brody's succinct description, "meet by chance, reconnect, couple off, split up, drink heavily, embarrass themselves, go away, come back" (Brody, 2016). His recent, seventeenth feature, *Jigeumeun matgo geuttaeneun teullida/Right Now, Wrong Then* (2016), is about a famous Seoul-based film director who arrives in the town of Suwon to screen and discuss his latest film. Due to a scheduling error, he finds himself with some downtime, sightseeing and spending time with a young woman who is an ardent fan of his work. They chat over coffee, visit her studio, and attend a dinner party hosted by her friends. The philandering, drinking, and a series of missteps do not turn out so well for him. In the second part of the film, the narrative replays itself again, in a kind of a wish-fulfillment fantasy tone that displaces the reality of the first part. What was wrong in the first part is right, and what was right . . . works out differently. Time acquires a very different trajectory when one gets a second chance, never literally doubling itself.

Daniel Kasman (2016) marvels at the playfulness of Hong's English-language film titles—*On the Occasion of Remembering the Turning Gate*, *Virgin Stripped Bare by Her Bachelors*, *Woman Is the Future of Man*, *The Day He Arrives*, *Hill of Freedom*—and Richard Brody (2016) points out a deeper invocation of French cinema in titles such as *Night and Day* (filmed in Paris), *Woman on the Beach* (a nod to Jean Renoir's film title), and *In Another Country*, which lists Isabelle Huppert in the lead role. In his varied but consistent, elliptical but reflexive work, Hong's modernist cinema positions the anxiety of routines, intellectual discourses, and sexual lapses against a larger canvas of cinema. He constantly flexes the inherent idiosyncrasies of cinema's ability to move and stop time, to map and cut space, and to recoil on itself again and again to find the structure of memory and imagination. Hong's work features distinct use of still images and sudden zooms, inhabiting the space as a temporary dwelling, with interruptions, quirky moves, and interjections of characters and actions. Sexuality and sexual frustrations are always subject to self-reflexivity, with the male character standing as a fulcrum of expositions and examinations, always incomplete in his endeavors. He deploys humor, abundantly used in his films, as a great tool for reflexivity. Brody calls his "an infra-cinema, in which the furiously meticulous attention to his characters' daily practices, the sharp-eyed focus on artists' routines, comes out the other side

(continued)

(continued)

a

b

Figures 7.12a & 7.12b In films such as *Hahaha* (2010) and *Right Now, Wrong Then* (2016),
Hong Sang-soo charts the relationship between the personal, artistic, and
political through urban characters' chance encounters and connections

to reveal grand vistas of a complete inner and outer world" (2016). Martin Scorsese's remark that "Hong's films unpeel like an orange" is most appropriate for a director whose innovations in narrative constructions and playful cinematic form make him a stand-out among the new generation of Korean filmmakers (Scorsese, 2007)

A major chapter in the experimentation and exploration of the film form can be attributed to the new waves in Taiwan cinema, whose international profile is much larger in art cinema than its domestic popular cinema. Over the past three decades, Taiwan's art cinema has been a bright presence at film festivals, in scholarly discourse and cinephile communities, and the auteurs Hou Hsiao-hsien, Edward Yang, and Tsai Ming-liang are among the most influential in global art cinema. Art cinema in Taiwan began with two films, both anthology films that marked a new phase in the construction of the narrative and the cinematic image. *Guang yin de gu shi/ In Our Time* (1982) and *Erzi de da wan'ou/The Sandwich Man* (1983) introduced radical changes in filmmaking practices in the country. Influenced by the literature of rural Taiwan (stories by Huang Chunming), the short films in this anthology took the early step to chart the movement from rural to urban society, critiquing the conditions of dependence on consumer culture and the neo-colonial dependence on the US. The scenes of life moved from rural areas to a city, and from tradition and community to a culture of speed and efficiency, but also of dependence and dislocation.

In the first short of the 1983 film ("the sandwich man" is literally translated from Chinese as "his son's big doll"), Hou acts as a sandwich man, dressing up clownishly as a billboard to advertise screenings at a local theater. When he loses his job at his employer's whim, he returns home without his costume, only to realize that his son does not recognize him without it. As the world around him is changing and the hustle and bustle of life accelerates toward a new future, the sandwich man must don his public, market identity even in his private life. The act of adapting to a new world, which will be inherited by the next generation, Hou suggests, requires compliance with the pressures of modernization. Hou employs his master-shot technique, holding

Figure 7.13 In Hou Hsiao-hsien's section of *The Sandwich Man* (1983), Hou plays a sandwich man whose job is to dress up clownishly as a billboard to advertise screenings at a local theater

(continued)

(continued)

the camera for long takes, allowing the spatial movements and relationships to reveal themselves in time. Hou's signature soundscapes of the nerves of life humming in the background calculatingly instill the perception that we are watching a culture in transition, demanding contemplation in content, style, and senses. Hou's film showed to Taiwanese cinema that a different space of cinematic practice was possible outside of the popular cinema and Hollywood's aggressive incursions. The pursuit of new style and constant questioning of the transitions to urban life inaugurated the first new wave of Taiwanese cinema.

The main force of innovation for the new wave was in Hou's evolving cinematic style—the long takes, master-shot images, and meticulous framing that reveal elements and relationships in time. He had abandoned the commercial goals of his filmmaking, taking the lead in establishing a distinct commitment to historical-autobiographical narratives embedded within deliberate critiques of the present. In the second phase of his career, the period of the first Taiwanese new wave (1983–1988), Hou develops his realist style, where long takes become a prominent mode to disclose and reflect on the present. His films in this period, *Tongnian wangshi/A Time to Live, A Time to Die* (1985), *Lian lian feng chen/Dust in the Wind* (1986), and *Bei qing cheng shi/A City of Sadness* (1989), are eminently realist narratives of the new Taiwanese cinema, characterized by long, slow takes and a master-shot aesthetic. These films blend personal memory and a nation's history, putting displacement, dislocation, and alienation center stage, and their influence on the changing film style and narrative commitment in Taiwanese cinema is immeasurable.

In 1987, the first new wave came to an end, as a group of filmmakers signed the Taiwan Cinema Manifesto for "another cinema," an alternative practice resisting commercial cinema and searching for a local Taiwanese identity and a new aesthetic. The center of the global art cinema movement shifts from the French New Wave and the Third Cinema movement to Taiwan. Hou and Edward Yang had already made a mark on art cinema, as innovative challengers to modernity's transitions, by experimenting with and shaping a globally influential aesthetic. Funding from the Central Motion Picture Company continued but in a progressively weakened phase, moving the film industry to seek funding from abroad. Hou kept in touch with filmmakers of the new generation, many of them educated abroad, while also convening film associations and political movements (Ti, 2008). He continued to make films, shifting to the third phase of his career: *Xi meng ren sheng/The Puppetmaster* (1993) is an examination of Taiwan's history; *Hai Shang Hua/ Flowers of Shanghai* (1998) closes in on the "flower houses" once prevalent in the city; *Qian xi man po/Millennium Mambo* (2001) is an elliptical chronicle of a young girl that ceaselessly blends Taipei's past and present, crystallizing the anxiety of the millennium moment; *Kôhî jikô/Café Lumière* (2003) was filmed in Japan as a tribute to Ozu; and *Le voyage du ballon rouge/Flight of the Red Balloon* (2007) is a tribute to the French New Wave and to Albert Lamorisse's unforgettable *Le ballon rouge/The Red Balloon* (1956).

In providing a critical account of Hou's films, Adrian Martin (2008b) reminds us of a thoughtful application of the task to "inhabit" the film, to map out the movements, spacing, and trajectories. Hou's films, he argues, may provide a different experience, but they direct us to a vital part of the aesthetic of global art cinema where narrative movement takes place underneath a pronounced experimentation with the capabilities of form or style. Hou's films invoke connections to the specific history of Taiwan, while they also beget responses that are abstract or metaphysical. The setting is tranquil and the pace is deliberately slow. The combination of long takes and master-shot *mise-en-scène* gives a measured rhythm to his films; the emphasis is on inviting the viewer into a universe to locate the possible coordinates of narrative elements in it, which are woven in elliptical, circular movements, enriching what simple storytelling can contain.

a

b

Figures 7.14a & 7.14b Hou Hsiao-hsien's signature master-shot *mise-en-scène* from *Flowers of Shanghai* (1998) and *The Boys from Fengkuei* (1983)

(continued)

(continued)

While he is focused on realism, the mediatory curtains of style take us closer to figurative meditations on the film rather than deciphering isolated elements. Reviews of Hou's films usually begin either with a sense of frustration or with a cinephilic immersion in the unique stroke of his visual style. For Adrian Martin, Hou's measure of strength comes from his ability to capture and enable the zeitgeist of the moment of transformation. In recording and analyzing history, Hou's cinema constantly tests itself, while his aesthetic style puts Taiwanese cinema on the world cinema map.

In focus 7.6   What time is it in world cinema? Tsai Ming-liang and *What Time Is It There?* (2001)

Two of the most well-known filmmakers of the second new wave of Taiwan's cinema (other than Hou, who continues to work) are Ang Lee and Tsai Ming-liang. The sharp difference between these two filmmakers illustrates the complex trajectories of the second new wave. We discuss in a different chapter the enormously versatile transnational scope of Ang Lee's work. Equally prolific, unlike Lee, Tsai's work remains firmly anchored within Taiwan and art cinema. He has produced a dozen features and many short films, and also contributed to several anthology films. His work has moved from theaters to art museums, stretching and animating the boundaries of cinematic image. His defiant experimentations with classical cinematic techniques make his transition to digital explosively interesting. The central focus of all his work has been the subjectivity of an individual in disjunctive, disruptive, and alienating global spaces. He maintains a primal connection to the primogenitors of the new wave in France, entirely mindful of the cross-cultural appeals in his narratives.

After working in television as a scriptwriter and director, Tsai made *Qing shao nian nuo zha/Rebels of the Neon God* (1992), the film that served as testing ground for his favorite themes: nihilistic, loner youths in Taipei, sex as a failed gesture toward fulfillment, the disintegrating family, Buddhist faith and contemporary life, and a recurrence of water. In *Vive L'amour* (1994), alienation links three young inhabitants (two men and a woman) in an apartment in Taipei, playing out their frustrations and the wayward dispersion of their desires. After filming a narrative of lives thrown asunder by their connection and immersion in water in *He liu/The River* (1997)—where Hong Kong director Ann Hui appears in the role of a film director—Tsai makes a musical-tragedy set in an apartment building in *Dong/The Hole* (1998). The film was part of an anthology series of feature films produced around the world to mark the end of the millennium. Again preoccupied with water, Tsai brings nightmarish dimensions of cities that cage in people, crippling any possibility of breaking free of their grip. His *Visage/Face* (2009), filmed at the Louvre at the invitation of a museum, is an ode to the inner struggles of filmmaking, recasting the travails of the artists from a distant chamber of perception.

Tsai's films have an abrupt, elliptical flow, with humor that peels off the existential absurdities in everyday situations. His realist mode makes the spatial geography of the setting as important as the discursive dispositions of the bodies, which oscillate between the pursuit of normal existence and hesitant efforts at pleasure and ecstasy (de Luca, 2011). Like Hou, he prefers master shots and long takes, mapping out the spatial parameters to narrate tales of despair, misfortunes, and alienation. The consistency of themes, figures, and styles position Tsai as an auteur mindful of the connections he makes in his films with the auteurs of the French New Wave, maintaining a multi-directional probing of issues and styles that concern him. Tsai's films have a quality of intratextuality and intertextuality where textual motifs, spaces, and temporal indices run through his films as though they are part of a shared loop of elements, moving together (Lim, 2007).

Our discussion of the auteurs of art cinema in Asia began with a need to reorient the generic pronouncement of an auteurist approach and frequent contributors to film festivals as "auteurs of world cinema" committed to cinematic modernity on a global scale. Instead, we emphasize a need to explore different modernities in the works of film directors from different parts of the world. Our discussion of Jia Zhangke, Hong Sang-soo, Hou Hsiao-hsien and Tsai Ming-liang suggests that a rejuvenated auteur approach that directs our attention to a specific connection between local and global modernity is best suited to understand the emergent filmmakers whose influence goes well beyond their local or regional context. As Adrian Martin says:

> It entails grasping in an artist's work, the overall complex or gestalt of style and content, sensibility and poetic gesture—in order, finally to probe, apply and extend that "very sensitive instrument" formed by a filmmaker's personal vision of the world, a *regard* (in the double sense of both a look and an attitude) that is both critical and loving. And it is my hope that writing about film can, in its own way, also carry on the "amorous vigilance" of that double regard which is so unique to cinema.
>
> (Martin, 2010)

Students of world cinema and cinephiles engaged in a discursive exchange in the public sphere develop a particular affinity for figures like Tsai. It is because they search for the contours of such gestalt by pursuing intratextual threads in their work. Art cinema's higher profile in world cinema is in part a result of the productive relationship between the auteurs of world cinema and students, viewers, and cinephiles.

Tsai's *Ni nabian jidian/What Time Is It There?* (2001) is a complex, challenging, and exciting work addressing precisely these ideas and providing many insights into the discourses of world cinema. Thematically and stylistically rich, the film is a veritable centerpiece from which one can make intra- and intertextual connections or develop observations on how a major director from Asian cinema maps "trans-Asian" coordinates with world cinema. *What Time* opens with Hsiao-kang's father at the kitchen table. Soon, we realize that the father has died and Hsiao-kang's mother grieves, conducts worship rituals, and hopes that his ghost will return. Covering the windows in black cloth to invite the spirit in the sanctum of her time zone, preparing meals for him,

(continued)

(continued)

and arranging the entire apartment to suit the ghost, she becomes obsessed with the idea that her husband may be reincarnated, perhaps as a cockroach or fish. Hsiao-kang sells watches on a skywalk in Taipei. A few days after his father's death, he meets a girl, Shiang-chyi, who insists on purchasing a dual-time-zone watch because she is leaving for Paris. Hsiao-kang is wearing the only watch of that kind so he gives it to her. After this brief and fleeting connection, she leaves for Paris and he stays in Taipei with his mother, both frustrated with longing and desire.

The film proceeds on two levels, in two cities. In Taipei, Hsiao-kang sells watches during the day and stays home in the night, cowering in his bed, fearful that his father's ghost might make an appearance. His grieving mother is obsessed with the reincarnation of her husband. It is a terrifyingly lonely existence for both of them; he is trapped in his fears and a closed world, she in her beliefs and obsessive rituals. Afraid to leave the bed because he may meet his father's spirit, Hsiao-kang pees in plastic bags and disposes of the urine outside the window. Longing for the girl in Paris, he buys a videotape of Francois Truffaut's *Les quatre cents coups/The 400 Blows*, and incessantly watches the film. He develops a comfort ritual of setting clocks, including those in a clock shop, to Paris time, channeling his desire and longing both through unsatisfying attempts at sexual encounters and manipulations of mechanical time. Meanwhile, in Paris, Shiang-chyi is frustrated by her loneliness and by being treated as a tourist. She tries to strike up a relationship with a woman but is rebuffed. Her bag is stolen when she dozes off in the Tuileries. On a visit to the cemetery she even meets Jean-Pierre Léaud—Antoine Doinel in *The 400 Blows*—who is there to charm the girls. Her bag is finally retrieved by a stranger who resembles Hsiao-kang's father.

There is a characteristic rigor to Tsai's visual style. He prefers long takes, the camera held back at a distance from the subjects to reveal the space that does not necessarily become active, nor inhabitable for movement. He creates a tableau in which the limits of the frame are open to extending beyond the frame. Sculptural figures in the house are illuminated with measured lights, usually from above, bringing the contours of bodies and objects in view without revealing their full spatial occupancy. As Hsiao-kang watches Truffaut's film in his dark room, his body is reposed in retreat in front of the screen, his eyes withdrawn into a space without coordinates, while the black-and-white images on the screen move like ghosts without an audience. Taipei in this film lives in the interior spaces of a troubled family. The images of the skywalk where he sells his watch remain in the foreground, bustling with activity while a long take centered on our protagonist signifies the anti-dramatic life of a loner in a busy city. Paris is emptied out without its markers, making Jean-Pierre Léaud's appearance ghost-like, like a flickering picture among moving images. The pace of the film is calculatingly slow, rolling along two sprawling metropolises in which the characters cannot find their anchors. Tsai's images may be placed in the galaxy of realisms that have emerged in world cinema, but his is a steadfastly stylized realism. The stylization and the uncontainable voluptuousness of his meticulous framing and long takes push Tsai's film into a kind of performance art, an orientation he would later pursue with his art installations.

The two narrative planes in Taipei and Paris are structured around the central figure of time, and a question mark following the title of the film already poses questions regarding this figure.

Figures 7.15a–7.15c In Tsai Ming-liang's *What Time Is It There?* (2001), the two narrative planes
in Taipei and Paris are structured around the figure of time that suggests
disjointed times and experiences in multiple modernities

(continued)

(continued)

Does Tsai intend to pose a question to the viewer, or is it a catachrestic gesture to bring our attention to the asynchrony in our global relations? If it is a question, is it directed toward a discovery of time elsewhere, or is it an unfurling of a different relationship to time itself? Hsiao-kang's efforts to set the clocks in Taipei to Paris time gives him the subversive satisfaction of being closer to Shiang-chyi's state of being, a small step toward communion with his object of desire. A dealer gives him an indestructible watch that he keeps hammering against the steel rails of the skywalk. The clock itself is indestructible but his gestures are driven with a desire to prove something else, to destroy the time-keepers for their failures to bring the worlds together. To be out of one's place is to find oneself in disjointed experiences of time. The severe loneliness and alienation of Hsiao-kang in Taiwan remove him from the materiality of his everyday life. Contemporary time promises a unified experience of global modernity, a synchronicity of experience that removes the separations of time zones. In effect, however, Tsai's film sets out to suggest otherwise—that we are part of a global system of disjointed times and experiences. In a world of dispersed trajectories of desires and connections, chronography is as divided as geography, perhaps more so. Hsiao-kang and Shiang-chyi are but two figures yearning to be in the same loop of time that forever eludes them. The thin thread that binds them is the shared condition of alienation, the status of a foreigner in the spaces they inhabit, both their own and foreign.

When Truffaut's film plays in Taipei, the protagonist of the film appears in Paris, now old and out of place, wooing Hsiao-kang's imagined paramour. While this is an adoring gesture toward the French New Wave whose magnetic spirit of experimentation Tsai channels in this film, it is notable that the imprint of time has made its mark on both figures. Truffaut's film is excavated from the street shops of Taipei and watched in a space haunted by an imagined ghost. The act of cinephilic admiration takes place in the dungeons of shrouded space of the everyday. And Jean-Pierre Léaud in Paris is an aged image of his youthful self, the spirit of which energized Tsai into filmmaking. While "the ghosts of previous new waves" haunt the streets and screens of Taipei, as Tweedie observes, they wear the scars of forces that push them away (2013: 37). Tsai's attempts at their resurrection are shot through with a sharp critique of forces that disassemble and marginalize bold and innovative experimentations of film form. The spectral bend of the narrative in this and other films by Tsai is quite in line with the diagnosis that African and Nigerian theorists propose about ghosts, where ghostly figures are aligned with the global syndrome of spectral figures and aesthetics. In this film, Tsai's shifts in time are orchestrated with the presence of ghosts who erupt from the folklore and spiritual belief systems. But the ghosts also come from art cinema. Both ghost figures are mediators, one in the movement of art cinema and the other in comparative studies of their emergence and their trajectories.

In assessing Tsai's indebtedness to the French New Wave, Mark Betz (2006) recognizes the modernist features of his work: the formal consistency, commitment, and continuity of actors and their on-screen personas; rigor and reflexivity in the visual style; and experimentation with narrative construction. But Tsai's committed auteur style is also rooted in reflecting on the specific experience of modernity in Taiwan. Tsai's iconic ghost figures, the persistence of faith (here symbolized by his mother, obsessed with the return of her husband's spirit), and the recurrence of motifs (food, water, bodily suffering) situates him in the local experience. The family dynamic-disintegration and the feeble attempts to put it together through spiritual means derive from the Confucian contexts, locating agency outside of the individual. The individual, the protagonist in Tsai's films, is homeless and lonely outside this context. In Tsai's films, one finds a negotiation or juxtaposition of dual modernity in the Taiwanese–Chinese identity, the crisis of which takes place against two different planes and across disjunctive time zones. From a different perspective, Yeh and Davis insist that Tsai's work has a "campy" character (2005: 223). The humor, arbitrariness, the specific deployment of the local idiom in gestures, objects, and music point toward an aesthetic that plays with the elements of his films. The self-reflexively lighthearted elements allow Tsai to work through a negotiation between marginality and tradition, between identity and its transitions. The presence of gay sexuality is woven into such elements, positioning for a campy absorption rather than a critique or confrontation.

With these considerations in mind, *What Time* becomes a nexus for multiple modernities. In framing the contentious debates around Tsai's films regarding European modernism and Asian–Confucian–Taiwanese national modernism, Betz (2006) situates Tsai's work in the realm of "transmodernity," modernity outside of the Eurocentric view that offers agency to other cultures. In Tsai's films, the multiple negotiations with local traditions, European art cinema, and a folk-cultural, self-reflexive style point toward such transmodernity or what is sometimes called a multicultural, multilevel modernity (Dussel, 2006). Tsai demonstrates a particular inflection of European modernity by negotiating with it from the vantage point of Asia. One sees formal innovations and thematic commitment of an auteur of world cinema, exemplifying the influence of Asian cinema on world cinema. Betz believes that Tsai's cinema allows us to re-examine the project of modernity in European cinema, re-situating it in the geopolitical shifts, rather than as a transcendent style (2006: 178). Tsai is not so much a modernist in the Eurocentric chronology of modernism, but a modernist who allows for a remapping of the global modernity from various vantage points in world cinema. Tsai's films are thus rich examples of the far-reaching influence of Asian cinema on world cinema.

Asian theoretical perspectives

The idea of cinema's universality gets diminished when we consider how the invention of cinema was received in different parts of the world in the late nineteenth century. The specificity of cinema's reception in different cultures makes for a fascinating archeology of the medium. In the West, cinema emerged in a soil readied by the edict of photographic realism. Like literature, cinema tuned into the promise of realism in representation. Yet, for a culture unaccustomed to the mechanical reproduction of images, the lifelike images appearing on the photographic paper and on the screen aroused suspicions of ghostly allure. Bracketing Western cinema's obsession with realism, Tom Gunning's masterful historical account of early cinema in the West demonstrates that early forms such as "spirit photography" and "magic theater" were suspicious of cinema as a realistic medium (Gunning, 1995). Except for the early, minor lure of seeing mysteries in cinematic images, however, realism and the indexical quality of the image held sway over the medium, influencing theoretical thinking for over a century.

Elsewhere in the world, this trajectory took varying turns. In India, cinema arrived in an energetic mix of folk traditions, mythologies, religious narratives, and multiple storytelling techniques. These art forms shaped the iconography of cinema as well as its relationship with spectators. The ingenuity or the specificity of "theory" of Indian cinema arises from this synergy. Realism did not have much appeal for its genesis. Cinema's passionate popularity among millions was pumped from the same well that breathed life into folk traditions, storytelling, and culturally-rooted forms of perceiving images. Cinema still maintains the mobility of folk traditions as it continues to travel in the countryside, despite the new technologies that have diversified and disseminated the medium, from theater to hand-held devices.

In Africa, cinema encountered a spellbinding mix of religion, native traditions, and belief systems that feared and revered the mystical elements in life. In addition, cinema existed under the cloak of colonialism, deepening suspicions of the medium until Africans gained control over it to narrate their own stories, construct their own iconography, and hold a mirror to themselves. The notion of realism was tainted with imported visions of dominance that held little appeal within the continent. Though African cinemas have evolved into complex and diverse formations, the conditions of their genesis continue to form the kernel of their identity.

Cinema's early reception in diverse Asian countries similarly encountered the existing modes of perceiving images and arts of expression. It is a layered account of the archeology that underscores parallel currents while also making the trajectory of cinema in each culture quite distinct. Intertwined histories of colonialism and ideological dominance in some periods make it very difficult to chart a coherent account of theoretical thinking in different cinemas of this region. As scholars unearth historical accounts of theoretical thinking, this project is also marked by the desire to label writings as "theoretical," acknowledging the influence of Western theoretical models, which arrived nearly at the same time as political and cultural conditions in the region began to experience change. This is also the moment that we identify as the beginning of the "new world cinema."

Debates on "film theories" and indigenous philosophies of image remain vibrant in all cinemas in the Asian region. Though many of the early writings remain inaccessible to the English-speaking world, there are increasing efforts to translate and present them to broader audiences. The discourses on film theories outside of European and English-speaking world remain more vibrant than ever, while the translation projects by the *Cinema Journal* and the workshops, conferences, and publications of the Permanent Seminar on the Histories of Film Theory remain exemplary in this regard.[4] Today, Chinese film theory consists of substantive scholarship, and an increasing amount of work published in Chinese-language journals has become available in English (Semsel et al., 1990; Fan, 2015).

Cinema's first encounters in China and Japan make for grounds of comparison as existing cultural forms encountered a new technology from the West that upset and transformed the forms of expressions and belief systems informing them. Though trajectories of film theories took different turns in both countries, their geneses held influence over the perception of cinema for quite some time. In China, cinema landed in the midst of traditions of theater, opera, and lantern shadowplays (*dengyinxi*). Film offered a different form of a shadowplay: a play-drama made of a new kind of shadows. Film became *ying xi* or "shadow play-drama." Film scholar Chen Xihe claims a distinct Chinese conception of film, seeing shadows and drama in a near-alchemical relationship:

> In Chinese, shadowplay *(ying xi)* is a word group consisting of a modifier and the word it modifies. Its key word is play, which means a drama; shadow, which means the image on the screen, is only the modifier of play. The basic understanding of the relationship of shadowplay to film is that play is the origin of film, but shadow is its means of presentation.
> (Chen, 1990: 193)

Drama was transformed by its projection on the screen, which in turn affected how play scripts were conceived. Traditional forms of drama (*xi*) changed from "ancient lantern shadowplay" (*dengyingxi*) to different forms of cinema: "electric shadowplay" (*dianguang yingxi*), "western shadowplay" (*xiyang yingxi),* or "moving shadowplays" (*huodong yingxi*) (Berry & Farquhar, 2006: 51). Audiences went to cinema from 1895 to 1933 to see marvelous spectacles of electric shadowplays, forming the kernel of their attractions to this new medium. Berry and Farquhar note that early Chinese cinema was "clearly a cinema of attractions, screened in public spaces (teahouses, markets, parks and theaters)," where "technology itself was part of the attraction" (2006: 51).

In formulating the foundational aesthetics of Chinese cinema, Chen (1990) argues that the image became a vehicle for narrating the story, and the script maintained its central power. Joined by Zhong Defang, he explains that image is a way of transforming the story, a way to modify its movement and its trajectory (quoted in Fan, 2015: 226). That cinema offers a symbiosis of the two is its distinctive feature and a specific approach of the Chinese film theory. Chinese film aesthetics, they contend, "cannot be classified into categories of formalism or realism" (Chen, 1990: 196). Chen thinks of the question of theorizing as a "speculative" matter. Chinese films and filmmakers come from a practical culture, placing the social function of film, performing drama, and storytelling above speculative and idealistic goals of filmmaking and viewing.

The concept of cinema as shadowplay faced its first challenge in 1979 when Bai Jingsheng wrote his influential article, "Throwing Away the Walking Stick of Drama" (in Semsel et al., 1990), bringing to attention the multidimensional aspects of film form beyond those of a play. He argued that the Chinese film theory was moving away from the traditionalist approaches rooted in the period when cinema arrived in the country. During four decades of Maoist influence, there was a "classical" film theory informed by socialist realism, aimed at political struggle, and based on the Soviet model. As this period came to an end, new thinking in film theory began to take shape (Ye, 1997).

Trained in the Beijing Film Academy, Chen and Zhong formulated their conception of Chinese film theory in 1985–1986, while also conceding the debate to the modernist theorists and filmmakers who were eager to work in the post-revolutionary period. Chen concedes that the new filmmakers working after the 1980s had "launched an attack on the traditional shadowplay" by embracing the modernist style of filmmaking (1990: 203).

Writing from the Hong Kong perspective, Emilie Yeh (2016) argues that Chen and Zhong's conception was misplaced as they privileged *xi* (fabrication, performance), concerned with cinema's dramatic effects and their attending ethos, instead of focusing on *ying* (the photographic image). She makes a case that cinema arrived in Hong Kong before it went to the Mainland. Cinema was practiced there as *ying hua* (photo pictures), used in educational and entertainment modes. The emphasis on play in *ying xi* overlooks cinema's role as "phantasmagoric adventure beyond a recurrence of live performance" (Yeh, 2016).

The emergence of systematic theoretical thinking in China occurs about the same time as Western film theory makes inroads in the country. Western scholarship becomes easily available to scholars while the exposure to European films widens through film festivals and other venues. In the spirit of conducting a dialog between Chinese and Western film theory, Victor Fan (2015) offers a new insightful conception of the Chinese film aesthetics. He invokes the term "*bizhen,*" often translated as "lifelike" or "approaching reality" (2015: 3). *Bizhen* recalls André Bazin's notion of the cinematic image, where the image brings us closer to the real, and gives a phenomenological apprehension of the real without representing the real itself. Fan offers a conception of *bizhen* as a key term of the Chinese theory of the image, whereby an image brings us closer to reality but maintains a distance from it. The potentiality of the image contains within it various affective states in comprehending the real of the image.

Fan's postulation of a Chinese concept of image through an insight obtained in Bazin's theories suggests that a dialog between different theoretical models is possible, indeed necessary. It also shows that increased interactions between different discourses in new world cinema brings indigenous theories to light—theories that were long hidden behind closed political systems as well as the inaccessibility of language.

In Japan, cinema met the magic lantern, the *gentō*, a sophisticated mode of storytelling in the 1890s, and one form of image projection merged into another without creating a shock (Gerow, 2010a: 27). In his masterly account of the early years of Japanese cinema and film theory, Gerow notes that the traditional *jidō gentō* (self-moving magic lantern) became part of carnival-like spectacles called "*misemono*" that traveled through the country. Japanese viewers were familiar with the discourse of realism of *misemono*, representing "the tension between knowledge of the object and the wonders of technique/technology" (Gerow, 2010a: 46). Early films were presented as performances with music and lectures. Audiences were accustomed to the presentation techniques and their association with the dramas of life. It was not until the arrival of the French detective serial *Zigomar* in 1911 that the culture experienced the arrival of cinema as a form distinct from the dramas and presentations of *misemono*, as fictional constructions meant to present imagined situations to audiences. The technique of making the fictional appear real contained the element of revelation about cinema; it felt different from the images of carnivals and magic lanterns. In this radical moment, according to Gerow, "cinema became foreign after it was familiar" (2010a: 62).

Once recognized as a foreign object, a popular form that exposed lower classes to unmediated influences and narratives, cinema became a centerpiece of Japanese modernity. Sensing the risk of presenting fictions to audiences, Japanese society sought to control the medium. This resulted in the so-called "Pure Film Movement," which used *benshi*, the narrator who controlled the storytelling process, while images were kept at a distance with the technique of long shots. Cinema was conceived as a social problem and film production was regulated.

Posing a counter-weight to the codes of the Pure Film Movement that restricted cinema through the 1920s, one of the earliest film theorists/critics, Yasunosuke Gonda, trusted the audience to determine the meaning of the film. During a period when reception and interpretation of a film were a matter of class control, Gonda's conception of cinema was focused instead on "content-centered" activity, where the audience was free to discover and interpret beauty on their own, by interacting with the image (2010: 24–36). The viewer's life was placed in the image and its flow, and perception and intuition mattered more than anything else. Film, for Gonda, was an "open text." He was witnessing a revolution and looking at cinema as a medium animated by the perception of the masses (Gerow, 2010b). The struggle between control and openness thus marked the difference in class positions in the Japanese film culture.

Japanese cinema was exposed to works outside of the country, especially those of European and American cinema, but theoretical thinking continued in the work of film critics and filmmakers. Gerow notes three phases: the principles of the Pure Film Movement in the 1910s; the Japanese *Nouvelle Vague* movement of the 1960s, when directors Nagisa Oshima, Yoshishige Yoshida, and Toshio Matsumoto wrote on cinema; and filmmaking in the 1990s, when Shinji Aoyama, Kiyoshi Kurosawa, and Makoto Shinozaki formed the second new wave. Their cinema was a response to the political and social conditions of their generations, including their interactions with the filmmakers from the West.

Japan's leading film critic, Tadao Sato (2010), takes account of Japanese theoretical works in his article, "Does Film Theory Exist in Japan?" Noting a number of film critics who wrote extensively on cinema, he questions the value of the so-called theoretical thinking that aims to emulate work published by "illustrious foreigners" (quoted in Sato, 2010: 22). Theory, he argues, should be based on experience and reflected in practice. Relating a number of anecdotes about directors' work on the set, he says that when a director explains a technique to his cinematographer, that in itself presents a valuable theory. For example, Kenji Mizoguchi's remarkable technique of long takes and compositions created a distinct figure of space that is richer than any theoretical musings. Sato argues that systematic, scholarly writing does not necessarily account for what theory is; instead, theory emerges from experience, practical skills, and insights.

Our account of Asian theory has been brief, partial, and hardly comprehensive but necessary to underscore the presence of indigenous traditions in each of the centers of world cinema. There are multiple such perspectives in all cinemas around the world, from Greece to Italy, from Korea to Russia. It is heartening to note a wider recognition of such perspectives and the broadening of debates in film studies. This recognition is less about the "purity" of theory than about the necessity of discovering theoretical traditions in various languages and cultures. Styles and cinemas are inspired at least in part by ways of thinking and seeing in specific cultural contexts. Our understanding of cinema never occurs in theoretical silos. Moreover, we need to question the epistemological privilege of one model over the other, and to be aware that the dominance of Western theoretical models is based on stronger patronage and institutional power.

The project of decentering theory is to recognize that there is much to learn from the less discussed theoretical models from different parts of the world. It is also to recognize interconnectedness between various theoretical traditions. Recognition of polycentric perspectives among different centers will only enrich our debates and discourses. Each of the five cinematic centers features an incredible diversity of thought, much of which still needs to be discovered. While this work continues to take place, to decenter the study of world cinema is to deny, once and for all, that Europe is "a unique source of meaning," that it is "the world's center of gravity," or "an ontological 'reality' to the world's shadow" (Shohat & Stam, 2002: 37).

Activity 7.1

Identify an Asian film festival in or near your region, and explore their recent program. How many films from Asian countries are included? Which Asian countries are represented? Compare this programming to the one by a major film festival such as Cannes, Venice, or Berlin. Based on what you observe, what can you say about the concept of Asia implied in the programming choices?

Activity 7.2

Identify five recent Hollywood blockbusters, and find out how they performed in the Asian markets by checking trade magazines such as *Variety*, *The Hollywood Reporter*, or *Screen International*. Then read up on the latest news about Asian cinema. What does the information you find illuminate about the relationship between Hollywood and Asian cinema?

Activity 7.3

Explore the websites of the Korean Film Council and UniJapan (a non-profit organization that supports and promotes Japanese films abroad), particularly their news and co-production sections. What news can you find about recent co-production ventures? Which industries are they co-producing with? Would you describe these co-productions as inter-Asian or trans-Asian?

Activity 7.4

What are the five top-grossing Chinese feature films in the recent years? Compare their revenues with Hollywood revenues in the Chinese market. What can you say about the sense of proportion, and the strength of the local product based on this comparison?

Activity 7.5

Identify three recent Hollywood blockbusters and find out how and in which ways they reference Asian and in particular Chinese audiences (stars, setting, plot, etc.)?

Activity 7.6

As discussed in this chapter in connection with the Fifth and Sixth Generation cinema, one of the driving forces in Mainland Chinese cinema has been the question of how to confront reality. One of the most important developments in this regard has been a documentary film movement, led by filmmakers such as Wu Wenguang (*Bumming in Beijing: The Last Dreamers*, 1990; *Dance With Farm Workers*, 2001), Wang Bing (*Crude Oil*, 2008; *Three Sisters*, 2012), and Li Hong (*Out of Phoenix Bridge*, 1997), among others. Watch one of these documentaries, and compare it to other documentaries you have seen. What is their approach to the genre of documentary? After reading the chapter's discussion on realism pertaining to the Sixth Generation filmmakers, what can you say about their use of realism?

Notes

1 For Yoshimoto (2006), for example, *trans-Asian* cinema denotes cinema of Asian nations engaged in a dynamic of their own. In these interactions, he believes, the identities in cultures and nations are not erased or generalized into some essences, but retained in "transformative and reflexive" practice. For Soyoung Kim (2006), the "trans-cinema" perspective also includes "trans-media" practices across borders in Asia. As a "curious, and unstable mixture" that includes screen projections and productions in multiple spheres, across digital technologies, and multiple formations of spectatorships, she uses "trans-cinema" to focus on connections within the cinemas of Hong Kong, China, and South Korea.

2 See, for example, Song Hwee Lim (2011), "Six Chinese Cinemas in Search of a Historiography," in Song Hwee Lim & Julian Ward (eds), *The Chinese Cinema Book*, London: Palgrave Macmillan, pp. 35–43; Yingjin Zhang (2012), "General Introduction," in Yingjin Zhang (ed), *A Companion to Chinese Cinema*, Malden, MA: Wiley-Blackwell, pp. 1–22; or Sheldon H. Lu (2014), "Genealogies of Critical Paradigms in Chinese-Language Film Studies," in Audrey Yue and Olivia Khoo (eds), *Sinophone Cinemas*, London: Palgrave Macmillan, pp. 13–25.

3 To read more about the controversy surrounding the film and its withdrawal from Cannes, see Da Lan (1999), "After Zhang Yimou's Withdrawal from Cannes," *Chinese Sociology & Anthropology* 32(2), 47–50.

4 See Translation/Publication Committee, *Society for Cinema and Media Studies*, www.cmstudies.org/page/comm_translation; and *The Permanent Seminar on Histories of Film Theories*, http://filmtheories.org

Bibliography

Ahn, Soojeong. (2012). *Pusan International Film Festival, South Korean Cinema and Globalization*. Hong Kong: HKU Press.

Andrew, Dudley. (2013). "Is Cinema Contagious: Transnationalism and the Case of Korea." *Cinema & Cie* 1, pp. 15–26.

Berry, Chris. (2003). "What's Big about the Big Film? De-Westernizing the Blockbuster in Korea and China." In Julian Stringer (ed), *Movie Blockbusters*. London: Routledge, pp. 217–229.

Berry, Chris. (2013). "Transnational Culture in East Asia and the Logic of Assemblage." *Asian Journal of Social Science* 41(5), pp. 453–470.

Berry, Chris & Mary Ann Farquhar. (2006). *China on Screen: Cinema and Nation*. New York, NY: Columbia University Press.

Bertozzi, Eddie. (2012). "A Still Life of the Wildest Things: Magic(al) Realism in Contemporary Chinese Cinema and the Reconfiguration of the *Jishizhuyi* Style." *Journal of Chinese Cinemas* 6(2), pp. 153–172.

Betz, Mark. (2006). "The Cinema of Tsai Ming-liang: A Modernist Genealogy." In Maria N. Ng & Philip Holden (eds), *Reading Chinese Nationalisms: Society, Literature, Film*. Hong Kong: Hong Kong University Press, pp. 161–172.

Bordwell, David. (2007). "Aesthetics in Action: Kung-Fu, Gunplay, and Cinematic Expression." In *Poetics of Cinema*. New York, NY: Routledge, pp. 395–411.

Brody, Richard. (2016). "The Hong Sang-soo Retrospective Is a Must-See." *New Yorker* (June 3). Available at: www.newyorker.com/culture/richard-brody/the-hong-sang-soo-retrospective-is-a-must-see. Accessed June 10, 2016.

Carroll, Rory. (2013). "Be Nice to China: Hollywood Risks 'Artistic Surrender' In Effort to Please." *The Guardian* (May 13). Available at: www.theguardian.com/film/2013/may/30/hollywood-china-film-industry. Accessed May 1, 2016.

Chan, Felicia. (2013). "Filming China: Zhang Yimou's Shifting Visual Politics." In Zheng Yangwen (ed), *The Chinese Chameleon Revisited: From the Jesuits to Zhang Yimou*. Newcastle: Cambridge Scholars Publishing, pp. 261–283.

Chen, Xihe. (1990). "Chinese Film Aesthetics and Their Philosophical and Cultural Fundamentals." In George S. Semsel, Xia Hong, & Hou Jianping (eds), *Chinese Film Theory: A Guide to the New Era*. New York, NY: Praeger Publishers, pp. 195–205.

Cheung, Ruby. (2016). *New Hong Kong Cinema: Transitions to Becoming Chinese in 21st Century East Asia*. New York, NY: Berghahn Books.

Choi, Jungbong. (2010). "Of the East Asian Cultural Sphere: Theorizing Cultural Regionalization." *China Review* 10(2), pp. 109–136.

Choi, Jungbong. (2012). "Of Transnational-Korean Cinematrix." *Transnational Cinemas* 3(1), pp. 3–18.

Choong, Kevin Teo Kia. (2005). "Old/New Korea(s), Korean-ness, Alterity, and Dreams of Re-Unification in South Korean Cinema." *Contemporary Justice Review* 8(3), pp. 321–334.

Chow, Rey. (1995). *Primitive Passions: Visuality, Sexuality, Ethnography, and Contemporary Chinese Cinema.* New York, NY: Columbia University Press.

Chow, Rey. (2003). "*Not One Less*: The Fable of a Migration." In Chris Berry (ed), *Chinese Films in Focus: 25 New Takes.* London: British Film Institute, pp. 167–174.

Ciecko, Anne Tereska (ed). (2006). *Contemporary Asian Cinema: Popular Culture in a Global Frame.* New York, NY: Berg.

Dai, Jinhua. (2014). "Temporality, Nature Morte, and the Filmmaker: A Reconsideration of *Still Life.*" Trans. Lennet Daigle. Available at: http://ihr.ucsc.edu/wp-content/uploads/2014/04/Still-Life-essay-Dai-Jinhua.pdf. Accessed October 20, 2015.

Davis, Darrell William & Emilie Yueh-yu Yeh. (2007). *East Asian Screen Industries.* New York, NY: Palgrave Macmillan.

DeBoer, Stephanie. (2008). *Coproducing the Asia Pacific: Travels in Technology, Space, Time and Gender.* Dissertation. University of Southern California Digital Library.

DeBoer, Stephanie. (2014). *Coproducing Asia: Locating Japanese–Chinese Regional Film and Media.* Minneapolis, MN: Minnesota University Press.

de Luca, Tiago. (2011). "Sensory Everyday: Space, Materiality and the Body in the Films of Tsai Ming-liang." *Journal of Chinese Cinemas* 5(2), pp. 157–179.

Desser, David. (2003). "Consuming Asia: Chinese and Japanese Popular Culture and the American Imaginary." In Jenny Kwok Wah Lau (ed), *Multiple Modernities: Cinemas and Popular Media in Transcultural East Asia.* Philadelphia, PA: Temple University Press, 2003, pp. 179–199.

Desser, David. (2006). "Hong Kong Film and the New Cinephilia." In Meaghan Morris, Siu Leung Li, & Stephen Chan Ching-Kiu (eds), *Hong Kong Connections: Transnational Imagination in Action Cinema.* Durham, NC: Duke University Press, pp. 205–222.

Dombrowski, Lisa. (2008). "Miramax's Asian Experiment: Creating a Model for Crossover Hits." *Scope* (February). Available at: www.nottingham.ac.uk/scope/documents/2008/february-2008/dombrowski.pdf

Duara, Presenjit. (2010). "Asia Redux: Conceptualizing a Region for Our Times." *The Journal of Asian Studies* 69(4), pp. 963–983.

Dussel, Enrique. (2006). "Transmodernity and Interculturality." *Poligrafi* 11(41/42), pp. 5–40.

Eleftheriotis, Dimitris. (2006). "Turkish National Cinema." In Dimitris Eleftheriotis & Gary Needham (eds), *Asian Cinemas: A Reader and Guide.* Honolulu, HI: University of Hawaii Press, pp. 220–229.

Eleftheriotis, Dimitris & Gary Needham (eds). (2006). *Asian Cinemas: A Reader and Guide.* Honolulu, HI: University of Hawaii Press.

Elsaesser, Thomas. (2009). "World Cinema: Realism, Evidence, Presence." In Lucia Nagib & Cecilia Mello (eds), *Realism and Audiovisual Media.* London: Palgrave Macmillan, pp. 3–19.

Fan, Victor. (2015). *Cinema Approaching Reality: Locating Chinese Film Theory.* Minneapolis, MN: University of Minnesota Press.

Forrest, Jennifer & Leonard R. Koos. (2001). *Dead Ringers: The Remake in Theory and Practice.* Albany, NY: State University of New York Press.

Gerow, Aaron. (2002). "Recognizing 'Others' in Japanese Cinema." *The Japan Foundation Newsletter* 14(2), pp. 1–6.

Gerow, Aaron. (2010a). *Visions of Japanese Modernity: Articulations of Cinema, Nation, and Spectatorship, 1895–1925.* Berkeley, CA: University of California Press.

Gerow, Aaron. (2010b). "The Process of Theory: Reading Gong Yasunosuke and Early Film Theory." *Review of Japanese Culture and Society* 22, pp. 37–43.

Gunning, Tom. (1995). "Phantom Images and Modern Manifestations: Spirit Photography, Phantom Images, Magic Theater, Trick Films and Photography's Uncanny." In Patrice Petro (ed), *Fugitive Images: From Photography to Video.* Bloomington, IN: Indiana University Press, pp. 42–71.

Hageman, Andrew. (2009). "Floating Consciousness: The Cinematic Confluence of Ecological Aesthetic in *Suzhou River.*" In Sheldon H. Lu & Jiayan Mi (eds), *Chinese Cinema: In the Age of Environmental Challenge.* Hong Kong: Hong Kong University Press, pp. 73–93.

Higbee, Will & Song Hwee Lim. (2010). "Concepts of Transnational Cinema: Towards a Critical Transnationalism in Film Studies." *Transnational Cinemas* 1(1), pp. 7–21.

Huat, Chua Beng. (2014). "Conceptualizing an East Asian Popular Culture." *Inter-Asia Cultural Studies* 5(2), pp. 200–221.

Hui, Wang. (2011). *The Politics of Imagining Asia*. Cambridge, MA: Harvard University Press.

Hunt, Leon. (2008). "Asiaphilia, Asianization and the Gatekeeper Auteur: Quentin Tarantino and Luc Besson." In Leon Hunt & Leung Wing-Fai (eds), *East Asian Cinemas: Exploring Transnational Connections on Film*. London: I.B. Tauris, pp. 220–221.

Iordanova, Dina. (2011). "East Asia and Film Festivals: Transnational Clusters for Creativity and Commerce." In D. Iordanova & R. Cheung (eds), *Film Festival Yearbook 3: Film Festivals and East Asia*. St Andrews: St Andrews Film Studies, pp. 1–33.

Iwabuchi, Koichi. (2002a). *Recentering Globalization: Popular Culture and Japanese Transnationalism*. Durham, NC: Duke University Press.

Iwabuchi, Koichi. (2002b). "Nostalgia for a (Different) Asian Modernity: Media Consumption of 'Asia' in Japan." *Positions: East Asia Cultures Critique* 10(3), p. 547–573.

Iwabuchi, Koichi. (2014). "De-westernization, Inter-Asian Referencing and Beyond." *European Journal of Cultural Studies* 17(1), pp. 44–57.

Jaffee, Valeria. (2004). "Bringing the World to the Nation: Jia Zhangke and the Legitimation of Chinese Underground Film." *Senses of Cinema* 32 (July). Available at: http://sensesofcinema.com/2004/fea ture-articles/chinese_underground_film. Accessed April 2, 2015.

Jameson, Fredric. (1998). "Notes on Globalization as a Philosophical Issue." In Fredric Jameson & Masao Miyoshi (eds), *The Cultures of Globalization*. Durham, NC: Duke University Press, pp. 54–81.

Jameson, Fredric. (2006). "History and Elegy in Sokurov." *Critical Inquiry* 33(1), pp. 1–12.

Jingsheng, Bai. (1990). "Throwing Away the Walking Stick of Drama." Trans. Hou Jianping. In George S. Semsel, Xia Hong, & Hou Jianping (eds), *Chinese Film Theory: A Guide to the New Era*. New York, NY: Praeger Publishers, pp. 5–10.

Kasman, Daniel. (2016). "Once More, With Differences: Hong Sang-soo's *Right Now, Wrong Then*." *MUBI: Notebook Feature* (June 24). Available at: https://mubi.com/notebook/posts/once-more-with-differences-hong-sang-soo-s-right-now-wrong-then. Accessed December 20, 2016.

Khoo, Olivia. (2004). "The Minor Transnationalism of Queer Asian Cinema: Female Authorship and the Short Film Format." *Camera Obscura* 29(1), pp. 33–57.

Khoo, Olivia. (2007). *The Chinese Exotic: Modern Exotic Femininity*. Hong Kong: Hong Kong University Press.

Khoo, Olivia, Belinda Small, & Audrey Yue. (2008). "Editorial: Transnational Asian Australian Cinema." *Studies in Australasian Cinema* 2(2), pp. 97–102.

Kim, Jin. (2004). "Blockbusters Fly Higher with 'Taegukgi.'" *The Korea Herald* (February 5). LexusNexus. Buffalo, NY: University at Buffalo Library.

Kim, Kyung Hyun. (2001). "Korean Cinema and Im Kwon-taek: An Overview." In David E. James & Kyung Hyun Kim (eds), *Im Kwon-taek: The Making of a Korean National Cinema*. Detroit, MI: Wayne State University Press, pp. 19–46.

Kim, M. (2000). "A Year of Money and Accolades for Korean Films." *The Korea Herald* (December 30). Available at: www.koreaherald.co.kr/SITE/data/html_dir/2000/12/30/200012300023.asp. Accessed December 22, 2016.

Kim, Soyoung. (2003). "The Birth of the Local Feminist Sphere in the Global Era: 'Trans-Cinema' and Yosongjang." *Inter-Asia Cultural Studies* 4(1), pp. 10–24.

Kim, Soyoung. (2005). "'Cine-Mania' or Cinephilia: Film Festivals and the Identity Question." In Chi-Yun Shin & Julian Stringer (eds), *New Korean Cinema*. New York, NY: New York University Press, pp. 79–94.

Kim, Soyoung. (2006). "From Cine-mania to Blockbusters and Trans-cinema: Reflections on Recent South Korean Cinema." In Valentina Vitali & Paul Willemen (eds), *Theorizing National Cinema*. London: British Film Institute, pp. 186–201.

Klein, Christina. (2003). "The Asia Factor in Global Hollywood." *Yale Global Online* (March 2003). Available at: http://yaleglobal.yale.edu/content/asia-factor-global-hollywood. Accessed November 5, 2016.

Klein, Christina. (2004a). "The Hollowing Out of Hollywood." *Yale Global Online* (April). Available at: http://yaleglobal.yale.edu/content/hollowing-out-hollywood. Accessed November 5, 2016.

Klein, Christina. (2004b). "Copywood No Longer." *Yale Global Online* (October 11). Available at: http://yaleglobal.yale.edu/content/copywood-no-longer. Accessed November 5, 2016.

Klein, Christina. (2004c). "Martial Arts and the Globalization of U.S. and Asian Film Industries." *Comparative American Studies: An International Journal* 2/3, pp. 360–384.

Knowledge at Wharton. (2016). "China's Film Industry: A Blockbuster in the Making." *Knowledge at Wharton* (February 17). Available at: http://knowledge.wharton.upenn.edu/article/lights-china-action-how-china-is-getting-into-the-global-entertainment-business. Accessed December 3, 2016.

Kreicer, Shelly. (1998). "*Sleepless Town* Review." *Chinese Cinema Site*. Available at: www.chinesecinemas.org/sleeplesstown.html. Accessed November 28, 2016.

Lau, Jenny Kwok Wah. (2007). "*Hero*: China's response to Hollywood Globalization." *Jump Cut* 49. Available at: www.ejumpcut.org/archive/jc49.2007/Lau-Hero/text.html. Accessed November 23, 2016.

Lee, Hyung-sook. (2006). "The Hong Kong Film Syndrome in South Korea." *Discourse* 28(2), pp. 98–113.

Lee, Sangjoon. (2012). "The Genealogy of Pan-Asian Big Pictures and the Predicament of the Contemporary South Korean Film Industry." *Transnational Cinemas* 3(1), pp. 93–106.

Lee, Sangjoon & Abe Mark Nornes (eds). (2015). *Hallyu 2.0: The Korean Wave in the Age of Social Media*. Ann Arbor, MI: University of Michigan Press.

Lee, Vivian P.Y. (2007). "Into/Out of the Critical Divide: The Indeterminacy of *Hero*." *Scope: An Online Journal of Film Studies* 9.

Lee, Vivian P.Y. (2009). "Karmic Redemption: Memory and Schizophrenia in Hong Kong Action Films." In *Hong Kong Cinema Since 1997: The Post-Nostalgic Imagination*. London: Palgrave Macmillan.

Lee, Vivian P. Y. (2011). *East Asian Cinemas: Regional Flows and Global Transformations*. London: Palgrave Macmillan.

Letteri, Richard. (2007). "Realism, Hybridity, and the Construction of Identity in Wang Xiaoshuai's *Beijing Bicycle*." *Southeast Review of Asian Studies* 29, pp. 72–89.

Lim, Bliss Cua. (2015). "A Pan-Asian Cinema of Allusion: Going Home and Dumplings." In Esther M.K. Cheung, Gina Marchetti, & Esther C.M. Gau (eds), *A Companion to Hong Kong Cinema*. Malden, MA: Wiley-Blackwell, pp. 410–439.

Lim, Dennis. (2010). "Parting Twin Curtains of Repression." *The New York Times* (July 30). Available at: www.nytimes.com/2010/08/01/movies/01spring.html. Accessed December 23, 2016.

Lim, Song Hwee. (2007). "Positioning Auteur Theory in Chinese Cinema Studies: Intratextuality, Intertextuality and Paratextuality in the Films of Tsai Ming-liang." *Journal of Chinese Cinemas* 1(3), pp. 223–245.

Lovatt, Philippa. (2012). "The Spectral Soundscapes of Postsocialist China in the Films of Jia Zhangke." *Screen* 53(4), pp. 418–435.

Lu, Sheldon Hsiao-peng. (1997). "Historical Introduction: Chinese Cinemas (1896–1996) and Transnational Film Studies." In Sheldun Hsiao-peng Lu (ed), *Transnational Chinese Cinemas: Identity, Nationhood, Gender*. Honolulu, HI: University of Hawaii Press, pp. 1–34.

McFarland, K.M. (2016). "Thought *Warcraft* Tanked? Nope—It Changed Blockbusters Forever." *Wired* (June 15). Available at: www.wired.com/2016/06/warcraft-and-the-future-of-blockbusters. Accessed December 3, 2016.

Magnan-Park, Aaron Han Joon. (2007). "The Heroic Flux in John Woo's Trans-Pacific Passage: From Confucian Brotherhood to American Selfhood." In Gina Marchetti & Tan See Kam (ed), *Hong Kong Film, Hollywood and the New Global Cinema: No Film is an Island*. New York, NY: Routledge, pp. 36–38.

Martin, Adrian. (2008a). "Review: Constantine Verevis, *Film Remakes*." *Velvet Light Trap* 61, pp. 60–62.

Martin, Adrian. (2008b). "What's Happening: Story, Scene and Sound in Hou Hsiao-hsien." *Inter-Asia Cultural Studies* 9(2), pp. 258–270.

Martin, Adrian. (2010). "What is Modern Cinema?" *16:9* (September). Available at: www.16-9.dk/2010-09/side11_inenglish.htm. Accessed May 12, 2015.

Mello, Cecilia. (2014). "Space and Intermediality in Jia Zhangke's *Still Life*." *Aniki: Portugese Journal of the Moving Image* 1(2), pp. 274–291.

Mitsui, Toru & Shohei Hosokawa (eds). (2001). *Karaoke Around the World: Global Technology, Local Singing*. New York, NY: Routledge.

Neves, Joshua. (2012). "Media Archipelagos: Inter-Asian Film Festivals." *Discourse* 34(2/3), pp. 230–239.

Noh, Jean. (2013). "Korean Film Exports Up 8.45 in 2012." *ScreenDaily* (February 11). Available at: www.screendaily.com/korean-film-exports-up-84-in-2012/5051843.article. Accessed November 1, 2016.

Nornes, Abe Mark. (2013). "The Creation and Construction of Asian Cinema Redux." *Film History* 25(1/2), pp. 175–187.

Ok, HyeRoung. (2009). "The Politics of the Korean Blockbuster: Narrating the Nation and the Spectacle of 'Glocalization' in 2009 *Lost Memories*." Available at: http://cinema.usc.edu/assets/096/15620.pdf. Accessed November 5, 2016.

Otmazgin, Nissim. (2012). "Geopolitics and Soft Power: Japan's Cultural Policy and Cultural Diplomacy in Asia." *Asia-Pacific Review* 19(2), pp. 37–61.

Otmazgin, Nissim & Eyal Ben-Ari. (2013). "Introduction: History and Theory in the Study of Cultural Collaboration." In N. Otmazgin & E. Ben-Ari (eds), *Popular Culture Co-productions and Collaborations in East and Southeast Asia*. Singapore: NUS Press.

Ping, Zhu. (2011). "Destruction, Moral Nihilism and the Poetics of Debris in Jia Zhangke's *Still Life*." *Visual Anthropology* 24, pp. 318–328.

Rayns, Tony. (2004). "The Strange Case of Kim Ki-duk." *Film Comment* (Nov/Dec), p. 51.

Reynaud, Berenice. (2007). "Zhang Yuan's Imaginary Cities and the Theatricalization of the Chinese 'Bastards.'" In Zhang Zhen (ed), *The Urban Generation: Chinese Cinema and Society at the Turn of the Twenty-First Century*. Durham, NC: Duke University Press, pp. 264–295.

Robertson, Roland. (1995). "Glocalization; Time-Space and Homogeneity-Heterogeneity." In Mike Featherstone, Scott Lash, & Roland Robertson (eds), *Global Modernities*. London: Sage, pp. 25–44.

Said, Edward. (1979). *Orientalism*. New York, NY: Vintage Books Edition.

Said, Edward. (1993). *Culture and Imperialism*. New York, NY: Vintage Books Edition.

Sato, Tadao. (2010). "Does Film Theory Exist in Japan?" Trans. Joanne Bernardi. *Review of Japanese Culture and Society* 22, pp. 14–23.

Scorsese, Martin. (2007). "Introduction to *Woman is the Future of Man*—New Yorker Video." Video introduction. Available at: www.youtube.com/watch?v=7-BttGmnVyw&feature=youtu.be. Accessed January 2, 2017.

Semsel, George S., Xia Hong, & Hou Jianping. (1990). *Chinese Film Theory: A Guide to the New Era*. New York, NY: Praeger Publishers.

Shaviro, Steven. (2004). "Shallowtail Butterfly." *The Pinocchio Theory* (February 2). Available at: www.shaviro.com/Blog/?p=256. Accessed November 28, 2016.

Shim, Ae-Gyung & Brian Yecies. (2012). "Asian Interchange: Korean-Hong Kong Co-Productions of the 1960s." *Journal of Japanese and Korean Cinema* 4(1), pp. 15–28.

Shohat, Ella & Robert Stam. (2002). "Narrativizing Visual Culture: Towards a Polycentric Aesthetics." In Nicholas Mirzoeff (ed), *The Visual Culture Reader*, 2nd edn. New York, NY: Routledge, pp. 37–59.

Spivak, Gayatri. (2007). "1994: Will Postcolonialism Travel?" In *Other Asias*. Malden, MA: Wiley-Blackwell, pp. 97–131.

Standish, Isolde. (1993). "Korean Cinema and the New Realism: Text and Context." *East-West Journal* 7(2), pp. 54–80.

Stephens, Chuck. (2004). "Local Heroes: The Many Faces of Korean Cinema's Perpetual Renaissance." *Film Comment* 40(6) (Nov/Dec), pp. 36–39.

Stevens, Carolyn S. (2007). *Japanese Popular Music: Culture, Authenticity and Power*. New York, NY: Routledge.

Teo, Stephen. (2007). *Director in Action: Johnnie To and Hong Kong Action Film*. Hong Kong: Hong Kong University Press.

Teo, Stephen. (2008). "Promise and Perhaps Love: Pan-Asian Production and The Hong Kong-China Interrelationship." *Inter-Asia Cultural Studies* 9(3), pp. 341–358.

Teo, Stephen. (2009). "Asian Film Festivals and Their Diminishing Dome: An Appraisal of PIFF, SIFF, HKIFF." In Richard Porton (ed), *Dekalog 3: On Film Festivals*. London: Wallflower, pp. 109–121.

Teo, Stephen. (2013). *The Asian Cinema Experience: Styles, Spaces, Theory*. New York, NY: Routledge.

Ti, Wei. (2008). "How Did Hou Hsiao-hsien Change Taiwan Cinema? A Critical Assessment." *Inter-Asia Studies* 9(2), pp. 271–279.

Tweedie, James. (2013). *The Age of New Waves: Art Cinema and the Staging of Globalization*. London: Oxford University Press.

Vandell, Daniel. (2014). "Transnational Remaking." In *Hollywood Remakes: Deleuze and the Grandfather Paradox*. London: Palgrave Macmillan, pp. 33–57.

Wee, Valerie. (2011). "Visual Aesthetics and Ways of Seeing: Comparing *Ringu* and *The Ring*." *Cinema Journal* 50(2), pp. 41–60.

Wilson, Rob. (2001). "Korean Cinema on the Road to Globalization: Tracking Global/Local Dynamics, or Why Im Kwon-taek is not Ang Lee." *Inter-Asia Cultural Studies* 2(2), pp. 307–318.

Wong, Cindy Hing-Yuk. (2015). "Creative Cinematic Geographies Through the Hong Kong International Film Festival." In Esther M.K. Cheung, Gina Marchetti, & Esther C.M. Yau (eds), *A Companion to Hong Kong Cinema*. New York, NY: Wiley-Blackwell, pp. 185–207.

Xu, Gary G. (2007). "Postscript: Remaking Asia." In *Sinascape: Contemporary Asian Cinema*. Lanham, MD: Rowman, Littlefield, pp. 151–158.

Yasunosuke, Gonda. (2010). "The Principles and Applications of the Moving Pictures." Trans. Aaron Gerow. *Review of Japanese Culture and Society* 22, pp. 24–36.

Ye, Hu. (1997). "Contemporary Film Theory in China." Trans. Ted Wang, Chris Berry, & Chen Mei. *Screening the Past* 3. Available at: www.screeningthepast.com/2014/12/contemporary-film-theory-in-china. Accessed June 25, 2017.

Yeh, Emilie Yueh-yu. (2016). "On Some Problems of Early Chinese Film Scholarship: News from Hong Kong." *Taiwan Cinema Studies Network* (December 15). Available at: http://twcinema.tnua.edu.tw/en/on-some-problems-of-early-chinese-film-scholarship-news-from-hong-kong. Accessed June 22, 2017.

Yeh, Emilie Yueh-yu & Darrell William Davis. (2005). *Taiwan Film Directors: A Treasure Island*. New York, NY: Columbia University Press.

Yoshimoto, Mitsuhiro (2006). "National/International/Transnational: The Concept of Trans-Asian Cinema and the Cultural Politics of Film Criticism." In Valentina Vitali & Paul Willemen (eds), *Theorising National Cinema*. London: British Film Institute, pp. 254–261.

Yoshimoto, Mitsuhiro. (2010). "Hollywood, Americanism and the Imperial Screen: Geopolitics of Image and Discourse After the End of the Cold War." *Inter-Asia Cultural Studies* 4(3), pp. 451–459.

Zeitchik, Steven & Jonathan Landreth. (2012). "Hollywood Gripped by Pressure System from China." *24 Frames: Los Angeles Times* (June 12). Available at: http://articles.latimes.com/2012/jun/12/entertainment/la-et-china-censorship-20120612. Accessed December 4, 2016.

Zhang, Benzi. (1998). "(Global) Sense and (Local) Sensibility: Poetics/Politics of Reading Film as (Auto)Ethnography." *Postmodern Culture* 8(2). Available at: http://pmc.iath.virginia.edu/text-only/issue.198/8.2.r_zhang. Accessed Nov 20, 2016.

Zhang, Yingjin. (2010a). "Transnationalism and Translocality in Chinese Cinema." *Cinema Journal* 49(3), pp. 135–139.

Zhang, Yingjin. (2010b). *Cinema, Space and Polylocality in a Globalizing China*. Honolulu, HI: University of Hawaii Press.

Zhang, Xudong. (2010). "The Poetics of Vanishing: The Films of Jia Zhangke." *The New Left Review* 63 (May–June), pp. 71–88.

Zhang, Zhen. (2007). "Introduction: Bearing Witness: Chinese Cinema in the Era of 'Transformation' (*Zhuanxing*)." In Zhang Zhen (ed), *The Urban Generation: Chinese Cinema and Society at the Turn of the Twenty-First Century*. Durham, NC: Duke University Press, pp. 1–45.

Zhou, Xun & Francesca Tarocco. (2007). *Karaoke: The Global Phenomenon*, London: Reaktion Books.

8 National formations

The transformative effect of globalization has radically redefined the status of the nation as a relevant economic, political, and cultural unit instead giving currency to the terms "world," "global," and "transnational" in descriptions of the current geopolitical map. Yet, we still divide the world by nations, and the nation retains its agency through institutions that facilitate its participation in the global sphere. In film studies too, studies of individual national cinemas are proliferating and expanding, policy is still informed by local film production, and national categories and labels continue to play a role in the production, exhibition, marketing, and understanding of films. *Nation* is not a unitary, romantic notion, a mere exercise in nostalgia and obsolescence, but a functioning, if radically transformed, entity. What we understand under "national" has changed profoundly, but it has anything but disappeared, and the understanding of national elements and their role is as important as ever.

National cinema

Although both cinema and nation are relatively recent phenomena in the larger scheme of history, they have always had intertwined and problematic functions in relation to one another and to the larger cultural sphere. On the one hand, cinema has been an international medium from its very beginning; as a visual medium, it has been seen as a universal language that transcends boundaries of nations and the limitations of languages. On the other hand, cinema has always had an important function in shaping, affirming, negotiating, or subverting the construction of nationhood and national identity, and played a key role in drawing national barriers (literal or imaginary). On a macroscopic level, the quite literal connection between nation and cinema can be traced in the overlap between the history of cinema and the modern nation-state. As Ashish Rajadhyaksha points out, we can periodize the time of celluloid, 1895–1990, as precisely the time of the rise and fall of the modern state: if the Spanish–American War of 1898 and the rise of the US as an imperial power coincides historically with the invention of celluloid, the collapse of the Soviet Union and the onset of globalization (as markers of the dissolution and transformation of the nation-state) also coincide with the gradual disappearance of celluloid (2012: 51)

In this way, the apparatus of cinema can be seen as a powerful technological presence linked to the nation-state, which validates the nation by providing both infrastructural and narrative models through which history is written and national identity created. The first American feature film, D.W. Griffith's *The Birth of a Nation* (1915), provides an epic and mythical account of the history of the American nation, a nation whose birth is predicated on a demarcation of the African American as an inferior Other against which white "superiority" is defined. In the 1920s Soviet Union, Lenin famously proclaims cinema to be "the most important of all arts," and uses it strategically to spread the message of the Revolution, to reunify and consolidate his shattered nation. Inspired by Lenin's lesson and realizing the enormous propaganda value of film, the German government of the 1930s skillfully manipulates the medium of film to objectify their fascist ideals; *Triumph of the Will* (Leni Riefenstahl, 1935), the most famous film of the period, quickly becomes a model for film propaganda among the Allies during the coming war. The post-war international new waves, such as Italian neo-realism, repulsed by how cinema was manipulated to serve nationalist projects, again deploy cinema in the service of nation building, this time to rebuild the destroyed nations and shattered national identities by remaining faithful to contemporary social reality. The post-war collapse of European empires, and the emergence of independent Third World nation-states, witnesses an explosion of the political Third Cinema movement and an emergence of various new national cinemas; the cinema of these new nations would again play a key role in both shaping the identities of new nations and providing a political and cinematic counter-narrative to Western metanarratives.

Nation-states have also provided financial and institutional support to film industries, playing a key role in the financing of films and facilitating traffic between national cinemas through specific agreements and structures. Despite international concerns and transnational circulation, the 1930s are marked by "cinema's nationalist turn," when every film was tied to specific linguistic and national communities, and cinema's Esperanto was divided into distinct national styles and thematic concerns (Andrew, 2010).[1] During this period, films are identified by national origins, cinema traffic acquires regional rather than world patterns and, as we discuss in Chapter 4, international film festivals become battlegrounds for national politics. During the heyday of art cinema's new waves in the 1960s and 1970s, nationalist geopolitics acquire a more commercial dimension, and national cinema labels promising exotic "otherness" are used as a marketing strategy to promote non-Hollywood cinema, along with the name of the director/auteur.

If looking at this brief "instant history" clarifies that cinema and nation have always had a very close if contentious relation to each other, the understanding of what constitutes "national cinema" has been no less difficult because national cinemas have performed different functions in relation to the state and because they are "national" in numerous ways. Until the 1980s, the dominant model of studying cinema remained the "national cinema" model, where various genres and auteurs are grouped together under the umbrella of national cinema. Tied to the aforementioned "national phase" in cinema, the idea of national cinema tends to focus on film texts produced within a particular territory, and often sees these texts as expressions of a national spirit and projections of national identity. Cinematic output is parsed along national borders, and cinemas of France, Germany, the Soviet Union, or the US are seen as having distinct industries, styles, and thematic concerns.

However, after the 1980s, as the interconnected and transnational patterns of national cinemas (that have always existed) began to assert themselves more prominently, the publication of a vast body of work emerged that challenged positivist, essentialist ideas of nationhood and national identity. Emerging from different but overlapping perspectives of anti-essentialist and postcolonialist criticism, these works have "shattered the theoretically naive and politically suspect beliefs in unified, ahistorical nations and national identities" (Eleftheriotis, 2002: 26). Their influence on the way film studies conceived of national cinema was extensive.

A standard point of departure for many of these anti-essentialist approaches to the concept of the nation is Benedict Anderson's groundbreaking study *Imagined Communities*, whose insights are still a starting point for any discussion of the nation. Anderson's work provides a vital insight for conceptualizing the nation as an active process arising out of various forms of national imaginaries and narratives of collectivities. Refusing to define a nation by a set of external, objective social facts, Anderson proposes a definition of the nation as "an imagined political community—and imagined as both inherently limited and sovereign" (Anderson, 2016/1983: 6). This seemingly simple thesis changes the course of study of nationhood in several aspects. Even more significant than his assertion that the nation is "thought out" or "created" is his argument that national consciousness is a product of material social changes in the nineteenth century, including communication and transportation technology, the development of specific linguistic cultures, and print capitalism. Thus, for Anderson, nationalism becomes secularized (as opposed to being based on cosmological or religious knowledge), as well as distinguished from the notion of the geographically and politically defined nation-state. It emerges not only in a geopolitical but in a *cultural* realm. The insight that national imaginings are always shaped *in and by a form* articulated in the cultural sphere, that nations are imaginary constructs whose existence depends on the apparatus of cultural fictions—and cinema becomes the most powerful of such an apparatus—becomes key for film studies and how it conceives the relationship between nation and cinema.[2]

For film studies, a key part of Anderson's insight has to do with the essential nature of form—in our case film form—in expressing national identity. Because it allows us to think of the nation beyond its geographical and political borders, in terms of national imaginaries, it shows how the irrepressible permeability of cinema across national borders begins to construct new modes of transnational imaginings. Shifting focus to the form of this imaginary, the consideration of national cinema has less to do with the body of films produced and circulating within a specific nation-state, and more to do with different *aesthetic* models or manifestations of national cinema. Post-war international new waves, such as Italian neo-realism, certainly deploy cinema in the service of nation building, but rather than characterizing the post-war Italian national cinema, they should be understood as part of the larger European art cinema model that flourished in the 1960s and 1970s and defined itself against Hollywood, both textually and in terms of distribution and exhibition channels. Similarly, the emergence of the Third Cinema movement during the post-war collapse of European empires, rather than a national movement, should be seen as an aesthetic model that rejects both Hollywood and European cinema and deploys an oppositional aesthetic in its politics of anti-imperial struggle. These models point to the extent to which national cinema production is predicated on a form of national imagining. In this case, the aesthetic models and cultural modes of production are distinct from those of Hollywood but are highly permeable and transcend national boundaries.

Understanding the nation as operating in the cultural realm above and beyond the nation-state thus brings into question the assumed internal coherence of national cinema. In one of the seminal articles on national cinema, Andrew Higson talks about "transnational" and "border crossing" to explain the tension implied in the imaginary coherence of national cinema (Higson, 1989). He argues that the question of national cinema should be approached not only in terms of films produced by and within a particular nation-state, but also in terms of distribution and exhibition, the range of specific audiences, and critical and cultural discourses circulating about the films. In other words, what the audiences *see* is just as important as what a film industry *makes*. Stephen Crofts, in "Reconceptualizing

National Cinema/s," takes the issues presented by Higson to refute the traditional notion of national cinema and offer an account of the global reach of national cinemas in terms of "the multiple politics of their production, distribution, and reception, their textuality, their relations with the state and with multiculturalism" (Crofts, 1993: 49). Far from undermining the significance of the nation-state, Crofts discusses various levels of permeability and hybridity of the nation-states that account for the complex web of interactions and interdependence of national cinemas. Most contemporary accounts of national cinemas, from Thomas Elsaesser's *New German Cinema: A History* (1989) to James Tweedie's *The Age of New Waves: Art Cinema and the Staging of Globalization* (2013) build on this approach to develop an understanding of the global interconnectedness of national cinemas and movements.

One of the consequences of expanding and reconceptualizing national cinema has certainly been an acknowledgement of a wider range of national cinemas, and we have seen the ever-widening spectrum of studies such as Iranian, Australian, Scandinavian, Turkish, Québecois, Philippine, Iranian, and various other cinemas. But this has also meant paying attention to popular, commercial cinemas within specific countries, which were too often ignored by previous studies that tended to focus only on national cinema produced for export—cinema that often defines itself against Hollywood, promising authenticity, creativity, and an exotic otherness not offered by Hollywood. Thus, *national cinema* was for a long time synonymous with *European art cinema*. Film festivals, a major site of circulation of national cinemas, have nurtured this aestheticizing of cultural specificity within the discourse of art cinema. Meanwhile, commercial cinemas that compete with Hollywood in domestic markets are not exported and thus less known, and are not considered by film cultures that define the critical terms of national cinema. Studies of popular cinemas and their ambivalent relation to the national have thus been an important methodological step. For example, Jyotika Virdi's analysis of popular Hindi film in post-independence India shows how Indian popular cinema, through specific historical and mythological genres, possesses a unique cultural history and deflects breakdowns in the concept of the nation (Virdi, 2003). Dimitris Eleftheriotis's study of European popular cinema shows how the model of national cinema in relation to European cinema has been particularly aggressive in drawing strict boundaries around the perceived characteristics of national cinema that have de facto excluded popular cinema or co-productions as "impure" and lacking national distinctness (2002: 33).

There is no doubt that along with such renewed approaches to the concept of national cinema, the impact of globalization has further pronounced the concept of the nation as inadequate. It has dissolved the nation-state as the primary unit of political, economic, and cultural difference, with transnational finance capital, deregulation of markets, mobility of labor, and the global penetration of communication networks contributing to the decidedly global nature of cinema. Despite these developments, and often because of them, the relationship between cinema and nation remains at the forefront of the debates in film studies, and national categories continue to come up in the critical discourse as well as in relation to sites of production, distribution, and reception. The idea of the nation remains an important concept in identity formation, offering some grounding in the shifting global world. National allegory remains an anchoring figure against which filmic texts articulate their locus in the world. Issues surrounding national film production and film culture continue to inform policy, and national labels are still key in international marketing and understanding of films. The national has in fact remained a major discourse strategy with which new cinemas are marketed, a form of branding that signifies and reinvents the local for global use. Rather than invoking an essentialist quality, national signifiers, as Thomas Elsaesser has argued in his study of contemporary European cinema, function as free-floating "second order references," branding the local for external use, and films themselves often self-consciously reflect not on national identity but rather on the "image that (one assumes) the other has of oneself" (2005: 71).

Equally important to a film text are the articulation of national imaginary and the allegorical formation of a nation, which serve as a frequent interpretive strategy of their own reality. The concept of "national allegory" has been one of the most controversial as well as persistent ways of understanding a cultural production of a nation, most emblematically and infamously represented by Jameson's (1986) proposal that all Third World texts are to be read as national allegories. While many scholars are wary of such an overarching theory, its dangers of generalization, theoretical orientalism, and a troubling appropriation of otherness, the concept of national allegory has nevertheless served as a productive and valid interpretive strategy. Films that resort to allegory to express their national identity or history abound, from Rainer Werner Fassbinder's *The Marriage of Maria Braun* (1979) and Theo Angelopoulos's *Ulysses' Gaze* (1997), to Emir Kusturica's *Underground* (1995), and they feature prominently in modern cinema. Ismail Xavier has argued that allegory as a mode of representation remains firmly inscribed in the dynamics of our time, even as the phenomenon of globalization has created a different historical conjuncture and a different context for its deployment (Xavier, 1999; 2012). That is, in the contemporary context of globalization, national allegory may question and deconstruct rather than affirm national identity, serving as an expression of social crisis, fragmentation, instability, and abstraction. Yet, it remains a significant structural presence and is useful, Xavier maintains, as long as we conceive of it not as a closed system, but rather as a relational dynamic. The politics of actually-existing nation-states aside, nation is still evoked or imagined, exists in a dialectical relation with globalization, and provides its essential dynamic. Whether it is to chart the possibility of forms of social life different from the patterns of global consumption, or whether it is to create a utopian space of collectivity as a political response to globalization, it is only through charting this dialectic that we can better understand the map of totality and dynamics of historical change (Xavier, 2012).

A persistent element of identity formation, the nation is also a continuously functioning category for film industries that rely in various ways on national institutional structures. It is precisely within and perhaps because of the profoundly transnational nature of film that many film industries have found it important to formulate a structural response to the national question, a formal way to assess national accountability or cultural ownership of a film. A telling example of such a strategy, Roy Stafford describes, is a cultural test introduced by the UK Film Council in 2007 that applies to any film production seeking public funding in the UK or not qualifying as an official co-production (2014: 97–105). To qualify as sufficiently "British," a production must score eighteen out of thirty-five points in a test whose scoring sections include categories of cultural content (setting, lead characters, subject matter, language), cultural contribution (representation of culture), cultural hubs (studio, post-production facilities), and cultural practitioners (director, scriptwriter, producer, cast, crew, etc.). This may result in sometimes obvious and sometimes surprising national labels, such as in the case of *Fantastic Mr. Fox* (2009). This is officially a British film since the cast and crew had many British members, music was recorded and post-production completed in London, and its cultural content (Roald Dahl's stories) was British. Films such as the sequel to *The Chronicles of Narnia* or *The Dark Knight* (2008) also qualified as British. Similarly, in 2013, much heated discussion about national ownership surrounded Alfonso Cuaron's *Gravity*, proudly claimed at the British Academy of Film and Television Arts (BAFTA) Awards as the most outstanding British film of 2013, despite the facts that the film was distributed by an American company (Warner Bros.), it featured American lead actors, director Alfonso Cuarón is Mexican, and the story was set in a decidedly non-national territory—space. However, the film was produced by a British producer, David Heyman; it was largely shot at the UK's Pinewood and Shepperton Studios; its visual effects were created by Tim Webber from the London-based Framestore company; its music was composed by a famous British film composer, Steven Price; and almost the entire film crew was British. "It is 98 percent British, we should put a flag in the ground and we should take pride in that fact," proudly stated Ben Roberts, director of the British Film Institute Film Fund, even asserting that Alfonso Cuarón is a long-time Londoner (quoted in Rankin, 2014).

Importantly, this flag-waving is functional and cannot be dismissed as a mere symbolic and retrograde claim of national identity. Certifying the film as British meant not only that the film was eligible for a U.K. tax break and had access to subsidies that can cover up to 25 percent of production costs, but it formed a significant assertion of cultural capital. Specifically, it served as the showcase and a glowing example of the golden period and powerful role of the British creative industries (U.K. creative industries are worth around £71 billion per year to the U.K. economy) in the face of both the overall economic recession and the aggressive domination of the U.S. film industry. It can be seen as part of a larger strategy of positioning the U.K. film industry on the playing field with other powerful industries, making it an attractive co-production partner and post-production hub in the hugely competitive and China-dominated global market.

These examples illustrate that the nature of film is profoundly transnational and a homogeneous national context is rarely possible for the production—and less so the reception—of a film. However, the discourse of the national, while radically reconceived, remains an important part of the dynamic of world cinema. Various articulations of the nation, affirmative or not, have a strong grip on how we understand and position ourselves in the world. The age of globalization and its complex interconnectedness has fundamentally changed and complicated the way we think of the national, and while its critical import is as relevant and pronounced as ever, it always has to be considered in the wider context of world cinema.

In focus 8.1   New Turkish cinema

After a period of grim crisis and recession throughout the 1980s and early 1990s, Turkish cinema has witnessed an incredible revival since the second half of the 1990s, becoming one of the most recognized national cinemas on the global stage. A new generation of filmmakers who have grown during the years of modernization and acquired a new approach to cinema are recognized at home and internationally: Nuri Bilge Ceylan, Zeki Demurkubuz, Yeşim Ustaoğlu, Semih Kaplanoğlu, Derviş Zaim, Reha Erdem, Emin Alper, and İnan Temelkuran, among others. Diasporic filmmakers like Fatih Akin and Ferzan Özpetek, as well as other minoritarian forms of cinema, such as women's cinema or Kurdish cinema, are very much a part of this phenomenon. These filmmakers have regularly appeared and garnered prizes at A-list international film festivals, putting an indelible stamp on contemporary world cinema.

While cinema in Turkey has experienced diverse periods, two developments carry a particular significance for contemporary Turkish cinema. One is a strong presence of popular cinema, referred to as "Yeşilçam cinema" (which translates as "pine-tree cinema," after the street in Istanbul where most film production companies were located) that emerged in the 1950s, when the transition from a single-party regime to multi-party democracy, plus fast economic growth, industrialization, urbanization, and mass migration to the cities brought a boost to the film industry. New tax and cultural policies, the establishment of studios, and the first film festival all contributed to the rise of popular cinema, which continued to flourish and expand during the 1960s and 1970s. Produced with rapid pace and popular with audiences at home and other Middle Eastern countries such as Iran, Iraq, and Egypt, Yeşilçam cinema was primarily a means of entertainment, dominated by genres of melodrama, comedy, and historical action.

The other development is the rise of political cinema in the 1970s, which developed in the midst of great social and political upheavals in Turkey, concurrently with other European new waves and political cinema of the Third World. Experimenting with social realism and neo-realism (like its European counterparts), this cinema was marked by a resistance to escapist, popular Yeşilçam cinema, addressing social problems and intensifying the debate surrounding national identity in Turkish cinema. Its strongest representative was the legendary director Yılmaz Güney. Both politically engaged and bearing popular appeal, his films such as *Umut/Hope* (1970), *Sürü/The Herd* (1978), and particularly *Yol/The Way* (1982; scripted by Güney and directed by Şerif Gören), a radical critique of Turkish society under oppressive military rule, are to this date considered the best films of Turkish cinema. They brought international visibility to Turkish cinema (*Yol* won the Palme d'Or in 1982), and Güney influenced a whole generation of auteurs who gained prominence in the 1980s and carried on his commitment to politically engaged, social-realist cinema (Dönmez-Colin, 2008; Suner, 2010).

Following the oppressive political and social climate in the 1980s that caused a deep crisis in the film industry, Turkish cinema has received a boost of energy since the mid-1990s. The opening of several film schools, advancements in technology and communications, various financial initiatives available to filmmakers (both through government loans and European funds), and the relaxation of censorship all contributed to a new mode of cinematic production and the emergence of what is seen as the new wave of Turkish cinema. This national cinema is very much part of the global transformations that include the impact of globalization and democratization, as well as the revival of nationalism. On the one hand, the tradition of Yeşilçam continues with popular genres, traditional (melodrama, comedy, nationalist film) and new ones (horror), a revival that has been nourished by new financing structures, new technologies, the expansion of the media industry and advertising, and a very close relationship between television and cinema, both in terms of financing and attracting new audiences. Turkish popular cinema, not unlike Hollywood, is marked by a star system, big budgets, and widespread promotion and distribution in Turkey as well as in European cities with a large Turkish diaspora. These films have mass audience appeal and earn considerable box office revenue, often challenging the success of Hollywood blockbusters. The top three box office earners in 2012, for example, were national productions: an epic action

(continued)

(continued)

film, *Fetih 1453/Conquest 1453*, by Faruk Aksoy, the romantic drama *Evim Sensin/You Are Home* by Özcan Deniz, and the comedy *Berlin Kaplanı/Berlin Tiger* by Ata Demirer.

Art cinema, on the other hand, as is the case in numerous national cinemas, largely circulates at international film festivals and relies on new international networks of distribution, along with financial support from the government. The development and reception of this cinema benefits greatly from the international film festival structure, but also no doubt — as we argue more broadly in the festival chapter — creates "new dependencies" at the level of both form and content, aiming for a product that is marketable to international cultural elites (Çelik, 2014). Unique and distinct as it is, new Turkish cinema's aesthetic of slow narration, minimalism, and poetical realism has to be seen in alignment and conversation with a larger "slow cinema" trend that has dominated the international film festival art cinema. Arguably the most acclaimed Turkish director and today one of the most respected names in world cinema is Nuri Bilge Ceylan. After winning several awards at film festivals for his *Uzak/Distant* (2002) and *İklimler/Climates* (2006), in 2008 he won the Best Director award at Cannes for *Üç Maymun/Three Monkeys*, and finally in 2014 the most prestigious festival award, the Palme d'Or, for *Winter Sleep*. Masterfully photographed, contemplative, and often set in a provincial town, Ceylan's films confront the issues of the past, displacement, belonging, and national identity, but his is also a highly existential and personal cinema that deals with larger philosophical questions. His stories, while profoundly grounded in local culture, history, and Turkish issues, carry universal appeal and frame these issues in a shared broader context of world cinema.

Preoccupations with a search for identity with regard to homeland, memory, displacement, trauma, alienation, migration from the village to the city, the crisis of masculinity, and the relationship between East and West in the context of Turkey's global positioning, are central not only to Ceylan — they are at the core of new Turkish cinema. If migration, exile, and displacement have been an integral part of Turkish economic and social history, in Turkish cinema, too, they are the crux of an identity crisis, sometimes presenting an impasse but also a beginning, a source of intellectual richness, a new language, and new consciousness. In his account of Turkish cinema, Asuman Suner (2010) argues that these are the central thematic concerns not only in art cinema but also in popular cinema, that the new wave of Turkish films revolve around the figure of a "spectral home," exploring through various forms and meanings the tensions and anxieties around the questions of belonging, identity, and memory in contemporary Turkish society.

Clearly situated in their national context, these narratives of exile and displacement have to be understood in their specificity as well as in relation to a wider context of world cinema. The identity of the new Europe, certainly, is based on this spatial and temporal intermingling and a fluid construction of home and identity that challenges national and cultural borders. But even more broadly, the fact that "the narratives of return" and hyphenated, disjunct subjectivities are among the most prominent in contemporary world cinema, from Morocco to Cuba to South Korea, speaks to their wider significance to the national imaginary.

New Turkish cinema thus points to the claim at the core of this book, that national cinema cannot be seen as an isolated phenomenon, but acquires its national identity

a

b

c

Figures 8.1a–8.1c In Nuri Bilge Ceylan's films, images of landscape are central to the narratives of displacement, alienation, belonging, and national identity: *Climates* (2006), *Three Monkeys* (2008), and *Winter Sleep* (2014)

(continued)

(continued)

within larger configurations of world cinema. Turkish cinema is specifically situated, a product of various internal economic, political, and cultural forces, and addresses the issues of national identity and history. But it is simultaneously a transnational phenomenon, not only a cinematic treatment of contemporary forces of globalization. It is nurtured by transnational networks of financing and distribution, modern technological changes (new delivery systems, computer graphics) and television, and by its profile in the expanding critical discourse—discourse that is shaped internally by film critics who construct the historiography and interpretation of Turkish cinema, and by a wider body of scholarship that pays attention to this cinema through the lens of their own frameworks and theories. Insofar as it shows a necessary embeddedness of national cinema within a larger network of world cinema, it can be seen as a prototype of the local/global dynamic of any national cinema.

In focus 8.2   New Argentine cinema

Another vital and effervescent national cinema is the cinema of Argentina, which has the largest film industry in Latin America. Despite the recent social, political, and economic crises,[3] the film industry in Argentina, paradoxically, is flourishing with new works by both young and established filmmakers who have worldwide critical recognition and public acceptance. Referred to as new Argentine cinema, this broad and diverse movement has produced the country's most exciting films. There is Adrián Caetano, whose *Pizza, birra y faso/Pizza, Beer, and Cigarettes* (1997), a film about the life of young social misfits who survive by stealing, helped jump-start the new Argentine cinema, and whose *Crónica de una fuga/Chronicle of an Escape* (2006), a story of four men who escape the military death squads in the 1970s, was a major domestic box office and critical success; Pablo Trapero, whose films, such as *Mundo grúa/Crane World* (1999), *Familia rodante/Rolling Family* (2004), and *Nacido y criado/Born and Bred* (2006), offer an astute critique of modern society—from the conditions of the working class to police corruption—in a social-realist style; and Juan José Campanella, whose *El secreto de sus ojos/The Secret in Their Eyes* (2009) won the Oscar for best foreign feature.

There are also Daniel Burman, whose films, such as *El abrazo partido/Lost Embrace* (2004) and *Derecho de familia/Family Law* (2006), represent central Buenos Aires, and whose style is often compared to that of Woody Allen; and Martin Rejtman, who came on the scene in the early 1990s with *Rapado* (1992), an offbeat comedy that made an assertive break from the political orientation that shaped much of Argentine cinema in the wake of dictatorship years, and whose long career established him as "one of the sharpest, savviest, and most humane comic sensibilities in contemporary cinema" (Nelson, 2014).

On a very different side of the spectrum, Lucrecia Martel's films, such as *La Ciénaga/The Swamp* (2002), *La niña santa/The Holy Girl* (2004), and *La mujer sin cabeza/The*

Figure 8.2a Israel Adrián Caetano's *Pizza, Beer, and Cigarettes* (1997) centers on a group of young social misfits who survive by stealing

Figure 8.2b In Juan José Campanella's *The Secret in Their Eyes* (2009), a judiciary employee (Ricardo Darín) and a judge (Soledad Villamil) investigate a rape and murder case that turns into an obsession for everyone involved

(continued)

(continued)

Headless Woman (2008), offer a piercing critique of the Argentine bourgeois class in a style that is complex, often abstract, and highly layered in its exploration of the micropolitics of location, gender, and sexuality. Also a radical departure from conventional narrative films, Lisandro Alonso's *La libertad/Freedom* (2001), *Los Muertos/The Dead* (2004), *Liverpool* (2008), and more recently *Jauja* (2014) feature lonely wanderers in remote hinterlands in a richly abstract, minimalist, and meditative style. Lucía Puenzo often focuses on queer or intersex characters to explore the standardization of the body in films such as *XXY* (2007) and *The German Doctor* (2013).

This incredibly diverse and prolific group of filmmakers cannot be called "a school" or a movement in the strict sense of the term. Their cinema is not aesthetically uniform, does not fit a set framework, and is profoundly multilayered. It includes art cinema circulating at film festivals, middle-brow commercial cinema, political documentary, activist film and video, and ongoing work by the older generation of filmmakers like Héctor Olivera, Fernando Solanas, and Leonardo Favio, who maintain deep connections with the Third Cinema movement. The filmmakers come from different regions of Argentina, set their films in different milieus, and examine different themes, but they are tied by Argentina's recent economic, social, and political history and share the spirit of commitment to political and critical representation of social and cultural issues.

While not explicitly polemical and displacing the allegorical universalism that defined the counter-cinema of the 1980s,[4] these films depict Argentina's social problems—unemployment, disaffected youth, immigrant life—with a unique aesthetic and unconventional narratives. Jens Andermann argues that this cinema, rather than embarking on a realist project or addressing explicitly Argentina's social and economic issues, constructs a different image of the present, a reflexive and critical point of view that is rather detached from contemporary political events and incorporates this "non-immediacy into reflexive, film-specific forms of narrative and staging" (2012: xiii). Some, most notably Martel's films (but also Albertina Carri and Lisandro Alonso), inhabit the dark, suffocating rural spaces that deconstruct the provincial middle- and upper-middle-class ideology.

a

b

Figures 8.3a & b Lucrecia Martel and Lisandro Alonso's films inhabit the rural spaces that serve to deconstruct the middle- and upper-middle-class ideology: Martel's *La Ciénaga* (2002) and Alonso's *Jauja* (2014)

More often, however, these films use the city as a primary location in which to stage various aspects of the social crisis, whether this crisis has to do with social margins, the torn-up domestic fabric of the middle-class society, sexual identity, or migrants and exiles. Importantly, as Tamara Falicov points out in her study of new Argentine cinema, the representations of urban space in this cinema are multilayered and include populations that have been traditionally unacknowledged on the Argentine screen, yet constitute a key part of the contemporary social milieu: working-class people, ethnic minorities, and immigrants from Bolivia, Paraguay, and Peru (for example, Caetano's *Bolivia* is about a Bolivian immigrant working in a Buenos Aires café). In this way, the new Argentine filmmakers break with the notion of Argentine exceptionalism and European superiority in relation to other Latin American countries, presenting "a new, more nuanced and varied image of the nation," and thus expand the notion of Argentine national identity and citizenship (Falicov, 2007: 137).

Such representations of urban spaces not only expose the restless instability in the traditional notion of Argentine national identity, but reorient and reposition Argentine cinema, both in terms of production conditions and at the level of textual expression, in an engaged relationship with other cinemas in the region and the world. As Tweedie argues in his global map of various new wave movements, the *mise-en-scène* that stages the interaction between the body, the objects, and urban space becomes

(continued)

(continued)

central to transnational new waves that register the consequences of economic and cultural globalization (2013: 1–10). In its orientation toward documenting a new cosmopolitan environment and its inhabitants, new Argentine cinema is thus part of a much larger dynamic of world cinema.

The state of film production in Argentina is but one sign of this interplay of specific, local forces and their place in a global context. Along with an outburst of refreshing creativity and original vision embodied by Argentina's filmmakers, Argentine industry has been supported by other factors that are unique to the Argentine situation due to its position as a "Europeanized" Latin American country: the growth of film schools (both private and state schools) that opened in Buenos Aires in the early to mid-1990s; the creation of film festivals that have served as a platform for filmmakers, particularly the Buenos Aires International Film Festival (whose profile as been consistently on the rise); and the expansion of state-run theaters, among other things.

In no small part, this revival was due to the Film Law, approved in 1994 and administered by the National Institute for Cinema and Audiovisual Fund (INCAA), which introduced a number of taxation schemes and provisions for exhibition regulations: screening quotas, taxes on box office revenue, and film broadcasting on television, among other measures. An autonomous entity with capacity to finance a great variety of projects, the INCAA contributed significantly to the development of an audiovisual industry that could compete worldwide, with support from state funds and private investment, and make cinema commercially viable. Although other international funds (such as the Hubert Bals Fund) also play an important role, most films in Argentina are made with the help of the INCAA's funds and loans—only one example that points to the importance of state support, even in the face of global integration and privatization, for the growth and sustenance of national cinemas. In many ways, the steady surge in production numbers speaks for itself: if only eleven films were released in 1994, the number increased to 45 in 2000, and rose to 172 in 2014, breaking all production volume records of the century (Marché du Film, 2015). The institute had a profound effect not only on the quantity of productions, but also on their formal appearance, their appeal to national and international audiences, and their relation to politics and history. As Falicov points out, if the 1960s generation worked outside of the studio system of the era, the new filmmaking is very much supported by the institute, and while the new Argentine filmmakers offer a critical vision of Argentine reality and consider themselves independent, "they nonetheless apply to the INCAA for funding, and thus they are working within the film establishment to make their films" (2007:127).

The rather indisputable success of the INCAA in the support of new Argentine cinema has been accompanied by a polarizing debate on the relationship between artistic quality and audience appeal—a debate that marks many landscapes of national cinema. Addressing the questions of what kind of national films should be supported in the post-economic crisis era, this debate revolves around the "industrial" or commercial auteurs on the one hand (Campanella, Fabián Bielinsky) and independent cinema on the other (Martel, Trapero, Rejtman, Alonso). Innovative filmmakers producing work that won the festival attention, the lament goes, did not translate into box office returns, and new Argentine cinema did not succeed in its own country; only about ten percent of films watched in Argentina are domestic products. The famed Third Cinema filmmaker Octavio Getino, for example, argued that while the new law fuels the production of low-budget art house movies exhibited almost exclusively on the festival circuit, these films are not subjected to the market pressure of audience appeal, and thus the lion's share of subsidies goes to blockbusters that are transnational ventures. In this scenario, Getino argued, lost are middle-brow films with artistic quality, sociopolitical critique, *and* audience appeal (quoted in Andermann, 2012: 2).

In her discussion of this chasm, Falicov suggests that it has been remedied somewhat by opportunities (such as corporate support of filmmaking projects) that have enabled new filmmakers to embark on more commercial, high budget projects. She points out that Bielinsky's first feature, *Nueve reinas/Nine Queens* (2000), a film that employs rather non-conventional, art cinema techniques, received considerable commercial success in Argentina, Spain, Brazil, Chile, and Mexico (2007: 143). The most important example of this phenomenon to date, however, is Damián Szifron's third feature, *Relatos salvajes/Wild Tales* (2014). A single-director anthology film that connects six separate stories under the theme of vengeance and violent eruptions of anger in the face of social injustices and abuses of power, the film has become a stunning critical success and an incredible box office and social phenomenon in Argentina.

(continued)

(continued)

c

Figures 8.4a–8.4c In *Wild Tales* (2014), Damián Szifron connects six separate stories under the theme of vengeance and eruptions of anger in the face of social injustices

A co-production of Argentina and Spain (with Pedro Almodóvar as one of the producers), *Wild Tales* premiered at the Cannes Film Festival in 2014 with an enthusiastic response. It was Argentina's submission for the Oscars, and was picked up by Sony Pictures Classics for theatrical release in the US. The film has broken all box office records in Argentina, becoming the first national film in history to surpass 100 million pesos ($12 million), and obtaining more than 40 percent of the box office for local films (Sarda, 2014). The film successfully addresses precisely this aforementioned gap between art and popular cinema. It has high production values and challenges the limits of its form and genre with a fragmented yet interconnected narrative, clever plot developments, intertextual references, and carefully choreographed shifts of tone. It combines dark comedy and tragedy with a piercing critique of contemporary Argentine moral and social landscape—all without barring commercial appeal.

New Argentine cinema is an evocative example of the importance and persistence of the national framework even as this framework is contested and has to be conceived in relation to the wider context of world cinema and transnational exchange. Discussing the relationship between nation and cinema in new Argentine cinema, Joanna Page explains that "recent Argentine films are implicated in a dual effort to chart the decline of the state and to question its legitimacy while reasserting national identity and rebuilding a sense of community mobilized around an idea of the nation" (Page, 2005: 312). Rather than antithetical, both of these impulses, she asserts, are firmly rooted in the Argentine social and economic experience, and both position the nation at the center of cinematic expression. Nation is thus registered in different ways; sometimes affirmed and sometimes ruptured, both specifically situated and globally intertwined. But it is there as an important element in a broader framework. To echo Falicov's metaphor, Argentine cinema can be described as "dancing a complicated tango," entangled with multiple partners—Hollywood cinema, European art cinema, cinema of its Latin American neighbors—as it maintains its own unique beat and rhythm.

Small and peripheral cinemas

The increasing interest in and significance of the idea of world cinema has resulted in a range of new studies of individual national and regional cinemas of Eastern Europe, Asia, Africa, and Latin America that has substantially expanded the traditional cinematic canon. In the 1990s and 2000s, the cinemas of Québec, Iceland, Scotland, Singapore, Taiwan, New Zealand, Cuba, and Burkina Faso, and a number of new movements from Eastern Europe—Romanian, Croatian, Slovenian, Bulgarian, Lithuanian, Estonian, and Turkish cinema, among others—are only a few examples that point to a growing significance of what has been termed "the cinema of small nations" (Hjort & Petrie, 2007). Of the films made globally every year, Iordanova (2015) estimates, about a quarter are made and released in the context of small national cinema, so understanding these cinemas is a necessary part of understanding the dynamics of global cinema.

Diverse, wide-ranging, and encompassing differently sized and formed cinematic traditions, the work in small cinema studies has accordingly been an important intervention in film studies, particularly for cinemas that are vibrant yet relegated to the margins both in film studies and the geopolitical world map. It has certainly contributed to a wider recognition of these cinemas but, more importantly, it has developed ways to conceptualize and think about the notion of "small" in the study of film, which has emerged as a productive analytical tool in understanding how the forces of national, regional, transnational, and global are reticulated in the cinematic sphere.

The concept of "small cinema" has been a rather elusive and fluid one, even as it is often employed as a clearly defined entity. While frequently invoked in the work of film scholars, it has figured "as a general intuition, rather than a clearly defined analytical tool," rarely offering a conceptual elaboration of the term and its necessarily relational nature: small is only small in relation to something (Hjort & Petrie, 2007: 3). What do we talk about when we talk about "small cinema"? *Small* can refer to a small country producing films, or to a country producing a small number of films. It can refer to certain production practices and strategies, such as reliance on national subject matter, literature, and history; or to distinct aesthetic and narrative approaches that stand in opposition to dominant practice frames. *Small* can designate the influence and visibility of a certain cinema, beyond the size of its territory or cinematic output. Danish cinema of the 1990s, for example, and the Dogme 95 movement in particular, may be considered small according to empirical variables of size, but large in terms of their intellectual and artistic influence, as they morphed into a global art house brand name that affected international and American independent cinema in profound and unexpected ways. *Small* has repeatedly been used to describe other phenomena and production practices that are not determined by geographical or cultural factors: experimental and avant-garde cinema, independent cinema, art house cinema, and political cinema have all been discussed as small, notwithstanding their national context. *Small* has also served as an identifier for regional and ethnic cinema, minoritarian cinema, or cinema that represents and addresses a specific social group.

Despite this fluidity of use, "small cinema" is most frequently deployed as a geographical and cultural marker. It is seen as cinema created by a particular nation or region, defined by its geography and culture. As Elsaesser puts it, small national cinema "stands in dialogue with the idea of the nation," "forges a feeling of belonging," and "refers to the historical imaginary" (2005: 20). Even as such a national framework may be problematic, for example in films that come from "small countries" but deal with universal themes (with geography as a mere backdrop), the national and regional affiliation remains important to their reception and understanding.

In fact, the context of origin or location plays a significant role in most small national cinema studies (Hjort, 2005; Hjort & Petrie, 2007; Lenuta, Falkowska, & Desser, 2015). Mette Hjort, one of the key scholars in small cinema studies, acknowledges the difficulty in establishing what counts as small, yet proposes four "measures of size" that she finds most helpful in thinking about small cinemas and the challenges they face: population, geographical scale, gross domestic product (GDP), and a history of rule by non-co-nationals—with GDP and a history of colonial rule being more determining factors. While *smallness* is a relative term always invoking comparisons, Hjort suggests that the presence and relation between these factors—the presence of all four measures, for example, will have a much deeper impact on the cinematic practice than the presence of only one or two—may help us better understand both the challenges and potential opportunities that small cinema filmmakers are likely to grapple with. Burkinabe and Irish filmmakers, for example, may be both small-nation filmmakers with something in common and something to gain from transnational alliances, but their challenges will be very different (Hjort, 2015: 1–5). Better examination of the relationship between matters of scale and cinematic practices can help identify the nature of challenges, the nature of power dynamics, and the politics of visibility and participation, but it can also lead to productive strategies and cultural resources that foster opportunities.

Beyond mapping the empirical or geopolitical aspects of small nationhood, the concept of small cinema is above all about the politics of visibility. A key aspect of the small cinema studies project is to foreground their discursive status and the relationship of small cinemas within their broader context. *Small* is not only an external and empirical variable of size. It is a discursive formation, and it is often this discursive terrain that will determine the dynamic of inclusion and exclusion of small cinemas on the world cinema map. That is, despite their presence and relative visibility on the global stage, small cinemas tend to be caught up in what Iordanova (2015: 261) has described as "the struggle for self-acceptance," or what Hjort and Petrie describe as "politics of recognition, the desire to see expressions of culturally inflected identities recognized as valuable both internally and externally" (2007: 25), a struggle to carve out a visible spot and stage oneself, to narrate oneself through film. It is the politics of recognition, the struggle for visibility in the emerging contexts of globalization, that often determines the positioning of small cinema in the broader sphere of world cinema.

Forces that affect which cinemas get noticed are certainly complex and multiple. These include financial pressures that barely allow filmmakers from small producing countries to fund their projects, demanding and expensive publicity machinery at major film festivals, and the reliance on transnational alliances and the state-sponsored mechanisms and retrospectives abroad that may help attract the critics and the media. There are also discursive factors in the media and academia that lead them to approach small cinemas with trepidation, often with preconceived notions about films from small countries, and fixed conceptual frameworks that determine the strategy of inclusion and exclusion. To examine the positioning of a small cinema on the global stage is therefore to examine the dialectic between political, economic, and institutional forces, and the dominant conceptual paradigms that define small cinemas and thus help shape the politics of recognition and cinematic mapping.

For Hjort and Petrie, the concept of small cinema is not meant to be a demeaning characterization, one that reduces these nations to the marginal position due to their small, suggestively insignificant size. Nevertheless, in the field of competing marketing forces where the number of films begging for a visible spot and the places they come from rapidly increases, the process of marginalization implied in the notion of small cinemas is difficult to escape. Consider one of the early provocations of this kind cited by Hjort and Petrie: Thompson and Bordwell's account of "smaller producing countries" during the silent era, in which they state that the cinemas of Mexico, India, Columbia, or New Zealand share some general traits. The specific features that Thompson and Bordwell identify with these "less prominent" national cinemas include the strategies of building local appeal by "using national literature and history as sources for their stories" and exploiting the locations of "distinctive natural landscapes" in order to differentiate their low-budget product from more polished and better positioned imports (2010: 65–66). This homogenizing posture points to a not-uncommon tendency in film studies, further perpetuated by the publicity machinery of film festivals, to see a group of films from a specific nation in terms of similar aesthetic and narrative commitments. It has serious implications for cinemas that are struggling with a politics of recognition that at worst makes them invisible, and at best sees them only through an essentializing lens of some preconceived national character or conceptual framework.

In the chapter on film festivals, we discussed the case of Iranian and Romanian cinemas on the world stage, whose presence and meaning was first generated by their presence at film festivals, then put firmly in place by the critical and academic discourse. In his discussion of Iranian cinema, Bill Nichols describes how film festivals produce a space where one can encounter films from unfamiliar contexts, thus opening up avenues to think about cinema outside of one's own position. His encounter with a cluster of films from Iran leads him to identify a "form of narrative structure that could be called inferential" (1994: 69), as he also locates distinct patterns of editing and composition. Romanian cinema has been similarly characterized as a rather uniform cinema, generating an exciting "new wave" due to the fact that the emergent generation of Romanian directors all received festival recognition within a short time span. Here also, this small cinema, despite the resistance its filmmakers have expressed to being perceived as a coherent group, is received in the short-hand of perception, as a group of films showing their "hallmark humor and deadpan style" or sharing "a penchant for long takes and fixed camera positions; a taste for plain lighting and everyday décor" (Roddick, 2007; Scott, 2008). There is no doubt that an early encounter with any cinema outside of one's context leads to setting patterns and structure on the as-yet-unknown and unfamiliar, a crucial process in that it "defines the act of making sense from new experience" (Nichols, 1994: 80). It is important to consider, though, how the persistence of such readings, aided by festival machinery, confers a notion of specific identity on cinemas struggling for recognition and visibility, and how categorizing our viewing experience into existing frames of interpretation also inevitably forces a homogenizing and reductive construction onto this cinema.

A useful insight into the dynamic of the politics of visibility is seen in Fredric Jameson's (1986; 2004) writing on small national cinema and Third World literature in a global context. His controversial thesis that Third World narratives necessarily assume an allegorical form places the construction of the nation and the marginal in a broader, global context, but also provides a rationale for reading marginal and diverse literatures as part of a larger totality, where all enunciative positions are always already part of the discourse of the dominant. Jameson clearly suggests that national identity of small, marginal nations is a product of their position in relation to the First World and its dominant discourse rather than some sort of internal reflection of national aspirations. In his tentative theory of small national cinema, he proposes three dominant features of national cinema: the presence of "collective assemblages" and groups as agencies (rather than individuals); the identification of a singular auteur that comes to represent this cinema outside of its borders; and a "stylistic distinction" that foregrounds particular elements as part of its national character (Jameson, 2004). Again, Jameson here considers films produced by small nations as part of a generalization that groups them together, as national allegories overtly couched in psychic or existential problems, and in a style that somehow bears the preconceived cultural specificity to the outside viewer. Seemingly generous in its inclusion of the cinemas of new small nations into a larger global framework, this perspective thus ends up further marginalizing the already marginal participants in world cinema, valorizing them as "the Other." Once situated thus, these cinemas have an option of either marketing themselves to what seems palatable and appealing to the larger audiences outside of their borders, or facing obscurity in the vast arena of world cinema.

We discuss in one of the case studies here how this rigid conceptual framework of small cinema determines in rather predictable ways the visibility of small national cinema. Such is the case with Slovenian cinema, whose new generation of filmmakers (Janez Burger, Maja Weiss, Jan Cvitkovič, Damjan Kozole, Igor Šterk, and Sonja Prosenc, among others) produced a large number of remarkable and very diverse films in the late 1990s and early 2000s. This group of films, even as they garnered some international film festival prizes and success at home, remains largely invisible outside their limited national and regional context. The only filmmaker whose work presents a blip on the international radar, and who is seen as the main representative of the Slovenian new wave, is Damjan Kozole. The success of his *Rezervni deli/Spare Parts* (2003), *Delo osvobaja/Labor Equals Freedom* (2005), *Slovenka/Slovenian Girl* (2009), and *Nočno življenje/Nightlife* (2016) can at least be partly attributed to the fact that these films lend themselves rather neatly to the small cinema and national allegory paradigm discussed here. Their straightforward, realist narrative style and the highly marketable, crime news-like social fables of human trafficking, prostitution, and unemployment translate more easily as familiar signifiers for descriptions of transitional East European societies such as Slovenia. This is but one example of how the enunciations of small cinema filmmakers are produced by the very discourse that recognizes them, and how the conceptual and discursive practices assign to the filmmaker the "national burden" of capturing the essence of national cinema if they are to be offered a visible spot on the map of world cinema.

Among other things, the processes involved in the cinematic mapping of small cinemas foreground the necessity of conceiving of *small* as a relational, rather than fixed and hermetic, concept. It is important to stress that the increasing visibility of small cinemas affects our understanding of world cinema beyond just expanding and complicating traditional cinematic canons. The concept of small always posits the engagement with national and cultural specificity within, and in relation to transnational and global frameworks. In fact, small nations can render the discrepant impact of globalization even more discernible. This is because many of them, having emerged out of the process of de-colonization, have a strong interest in nation building and national identity on the one hand, and have a stronger dependency on external markets to sustain themselves under the economic and political pressures of globalization on the other.

Thus, the concept of small is not about positing traditional binaries, nor is it about a mere gesture of inclusion. Rather, as Iordanova et al. argue, it is about shifting the perspective, displacing the traditional paradigms of world cinema, "turning history on its head by making the periphery the center of our study" (2010: 6) and thus conceiving the map of world cinema from a peripheral point of view. If we are to turn attention to small cinemas, we should not study them as cases on their own, as a phenomenon deserving recognition merely because they are small—a gesture aligned with identity politics. Small cinemas are important not because of their size but because they reveal the processes that determine the politics of mapping world cinema and urge us to see this map from a different perspective.

The fluidity and multiple meanings of the notion of small point to the concept as a dynamic and relational one, contributing to varying patterns of dominance in multiple spheres, including the geopolitical, textual, industrial, ideological, or discursive. It is this emphasis on a relational framework that may be the most significant import of small cinema studies—an insistence that a specifically situated context of small national cinema is not just a key part of world cinema, but forms a perspective that always watches and understands across its own borders, is always aware of the larger forces shaping and shaped by its own existence.

In focus 8.3   The politics of visibility in Palestinian cinema

In his introduction to a study on Palestinian cinema, Hamid Dabashi writes, "The world of cinema does not quite know how to deal with Palestinian cinema precisely because it is emerging as a stateless cinema of the most serious national consequences" (2006: 7). Dabashi here points to the paradox that is at the core of the very notion of Palestinian cinema. Palestine as a nation very much exists on screen. Despite its diversity and disparity, Palestinian cinema is a vibrant, increasingly prolific cinema based on the assertion of collectivity, a unified national entity, a shared language, shared past, and shared identity. However, Palestinian cinema is a stateless cinema in that it is "structurally exilic," produced either in the internal exile in the occupied Palestinian territory or suffering erasure in other countries (Naficy, 2006: 95). It represents socially, economically, and geographically a fragmented community of ten million Palestinians worldwide, whose nation is simultaneously a concretely felt reality and an abstract construct, an entity that officially does not exist and whose status has been silenced and denied.

When the second Intifada was still raging, the Nazareth-born filmmaker Elia Suleiman's film *Yadon ilaheyya/Divine Intervention* (2002) was submitted to the Academy as the Palestinian entry for Best Foreign Language Film. The Academy rejected the film on the grounds that "Palestine is not a country." For Suleiman, as for most other filmmakers who identify as Palestinian (most of whom live, are trained, and work abroad), a relationship with Palestine is thus not a matter of a simple positivist assertion of national identity, but a symbolically loaded, ethical, and political prerogative.

Its existence thrown into question by external denial, the stateless status of Palestinian cinema is also imposed by internal difficulties. The elements that make any national cinema possible and sustainable are absent in Palestine: no national funding; no production companies; no equipment, crews, or institutions to train them; lack of basic film shooting conditions (movement and access in the Palestinian territories are severely restricted); lack of distribution; and no movie theaters. Al-Kasaba Theatre in Ramallah is the only functioning multipurpose cinema venue. In the face of a

(continued)

(continued)

complete absence of industrial and economic infrastructure, Palestinian cinema is almost entirely dependent on outside sources—largely European and American, and to some extent Israeli—for financing, resources, and circulation, as well as for recognition and visibility.

This invisibility, erasure, and lack on various levels not only questions the existence of Palestinian cinema as national cinema, but strongly frames the question of its identity around the issue of visibility. If the history of Palestinian struggle has to do with "the desire to be visible" (Said, 2006: 3), the history of Palestinian cinema, too, is based on the politics of visibility and recognition. While the struggle for visibility demarcates any small cinema, as we argue in the introduction to this section, it is particularly emblematic, pronounced, and explicitly political in the case of Palestinian cinema.

Given the paradox at its core, Palestinian cinema has been shaped profoundly in relation to the outside, whether this external context has to do with financing, infrastructural support, audiences or, equally important, the interpretive framework that defines it; namely, the fact that its visual identity in the media is rigidly linked to threat, terrorism, and violence. As Said says, "On the one hand, Palestinians stand against invisibility, which is the fate they have resisted since the beginning; and on the other hand, they stand against the stereotype in the media: the masked Arab, the *kufiyya*, the stone-throwing Palestinian" (2006: 3). Palestinian cinema is therefore in a precarious position of not being able to speak, and if it does speak, this speech act is strained and conditioned first by the urgency to assert one's existence and visibility, to reclaim an erased identity, and then by the ethnographic and expository task of providing a counter-narrative, counter-identity to an imposed identity of violence and terrorism. Aware of such an impasse, Palestinian films often foreground the issue of narration. They are "about the act or gesture of narrating itself," consciously addressing the difficulty, often outright impossibility of narrating itself when one is both silenced and intensely spoken for by the reductive outside context (Mokdad, 2012: 193).

The imperative to document the Palestinian struggle, to depict the life under Israeli occupation, and to assert cultural identity, makes a relationship between image and reality in Palestinian cinema a heavily politically inflected one. Cinema becomes a means of making visible what has been silenced as well as a tool of resistance. The political inflection has been a consistent element in most Palestinian films since the 1960s. But the nature of this politics, the approach to how the cinematic medium can articulate it, has shifted since the 1980s, which is the period to which Palestinian cinema as we know it today is generally traced. That is, against the background of the Arab defeat in the 1967 war, the main concern of Palestinian cinema of the late 1960s and 1970s, largely in a documentary form, was to assert a homogeneous identity; to provide testimony, evidence, and collective memory; to map the Palestinian landscape; to construct an imaginary and lost past; to describe and chronicle its victimization; and to call for international spectators' sympathy and identification. After the 1980s, with an emergence of a larger wave of Palestinian filmmaking, many of the conventions that marked Palestinian film narratives begin to be challenged, charting in a more nuanced and scrutinizing way the relationships between the personal and national, actual and imaginary space, and the act of narration and silence.

Instrumental to the revival of Palestinian cinema in the 1980s is Michel Khleifi, who returned to his native Palestine after living in Belgium for a decade with an active desire to revitalize his nation's cinema. His debut feature *Al Dhakira al Khasba/Fertile Memory* (1980), a film about the struggles of two women living in the West Bank, and *Urs al-jalil/Wedding in Galilee* (1987), a story about a mayor of a West Bank village under Israeli curfew who tries to hold a traditional wedding celebration for his son, launched the Palestinian new wave, presenting a breakthrough in Palestinian filmmaking. Filmed in a neorealist style that blurs the boundaries between fiction and documentary, both films center on female protagonists to represent the oppressive life under the Israeli rule as well as the gendered nature of traditional Palestinian society. The elements that have been central to Palestinian cinema continue to permeate Khleifi's films: the importance of mapping geographical space for Palestinian memory and national identity, the challenges of narrating history and its trauma, displacement, exile, and the narrative of return. But Khleifi also forges a more innovative approach to representation of trauma, where the films not only narrate traumatic memory and map Palestinian space, but also work through its paradoxes, as well as the paradoxes of the cinematic medium that aims to represent it.

Khleifi's films, financed by German and Dutch sources, garnered considerable international festival recognition, and opened the door to other filmmakers who emerged in the 1990s. Rashid Masharawi's *Hatta Ishaar Akhar/Curfew* (1994), about the military-curfew-defined life of a Palestinian family in occupied Gaza, and *Haïfa* (1995), a story of a "village idiot" who aspires to return to his hometown, were released against the background of the Oslo Accords that spelled the end of the Intifada. Focusing on individual life stories, personal struggles in Masharawi's films also function as allegories for "the loss of collective hopes" and a desperate downward spiral of national aspirations (Gertz & Khleifi, 2008: 106). They refrain from mapping the larger Palestinian landscape, a strategy that imbues Khleifi's films, and use the spatial figure of a battered house to articulate frustrations borne out of continuously diminishing space, confinement, lack of mobility, and stasis. The intertwining of space, memory, nation, and identity is also a central theme for Ali Nassar, whose *Shvil Hahalav/The Milky Way* (1997) and *Bahodesh Hath'i/In the Ninth Month* (2002) both depict daily life in an Arab village and use the figure of a destroyed house to speak about the fate of Palestinians and their derailed national aspirations.

The problematic aspects of the representation of space, traumatic memory, and narrative are articulated most critically in the films of Elia Suleiman, considered by many to be the most important and compelling Palestinian director. In *Chronicle of a Disappearance* (1996) and *Divine Intervention* (2002), Suleiman casts himself as a silent, deadpan, Buster Keaton-like figure, one who functions as a witness to the suffocated yet heavily charged pulse of public and private spaces in Nazareth, Jerusalem, and Ramallah. A powerful and salient presence, brimming with detached humor and irony, his alter ego is an alert and observant witness, one through which the spectator gains a wealth of indiscriminate information, yet a witness who remains ironically distant and refuses to articulate, make sense of, or chronicle the episodic and fragmented scenes.

(continued)

(continued)

a

b

Figures 8.5a & 8.5b Michel Khleifi's films, such as *Fertile Memory* (1980) and *Wedding in Galilee*
(1987), map the Palestinian space and narrate traumatic memory in a
neorealist style that blurs the boundaries between fiction and documentary

He is a silent witness who refuses to speak, nor does he evoke our sympathy or
identification.

In her analysis of Suleiman's films, Linda Mokdad (2012) argues that Suleiman's
silence, the act of witnessing, rather than signs of passivity, express active agency,
which demands engagement yet resists catering to spectator's expectations, and
resists translating the unspeakable into easy language.

Figures 8.6a & 8.6b Elia Suleiman's alter ego as a silent yet alert witness in *Divine Intervention* (2002). Suleiman's Post-it Notes in *Divine Intervention* mirror his strategy of refusing to assemble fragmented scenes into a coherent, unified narrative

By refusing to play into "the codification of Palestinian dispossession" Suleiman makes us complicit as spectators, and forces us "to consider our role as witnesses to the visualization of Palestinian suffering and dispossession" (Mokdad 2012: 198). Silence in Suleiman's films thus persists as an eloquent gesture, not as a negation of something but rather as a deliberate positioning from which to understand the conditions of Palestinian people.

Aligned with his approach to silence is Suleiman's construction of space, whereby his careful bracketing of cinematic space constructs both a representational mode and a figurative locus to articulate the cinema of exile and alienation. Foregrounding the

(continued)

(continued)

a

b

Figures 8.7a & 8.7b Frustrated speech and suffocated space in Elia Suleiman's *Chronicle of a Disappearance* (1996)

troubled relationship between knowledge and visuality, Suleiman's cinematic space is often de-centered, fragmented, obscured from view, and marked by long shots that make it difficult to decipher objects, characters, and actions.

Suleiman commands the view of the space through a stationary shot, as if to make a commitment to what is in front of the camera, while the world around it is important only insofar as it relates to this space. This figurative construction charts what Suleiman calls a "non-space," a space of imagination of a locus that cannot be

Figures 8.8a & 8.8b Suleiman's cinematic space (*Divine Intervention*, 2002) is often de-centered, obscured from view, making it difficult to decipher objects and actions

pinned down and insists on being external to physical space. He is always positioned outside of it, observing an entity that has been denied to him. "Memory and identity are tied to space, but not necessarily to a real space," notes Suleiman in an interview (2000: 96). The troubled and chaotic status of Palestine becomes for Suleiman a critical foundation for the construction of not real but imaginary space, one that can be deployed as an investigative tool for the twisted problems of reality, borders, identity, and politics.

(continued)

(continued)

The 2000s saw added expansion and diversification in Palestinian production. Michel Khleifi, Rashid Masharawi, and Ali Nassar have all continued to make films, with new filmmakers on the scene—many of them documentary (Nizar Hassan and Mai Masri, among others)—who further bolstered the reach and visibility of Palestinian cinema. Hany Abu-Assad's *Al qods fee yom akhar/Rana's Wedding* (2002), *Paradise Now* (2005), and *Omar* (2013) chart a different relationship between suppression and defiance, but also represent a threshold for Palestinian cinema in that they are Arab-funded, and became the most internationally visible Palestinian films. *Paradise Now* was the first Palestinian feature nominated for the Oscar, and *Omar* continued the trend by making it into the final five nominees in the foreign language category. Importantly, women filmmakers emerge for the first time. Annemarie Jacir's *Milh Hadha al-Bahr/Salt of This Sea* (2008), about a third-generation Palestinian living in America on a quest to reach her home in Jaffa, received remarkable international exposure and success. Najwa Najjar, who works both in fiction and documentary, achieved sizeable exposure with *Al-mor wa al rumman/Pomegranates and Myrrh* (2008) and *Eyes of a Thief* (2014).

These filmmakers are not only prolific in their output but they have also been actively engaged in building the infrastructure that would sustain Palestinian cinema as national cinema. Suleiman returned to Jerusalem in 1994 to help develop the Film and Media Department at Birzeit University. In 1996, Masharawi founded the Cinema Production and Distribution Center in Ramallah to promote film production, and he began a project called Mobile Cinema, setting up mobile screens and tent theaters in refugee camps to build a relationship between Palestinian audiences and their films. Since 2013, Suleiman has served as Artistic Advisor to the Doha Film Institute, an important presence in the support and visibility of Arab cinema.

Suleiman asserts that in filmmaking, what matters is "to be able to position oneself in relation to the world, to give a spatial support for your perception of the world" (2000: 96). With this statement, he points to the key dynamic of small, peripheral cinema, the fact that small cinema is not about size but about its place in the world, its situatedness in the nexus of power relationships that shape cultural, political, and cinematic spheres. For Palestinian cinema, which is "a cinema of nowhere" to use Suleiman's terms, positioning oneself in relation to the world depends not so much on telling a story of Palestine, but rather on forging a politics of space and politics of counter-visuality that renders visible and reclaims what has been denied and silenced.

In focus 8.4   Slovenian cinema as small cinema

One of the distinct characteristics of contemporary Slovenian cinema is that it is a "small" cinema, in the scheme introduced in Hjort and Petrie's work on "the cinema of small nations" (2007), with a population of about two million people and about eight features produced annually. Since the mid-1990s, the work of the young generation of Slovenian filmmakers, such as Jan Cvitkovič, Janez Burger, Damjan Kozole, Igor Šterk, Hanna Slak, Maja Weiss, and Sonja Prosenc, started receiving considerable festival exposure and international recognition, suggesting a cinematic renaissance and the emergence of a new wave. Some of the films—Damjan Kozole's *Rezervni deli/Spare Parts* (2003) and *Slovenka/Slovenian Girl* (2009), and Vinko Mönderndorfer's *Pokrajina št. 2/Landscape no. 2* (2009)—have been released in the US and in international markets to relatively wide acclaim.

Slovenian cinema also makes its presence felt in the form of retrospectives and screenings of individual films from Cannes and Barcelona to New York and Los Angeles, and has become a dynamic participant in the regional and global networks. Despite its presence on the international stage, Slovenian cinema is largely absent from a conceptual map of world cinema, where it remains marginal at best, even as other small cinemas have begun to surface on the radar of discourse. Caught up in the politics of recognition typical of many small nations, it can thus be seen as emblematic of the dialectic between political, institutional forces, and the dominant conceptual paradigms that define small cinemas in the broader context of world cinema. Its struggle is not only about visibility, but also a struggle against reduction to essential narrative and aesthetic qualities that can be easily traced to the established political and ideological framework of the nation.

Even though Slovenian cinema has a long and unique history within the broader context of former Yugoslavian cinema, it emerges as a distinct national cinema in the mid-1990s, with the founding of the Slovenian Film Fund in 1994 (succeeded by the Slovenian Film Center, or SFC, in 2011), which replaced the Ministry of Culture as the new state-funding agency for film production. The SFC significantly promoted the emerging new talents of the early 1990s (most of them young first-time directors), backed the debut works of more than twenty filmmakers in its first decade, and significantly increased the pace of film production. In the two decades following its founding, over one hundred theatrical feature films were produced, most of them either entirely or partly financed by the Center, with over thirty films as co-productions. In addition to film financing, the SFC is also charged with promoting Slovenian cinema abroad: it has presented films at major international festivals, and organized retrospectives in many European countries plus Canada and the US.

The central position of the agency can be considered a benchmark for Slovenian cinema, for until the 1990s Slovenia was practically the only Central European country that had failed to produce a significant body of cinematic art and was literally stuck when it came to filmic production. Now, the festival successes and visibility of the new generation of young Slovenian filmmakers have urged film critics to reconsider Slovenian cinema as a national cinema distinct from the former post-Yugoslav cinema, a broad umbrella under which Slovenian films were traditionally placed. Further, considering the number of cinemas in Slovenia (close to 100), films like *Outsider* (Andrej Košak, 1997), *V leru/Idle Running* (Burger, 1999), *Kajmak in marmelada/Cheese and Jam* (Branko Đurić, 2003), *Petelinji zajtrk/Rooster's Breakfast* (Marko Naberšnik, 2007), *Čefurji raus!/Chefurs Raus!* (Goran Vojnovič, 2013), and *Šiška Delux* (Cvitkovič, 2015) have attracted a substantial audience in Slovenia, often outperforming the most successful Hollywood blockbusters.

The quantity and quality of film production notwithstanding, the precarious place of contemporary Slovenian cinema is a telling example of a discursive construct of small

(continued)

(continued)

national cinema, where the conceptual practices privilege filmmakers who more readily fit within the national allegory framework and capture the "essence" of national cinema in their appeal to audiences outside of their borders. Despite its variety, one Slovenian filmmaker—Damjan Kozole—has emerged on the radar of world cinema as a singular auteur who represents Slovenian cinema on the world stage. His films have received the largest festival recognition and praise, as well as international distribution. *Rezervni deli/Spare Parts* (2003), a drama about human trafficking, was included in the list of "10 key films of the New Europe" in the June 2008 issue of *Sight and Sound*, and has been analyzed in several broader thematic studies on the cinema of migration (Brown et al., 2010; Loshitzky, 2010). He was the sole Slovenian contributor to the Zentropa omnibus production *Visions of Europe* (2004), and his *Slovenka/Slovenian Girl* (2009), having achieved success at many international film festivals, became one of the very few Slovenian films to receive distribution in the US.

In contrast to most new wave films that do not directly invoke the contemporary political context of Slovenia and its integration into the European Union, in Kozole's films this new reality provides a potent and critical backdrop. This is present in both *Spare Parts*, which directly addresses human trafficking and the question of borders in the New Europe, and in *Slovenian Girl*, which tackles the question of prostitution within the setting of the capital, Ljubljana, in 2008, the year of the Slovenian presidency over the European Union.

Kozole's realist narratives of the invisible human trafficking business and prostitution carry appeal for the international market partly because of their "crime news" marketability (giving the impression of interesting and controversial "action" in an otherwise relatively peaceful and non-eventful country) and partly because their realist aesthetic, combined with images of poverty, crime, and underground worlds, translates rather easily into a familiar signifier for supposedly genuine descriptions of transitional societies such as Slovenia. In contrast to their welcoming international reception, the films received a harsher response at home, often accused of stereotyping and simplifying social issues to appeal to wider audiences. Beyond its undisputable critical value, the work of Damjan Kozole thus becomes exemplary in how the enunciations of filmmakers from "small new nations" are produced by the very discourse that recognizes them, and how it captures the kind of crises that easily embed an allegory of the nation into the film narrative.

In contrast to Kozole's work, the majority of films of the Slovenian new wave are strongly marked by a distance from the familiar aesthetic and ideological matrices that characterize the discourse of cinema of small nations, and remain—perhaps precisely for this reason—invisible in comparison. On the polar opposite side of this spectrum are films that are successful with domestic audiences, but have virtually no presence outside of Slovenia and completely elude the international festival and critical radar. Films such as *Outsider*, *Jebiga/Fuck It* (Miha Hočevar, 2000), and *Kajmak in marmelada/Cheese and Jam*, and more recently *Petelinji zajtrk/Rooster's Breakfast*, *Čefurji raus!/Chefurs Raus!*, *Šiška Delux*, and *Pojdi z mano/Come Along* (Igor Šterk, 2016) have attracted more than impressive audiences and have often outsold the biggest

a

b

Figures 8.9a & 8.9b Damjan Kozole's *Spare Parts* (2003) and *Slovenian Girl* (2009) tackle the problems of human trafficking and prostitution in a realist aesthetic

Hollywood blockbusters, an impressive fact given that Hollywood traditionally wins the box office receipts for eight or nine of the top ten films in most European countries every year. Branko Đurić's popular comedy *Cheese and Jam* set an all-time box office record for Slovenia in 2003 with almost 140,000 tickets (Hollywood films sell an average of 100,000 tickets), a record then broken in 2007 by Naberšnik's romantic comedy *Rooster's Breakfast*, which became the most successful film in Slovenian film history (about 180,000 admissions), second only to *Troy* (2004) and *Titanic* (1997).

(continued)

(continued)

Figure 8.10 One of the biggest domestic hit comedies, *Cheese and Jam* (2003). Image courtesy of the Slovenian Film Center

The film was not only a popular but also a critical success in Slovenia; it won five major awards at the 10th Festival of Slovenian Film, received an overwhelmingly positive critical reception, and was Slovenia's 2009 Academy Awards submission in the Best Foreign Language Film category.

Yet, this commercially successful film in Slovenia was barely a blip on the international radar. *Rooster's Breakfast* revolves around the story of Gajaš, elderly owner of a car repair shop, who loves to drink, play cards with his buddies, and dream about meeting pop star Severina; and Djuro, his young and attractive apprentice, who falls in love and has an affair with a beautiful married woman. The film is a love story, set in a very small rural town, where people live quiet, slow, and imperceptible lives, but where their own hidden passions eventually result in a series of dramatic events. Besides the fact that the film is beautifully written and shot, there are several aspects of it that can help explain why this portrait of a time and place had such popular appeal: its piercing humor; great performances; its nostalgia for the past; the role of Severina, whose song for the film became one of her biggest hits; and the fact that the film is an adaptation of a novel by Feri Lainšček, the most popular writer in Slovenia. It also helped that the film had one of the biggest marketing campaigns for a domestic product, with advertising that began eight months before the film opened in theaters.

But the very elements that characterize this film's success at home are also the elements that contribute to its international invisibility. It is not only that the film's vernacular language and humor, its portrait of a local community, and its popular as well

Figures 8.11a & 8.11b A box office record was broken by Marko Naberšnik's *Rooster's Breakfast* (2007), which became the most successful film in Slovenian film history

as historical references get entirely lost in translation, but the very premise of the film and its generic framing make it difficult to place it in the critical discourse that shapes our reception and understanding of Eastern European "small cinema." Avoiding explicit and familiar political context, Naberšnik constructs a rather universal narrative that is nevertheless embedded in and reflects specific local and regional traditions, in a style of storytelling that invokes neither the conventions of art house cinema nor those of the

(continued)

(continued)

mainstream cinema. His films do not offer anything specifically exotic, odd, or particularly "Slovenian" to the outside world.

Positioned in between these two poles—of internationally visible cinema as national allegory and domestically popular but internationally invisible films—is the group of filmmakers whose work most strongly represents the new wave. For filmmakers like Igor Šterk (*Express, Express*, 1996; *Ljubljana*; *Tuning*, 2005; and *9:06*, 2009), Jan Cvitkovič (*Kruh in mleko/Bread and Milk*, 2001; *Odgrobadogroba/Gravehopping*, 2005; *Archeo*, 2011), Janez Burger (*Idle Running*, 1999; *Ruins*, 2003; *Circus Fantasticus/Silent Sonata*, 2010), Maja Weiss (*Varuh meje/Guardian of the Frontier*, 2002; *Installation of Love*, 2007), Vlado Škafar (*Dad*, 2010; *A Girl and a Tree*, 2012; *Mama/Mother*, 2016), and Sonja Prosenc (*Drevo/The Tree*, 2014), it is not the specificity of the national context and its representation in a wider sphere that matter, but rather the specificity of the medium of cinema itself. Their work, while not entirely devoid of its regional, national context, is intensely personal and intensely cinematic, concerned with the ability of the cinematic language to embody individual as well as collective consciousness. This is significant in the context of Slovenian history (as well as many other Eastern European nations), where art, particularly literature, has been pressed into the service of expressing the ideology of the nation. Cvitkovič's *Archeo* and Burger's *Silent Sonata*, for example, are both visual poems, effectively silent films, bypassing conventional storytelling and relying on a different spatial and temporal realm to communicate sensibilities, atmosphere, and perspectives that crucially inform our social reality yet cannot be articulated through words. Here, cinema is freed from the constraints of national narratives and taken into the realm of language and form, toward an idiom that cannot be captured by a preconceived regional essence of cinema.

Using a different path but pursuing a similar goal, genre films are emerging for the first time in Slovenian cinema that both deploy and subvert genre conventions, inflecting global genres with local significance. Announcing this trend were the action horror film *Idila/Idyll* (Tomaž Gorkič, 2011) and noir thriller *Psi brezčasja/Case: Osterberg* (Matej Nahtigal, 2015), a detective story that blends film noir, Asian thriller,

Figure 8.12 The primal family in Jan Cvitkovič's poetic *Archeo* (2011)

Figure 8.13 Sonja Prosenc's *The Tree* (2014) uses visual elements, such as this large wall surrounding the house's concrete yard, to tell its elemental story about a family confined in their home

Figure 8.14 Vlado Škafar's beautiful cinematic poem *Mama* (2016). Image courtesy of the Slovenian Film Center

(continued)

(continued)

and television police drama. They were followed by more examples of genre and genre-bending films such as the youth adventure drama *Pojdi z mano/Come Along*, and psychological crime drama *Pod gladino/Buoyancy* (Klemen Dvornik, 2016). These films deftly mediate the line between commercial and art cinema, and turn to popular genre conventions not merely as a means to an end. Instead, they explore how the rather universal generic conventions can be deployed and bent to reflect on the reality of a specific socio-cultural sphere.

Vying for international recognition, Slovenian cinema, like many other small cinemas, remains productive and popular with home audiences. As those few films that fit the expectations and the dominant conceptual categories gain recognition, most remain invisible despite their remarkable diversity and grasp on the popular imagination of the country. Importantly then, returning to the films themselves can show the diversity of small cinemas, and the fact that not all cinematic practices can be traced to the same dominant models of world cinema. It can also reveal the economic, institutional, and discursive factors that determine a film/filmmaker/national cinema's visibility on the map of world cinema.

Activity 8.1

Watch some post-1990s films from Latin America, such as *Central Station* (Walter Salles, 1998), *Amores perros* (Alejandro González Iñárritu, 2000), *City of God* (Fernando Meirelles, 2002), *The Secret in Their Eyes* (Juan José Campanella, 2009), *The Maid* (Sebastián Silva, 2009), *No* (Pablo Larrain, 2012), and *Gloria* (Sebastián Lelio, 2012). How do these films address the concept of national allegory? How do they define and approach the concept of the nation differently? In what ways do they articulate national, regional, or global dynamics?

Activity 8.2

Watch a recent foreign film, and explore its production and distribution background. Can you identify the nationality of the director and cast? Who are the production companies involved in financing the film? After you gather this information, consider what makes the film "national," and in what ways the film complicates national labels, either in its narrative, style, or production background.

Activity 8.3

Check the list of the ten best foreign films on your preferred streaming service. What countries do they come from? Are some national cinemas better represented than others, and can you speculate as to why? Looking at the films' descriptions, are most on the list art films, or are they popular/genre films? Identify any other patterns you find on the list, and consider what they may suggest about the reception of other national cinemas.

Activity 8.4

Choose one example of small cinema, such as the cinema of Denmark, Ireland, Iceland, Bulgaria, Taiwan, New Zealand, or Cuba, among many others. Explore their recent film production and try to determine the factors that designate this cinema as "small." How many films does it produce annually? What are its size, population, and GDP? What are its film institutions? What cinematic traditions is it connected to? How would you describe its presence and visibility in world cinema?

Activity 8.5

Many small national cinemas emerged in the 1990s after the dissolution of the Soviet Union from the Baltic, Central Asian, and East/Central European states: the cinemas of Estonia, Latvia, Lithuania, Kazakhstan, Kyrgyzstan, Belarus, Armenia, and Ukraine, among others. Explore and compare the recent production output from five of these states. Which of these small cinemas seem to have a bigger corpus of films? How do they assert themselves on the international scene? Considering that during the Soviet period there was little distinction between Russian and, let us say, Ukrainian or Estonian films, what are the ways in which these cinemas attempt to separate themselves from the shadow of the Soviet Union?

Activity 8.6

Identify the Academy Awards nominees for Best Foreign Language Film for the past five years. How many of these nominated films come from what we would label as small national cinema? Which countries do they come from? Do some national cinemas get considerably more exposure than others? What might be the reasons?

Notes

1 See, for example, Dudley Andrew's discussion of "the national phase" in cinema in "Time Zones and Jetlag: The Flows and Phases of World Cinema," in Nataša Đurovičova & Kathleen Newman (eds), *World Cinema: Transnational Perspectives*, New York, NY: Routledge, 2010, pp. 59–89.

2 See, for example, Lotte Eisner's *The Haunted Screen: Expressionism in the German Cinema and the Influence of Max Reinhardt*, originally published in 1952. Eisner's book is a seminal analysis of the golden age of German cinema of the Weimar Republic, one of the earliest comprehensive studies of national cinema that remains relevant to the scholarship of national cinema today. Contextualizing early German cinema within both broader tendencies in German society and German artistic traditions, Eisner effectively demonstrates the relationship between national imaginings and their material/historical conditions. This close connection between specific history and the workings of the imaginary reveals the significance of seeing films as historical documents, even (or precisely) when they appear most fictional and ahistorical.

3 After a successful run in the 1990s, the economy in Argentina reached its breaking point in 2001. The economic meltdown resulted in massive unemployment, poverty, political turmoil, and riots, the fall of the government, and default on the country's foreign debt.

4 In 1983 Argentina emerged from a decade of military dictatorship and went through a process of democratization and enormous renewed cultural production, which included filmmaking. Filmmaking in this period was closely tied with the redemocratization process and refashioning of national consciousness. These films stood in opposition to Hollywood, resembling "counter-cinema" in their political modernism and allegorical narratives about the nation's plight. Many of the films then attracted international attention and received wide distribution public acclaim in the US and Europe: Luis Puenzo's *La historia oficial/The Official Story* (1986), María Luisa Bemberg's *Camila* (1984), Eliseo Subiela's *Hombre mirando al sudeste/Man Facing Southeast* (1986), and Fernando Solanas's *Tangos, el exilio de Gardel/Tangos, the Exile of Gardel* (1985) are all outstanding films with high production values while also addressing sociopolitical issues.

Bibliography

Andermann, Jens. (2012). *New Argentine Cinema*. New York NY: I.B. Tauris.

Anderson, Benedict. (2016). *Imagined Communities: Reflections on the Origins and Spread of Nationalism*. Revised edition (originally published in 1983). New York, NY: Verso.

Andrew, Dudley. (2010). "Time Zones and Jetlag: The Flows and Phases of World Cinema." In Nataša Đurovičova & Kathleen Newman (eds), *World Cinema: Transnational Perspectives*. New York, NY: Routledge, pp. 59–89.

Brown, William, Dina Iordanova, & Leshu Torchin (eds). (2010). *Moving People, Moving Images*. St Andrews: University of St Andrews.

Çelik, Tülay. (2014). "International Film Festivals: A Cinema Struggling to Exist Between New Resources and New Dependencies." In Murat Akser & Deniz Bayrakdra (eds), *New Cinema, New Media: Reinventing Turkish Cinema*. London: Cambridge Scholars, pp. 205–226.

Crofts, Stephen. (1993). "Reconceptualizing National Cinema/s." *Quarterly Review of Film and Video* 14(3), pp. 49–67.

Dabashi, Hamid (ed). (2006). "Introduction." In *Dreams of a Nation: On Palestinian Cinema*. Preface by Edward W. Said. New York, NY: Verso.

Dönmez-Colin, Gönül. (2008). *Turkish Cinema: Identity, Distance and Belonging*. London: Reaktion Books.

Eleftheriotis, Dimitris. (2002). *Popular Cinemas of Europe: Studies of Texts, Contexts and Frameworks*. New York, NY: Bloomsbury Academic.

Elsaesser, Thomas. (1989). *New German Cinema: A History*. New Brunswick, NJ: Rutgers University Press.

Elsaesser, Thomas. (2005). *European Cinema: Face to Face with Hollywood*. Amsterdam: Amsterdam University Press.

Falicov, Tamara. (2007). *The Cinematic Tango: Contemporary Argentine Film*. New York, NY: Wallflower Press.

Gertz, Nurith & George Khleifi. (2008). "Without Place, Without Time: The Films of Rashid Masharawi." In Nurith Gertz & George Khleifi (eds), *Palestinian Cinema: Landscape, Trauma and Memory*. Edinburgh: Edinburgh University Press, pp. 101–119.

Giukin, Lenuta, Janina Falkowska, & David Desser (eds). (2015). *Small Cinemas in Global Markets*. London: Lexington Books.

Higson, Andrew. (1989). "The Concept of National Cinema." *Screen* 30(4), pp. 36–47.

Hjort, Mette. (2005). *Small Nation, Global Cinema: The New Danish Cinema*. Minneapolis, MI: University of Minnesota Press.

Hjort, Mette. (2015). "Small Cinemas: How They Thrive and Why They Matter." *Mediascape: UCLA Journal of Cinema and Media Studies*, pp. 1–5.

Hjort, Mette & Duncan Petrie (eds). (2007). *The Cinema of Small Nations*. Bloomington, IN: Indiana University Press.

Iordanova, Dina. (2015). "Unseen Cinema: Notes on Small Cinemas and the Transnational." In Lenuta Giulkin, Janina Falkowska, & David Desser (eds), *Small Cinema in Global Markets*. New York, NY: Lexington Books, pp. 259–269.

Iordanova, Dina, David Martin Jones, & Belen Vidal (eds). (2010). *Cinema at the Periphery*. Detroit: Wayne State University Press.

Jameson, Fredric. (1986). "Third-World Literature in the Era of Multinational Capitalism." *Social Text* 5(3), pp. 65–89.

Jameson, Fredric. (2004). "Thoughts on Balkan Cinema." In Atom Egoyan & Ian Balfour (eds), *Subtitles: On the Foreignness of Film*. London: MIT Press, pp. 231–258.

Loshitzky, Yosefa. (2010). *Screening Strangers: Migration and Diaspora in Contemporary European Cinema*. Bloomington, IN: Indiana University Press.

Marché du Film. (2015). *Focus: World Film Market Trends*. Marché du Film. Festival de Cannes.

Mokdad, Linda. (2012). "The Reluctance to Narrate: Elia Suleiman's *Chronicle of a Disappearance* and *Divine Intervention*." In Lina H. Khatib (ed), *Storytelling in World Cinema, Vol. 1*. New York, NY: Columbia University Press, pp. 192–203.

Naficy, Hamid. (2006). "Palestinian Exilic Cinema and Film Letters: On Palestinian Cinema." In Hamid Dabashi (ed), *Dreams of a Nation: On Palestinian Cinema*. New York, NY: Verso, pp. 90–104.

Nelson, Max. (2014). "The Noise Made by People: The Films of Martin Rejtman." *Cinema Scope*. Available at: http://cinema-scope.com/features/tiff-2014-two-shots-fired-martin-rejtman-argentin achilegermanynetherlands-contemporary-world-cinema. Accessed March 5, 2017.

Nichols, Bill. (1994). "Global Image Consumption in the Age of Late Capitalism." *East-West Film Journal* 8(1), pp. 68–85.

Page, Joanna. (2005). "The Nation as the Mise-en-Scene of Filmmaking in Argentina." *Journal of Latin American Cultural Studies* 14(3), pp. 305–324.

Rajadhyaksha, Ashish. (2012). "A Theory of Cinema That Can Account for Indian Cinema." In Lúcia Nagib, Chris Perriam, & Rajinder Dudrah (eds), *Theorizing World Cinema*. New York, NY: I.B. Tauris, pp. 45–60.

Rankin, Jennifer. (2014). "After *Gravity*, is the British Film Industry Rocketing or Crashing to Earth?" *The Guardian* (28 February). Available at: www.theguardian.com/film/2014/feb/28/gravity-british-film-industry-rocketing-crashing-earth. Accessed November 25, 2016.

Roddick, Nick. (2007). "Eastern Promise." *Sight and Sound* (October). Available at: www.sightandsound/feature/49399. Accessed December 1, 2016.

Said, Edward W. (2006). "Preface." In Hamid Dabashi (ed), *Dreams of a Nation: On Palestinian Cinema*. New York, NY: Verso.

Sarda, Juan. (2014). "Damián Szifron talks *Wild Tales*, New Sci-fi Film." *Screen Daily* (September 30). Available at: www.screendaily.com/features/interviews/szifron-talks-wild-tales-new-sci-fi-film/5078105.article. Accessed November 15, 2016.

Scott, A.O. (2008). "New Wave on the Black Sea." *New York Times* (January 20). Available at: www.nytimes.com/2008/01/20/magazine/20Romanian-t.html. Accessed December 11, 2016.

Stafford, Roy. (2014). *The Global Film Book*. New York, NY: Routledge.

Suleiman, Elia. (2000). "Cinema of Nowhere." *Journal of Palestine Studies* 29(2), pp. 95–101.

Suner, Asuman. (2010). *New Turkish Cinema: Belonging, Identity and Memory*. New York, NY: I.B. Tauris.

Thompson, Kristin & David Bordwell (2010). *Film History: An Introduction*. 3rd edn. New York, NY: McGraw-Hill.

Tweedie, James. (2013). *The Age of New Waves: Art Cinema and the Staging of Globalization*. London: Oxford University Press.

Virdi, Jyotika. (2003). *The Cinematic ImagiNation: Indian Popular Film as Social History*. New Brunswick, NJ: Rutgers University Press.

Xavier, Ismail. (1999). "Historical Allegory." In Toby Miller & Robert Stam (ed), *A Companion to Film Theory*. New York, NY: Blackwell Publishing, pp. 333–363.

Xavier, Ismail. (2012). "On Film and Cathedrals: Monumental Art, National Allegories and Cultural Warfare." In Lúcia Nagib, Chris Perriam, & Rajinder Dudrah (eds), *Theorizing World Cinema*. New York, NY: I.B. Tauris, pp. 25–45.

9 Transnational formations

Cinema has been a transnational medium from the very beginning, from immigrant talent in Hollywood to cross-border influences of directors on one another. But the concept of transnationalism has gained particular relevancy in the global age, even though it has often been deemed banal and privy to easy appropriation in marketing. Economic, political, and cultural relationships that underlie cinematic production, distribution, and consumption are increasingly transnational. Discrete national frameworks, clearly defined national policies, economies, and cultures—even if they were always problematic—are no longer a valid point of reference. Financing is multinational, and cultural political bodies that provide funding for film are no longer bound within a nation-state. Networks of distribution and exhibition are transnational, as are flows of circulation enabled by new technologies such as digital media and online streaming. A film viewer's encounter with film is more transnational than ever: the incredible rise of film festivals and the increased mobility of and access to films have given rise to a cosmopolitan cine-literacy, spectators with rich visual currency capable of reading films beyond their nationally and culturally specific frameworks. Cultural representations on screen are transnational as well. They increasingly interrogate assumptions, myths, and associations of national identity, and their approaches to film form and genres unravel the distinctions that produced traditional national cinematic canons.

Transnational cinema

For reasons noted previously, "transnational" has become widely used in film studies to approach and study film and its related phenomena. Addressing various components of the interconnected world-system with a high degree or elasticity, the concept of transnationalism "enables us to better understand the changing ways in which the contemporary world is being imagined by an increasing number of filmmakers across genres as a global system rather than as a collection of more or less autonomous nations" (Ezra & Rowden, 2006: 1). Transnational cinema studies address numerous manifestations of this new reality: some examine the transnational flows that define the interactions between cinematic output and the consumption patterns of the diaspora; others study the mobility of filmmakers and their transnational mode of work; still others explore the new dimensions of global cinephilia, or transnational critical approaches. For all of them, the concept of transnationalism allows for a better understanding of the complex and interwoven network of economies, cultures, and aesthetic forms, which avoids the traditional divisions that have informed our understanding of film industries and systems of representation.

The concept of transnationalism has gained such powerful currency in academia that transnationalism is often heard as a mantra, used repeatedly and generically without specific contextual connections. As Higbee and Lim point out, perhaps the biggest danger in deploying the concept of the transnational is its pervasiveness and popularity as a descriptive marker, so that it tends to be used as "a shorthand for an international or supranational mode of film production whose impact lies beyond the bounds of the national," often dismissing the intricate and always contextually specific dynamic and implications of the term (2010: 10). Because of the generalizing tendencies of the term, they urge for a "critical transnationalism" as a methodology, not merely as a descriptive label. As a methodology, critical transnationalism is mindful of the specific and historically-situated interplay in a filmic production between local and global forces that may not always fit the abstract conceptual model of transnational, and usually extends beyond the mere transnational circumstances of production. Moreover, considering the transnational as a methodology should also imply a self-reflexive examination of our subjective position vis-à-vis the cinematic text, the "cross-border looking relations" defined by unequal power relations, different historical contexts, and different systems of knowledge.[1] Here, the focus is not only a transnational text, its aesthetics, and its circumstances of production and circulation, but also the "transnational gaze" that is mobilized and reflected in it.[2]

Higbee and Lim's concept of "critical transnationalism" is of particular importance and aligned with this book's approach to world cinema, as it is mindful of the specific and historically-situated interplay of elements in films, both on textual and extra-textual levels. It requires mapping specific relations to disclose how films are produced, distributed, received, and speak across national borders. Critical transnationalism is also a useful strategic method to disclose the complex interplay at work between unequal power relations, different historical contexts, and cross-cultural systems of knowledge. Critical transnationalism is not a label but a tool to understand a film's place in world cinema by examining its various levels of border-crossing relationships. Because it both "transcends the national and presupposes it," transnational engages with the dynamics of cosmopolitanism while maintaining the significance of national or regionally specific contexts (Ezra & Rowden, 2006: 2). It retains the importance of the specific local or national culture, but always in a relation to a wider system, which it both depends on and contributes to.

On one level, critical transnationalism helps us account for the so-called "borderless" and highly mobile state of cinema, while also unraveling its underlying paradox. The processes of globalization and advances in digital technology have erased traditional cinematic borders and increased the mobility of cinema. Films from countries that had a relatively limited reach now command large global audiences. The contemporary "culture of access," where filmmakers can bypass official networks of financing and distribution, and consumers are no longer limited to theatrical distribution, has dissolved national boundaries as both ideological and economic forces that control production, distribution, and representation (Ezra & Rowden, 2006: 6). But similar to human mobility, cinematic mobility is very uneven and determined by different economic and geopolitical factors. While some films cross boundaries with great ease (either due to access to strong distribution networks, high production values, marketing campaigns, or global appeal), many films even from strong film-producing countries fail to reach audiences outside their own national or regional borders. The concept of critical transnationalism can be productive in explaining both this cinematic borderlessness or mobility, and new divides and borders that have less to do with nation-states and more with the politics of inclusion and exclusion determined by highly uneven access to technology, financing, and distribution networks.

On another level, critical transnationalism addresses the hybrid nature of most cinematic cultures by moving beyond the problematic dichotomies between local/global, or specific/universal that underlie most traditional studies of national cinemas. In this dichotomy, the local and specific are traditionally associated with national cinema, whether related to production and distribution practices or narrative and aesthetic modes of address. Meanwhile, Hollywood stands for the universal and global, denoting its global reach and dominance in terms of production and reception, as well as its reliance on a universal mode of address in order to appeal to global audiences. An extension of this binary is the dichotomy between art cinema—always associated with "foreign film" and national cinema—and the US as a site of commercial, entertainment cinema. The concept of transnationalism allows us to go beyond this problematic binary not only in that it takes into account the permeability of national borders in a global cinematic landscape, but also because it unravels the strict dichotomy between Hollywood cinema and its others.

Cinema has been a transnational and hybrid medium from its inception, and even the classical Hollywood period is inconceivable without the "foreign" influence, either in terms of film movements or European directors, such as Fritz Lang, or Charlie Chaplin working in Hollywood. Such hybridizing tendencies, as Ezra argues, are ever more pronounced in a contemporary context, where European art cinema or Asian popular cinema have an enormous influence on Hollywood film directors (consider the influence of European auteur cinema on the work of directors such as Woody Allen or Wes Anderson, or the importance of Asian martial arts films on the films of Quentin Tarantino), and when directors such as Ang Lee, Alfonso Cuarón, and Alejandro González Iñárritu have become an essential part of the Hollywood canon (Ezra & Rowden, 2006: 2). As well, the traditional dichotomy between national as art house cinema and Hollywood as commercial entertainment collapses when we consider the fact that on the one hand the majority of the world's film industries are defined not by art films but popular entertainment genres very similar to Hollywood (for example, Bollywood, Nollywood, and Korean blockbuster), and on the other hand the fact that the biggest box office successes with global dissemination are often "foreign" films (Ang Lee's *Crouching Tiger, Hidden Dragon*, Zhang Yimou's *Hero*, or Bruce Lee and Jackie Chan films).

The transnational, migratory dynamic of cinema, certainly an aspect of its production, circulation, and mutual sphere of influences, is also reflected in the themes and narrative character of filmic texts that explore the effects of migration, exile, and diaspora on contemporary subjectivity, and rethink traditional assumptions about an "imagined community." Ezra and Rowden explain that "transnational consciousness" is marked as much by the worldly figure of the cosmopolite as it is marked by a sense of loss, homelessness, displacement, deterritorialization, and alienation (2006: 7). Problematizing the idea of homeland, the importance of location, and of national and cultural identity, many of these films thus "house" their narratives in what Marc Augé calls the "non-places" of postindustrial landscape (airports, highways, hotels, cyberspace), those in-between and transitional spaces that come to constitute our permanent conditions and relationships (2009). In other words, critical transnationalism must not only account for those cosmopolitan residents who, thanks to the global culture of convergence and mobility, are "at home everywhere," but include those who are the byproducts of this global culture who are "at home nowhere," immobilized, imprisoned, having to face ever more tightening restrictions and ruthless, if invisible, borders (Ezra & Rowden, 2006: 9).

Implied in the method of critical transnationalism is sensitivity to the significance of the local, which becomes particularly urgent in an era when national cinema has lost its relevance and when cosmopolitan, mobile filmmakers produce transnational films with universal themes that address global audiences and the global imaginary. A bias toward films that have a transnational dimension and the popularity of everything with a transnational flavor does not only obscure a significant body of films that continue to be financed, distributed, and consumed on a local/national level, but also fails to address the effects of globalization on the local strands of filmmaking within specific national cinemas.

In the case of Iranian cinema, Shahab Esfandiary (2012) argues, the complex process of globalization has consequences that go far beyond the domain of transnational cinema and its renowned filmmakers. He reminds us that transnational filmmakers in Iran, while certainly most visible, constitute only a small fraction and dimension of Iranian cinema, and that transnationalism in Iranian cinema has produced rather conflicting effects. It has created a situation where the exemplars of national cinema on the global stage like Mohsen Makhmalbaf and Abbas Kiarostami have lost touch with the local audiences that first made them famous, while their status as transnational auteurs has resulted in the emergence of "sacred defense cinema" that positions itself strongly against the assimilation of Iran into a homogenized culture of global capitalism (Esfandiary, 2012). In this example, transnationalism is not a mere label that celebrates the transnationalism of contemporary Iranian cinema, but a method that reveals the power relationships and specific dynamic that propel some filmmakers or styles into global visibility, in turn making invisible and transforming other local cinematic expressions.

For critical transnationalism, it is thus always important to ask: how does a film become transnational? This means considering the different manifestations of transnational, the various ways in which films cross frontiers and become transnational, beyond economic and geographic criteria. In his study of Latin American transnational cinema, Paul Julian Smith (2012) offers a useful insight into the different transnational positions that films occupy in their production, circulation, and textual fields. First, the commercial genre films often circulate locally but are transnational in that they employ the narrative and filmic techniques of genres that are readily accessible to international viewers. That is, they use global genres such as comedy, western, action, or horror, but rely in other ways on plot, narrative elements, casting, or other subtexts that are directed specifically to local or regional audiences and remain hidden from foreign audiences. These films, while working with transnational genres and boasting high production standards, tend to be commercial successes in their local or regional contexts, but, because they resist easy translation, do not perform well outside of local theatrical markets and are in fact rarely seen abroad. As Smith puts it, a high level of specificity is "superimposed on a generic transnational base, forming an 'assemblage' of multiple plateaux that affect each other mutually and are difficult to interpret, at once geographically and historically" (2012: 70).

Second, films that circulate in international festivals become transnational on a different level. They reject genre templates and could be seen as "localist" in that they are rather firmly rooted in a specific place and time, but become transnational because they circulate in the international film festival sphere, and receive significant foreign input into their production process, and also because of their cinematic and narrative alignment with the auteurist art cinema conventions that have come to define the so-called "festival film." In this way festival films, while displaying an autonomous aesthetic and a high degree of specificity, are transnational in production, distribution, and aesthetics.

Third, the most overtly transnational is what Smith calls the "prestige film." Films such as *Babel*, *Gravity*, or *Snowpiercer* signal border-crossing in a highly dispersed financing and production model, an international cast, an ambitious global distribution, and a mode of address that, framed within a global audience imaginary, tends to avoid specific cultural contexts and referents while it aims for universal relevance. While these various trans-border levels can be seen as distinct, they mutually affect or even undercut each other. It is thus important to recognize the particularities of national and cultural context within the practice of transnational filmmaking.

At the core of all these different dimensions of critical transnationalism is an argument that transnational is not just a condition of its production, circulation, and reception, nor a mere textual or aesthetic quality of a film. It is above all a methodology, a mode of inquiry, a way of understanding film not as a fixed object but as part of historical flux that changes and varies with different circumstances and perspectives. For Dudley Andrew, this is the most fundamental approach to world cinema:

> The transnational dimension shows every film to have access to a past and a future extending beyond the flicker of its original projection, its local moment . . . And so we should not treat a film for what it is but instead phenomenologically, for the way it has come into being and for what it has meant in its successive appearances.
>
> (Andrew, 2013: 19)

The transnational dimension of, let us say, Bong Joon-ho's *The Host* (2006) means that the understanding of the film will change dramatically as this film, which set the national box office record in Korea, gets absorbed into various transnational waves and discourses, from its festival appearances in Cannes, Toronto, and Tokyo to its theatrical premieres in Japan, Singapore, Australia, Hong Kong, the UK, and the US, and its enthusiastic embrace by film critics, cinephiles, and filmmakers (such as Tarantino) alike who endowed the film with a cult status and propelled Bong Joon-ho into a world cinema canon. A local genre film that speaks to Korean conflict over the U.S. occupation to its local audiences, *The Host* became a regional blockbuster because it projects a broader regional concern about U.S. dominance, and an international hit because it frames local concerns with the more universal stylistic elements of a global blockbuster. In each of these contexts, the film acquired a different transnational dimension. Rather than a fixed characteristic with a static meaning in a film, the transnational instead has to be understood on the basis of its "developing significance" (Andrew, 2013: 26).

Film studies must therefore resist using transnationalism as a macroscopic lens, a slippery signifier that applies to any and all films made and circulating in a contemporary global context. Instead we must rely on the insights of critical transnationalism to deploy it in a microscopic way as a strategy that uncovers specific alignments of the local and global in a film's production, circulation, and textuality. Given the complexity and multidimensionality of the term, it is important to note that the two case studies of transnational cinema chosen here may seem most "exemplary" in that they flesh out transnationalism and its relational dynamic in its various aspects, sometimes obvious and sometimes less so. They disclose the transnational as a dynamic that transcends the local/global binary and is grounded in multiple sites simultaneously, whether this multiplicity has to do with locations, cultures, identities, aesthetic models, or other affiliations. Such multiplicity is present in most contemporary films, and our challenge is not merely to slap a transnational label onto it but critically analyze how its elements are negotiated and positioned in relation to each other.

In focus 9.1   The transnational cinema of Ang Lee

Taiwan's Ang Lee presents the most perplexing and enigmatic case when it comes to the question of transnationalism. He is seen as a national auteur, a diasporic film-maker working abroad, a recruit for Hollywood cinema, and a truly transnational auteur all at once. Ang Lee has established himself as the most versatile and commercially successful auteur of the new Taiwanese cinema, which includes filmmakers like Hou Hsaio-hsien, Edward Yang, Stan Lai, and Tsai Ming-liang. While the directors in this group largely circulate in the art cinema festival circuit, Lee's embrace of popular genre forms has expanded his commercial appeal and made him not only one of the most bankable Asian directors, but one of the most prominent names in transnational filmmaking.

His diasporic status—born in 1954 in Taiwan, Ang Lee relocated to the US in 1975 and studied film at New York University—and transnational mode of production places him firmly "within the framework of transnational film production and mar-keting" (Pidduck, 2006: 394). Lee's career has always been shaped by the forces of Western capital, a renewed market for international art cinema in the 1990s, as well as transnational collaborations, particularly Lee's long-time partnership with American producer and writer James Schamus and his company Good Machine (Pidduck, 2006: 394). Beyond his diasporic status and transnational production practices, Lee's trans-national profile is further bolstered by his deployment of both Chinese and Western popular genres to address culturally diverse audiences, and his cinematic explorations of personal identity as a fluid and hybrid construction that often transgresses all kinds of borders— spatial, cultural, ethnic, moral, and sexual.

Lee's film career began with a trilogy of Taiwanese/American family melodramas, known as the "father knows best" trilogy: *Tui shou/Pushing Hands* (1991), a story about an elderly Chinese teacher who emigrates to New York to live with his son's family; *The Wedding Banquet* (1993), a film about a gay Taiwanese immigrant in the US who marries a mainland Chinese woman to appease his parents; and *Yin shi nan*

a

b

c

Figures 9.1a–9.1c Ang Lee's "father knows best" trilogy: *Pushing Hands* (1991), about an elderly
Chinese teacher who emigrates to New York to live with his son's family;
The Wedding Banquet (1993), about a gay Taiwanese immigrant in the
US who marries a mainland Chinese woman to appease his parents; and
Eat Drink Man Woman (1994), set in contemporary Taipei, featuring a
widowed Chinese chef whose three daughters, each in their own way,
present a challenge to traditional Chinese cultural norms

nu/Eat Drink Man Woman (1994), set in contemporary Taipei and featuring a widowed Chinese chef whose three daughters, each in her own way, present a challenge
to traditional Chinese cultural norms. The trilogy achieved considerable box office
success and critical acclaim in Taiwan and abroad, and seeded Lee's international
reputation.

(continued)

(continued)

Although these films are often seen within his "national cinema director" phase and are considered separately from his later, Hollywood-based film oeuvre, Lee scholars argue that unlike his new Taiwanese cinema colleagues, Lee's work has carried a transnational and diasporic imprint from the very beginning. For Julianne Pidduck, the trilogy already "establishes themes that have become associated with Lee's oeuvre as a whole: family and coming of age social dramas, intergenerational and cross-cultural conflicts, and tensions between cultural traditions and modernization," themes that center on diasporic experience, displacement, and hybrid identities (2006: 394). Similarly, Song Hwee Lim's study of Lee contends that while Lee's early films benefited from national schemes of sponsorship (Taiwan's Central Motion Picture Corporation), they "simultaneously belong to a national and a diasporic cinema" (2012: 131). Apart from their themes, their diasporic nature should also be considered, Lim suggests, due to Taiwan's own "jagged modern history" in relation to the national and the diasporic. Lee's early work thus already conflates boundaries between the national and diasporic or the transnational, and raises important questions about how to understand the transnational imaginary and the nature of accented cinema.

The transnational signature in Lee's work becomes even more clearly pronounced with his entry into English-language film and literary adaptations from cultural and historical contexts far removed from his own: eighteenth-century England in *Sense and Sensibility* (1995), 1970s American suburbia in *The Ice Storm* (1997), the American Civil War in *Ride with the Devil* (1998), and rural North America in *Brokeback Mountain* (2005). Lee's cinematic adaptation of literary works so grounded in cultural and historical specificity is guided less by a faith in the source material and more by an interest in reworking the material in order to capture the idiosyncratic nature of national, cultural, or gender identity. Spanning a broad range of contexts, these adaptations are nevertheless remarkably consistent and centered on familiar issues in Lee's films—the figure of the father, outsiders, racial and ethnic tensions, love and marriage, gender and sexual orientation—and thus continue the transnational motifs already present in the "father knows best" trilogy.

The discourse of transnationalism culminates, however, with his Chinese-language epic *wuxia* film, *Crouching Tiger, Hidden Dragon* (2000), by many accounts seen as an exemplary case of transnational cinema.[3] A phenomenal commercial and critical grand slam worldwide, the film earned more than $200 million, far exceeding the success of any other Chinese-language film in Asia, and becoming the highest grossing, and most influential, foreign language film in the US.[4]

Groundbreaking in terms of its impact on international film, *Crouching Tiger* is also a productive example of the mediation between the local and global in transnational cinema, its constellation of local and global elements making it powerful and problematic all at once. On the one hand, the film can be seen as a "resolutely local film—that is, a product of China's unique history, culture, values, and aesthetic traditions" (Klein, 2004: 18). Based on one of the novels in the *Crane Iron Pentalogy* by Wang Du Lu set in the classical Qing dynasty, the film tells a story of a great warrior in pursuit of a legendary sword that he gave as a gift to his dear friend, which was stolen by a mysterious and rebellious female martial arts fighter.

Figures 9.2a & 9.2b Ang Lee's film *Crouching Tiger, Hidden Dragon* (2000) reworks the *wuxia pian* genre to appeal to the global market, with a female martial arts fighter, iconic Chinese landscapes, and detailed period costume and décor

Spoken in Mandarin, starring renowned Chinese actors, featuring iconic Chinese landscapes, detailed period costume and décor, and a thematic concern with a conflict between individual freedom and communal responsibility embedded in the ancient martial arts world, the film certainly has no shortage of the signifiers of Chineseness. That the film was released on the heels of Hong Kong's realignment with China and its cooptation into the Chinese film industry added yet another layer to its specific regional situatedness.

On the other hand, the film can be seen as a resoundingly global product both in production, marketing, and distribution, as well as thematically and aesthetically. Made by a Taiwanese director educated and based in New York and co-produced by five different companies in four regions,[5] the film employed personnel from Mainland China, Malaysia, Hong Kong, Taiwan, and the US, achieved global distribution, reworked the *wuxia pian* genre and the historical specificity of the narrative for a broad appeal,

(continued)

(continued)

and constructed a mythical and timeless picture of China. As such, the film's global identity signifies not national or cultural specificity but an appropriation of this specificity for the global gaze and consumption. Its appropriation and hybridity, in many ways an inevitable part of any cinematic product made to appeal to global audiences, inflamed passionate debates about the film's authenticity, questionable representation of Chinese history, stereotyping, and pandering to the gaze of the West.[6] Such criticism, Kenneth Chan points out, not at all uncommon with foreign films that succeed in Hollywood, reveals as much about the nature of global cinematic product as it does about "a cultural anxiety about identity and Chineseness in a globalized, postcolonial, and postmodern world order" (Chan, 2009: 76).

Considering many arguments on both sides of the local/global relationship, both Klein and Chan suggest that Lee's ambiguous configurations on all levels of cinematic representation (genre norms and national, cultural, or gender identity) should be understood as an important part of an increasingly transnational self and nation in contemporary China and Taiwan, and moreover as a key component of a film that successfully navigates the transnational cinematic framework without reducing itself to a global pudding. For these scholars, transnational in cinema is not a simple border-crossing gesture—in Lee's case, between tradition and modernity, ethnicities, generations, sexuality, East and West, and European art house, Hollywood, and Asian popular genres. Rather than identifying the film in singular, either/or terms, transnational and diasporic means that the film is "oriented along multiple axes of affiliation," simultaneously grounded in multiple locations, ethnicities, and aesthetic traditions (Klein, 2004: 38). To use Lim's term, transnational and diasporic cinema speaks in "multiple tongues," where speaking in tongues both challenges the concept of binaries

Figure 9.3a Richard Parker the Bengal tiger and Pi (Suraj Sharma) stranded at sea in Ang Lee's *Life of Pi* (2012)

(Hollywood as global, national as local, for example) and makes us consider film language as equally particular and capable of speaking across cultural and formal particularities (2012: 143).

Clearly aware of the significance and implications of transnational imprint in his films, Ang Lee takes it a step further and weaves its discourse into the very plot and narrative structure of his recent 3D cinematic adventure, *Life of Pi* (2012). Topping the charts in Mainland China, Taiwan, and India, receiving eleven nominations and four wins at the Oscars, *Life of Pi*, as most other Lee's films, carries its transnational identity on its sleeve. It is based on the novel by a French-Canadian author, Yann Martel; shot in Taiwan, India, and Canada with a mostly non-American cast; co-produced by eight different companies in the US, Taiwan, and UK; and was released globally in various languages: English, French, and Tamil.

Its transnational address, however, is also articulated by its border-defying and layered narrative and aesthetic form. A relatively simple story of a young man who survives a harrowing shipwreck and months in a lifeboat with a large Bengal tiger turns in Lee's hands into a complex cinematic meditation on the nature of storytelling, and the relationship between religion and faith, fiction and reality, animal and man.

Lee deploys a complex story-within-a-story with an open ending, combining his long-time concern with the fluid nature of geographical and cultural boundaries with the fluid boundaries of digital cinema. In other words, Lee's musings on the dislocation and relocation that mark a diasporic identity and transnational cinema are, in this film, mapped onto the very nature of digital cinema, which more than ever before suspends the boundary between reality and fantasy, indexicality and computer-generated special effects. The film's open ending, its structure that works like the surface of the ocean—tangible and real in its own right yet serving only to reflect the sky

Figure 9.3b The reflexivity of the ocean in *Life of Pi*, at once tangible and real yet serving only to reflect other objects, is like Pi's storytelling, which blurs reality and fantasy

(continued)

(continued)

and other objects upon it—encourages diverse online communities and audiences to "decode" the film in various ways and modify its cultural material according to their own context (Ziheng, 2015).

The diversity of interpretations enabled by the film thus mirrors the film's central question of "what is real and what is not," which stories can be believed and which ones are implausible. The multiple stories do not cancel each other out, but exist simultaneously, speak to and inform each other, constructing a new meaning that transcends yet includes all of them. Like Richard Parker, the Bengal tiger in the film who is at once a magnificent digital creation and a palpable, real beast, this multiplicity is at the core of the film's transnational being.

In focus 9.2   The transnational cinema of Alejandro González Iñárritu

Together with Alfonso Cuarón and Guillermo del Toro, Alejandro González Iñárritu is one of the most globally recognized Mexican directors. This group of filmmakers, often dubbed "the three amigos," pioneered the new Mexican cinema and have worked their way into and put an indelible stamp on the international flavor of Hollywood since the late 1990s, each with their own distinct style. As opposed to Carlos Reygadas, Amat Escalante, or Julián Hernández, who largely circulate in the art cinema festival sphere, these filmmakers are seen as exemplars of transnational aspirations in Mexican cinema. While they carefully cultivate their collective Mexican identity and act as ambassadors for the national film industry, "they have had unprecedented international success and have crossed linguistic, national, and generic borders, cutting through traditional divisions created by film markets" (Shaw, 2013: 2). They have developed a global cinematic style that incorporates elements of both mainstream and art cinema, with a mode of address framed within a global imaginary and aimed at widespread market circulation.

Iñárritu's first feature, *Amores perros/Love's a Bitch* (2000) emerged when most Latin American films found it difficult to make an impact in their home markets, which were dominated by telenovelas. Only a handful of features were produced in the late 1990s, and the Mexican film industry was in the midst of the worst crisis since the 1930s (Elena & Lopez, 2012). A hit both in Mexico and abroad, and receiving commercial and critical acclaim, *Amores perros* thus signaled a revival of Mexican cinema.[7] Although *Amores perros* may not be regarded as a transnational feature given Iñárritu's later body of work—it was produced by Mexican production companies Zeta Film and Alta Vista Film, with a Mexican cast and crew—the film already weaves the cultural specificity of certain aspects of Mexican culture into its transnational texture. The pulse of contemporary Mexico City is captured in a style that recalls recognizable global visual models, the graphic immediacy of Hollywood (for example, the films of Tarantino), and international art cinema, and the story is framed within a rather prevalent contemporary film form of network narrative.[8]

Figures 9.4a & 9.4b In *Amores perros* (2000), Alejandro González Iñárritu draws on the parallels between dogs and their human owners to explore the dark forces of carnal violence

As such, D'Lugo argues,

Amores perros needs to be read not simply as a product of a revived Mexican cinema, but as a pointed interrogation of the position of Latin America's increasingly urbanized culture situated as it is in the slipzone between communities on the margins and mass mediated, global culture.

(D'Lugo, 2012: 222)

(continued)

(continued)

By the time he made his second feature, *21 Grams* (2003), Iñárritu was based in the US and making his films in English, in a style that combines the conventions of post-classical Hollywood and independent art cinema into a fashionable international film language. As Shaw explains, *21 Grams*, a film about a tragic car accident that brings together the lives of three characters, "positions itself firmly within the codes of American independent filmmaking" with its innovative cinematography and fragmented, non-linear narrative that carries the stamp of his script writer, Guillermo Arriaga (2013: 113). While such a multi-thread, multi-protagonist narrative has become one of the most pronounced aspects of Iñárritu and Arriaga's authorial signature, it is by no means a singular phenomenon. Arriaga and Iñárritu adapt a postmodern narrative that is both symptomatic and representational of a global network society.

In fact, scholars who study this postmodern narrative form—sometimes referred to as "fractal films, " "smart films," or "thread structure," but more often as "network narrative"—argue that it is part of a dominant trend in post-classical Hollywood and transnational art cinema, a cinematic mode that is both a symptom and effective representation of the postmodern, global "network society." [9] Paul Kerr (2010), for example, points out that while the form of network narrative such as the one in *Babel* has several historical antecedents, it becomes a prevalent trope in both art and commercial cinema after the 1990s. The reasons for this are partly based on zeitgeist: the transnational context marked by the culture of fragmentation, internet, connectivity, and networking, where resources, people, and work processes are both globally integrated and locally fragmented. The ubiquity of the network narrative is also preconditioned by industrial factors, such as the popularity of shorter and interactive media forms (music videos, video games, internet surfing), the impact of television serials and indie movies that deploy the fragmented format, and the mainstreaming of network narratives by festivals' globalizing of national art cinema (Kerr, 2010).

This trademark transnational cinematic aesthetic, particularly the form of the network narrative, culminates in *Babel* (2006), Iñárritu's third feature and the last of his collaborations with Guillermo Arriaga. *Babel* speaks to the dynamic of transnationalism not only in terms of its production context, cast, crew, and setting, but it rather explicitly addresses the theme of globalization and border-crossing within the narrative. Transnationalism is anything but subtle in this film, so it is no surprise that it is one of the most celebrated and frequently used examples in discussions of the transnational in film. The film was co-produced by a Mexican production company, Zeta Films, American companies Media Rights Company, Paramount Vantage, and Anonymous Content, and French company Central Films. Made by a Mexican director in Hollywood, the film features transnational stars: Brad Pitt, Cate Blanchett, Gael García Bernal, and Rinko Kikuchi, among others. Its narrative crosses borders in various aspects: geographically, between Mexico, the US, Morocco, and Tokyo; linguistically, between six languages (Arabic, English, Spanish, Berber, Japanese, and sign language); and in its score, between Western club music, classical orchestral compositions, and Mexican *norteño* tracks.

Similarly to *Amores perros* and *21 Grams*, *Babel* presents four separate yet interconnected narrative story strands: that of an American couple, Susan and Richard, vacationing in Morocco; their two young children back in the US with their Mexican nanny, Amelia; a Moroccan boy, Yussef, who accidentally shoots Susan with a hunting rifle; and a mute, troubled Tokyo teenager, Chieko, whose father gave the rifle to his Moroccan guide as a gift.

As is often the case in network narratives, a single object, a gun, originally owned by Chieko's father and given to his Moroccan guide, then used by a young Moroccan shepherd who accidentally injures Susan, links separate story lines. These separate yet interconnected story lines allow Iñárritu to set up effectively the thematic of a global world, where the result of temporary and less-temporary encounters of people with different national identities and cultural backgrounds is a far cry from a global utopia and mutual understanding. The experiences these encounters lead to highlight differences

a

b

(continued)

(continued)

Figures 9.5a–9.5d Four separate stories interconnect in *Babel* (2006): that of an American couple, Susan and Richard, vacationing in Morocco; their two young children back in the US with their Mexican nanny, Amelia; a Moroccan boy, Yussef, who accidentally shoots Susan with a hunting rifle; and a mute, troubled Tokyo teenager, Chieko, whose father gave the rifle to his Moroccan guide as a gift

and similarities, communication and miscommunications, divergences and connections, universality and particularity all at once.

A key aspect of this global dynamic, one that is emphasized throughout this book, is the unequal power relations that *Babel* draws out not only within the narrative but in its broader representational system. Just like the global, network society designates not evenly distributed heterogeneous flows but unequal geopolitical power relations, so too in *Babel* the transnational connections are construed by clear hierarchical structures. On the one hand, these unequal power relations are a deliberate and driving force of the narrative, where the US and Tokyo are clearly on the "winning" side, and most of the tragic consequences of the chain of events are suffered by the Moroccan boy, Yussef, and his family, and the Mexican nanny, Amelia. Yussef and Amelia have the benefit of solid familial bonds (as opposed to Susan and Richard, or Chieko, who are all in the midst of a family crisis), but are deprived of sociopolitical structural support. Their innocent and well-intended actions are thus necessarily interpreted as threats within the frameworks of Islamic terrorism and an immigration crisis in the US.

Perhaps not so deliberately, these unequal power relations are inscribed in the very ideological configuration of the film. As several critics point out, the globalization of

a

b

(continued)

(continued)

c

d

Figures 9.6a–9.6d The familiar cinematic tropes associated with *Babel's* locations: the U.S./
Mexico border; the marital angst of the middle-class American couple; the
hyper-modern and urban culture of Japan; and the poor and rural Morocco

national cinema means not only incorporating multiple locations, languages, and cultures, but a process of "deculturalization," of making these cultures consumable by using familiar cinematic tropes associated with a certain locality and archetypal characters (Shaw, 2011; Kerr, 2010). Thus, *Babel* deploys the rather familiar tropes of the U.S./Mexico border, the marital angst of a middle-class American couple, the urban identity of a Japanese teenager, and Moroccan poverty. In this picture, Mexico and Morocco are rural and poor, while Japan is marked by hyper modernity: urban fashion, clubs and trendy cafés, the latest technology, and modern cityscapes.

What is more, *Babel* "privileges North American point of view, even when it appears not to," building the main point of identification with the characters of Susan and Richard, and putting the grunt of blame for the tragic series of events and irresponsible behavior on both the Mexican nanny (who, in the absence of alternative childcare, makes a hazardous decision to take the kids across the border), her nephew, and the Moroccan boy who also irresponsibly, albeit with innocent intent, uses the gun (Shaw, 2011: 15). This perspective, Shaw concludes, results in the construction of the tourist gaze that facilitates and appropriates the world of the other, and even as *Babel* tries to address and deconstruct this tourist gaze, it "ultimately relies on images of otherness as familiar to the tourist as to the film spectator" (2011: 22). In this criticism, *Babel* fails to embed within the film text the self-reflexive critique of the very global inequality that the film purportedly exposes by its juxtaposition of the global north and south.

Beyond its narrative and ideological structure, the social relations in the transnational context of network narrative are also mirrored in the social relations embedded in its mode of production. Both Shaw and Kerr point out that despite its transnational production context, principal financing for *Babel* came from the three American companies, thus "*Babel*'s global reach is, in large part, conditioned by a North American perspective" (Shaw, 2011: 14). This privileged perspective incorporates the local specificity into a global language of art house cinema, while also appropriating the resources and skills of the diasporic and migrating artistic talent of the globalized media firms into making an accessible global product (Kerr, 2010: 48).

For his next venture, *Birdman* (2014), which received nine Oscar nominations and won the Best Picture award, Iñárritu turns entirely to the emerging trend in the global cinematic aesthetic of a single, uninterrupted shot aligned with a "slow cinema" movement, but here it is used as a gimmick to produce a wow effect. Along with Alfonso Cuarón's *Gravity* (2014), and Guillermo del Toro's *Pacific Rim* (2013), the success of *Birdman* is a potent example of global cinematic aesthetic, its transnational appeal tied to new models of funding, production, and distribution strategies, and the power of the international film festival circuit.

Produced by American companies Fox Searchlight and New Regency for a relatively modest $18 million, with an all-star cast (Michael Keaton, Ed Norton, Naomi Watts, and Emma Stone, among others) and a lauded technical crew, *Birdman* stages, quite literally, a story about a neurotic actor past his prime, Riggan Thomson, famous for his action movie series *The Birdman*. While on a quest to prove his artistic merits by producing a Broadway play, his obsession with transcending commercial success and achieving critical acclaim produces a full-fledged identity crisis, his crushed ego tormented repeatedly by the inner voice of Birdman. Defying genre distinctions, presented as a single, continuous take, masterfully choreographed, with echoes of magical realism, the film lays out serious, dense themes that are at the center of film theory: relationships between theater and cinema, stage and screen, realism and formalism, popular appeal and critical acclaim, reality and fiction, and acting and being, to name a few. Once laid out, however, these themes implode and deflate under the weight of the actor's mid-life identity crisis and his (ambiguous) act of transcendence. The film thus mirrors Riggan's fragile and ultimately failing tightrope walk between artistic legitimacy and popular appeal, enacting the traits of the identity crises of many a national cinema auteur on a quest for global acclaim.

Diasporic and postcolonial cinema

The mid-twentieth century witnessed geopolitical transformations on a vast scale as Western colonialism began to unravel and several nations gained independence, asserting their agencies and experiencing new identities in their relationship to the world. The British disengagement from its second empire of the nineteenth and twentieth century, and the various decolonization movements in the 1960s and 1970s in Africa, Latin America, and elsewhere, triggered political, economic, and cultural transformations that profoundly changed the international order and with it our understanding of the world. Previously-colonized nations and communities reclaimed their territories, their histories, and their languages through liberation movements that were based on national self-determination, resistance against colonialism, and the establishment of independent nation-states. A postcolonial phase can be broadly understood as the state of affairs representing the aftermath of colonialism, the experience of independence, memories of colonialism, and the formation of new, postcolonial identities. It implies the process of overcoming colonialism but also the difficulties of doing so, as emerging nations experience new struggles and forms of domination that include economic and cultural imperialism. Postcolonial studies engage these ambiguities and investigate how the ambivalent legacy of the Enlightenment and various trajectories of modernity are experienced from different cultural and historical perspectives.

The postcolonial phase, while imbuing all cultural representation with a political nature, also influenced a broader analysis of cultural production of all nations, insofar as the encounter with the Other and experience of the present weighted by a colonial past were no longer exclusive to the nations in the global south but also marked nations that were once colonial powers and now had to encounter a radically transformed world. The subsequent decades would be defined by newly conceived political, economic, and cultural relationships, further challenged by large-scale migrations and formations of diasporic communities outside of national borders. Like postcolonial identities, diasporic identities too were straddled between two worlds, home and host country, rendering cultural experience and exchanges (of people, capital, commodities, and information) profoundly complex and inextricably interlinked. The speed, frequency, and intensity of this interchange resulted in remarkable transformations in the fields of economics, politics, and culture. Various forms of dislocation and migration have been extensively explored in literature and film, and while they have been the main concern of postcolonial thought and multidisciplinary diaspora theories, we are still struggling to develop adequate terms for these complex sociocultural phenomena.

What we can say for certain is that particularly since the massive transformations in the era of globalization, the concepts of the postcolonial and diasporic are closely intertwined and both are implicated in the broader dynamic of transnationalism. As the distinctions between postcolonial, diasporic, and transnational subjectivities become less rigid, cultural production as well can be read as simultaneously postcolonial, diasporic, and transnational, suggesting not a simplification or reduction but a layered complexity.

As a term, *postcolonial* has been widely adopted since the 1980s to designate work thematizing issues that emerge from colonial relations and their aftermath. Denoting the stage after the demise of colonialism, it is associated with Third World countries that gained independence after the Second World War, but also refers to Third World diasporas within the First World. A complex amalgam of diverse currents, postcolonial theory built on the work on anticolonial thinkers such as Aimé Césaire and Frantz Fanon, whose powerful analyses of colonialist imaginary and of the relations between imperialism, identity, and nationalism provided a theoretical blueprint for Third World anticolonial thought as well as political struggle in the 1960s and after. Building from their insights, foundational texts such as Edward Said's *Orientalism* (1978) and Homi Bhabha's *Nation and Narration* (1990) examined cultural representations that provide the core of imperialist enterprise, and the hybrid nature of the colonial exchange. While the nationalist discourse of the 1960s relies on a clear binary distinction between the First and Third World, the oppressor and the oppressed, postcolonial thought questions such rigid paradigms and secure boundaries, emphasizing instead multilayered and hybrid subjectivities that spring as the result of geographical displacement and all kinds of mixing (linguistic, biological, economic, religious, etc.). Such postcolonial hybridity and multiple displacements are the subject of a diverse range of postcolonial films: *Chocolat* (Claire Denis, 1988), *Once Were Warriors* (Lee Tamahori, 1994), *La Haine/Hate* (Mathieu Kassovitz, 1995), *Chinese Box* (Wayne Wang, 1998), *Monsoon Wedding* (Mira Nair, 2001), *The Edge of Heaven* (Fatih Akin, 2007), and *Jindabyne* (Ray Lawrence, 2007), among others.

Postcolonialism, although a profoundly heterogeneous body of debate that successfully addresses the issues of deterritorialization, the constructed nature of national identity, and the limitations of nationalist discourse, is often approached with skepticism. Its investment in nationality as a master trope and primary grounds of resistance, among other disadvantages, has led many scholars to question its analytical purchase and replace it with "diaspora" as a more productive term to capture the social complexity of cultural diasporas, or situations that are not defined by imperial or colonial histories. Robert Stam, for example, has outlined numerous disadvantages of the term: the "post" in the postcolonial is a rather vague designation of perspective that can refer to either the ex-colonized (Algerian, Indian, Philippino), the ex-colonizer (French, British, Spanish), or a displaced hybrid in the metropole (Algerian in France; Indian in the UK); since most of the world is now in a postcolonial context, the "post" might also blur the differences between France and Algeria, the US and Iraq, or the US and Brazil (Stam, 2007). Finally, "post" implies that colonialism is over, obscuring the global inequality often hidden under the celebratory discourses of transnationalism, obscuring the debilitating and enduring residues of colonialism, or effacing the effects of cultural and economic colonialism that remains rampant long after the geopolitical oppression has ended.

On the other hand, the term remains useful in its emphasis on mixed, multilayered identities, already present under colonialism but further complicated by various forms of displacements in the post-independence era. It offers a theoretical framework of hybridity that refuses rigidly opposed lines of identity or aesthetic formations (distinctions, let's say, between First and Third Cinema), while being mindful of the celebratory implications of hybridity that fail to take into account unequal power relations and forced assimilation. As Stam emphasizes, relations in a postcolonial context are hybrid and syncretic, but this hybridity is "power laden and asymmetrical," and the difficult questions about how race, class, and neocolonial power relationships refigure in this hybridity are as urgent now as ever (2007: 103). Thus, rather than understanding the postcolonial as a term designating a temporal period, much of the project of postcolonial studies revolves around *postcoloniality* as a social condition in relation to various forms of domination (economic, cultural, geopolitical) and transnational migration, and as such can be employed within varying contexts of political struggle and imperial domination.

Closely aligned and intertwined with the postcolonial is the concept of diaspora, and diaspora studies. Literally meaning "scattered through" or "across," *diaspora* denotes physical and psychic dispersion (forced or voluntary) of a group of people from their country of origin. If *diaspora* originally referred to the dispersion of the Greeks after the destruction of Aegina, to the Jews after their Babylonian exile, the Armenian expulsion, and the slave trade and forced migration of West Africans in the sixteenth century, the process of dispersion occurs on a massive scale today. The twentieth century is often referred to as "the century of migration," defined by massive movement across borders, only accelerated by a complex conjuncture of factors such as globalization of capital and the labor market, transportation and communication technologies, transnational media, ethnic strife, civil war, climate change, and other population pressures. Global migration has affected an estimated 180 million people, first-generation migrants constitute over three percent of the population, and if diasporas today were to constitute a nation they would be one of the world's largest nations. For this reason, the experience of diaspora and the concept of diaspora have emerged since the 1980s as a powerful way to address issues surrounding nation, transnationalism, displacement, and migration. Often used synonymously with "refugee," "exile," "guest worker," and "immigrant," the name "diaspora" has been used to describe migrant communities, but has also served as an important theoretical concept to understand larger socioeconomic and political processes underlying contemporary patterns of migration, processes that include various forces of global modernity: capitalism, postcoloniality, nationalism, racial formations, etc.

A conceptual frame rather than an essentialist category, diasporic critique brings into question the centrality of a fixed home, fixed origins, and the role they play in the formation of nation, race, and identity. Diasporic space is understood as an entangled space in relation to which "home" is not only lost (thus evoking nostalgia) or transcended but becomes a placeholder, both an idealized and contested site for cultural memory, identity, and desire for home. Almost by definition, since *diaspora* conjures a deterritorialized area, it contests traditional constructions of nationhood, national identity, modernity, and citizenship, instead emphasizing subjectivity not as a fixed and hermetic process, but as something porous and mutable, ambivalent and contingent. Importantly, this notion of displacement goes well beyond the geographical territories and figures into various other spaces; its "politics of location" denote gendered spaces of class, race, ethnicity, sexuality, and age. Its movements imply shifting cultural, linguistic, and psychic boundaries. According to Avtar Brah, the concept of diaspora embodies "border crossings across multiple positioning," which can be territorial, political, economic, linguistic, cultural, and psychological (2005: 201). Brah also argues that these are not minority identities located at peripheries; rather, through the process of decentering they challenge the marginalization impulses of the dominant culture.

Diasporic filmmaking, which constitutes a vast transnational film movement and film style located within multiple sites of diaspora space, broadly refers to a diverse spectrum of filmmaking of any dispersed community living away from its country of origin, including imperial/colonial and cultural/hybrid diasporas: German emigres to Hollywood in the 1930s, *beur* cinema in the 1970s France, contemporary Turkish–German cinema, Maghrebi French cinema, black and Asian British cinema, or cinema of Indian diasporas, among many others. Jigna Desai writes that as a category, diasporic cinema provides a conceptual model that subsumes the national and transnational sites but traverses them, accommodating the complex sites of diaspora and spanning "the spatial continuum of cinemas from minority and regional, to national and transnational cinemas" (2013: 207). As an analytical model, it thus cannot be examined through a single frame and is necessarily dynamic, shifting between various spatial, temporal, and political sites.

While diasporic cinema has always been key in articulating the cultural, economic, and social dimensions of displacement and migration, cinematic representations of diasporic experiences have assumed a prominent position since the 1980s. At that moment, due to many economic and cultural factors related to globalization, a critical mass of diasporic filmmakers gained access to production, achieved visibility and critical acclaim, and repositioned the diasporic as well as postcolonial perspective from the margins to the center of cinematic narratives. In one of the first studies to take into account and map the contributions of diasporic and exilic films, *An Accented Cinema: Exilic and Diasporic Filmmaking*, Hamid Naficy deploys the term "accented cinema" to discuss the work of filmmakers such as Jonas Mekas, Atom Egoyan, Michel Khleifi, Mira Nair, Trinh T. Minh-ha, Elia Suleiman, Mitra Tabrizian, and Ann Hui, among many others. These filmmakers, Naficy writes, are the products of the "dual postcolonial displacement and postmodern or late modern scattering" and have become "the subjects in world history" because of this displacement from the margins to the center (2001: 11).

On a more superficial level (and running the risk of essentializing diasporic subjectivity and filmmaking), diasporic films can be identified as those made by filmmakers whose situatedness in the interstices of culture and film practice, their "accented status" as Naficy argues, will determine their approach to the film practice and aesthetics. Such accented style, he describes, is often characterized by qualities such as an open- or closed-form visual style; a fragmented, multilingual, self-reflexive narrative structure, and ambiguous and lost characters. Further, diasporic cinema engages the themes associated with colonialism, nationalism, and global capitalism through representations of diasporic journeying, dislocation, and loss, which frame these issues within larger questions of origins, memory, historicity, movement, and dislocation. Finally, diasporic cinema is identified as such not only on the basis of a filmmaker's position and film's content, but also its mode of production and circulation. In Naficy's study, most of these films, simultaneously local and global, are located outside dominant cinematic production practices, outside of major national cinemas and industries, and it is their marginalized mode of production, as much as their style and subject matter, that defines them as interstitial and "accented." It is important to note here the immediately problematic nature of the term "accented," which marks a foreign discourse as a deviation from all other accents that are absorbed within the mainstream and therefore deemed normal or "unaccented" (to use the linguistic comparison, why is American English with a southern drawl not considered as accented as American English spoken by a Chinese man or woman?)

While Naficy identifies accented filmmaking as a site of resistance and marginality in relation to dominant filmmaking, in terms of narrative approaches, style, and production practices, it should be emphasized that diasporic cinema—as opposed to, let us say, Third Cinema and other 1960s cinema of political engagement—is often located within and assumes the privileges of hegemonic cinema. It encompasses complex fields of power and straddles multiple film cultures, simultaneously resisting as well as working within dominant ideologies and cultural practices. As Desai argues in her study of Indian diasporic cinema, understanding accented films purely in terms of resistance to dominant paradigms and cinemas often fails to recognize "their location within, privileges from and impact on hegemonic cinemas such as Hollywood and Bollywood," and their political and economic privileges of being positioned in the global north in relation to their postcolonial homeland nation-states (2013: 209). Further, an increasingly decentralized film landscape and cultural diversity have repositioned the concerns of diasporic cinema. Qualities of marginality, the exotic, cultural otherness, have become mainstream and commodified, so the increased value of diasporic filmmakers should be understood not despite but because of their direct engagement with marginality and cultural difference.

While for Naficy the filmmaker's diasporic status is an important consideration that determines the position of a film as migrant or diasporic, this potentially excludes a rich body of work that addresses the subject matter but is made by filmmakers not considered migratory or diasporic. A more useful frame of reference here is Brah's concept of "diaspora space" as a conceptual category that considers the intersection and convergence of migrants and natives:

> The concept of diaspora space (as opposed to diaspora) includes the entanglement, the intertwining of genealogies of dispersion with those of "staying put." The diaspora space is the site where the native is as much a diasporian as the diasporian is a native.
>
> (2005: 209)

In fact, migration, diaspora, and cultural diversity define the global multicultural cities so much, and are so central to the present-day imaginary, that they occupy a central position in various kinds of films made by filmmakers with vastly different backgrounds. For this reason, the concept of diaspora cannot be tied to the identity of a filmmaker, but rather accommodates a plurality of production models and styles that articulate diasporic experiences. For example, a 2015 Palme d'Or winner, *Dheepan*, is directed by French filmmaker Jacques Audiard but explores the destabilizing effects of an enforced diasporic life through the story of a Tamil Tiger soldier who flees the Sri Lankan civil war and settles in the Paris suburbs.

Also problematizing the concept of diasporic cinema, Song Hwee Lim maintains that accented cinema has to be rethought both to avoid the binary distinction between "accented" and "unaccented" as the dominant norm, and to avoid the hierarchical concept of the migratory route from the Third World to the First World (Lim, 2012). For example, the work of Taiwanese diasporic filmmakers such as Ang Lee is often split between his "national" phase in Taiwan and diasporic phase after he relocates to the US. Lim argues that when we take into account the Taiwanese history of double colonization (first by the Japanese then the mainland Chinese regime), we can understand the body of work produced in Taiwan and its cinematic institutions as an example not of national cinema but "a hegemonic cinema that is at once national and diasporic, indeed a national cinema in diasporic/exilic form" (2012: 133). Lim's study highlights migratory routes, relations of power, and hegemonies that are not structured between the First and Third Worlds but rather travel within the Third World, and points to accented cinema as not merely an interstitial and marginal mode of production but occupying a hegemonic position and relying on state sponsorship. For Lim, such an expanded notion of accented cinema can better consider a broad variety of migratory routes and power dynamics, and is key to understanding work by filmmakers such as Malaysian-born Tsai Ming-liang, who is based in Taiwan but speaks about Chinese population and its languages in Malaysia, or Wong Kar-wai and Nuri Bilge Ceylan, who are based in their homelands but whose work exhibits diasporic concerns and styles.

More recently, Naficy himself has written about a more intertwined relationship between diasporic and mainstream cinema, whereby features that were commonly associated with diasporic cinema—cultural and linguistic multiplicity, fragmentation, dispersion of story sites—increasingly characterize contemporary mainstream narratives and inflect mainstream cinema with an accent (Naficy, 2010). The dynamism of globalization, Naficy says, implies a multidirectional flow of influence, whereby accented film practices have a reciprocal impact on mainstream modes of production, as in the cases of Mexican film-makers (Alejandro González Iñárritu, Alfonso Cuarón), Indian filmmakers (Mira Nair, M. Night Shyamalan), and many other directors currently working in Hollywood.

But this conception still relies on the distinction between accented and mainstream cinema, even as it refashions the relationship between the two. We have to undo entirely the binary between "accented" and "unaccented" that is traditionally at the core of diasporic cinema. Thus, when we consider the career trajectories of filmmakers like Ang Lee, Alejandro González Iñárritu, Mira Nair, Wong Kar-wai, Fernando Meirelles, or Paul Verhoeven, they are not so much examples of accented filmmakers gaining admission into the mainstream, of inflecting Hollywood with an accent, as Naficy would have it. Rather, their work signals their ability to "speak in multiple tongues" at once, to use Lim's term, where Hollywood is just as accented, specific, and situated as any other tongue (Lim, 2012: 144). It is such speaking in multiple tongues, where all cinemas are at once specific, situated, and able to communicate and operate beyond their specific contexts (national, cultural, linguistic, formal) that stands at the core of the diasporic project, and also aligns it with the broader transnational approach emphasized in this book.

The two case studies of diasporic cinemas that follow are only select examples, representative in a limited way, and were chosen not only because of their size and complexity (Indian and Chinese diasporas are the world's largest) but because they illustrate effectively the main issues that mark the study of diasporic and migratory cinema discussed in this chapter. Although they center on diasporas under a national (problematic as it is) framework, it is important to note that this is merely one way to approach the study of diasporic cinema. Another important way to map a case study, for example, would be to study the work of diasporic women filmmakers, within or across national boundaries, to see how they inscribe the diasporic narratives with feminist and queer perspectives, and thus challenge the conventional, heteronormative, and nation-oriented, diasporic imaginary. In fact, as is argued in cases of both Chinese and Indian diasporic cinema, despite the fact that they are discussed under the umbrella of national identity, they complicate the notion of diaspora by both gendering it and queering it. That is, they align the diasporic perspective not with the focus on national or ethnic identity and its displacement, but with the displacement of other forms of identity such as gender and sexuality.

In focus 9.3   Chinese diasporic cinema

Chinese cinema presents one of the biggest challenges to the national cinema model, and the scholarship on Chinese cinema has been at the forefront of transnational and diasporic approaches to national cinema studies (Lu, 1997; Zhang, 2002; Wang, 2011; Bergen-Aurand et al., 2015). For one, as we discuss in the chapter on Asian cinema, few places have a more complicated relationship to the national than the combined formation of the People's Republic of China, Hong Kong, Taiwan, and the Chinese diaspora. The split of China into different geopolitical entities since the nineteenth century; the relations between competing local "Chinese cinemas;" the globalization of the film industry since the 1990s; the negotiations of the concept of "Chineseness"

(continued)

(continued)

and "China" in the film discourse itself; and the examinations of national, cultural, and gender identities of communities in the Mainland, Taiwan, Hong Kong, and the Chinese diaspora. These are merely some factors, as Lu explains, that make the Chinese example "paradigmatic of the situation of world cinema at the present time" and point to the necessity of a transnational approach to the study of national cinema (1997: 3).

There are approximately 50 million people of Chinese ancestry living outside of China, and this "diaspora community" (a problematic notion in that it assumes some level of unity) has been built over centuries of numerous migration flows, from the great south Chinese exodus in the late nineteenth century to the more recent flows resulting from China's opening to the global economy, the return of Hong Kong to Chinese rule, and the Tiananmen Square uprising. These communities, already distinguished before migration, are still divided by region, class, language, nationality, and type of migration, with local identities (Taiwanese, Singaporean) often constructed in opposition to larger diasporic identities.

Compared to this long and complicated history of migration, the history of Chinese diasporic cinema is a relatively short one, and Chinese diasporic cinema is dominated by recent migrant filmmakers in the West who have established a reputation outside of Mainland China, Hong Kong, and Taiwan: Wayne Wang, Ang Lee, Evans Chan, Mina Shum, Clara Law, and Dai Sijie, among others. It also includes ethnic Chinese filmmakers in Southeast Asia, Singaporean filmmakers (Eric Khoo, Royston Tan), and Malaysian filmmakers (Tan Chui Mui, James Lee). While common diasporic themes—journeys, divided families, displaced individuals, economic migration—are their concerns, their work is also marked by incredible fluidity in regard to diasporic approach. They are not only engaged in an ongoing negotiation of ethnic representation but, as Marchetti notes, "The same filmmaker may be at various points, a Chinese exile, a Hong Kong emigre, an American immigrant, Mandarin speaking, a sojourner, a naturalized citizen, Asian American . . . Ties to China may be strong, broken, or ignored" (2012: 4).

More importantly, national or ethnic identity—a key structural principle of diaspora—may not even be their organizing principle, and they foreground instead the formation of other, non-national, identities. Lim argues that in the study of Chinese diasporic cinema, it is thus important to displace some core assumptions of the concept of diaspora and to trace a "minor Chinese film historiography" that would account for films made in any corner of the world that challenge the concept of Chinese-language cinema, construct contemporary subjectivities not based on national identity, or foreground ruptures within pan-Chinese identity (Lim, 2011). Films such as Hou Hsiao-hsien's *Café Lumière* (2003), set in Tokyo, speaking Japanese, but addressing postcolonial relations between Japan and Taiwan; films of Tsai Ming-liang, a Malaysian based in Taiwan; or films like Alice Wu's *Saving Face* (2004), set in New York City and exploring lesbian love within the context of the Chinese American immigrant community, are positioned very differently and as such articulate the various layers of the Chinese diasporic experience.

Diverse, plural, and multifaceted as they are, Chinese diasporic cinema(s) demonstrate that the fluidity of diasporic subjectivity goes well beyond the notion of hyphenated identity or double occupancy: the Chinese American being simultaneously this and that, here and there. In *Chan is Missing* (1982), a debut feature by Hong

Figures 9.7a & 9.7b In Wayne Wang's *Chan is Missing* (1982), two San Francisco Chinatown cabdrivers, Jo and Steve, are searching for Chan, an acquaintance who vanished with their money. Chan becomes a marker for diasporic identity that is fluid, defined by absence and constant negotiation

Kong-born, San Francisco-bred director Wayne Wang, two San Francisco Chinatown cabdrivers, Jo and Steve, are in search of Chan Hung, an acquaintance who, having just recently arrived from China, vanished with their money.

Driving through Chinatown, they collect rather rich yet often conflicting information about Chan, and the more they find out about him, the less they know, and the more abstract his sketch becomes. Chan is too Chinese and not Chinese enough; has ties to Communist China, and is a fierce anti-Communist; he is an inventor and a murderer. *Chan is Missing* shows us that diasporic identity is not only a projection, a construction, but also fundamentally shapeless and fluid, defined by absence, defying fixed

(continued)

(continued)

notions of ethnic identity, cultural assimilation, or language. As Peter X. Feng (2002) argues, what it means to be Chinese American is not only a multilayered and complex question, an uneasy encounter between two cultures, but also constantly in the process of becoming and negotiation.

Recommended films

Wayne Wang: *Chan is Missing* (1982), *Dim Sum: A Little Bit of Heart* (1985)

Evans Chan: *To Liv(e)* (1992), *Qingse ditu/The Map of Sex and Love* (2001)

Mina Shum: *Double Happiness* (1994), *Drive, She Said* (1997), *Long Life, Happiness & Prosperity* (2002)

Clara Law: *Wonton Soup* (part of *Erotique*, 1994), *Floating Life* (1996), *The Goddess of 1967* (2000)

Dai Sijie: *Chine, ma douleur/China, My Sorrow* (1989), *Tang le onzième/The Eleventh Child* (1998)

Eric Khoo: *Mee Pok Man* (1995), *12 Storeys* (1997), *Be with Me* (2005)

In focus 9.4   Indian diasporic cinema

Not unlike the challenges presented by the issues of the Chinese diaspora, the task of writing about a community as vast as an Indian diaspora is just as daunting and necessarily runs the risk of simplification and reduction of an incredibly complex phenomenon. Along with the Chinese, the Indian diaspora is the world's largest, constituting over 25 million people spread around the globe. The enormity and diversity of this complex social formation, various patterns of migrations, and the troubled idea of India within its own territory are only some of the factors that make it impossible to conceive of this as a "community" in a unifying way.

Broadly, the Indian diaspora in the global north and south is seen as part of the larger historical forces that shaped global modernity, framed as a "transnational formation established and shaped by postcoloniality, racial formations and capitalism" (Desai, 2013: 207). As with many other diasporic communities, there are big differences between earlier and newer forms of migration that are the product of different historical conditions. If migration during the British colonial rule in the nineteenth century occurred largely within forms of indentured labor or voluntary exile to places like Fiji, Africa, Malaysia, the Middle East, South America, and many parts of the Caribbean, the recent patterns are also dominated by professionals and elites who migrate to metropolitan centers for economic reasons. This so-called "model minority," part of the post 1980s patterns of global migration and hypermobility, not only contributes to a different kind of visibility and importance of the Indian diaspora around the world, but is often invested in and shapes the motherland in palpable and important ways. Scholars of the Indian diaspora write about the many ways in which Indian diasporas in the West have been shaping the Indian nation-state since the adoption of neoliberal policies in the 1990s, the importance of the so-called NRIs (non-resident Indians) for the politics and economy of the country, the ways in which the nation-state has been incorporating diasporic people as members of the nation and claiming the Indian diasporic as a non-resident Indian who is offered "privileges of heightened citizenship in exchange for his economic and political capital" (Desai, 2008: 347). This influence, as we extensively discuss in the chapter on Indian cinema and Bollywood, includes its role in shaping Indian popular cinema.

While Indian diasporic communities are dispersed all over the world, and therefore the genealogy of Indian diasporic cinema would include various contexts and sites (for example, there are ever-growing communities in New Zealand, Australia, and Ireland, among others), the cinematic production that has made the biggest impact is related to the more recent migrations to the West, specifically the UK, the US, and Canada. Most scholarly accounts of Indian diasporic cinema are thus focused on what Desai calls the feature film production of "the Brown Atlantic" (2013). The way these films are produced, circulated, and received has shaped in significant ways both the public culture of the diaspora and its host nations.

The Indian diasporic cinema in Britain is an outcome of the colonial legacy and an overall rise of minority cinema within British postcolonial diasporic communities after the post-war economic expansion in Great Britain. It has roots in and is aligned with the rise of "black politics" of Asian and Afro-Caribbean groups that began in the late 1960s, went through similar experiences of marginalization and social exclusion, and started achieving access to citizenship and self-representation (Mercer, 1987). As Stuart Hall puts it, black subjects became "the bearers, the signifiers of the crisis of British society in the 1970s," a crisis that was punctuated by race and that becomes the mark and subject of black British cinema (Hall et al., 1978). Strategically beneficial but also problematic, this "politics of black" often functioned as a unifying paradigm for diverse histories and communities, conflating African, Afro-Caribbean, and Asian minorities in Britain. It was not until the late 1980s that the Indian diaspora gained a more distinct identity, when a notable group of filmmakers who were part of it—Hanif Kureishi, Gurinder Chadha, Pratibha Parmar, and Meera Syal—came to prominence and became transnationally recognized.

Their international visibility and success, Desai points out, is closely linked to the growth of the neoliberal markets that were shaping the rise of British independent cinema in this period, and venues such as Channel 4 that promoted their work (Desai, 2013). Films such as *My Beautiful Laundrette* and *Sammy and Rosie Get Laid* (Stephen Frears, 1986 and 1988), written by Kureishi; Pratibha Parmar's *Khush* (1992); Gurinder Chadha's *Bhaji on the Beach* (1993); Udayan Prasad's *My Son the Fanatic* (1997); and Ayub Khan-Din's *East is East* (1999) were significant not only because they represented a threshold moment for the self-representation and international visibility of the Indian diaspora, but they also represented potent critiques of the nation-state, national cinema, racism, and colonialism. They mark an important moment for diasporic cinema in that they distance themselves from the dominant paradigm of Bollywood, firmly

(continued)

(continued)

situate themselves in the diasporic experience of South Asians in Britain, and offer cutting-edge approaches to the issues of racism, hospitality, and assimilation. They complicated the notion of diaspora, rendering its issues in a complex way that goes beyond the nostalgia for the homeland and obsession with the nation. Often focused on unconventional gender and inter-racial relationships, they connected the diasporic perspective not with national identity but with the displacement of heteronormativity, through queerness and feminism (Desai, 2013: 214).

a

b

c

Figures 9.8a–9.8c Stephen Frears's *My Beautiful Laundrette* (1986), Gurinder Chadha's *Bhaji on the Beach* (1993), and Ayub Khan-Din's *East is East* (1999), all situated in the diasporic experience of South Asians in Britain, represent a threshold moment for the self-representation and international visibility of the Indian diaspora

Like their British counterparts, the diasporic filmmakers in the US and Canada— Deepa Mehta with *Sam and Me* (1991), *Fire* (1996), *Earth* (1998), *Water* (2005), and *Beeba Boys* (2015); Mira Nair with *Mississippi Masala* (1991), *Monsoon Wedding* (2001), *The Namesake* (2006), and *The Reluctant Fundamentalist* (2012); and Srinivas Krishna with *Masala* (1991) and *Lulu* (1996)—similarly emphasize the transnational nature of diaspora and the intertwining of diaspora and postcolonial migration with gender and sexual politics. Hardly nostalgic, Mehta and Krishna's films, for example, are deeply reflective and critical both of the experience of Indians in Canada and their complex historical and cultural heritage. Mehta's trilogy *Fire*, *Earth*, and *Water* is set in India but it confronts head-on the pernicious heritage of gender, class, and cast relations, issues that are at the core of her diasporic critique and at the core of her controversial status and reception in India.

As a second-generation diaspora, their concern is less with the relationship between the homeland and the host country and more with "differences and conflicts within diasporic communities," "[u]tilizing generation, class, sexuality and gender," rather than nation, as sites of difference and identification (Desai, 2013: 215). Even though their films are sometimes set in India, they are marked by transnational models of production and exhibition, a cosmopolitan sensibility, and are thus uniquely positioned to appeal to broad audiences. Desai argues that Nair and Mehta's films are consciously constructed for multiple audiences in India and the West, and while they have a contested relationship with both Bollywood and Hollywood, they are aligned with Western liberalism and rooted in the generic and narrative traditions of Western cinema. While such positioning may invite criticism regarding their assimilationist tendencies, Desai

(continued)

(continued)

contends that "it is precisely these aspects that also allow them to shift scales and reach South Asian, British and global audiences while participating in complex discourses about cultural and national belonging from a gendered and racialized subject position" (2006; 2013: 217). As was argued in the introduction to this section, this urges us to understand diasporic cinema as not merely marginal, resisting the dominant paradigms, but rather as existing in a tangled yet close relationship to the mainstream.

Desai's argument about the global positioning of Indian diasporic cinema points to an important and unique aspect of the Indian diaspora: the extent to which it has influenced Bollywood cinema on the one hand, and the influential role of Bollywood in the construction of Indian diasporic identity on the other. Both diasporic cinema and

a

b

c

Figures 9.9a–9.9c Deepa Mehta's trilogy *Fire* (1998), *Earth* (1998), and *Water* (2005) is set in India but confronts the heritage of gender, class, and cast relations that are at the core of her diasporic critique

Bollywood can function as indices of the globalization of the Indian nation-state since the 1980s. The Indian film industry has always targeted audiences around the world, and Hindi films have been popular in Afghanistan, Iran, the Middle East, and Russia ever since the 1940s. But since the 1980s, special efforts have been made by Indian filmmakers to appeal to diasporic audiences, who turned out to be a lucrative market for Hindi cinema. This changed the outlook and orientation of Indian cinema quite radically. Popular films such as *Dilwale Dulhania Le Jayenge/The Brave-Hearted Will Take Away the Bride* (Aditya Chopra, 1995), *Pardes* (Subhash Ghai, 1997), *Ab Ab Laut Chalen/Come, Let's Go Back* (Rishi Kapoor, 1999), and *Mujhse Dosti Karoge!/Will You Be My Friend?* (Kunal Kohli, 2002) are all centered on characters living in the West, but they build rather intense nostalgia for the homeland and its values. Whereas diasporic films such as *East is East* or *Bend It Like Beckham* address the diasporic experiences in all their complexity, Bollywood narratives use those experiences as a structuring principle for the assertion of homeland and "traditional" Indian values, incorporating and claiming the diaspora as an integral part of national imaginary.

This influence, of course, works both ways. If diasporic communities contribute to the reorientation of Bollywood cinema, Bollywood cinema in turn plays a key role in bringing together the vastly diverse and dispersed Indian diaspora. Hypermobility, globalization, and developments in communication technologies and media have made Bollywood into a force that constructs a rather homogeneous "imagined community" among the otherwise very diverse diasporic communities in New Zealand, Europe,

(continued)

(continued)

Canada, and the US. Not India, but rather Hindi cinema is the main connecting point for dispersed diasporas, and to an extent shapes a global Indian imaginary that functions as a binding agent with the power to traverse generational, cultural, and class fissures of this incredibly polycentric community.

Recommended films

Deepa Mehta: *Sam and Me* (1991), *Fire* (1996), *Earth* (1996), *Water* (2005), *Beeba Boys* (2015)

Mira Nair: *Mississippi Masala* (1991), *Kama Sutra: A Tale of Love* (1996), *Monsoon Wedding* (2001), *The Namesake* (2006), *The Reluctant Fundamentalist* (2012)

Gurinder Chadha: *I'm British, But . . .* (1989), *Bhaji on the Beach* (1993), *Bend It Like Beckham* (2002), *Bride and Prejudice* (2004), *It's a Wonderful Afterlife* (2010)

Ayub Khan-Din: *East is East* (1999)

In focus 9.5   European migratory cinema: undoing diasporas

The late 1980s and 1990s are a transformative and defining period for the European political, economic, and cultural landscape as well. The 1990s were marked by the integration and re-centering through the constitution of one common Europe: the creation of a single European market in the late 1980s, the signing of the Maastricht Treaty in 1992, the circulation of the Euro as the new common currency, and the enlargement of the European Union (EU) to twenty-seven countries in 2007. However, this re-centering was paralleled by the traumatic reconfiguration and fragmentation of spatial boundaries in the former Eastern bloc: the fall of the Berlin Wall in 1989, the break-up of the Soviet Union, the disintegration of Yugoslavia and the ensuing war, and the formation of an unprecedented number of nation-states throughout Central and Eastern Europe. The unified, borderless new Europe (both a vision and a concrete geopolitical entity) and the utopian ideological model of cosmopolitan European citizenship are paralleled and challenged by the phenomenon of massive migration and waves of refugees that have been exponentially increasing the immigrant populations in the EU. Although Europe has historically evolved through a process of absorbing and assimilating diverse ethnic, religious, and national groups, this massive and ever-intensifying phenomenon has placed immigration at the core of anxieties about "Europeanness" and new European identity.

New patterns of migration have occurred against the background of older, more established European diasporas, and not only intensified the phenomena related to migration but urged an entirely new understanding of the concept of diaspora and diasporic cinema. That is, the older, rather settled European diasporas—the Turks in Germany; the Algerians in France; Jamaicans, Indians, and Pakistanis in the UK—are mature diasporas whose voices have been steadily and definitively shaping the European cultural landscape, and the cinematic output and texture of countries like France, Germany, and the UK. They have produced diasporic cinema in the more traditional sense: black and Asian British films, *beur* and *banlieue* cinema in France, Turkish German cinema, and Hispano-American cinema in Spain, among others.

Now, these mature diasporas are accompanied by multiple new influxes, and as opposed to rather compact migrant communities in countries like Germany and France, the new migratory patterns are much more convoluted, and demographic shifts much more ambivalent. If *diaspora* assumes a certain unity in dispersion based around the concept of the home nation and host country, the current discourse of migration and hybridization in Europe often defies the notion of diasporic community. For example, Eastern European countries, which were traditionally Europe's Other, and classical countries of emigration (the former Soviet Union, Poland, Romania, Bosnia), are now on the receiving end and have themselves become desired destinations for migrants from China, Africa, South America, and—recently on a massive scale—the Middle East and Syria, among other things blurring the distinction between self/other and guest/host. The widespread globalization, climate change, and financial crisis of 2008 has propelled further and complicated even more the migratory dynamic, and with it the nature of new European cinema that is shaped by as much as it depicts these complex transformations.

Like the radically changing landscape of contemporary Europe, filmmaking, as well, exists in a perpetually shifting and less permanent dynamic that makes labels like "national" or "diasporic" problematic, to say the least. The European film industry is defined by increasing mobility and interwoven structure in terms of funding, production practices, and distribution (Jäckel, 2010). Important films that address diasporic themes and migration are made in many different countries, by directors not considered migrants themselves: for example, Nuri Bilge Ceylan in Turkey or Jean-Pierre and Luc Dardenne in Belgium. Even filmmakers who may be considered migratory are often not part of diaspora communities but move fluidly from country to country depending on the nature of the project. As Iordanova argues, in current European cinema "film professionals function in a supranational context where they migrate on what we call a 'per project' basis . . . As their migrations are project-based enterprises, they are more adequately described as 'transnationally mobile filmmakers'" (2010: 65). Filmmakers like Emir Kusturica, Agnieszka Holland, Maja Weiss, or Sergei Bodrov may have ties to their countries of origin but their projects are set in various locations and financed by various pan-European arrangements. Migration, diaspora, hybridity, intermingling, issues of "otherness" are so central to the European imaginary and define so profoundly European cultural space and cinematic production that the traditional concept of diaspora simply cannot capture its pulse and its significance.

Indeed, many key European productions that have emerged since the 1990s would not be considered diasporic, yet place the issues of borders, journeying, immigration, and strangers at the foreground of a troubled European identity. One of the most widely written-about films on this topic, *La Haine/Hate*, with black, Jewish, and Moroccan protagonists, is an unsettling portrayal of racial and cultural hostility in modern-day France and the low-income *banlieue* districts of Paris. *La Promesse/The Promise* (Luc

(continued)

(continued)

Figure 9.10 Mathieu Kassovitz's *La Haine* (1995), a film about racial and cultural hostility in the *banlieue* districts of Paris

and Jean-Pierre Dardenne, 1996), set in the industrial suburbs of Liege, Belgium, centers on a father–son duo who smuggle, house, and exploit illegal immigrants from Africa and Eastern Europe. *Nordrand/Northern Skirts* (Barbara Albert, 1999) follows a group of people displaced by the Balkan war whose lives intersect in the bleak industrial outskirts of working-class Vienna.

Also using the Balkan war as a backdrop, *Divni ljudi/Beautiful People* (Jasmin Dizdar, 1999) presents interwoven stories of Bosnian refugees settled in London. Another drama about illegal immigrants in London is *Dirty Pretty Things* (2002) by Stephen Frears. Also a British production, Michael Winterbottom's *In This World* (2002) follows two young Afghan refugees from a refugee camp in Pakistan to London. *Rezervni deli/Spare Parts* (Damjan Kozole, 2003) is about two smugglers in Slovenia transporting illegal migrants, who are often killed and their organs are sold for money. Fatih Akin's *Gegen die Wand/Head-On* (2004) and *Auf den anderen Seite/The Edge of Heaven* (2007) are both significant works on Turkish immigrants in Germany, and Abdellatif Kechiche's *La faute à Voltaire/Blame It on Voltaire* (2000) and *La graine et le mulet/The Secret of the Grain* (2007) on the Maghrebi immigrants in France. Aki Kaurismäki's *Le Havre* (2011) tells a beautiful story of a shoe-shiner in the French port city of Le Havre who tries to save an immigrant child. A 2015 winner of the Palme d'Or at Cannes, *Dheepan* (Jacques Audiard, 2015) is about three Tamil refugees who flee war-torn Sri Lanka and come to France. *Mediterranea* (Jonas Carpignano, 2015) follows two African refugees on their trek from Burkina Faso to Italy.

Even in works whose subject matter is not necessarily immigration—for example, an anthology film, *Visions of Europe* (2004), which brings together many European filmmakers to contemplate on the concept of the EU—the issues of "otherness" and immigration become fundamental to the broader question of Europe.

Official political discourse has been largely anti-immigration and enforcing of the notion of Fortress Europe (a term applied to the discourse of E.U. immigration

Figure 9.11 Aki Kaurismäki's *Le Havre* (2015) is about a shoe-shiner in the French port city who tries to save an immigrant child

Figure 9.12 Jacques Audriard's *Dheepan* (2015), about Tamil refugees from Sri Lanka in France, is one of many European productions that place the issues of borders and immigration at the center of troubled European identity

policies and legislation targeting immigrants, and the rise of ultranationalist, right-wing parties in European countries). In contrast, these films provide a nuanced alternative to the media and public discourse on migrants that often demonizes them. They are

(continued)

(continued)

intriguing insights into how Europe's new sociocultural space has been shaped by the experience of displacement, diaspora, exile, homelessness, and border crossing, which challenge the traditional notions of Europeanness as well as the classic "Others" of Europe (Jews, the Roma, refugees from Eastern Europe), now replaced by new "Others" from Africa, Asia, and the Middle East.

Rather than diasporic, these films are discussed under terms such as "journey," "migratory," "cross-border," or "immigration" films (Loshitzky, 2010; Berghahn & Sternberg, 2010; Ballesteros, 2015). In her study of such films, Iordanova proposes the term "cinema of the metropolitan multicultural margin" to capture both these films' textual characteristics and their condition of production and reception (2010: 57). They may be made in a national context, but they travel across Europe and map the hybrid and contested territory of the European metropolis. Many of them center on the peripheral spaces, ethnic enclaves of the multicultural global city, and while they may make immigration their main subject, they chart in a broader way the problematic of this hybrid collective space, embodying the perspective of and giving voice not only to immigrants but also to other marginal, similarly voiceless social groups (Iordanova, 2010).

In a similar vein, Thomas Elsaesser dubs such works "films without a passport," not only because their production and circulation transcends national boundaries and because they interrogate the idea of the nation, but also because they forge a different process of identification for the spectator, a different perception of space and boundaries, and a different understanding of history (2005: 20). While most films mentioned here embrace the documentary-like technique and a realist format to some extent in order to convey a sense of reality, their representational mode often challenges generic conventions, narrative traditions, and styles of a particular film culture. Journeying and heightened mobility is their cinematic approach, not merely their subject matter. A film about African migrants in Italy, *Mediterranea* (2015), for example, uses the grainy, hand-held, observational style associated with the documentary mode, but its tightly framed shots and elliptical jump-cut editing, among other techniques, also work to decontextualize its images, displace the viewer, and prevent easy identification with the characters. Rather than building empathy and superficial acceptance of the Other, these films often deconstruct familiar frameworks of identity, collapse the opposition between self/other and host/stranger, and forge an awareness of otherness as an element already at the core of European identity.

Finally, the context of convoluted patterns of migration in Europe and cinematic representations of migration in new European cinema foreground the necessity of a transnational way of studying films perhaps more forcefully than some other contexts, the practice of what Iordanova calls "watching across borders," which traces "the cycle of film production, dissemination and reception as one dynamic process that rises above national boundaries" (2010: 61). This methodology, necessary to study the dynamic of new European cinema or any other diasporic cinema, is at the core of this book, and constitutes the basic characteristic of world cinema. Whether the context

Figures 9.13a & 9.13b Meditteranea's narrative of displacement deploys tightly framed shots and elliptical jump-cut editing to displace the viewer and prevent easy identification with the characters

is that of a national, transnational, or diasporic cinema, we should not embrace and deploy these labels as a means to an end, but rather disclose how the various elements and relationships are embedded within a specific film, and how the film positions itself in the larger context of world cinema.

Transnational women's cinema

Patricia White's insightful study of global women's filmmaking in the twenty-first century begins with an observation that "though still drastically underrepresented, women directors are increasingly coming into view within the current circulation of world cinema" (2015: 4). Indeed, even though the presence of women filmmakers in world cinema is anything but new, the expanding festival network, shifts in global production, circulation, and reception of films, and new financing and marketing structures have markedly widened the opportunities and strengthened the visibility of a new generation of women directors, resulting in an increased awareness of the representation and participation of women at all levels of the film industry. Professional organizations such as Women in Film and Television International, the European Women's Audiovisual Network, New York-based Women Make Movies, and LA-based Alliance of Women Directors offer rich resources and facilitate global networks of women's initiatives. Numerous film festivals around the world devoted to women's cinema have established a strong presence on the festival network: the Seoul International Women's Film Festival (South Korea), Festival International de Films de Femmes in Creteil (France), Cologne International Women's Film Festival (Germany), Athena Film Festival in Chicago (US), Mujeres en Foco in Buenos Aires (Argentina), Women Make Waves Film Festival in Taipei (Taiwan), Women's Panorama in Zanzibar, and Mumbai Women's International Film Festival (India), to mention only a few.

Most national cinemas, traditionally driven by male auteurs, now boast internationally recognized women directors: Rakhshan Bani-E'temad, Samira Makhmalbaf, Marjane Satrapi, and Shirin Neshat in Iran; Lucrecia Martel and Celina Murga in Argentina; Isabel Coixet, Icíar Bollaín, and Gracia Querejeta in Spain; Aida Begić and Jasmila Žbanić in Bosnia and Herzegovina; Xu Jinglei, Li Yu, Zhao Wei, and Sylvia Chang in China; Naomi Kawase, Miwa Nishikawa, Yang Yong-hi, and Yuki Tanada in Japan; Nadine Labaki, Danielle Arbid, and Maryanne Zehil in Lebanon; and Annemarie Jacir and Najwa Najjar in Palestine, to point out a few. Many international film festivals today claim close to fifty percent representation by women filmmakers, and several countries—such as France, Norway, Sweden, and Lebanon—claim an almost equal representation of women in their film industry, while women's participation in the industry and at festivals in most BRICS countries (Brazil, Russia, India, China, and South Africa) has increased to a healthy thirty percent.[10] In light of these encouraging developments, film website Fandor, in its spotlight on women filmmakers that pays tribute to a varied and rich group of directors, argues that in many ways we should no longer differentiate between "directors" and "female directors."

This increased presence and visibility, however, in no way diminishes the fact that women directors and women's voices are still significantly underrepresented on all levels of the filmmaking world. What do we make of the fact that in Hollywood, the reputation of mainstream filmmakers like Kathryn Bigelow or independent ones like Ava DuVernay or Kelly Reichardt notwithstanding, the percentage of women directors stands at an appalling seven percent, and that out of the hundred highest grossing films, a mere 1.9 percent are directed by women? That in all Oscar history, only four women have been nominated for Best Director, with over three decades separating the first woman nominee in 1976, Lina Wertmuller, and the first—and only—winner in 2010, Kathryn Bigelow? And if we dismiss Hollywood as too constrained by mainstream industry dictats and therefore lacking diversity of all kinds, not just of gender, what do we make of the fact that prestigious international film festivals such as Cannes, which claim to represent the best of world cinema and pride themselves on inclusivity, hold similarly appalling track records, with many editions of the festival (in 2012, for example) featuring not a single female director in the main competition? The only woman director to win the prestigious Palme d'Or, Jane Campion, when appointed as the first female jury president in 2014 expressed outrage about such a dearth of women directors and dubbed Cannes' unbalanced representation as "the old boys' network" (quoted in Higgins, 2015). Even at Sundance, which prides itself on gender equality, women have represented less than a third in narrative and documentary production featured in the festival since 2002.[11]

Such glaring statistics, White argues, beyond highlighting the underrepresentation of women filmmakers, point to the fact that the significance of their participation in world cinema is often misrecognized, and that women directors are ambiguously recruited to the project of world cinema, whose dominant conceptualization is still organized around national movements, waves, and traditionally masculine *cinema d'auteur*. While there has been considerable remapping of world cinema, the questions of gender and the issues they raise in terms of representation, visibility, aesthetics, and politics "have yet to structure such inquiry significantly" (White, 2015: 6). It is thus important to contextualize the concept of women's cinema, both as a practice and a critical discourse, and see it not only as a significant element in world cinema, but one that exposes and reconfigures the very logic that structures its map. That is, the inclusion of women filmmakers is not a matter of filling a gap, nor is it a mere nod to their increasing visibility. It is to give voice to a structural silence in film history to reveal both the gendered dynamic of transnational processes in world cinema, as well as the profoundly transnational dynamic of women's filmmaking. What makes women's cinema a matter of study is a complex network of different voices expressed across the global spectrum—some repressed, some enabled by funding, some privileged, some more visible than others. They should be brought together not because they are women but because they represent and bring to light the profoundly uneven structures of access, financing, representation and visibility that chart the contours of world cinema.

As layered in its evocation and dense in its complexity as the concept of "world cinema," women's cinema as well is a notoriously difficult and slippery concept to define. It can refer to films made by women, films made for women, films made about women, or any combination of the three. It can invoke feminist aesthetics, feminist modes of practice, or a mode of consumption. It evades and traverses generic, national, aesthetic, political, and cultural boundaries, yet involves and subsumes all of them. It can intersect with or distance itself from feminist film theory and the theoretical concept of women's cinema. A complex discursive and institutional construction engaging various constituencies—audiences, filmmakers, critics, scholars—women's cinema is a "hybrid concept, arising from a number of overlapping practices and discourses, and subject to a baffling variety of definitions" (Butler, 2002: 2). Rather than trying to define it, we highlight some key ways in which the issues surrounding women's cinema and feminist film criticism intersect with and inform the discourse of world cinema.

While women have been an important part of the cinematic landscape since the early days of cinema, on sides of production and reception, the idea of women's cinema is a more recent phenomenon in film theory, emerging in the late 1960s when feminist issues animated the social and cultural sphere. The activism of women's liberation movement, the feminist wave in film studies, the emergence of women's film festivals and film journals that embarked on an archaeological project to unbury the history of female auteurs such as Dorothy Arzner, Agnès Varda, and Germaine Dulac, all shaped the development of women's cinema into a political counter-cinema whose aim was to challenge the patriarchal system, the language it is built upon, and the sexist structure of filmic representation.

What this political stance encompassed, however, and how it was defined, soon became a matter of contention. Early film feminism and film practice often stressed the importance of political activism, the practical goals of consciousness raising, the critique of media and filmic representation of women through negative stereotypes, and the need to recover and construct positive, realistic images of women. By the end of the 1970s, however, such focus on the "image" of women and issues of representation came to be seen as naïve, merely corrective, and feminist theorists such as Laura Mulvey and Claire Johnston emphasized that in order to deconstruct cinema's patriarchal ideological premises, we need to move beyond the imagistic content—positive, negative, realistic, or distorted—and instead turn to vigorous interrogation of the form and language it is based on. That is, the focus of feminist analysis became the very cinematic apparatus, the socially and sexually charged nature of the medium, and the gendered nature of vision itself.

But if Mulvey and Johnston stand on common ground in their basic understanding of feminist critique, they differ in their vision of women's cinema, and their difference in many ways informs a larger split that has marked—and still does—the discourse of women's counter-cinema. In her impassioned critique of gendered visual dynamics and codes of representation in mainstream narrative film that reproduce a binary structure of male looking and female to-be-looked-at-ness, Laura Mulvey dismisses outright the possibility of a feminist film practice that exists within the mainstream narrative and its heavily gendered mechanisms of pleasure and the male gaze. Her hugely influential "Visual Pleasure and Narrative Cinema" (1975) argues that women's cinema as oppositional cinema must be avant-garde, and adopt a deconstructive, denaturalizing, and reflexive mode, and this breaking down of the codes of classical narrative cinema for Mulvey necessarily implies also the destruction of pleasure that these codes are based upon.

In her canonical "Women's Cinema as Counter Cinema," Claire Johnston (1973) argues similarly for the oppositional stance of women's cinema, but maintains that it can grow within the contradictions of mainstream Hollywood cinema and exist in a relationship with politics and entertainment. For her, politics is not mutually exclusive with entertainment and pleasure; rather, the two inform each other in a two-way process. White notes that in today's climate, when many more women have access to and participate in mainstream cinema, it is particularly important to keep in mind both "Johnston's insistence that politics accompany pleasure and Mulvey's emphasis on a feminist film practice" (2015: 5). Thus, in the early feminist discourse on women's filmmaking, there is an imperative for women's cinema to be a political cinema. However, what constitutes politics, how it addresses the dynamic of pleasure and entertainment, and what form or aesthetic it should assume to deconstruct imposed paradigms are all matters of contention.

If 1970s conceptions of women's cinema were largely dominated by calls for counter-cinema that mounts a critique of patriarchal ideology through deconstructing its language and form, 1980s feminist theory reframes the conflict between oppositional politics and aesthetics of women's cinema to account for the diversity in women's cinema practice. Addressing the contradiction at the core of the debate on women's cinema—the critical negativity of its theory and affirmative stance of its politics—Teresa de Lauretis argues that the subject of feminism is constructed not merely through content, formal codes, or a prescribed "feminine aesthetic," but rather through a mode of address that makes visible and addresses the female spectator who is multiple and diverse, embodying different positions of class, race, nationality, and sexuality (1987). Emphasizing the social experience of cinema, de Lauretis is less concerned with the division between avant-garde and narrative cinema and more attentive toward the reception politics, with cinema as social technology. Similarly to de Lauretis, other feminist scholars acknowledge the more intertwined relationship between women's cinema and mainstream traditions, and distance themselves from a narrowly defined political women's cinema to account for the expansiveness of contemporary women's filmmaking in the post-1980s landscape.

The diversity of women's filmmaking practices and new structures and networks that support films made by, for, and about women in the post-1980s era not only expose the prescriptive political and aesthetic frameworks of early feminism, but also its Western-centric positioning that assumes a faulty universality. Spivak's work, concerned with the suffering of the "subaltern," condemns Western feminism for creating a discursive homogenization of women's suffering, assuming a universal elitist posture that is both produced by and for white, middle-class women. Women in South Asia, for example, face different types of oppression and exploitation in the context of the postcolony (Spivak, 1988). Spivak's provocative question "Can the subaltern speak?" questions the universal assumptions embedded in the issues of women's voice and agency, urging for a feminist critique that is grounded in and relevant to a specific sociocultural background and conditions.

A part of Third World feminism, the critique of the middle-class and white hegemony of feminism by scholars like Spivak and Chandra Talpade Mohanty stressed the cultural specificity and historical differences in feminist discourses outside of Western-oriented paradigms. They show that the way we conceive of and think about women's cinema has to change to make space for more flexible, comparative, interdisciplinary, and historically-situated methods. Accordingly, feminist film theory has expanded and become firmly integrated in various new directions in queer, postcolonial, or diasporic film studies—in fact any studies that foreground the questions of power, relationality, agency, and visibility. Intersectional feminism, for example, emerging in the late 1980s (the work of Kimberlé Crenshaw, for instance), questioned the white, middle-class, heterosexual foundation of Western feminist theories and practices, insisting that cultural patterns of gender oppression intersect with and need to be explored along with race, ethnicity, and class.

The work in transnational feminism by scholars such as Ella Shohat, Trinh T. Minh-ha, Lingzhen Wang, Patricia White, and Alison Butler also calls for a transnational, relational methodology to address the multiplicity of constituencies, forms, and concerns in contemporary women's cinema. The newly emerged studies of women directors within national and regional cinema studies highlight women's work not as an "addition" or inclusion into the canon but as a way to investigate the ways in which the concepts of the nation, collectivity, and transnationality are always already gendered.

This relational methodology and transnational approach is key, for example, to Alison Butler, who argues that due to its sheer expansiveness and diversity, contemporary women's cinema "exceeds even the most flexible definition of counter-cinema" (2002: 12). She thus proposes women's cinema not as counter-cinema but as "minor" cinema, a term used by Gilles Deleuze and Félix Guattari when speaking of literature of a marginalized group written within a major language. Butler deploys "minor" as a productive term insofar as it calls attention to the displacement or deterritorializing mode of women's cinema. That is, as a minor cinema, women's cinema is not based on its gendered subjectivity, but rather on its never-quite-at-home position in any of the discourses it inhabits. Existing both outside and within contemporary mainstream culture, it is "neither included within nor excluded from cultural traditions, lacking a cohesive collective identity but not yet absolutely differentiated from each other" (2002: 22). Minor thus has to do with conceiving women's cinema as existing within, struggling against, and attempting to change the discourses that dominate it.

Butler's idea of women's cinema as minor cinema resonates in many important ways with the concept of transnationalism as discussed in this book. First, it considers women's cinema outside of ghettoized, interstitial, and marginal spaces in the national context, and opens up a more heuristic play of transnational configurations. Further, it foregrounds the issues of borders, belonging, otherness, and displacement—issues at the core of transnational cinema—as inherently gendered issues. Several recent feminist studies insist that the increasing presence of women filmmakers on the world cinema stage cannot be seen as a mere presence of an "alternative voice." For Marciniak et al., for example, transnational feminism is

> not a decorative addition or an optional perspective that can be applied to studies of transnational media but an acknowledgement that transnational processes are inherently gendered, sexualized, and racialized.
>
> (2007: 4)

Women's cinema is particularly well placed to take on the dilemmas of transnational cinema that revolve around themes of borders and border identity, displacement, fragmentation, and otherness. Beyond that, however, transnational feminism presents an epistemological shift that establishes the issues of transnational women's cinema as a necessary framework for understanding the dynamics of a transnational imaginary.

Finally, the transnational framework maps feminist practice in a global context without losing sight of the spatial and temporal situatedness of a specific feminist practice. Common threads, alliances, and connectivity are mapped together with disjunctions, differences, and uneven relationships. Whether it is Spivak's concept of "strategic essentialism," referring to the ways in which marginalized groups may temporarily put aside local differences to forge a sense of collective identity for political interests, or Mohanty's notion of "politics of engagement" across cultural differences but with alliances between women, transnational approaches to women's cinema are always mindful of a contentious relationship between globalizing forces aligned with "universal" feminism or the more plural category of "women's cinema," and the "politics of location" which may resist these same forces.

According to Lingzhen Wang, transnational feminism "helps to chart both the linked historical analogies and the different perspectives of disempowered and marginalized groups" (2011: 14). Advancing a similar argument about transnational methodology, White stresses that feminism has been profoundly reshaped by transnational perspectives and realities, and that while this new context intersects with feminists' models of affiliation and connectivity, it should account for historical specificity and differences (politics of location), as well as similarities and affiliation in otherwise diverse and asymmetrical relations. Such "gendered cartographies of knowledge," she contends, have to be attentive to the ways in which "women's works are encountered in relation to each other, to their competing histories and discursive surrounds" and their various constituencies (2015: 19).

Rather than perceiving women's cinema as containing fixed intrinsic and generic values, these new approaches stress a need to engage with women's cinema as historically constituted, specifically situated and existing within a larger, transnational network of women's cinema. Women across geopolitical divides confront different demands and conditions, and the way they engage with historical forces and how they deploy gender to address these forces will vary, requiring that we always keep in mind both the specificity of a context and its relationship to the larger network of world cinema. Finally, studies in women's cinema show that approaching world cinema through paradigms that go beyond national frameworks is a crucial, not just alternative step in moving beyond the nation-oriented imaginary and mapping the nature of the transnationalism of contemporary cinema. Drawing the map of world cinema through the intersection of women's cinema, within and across national borders, is a necessary and important part of understanding the local/global dynamic that steps out of the narrow confines and traditional coordinates of film studies.

In focus 9.6 Women's anthology films: *Breakfast, Lunch, Dinner* (2011)

Made of multiple short films commissioned for a project that centers on a shared, central theme, anthology film is a distinct and ever more visible film form. It presents an interesting test case for transnational methodologies discussed in this book, in that it brings together filmmakers from various contexts and backgrounds and urges us to see and understand their work in relation to each other. Most anthology films produced over the past two decades are transnational projects: they bring together directors from various countries, are co-financed by various transnational agencies, are launched as part of international film festivals, and project a worldview that forges a vision beyond national, regional, and cultural borders.

Quite a few of these are women's anthology films. *Seven Women, Seven Sins* (1986) re-visits the codes of Christian ethics and presents an allegorical critique of the notion of sin and its strategic exclusion of women's subjectivity. *Neke druge priče / Some Other Stories* (2010) brings together filmmakers from five Balkan countries to focus on women's experience of pregnancy. *Ten, Ten* (2008), produced by the International Women's Film Festival in Seoul, portrays the city as a burying ground for women's memories and a tableau that charts their inter-subjectivities. *Erotique* (1994) is a four-pronged negotiation of women's sexuality and the (im)possibility of its representation. Asserting the specificity of their directors' enunciative positions with a mode of address embedded within a global discourse on women's experiences, these anthologies serve as particularly productive examples of transnational women's cinema as discussed in this chapter. From the vantage point of their cultural specificities, accounting for the particularities of their subject positions, these directors address a transnational women's imaginary in a collective film form that calls for new configurations of the restrictive frameworks of national cinema and authorship.

One such anthology film that engages with transnational women's imaginary is the pan-Asian *Breakfast, Lunch, Dinner* (2011), directed by Wang Jing (China), Anocha Suwichakornpong (Thailand), and Kaz Cai (Singapore). Representing women's experiences in three different Asian cultures, the film uses the three meals of a day as the connective tissue for its episodes that explore the complexities of love through different cultural perspectives. Publicized as "three stories of love in three Asian cities,"

(continued)

(continued)

the film uses interesting intratextual linkages between three different cultural contexts, constructing a continuous thread of time between them, where the sharing of meals in separate lives suggests a shared subjectivity and existential disposition.

The film begins in Nanjing with a woman and her boyfriend having breakfast, continues in Bangkok with a girl who skips school to have lunch and watch a movie with her friend, and ends in Singapore with an old woman who reflects on her past over supper. The female lead in each of the shorts is named Mei, and each short film figures in some form the death of the Prime Minister of Pakistan, Benazir Bhutto, the news of which trickles over radio and newspapers.

In the *Breakfast* episode, the radio announcer laments the tragic fate of women, and in *Lunch* a Thai woman wonders if her country will ever have a woman Prime Minister again.

a

b

Figures 9.14a–9.14c Three different settings and versions of the character Mei in a women's anthology film, *Breakfast, Lunch, Dinner* (2011)

This invocation of Bhutto is not without provocation, as it is the death of one of Asia's most prominent public leaders, a woman who led a Muslim country and whose national and global identity stood as an accomplishment for women's struggle against orthodoxy and traditional values. The news of her death serves in the film both as a moment of reflection on the state of women and a recognition that the gender threshold remains a transnational ideal for East Asian women. Another thread of explicit connection between the shorts comes in the form of a question, "Will you marry me?" It is a question that never gets answered, either disrupting the narrative or merely filling up empty moments in a conversation, thus bringing up the notion of romance as well as the futility of framing it within its conventional lexicon.

In Wing Jing's first episode, *Breakfast*, Mei travels by train to visit her boyfriend, who is distant and disinterested in anything except his own desires. While waiting for his roommate to leave the apartment, they have breakfast, a bland affair filled with idle talk, uneasy tension, and increasing disconnect between the couple. Mei, bored by the interaction (and ultimately walking away from it), gazes at the birds in a sanctuary, flashing the only smile in the narrative. "Wish we could be like the birds," she says, "migrate to warmer regions in the cold season," pointing to their trapped corporeality, limited both by imposed desires and the lifeless, cold, and confining spaces of the city of Nanjing. Anocha Suwichakornpong's *Lunch* brings together two teenagers, Mei and her boyfriend, who skip their classes to have lunch and spend an afternoon together. In a more lighthearted tone than *Breakfast*, their conversation about friendship and sexual experiences is carefully controlled by Mei's voice, who seems skeptical and careful not to take on any experience that may define her. In her conversation with the boy, Mei quizzes his assumptions on sexuality while maintaining a cautious distance from a relationship that is purely based on it.

(continued)

(continued)

Kaz Cai's *Dinner*, the most poetic and complex of the three shorts, takes place over three nights as graceful elderly Mei, introduced in the gentle golden light of a park, prepares traditional Otak-Otak, a spicy fish paste wrapped in bread. Each night she sits on a bench facing an uninhabited house built in 1924, with a church wall behind her, and each night, a young male worker from a bakery greets her on his rounds to distribute bread. As Mei fixes her contemplative gaze on the house in front of her, she sees, in moments of magic realism, a young woman on the balcony of the house waiting for someone—possibly a memory of her own youth, or a fantasy of a life she never had. On the third night, Mei's magic-realist gaze brings a young uniformed British naval officer next to her on the bench. Speaking in English, she asks him if he is waiting for someone. Alternating between Mei of 1924, who may have been in love with him, and Mei who speaks as an older woman reflecting on her past, she exists simultaneously in two time frames, bringing together two historical moments of her nation.

The British man inserts the colonial presence of his nation into the narrative, coated with a gesture of love for the native woman. As he proposes to her, the two of them kiss, merging memory and fantasy into a single image. For Cai, the national imaginary of Singapore is impossible to conceive of without the burden of colonial memory and fantasy, pain and pleasure.

It seems that the different subject positions of Mei from all three episodes converge on this final reflective moment on the bench. The intratextual linkages and merging of the female protagonists' subjectivities function not merely as a textual strategy and the connective tissue for the anthology, but they result in the blurring of any directorial stamp that, while still discernible, fades into the background to reveal a more fluid transnational cinematic collaboration and a new way of posing subjectivity that belongs to neither the only-local nor purely-global. The anthology film is thus a particularly cogent articulation of transnationalism in women's cinema. It is risky, no doubt, and perhaps naïve to approach these films as addressing a transnational women's imaginary, as constructing a discourse that appeals to a "universal" women's condition. Yet, the anthology film form suggests that it is possible and in fact essential to recoup a transnational imaginary in women's cinema that forms connections, alliances, and alignments in otherwise diverse texts and enunciations in world cinema.

In her account of the importance of the short film form for women filmmakers in Asia, Olivia Khoo points out that women's anthologies "engage strategies of both national and transnational connection," mindful of local specificities of gendered and sexual identities yet considering regional or transnational solidarities among women filmmakers (2014: 51). Such "minor transnational" filmmaking, as she terms it, is significant in that it both positions the otherwise marginalized local voices in a larger transnational network beyond limited national cinema formations, but also outside the realm of traditional authorship, which is still closely connected to arthouse feature filmmaking. Khoo reminds us that while the privileged cultural value of feature filmmaking marginalizes other forms of production, women filmmakers in Asia are actively working within a range of other, minor forms of production and collaborating transnationally "in political as well as aesthetic terms, from inception and production to circulation, distribution and exhibition" (2014: 51). By establishing connections between women

a

b

Figures 9.15a & 9.15b In a dinner episode of *Breakfast, Lunch, Dinner*, Mei exists simultaneously in two time frames, bringing together two historical moments of her nation

filmmakers and their work, Khoo argues, the notion of female authorship is politicized rather than individualized.

Paying similar attention to the risk of essentialism and a universalizing approach to women's cinema while remaining mindful of the transnational reverberations of women's filmmaking, Spivak (1985) proposes "strategic essentialism" as an analytical frame within which to understand the enunciating positions of women's films. In Spivak's articulation, strategic essentialism as a methodological approach preserves

(continued)

(continued)

both the discontinuities between subjectivities, their dispersal in different discursive engagements, and the commonalities between them, yielding a perspective that can problematize both. Strategic essentialism discloses transnationalism itself as a strategy—both in terms of reading and filmmaking practices, as a mode of authorship and a mode of analysis—that establishes connections and political links among a diverse group of texts and enunciative positions, discovers unity among multiple dispersed voices, and makes visible what are otherwise marginal circuits.

This approach seems built into the very premise of women's anthology films such as *Breakfast, Lunch, Dinner*. Three distinct Asian women filmmakers, three distinct and locally- based episodes, three distinct protagonists and experiences, all aligned with a common subjectivity and a discernible network. As such, it envisions women's cinema as a methodology that retains the importance of the local even as it is consciously positioned in a transnational dynamic and evokes the transnational echoes of women's memory and trauma.

In focus 9.7   Transnational Balkan women directors: Aida Begić's *Djeca/Children of Sarajevo* (2012)

The argument that emerging transnational configurations of women's filmmaking has been reshaping the discourse of world cinema reveals itself in a particularly interesting light in the context of Balkan cinema, one among many small national cinemas that came to prominence on the world stage in the 1990s. A large group of films that emerged in the 1990s and made Balkan cinema visible, however, were not only all made by male directors but presented, without the slightest hint of ambiguity, a hyper-masculine and patriarchal image of a nation, constructed in a thematic and stylistic framework that appealed to international audiences.

After more than a decade of silence, a new generation of filmmakers from former Yugoslav nations with basically no history of women's filmmaking (particularly Bosnia) are bursting onto the scene, achieving recognition at A-list international film festivals and considerable success at home: Maja Weiss, Jasmila Žbanić, Aida Begić, Sonja Prosenc, Marina Andree Škop, Aneta Lesnikovska, Teona Strugar Mitevska, and Andrea Štaka, to name only a few. On the most superficial level, their presence on the international stage fulfills a very significant lack, and serves as a corrective to the 1990s cinematic image of the region that was constructed through an ideological lens of Balkanization, offering a perception of "authenticity" cloaked in a preconceived framework of local style. These films thus provide a crucial reflection on the post-war, transitional reality of the nations in the region. Quite a few scholars discuss how, during the 2000s when this cinema emerged, the changed political and ideological landscape profoundly influences the cinematic landscape (Iordanova, 2001; Longinović, 2005; Pavičić, 2010). As Pavičić explains, the process of political and economic reforms "that is usually called by a blurry, seductive term 'normalization'" was reflected in what he calls "films of normalization," which show a clear rejection of the previous stylistic dominant of self-Balkanization (2010: 44). They tend to deploy realistic, everyday, and often urban settings, characters capable of transformation "who have to surpass traumas and obstacles inherited from the past" and "take an active attitude to problems, trying to sort out a better future for themselves" (Pavičić, 2010: 47). As such, these films implicitly illustrate the dynamics of transitional society and endorse the values of liberal capitalism that define the larger sphere of the EU.

While one could argue that women's films that emerge in this period are undoubtedly an important part of this "cinema of normalization," they also present a unique intervention that goes well beyond correcting the previous stylistic dominant. Transnational in their production background, they also construct a critical transnational imaginary both through their textual and extra-textual practices that negotiates the relationship between a specific local enunciation and its positioning in the transnational sphere, urging us to rethink the processes by which the discourse of the national is integrated into the larger sphere of world cinema. The work of women filmmakers like Jasmila Žbanić and Aida Begić seems to circle precisely around the divide between the postulates of universal feminism and problems posed by specific local conditions. This divide, so crucial to the discourse of transnational feminism, determines their reception as well as their textual politics. The films received a positive reception and were embraced by international audiences because they talked about the specific conditions of Balkan women in universal terms that in many ways addressed and catered to the expectations of women cinema that circulates on a global stage. However, their aesthetic, while commanding the attention of the international gaze, also displaces and questions it, complicating the viewer's ethnographic engagement with the image, and retaining the critical relationship between the locally specific enunciation and the transnational context in which it circulates.

The problem of transnational identity is explicitly mapped onto the question of women's subjectivity in Begić's sophomore feature, *Djeca/Children of Sarajevo*. As an auteur, Begić herself is very much a part of and sustained by the transnational art cinema network and festival circulation: her graduation short *First Death Experience* was selected for the Cinéfondation in 2001, her first feature, *Snijeg/Snow* (2008), won the Critic's Week Grand Prix, and *Djeca/Children of Sarajevo* (2012) was selected for the *Un Certain Regard* competition.

A co-production between Bosnia, Germany, France, and Turkey, *Children* revolves around the 23-year-old Rahima who, having lost her parents in the war, is now committed to keeping her 14-year-old diabetic brother Nedim out of the hands of the state and the orphanage where she herself grew up. They live in her tiny, sparse apartment, where Nedim is forced to spend much of his time outside of school by himself, and is becoming entrenched in a life of full-blown criminal activity, while his older sister works long hours at a local restaurant, trying to make ends meet. Rahima, with a troubled background herself, is determined to protect her family, which proves to be more than a simple challenge. Various tensions, the social stigma that comes with their orphaned status, and Rahima's recent decision to wear a headscarf all exacerbate their situation.

(continued)

(continued)

Children is set in a contemporary Sarajevo that has clearly transitioned from the devastation of the war and become an active participant in the global economy. The Sarajevo party and restaurant scene, music, shops, the pervasive presence of technology in the film (iPhones and videogames, for example), and the new divisions of labor are clear markers in the film of the "Bosnian Dream," a dominant post-war public and political discourse that revolved around the need and ability to reconstruct Bosnia through its tourist potential, foreign investment, the process of privatization, the creation of a free market, an "open city" initiative, and gender and youth empowerment. The fact that the Bosnian pre-war economy was flourishing, with its industry one of the strongest in the region, made this "dream" less dreamy and in fact quite realistic and tangible.

In contrast to this utopian vision, the reality of contemporary Sarajevo revealed in Begić's film is one of a wounded city and devastated economy, and shattered identities, a result of the war and the global economic crisis, made even more so by criminal privatization processes and corrupt government schemes. The film offers only brief and distant flashes of villas, fancy cars, government officials, and the upscale space of the City Opera restaurant where Rahima works. Its spaces exist in stark contrast to this flashy surface, whether it is the underground, stuffy space of the restaurant kitchen, the dark, destroyed alleys covered with graffiti, or the modest and barely functioning apartment where Rahima and her brother live. This is Sarajevo where war is not a matter of traumatic memory, a matter of a repressed past, but something that still defines the present-day reality. The amateur home video footage of the war that Begić intersperses with the present action is not a mark of the past that still haunts the present, but rather serves as a bridge or an interpretive frame through which to understand the present. The woozy hand-held camera that characterizes these home videos is not unlike Begić's shaky hand-held camera that persistently follows Rahima behind her shoulder. With a Blair Witch-like effect, it constructs the space as not only

a

Figures 9.16a–9.16c Aida Begić's *Children of Sarajevo* (2012). The film's dark, underground spaces and destroyed alleys covered with graffiti construct the cinematic space as unstable and threatening

claustrophobic but unstable and threatening, with a constant sense of the unknown lurking just beyond the tightly constructed frame.

One of the most pronounced features of the film is its soundscape, which transforms everyday urban sounds—airplanes, clattering pans, vacuum cleaner, creaking water pipes, hammering, and drilling—into the sounds and signifiers of war. The fireworks that the teenagers throw in the run-up to New Year's Eve sound like bomb explosions, the clanging and screeching of the construction work in the neighboring apartment

(continued)

(continued)

recalls the arrival of the tank, and the vacuum cleaner echoes the bombing raid alarm. Both Begić's visual technique and the use of sound endow everyday domestic objects with an intangible sinister quality, and result in an alienation and disorientation where familiar territory becomes unsettled and unknown.

The persistent tracking shots that survey Rahima's movement through Sarajevo's landscape establish a physical setting and referential world only to overcome it by charting an inner movement, an embodied knowledge of trauma and displacement, a kind of emotional cartography that is simultaneously bonded to the real space and sensitive to the inner world of affect. We can see this style as one that aligns with "new realism" described sometimes as phenomenological realism, sensory realism, or the "post-photographic" (Elsaesser, 2009), an aesthetic that is very much a part of a larger trend in world cinema and can be seen in films by Béla Tarr, Carlos Reygadas, Apichatpong Weerasethakul, or Kelly Reichardt. Begić's aesthetic connects with this larger trend, yet establishes it as a both locally specific and grounded in female subjectivity.

For the main character, Rahima, her successful navigation through this ambiguous territory is enabled by the process of labor, which assumes a paradoxical function in the film. Rahima, in many ways a pregnant example of the relationship between domestic household labor and wage labor in a capitalist society, is defined by financial and emotional economies. Not only her domestic and professional labor, but also every minute bodily gesture, is defined by movement, purpose, and a sense of production. We never see her idle or engaging in "fun" or leisurely activities. Despite her constant movement between different activities in public and private spaces, these spaces become homogeneous and unified through her perpetually engaged and moving bodily presence. Begić's camera, serving as an extension of Rahima's body and committed to her point of view, only reinforces this role of labor as it echoes her every move with a restless, always-on-the-go ethos.

Rahima's various forms of labor mark her participation in and bondage to the global economy, and it is labor—according to the Marxist dictum—that binds her and alienates her as a subject both from her personal life and from the engagement in the political discourse. However, the film also inverts this dictum and establishes labor as something that liberates her (from life) and is key to the construction of her agency. In a scene that seems almost out of place in a narrative, which is also the only scene where she explicitly expresses her subjectivity as a woman, a man in a car stops her to ask for directions to the beach and invites her to join him. She replies, "Sorry, I forgot my parasol." When he still insists after she explains she has to go to work, she asserts that "work liberates me from life." The answer, rather than directly addressing the man's question and his invitation, serves as an enunciation of the film's discursive position on the function of labor and production. If work is something that marks the erasure of her subjectivity, it is also formative of it, essential to her self-recognition and self-definition.

Tied to this enunciation, Rahima's headscarf serves not so much to signify her Muslim identity, but becomes in the film a material embodiment of the paradox of identity that mediates the dynamic between the local and global, the individual and universal. Rahima's decision to start wearing a headscarf gives rise to numerous tensions

Figures 9.17a & 9.17b "Work liberates me from life," says the protagonist Rahima, asserting labor as both key to her agency and marking her bondage to the global economy

in the film, and even her closest friends, family members, and co-workers have a difficult time accepting and understanding it. Her boss remarks, "Put some make-up on. Just because you're covered doesn't mean you're dead." Her brother, after being bullied at school, angrily accuses her that "no one messed with me until you started wearing a headscarf." Even her best friend deems it a gesture that has nothing to do with "finding faith," somewhere between too radical and unnecessary. The headscarf becomes in the film a sign of her subjectivity that is both singular and bonded to the wider context. It is a marker of a home-grown practice and religion that finds itself redrawn and

(continued)

(continued)

deemed threatening by the outside Islamic forces. At the same time, it serves as a material expression of her agency that resists being coopted by the discourses that define it. Fully aware of the narrow and ambivalent political ramifications of wearing a headscarf, Rahima insists on wearing it, yet dismisses the gesture as purely personal, merely something that "covers her crooked ears." Rahima wears it, yet never *just* wears it. She, and the camera with her, caresses it, keeps readjusting it, touches it, obsessively, as if to affirm and reaffirm its specific materiality while acknowledging its wider significance.

a

b

Figures 9.18a & 9.18b Rahima's dream, where she chases a perpetually-out-of-range cloaked figure with a mirror face, recalls Maya Deren and Alexander Hammid's *Meshes of the Afternoon* (1946), aligning the film with, as well as problematizing its position in, the politics of women's cinema

The paradox and inner conflict evoked by the headscarf is most present in a dream sequence that directly aligns the film and its expression of female subjectivity to Maya Deren and Alexander Hammid's iconic *Meshes of the Afternoon* (1946), with Rahima chasing a perpetually-out-of-range cloaked figure with a mirror face. The hyper-signification that characterizes the dream establishes the headscarf as a fetishistic object, one that both positions Begić's voice within the larger history and politics of feminist cinema, and one that elicits a very specific personal and cultural biography. In a world where all other objects, as well as bodies, become deracinated and transformed into a transnational commodity, where global movements of capital and culture mutate the shifts between commodity and singularity, the scarf becomes a sign that cannot be reducible to exchange even as it evokes it. It is at once an object that encodes social history, an object that works as a repository of culture and memory threatened to be erased in the global economy, but also one that is highly personal, with a power to release meaning that is specific, individual, and locally situated.

Rahima in this way functions as a stand-in for Begić and her subjectivity as a woman auteur, a Bosnian woman filmmaker whose presence on the map of world cinema is formed both by the singularity of female authorship as well as its inherently transnational nature, its participation in the transnational economy that defines the new cinematic landscape. Working in a country where most cultural institutions are destroyed and the annual film budget is $1.5 million (including features, documentary, and short films), this dynamic of transnational imaginary is revealed as essential to her process of production.

Activity 9.1

Consult Iain Robert Smith and Constantine Verevis's book, *Transnational Film Remakes*. Watch one such remake (*The Girl with a Dragon Tattoo*, or *Oldboy*) and consider the various ways in which film adaptation works or does not work across cultural borders. What elements remain the same, which ones are simply transposed, and which ones do not translate? To what extent does a remake engage in the process of "deculturalization," discussed in the case of *Babel*?

Activity 9.2

Consider the example of a famous Danish director, Lars von Trier. Based in Denmark, he is known for his fear of flying and reluctance to travel, yet most of his films are seen as profoundly transnational. Watch and research two of his more recent films (*Dancer in the Dark*, *Dogville*, or *Melancholia*) and try to identify in his films all the various dimensions of transnationalism discussed in the chapter.

Activity 9.3

Study a film that revolves around the condition of postcoloniality: for example, Cameroon-born French director Claire Denis's *Chocolat* (1988) and *White Material* (2009), Mauritius-born and Paris-based filmmaker Abderrahmane Sissako's *Bamako* (2006), Senegalese Ousmane Sembène's *Xala* (1975), or Filipino director Kidlat Tahimik's *Perfumed Nightmare* (1977). How do these films approach the issue of postcolonial identity? How do they construct the relationship between the colonial past and postcolonial present? What do they say about the relationship between the colonizer and the colonized?

Activity 9.4

Compare two examples of diasporic films from Europe, one made by a diasporic filmmaker (for example, Fatih Akin's *The Edge of Heaven*) and one made by a film-maker not considered migratory but dealing with diasporic and migrant issues (for example, Aki Kaurismäki's *Le Havre*, or the Dardenne brothers' *La Promesse/The Promise*). Can you discern differences in the way they approach the issues of the Other, identity, migration, or diaspora?

Activity 9.5

Gurinder Chadha's *Bend It Like Beckham* (2002) was a breakout British hit and became one of the most celebrated examples of diasporic cinema. Watch the film, and consider how it positions the relationship between the first-generation diaspora (parents) and second-generation diaspora (children). What are the primary concerns for one, and how are those concerns different for the other? How does the film mediate between the two? In what ways do gender and class inform diasporic identities in the film?

Activity 9.6

Explore the website of Women Make Movies (www.wmm.com), one of the most important feminist media arts organizations, based in New York. What latest news can you find about the status of women in the industry? What are the most surprising facts you can find, and why do you find them surprising? Check its catalogue, especially the new releases. What countries are represented? What kinds of films are represented?

Activity 9.7

Check the website of Films de Femmes, the international film festival in Creteil, which is the longest-running film festival of women's cinema. Explore its competition program and winners for the last three years. Do you recognize any of the filmmakers? Explore their profiles and the circulation/distribution of their films.

Activity 9.8

Identify the women filmmakers in your country or region (or any country whose industry you may be interested in learning about), both in the mainstream and art cinema and independent sectors. Explore their careers and their body of work. How does their visibility at home compare to their international reputation? What does their work reveal about the representation of women in the film industry of the country?

Activity 9.9

Explore a career of a woman director working in the mainstream, such as Kathryn Bigelow or Nora Ephron. Watch at least two of their films, and read some articles on their work. What are the advantages or disadvantages of considering their work under the umbrella of "women's cinema"? How does their work inform or revise the contentious issue discussed in this chapter concerning the relationship between mainstream, entertainment cinema and women's cinema? How do you think these directors would defend—or not defend—their position as women auteurs?

Activity 9.10

Watch Ana Lily Amirpour's debut feature film *A Girl Walks Home Alone at Night* (2014), which premiered at the Sundance Film Festival and was considered one of the best independent films of 2014. Made by an American Iranian woman filmmaker, and tagged as an "Iranian vampire western," the film defies various kinds of boundaries and can be seen as a rich case study to explore the intersections between national, transnational, diasporic, and women's cinema, as well as the intersections between art and genre/commercial cinema. How does your understanding of the film change whether you see it through transnational, diasporic, or women's cinema frameworks?

Notes

1 "The cross-border looking relations" is a term used by Robert Stam and Ella Shohat in "Transnationalizing Comparison: The Uses and Abuses of Cross-Cultural Analogy," *New Literary History* 40 (2009): 474.

2 For a more extensive discussion on the critical and pedagogical implications of the concept of transnational, see Katarzyna Marciniak and Bruce Bennett, *Teaching Transnational Cinema: Politics and Pedagogy*, New York, NY: Routledge, 2016.

3 A transnational framework is deployed in some way or other in most studies of the film, but that *Crouching Tiger* is "a major case of transnational cinema" is argued, among others, by Sheldon Lu in *Chinese Language Film: Historiography, Poetics, Politics*, University of Hawaii Press, 2004.

4 Among many other prestigious awards, the film broke records at the Academy Awards, where it was nominated in ten categories and became the first Chinese-language film to be nominated for Best Picture.

5 The film was co-produced by Asia Union Film & Entertainment and China Film Co-Production Corporation in Mainland China; Columbia Pictures, Sony Pictures Classics, and Good Machine (James Schamus' production company) in the US; EDKO Film in Hong Kong; and Zoom Hunt International Productions and United China Vision in Taiwan.

6 See, for example, Kenneth Chan, 2009. Here, Chan explains that audience response to the film in Mainland China was a lot more reserved than elsewhere in the region. The main complaints had to do with reappropriation of *wuxia pian*, considered by most a sacrosanct genre; the actors' lack of real martial arts skills; inaccurate representation of Chinese history, costumes, and setting; and questionable pronunciations, among other things.

7 After winning the main national film award in Mexico, the Ariel, *Amores perros* was nominated for an Oscar, and received awards at the Cannes, Tokyo, Chicago, São Paulo, and Edinburgh film festivals.

8 "Network narrative" is a term introduced by David Bordwell for multi-narrative, multi-protagonist films that trace the fragmented experiences of several characters through colliding, intersecting stories. Some examples discussed by Bordwell are Robert Altman's *Short Cuts* (1993), Michael Haneke's *71 Fragments of a Chronology of Chance* (1994), Quentin Tarantino's *Pulp Fiction* (1994), or Wong Kar-wai's *Chunking Express* (1994). Some older examples that are considered historical antecedents of this form would include Minoru Murata's *Souls on the Road* (1921), Akira Kurosawa's *Rashomon* (1950), Kenji Mizoguchi's *Street of Shame* (1956), or Krzysztof Kieślowski's *Dekalog* (1989). See Bordwell, 2016.

9 For a discussion of this narrative form, see for example Bordwell, 2016; Kerr, 2010, pp. 37–51; and Everett, 2005, pp. 159–171.

10 France has traditionally had gender equality in film production, while many Nordic countries have recently tried to achieve it by introducing gender equity quotas. According to Anna Server of the Swedish Film Institute, "In 2014 we had 50 percent female directors, 55 percent female scriptwriters and 65 percent female producers, but in the past three, we have had 43 percent female directors, 49 percent scriptwriters and 53 percent producers. Women creatives also take home 69 percent of the trophies at film awards ceremonies in Sweden." *Agnes Film*, "Supporting Women and Feminist Filmmaking" http://agnesfilms.com/reviews/reviews-2/women-honored-at-the-68th-cannes-film-festival; for women's representation in the BRICS countries, see *Gender Equality, Heritage and Creativity*, UNESCO, 2014.

11 The exception to this was 2013, when half the films in the festival's dramatic section were directed by women.

Further reading, transnational cinema

Chung, Hye Seung & David Scott Diffrient (2015). *Movie Migrations: Transnational Genre Flows and South Korean Cinema*. New Brunswick, NJ: Rutgers University Press.

Đurovićova, Nataša & Kathleen Newman (eds). (2010). *World Cinema, Transnational Perspectives*. New York, NY: Routledge.

Khoo, Olivia, Belinda Smaill, & Audrey Yue (eds). (2013). *Transnational Australian Cinema: Ethics in the Asian Diasporas*. Lanham, MD: Lexington Books.

Lu, Hsiao-peng & Sheldon H. Lu (eds). (1997). *Transnational Chinese Cinema: Identity, Nationhood, Gender*. Honolulu, HI: University of Hawaii Press.

Prime, Rebecca (ed). (2015). *Cinematic Homecomings: Exile and Return in Transnational Cinema*. New York, NY: Bloomsbury.

Rivi, Luisa. (2007). *European Cinema After 1989: Cultural Identity and Transnational Production*. New York, NY: Palgrave Macmillan.

Smith, Iain Robert & Constantine Verevis (eds). (2017). *Transnational Film Remakes*. Edinburgh: Edinburgh University Press.

Further reading, diasporic cinema

Khoo, Olivia, Belinda Smaill, & Audrey Yue (eds). (2013). *Transnational Australian Cinema: Ethics in the Asian Diaspora*. Lanham, MD: Lexington Books.

Marks, Laura. (2000). *The Skin of the Film: Intercultural Cinema, Embodiment, and the Senses*. Durham, NC: Duke University Press.

Martin, Michael T. (1996). *Cinemas of the Black Diaspora: Diversity, Dependence, and Oppositionality*. Detroit, MI: Wayne State University Press.

Further reading, women's cinema

Chandra, Mohanty. (2003). *Feminism Without Borders*. Durham, NC: Duke University Press.

de Lauretis, Teresa. (1984). *Alice Doesn't: Feminism, Semiotics, Cinema*. Bloomington, IN: Indiana University Press.

Gledhill, Christine & Julia Knight (eds). (2015). *Doing Women's Film History: Reframing Cinemas, Past and Future*. Urbana, IL: University of Illinois Press.

Grewal, Inderpal & Caren Kaplan (eds). (1994). *Scattered Hegemonies: Postmodernity and Transnational Feminist Practices*. Minneapolis, MN: University of Minnesota Press.

Kaplan, Caren, Norma Alarcon, & Minoo Moallem (eds). (1999). *Between Woman and Nation: Nationalisms, Transnational Feminisms, and the State*. Durham, NC: Duke University Press.

Kaplan, E. Ann (ed). (2008). *Looking for the Other: Feminism, Film, and the Imperial Gaze*. New York, NY: New York University Press.

Mayne, Judith. (1990). *The Woman at the Keyhole: Feminism and Women's Cinema*. Bloomington, IN: Indiana University Press.

Shohat, Ella. (1997). "Post-Third-Worldist Culture: Gender, Nation, and the Cinema." In Jacqui Alexander & Chandra Mohanty (eds), *Feminist Genealogies, Colonial Legacies, Democratic Futures*. New York, NY: Routledge, pp. 183–212.

Shohat, Ella. (2006). *Taboo Memories, Diasporic Voices*. Durham: NC: Duke University Press.

Trinh, T. Minh-ha. (1989). *Woman, Native, Other: Writing Postcoloniality and Feminism*. Bloomington, IN: Indiana University Press.

Bibliography

Andrew, Dudley. (2013). "Is Cinema Contagious? Transnationalism and the Case of Korea." *Cinema & Cie* 1, pp. 15–26.

Augé, Marc. (2009). *Non-Places: An Introduction to Supermodernity*. Trans. John Howe. New York, NY: Verso.

Ballesteros, Isolina. (2015). *Immigration Cinema in the New Europe*. Chicago, IL: University of Chicago Press.

Bergen-Aurand, Brian, Mary Mazzilli, & Hee Wai-Siam (eds). (2015). *Transnational Chinese Cinema: Corporeality, Desire, and Ethics of Failure*. London: Bridge Publications.

Berghahn, Daniela & Claudia Sternberg (eds). (2010). *European Cinema in Motion: Migrant, Diasporic Film in Contemporary Europe*. New York, NY: Palgrave Macmillan.

Bhabha, Homi. (1990). *Nation and Narration*. New York, NY: Routledge.

Bordwell, David. (2016). *The Way Hollywood Tells It: Story and Style in Modern Movies*. Los Angeles, CA: University of California Press.

Brah, Avtar. (2005). *Cartographies of Diaspora: Contesting Identities*. New York, NY: Routledge.

Butler, Alison. (2002). *Women's Cinema: The Contested Screen*. New York, NY: Wallflower Press.

Chan, Kenneth. (2009). *Remade in Hollywood: The Global Chinese Presence in Transnational Cinema*. Hong Kong: Hong Kong University Press.

de Lauretis, Teresa. (1987). "Rethinking Women's Cinema: Aesthetics and Feminist Theory." In *Technologies of Gender: Essays on Theory, Film, and Fiction*. Bloomington, IN: Indiana University Press, pp. 127–158.

Desai, Jigna. (2006). "Bollywood Abroad: South Asian Diasporic Cosmopolitanism and Indian Cinema." In Gita Rejan & Shailja Sharma (eds), *New Cosmopolitanisms: South Asians in the US*. Los Angeles, CA: Stanford University Press, pp. 115–137.

Desai, Jigna. (2008). "Bollywood, USA: Diasporas, Nations and the State of Cinema." In Susan Koshy & Rajagopalan Radhakrishnan (eds), *Transnational South Asians: The Making of a Neo-Diaspora*. London: Oxford University Press, pp. 345–367.

Desai, Jigna. (2013). "The Scale of Diasporic Cinema: Negotiating National and Transnational Cultural Citizenship." In K. Moti Gokulsing & Wimal Dissanayake (eds), *Routledge Handbook of Indian Cinemas*. New York, NY: Routledge, pp. 207–218.

D'Lugo, Marvin. (2012). "*Amores Perros/Love's a Bitch*." In Alberto Elena & Marina Diaz Lopez (eds), *The Cinema of Latin America*. New York, NY: Columbia University Press, pp. 221–230.

Dwivedi, Om Prakash. (2014). "Introducing the New Indian Diaspora." In Om Prakash Dwivedi (ed), *Tracing the New Indian Diaspora*. New York, NY: Rodopi, pp. x–xiii.

Elena, Alberto & Marina Diaz Lopez (eds). (2012). *The Cinema of Latin America*. New York, NY: Columbia University Press.

Elsaesser, Thomas. (2005). *European Cinema: Face to Face with Hollywood*. Amsterdam: Amsterdam University Press.

Elsaesser, Thomas. (2009). "World Cinema: Realism, Evidence, Presence." In Lúcia Nagib & Cecilia Mello (eds), *Realism and the Audiovisual Media*. New York, NY: Palgrave Macmillan, pp. 3–19.

Esfandiary, Shahab. (2012). *Iranian Cinema and Globalization: National, Transnational, and Islamic Dimensions*. Chicago, IL: University of Chicago Press.

Everett, Wendy. (2005). "Fractal Films and the Architecture of Complexity." *Studies in European Cinema* 2(3), pp. 159–171.

Ezra, Elizabeth & Terry Rowden. (2006). "General Introduction: What Is Transnational Cinema?" In Elizabeth Ezra & Terry Rowden (ed), *Transnational Cinema: The Film Reader*. London: Routledge, pp. 1–12.

Feng, Peter X. (2002). "Being Chinese American, Becoming Asian American: Chan Is Missing." In Peter X. Feng (ed), *Screening Asian Americans*. New Brunswick, NJ: Rutgers University Press, pp. 185–216.

Hall, Stuart, Chas Critcher, Tony Jefferson, John Clark, & Brian Roberts. (1978). *Policing the Crisis: Mugging, the State, and Law and Order*. London: Macmillan.

Higbee, Will & Song Hwee Lim. (2010). "Concepts of Transnational Cinema: Towards a Critical Transnationalism in Film." *Transnational Cinema* 1(1), pp. 7–21.

Higgins, Charlotte. (2015). "Cannes Contender Jane Campion Gives Clarion Call to Women Directors." *The Guardian* (May 15). Available at: www.theguardian.com/film/2009/may/15/jane-campion-cannes-film-festival. Accessed March 1, 2017.

Iordanova, Dina. (2001). *Cinema of Flames: Balkan Film, Culture and the Media*. London: British Film Institute.

Iordanova, Dina. (2010). "Migration and Cinematic Process in Post-Cold War Europe." In Daniela Berghahn & Claudia Sternberg (eds), *European Cinema in Motion: Migrant, Diasporic Film in Contemporary Europe*. New York, NY: Palgrave Macmillan, pp. 50–75.

Jäckel, Ann. (2010). "State and Other Funding for Migrant, Diasporic and World Cinemas in Europe." In Daniela Berghahn & Claudia Sternberg (eds), *European Cinema in Motion: Migrant, Diasporic Film in Contemporary Europe*. New York, NY: Palgrave Macmillan, pp. 76–96.

Johnston, Claire. (1973). "Women's Cinema as Counter Cinema." In Claire Johnston (ed), *Notes on Women's Cinema*. London: Society for Education in Film and Television.

Kerr, Paul. (2010). "*Babel's* Networked Narrative: Packaging a Globalized Art Cinema." *Transnational Cinema* 1(1), pp. 37–51.

Khoo, Olivia. (2014). "The Minor Transnationalism of Queer Asian Cinema: Female Authorship and the Short Film Format." *Camera Obscura* 84, pp. 33–57.

Klein, Christina. (2004). "*Crouching Tiger, Hidden Dragon*: A Diasporic Reading," *Cinema Journal* 43(4), pp. 18–42.

Lim, Song Hwee. (2011). "Six Chinese Cinemas in Search of a Historiography." In Song Hwee-Lim & Julian Ward (eds), *The Chinese Cinema Book*. London: Palgrave Macmillan, pp. 35–46.

Lim, Song Hwee. (2012). "Speaking in Tongues: Ang Lee, Accented Cinema, Hollywood." In Lúcia Nagib & Rajinder Dudrah (eds), *Theorizing World Cinema*. New York, NY: I.B. Tauris, pp. 129–144.

Longinović, Tomislav. (2005). "Playing the Western Eye: Balkan Masculinity and Post Yugoslav War Cinema." In Anikó Imre (ed), *Eastern European Cinema*. New York, NY: Routledge, pp. 35–47.

Loshitzky, Yosefa. (2010). *Screening Strangers: Migration and Diaspora in Contemporary European Cinema*. Bloomington, IN: Indiana University Press.

Lu, Sheldon. (1997). *Transnational Chinese Cinemas: Identity, Nationhood, Gender*. Honolulu, HI: University of Hawaii Press.

Lu, Sheldon. (2004). *Chinese Language Film: Historiography, Poetics, Politics*. Honolulu, HI: University of Hawaii Press.

Marchetti, Gina. (2012). *The Chinese Diaspora on American Screens: Race, Sex, and Cinema*. Philadelphia, PA: Temple University Press.

Marciniak, Katarzyna & Bruce Bennett (eds). (2016). *Teaching Transnational Cinema: Politics and Pedagogy*. New York, NY: Routledge.

Marciniak, Katarzyna, Anikó Imre, & Áine O'Healy (eds). (2007). *Transnational Feminism in Film and Media*. New York, NY: Palgrave Macmillan.

Mercer, Kobena (ed). (1987). *Black Film, British Cinema*. London: Institute of Contemporary Arts.

Mulvey, Laura. (1975). "Visual Pleasure and Narrative Cinema." *Screen* 16(3), pp. 6–18.

Naficy, Hamid. (2001). *An Accented Cinema: Exilic and Diasporic Filmmaking*. New Brunswick, NJ: Princeton University Press.

Naficy, Hamid. (2010). "Multiplicity and Multiplexing in Today's Cinema: Diasporic Cinema, Art Cinema, and Mainstream Cinema." *Journal of Media Practice* 11(1), pp. 11–20.

Pavičić, Jurica. (2010). "Cinema of Normalization: Changes of Stylistic Model in Post-Yugoslav Cinema after the 1990s." *Studies in Eastern European Cinema* 1(1), pp. 43–56.

Pidduck, Julianne. (2006). "The Transnational Cinema of Ang Lee." In Dimitris Eleftheriotis & Gary Needham (eds), *Asian Cinemas: A Reader and Guide*. Honolulu, HI: University of Hawaii Press, pp. 393–405.

Said, Edward. (1978). *Orientalism*. London: Vintage.

Shaw, Deborah. (2011). "*Babel* and the Global Hollywood Gaze." *Situations: Project of the Radical Imagination* 4(1), pp. 11–31.

Shaw, Deborah. (2013). *The Three Amigos: The Transnational Filmmaking of Guillermo del Toro, Alejandro González Iñárritu, and Alfonso Cuarón*. Manchester: Manchester University Press.

Smith, Paul Julian. (2012). "Transnational Cinemas: The Cases of Mexico, Argentina and Brazil." In Lúcia Nagib & Rajinder Dudrah (eds), *Theorizing World Cinema*. New York, NY: I.B. Tauris, pp. 61–77.

Spivak, Gayatri Chakravorty. (1985). "Subaltern Studies: Deconstructing Historiography." In Donna Landry & Gerald Maclean (eds), *The Spivak Reader*. New York, NY: Routledge (1996), pp. 203–236.

Spivak, Gayatri Chakravorty. (1988). "Can the Subaltern Speak?" In Cary Nelson & Lawrence Grossberg (eds), *Marxism and the Interpretation of Culture*. Chicago, IL: University of Illinois Press, pp. 271–315.

Stam, Robert. (2007). "Third World and Postcolonial Cinema." In Pam Cook (ed), *The Cinema Book*, 3rd edn. London: British Film Institute, pp. 97–104.

Stam, Robert & Ella Shohat. (2009). "Transnationalizing Comparison: The Uses and Abuses of Cross-Cultural Analogy." *New Literary History* 40(3), pp. 473–499.

Wang, Lingzhen (ed). (2011). *Chinese Women's Cinema: Transnational Context*. New York, NY: Columbia University Press.

White, Patricia. (2015). *Women's Cinema, World Cinema: Projecting Contemporary Feminisms*. Durham, NC: Duke University Press.

Zhang, Yingjin. (2002). *Screening China: Critical Interventions, Cinematic Reconfigurations, and the Transnational Imaginary in Contemporary Chinese Cinema*. Michigan, IL: Michigan Center for Chinese Studies.

Ziheng, Alex Jiao. (2015). "The Global Connectivity of *Life of Pi*." Blog post. Available at: www.academia.edu/4463869/The_Global_Connectivity_of_Life_of_Pi. Accessed August 20, 2015.

10 Polyvalent world cinema

James Cameron's *Avatar* (2009) remains one of Hollywood's most successful blockbusters, perceived as a game-changer in cinematic history. A spectacular science-fiction adventure, the film quickly achieved global popularity, drew the attention of diverse audiences, and generated an endless variety of interpretations. The film was released in a range of formats and screens, from IMAX to 3D. It gained over $2 billion in its first eight weeks, and for quite some time it was also one of the most pirated Hollywood productions. It is a test case of a film whose impressive cinematic wizardry and state-of-the-art 3D technology created diverse responses from around the world, opening numerous, specifically situated interpretive worlds. Politicians, opinion writers, broadcasters, video artists, and reviewers all chimed in, offering distinct positions on the film's narrative. Academic scholarship, too, created a labyrinthine discourse on analyses and meta-analyses of the film's reception.

A fantasy tale at its best, the centerpiece of Cameron's film is the alien world of the evolved species of the Na'vi—the tall, blue-skinned humanoids inhabiting the planet Pandora. American technological enterprise lands on the planet to harness a vital resource, a mineral that is the key to solving an energy crisis on Earth. In an attempt to infiltrate the natives' world, they produce Na'vi–human hybrids called avatars. *Avatar*'s hero is Jake, a paraplegic marine who is given the chance to walk again if he proves successful in his mission to convince the Na'vi people to relocate their home. After living with them, Jake falls in love with the chief's daughter, Neytiri. Soon, Jake's divided loyalties—between Neytiri's people and his own bosses—become apparent. Having seen the Na'vi world from within, Jake motivates them to stage a rebellion against the aggressors to reclaim their land and resources.

The film charged nearly every space on the political spectrum. The political right, particularly in the US, considered the film to be an affront to the values of the nation and its primogenial right to establish justice outside of national borders. Its faintly couched critique of the American military might, particularly the aggressive moves abroad after the 1990s, the uncomplicated caricature of the greed of the American corporate world, and the destructiveness of technological advances, struck many as anti-American. Added to this, the blatant environmental message of the film, its sharp juxtaposition of the natives' purity with the corruption of American power, stoked the mantras often chanted by nature-devotees on the left and derided by the right. On the other side of the spectrum, the political left launched a multipronged attack on the film, seeing it as a testament to corporate capitalism, the destruction of the environment, and utter disregard for indigenous cultures and resources in other parts of the universe. The film's aggressive posture wrapped in the cloak of cinematic and technological marvel laid bare the charge of colonialism. Annalee Newitz (2009) accused the film of "imaginatively revisiting the crime scene of white America's foundational act of genocide." *New York Times* columnist David Brooks (2010) critiqued the film's "racial fantasy" and cultural imperialism that valorizes the purity of native lives while posturing the white protagonist as a prototypical "White Messiah" who falls for the simple exoticness of the natives, masters their way of life, raises his consciousness, and single-handedly triggers a rebellion against the corrupt corporations.

Despite or precisely because of this context of cultural imperialism, the film not only affirmed the dominant capitalist ideology, but also captured "the resistant imagination from below" (Loshitzky, 2012: 153). The rebellion of the native Na'vi to protect their resources struck a strong chord with millions around the world, affirming their beliefs that aggressive Western powers needed a rebuke of this kind. The narrative trajectory of the film offered a relief in favor of environmental protection, the preservation of native cultures, and the urgency of rebellion against corporate invaders. The film's narrative movement toward a successful rebellion of the Na'vi galvanized the imagination of oppressed and dispossessed groups who saw in the film a reflection of their own struggles. Bolivia's President Evo Morales, himself a member of the country's indigenous Aymara community, and a farmer and labor activist, praised the film for its "profound show of resistance to capitalism and the struggle for the defense of nature" (Huffington Post, 2010). In Palestine, the film mobilized people for action, including some Israeli–Jewish groups who protested against the Wall in the West Bank. Dressed up as blue-skinned Na'vi characters from the film, Palestinian activists, peasants, and resistance members marched in a nonviolent protest.

They cherished in their minds the images of a homeland lush with resources, blessed by the riches of nature, and showered by the elements—visions of home that resonated with

Figure 10.1 Palestinian protesters in the West Bank, dressed as the blue Na'vi from *Avatar* to protest against the Israeli occupation and the construction of a barrier in the town of Bil'in near Ramallah. Image courtesy of AFP/Stringer

their collective imagination of the Palestinian landscape prior to Zionist settlement, and connected its pillage to their history of dispossession and discrimination. Yosefa Loshitzky (2012) notes that the Palestinian adoption and appropriation of the film, particularly the identification of people who live in arid land with the lush, resource-rich, Edenic environment of Pandora, makes for a potent example of a locally situated and political reading of a global Hollywood blockbuster, so often derided for its conformist, imperialist views.

In a telling instance of the power and subversive potential of the film, Chinese authorities made a decision to limit the exhibition of it to select theaters, presumably to make room for films from its own industry. The film's reputation likely preceded its release and fueled the Chinese government's anxiety over its own brutal practices of property development and evictions (Macartney, 2010; Jenkins, 2010a). Biologists heaped praise on the film for the wonderment it caused among audiences about endless biodiversity. Religious debates brought accusations of pantheism, animism, and paganism. Slavoj Žižek (2010) launched a strong attack from the left, calling the film a fantasy perpetuating the cruel realities of environmental exploitation, playing out a cathartic relationship to the real conditions of suffering, and in turn enabling ignorance even from the most socially conscious left. Henry Jenkins (2010b) reported that among younger audiences, *Avatar* provided fuel to imaginative activities on the Internet and local media. Accounts of protests against corporate-state power inspired by the film persisted for quite some time, making the film a unique case of a Hollywood blockbuster with global ambitions that generated endless local and politically inflected responses from around the world.

Academic scholars engaged in debates and analyses of specific features of the film that aroused diverse torrents of responses. Thomas Elsaesser (2011) attributes the power of the film to its textual dexterity in combining an affirmation of the practice with its critique; the reality and its erasure; the claim to truth and its denial. He sees the film as a perfect emblem of Hollywood's tendency to coopt multiple responses to its films as a strategy to maintain global dominance and appeal. For Catherine Grant (2010), *Avatar* is "*polysemic text par excellence*," a deft integration of allegories on multiple levels, engaging the viewer into a reflexive posture of presenting a problem and providing a solution to it. The film invites the viewer into allusions of a world on the screen, which in turn offers another world that is "kept out of view," a world of interpretations. The fecundity of *Avatar*'s numerous interpretations arises from the allegorical readings it produces among readers.

The vibrant debates surrounding *Avatar* disclose fundamental principles of reception and understanding of films in world cinema. As films travel across cultural spaces and borders, they are charged with belief systems, conditions of reception, and imperatives of the moment, whether political, ethical, or cultural. Differentiated meanings of films arise from a heuristic mix of forces at work, shaping the popularity and values of their construction. Audiences in different places on the map reject films, welcome them with jubilation, or criticize them with fervor. Like literature, poetry, art, and language, each film is a traveling signifier in search of signification. In addition, the unparalleled universe of significations created by Cameron's blockbuster film is unique for its visibility in world cinema. The propulsive power of Hollywood's machine, accelerated by the technological feats of the film, make *Avatar* a paradigm case of popularity in world cinema, a sign typifying the global presence of film and the possible diversity of interpretations across the map. Scholars turn their attention to the textual mechanics of the film to trace the genesis of critical energy that generated such a wide spectrum of responses and interpretations.

This attention needs to be combined with an awareness, however, that numerous films are deprived of such critical attention as they circulate in relatively limited spheres and with the complex taxonomy of textual constructions. The enormous power of the Hollywood machine that fueled *Avatar*'s global presence eludes most films of world cinema. Yet, the global popularity of *Avatar* only confirms an axiom of film studies: each film is a polysemic text capable of eliciting diverse responses across borders. To accept the reality of world cinema is also to accept the capacity of films to create multiple interpretive worlds.

The premise of world cinema, similar to that of world literature and comparative literature, is that we read texts produced outside of our own world and energize the discourse with the multiplicity of our efforts. Film studies already recognizes this, from reception to fan culture studies. In this book, we advocate the concept of a cinematic center with an essential feature—a tradition of scholarship of reading images embedded in a specific context. We maintain that Western Anglo-American scholarship, valuable as it is, cannot claim hegemony over other discourses from different cultural contexts. Sadly, a truly polycentric account that includes writings outside of the English language remains limited due to the lack of access to texts and their translations. Brief as it has been, our effort to include such multiple perspectives emphasizes a need to make up for this gap in film studies, and recognizes such perspectives beyond the cinematic centers discussed here.

We want to return to the locus of the viewer since it is the viewer's perspective that illuminates the multiple germinations of discourses, marking the final step in decentering the prevailing cinematic models. All readings of films, whether by critics, scholars, or viewers, are produced from specific geo-cultural coordinates in world cinema. Each interpretation is charged with an active apparatus that is a constellation of cultural, political, experiential, and cognitive factors. Each film is thus a "polyvalent" film, carrying multiple valences of interpretations. The notion of polyvalence fuels tremendous energy in reading films in transnational contexts. Various theories in world cinema, such as the cinema of periphery or migrant cinema, attempt to reorient the lens of reading films through specific perspectives and provide justifications of polyvalence in world cinema. Our emphasis on indigenous theoretical perspectives in each of the centers recognizes this and gives credence to the effort of decentering Eurocentrism.

The idea of valences comes from two sources. First, the elements in chemistry are characterized by specific charges—valences—that give them certain capabilities and properties. Each element interacts with the other, picking up the charge/s of what they come in contact with, forming a new entity. The second meaning of *valences* goes beyond descriptive use. In his recent work, Fredric Jameson takes up the notion of valences as an investment of agency (2009: 38–48). He proposes that dialectical thought may be engaged in reversals of valences by transforming the values and functions to uncover the possibilities of reading history. To shift the valences is to change the trajectory of thought and render it effective for the political force in the present. This mechanism is at work in various interpretations of *Avatar*, as the viewers invest it with politically charged readings, illustrative of both the locus of the viewer in the larger geo-cultural sphere, and the agency of the viewer to make the film viable for specific political purposes.

Retaining the notion of valences as an agency is to recognize that readings of films are charged by interpretive apparatuses of the viewers. It goes beyond the descriptive meaning of *polyvalence* where the existence of multiple meanings is a given. The three models we propose—cognitive mapping, worldliness, and worlding—are borrowed from world and comparative literature, though film studies scholars have used them in select instances. Theories of cognitive mapping, worldliness, and worlding demonstrate how our encounters with texts—in our case, films—disclose the interpretive avenues opened up by the text and guide this interpretation to analyses of power in different forms. The following account of polyvalent cinema provides a partial view of some of the available current models in the studies of literature, cinema, and the arts. Developed in multiple theoretical perspectives in critical theory, these methods, however partial, are heuristic enough to begin a discourse on polyvalence in film studies.

Cognitive mapping

When we watch films, especially films from other cultures, we perceive an environment, a space outside of our experiential world. To watch a film that originates from a location other than our own is to be aware of two spatial worlds. It is a form of travel and traversal across maps. According to Tom Conley, "A film can be understood in a broad sense to be a 'map' that plots and colonizes the imagination of the public it is said to 'invent' and, as a result, to seek to control" (2007: 17). An eloquent poet of this process, Roland Barthes (1986) likened the experience of geography of a film to a state of hypnosis, a transport of reverie into the spaces offered in a theater. As we enter a world of affective invitations of the film, there is an ever-present negotiation with the spaces of the film, which are also ideological, societal spaces. Films become maps we navigate to find our relation to the spaces in front of us. Our perception of the cinematic space and efforts to relate our space to the space on the screen leads to "cognitive maps," maps formed in our minds that locate our place in the world.

In an essay that defines the influential concept of "cognitive mapping," Fredric Jameson (1988) takes a cue from Kevin Lynch's book, *The Image of the City* (1960). There, Lynch describes the dilemmas posed by large, sprawling cities. The residents of that city find it difficult to locate their position in relation to the city-spaces around them. To overcome the large spaces they inhabit, the residents attempt to locate their orientation by constructing its cognitive/mental representation. A cognitive map is not a physical map, but a representational map, a perception of that space. A cognitive map represents the impossibilities of total space comprehension based on an individual's experience in that environment. To improve Lynch's concept, Jameson proposes that cognitive mapping involves three elements: the individual subject, the real, and the imaginary projection. In his broader interpretive framework, Jameson argues that our conception of cultural space is a symptom of economic realities. Focusing on spatial issues allows us to get to the kind of distortions and omissions caused by the world-system, specifically global capitalism (1992: 4). What Jameson defined earlier as "postmodernism" has morphed into a neoliberal global capital culture, with its various manifestations and censorships in the areas of cultural production. The vast totality of the world-system, and the relationship of the individual to that system, is impossible to grasp. Cognitive mapping, the representation of the totality of the world–system, thus becomes a pedagogical and political tool in approaching globalization, a way to attend to the distortions, and reorient the individual to the collective, the local with the global.

Dudley Andrew's pedagogical instruction to "examine the film as map—cognitive map—while placing the film on the map," is based on the thesis that "films project cognitive maps by which citizens understand both their bordered worlds and the world at large" (2004: 16-17). In film studies, the concept of "cognitive mapping" appears as a tool of analysis where representation in the film itself is said to cognitively map the larger totality. It becomes, for the most part, a descriptive device to access the complexity of films. Alejandro González Iñárritu's *Babel* (2006), in its multiple narratives set in four geographical locations around the globe, approximates the totality of global reality, or represents a "simplified reduction of totality" (Silvey, 2009). Similar ensemble films, such as Robert Altman's *Short Cuts* (1993), Paul Thomas Anderson's *Magnolia* (1999), Michael Haneke's *Code inconnu: Récit incomplet de divers voyages/Code Unknown* (2000), and Paul Haggis's *Crash* (2004), offer narratives that emphasize the interconnectedness of people, "prompting us to consider the world as a map or a system" (Silvey, 2009). Lorraine Sim (2012) argues that "such films can also be understood to serve a conceptual and cathartic function" by providing cognitive maps of a larger reality that "the individual may not be able to realize in actual life." These analyses take up Jameson's thesis that we experience films in relationships they provide rather than their content.

These films illustrate what Jameson means by the descriptive use of cognitive mapping; that is, they are textual representations that grasp their own location in the larger world-system. An imperial example of cognitive mapping takes place in the narratives of the Hollywood blockbuster franchise of the Jason Bourne film series: *The Bourne Identity* (2002), *The Bourne Supremacy* (2004), *The Bourne Ultimatum* (2007), *The Bourne Legacy* (2012), and *Jason Bourne* (2016). The narratives move an American secret agent through a space from where he maps the world and situates himself across continents. The films project accelerated movements of a person who is in command to move across global space without regard for national or regional boundaries. His field of action knows no limits and his conception of the global space is the space of neoliberal capital, with its technological power and untrammeled aggression. Each place becomes "a spectacle, a signifier of the film's subject, a metaphor for the state of mind of the protagonist" (Aitken & Zonn, 1994: 17).

But Jameson also uses cognitive mapping in prescriptive terms. That is, a viewer's analysis of figurations in films both discloses and conceals relations to the systemic totality. Since mimetic, complete totality is never achieved by cognitive maps, the total aesthetic experience of space is always a result of repression, containment, and other strategies of invisibility. In illustrating this problem succinctly, Albert Toscano and Jeff Kinkle argue that the aesthetic of cognitive mapping, laying bare its mechanisms, brings those elements into visible realm: "It is the task of the critic to tease out the symptoms of, at one and the same time, the consolidation of a planetary nexus of capitalist power and the multifarious struggles to imagine it" (2015: 20). The viewer's approach to cognitive mapping involves a focus on how the text prevents our understanding of social totality and how it directs it in a certain way. The viewer's subjective experience in locating her position in the larger spaces that are not representable provides one understanding of cognitive mapping, but Jameson also considers cognitive mapping to indicate the relationship of the represented space to the larger totality of the multinational, global, late capitalist system. Individuals attempt to grasp their place by cognitively mapping the spaces around them, while the textual representations are attempts to grasp their own locations in the large world-system.

While abstraction in the notion of totality in Jameson's work remains controversial (Tally, 1996), it is possible to take specific steps toward its pragmatic interpretation. Let us return to one of our earlier propositions, that a comparative framework in cinema is possible, even necessary in the age of neoliberal globalization, when all cinemas around the world are "differential encounters with capitalism" (Willemen, 2005: 99). The conception of totality advocated by Jameson confronts us with one of its material forms— a singular march of capital as a dominant force that shapes culture, including cinema.

One of the central arguments of this book is that the conditions of neoliberal globalization shape cultural production, including filmmaking. The idea of cognitive mapping aligns with our project of mapping in world cinema and Jameson's thesis that representations of space and spatial relationships are a symptom of the global economic system. In its insistent positioning of the local with the global, a cognitive map is a determining index of the imperatives of conditions created by the system of neoliberal—cultural, historical, and economic—capital. With cognitive mapping, we leave behind the consideration of the national as a site caught between the global and the local and open to contestatory claims. The experience of film narratives as instances of cognitive maps offers us a diagnosis of the present.

Studies of cognitive mapping in cinema emerging from different parts of world cinema testify to the usefulness of the concept to track the negotiation of the narratives with the dispersions and disjunctions of the social geographies of neoliberal present. For example, the spatial itineraries in the narratives of María Inés Roqué's *Papá Iván* (2000), Albertina Carri's *Los Rubios/The Blonds* (2003), and Nicolás Prividera's *M* (2007), along with slow, observational modes of filmmaking in Lucrecia Martel's *La Ciénega/The Swamp* (2001), have allowed Argentinian cinema to map the internal trajectories of alienation, while also insisting on constructing a referential present that connects the films to broader economic realities (Andermann, 2012: 114, 173). Cognitive mapping orients the film's narrative to the global totality in which the subjects find their locus, while it also directs us to utopian possibilities in the narrative. As Brian L. Ott and Gordana Lazić (2013) put it in their analysis of cognitive mapping in Jens Lien's Norwegian film *Den brysomme mannen/ The Bothersome Man* (2006), the concept allows the critic to examine the film's orienting impulses, placing it in a network of relationships by satirizing it, while rhetorical hints at the future direct the film to the utopian impulse of Jameson's idea.

Intense debates have developed around the concept of cognitive mapping. Unmoored from these controversies, it is important to note that the concept remains relevant in the age of globalization (Cevasco, 2012: 87). Examining a film as a cognitive map is to locate it in relation to the world-system, other cultures and peoples, and the maps projected by films from other parts of the world. The insistence on totality is an effort toward political justice and toward the placing of voices on different registers of power on a comparable scale. Examining films as cognitive maps allows us—the students, critics, and scholars—to overcome the ideological myopia experienced from within one's own local experience. It allows us to imagine the limits of that experience as much as the possibilities of its expansion.

Filmmakers of Third Cinema, entirely mindful of their location in relation to the global structures of filmmaking, utilized both of these impulses of cognitive mapping. The political charge of their manifestos stemmed from the necessity of establishing an affective relationship with their audiences by bringing their own worlds onto the screen, but they also insisted on being aware of the world outside of their borders that defined their practice, making it essential to formulate a program of resistance. Jacob Nilsson (2013) argues forcefully about the inherent value of cognitive mapping in orienting Third Cinema to world cinema while also providing it with an ability to imagine a utopian future by critiquing the inadequacies and injustices of their present life. If cognitive mapping allows you "to think of the outside" (Cevasco, 2012: 87), each reading of the film is an attempt to conceive of the larger system, an effort to produce a map of that totality. Cognitive mapping is thus a tool of mapping the polyvalence of a film.

Worldliness

The act of mapping is an imperial gesture, implying an odious colonialist desire. Necessary in the trajectory of modernism in the West, maps are products of imagination. The situated specificity of subjects is more urgent for those who want to write their own narratives. The notion of worldliness, developed first in the work of Edward W. Said (1983) and then Achille Mbembe (2000), attempts to reorient the perspective from a global imagination to the situational specificity of the reader, the viewer, and the critic. Creative works are shaped by "circumstantial reality" of their creativity. Texts have "ways of existing, both theoretical and practical, that even in their most rarified form are always enmeshed in circumstance, time, place, and society—in short, they are in the world, and hence worldly," says Said (1983: 35). "Worldliness" of the text comes from the self-conscious efforts of the creators to embed the conditions of their production into their work, while "worldliness" of the critic comes from the act of placing the text and interpretation in its specific historical, cultural, and political conditions of reading. Said makes the act of reading an ethical and political act, where each work of art lives a life in the conditions of its reception, and where one must be mindful of the conditions in which the reading takes place. Reading a text itself is part of a text's being in the world.

It is clear that worldliness marks a distance from theory that is uninterested in the conditions of the text's being, and considers it unethical to ignore the efforts involved in the production of texts, often violent and full of struggles. Worldliness implies a responsibility of the critic, faith in human agency, and an ability to affect the discourse. Theory has a political utility when it is connected to public life and invests value in it. Worldliness creates multiplicity in the discourse of interpretation, as each act of criticism constitutes and puts to work its own worldliness. The aim of reading and criticism, for Said, is to create "resistance and heterogeneity of civil society," an aim that eludes theorists placed in the firmaments of their academic discourse (1983: 25).

The act of reading is never value-free; rather, it implies commitment through situated criticism that is "skeptical, secular, reflectively open to its own failings" (Said, 1983: 26). Arguing against the limitlessness of interpretations, a fond belief in liberal pluralism, Said asserts that interpretations are guided by their "worldliness," their solicitation of "the world's attention" (1983: 40). The text's meaning is not generated by ahistorical theoretical apparatus, but has to firmly place the text in the networks of power and mechanisms of visibility. Readings produced by worldliness speak of the location of the critic, the conditions of reception, and the play of power that shapes each step in the process. Said extricates the text from the burden of theories produced in the outmoded or hegemonic structures in the West or in the hands of power. The act of defining the contours of the world in which the text exists, and where and how it is received, constitutes the worldliness of these gestures. The concept validates the acts of molding the text's receptions and readings to suit the particularities of conditions on the local level, thus directing us to a postcolonial discourse of uncovering silences and injustices.

In a globalized world that operates with its own system of knowledge, categories, and hierarchies of power, Achille Mbembe (2000) discovers that the modalities imposed by the West have confined Africa to the margins of the world, denying it the ability to write itself onto the global space and time. He sets out to "write the world from Africa" and "to write Africa into the world," an effort which leads him to modify Said's worldliness into a political act of defining the encounter on several levels (Weaver Shipley, 2010: 656). Worldliness is an act of empowering and engaging with the creation and criticism of culture:

Worldliness, in this context, has had to do not only with the capacity to generate one's own cultural forms, institutions, and lifeways, but also with the ability
to foreground, translate, fragment, and disrupt realities and imaginaries originating
elsewhere, and in the process place these forms and processes in the service of one's
own making.

(Mbembe & Nuttall, 2008: 1)

Here, worldliness is defiance against the efforts to marginalize Africa and its cultural production, allowing it to mark its distinctiveness on its own terms. Destabilization of existing methods of defining worlds and cultures is therefore a prerequisite to worldliness. As
our discussion of Nollywood makes clear, worldliness involves different life-worlds of
texts and textualities, from cultural and religious practices to technological and economic
transformations in popular culture (Garritano, 2014).

The perspective of worldliness, argues Kenneth W. Harrow (2016), allows African
spectators to formulate their own notions of political engagement and subjectivity in
various spheres of filmmaking, from Nollywood's film genres to the work of global
auteurs, and to write their own itineraries in world cinema. The discourse of worldliness is written by the efforts of every filmmaking practice to write itself into world
cinema. This does not deny the interpretations of African cinema produced elsewhere,
but it claims the space of worldliness of Africa's own discourse as one among many in
world cinema.

While Mbembe's conception of worldliness aims to reclaim a space for African identity
through cultural production including film, the most notable discussion of the idea has
remained in the context of Nollywood. Indeed, a relatively new but formidable component in world cinema necessitates the assertion of worldliness at the moment. It pushes
back against any attempt to classify Nollywood or other currents of African cinema as
existing outside the legitimacy accorded by the canons of film theory. To this extent,
worldliness has the potential to re-situate discourses of various other cinemas in the world,
from Bhojpuri cinema in India to Native American film production in the US and Maori
filmmaking in New Zealand. Since worldliness defies distance from the apolitical dimension of theoretical work, the act of creating worldliness produces ethically and politically
responsible film criticism.

Although Said's notion of worldliness is more influential in world literature and has
not been frequently deployed in film studies, his insights remain guiding posts for critics
and viewers (Arac, 2013). Said called for a "decentered or multiply-centered world" that
would allow for cultural texts to migrate from one cultural realm to another, making it
possible for critics to encounter texts across borders (Arac, 2013: 119). While worldliness as a concept for critical practice remains marginal in film studies, a brief illustration of Said's own sense of responsibility in situating the text in its political contexts
comes from his review of Costa-Gavras's film *Hanna K* (1983). The film is a story of
Hanna Kaufman, an American attorney married to an Israeli lawyer, Joshua Herzog.
Hanna defends the right of a Palestinian man accused of being a terrorist to claim his
family property in Israel. Hanna battles her husband in court as her life continues to be
threatened by the state. The film was criticized for its flippant treatment of a volatile
political issue, despite its achievement as the first mainstream Hollywood film to depict
Palestinian struggles. Said regards the film for its value in representing Palestinian characters in full human dimension, without neglecting to represent the military power of
their adversaries. For Said, the film's focus on "lived experience" brings it closer to the

circumstances of Palestinian everyday reality. Fully aware that the film caricatures the conflict in many ways in a rather untidy aesthetic, Said's focus is on the "worldliness" of the characters that have been denied representation on par with other human characters in the region. It is the perceived value of the representation of Palestinian life whose existence is recognized in the narrative, not the aesthetic achievements, that makes the film politically viable for him.

Worlding/world-making

"To see a world in a grain of sand," begins William Blake's poem "Auguries of Innocence," suggesting worlds of possibilities in every human experience (Blake, 2004). Philosopher Stanley Cavell begins his book on film, *The World Viewed*, with an epigraph from Henry David Thoreau: "Why do precisely these objects which we behold make a world?" (1979: i). What is this "world" made of? Does it show up in films? The two quotes evoke the experience of the world produced by watching films. With each film viewing, a viewer sees and constructs many worlds: a world of characters, spaces, movements, values, and affects unfolding on the screen; a world created by the filmmakers interacting with the world in which the viewer watches the films; and a world that the viewer creates through that experience, merging, folding, and transposing the world of objects and beings of one's own experience onto the world captured by the camera.

What we call "world cinema" is an abstraction. It is a theoretical projection, an attempt to map what we know onto a reality we know, where cinema circulates and viewers live. When a viewer watches a film in some corner of this globe, it is an opportunity to give meaning to that experience, a moment to "create worlds." Thus, viewers from around the world constitute their plural worlds through their act of watching films. What distinguishes the current moment in world cinema are the widely expanded opportunities in this world-creation.

Film studies have long been concerned with the question of world-making in films, even if on the margins. Film scholar V.F. Perkins maintains that "the priority in thinking about cinema" is to advance "our grasp of what is involved in worldhood of fictional worlds" (2005: 5, 32). Watching films, for Perkins, is to be aware that the world in front of you has specific perspectives, and is also connected to the world outside the theater, the bigger picture. To watch a film is to disclose the world from a specific perspective. For Cavell, too, we encounter a world on the screen that magically interacts with the world outside the theater. Films do not present us a world, but instead place us at a distance from the world of our experience (Cavell, 1979: 40–41). Cavell draws the essence of this view from the Thoreau epigraph: like philosophy, films direct us to a world of thought—exploring the unseen—to think of our worlds. Cinema and philosophy help us understand the world as a representation.

Cavell's inspiration comes from philosopher Martin Heidegger, whose meditations on the work of art offer one of the most difficult and widely known conceptualizations of the "world." His essay "The Origin of the Work of Art" (1971) proposes that our encounter with art discloses the world. Heidegger approaches art or aesthetic experience as an examination of the process of perception, and as a discovery of our relationship to the objects around us. The world of our being encounters the being of the work of art in a dialectical interaction. This encounter reveals something unique about us as much as about the work of art. The work of art brings a world to us, disclosing new possibilities of understanding another existence, that of its own making and being. This continuous interaction between us (the world we know) and the work of art (the world it brings to us) creates a new world of encounter.

Heidegger's terminology and philosophy are formidable and dense for a brief introduction. His work is centered on the main issue of how human beings understand and come to grips with the meaning of their existence as they grasp their view of the surroundings, the objects, and the horizons/limits. It is a process-philosophy, a phenomenology of existence. It is not that we know the world as subjects and objects, but that the relationship is mutually entwined, disclosing both in a process of existence. What we learn from Heidegger is that art opens up our world, allowing us to understand ourselves as much as showing us the regions, contexts, limits, and possibilities of things around us. The "world" for Heidegger is the possibility in which all objects including our own existence make sense to us. The world is the existence we inhabit, and the existence of the world includes us. Our worlds are continually formed and shaped by our existence. In Heidegger's philosophy, "being-in-the-world" or *Dasein* are also part of worlding. The world is not a map or a space. It is a "mystery" (Heidegger, 1988: 166). We continuously make worlds while the worlds make us.

It is important to recognize that Heidegger's philosophy opens up a different way of thinking, a different way of using language, and understanding a film experience. The world of film—watching the cinematic narratives unfold, meeting new characters, exploring new spaces, and experiencing aesthetic elements on the screen—gives us a sense of "being-in-the-world." Our world is neither a collection of objects and things nor a product of our imagination. "The world worlds," says Heidegger, emphasizing a gerundive and generative process of making worlds (1971: 43). That is, the world is never there for us; rather, the world has the transformative power of remaking and re-worlding. This is a crucial feature of our encounter with art, including cinema.

Turning a noun, *world*, into a verb, *worlding*, Heidegger indicates an activity of making worlds in our encounters with art. Encountering a work of art is an act of giving intelligibility to our world, and "worldliness is a capability of my being" (Cheah, 2016: 99). The use of Heidegger's concepts and terminology shifts from his philosophy to studies of literature, film, and the arts. We are always active in making the worlds, worlding the world, while the world itself is engaged in worlding or re-worlding itself. While the debates surrounding the uses of "worlding" are quite extensive, we want to note a few essential points. Heidegger emphasizes the experiential, aesthetic experience of the world and worlding. The world is not a container of things. It is also not a spatial map that we inhabit. The world is not constructed by us, but a process of which our being is an essential part. Each one of us watches films or reads literature to make our own worlds, while we remake the worlds of and in the films.

While Heidegger informs much of the theorization and discussion of worlding and worldliness in film and literature studies, the ideas of making plural worlds or disclosing possible worlds constitute a complex field of intersecting philosophical perspectives. The most notable of these efforts is Daniel Yacavone's book *Film Worlds: A Philosophical Aesthetics of Cinema* (2015). His primary thesis is that films make worlds and we interpret these worlds as viewers and as a community of viewers. Combining the cognitive-symbolic aspects of filmmaking with the phenomenological-interpretive aspects of film experience, he presents the dual aspects of cinematic world-making. Synthesizing cognitive-symbolic perspectives with aesthetic-hermeneutic dimensions of film worlds, Yacavone presents a comprehensive theory of perceiving and making film worlds. He theorizes three kinds of cinematic responses to the "world-in-film": cognitive-diegetic, sensory-affective, and formal-aesthetic.

While his is a vitally important and necessary work in film studies, our effort focuses primarily on viewers and their world-making in encounters with cinema. We need to re-adjust Yacavone's perspective back to the viewer and examine the role of agency in making worlds possible in "worlding films." The activity of making worlds from within your own world takes precedence over cognitive views, recognizing the dynamism of the encounter with films. In elucidating the concept of world in relation to world literature, Pheng Cheah provides a masterly treatise on "world" and "worlding" in Heidegger that carries direct implications for the act of worlding in world cinema. Rather than an objective presence or a spiritualist conception, says Cheah, "the world is held together by temporality" (2016: 97). Such a world cannot be "regulated for oppressive economic and political ends" in the same way as the spatial world. The process of worlding also allows us to relate to the Other and the unknown through works of art. Our experience of the works of art is part of the "force of worlding," and what Cheah says about literature is equally valid in the case of film:

> Literature creates the world and cosmopolitan bonds not only because it enables us to imagine a world through its powers of figuration, but also, more importantly, because it arouses in us pleasure and a desire to share this pleasure through universal communication.
>
> (Cheah, 2008: 27)

In watching films, we do not perceive the world as such, nor its physical properties or contours, but we produce an imagination of a world. To echo Cheah in the context of world cinema, we are engaged in creating multiple worlds while watching films, negotiating with the worlds of the others, ethically connecting to them, making them part of our own world, while also partaking in a process of their world-making. Watching films to create worlds is cosmopolitan activity par excellence.

The notion of "worlding" inspired by Heidegger has taken hold in world literature and cultural studies. When we "world the world," we do not bring it anywhere near the world created by globalization. In fact, to think of world cinema as a mere mechanism of circulation is to aid in "globalization's unworlding of the world" (Cheah, 2008: 193). Worlding transforms the known worlds imposed on us and also the worlds of our everyday experience by crafting alternative worlds delimited by our situations and agency.

The notion of "worlding the world" suggests a world-in-the-making, an engaged process involving our existence and the objects in that existence, while the "force of worlding" that engages us with objects of art, literature, or cinema suggests an agency in the concept of "worlding." Addressing the urgency of pedagogy in reading world literature, Rob Wilson (2007) formulates a manifesto-like statement on worlding. Synthesizing thought in cultural studies and addressing Heidegger's legacy, he invests a self-reflective agency in the act of worlding. Worlding for him is a process of imagination that reciprocally engages with literature to think of "worlds" in "situated practices" (2007: 220). We make worlds in reading world literature, tracing horizons of this world into our own, framing the discourse in our temporal coordinates against the imposed spatial boundaries. The worlds offered to us in literature (and film) are reconstituted in our own worlds, mapped and marked in our own life-worlds, our own contexts. The self-reflective process may, at any moment, enlarge our worlds, and transpose them to the outside worlds so that, like Thoreau, we go beyond the things in front of us to imagine worlds.

Taking a cue from the key works by Gayatri Chakravarty Spivak, scholars in world literature and comparative literature engage in efforts to re-inscribe the act of "worlding" as a political gesture in reading literature, the arts, and cinema. Spivak calls for worlding of the Third World in much the same way Mbembe calls for a re-conception of worldliness in writing on African cultural production. The act of worlding our worlds, re-framing the experience offered to us in our own temporal-political coordinates, is a decisive gesture against colonialism, Eurocentrism, and globalization (Spivak, 1985). The dominant powers are always engaged in circumscribing the contours of our world; our worlds are "re-worlded" by these powers. Our act of worlding thus functions as a counter-strategy, a gesture of resistance to the dominant discourses and interpretations (Koptiuch, 1991; Robbins, 2011). Our acts of reading films to world their worlds destabilize the existing worlds and "open up reality to interpretation" (Cheah, 2016: 311).

William Blake's abstraction puts a new life to our proposition. There is no single world cinema, no complete reality to be perceived or accounted for. Instead, there is a possibility of seeing a new world in each grain of sand. Each experience of a film is an interruption in the life-world, in the way we perceive and make our own world. It is a fortuitous opportunity to remake our worlds. We see in each experience the world taking a new shape. In each interpretation, the world is re-worlded. The viewer can remake the worlds of cinema by inflecting these worlds with her/his own, by re-situating them in an act of worlding, making the horizons of the local pertinent borders against the world that announces its totality. Reading films in multitudinous spaces of world cinema is therefore not about being consumed by the world's endless horizons, but an act of ethical responsibility, an opportunity to bend the force of globalization against itself, and to use its resources and technology to generate multiple worlds.

The questions we raise in this book—from decentering the current models to re-orienting our current efforts to the reality of world cinema in the age of globalization where the plurality of cultures is caught in a mixed state of marginalization and blessedness of the pilfering resources of production and dissemination—are underlined by the recognition that world cinema must begin with the viewer, that it originates in the encounters with films. The castles of theory where thinking fortifies itself are mere markers in the field where viewers make their own worlds. It is as important to take films to the viewers as it is to tune into their experiences of cinema. Charging and re-charging our valences to the system of world cinema will inflect that discourse with the desired plurality this world contains and demands.

Bibliography

Aitken, Stuart C. & Leo E. Zonn. (1994). "Re-Presenting the Place Pastiche." In Stuart C. Aitken & Leo E. Zonn (eds), *Place, Power, Situation and Spectacle: A Geography of Film*. Lanham, MD: Rowman and Littlefield, pp. 3–27.

Andermann, Jens. (2012). *The New Argentine Cinema*. London: I.B. Tauris.

Andrew, Dudley. (2004). "An Atlas of World Cinema." *Framework: The Journal of Cinema and Media* 45(2), pp. 9–23.

Arac, Jonathan. (2013). "The Worldliness of World Literature." In Theo D'haen, David Damrosch, & Djelal Kadir (eds), *The Routledge Companion to World Literature*. New York, NY: Routledge, pp. 117–125.

Barthes, Roland. (1986). "Leaving the Movie Theater." In *The Rustle of Language*. New York, NY: Hill & Wang, pp. 345–346.

Blake, William. (2004). "Auguries of Innocence." In *The Pickering Manuscript*. Whitefish, MT: Kessinger, p. 15.

Brooks, David. (2010). "The Messiah Complex." *New York Times* (January 7). Available at: www.nytimes.com/2010/01/08/opinion/08brooks.html. Accessed May 2, 2017.

Cavell, Stanley. (1979). *The World Viewed: Reflections on the Ontology of Film*. Enlarged edition. Cambridge, MA: Harvard University Press.

Cevasco, Maria Elisa. (2012). "Imagining a Space That is Outside: An Interview with Fredric Jameson." *Minnesota Review* 78, pp. 83–94.

Cheah, Pheng. (2008). "What Is a World? On World Literature as World-Making Activity." *Daedalus* 137(3), pp. 26–38.

Cheah, Pheng. (2016). *What Is a World? On Postcolonial Literature as World Literature*. Durham, NC: Duke University Press.

Conley, Tom. (2007). *Cartographic Cinema*. Minneapolis, MN: University of Minnesota Press.

Elsaesser, Thomas. (2011). "James Cameron's *Avatar*: Access for All." *New Review of Film and Television Studies* 9(3), pp. 247–264.

Garritano, Carmela. (2014). "Introduction: Nollywood: An Archive of African Worldliness." *Black Camera* 5(2), pp. 44–52.

Grant, Catherine. (2010). "Seeing through *Avatar*: Film Allegory 101." Film Studies for Free (January 27). Available at: http://filmstudiesforfree.blogspot.com/2010/01/i-see-you-on-avatar-and-allegory.html. Accessed May 15, 2017.

Harrow, Kenneth W. (2016). "African Cinema in the Age of Postcolonialism and Globalization." In Yannis Tzioumakis & Claire Molloy (eds), *The Routledge Companion to Cinema and Politics*. New York, NY: Routledge, pp. 387–397.

Heidegger, Martin. (1971). "The Origin of the Work of Art." In *Martin Heidegger: Poetry, Language, Thought*. Trans. Albert Hofstadter. New York, NY: Harper Perennial, pp. 15–86.

Heidegger, Martin. (1988). *The Basic Problems of Phenomenology*. Trans. Albert Hofstadter. Bloomington, IN: Indiana University Press.

Huffington Post. (2010). "Evo Morales Praises *Avatar*." *Huffington Post* (January 12). Available at: www.huffingtonpost.com/2010/01/12/evo-morales-praises-avata_n_420663.html. Accessed April 10, 2017.

Jameson, Fredric. (1988). "Cognitive Mapping." In Cary Nelson & Lawrence Grossberg (eds), *Marxism and the Interpretation of Culture*. Chicago, IL: University of Illinois Press, pp. 347–360.

Jameson, Fredric. (1992). *The Geopolitical Aesthetic: Cinema and Space in the World System*. Bloomington, IN: Indiana University Press.

Jameson, Fredric. (2009). *Valences of the Dialectic*. London: Verso.

Jenkins, Henry. (2010a). "What the Chinese Are Making of *Avatar*." Confessions of an Aca-Fan: The Official Blog of Henry Jenkins (March 12). Available at: http://henryjenkins.org/2010/03/avatar_and_chinese_fan_culture.html. Accessed March 10, 2017.

Jenkins, Henry. (2010b). "*Avatar* Activism and Beyond." Confessions of an Aca-Fan: The Official Blog of Henry Jenkins (September 22). Available at: http://henryjenkins.org/2010/09/avatar_activism_and_beyond.html. Accessed March 10, 2017.

Koptiuch, Kristin. (1991). "Third-Worlding at Home." *Social Text* 28, pp. 87–99.

Loshitzky, Yosefa. (2012). "Popular Cinema as Resistance: *Avatar* in the Palestinian (Imagi)nation." *Third Text* 26(2), pp. 151–163.

Lynch, Kevin. (1960). *The Image of the City*. Cambridge, MA: MIT Press.

Macartney, Jane. (2010). "Confucius Says No to Subversive Blockbuster *Avatar*." *The Times* (January 19). Available at: www.thetimes.co.uk/article/confucius-says-no-to-subversive-blockbuster-avatar-kjq6rb2d7vn. Accessed April 1, 2017.

Mbembe, Achille. (2000). "At the Edge of the World: Boundaries, Territoriality, and Sovereignty in Africa." Trans. Steven Rendell. *Public Culture* 12(1), pp. 259–284.

Mbembe, Achille & Sarah Nuttall. (2008). "Introduction: Afropolis." In Sarah Nuttall & Achille Mbembe (eds), *Johannesburg: The Elusive Metropolis*. Durham, NC: Duke University Press, pp. 1–36.

Newitz, Annalee. (2009). "When Will White People Stop Making Movies Like *Avatar*." io9 (December 18). Available at: http://io9.gizmodo.com/5422666/when-will-white-people-stop-making-movies-like-avatar. Accessed May 1, 2017.

Nilsson, Jacob. (2013). "Concept-Cognitive Mapping: Third Cinema as Cartography of Global Capitalism." *Cinéma & Cie: International Film Studies Journal* 1, pp. 87–96.

Ott, Brian L. & Gordana Lazić. (2013). "The Pedagogy and Politics of Art in Postmodernity: Cognitive Mapping and *The Bothersome Man*." *Quarterly Journal of Speech* 99(3), pp. 259–282.

Perkins, V.F. (2005). "Where Is the World-Horizon of Events in Movie Fiction." In John Gibbs & Douglas Pye (eds), *Style and Meaning: Studies in the Detailed Analysis of Film*. Manchester: Manchester University Press.

Robbins, Bruce. (2011). "The Worlding of the American Novel." In Leonard Cassuto, Clare Virginia Eby, & Benjamin Reiss (eds), *The Cambridge History of the American Novel*. Cambridge: Cambridge University Press, pp. 1096–1107.

Said, Edward W. (1983). *The World, the Text, and the Critic*. Cambridge, MA: Harvard University Press.

Silvey, Vivien. (2009). "Not Just Ensemble Films: Six Degrees, Webs, Multiplexity and the Rise of Network Narratives." *Forum: The University of Edinburgh Postgraduate Journal of Culture and the Arts* 8, n.p.

Sim, Lorraine. (2012). "Ensemble Film, Postmodernity, and Moral Mapping." *Screening the Past* 35. Available at: www.screeningthepast.com/2012/12/ensemble-film-postmodernity-and-moral-mapping. Accessed May 1, 2017.

Spivak, Gayatri Chakravarty. (1985). "Three Women's Texts and a Critique of Imperialism." *Critical Inquiry* 12(1): pp. 243–261.

Tally, Robert. (1996). "Jameson's Project of Cognitive Mapping: A Critical Engagement." In R.G. Paulston (ed), *Social Cartography: Mapping Ways of Seeing Social and Educational Change*. New York, NY: Garland Science, pp. 339–416.

Toscano, Albert & Jeff Kinkle. (2015). *Cartographies of the Absolute*. Alresford: Zero Books.

Weaver Shipley, Jesse (ed). (2010). "Africa in Theory: A Conversation Between Jean Comaroff and Achille Mbembe." *Anthropological Quarterly* 83(3): pp. 653–678.

Willemen, Paul. (2005). "For a Comparative Film Studies." *Inter-Asia Cultural Studies* 6(1), pp. 98–112.

Wilson, Rob. (2007). "Afterword: *Worlding* as Future Tactic." In Rob Wilson & Christopher Leigh Connery (eds), *The Worlding Project: Doing Cultural Studies in the Era of Globalization*. Santa Cruz, CA: North Atlantic Books, pp. 209–223.

Yacavone, Daniel. (2015). *Film Worlds: A Philosophical Aesthetics of Cinema*. New York, NY: Columbia University Press.

Žižek, Slavoj. (2010) "*Avatar*: Return of the Natives." *New Statesman* (March 4). Available at: www.newstatesman.com/film/2010/03/avatar-reality-love-couple-sex. Accessed April 1, 2017.

Index